AN ARTHUR FROMMER PUBLICATION

1980-81 EDITION

ISRAEL

ON $20 A DAY

By ARNOLD SHERMAN
and SYLVIA BRILLIANT

FP A FROMMER/PASMANTIER BOOK

Published by Frommer/Pasmantier Publishers
A Simon and Schuster Division of
Gulf + Western Corporation
380 Madison Avenue
New York, NY 10017

ISBN: 0-671-25490-1
Library of Congress Catalog Card Number: 80-50445

Manufactured in the United States of America

Cover photo by E. Streichan/Shostal Associates

*Although every effort was made to ensure the accuracy
of price information appearing in this book,
it should be kept in mind that prices
can and do fluctuate in the course of time.*

CONTENTS

MAPS

New Currency Alert

In March 1980 the Israeli Government changed the main unit of Israeli currency from the lira or pound to the shekel. 10 old lira now equal one shekel, and there are 100 agorat to each shekel. Shekels will be issued in the following note denominations: 1, 5, 10, and 50; agorat (or 1 agora) coins will be in units of 1, 5, 10, plus a half-shekel coin.

The lira will be phased out by June 1980, but it will take some time before the changeover is fully effected.

Since the government has not officially announced the abbreviation as we go to press we have denoted shekels as 'SH' throughout this book. The rate of exchange has been based on 3.4 shekels to one dollar.

Preface

A VETERAN ISRAELI recently explained that if a single generalization can be applied about one of the world's newest/oldest, most controversial and enigmatic countries, it is that Israel categorically rejects all attempts at definition or classification. It is a warm, temperate country, comprised of arid desert areas. But even the summer winds in the Galilee are cool, and while frolickers bask in the subtropical sun of Eilat, Mount Hermon in the north remains streaked with snow.

It is a nation where a 2,000-year-old language has been successfully resurrected. The vast majority of Israelis are distinctly polyglot, speaking Arabic, Yiddish, English, French, German, Rumanian, Polish, Hindi, and Russian. It is a land of almost insufferable impoliteness and schizophrenic motoring, and yet, the Israelis can be the warmest of all hosts.

The mood in the country is constantly changing. In the beginning there was a grim determination—born partially out of the horrors of World War II—to hang on, to protect every sand dune, to force life out of the desert. Then conditions grew more stable. Israelis became a little more like other people. Television, the good life, and a certain cockiness were infused into the overall picture. This was particularly apparent during the heady days after the Six-Day War in 1967. Suddenly, Israel was no longer a struggling state hanging on tenaciously to its hard-won independence. Land areas had more than trebled. Infusions of new immigrants swelled the country's Jewish population. The economy was burgeoning and tourism was increasing at a rate greater than ever before.

Israel, with its artifacts, excavations and kibbutzim, always had a lot to offer. After the 1967 war, it had more. Most important of all, there was united Jerusalem, the Western (Wailing) Wall, the Levantine veneer of the Old City. For the Christian, Israel became a synonym for the entire Holy Land. Both sides of Jerusalem were joined together. Barbed-wire fences and the Mandelbaum Gate border post became things of the past. Bethlehem, once virtually inaccessible from Israel, was only minutes away from the Israeli capital. Jericho, believed to be the oldest city in the world, and Hebron, where the ancient Hebrew patriarchs were buried, were open to visits. In the north, the Golan Heights provided a double meaning: tranquility in the Galilee and a new area for tourist inspection.

In the opposite direction, there was a new accessibility to the great historic wilderness called Sinai. Eilat, once considered by Israelis as the end of the world, awoke one morning with a deep and dependable tourist hinterland. The craggy isolation of the Santa Katarina Monastery, at the base of Mount Sinai where Moses was believed to have received the Ten Commandments, provided an unforgettable experience. Command cars, jeeps, buses, and airplanes began penetrating the desert that had once sustained the ancient Israelites during their 40-year odyssey.

In those days, the mood was optimistic. No one any longer questioned the premise that Israel was on the map for good. World economies were booming, and there was a tremendous quantity of expendable wealth. The major items were hotel accommodations and airline space, and an empty hotel room in July was as rare as summer rain in the desert.

But the country experienced a sharp change in fortune in October, 1973. The completely unexpected Yom Kippur War had a sobering effect on the entire nation. The price was steep. Over 2,500 young men were killed, losses proportionately higher than the casualties the United States sustained during the entire Vietnam War. While the war ended with Israel closer to Cairo and Damascus than ever before, the initial setbacks and the high cost in lives shook the nation's confidence, plunged the people into despair, and tarnished the image of national heroes. In a backlash voters turned against the Labor party, which had led the state since its foundation, and elected a new government dominated by the right-of-center Likud.

A few weeks after he assumed office in 1977, Prime Minister Menachem Begin asked President Ceausescu of Rumania to arrange a meeting with President Sadat anywhere in the world. This set in motion a series of events highlighted by President Sadat's dramatic visit to Jerusalem, the conclusion of a framework for the Middle East peace agreement in Camp David, and the treaty with Egypt in March 1979 terminating 30 years of war between the two countries. Accordingly, Israel withdrew from about two-thirds of the Sinai to a line from El Arish to Ras Muhammad, and undertook to pull back to the international border by 1982. In the meantime, Israel controls tourist areas in Sinai, including the beach resort at Yamit on the Mediterranean coast, and the skin-diving resorts on the shore of the Gulf of Aqaba down to Sharm-el-Sheikh. Mount Sinai, with the Santa Katarina Monastery, reverted to Egypt; with the state of peace it remains open to tourists from Israel.

Inflation. Israel's inflation hit a record high in 1979, exceeding an annual rate of over 100%, and costs are continuing to spiral. But tourists are only marginally affected, because the steady currency devaluation gives them an ever-increasing number of shekels for their dollar. At the start of 1979, when the lira was still in circulation, the dollar fetched IL.19, and by the end of the year nearly IL.35. The rate is now determined by supply and demand, since the Likud government has abolished the foreign currency controls that had been in force for 30 years. The reform has effectively eliminated the black market that flourished when the exchange rate was fixed administratively by the government.

Security. No one can gloss over the security implications of the Middle East. No one can deny that there have been some outrages committed against tourists. No one can predict what the future will hold. But there are certain evident facts. Of the over 14-million travelers who have already visited the country, incidents in which tourists have been involved are so few that it would take a platoon of decimal points to calculate the actual figure. And this should be considered in context with the fact that the streets of Israel are among the safest in the world, violent crime is blessedly low, and security precautions, at all stages of the tourist's journey, are exceptionally high and effective. This does not mean that incidents cannot occur, and it certainly doesn't infer that certain precautions shouldn't be taken; elementary common sense proscribes wandering in the Golan Heights at night, taking unescorted trips to the northern border areas or West Bank, or women hitchhiking alone.

Fundamentally, though, despite the screaming headlines, Israel is probably a good deal safer than most other parts of the world. If you don't believe us, just ask any young woman strolling down Tel Aviv's Dizengoff Street at three in the morning for verification.

And now enough general remarks. The real issue has nothing to do with politics or security. The major challenge is to obtain maximum value for your dollar or, in other words, to see Israel on $20 a day.

Introduction

ISRAEL ON
$20 A DAY

Along General Lines

ISRAEL IS NOT an inexpensive country. A brittle economy and inflationary trends of over 100% a year have pushed consumer prices skyward. An
Israeli-made raincoat or bathing suit often costs more in Tel Aviv than in New
York. A meal in one of the country's better restaurants will peak at $10. The
price of a room in a luxury hotel would not only devour our $20 allotment, but
eliminate meals the next day.

And yet, paradoxically, the very seriousness of the situation, and the high
competition for tourist dollars, have produced a reaction which is working for
the overseas traveler. Some four-star hotels have reduced their off-season prices
in an effort to attract higher occupancies. There has been a proliferation of
clean, unpretentious restaurants serving acceptable meals at rock-bottom costs
(about $4). The seaside resorts of Netanya and Nahariya are squarely devoted
to the postulate of popular tourism. Kibbutz guest houses, providing clean,
comfortable lodging and wholesome, tasty food, are attracting ever larger
numbers of people. Some of the kibbutzim (collective farm settlements) even
have arrangements where you can offset the cost of room and board with good,
honest toil.

So while the postulate of $20 a day is not easy, it certainly is not impos-
sible. It requires a certain ingenuity, a willingness to experiment, and a spirit
of adventure, but the practicalities are all there.

The aim of this book is to show you how to function in Israel at the lowest
of costs: first, because we think more and more people should be encouraged
to travel in Israel, and second, because we believe low-cost Israel is the most
interesting Israel. For Israel is an informal and vigorous country that bears
little resemblance to the staid luxury-class hotels in which the higher-living
tourists will be staying.

THE $20-A-DAY STANDARD—WHAT IT MEANS: The $20-a-day
budget (for room and meals) in Israel is based on necessary expenses per person
per day—and there's nothing impossible or gimmicky about that goal. You can
stay in comfortably unostentatious hotels, hostels, or hospices, and you'll find
that there are many such places in each and every area this book covers. That
leaves adequate money for lunch, dinner, and occasional splurges.

Budget restaurants are no problem in Israel, because of the prevalence of traditional oriental cuisine, which is inexpensive. You'll find, by the way, that the hot summer weather will decrease your appetite for the meat-and-potatoes type of meal, and that you'll be eating more and more dairy, vegetable, and salad meals—which are healthy, plentiful, and relatively inexpensive.

People traveling alone will, of course, have to pay more per person for a room than two people traveling together. But couples will find many good-quality hotel rooms with private facilities available in all seasons of the year within their budget.

You will notice that we have also mentioned some restaurants and hotels slightly out of budget range. These are to be considered "splurges"—and particularly worthwhile ones. They all represent considerable value for the money, worth the extra expenditure should you be able to save elsewhere.

A WORD ABOUT PRICES: Rates quoted in dollars in this book for hotel rooms graded by the Ministry of Tourism will, the government assures us, remain valid until February 28, 1981, when they will be reviewed. Prices quoted in Israeli shekels are liable to be higher than recorded here because of steep inflation in Israel—approximately 85% predicted for 1980. Bear in mind, though, that things will not really be more expensive for you, even though Israeli prices are up.

Seasonal Prices

Most of Israel's hotels have standard rates throughout the year. In some resort areas, such as Metulla, Nahariya, and Safed, rates in July and August, and during Jewish holidays, are a few dollars or between 15–20% higher. Some hotels have low-season rates from mid-November to the end of February. All of these irregularities will be mentioned in the relevant chapters and/or hotel write-ups. In East Jerusalem rates jump 20–25% during Easter week. Some hotels and restaurants also up the rates for Passover.

Additional Charges

When figuring costs be sure to include the 15% service charge which all hotels add to your bill. Cafes and restaurants will charge both 12% VAT and a service charge, unless operated within the hotel you're staying at, and payment is in dollars. In the latter case, only service charge is included. If you convert your dollars into shekel travelers checks, you can pay your hotel bill with the latter and you'll still be exempt from paying VAT. If you pay in Israeli currency (cash), however, VAT will be added to your bill. And do set aside SH30 ($8.82) for the airport tax you must pay when you leave the country.

HOTEL MISCELLANY: Hotels are in five categories, graded according to facilities, location, size, etc. Rates are fixed in dollars, and are government controlled in hotels approved by the Ministry of Tourism. Unless otherwise stated, the rates quoted in this book are for bed and breakfast during the summer season of from March 1980 until February 28, 1981. Most three-, and all four- and five-star hotels are far above our range. Three-star hotels with lower rates have been included, along with one- and two-star hotels. We have also listed officially ungraded hotels which do not meet the standards demanded by the government, but which may suit visitors on a very tight budget. Judea and Samaria hotels are not officially graded, since they are not members of the Israel Hotel Association.

A 50% reduction will be allowed for children up to the age of six, and a 30% reduction for children up to the age of 12, when occupying the same room as their parents.

If you are coming to Israel in high season, you're advised to book accommodations in advance. However, if you haven't done that, head for the **Israel Government Tourist Information Office,** conveniently located in the arrivals hall of the Ben-Gurion Airport.

Rooms in private homes, yet another option, are inspected by the Ministry of Tourism and have to be kept up to a specified standard.

THE ORGANIZATION OF THIS BOOK: This book is a travel guide for the general sightseer as well as a budget handbook on inexpensive and moderately priced hotels, restaurants, and nightspots.

The general sightseeing information is presented with commentary, anecdotes, and personal experiences, in the belief that this is a more human method of communication than the encyclopedic listing of facts and dates. In many instances, you'll have to put up with opinions—but there you have the choice of agreeing or disagreeing, which is something you can't do with facts and dates.

Chapter I will hopefully help you get more out of your trip by briefing you on the many different facets of today's Israel—its land, people, customs, places, and interests. As the chapter also includes "mini-data" on packing, visas, language, and currency; temperatures, telephones, and times; weights, measures, and so forth, it may well save you many frustrations after you arrive. Two sections outline special events, activities, and incentive discounts offered only to tourists and/or students. And there are notes about where to find special help, in case it's ever needed.

Chapter II takes you through the transportation maze. Here you find plane fares to Israel, as well as discounts and money-saving plans which are available to you. In this chapter we also discuss transportation within Israel—by train, bus, taxi, and plane service. A special section cites the many low-cost student opportunities for travel to and within Israel.

Chapters III through X deal with the budget hotels, restaurants, nightspots, tours, and sightseeing attractions of Israel and the Holy Land. Within each of these chapters you'll find discussions of scores of secondary towns and resorts as well as the major cities.

Chapter XI is called "Israeli Adventures" and deals with off-the-beaten-path activities and exotica—and just plain adventures. Here's an idea of what's involved in this chapter: hitchhiking, vacation villages, language schools, remote sightseeing areas, sports, camping sites, youth hostels, Christian hospices.

The kibbutzim (collective farms) of Israel are under scrutiny in *Chapter XII,* and information is given on how to stay on a kibbutz, either as a paying guest or by earning your keep.

Chapter XIII delves into shopping in Israel, including what's unusual and/or a special bargain, plus some notes on how to determine if items are fake or genuine. We offer pointers on the art of bargaining with Bedouins and Arabs, and on which markets or towns have better prices for which wares.

Chapter XIV, finally, offers capsule vocabularies of both Hebrew and Arabic that should be sufficient for your needs.

THE FUTURE OF THIS BOOK: In time, *Israel on $20 a Day* hopes to become a clearing house for the low-cost hotel and restaurant finds of its readers. If you've come across any particularly appealing hotel, restaurant, beach, shop, or bargain, please don't keep it to yourself. We'll send free copies of the next edition of this book to readers whose suggestions are printed in "Readers' Selections" sections to be included in that edition. Send your comments and finds to: Arthur Frommer, Inc., 380 Madison Avenue, New York, N.Y. 10017.

THE $15-DOLLAR-A-DAY CLUB: In this book we'll be looking at how to get your money's worth in Israel, but there is a "device" for saving money and determining value on *all* your trips. It's the popular, international $15-a-Day Travel Club, now in its 16th successful year of operation. The Club was formed at the urging of numerous readers of the $$$-a-Day and Dollarwise Guides, who felt that such an organization could provide continuing travel information and a sense of community to value-minded travelers in all parts of the world. And so it does!

In keeping with the budget concept, the membership fee is low and is immediately exceeded by the value of your benefits. Upon receipt of $10 (U.S. residents), $12 (Canadian and Mexican residents), or $14 (other foreign residents) in U.S. currency to cover one year's membership, we will send all new members, by return mail (book rate), the following items:

(1) The latest edition of *any two* of the following books (please designate in your letter which two you wish to receive):

Europe on $15 a Day
Australia on $15 & $20 a Day
England and Scotland on $20 a Day
Greece and Yugoslavia on $15 & $20 a Day
Hawaii on $25 a Day
Ireland on $15 a Day
Israel on $20 a Day
Mexico and Guatemala on $10 & $15 a Day
New Zealand on $15 & $20 a Day
Scandinavia on $20 a Day
South America on $15 a Day
Spain and Morocco (plus the Canary Is.) on $10 & $15 a Day
Turkey on $10 & $15 a Day
Washington, D.C. on $25 a Day

Dollarwise Guide to the Caribbean (including Bermuda and the Bahamas)
Dollarwise Guide to Canada
Dollarwise Guide to Egypt
Dollarwise Guide to England and Scotland
Dollarwise Guide to France
Dollarwise Guide to Germany
Dollarwise Guide to Italy
Dollarwise Guide to Portugal (plus Madeira and the Azores)
Dollarwise Guide to California and Las Vegas
Dollarwise Guide to New England
Dollarwise Guide to the Southeast and New Orleans
(Dollarwise Guides discuss accommodations and facilities in all price

ranges, with emphasis on the medium-priced.)

The Caribbean Bargain Book
(A one-of-a-kind guide to the "off-season" Caribbean—mid-April to mid-December—and the fabulous resorts that slash their rates from 20% to 60%; includes almost every island group in the Caribbean, and the Bahamas too.)

Where to Stay USA
(By the Council on International Educational Exchange, this extraordinary guide is the first to list accommodations in all 50 states that cost anywhere from $3 to $20 per night.)

(2) A copy of **Arthur Frommer's Guide to New York,** a newly revised pocket-size guide to hotels, restaurants, night spots, and sightseeing attractions in all price ranges throughout the New York area.

(3) A one-year subscription to the quarterly Club newsletter—**The Wonderful World of Budget Travel** (about which more below)—which keeps members up-to-date on fast-breaking developments in low-cost travel to all areas of the world.

(4) A voucher entitling you to a $5 discount on any Arthur Frommer International, Inc. tour booked by you through travel agents in the United States and Canada.

(5) Your personal membership card, which, once received, entitles you to purchase through the Club all Arthur Frommer Publications for a third to a half off their regular retail prices during the term of your membership.

Those are the immediate and definite benefits which we can assure to members of the Club at this time. Further benefits, which it has been our continuing aim to achieve for members, are announced to members in *The Wonderful World of Budget Travel (WWBT)*. An eight-page, full-size newspaper, *WWBT* carries such continuing features as "The Traveler's Directory" (a list of members all over the world who are willing to provide hospitality to other members as they pass through their home cities) and "Share-a-Trip" (offers and requests from members for travel companions who can share costs); worldwide travel news and feature stories by our acclaimed expert travel writers; plus tips and articles on specific plans and methods for travel savings.

If you would like to join this hardy band of international budgeteers and participate in its exchange of travel information and hospitality, simply send your name and address, together with your membership fee of $10 (U.S. residents), $12 (Canadian and Mexican residents), or $14 (other foreign residents) in U.S. currency to: $15-a-Day Travel Club, Inc., 380 Madison Avenue, New York, NY 10017. Remember to specify which *two* of the books in section (1) above you wish to receive in your initial package of members' benefits. Or, if you prefer, use the last page of this book, simply checking off the two books you want and enclosing $10, $12, or $14 in U.S. currency.

Chapter I

MINI-DATA ON MODERN ISRAEL

1. Israel—What It's All About
2. The Basics
3. Especially for Tourists—I.G.T.O.
4. Especially for Students
5. Entertainment in Israel
6. Israeli Foods
7. Packing
8. Books About Israel

BEFORE YOU JET OFF to Israel, do yourself a favor and bone up on the country—it will save you valuable time upon arrival. Much of the information you'll need is packed into this chapter in the form of how-to's, facts and figures. Equally important to understand before you set out, however, is what it is in Israel you're looking for. Israel is a land which represents many different things to many different people, and specific things to all. If you don't plan your trip according to your own personal system of evaluation, you might realize too late that you've missed something you especially wanted to see. Many newcomers to Israel are talked into must-see/must-do deals which prove less meaningful to them than if they had approached the "Promised Land" more personally. Hopefully, this chapter will help you out on this score too.

1. Israel—What It's All About

Most tiny countries have a uniform topography. They're either sandy or rocky, mountainous or flat, high or low, lush or arid. The people who live in such small countries may vary greatly, but usually they possess certain "national" characteristics. Their foods and fashions, customs and cussing, wares and wants possess a thread of similarity.

About the only thing Israel has in common with such countries is size: it is tiny. And about the only thing *all* Israelis have in common is that they're Israelis.

THE LAND: Traveling north to south, east to west, you can't help marveling at the changes in the land: stretches of sandy shores . . . lush and rich valleys and mountainsides . . . rambling foothills and flat plains . . . skybound snow-

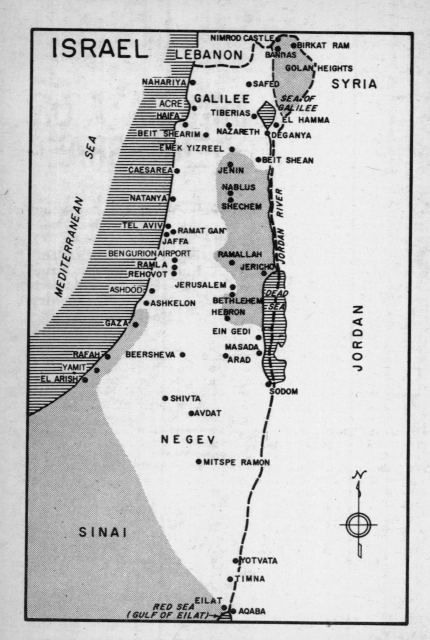

capped peaks . . . body-parching hot wilderness climbing from the mineral-saturated waters of the Dead Sea, lowest and possibly stillest spot on earth . . . lifeline oases in desert regions that vary from shifting sands to hard, cracked mud to the awesome and frighteningly beautiful multicolored crags and crevices of Sinai. So you can't really say Israel is uniform! But wherever you go, one thing is for certain: there you'll find traces and remnants of uncountable centuries of civilization.

THE PEOPLE: Israel's peoples match their land in variety. They vary greatly in looks, customs, speech, personalities. Their particular needs are as devastatingly different as the countries from which they came, whether they arrived to stay in Israel last week, last year, five or six generations ago—or if they happen to be of the few who are descended from "original" stock.

True, with difference comes divergence. Quite astounding progress has been made to bring them together; but Israel is still a country of assorted peoples—and this, to us, is a positive feature of the country. Hebrew—the language excavated, reconstructed and reclaimed after thousands of years of disuse—has probably done more to unite the people than anything else. And the fact that 85% of Israelis are Jewish is also a strong bonding element—whether the individual translates his or her Judaism into strict and orthodox adherency or into a sort of nationalism separate from any religious ideology. The parliamentary democracy of Israel gives all citizens a voice in government (which gets a bit confusing at times), and race, creed, or color set no limitations on citizenship—another point of growing unity, as is compulsory military service for both sexes. Then, too, every effort seems to be made to provide the best possible education, housing, medical, sanitation, technical, and spiritual services and rights for everyone. Of course, any "melting pot" has its tensions, and Israel has its share.

AESTHETICS, RELIGION & NATIONALISM—ISRAEL'S BOON & BANE: Israel is special, if not sacred, to more faiths than any other land mass in the world. Today, to at least 15 different Jewish sects, several Christian sects, Moslems, Druze, Bahais, Samaritans, Circassians, Karaites, Bedouin, and on and on and on, Israel is holy, and although many of the groups claim the land as "their own," the differing faiths are practiced side by side. This calls for daily tolerance, not just of those who adhere to creeds different from yours, but of those who supposedly practice what *you* preach! For instance, there are Jews who visit Israel and return home shaking their heads in woe because it isn't "Jewish" in the way they personally practice or understand Judaism. A Yemenite will tell these visiting Jews that items such as gefilte fish are "gentile" foods—most confusing! Christians traveling in Israel are often perplexed by certain Israeli Christian groups, those who charge entrance fees at holy shrines, those who subdivide famous churches (with actual lines of demarcation on walls and floors) among different sects of Christianity. Protestants are often amazed to find most holy places tended by Catholics; Catholics are surprised to find their Israeli counterparts functioning as they did hundreds (or thousands) of years ago, instead of following modern practices that have spread to most parts of the Catholic world.

And then there's nationalism, which translates here to Zionism. Yes, Israel is the Jewish homeland, fired with a national spirit akin to religious fervor, yet equally secular and political. Many people visit the country today to express or increase their Zionist feelings. Though Israel was founded by dint of Zionism, the form it takes these days disappoints those Zionists who have been removed from the tide of daily life in Israel. Zionism has changed through the years among Israelis themselves, perhaps not so much among those who are Zionists only in spirit. That is not to say that Israelis do not welcome visiting Jews to their country (as a matter of fact, they consider such a visit "a natural action for any Jew"); it is to say, rather, that they welcome everyone to their land, happily, but without great fuss. Israel has come of age.

THE SPIRIT OF ISRAEL: Religion aside, Israel is a country for the young in heart and in spirit. It's been built by youthful energies. It thrives on youth, from the pride of a young mother in her sabra (native-born) son, to the zest with which a 50-year-old reservist races across an infiltration course. A friend of ours, a middle-aged New York artist, made several trips to Israel, each time extending her visit, until at last she came to stay. In Manhattan, she confided, she felt age closing in about her. In Israel, riding about the countryside or visiting friends on a kibbutz, she felt ten years younger.

Perhaps what gives Israel this particular youthful spirit is not so much the young people themselves and what they accomplish, but the feeling of perseverance, optimism, and idealism—traditionally associated with youth—that infused every facet of Israeli life.

2. The Basics

VISAS: They're given free to U.S. citizens, without prior application, when they enter Israel and show valid U.S. passports. Good for three months, the tourist visa can be extended for another three consecutive months at any office of the Ministry of the Interior. To work, study, or settle in Israel, you need the proper permit before arrival. If you plan to visit Arab countries, ask for a separate visa (if your passport is stamped by the Israelis, that stamp will close most Arab-world doors). Americans need no smallpox certificate unless they've spent the 14 days immediately prior to entering Israel in a country where there's been a recent smallpox outbreak (same applies for Europeans or Canadians).

CURRENCY AND COSTS: The Israeli unit of currency is now the shekel. It is divided into 100 *agorot,* sometimes called *grush, prutot,* or *piastre.* Through this book we shall use the terms shekels and agorot when speaking of Israeli currency. As we went to press a symbol to denote shekels had not been decided, and so throughout this book we have used the abbreviation "SH."

Foreign currency can be exchanged at banks, travel agencies, most hotels, and at shops that cater especially to tourists. Special bank offices are open round-the-clock near custom-clearance desks at all ports of entry into Israel, giving you a chance to change money before getting a bus or taxi to your first destination.

Finally, while the Israeli shekel plummets downward, oil hikes are forcing airfares in the opposite direction. As of this writing, the fares quoted in Chapter II are valid and up-to-date. The latest details are easily obtainable from any reputable travel agent or international airline.

LANGUAGE: English is Israel's major international language. Street and road signs are in English, Hebrew, and Arabic. English will suffice in virtually every shop, restaurant, and hotel in the three major cities, as well as most other places. If, however, you chance to encounter a storekeeper who speaks only Russian, Polish, Yiddish, or one of the 17 or so other relatively common languages, just look for his 12-year-old son, who's studying English in school.

If you find yourself groping for another language, try French, German, or Yiddish. Most Israelis with Slavic origins know French, and most of the Israelis of North African birth—the thousands and thousands who come from Morocco, Algeria, and Tunisia—also speak fluent French.

But Hebrew is the national language, followed by Arabic. You can use our glossary at the back of the book as a crutch, and you'll find that your stabs at speaking Hebrew will be warmly appreciated. For predominantly Arab areas, we've added an Arabic glossary, too.

A Note About English Spellings

You will doubtless notice when traveling in Israel, or just reading about it (in this book as well as any other), that the English spellings of Hebrew or Arabic place names is haphazard, to say the least. That's because the Hebrew and Arabic alphabets are different from the English alphabet and transliterating the Hebrew or Arabic characters into English characters does get a bit hairy. Thus you see a town like Netanya spelled "Natanya" or "Natania." Or Eilat, "Elath," or Ashkelon, "Askqelon." And on and on. The basic rule to follow is: if it sounds the same as the place you're looking for, it is the same—forget about the exact spelling.

CLIMATE: The range of average temperatures (average low and average high) in Israel, stated in terms of Fahrenheit degrees, follow:

	Jan.	March	May	July	Sept.	Nov.
Jerusalem	45-57	52-66	61-80	67-83	66-82	54-66
Tel Aviv	48-66	55-71	60-79	71-87	70-83	55-75
Haifa	51-62	55-70	62-76	71-83	72-83	59-70
Tiberias	54-69	57-79	68-92	77-98	72-96	62-77
Eilat	52-72	67-75	73-97	80-105	80-100	59-82

Actually, Israel uses the Centigrade system, which, because the numbers are smaller, often deceives Americans into thinking that it doesn't get all that hot in Israel.

If you're a scientifically minded type who wants to know that exact Fahrenheit equivalent, multiply the Centigrade reading by 9, then divide by 5, and add 32 degrees. But when you get Centigrade temperatures over 40 degrees, forget about converting—just stay out of the sun.

The Israeli seasons are somewhat different from those in America and Western Europe. To start with, the Israeli winter doesn't normally involve snow—although there are occasional flurries every couple of years in Jerusalem and the Upper Galilee, and Mount Hermon on the Golan Heights is snow-covered. Winter in Israel starts with some showers in October, and continues through a time of periodic heavy rainfalls from November to March. In most parts of the country, you need sweaters and medium-weight coats during the winter. Swimming is out in the Mediterranean during this time, except during occasional heat waves, although you can definitely swim in Eilat and the Dead Sea in the winter.

From March to September, it seldom rains at all. Nevertheless, at the beginning of March the entire country seems to turn green; in the months that follow the heat gathers intensity, reaching its peak in July and August, when the only relatively cool spots are Jerusalem and the high mountains around Safed (where you'll sometimes need a sweater in the evenings). The landscape is dry and parched by late August, but by September the temperatures are falling off a bit. The October rains are the herald of a new winter's arrival.

Generally, Israel's Mediterranean climate is somewhat similar to that of southern California: days of brilliant sunshine, intense summer heat, breezy nights, the coastal winds of winter. However, California doesn't know about the hot and dry easterly winds that often plague Israel at the beginning and end of the summer, usually May and September. These are the easterlies, the *khamseen,* from the Arabic word meaning "fifty," since the wind was traditionally believed to blow for fifty days a year; thankfully, it doesn't.

WEIGHTS & MEASURES: We've already discussed the conversion of Centigrade readings into Fahrenheit, and there are several other measuring units using the metric system that you'll want to understand.

For example, liquids in Israel are sold by the liter—which is, roughly, about one quart. In purchasing gasoline, remember that four liters are about equivalent to a gallon.

Solids are weighed in grams and kilograms. Israelis call the latter simply "kilos." One kilogram, 1,000 grams, equals 2.2 pounds.

Distances: signs and maps are measured in kilometers, one kilometer being equivalent to .62 miles. The simplest method of conversion from kilometers to miles is to multiply the kilometers by six tenths, or 60%. Thereby, for example, 300 kilometers become 180 miles.

You may notice that when tracts of land are described, they are measured in dunams. A dunam is roughly a quarter of an acre.

ELECTRICAL EQUIPMENT: The electric current used in Israel is 220 A.C., 50 cycles. If you bring an electric shaver, iron or non-transistor radio, you can buy an inexpensive transformer in Israel to convert the current to the American voltage cycle. Or you can buy 220-voltage equipment at special shops in New York that can be directly used in Israel.

"DUTIFUL" CUSTOMS: You can bring $75 worth of tax-free gifts into the country. You can also bring in a carton of cigarettes, one bottle of liquor, and a reasonable amount of film. When you leave you can convert up to $3,000 back into foreign currency at the airport, so keep your bank receipts.

POSTAL NOTES: Post offices, identified by a blue sign with a white leaping deer, are open from 8 a.m. to 6 or 8 p.m. (on Fridays from 8 a.m. to 2 p.m.). The smaller branch offices close in the middle of the day, from 12:30 to 4 p.m., when nearly every sensible citizen takes a short nap.

Nowadays, an air-letter costs SH1.20 (35¢) to the States and Europe. A regular U.S.- or Europe-bound letter in an envelope requires SH2 (59¢) air mail postage for the first ten grams. The average envelope within Israel runs SH.27 (8¢). An air-mail postcard is SH.95 (28¢) to the U.S.A., SH.80 (24¢) to Europe.

TELEPHONES: Large quantities of patience and understanding are necessary when trying to make telephone connections in Israel. It's not that the equipment's bad—it's fully automatic, and all phones have direct-dial—it's just that there are fewer lines and phones in comparison to what most tourists have back home. So you can spend several minutes just trying to get a clear line and dial your number. Aside from that, you'll find the process similar to Stateside telephoning.

To save money, try making all your calls from public telephones—which can be found in street booths, in hotels, in many restaurants and most public places, as well as in all post offices. You'll need special tokens to operate most phones, and we suggest you stock up at a post office, where they're SH.25 (7¢) each. A public telephone **local call** requires one token for unlimited time; many hotel and restaurant phones are connected to time-tallying meters. For a **zonal call,** the charges mount according to distance, duration, and time of day. A long-distance—**inter-zonal**—call requires an area code plus number, and also costs according to distance, duration, and time of day. If you can't find a number in the English telephone directory, dial 14 for **information,** although you'll be charged for it, unless it is not listed. For information on **international direct dialing** phone 195.

For the **time** dial 15; for **weather** dial 03-625231. Dialing 100 reaches the **police,** and 101 gets **first aid.** Dialing 14 will let you know the hours when the **Sabbath** and/or Jewish **holidays** start and end (this information can also be found in the newspapers). **Airport arrivals** can be checked by dialing 03-614656 and **departures** at 03-971461.

Except when making local calls, Israel's phone system requires an area code before the actual number. Tel Aviv and the airport are 03; Jerusalem is 02; Haifa 04, and Netanya 053. Other codes are easily obtainable from the map in the phone book.

PHOTOGRAPHY: The variety of colors, landscapes, dwellings, and peoples make Israel a shutterbug's paradise. Fortunately, all sorts of film can be bought almost anywhere in the country, to refuel cameras of folks who find they just can't snap the pictures fast enough. However, as film is more expensive in Israel than in the U.S., budgeteers will probably prefer to bring extra rolls with them. As for developing, Israel is geared to process color and black and white, but most tourists mail or tote exposed film home for that. Since the sun's so bright, and reflections tend to get glaring, many "pro" photographers use special filters to soften such effects. If you're really a photography fanatic, we suggest you investigate this, and other special photographic conditions in Israel, before leaving home—a Stateside Israeli Government Tourist Office or Israeli Consulate can guide your research, and there are several books about it. Aside from that, there are only three restrictions on picture-taking in Israel: certain military areas—which are plainly marked in several languages as no-photo territories; aerial photography over inland routes without special permission; certain people—who use their own sign language (usually hands over face) to let you know they don't want to be photographed. Most of the time, such people are simply following a religious interpretation linking photos to "graven images," although sometimes they are actually afraid that a photo can capture or control some of their personal essence or soul.

TIME: In Tel Aviv, it's seven hours later than it is in New York (unless New York is on Daylight Saving Time, in which case the difference is six hours).

BUSINESS HOURS: The banks are open from 8:30 a.m. to 12:30 p.m. and from 4 to 5:30 p.m.—except on Wednesdays, when they're closed all afternoon. On Fridays, the hours are 8:30 a.m. to noon.

Some shops keep to a schedule of 8 a.m. to 1 p.m. and 4 to 7 p.m., Sunday through Thursday; they generally close for the Sabbath by 2 or 3 p.m. on Fridays and don't re-open until Sunday morning.

You can visit government offices on weekdays, usually from 7:30 or 8 a.m. Some offices are closed to the public on Fridays, and all are closed on Saturdays; they are open during summer weekdays till 1 or 3 p.m.; in winter months they remain open until 2 or 4 p.m.

In Bethlehem, Nazareth, Ramallah, and other Arab or Christian cities, the Israel Government Tourist Offices are open Saturdays and closed Sundays. Otherwise, I.G.T.O. doors are open from 8 a.m. to 6 p.m. daily during the summer, till 5 p.m. during the winter. On Fridays, they close at 3 p.m. in summer, 2 or 3 p.m. in winter.

THE SABBATH IN ISRAEL: The Bible states that the seventh day is one of rest—a time when no fires are lit, no money handled, no business transacted and so forth. So that's the way it is in most of Israel, where the Sabbath is celebrated on Saturday. By two or three of a Friday afternoon (the Israeli Sabbath begins at sundown), most shops have closed for the day; buses and trains stop running an hour later, and the movie houses are closed at night with the exception of a few maverick movie theaters in Tel Aviv. Then, on Saturday, almost all shops are closed (except a few cafes plus Arab or Christian establishments), and nearly all transportation stops (only Haifa has bus service at this time, and only taxis or small sherut companies ply in or between cities). Most admission-free museums ordinarily open for part of the Sabbath; entrance tickets, when required, must be bought in advance. Many strictly kosher restaurants follow this same no-money-handling rule, accepting only advance prepaid orders for Sabbath meals, which will often be served cold (cooked in advance). Also, do watch for signs in restaurants or hotel dining rooms asking you not to smoke on the Sabbath, so as not to offend some Orthodox guests.

If you want to drive on Saturday, it's up to you. About the only people who'll try to stop you are the ultra-religious Jews, such as those in Jerusalem's Mea Shearim section. There they tend to get rather heated about those who break their particular interpretation of the Sabbath. However, if you steer clear of such areas, you'll find that some Israelis do indeed take to the roads on Saturdays—going on picnics, to the beaches, to visit friends and family. Almost all gas stations are open on the Sabbath. Precise Sabbath commencement information is available from local newspapers.

Israelis work six days a week, and as most everything is shut down on Friday nights, they make Saturday nights their stay-up-late-and-have-a-party time. By sundown transportation services resume, and movie houses begin selling tickets for evening shows. By dark, all entertainment places are usually packed full, including the many sidewalk cafes in all cities. Come Sunday morning, all these folks return to work again, waiting for another Saturday night to roll around.

ISRAEL'S UNUSUAL CALENDAR(S): If awards were given for "daily" confusion, or for having the maximum number of holidays a year, Israel would probably win them all. First, the country "officially" operates on two separate systems for determining day, month, and year: The Jewish Calendar (charted from Creation, which they date, as of this writing late in 1979, as 5740 years ago) and the Gregorian Calendar (a Christian system named for Pope Gregory XIII, and used in most countries, including the U.S.). Recognized, but "unofficial," are even more dating systems—such as the Julian (Julius Caesar) Calendar, which runs 13 days behind the Gregorian; or the Moslem Era, dating from 622 A.D., when the Prophet Mohammed hied from Mecca to Medina. Not only do these calendars disagree about the date, but also about whether time is measured by sun, moon, or a combination, and when the year should start and end. (We've never calculated how many New Year celebrations occur each year in Israel, but we do know of at least three Christmases.)

Holidays

Jewish holidays can disrupt a tourist's visit due to restrictions on public transportation, entertainment, and commerce. Here is a list of the major religious holidays, with the season or month in which they occur:

Rosh Hashanah (Jewish New Year) is the start of the High Holy Days. Since the calendar starts in September or October, that's when the New Year falls. It is a two-day religious festival, not an occasion for revels but rather for solemn contemplation and prayer.

It culminates with **Yom Kippur** (the Day of Atonement), which is the most solemn of all Jewish holidays. Observant Jews spend nearly the whole day in synagogue. Places of worship are crowded, but the large synagogues reserve seats for tourists, and some of the larger hotels organize their own services. Yom Kippur is a fast day, but hotel dining rooms serve guests who wish to eat. Everything comes to a standstill. There is no vehicular traffic, beaches and swimming pools are deserted, restaurants, cafes, and entertainment places are closed—even television and radio stations suspend broadcasts.

Closely following Yom Kippur is **Succoth,** a seven-day period for recalling how Moses and the Children of Israel dwelled in "booths" as they left Egypt to wander in the desert. Observant families have meals and services in specially built, highly decorated yet simple huts, located outside in gardens or on balconies. Succoth is also a harvest festival (the Feast of the Tabernacles) and thus a kibbutz favorite. On the first day of Succoth Sabbath-like restrictions are observed. It culminates with **Simchat Torah,** when Jews rejoice that they have the Torah (the Law); street festivities in Jerusalem and Tel Aviv mark this day. On Simchat Torah, cantors read the final verses of the Torah (the first five books of the Bible), and then start again at its beginning.

Pesach, or Passover, which occurs in the spring, has further restrictions. No bread, beer, or other foods containing leavening are obtainable for eight days, and hotel and restaurant meals may cost more because of the culinary complexities. The first night is devoted to a seder, a family meal and ritual recalling the exodus of the ancient Israelites from Egypt. Many hotels and restaurants have special seders for tourists (the I.G.T.O. can direct you). The first and last days of this holiday are Sabbath-like affairs, which means the country more or less closes down.

The last religious holiday with restrictions is **Shavuoth,** the harvest celebration of Pentecost that occurs in May or June. A joyous time, it is a special favorite of agricultural settlements. It is often marked by special plays, entertainment, and children dressed in white, wearing floral crowns. Since it also recalls the receipt of the Ten Commandments, plus the bringing of the "first fruits" to the First Temple, it is observed as a religious holiday.

Semi-religious holidays, where Sabbath-like prohibitions do not apply:

Chanukah, which falls in December, celebrates the victory of the Maccabees over Syrian-Greeks and the consequent rededication of the Temple in 164 B.C. The menorah, the symbol of this holiday, is lit nightly for the eight nights of the festival.

March ushers in the Feast of Lots, **Purim,** remembering the time (Fifth century B.C.) when Queen Esther saved her people in Persia. This is an exciting time (so too the food) when folks dress up in fancy costumes, have parties, parade in the streets, give gifts, and generally make merry.

Ending 33 days of mourning, **Lag b'Omer,** in May, is the chief happy celebration for the Hasidim, who leave Jerusalem and other cities at this time to sing and dance around bonfires at the Meron tomb of the mystical Rabbi Shimon Bar Yohai, in the Galilee. Children around the country also sing, dance, and light bonfires.

The Israeli Arbor Day—**Tu b'Shevat**—comes in January or February, with thousands of schoolchildren singing, dancing, and traipsing off to plant trees all over the country.

The fast day of **Tisha b'Av,** in July or August, is a time set aside to remember the destruction of the First (587 B.C.) and Second (70 A.D.) Temples.

NEWSPAPERS, RADIO, & TV: At most newsstands in Israel, you'll find publications in many languages, from Israel and around the world. Though many tongues are used by the local press, only one paper is printed in English—the *Jerusalem Post,* a daily which sells for SH1.40 (41¢); SH2.20 (65¢) for the Friday "weekend" edition that comes complete with magazine section. Also in English is the *International Herald Tribune.* It's usually available the same day it's printed, always by the next day.

For latest-news addicts, the radio Voice of Israel broadcasts six 15-30 minute English-language news summaries daily, at 7 a.m., 2, 6, 8, and 10 p.m., and 12:30 a.m. It's usually easy to tune in on one of the frequent broadcasts of Britain's BBC or the Voice of America. Turning the radio dial can be fun in Israel: you'll find great diversity in music, news, plays, and moderated shows in several languages, from several countries, on three different wave lengths.

Television is young, but active. You might enjoy viewing the several hours of commercial-free shows daily. Many presentations are pre-packaged from England, France, and the U.S., and you can often catch English-language films. (The Hebrew and Arabic news broadcasts are fun too, even if you don't understand them.) Programming usually consists of the following: one hour of children's entertainment from 5:30–6:30 p.m.; Arabic shows and news from 6:30–8 p.m.; and a mixture of news, and Hebrew and English programs until midnight.

WHERE TO GO FOR SPECIAL HELP: For numbers to call in the event of a genuine emergency, turn back to the "Telephone" section above. Most telephone operators and police personnel speak English and will assist you in finding any special help you may need, if not helping you themselves. Hopefully, you'll never need emergency assistance.

You might, however, need or want something for sunburns or minor physical discomforts, in which case you'd look for one of the many **pharmacies,** or chemist shops, in all towns and cities. In Israel, unlike in the States, pharmacists are allowed to advise about medicines and medications, and can sell you many items that would require a prescription in the U.S. In fact, unless the medicine you require is in the addictive-drug category, you can buy it by simply asking in most pharmacies.

If you need a pill at night, Friday afternoon, or on Saturday, when drug-stores are closed, don't panic: check the *Jerusalem Post* or the door of the nearest pharmacy for a list of pharmacies on round-the-clock emergency duty in your area.

If a pharmacy can't fill your medical needs, the **Israel Medical Association** can suggest a local medical doctor. Then there's the **Magen David Adom** (Israel's Red Shield), and numerous modern hospitals and clinics. There are plenty of American doctors around too, and the U.S. Embassy can suggest several for whatever ails you.

Your country's **embassy** is ready to help with any passport or visa problem, any legal matters, any business or financial queries—actually, it's there for most any kind of help you need.

AND THEN SOME: Barber shops and **beauty parlors** abound in the cities and towns, ranging from expensive to cheap, with elegant or plain-basic styling. Hotel shops are more expensive, but you can at least be sure the stylist will understand your language and trim, curl, or color as you dictate. . . . If you're one of the thousands of parents who bring their children along to Israel, the time may come when you want a **babysitter.** On the spur of the moment you'll never find one, but if you plan a day or two in advance, your hotel will try to help arrange this service. . . . **Dry cleaning** and **laundry services** are available almost everywhere—see below for more details. . . . To **tip** or not is up to you in Israel, where tipping has become established practice in some of the more touristy places, but is unknown in most others. You may want to know that wherever you eat, drink or sleep, you pay a mandatory service fee anyway.

3. Especially for Tourists—I.G.T.O.

Being a tourist today in Israel is lots more fun and interesting than ever before, thanks mostly to the many services of the Israel Government Tourist Offices (I.G.T.O.). They exist for one purpose only: to serve the tourist. Located in almost every city and nearly all major sightseeing destinations, they can provide you with details and advice concerning hotels, tours, events of current interest, shopping, almost any other matters which concern you, including dealing with complaints against those bearing their emblems. Branches are opened from 8 a.m. to 6 p.m., Fridays until 3 p.m. The following listing gives addresses, area codes and telephone numbers of the I.G.T.O. offices in Israel. The Haifa Port facilities, incidentally, are open only when passenger ships dock.

Jerusalem	24 King George St.	Tel. 02-241281/2
	Jaffa Gate	Tel. 02-282295/6
Tel Aviv	7 Mendele St.	Tel. 03-223266/7
Haifa	18 Herzl St.	Tel. 04-666521/3
	Haifa Port, Shed 12	Tel. 04-663988
	Shed 14	Tel. 04-645692
Ben-Gurion Airport	Main Hall	Tel. 03-971485
Tiberias	8 El Hadeff St.	Tel. 067-20992
Beersheba	120 Herzl St.	Tel. 057-36001
Eilat	New Commercial Center	Tel. 059-2268
Safed	Municipality Building	Tel. 067-30633

Bat Yam	Ben-Gurion Rd.	Tel. 03-889766
Nazareth	Casanova St.	Tel. 065-73003
Ashkelon	Afridar Commercial Center	Tel. 051-32412
Arad	Commercial Center	Tel. 057-98144
Bethlehem	Manger Square	Tel. 02-742591
Netanya	Ha'atzmauth Square	Tel. 053-27286
Nahariya	Egged Bus Station	Tel. 04-922126

Each year, I.G.T.O. comes up with new and exciting events and plans (check with the I.G.T.O. each place you go), and also repeat some favorite events each season:

MEET THE ISRAELIS: I.G.T.O. sponsors a program whereby you can meet Israelis in their homes and share a cup of tea with the family. The idea is to bring together people of similar interests and backgrounds. If, for example, you're an architect and want to talk shop with an Israeli architect, you need only apply to the I.G.T.O., which will set it up for you.

FOLKLORE EVENINGS: The spirit of both modern and ancient Israel is reflected in song and dance at these weekly sessions in Israel's large cities. Folklore Evening in Jerusalem is generally Wednesday at the Khan. The situation is similar in Tel Aviv, Friday evenings at the Z.O.A. House. Check with the Tourist Information Office for details.

VISITORS' FORUM: For the thousand-and-one questions that most visitors want to ask, I.G.T.O. offers weekly question-and-answer sessions. A panel of local experts does the answering. Between March and October, the Forums are held every two weeks in the three main cities (from November to February, they are scheduled less regularly). There is no entrance fee. Check with I.G.-T.O. in each city for time, place and date.

PLANT A TREE: To many people, Israel was first associated with the act of dropping coins into a rectangular blue and white box. There were thousands of such boxes and the coins went toward planting trees in Israel. As a result of all those coins, as well as other donations and the labor of many workmen, the **Keren Kayemet** (Jewish National Fund) has planted about 130 million in Israel.

Some tourists come to Israel with their certificates in hand, with the expectation that they can look upon the tree they donated for planting. Unfortunately, it doesn't work that way, unless perhaps you gave thousands of dollars and they planted a grove in your name.

Once in Israel, however, you *can* plant a tree—and with your own hands—and feel some connection with the physical development and beauty of the country. This emotional outlet for sightseers was established by the Jewish National Fund. It costs $5 a tree, and the J.N.F. will tell you how it's done.

You have a choice of five main forests: **Mount Birya**, near Safed; **Balfour**, close to Nazareth; the **Jerusalem Peace Forest**, overlooking United Jerusalem; the **American Bicentennial Park** on the road to the famous Soreq Cave; and at **Golani Crossroads** on Nazareth–Tiberias Highway. You will be given a certificate and a badge. Check with the Keren Kayemet directly: in Jerusalem, at the head office, King George and Keren Kayemet Sts., tel. 02-635261; in Tel Aviv, 96 Hayarkon St., tel. 03-234449.

DISCOUNTS: Alone, or in cooperation with other organizations, I.G.T.O. has arranged some very nice special discounts for tourists in Israel. Instead of paying to enter each archeological site or national park, you can buy a $3.50 ticket at the office of the **National Parks Authority,** 3 Khet St., Hakirya, Tel Aviv (tel. 03-252281). It will get you into all 29 sites and parks during any two-week period. The above rate is for adults of 18 or over. Children or students pay for entry in each national park or site from SH.80 (24¢) to SH1.80 (53¢).

V.T.S.: If you happen to spot a sweet little lady wearing a badge imprinted with "V.T.S.," you know immediately she's your friend—a member of Israel's Voluntary Tourist Service. You'll find these helpful volunteers at the Arrivals Hall of Ben-Gurion Airport Sunday through Thursday (except Jewish holidays) from 5 to 10 p.m., and at major hotels from about 6 to 8:30 p.m. They are ready to offer assistance in locating friends or relatives, arranging home hospitality, answering any questions, etc. And should a tourist fall ill and be hospitalized, members of V.T.S. tend to his or her daily needs. V.T.S. has offices in Tel Aviv at 28 Bialik St., tel. 03-50919; in Jerusalem at Jaffa Gate, tel. 02-288140; in Haifa at 10 Ahad Haam St., Hadar, tel. 04-665645, and in Eilat, tel. 059-2344. These offices are open from 8:30 a.m. to 1 p.m., daily except Saturdays and Jewish holidays.

4. Especially for Students

The discounts offered to students traveling in Israel are unequalled anywhere else in the world. Students are treated royally, via an elaborate program of reductions that lower the tab in youth hostels and hotels, on buses and trains, car rentals, even in swimming pools, restaurants and sundry places of entertainment. Your passports for these savings are, first, the **International Student Identity Card** (available in the U.S. from the Council on International Educational Exchange, William Sloane House, 354 West 34th Street, New York, N.Y. 10001, tel. 695-0291; the fee is $3, and you must present proof of full-time student status; write for information) and the **International Youth Hostel Card** (available in the U.S. from American Youth Hostels, Inc., Delaplane, Virginia 22025; the fee is $7 or $14, depending on your age; write for information).

When you arrive in Israel, make your first stop at **ISSTA,** the Israeli National Student Travel Association, which offers a never-tiring helping hand to students and does an excellent job of looking after visiting young people. ISSTA offices in Israel: Tel Aviv, 109 Ben Yehuda St., tel. 03-274164/5; Jerusalem, 5 Eliashar St., tel. 02-231418; and in Haifa, Beit Hakranoth, 16/20 Herzl St., tel. 04-669139. Hours are usually 9 a.m. to 1 p.m. and 3 to 6 p.m.; offices close on Wednesday and Friday at 1 p.m. and all day Saturday. ISSTA's range of student activities—and they are plentiful—can be found at the end of Chapter II. By the way, in the United States, ISSTA is represented by **CIEE/ SOFA Student Travel Services** at the above-listed CIEE address, it might be worth your while to contact them before planning your trip.

If you've arrived in Israel equipped with the above-mentioned cards, then you can go directly, without any further ado, to the central train and bus stations in any of the three major cities to receive discounts on their routes throughout the country. You can also get a 10% discount on car rental from various companies.

And, should a student really need someone to talk to, he or she can call one of Israel's many colleges or universities and ask for the **Foreign Student Advisor.**

In the following chapters, we list the student facilities available in each particular area, and in Chapter XI we present a complete list of youth hostels in Israel—but since this is not a student book per se, we cannot present *all* the relevant data students and young people ought to know. Incidentally, students should always show student cards when requesting reductions. This tack might work even in cases where an establishment is not advertising student discounts. For this we recommend you get a copy of the *Whole World Handbook,* prepared by the Council on International Educational Exchange, which presents a complete round-up of information about travel, study and work for students and young people in Israel (and the rest of the world). The book is available at bookstores—or we'll be glad to send you a copy (see the last page of this book).

5. Entertainment in Israel

In this area, Israel has loads to offer, with something for every personality and pocketbook. Movie houses can be found in every city and town, and films are part of the standard fare at kibbutzim and desert camping villages. Some city cinemas go so far as to have non-stop shows; others have two or three presentations daily. Nighttime shows are usually at 7 and 9 p.m., but it's always best to check. You can pay SH7.50 ($2.20) or more, depending on the film and where you sit. By the way, the films often are in English, with Hebrew and French subtitles, so you'll seldom find a language barrier.

For live performances, you've a batch to choose from—including large and small companies ranging in quality from amateur to professional. Theater productions—plays and musicals—vary from the latest Broadway hits to new works, old favorites and classics. Most productions are in Hebrew, although some smaller companies stage productions in English or Yiddish. There are also several dance groups and companies performing everything from classical ballet to modern jazz and folk dances, and then there's the **National Opera** company in Tel Aviv. (For specific data on the Opera House, check their box office at 1 Allenby Rd., tel. 03-57228, Friday's *Jerusalem Post,* or billboards.)

Israel has an excellent reputation for producing fine music and musicians. If you can get a seat for an **Israeli Philharmonic Orchestra** concert, grab it. If not, try for tickets to any of the several other orchestra or chamber ensemble performances. If the classics are not exactly your cup of musical tea, ask I.G.T.O. or local ticket agencies about folk music and other types of concerts that are also part of the usual bill of entertainment fare in Israel.

During July and August, as well as the Passover season, you can enjoy the Israel Festival and the **Ein Gev Music Festival.** Each summer, the Israel Festival offers musical and dramatic performances by leading internationals, presented throughout the country. But there's something extra-special about taking it in under the stars in the restored Roman amphitheater at Caesarea, where you feel occasional breezes from the nearby Mediterranean and realize that you're sitting here like folks did ages ago—King Herod, for one. In springtime at Ein Gev, a kibbutz on the Galilee shore, a big, fancy auditorium houses most performances of the Ein Gev Music Festival.

Other festivals in Israel aren't quite so well known or established, but again, check with I.G.T.O. to see what's up. The **International Harp Contest** is held every three years in Israel, and you won't want to miss the international choir festival, the **Zimriya,** another once-in-three-years event.

There are concerts of light, classical and pop music held at the Yarkon Park at Rokach St. near Tel Aviv's Exhibition Grounds on Tuesday and Saturday evenings during July and August. Programs begin at 8:30 p.m. on Tuesday and 9 p.m. on Saturdays and last for about two hours. No fee, and you sit on the grass. These concerts are usually advertised on billboards. There is also folk dancing in front of Tel Aviv's City Hall on Saturday evenings beginning about 8:30 p.m. during July and August.

Some people would rather do their own singing and dancing, and Israel has places for that, too: nightclubs, discos, community houses and so forth. Some are tailored to youngsters, serving no alcoholic beverages; others have crowds of mixed ages, and serve alcohol as a general rule. There are floor shows in many places, with entertainers who juggle, clown, sing and dance, mime, make magic, even strip.

Then there is the **Jerusalem International Book Fair,** held every two years in the city's Binyanei Ha'uma Convention Centre, and lasting one week. It attracts dealers, publishers and authors from all over the world.

Also in Jerusalem, a week-long **Arts and Crafts Fair** is held in Hutzot Hayotzer Plaza during the spring. Amateur artists and craftsmen exhibit their works in booths.

In Tel Aviv during the spring, an **Arts and Crafts Fair** and a **Book Fair** are held for one week. The large plaza in front of the Municipality Building holds the Book Fair where publishers display a vast number of books at reduced prices. The Arts and Crafts Fair is held at the same time on Chen Blvd. which is festooned with colored lights.

There are more museums than seem possible in such a small land. Small galleries abound, and there are a number of thriving artists' colonies around the country. Key colonies are in Ein Hod, Safed, Jaffa, and Jerusalem; at each you can visit artists' homes and studios.

SPORTS: If you're a doer rather than a watcher, you'll find it possible to combine sporting activities with much of your sightseeing. The summer is terrific for water sports in seas, lakes, springs, and pools. Skin-diving enthusiasts can flipper through what's often called the world's greatest underwater scenery in the Red Sea at Eilat or Sharm-el-Sheikh. Fully stocked sporting centers flourish around those areas, where all equipment, as well as underwater guides and instructors, can be hired. Above-water sports—skiing, boating, surfing, swimming—also thrive around Eilat, plus all along Israel's strip of golden Mediterranean beach, at the Sea of Galilee, and in the many public or hotel pools scattered all over the land.

Basketball runs a close second to soccer as the nation's most popular sport; games are frequent, and I.G.T.O. and ticket offices can provide the when-where details. More on sports in Chapter XI.

PARKS: There is an abundance of archeological sites and National Parks throughout the country and, with the exception of Masada, they are open as follows: April–September, 8 a.m. to 5 p.m.; October–March, 8 a.m. to 4 p.m. Friday and holiday evenings, the parks close one hour earlier. High holidays, they close two hours earlier and, on Yom Kippur are completely shut. Masada hours are 7:30 a.m. to 3:30 p.m. year round except Yom Kippur. For further information: National Parks Authority, 3 Khet St. Hakirya, P.O. Box 7028, Tel Aviv, tel. 03-252281.

6. Israeli Foods

For most travelers, Israeli foods are an altogether novel experience. With the country's population swelled by immigrants from 70 countries, it is only natural that a rather diverse cuisine should have developed through the years.

We can group the cooking into three main types: **European** (which means Polish, French, German, Viennese and Hungarian), **dairy-vegetarian** (including the traditional Jewish dishes) and **oriental** (originating not in the Orient, but in the Middle East and the Levant). Nearly all hotels and a good number of restaurants are kosher.

Breakfast is likely to be the most startling meal of the day. Time was when the hardy settlement workers had to pack away a 5 a.m. feast sufficient for the next seven hours in the fields. Tourists may not have quite so arduous a day ahead of them, but Israeli hotels do serve up overwhelming breakfasts. Many hotels have buffet tables laden with fresh vegetables, various cheeses, boiled eggs, olives, herring, sardines, etc., with coffee and rolls in accompaniment.

Lunch and dinner vary according to taste and pocketbook, often accentuating dairy products and vegetables. Israeli meat is plentiful, but substandard compared with American cuts. Poultry, however, is good and evident everywhere.

Here's a description of the more common local foods:

Pitta: A flat, pancake-shaped Arab bread, chewy and split in the middle.

Felafel: Sold like hot dogs by street vendors, felafel consists of small balls of deep-fried ground chick peas, spiced with peppers, plus salad, cole slaw, tchina, and condiments and eaten within the split pitta.

Humus: A paste made from ground chick peas and olive oil.

Tchina: Like humus, but made from ground sesame seeds, giving it a peanut-butterish sort of taste.

Eshel, leben: Like sour cream, only thinner.

Shamenet: Like sour cream, only thicker.

Kabab: Chopped and spiced lamb or turkey broiled on a skewer.

Shashlik: Pieces of lamb or beef or turkey, charcoal-broiled on a skewer, flavored with onions and tomatoes.

Bamia: Okra prepared with a thick, juicy tomato sauce.

Shwarma: Lamb or turkey, grilled on a spit and served in small pieces.

And don't forget that when you order coffee in a cafe, you might get one of four varieties. Be specific: there's Turkish coffee, thick and sweet; Nescafe, sometimes called Nes; ragil (regular); and botz (literally mud), which is coffee grounds with boiling water poured on top.

One last note, Israel is a hot country and sanitary conditions should be observed. Wash all fruit and vegetables and resist meat from outdoor street stands when in doubt.

7. Packing

Everything you'll need in Israel you can buy right there, but if you prefer to come prepared, here's a list of items you'll find useful or necessary: a stopper for sink or tub, as many hotels don't have them; a plastic bottle of soap liquid for your wash-and-wears; tissues to carry at all times, as many public restrooms lack paper or at least the kind you're used to. Add sun-screening lotion, sunglasses and a shade hat and consider all three utterly vital necessities. Insect repellent is another item we wouldn't travel without, especially if we're headed for the Dead Sea or desert regions. If you're planning on long walks or hiking, a canteen will come in handy. Cosmetics and personal toiletries come next, and a plastic bottle of astringent can be mighty welcome when you're touring around. Some travelers include a supply of tablets for relief of miscellaneous aches and upsets. Then they stuff in some extra rolls of film, safety pins, and a small sewing kit. Again, you can buy all such things in Israel, but the prices are quite high on some of these items, whether locally made or imported.

As for clothing, there are no hard and fast rules on what is or isn't proper gear. You'll see almost everything, from ancient dress to modern fads and fashions, so let comfort guide your personal selection of styles. However, do try to select fabrics that you can personally wash and dry, because that's the best way to keep clean in this land where laundry services usually take about a week and cost like crazy. Dry cleaning is expensive, too (especially in hotels), and can take up to 10 days, unless you up the ante for "express" service of one or two days. So it's really best to take easy-wash and quick-dry fabrics, plus a few plastic clothespins with hangers attached. You'll find clothing for all climates in such fabrics.

Speaking of fads and fashions: jeans, shorts and the like are acceptable, but not everywhere—bring along a long-sleeved shirt or modestly long skirt to wear when visiting synagogues and other religious places. Without such coverings, you'll not be allowed to enter and/or will seem offensive.

Whatever else you pack will depend on the season, but try to travel light, with just one suitcase per person. Keep in mind too: even those on a tight budget do shop along the way.

SUMMER: The hot weather of summer usually lasts from mid-May to the beginning of October. The evenings are cool or reasonably cool. Jerusalem, Safed and the inland regions are dry. It is moist along the coast. Eilat and the deserts are very dry. You will be happy to wear a sweater or jacket in Jerusalem after the sun goes down. The days are hot all over.

Nevertheless, there are a few precautions you should take: and the most important of these is to remember that the sun is unusually strong—so wear a hat!

Secondly, take clothes that are "cool" and will allow your body to breathe. This is very important, because you will perspire a lot. And because of the lack of humidity, you will hardly be aware of it—*if* your clothes allow the moisture to evaporate. Arnel and nylon fabrics may be non-wrinkle, but they are also non-breathing. Cotton with a combination of dacron and rayon is much to be preferred.

When we refer to "cool" clothing, we don't mean that you should take many sun-dresses; in fact, dresses that expose much of your body to the sun cancel out the protection of wearing a hat. Rather, sleeveless or loose short sleeves that will cover your shoulders fit the requirement. Even the olive-skinned person who tans easily can burn in this sun, so use common sense to protect yourself. We found that salt tablets often helped to beat the heat.

WINTER: From November through early March is "winter" in Israel. Not winter as you know it, with heavy coats, mufflers, snow-wear and cozy fires, but rainy-season-winter—more like a chilly April. It's a good idea, in that time of year, to bring several sweaters of different weights, so that you can peel them off or pile them on, depending on the day and the location. Jerusalem tends to be chilly in winter, while Haifa and Tel Aviv often have spells of warm spring-like weather in December and January.

Of course, your staple apparel for winter is a good waterproof raincoat, a rain hat, an umbrella and a pair of sturdy, comfortable boots. For women, a pair of warm slacks and socks can also give you a much-needed extra layer of warmth in an unheated Jerusalem hotel. And finally, a wool or knit ladies' suit, or corduroy skirt and jacket, can be used for all occasions—touring, evening out, traveling—depending on whether you wear a sweater or an evening blouse with the outfit.

IN HER SUITCASE, TAKE:

    one pair walking shoes
    one pair sandals
    one pair rubber sandals
    4 sleeveless drip-dry blouses
    2 cotton skirts
    3 daytime dresses (drip-dry)
    one bathing suit
    one bathing cap
    2 pair slacks
    one wool sweater (also doubles for evening wear)
    one pair medium-heel shoes
    one dark-colored cotton dress for evening
    one cotton sun hat (for beach and city)
    underwear
    sunglasses
    pharmaceuticals, including salt tablets, aspirin, suntan cream, zinc oint-
    ment (for sun blisters), toothpaste, talcum powder and personal items.
    5 folding plastic hangers, 4 plastic combination clothespin hangers, one
    stretching clothes-line.

IN HIS SUITCASE, TAKE:

    one pair sneakers (or sandals)
    one pair rubber sandals
    one pair walking shoes
    one bathing suit
    5 drip-dry shirts
    3 pair slacks
    one pair shorts
    one tie (you may never need it, but just in case)
    one sports jacket
    underwear
    sunglasses
    sun hat
    personal items, such as brush, shoe polish, shaving equipment.

8. Books About Israel

For tourists who take their traveling seriously and want to bone up on Israel, there are several good books that can greatly add to the enjoyment and appreciation of your stay.

One need hardly mention such best sellers as *Exodus* and *The Source*. Werner Keller's *The Bible as History* reads like a suspense novel, although it's actually an archeological survey of the biblical remnants uncovered in Israel and the surrounding countries. A fascinating, well-written book. *A History of the Holyland*, edited by Michael Avi-Yonah, is another good selection. You'll also see Josephus' *The Jewish Wars* on every English-speaking Israeli's bookshelf. Ruler of the Galilee during Roman times—and a sometime traitor—he was also an historian who provided historical commentaries and anecdotes about almost every area you'll see in Israel. In fact, his section on the Masada battle is the most often quoted of all historical texts, in terms of factual accuracy. More recently, Yigal Yadin wrote two very readable accounts about Bar Kochba and Masada, detailing history, archeology and excavated finds; each is handsomely illustrated. His latest book now deals with the ancient site of Hatzor.

Also check out:

Footloose in Jerusalem, by Sarah Fox Kaminker, a series of guided walking tours in Jerusalem; *The Arab-Israel Conflict: Its History in Maps,* by Martin Gilbert, tracing the history of the conflict from the turn-of-the-century to the present day; *A Life,* the autobiography of Jerusalem's famous mayor, Teddy Kollek, written with his son, Amos; *The Israel I Love,* by Noel Calef; *The Natural History of the Land of the Bible,* by Azaria Alon; *The Autobiography of Abba Eban; The Rabin Memoirs,* by Itzhak Rabin; *The Revolt,* by Prime Minister Menachem Begin; *My Life,* by Golda Meir; *Story of My Life,* by Moshe Dayan; and Samuel Katz' *Battleground—Fact and Fantasy in Palestine.*

Finally, for humor, you'll enjoy *The Chronicles,* a two-volume set of Bible history articles written in modern tabloid-newspaper jargon, with misleading or overdone headlines, plus a few scandalizations. Of course, the doyen of Israeli humorists remains Ephraim Kishon of *Sallah Shabbati* fame.

Chapter II

GETTING THERE

1. By Plane
2. Traveling Within Israel
3. Student Travel

THE STATE OF ISRAEL is located on the far eastern end of the Mediterranean, no less than 6,000 nautical miles from New York. By all rights, it should cost a small packet to travel to Israel; and the widespread belief that a trip to Israel definitely is expensive has stopped many tourists—particularly the budget tourist—from ever dreaming of attempting the trip.

The fact is that under certain circumstances it costs less to fly to Israel than to fly to Rome or Athens! And with that provocative statement, we begin our study of the cheapest ways to get to the place under discussion.

1. By Plane

Air fares are in a constant state of flux, buffeted by free-enterprise entrepreneurs such as Freddie Laker, and by spiraling oil prices; one forces prices down, and the other, of course, makes them shoot up nearly every month. The following fares, therefore, from El Al are guidelines and correct *only* at press time.

Before you travel check which fare gives you the best value; look into fares from Europe to Israel (to get there take advantage of cheap flights between New York, or Los Angeles, and London); by the time you plan your trip perhaps Laker will have *Skytrain* crisscrossing Europe, which he is planning to do in early 1981—this will undoubtedly force other airlines to bring down their prices. The time of year that you travel can have a bearing on costs, as you will see.

The Economy Apex and Economy Group fares are divided into the following seasons: Basic—November 1 to March 31; Shoulder—April 1 to June 19 (June 30 from Israel), August 1 (September 16 from Israel) to October 31; Peak—June 20 to July 31 from the U.S.A., July 1 to September 15 from Israel.

Youth, Budget, and Individual Excursion fares are broken down as: Basic—August 1 to June 19 from U.S.A. September 16 to June 30 from Israel; Peak—June 20 to July 31 from U.S.A., July 1 to September 15 from Israel.

Economy 6-to-60-Day Apex Fare

At $782 (basic), $917 (shoulder), and $986 (peak), this is the cheapest roundtrip fare to Tel Aviv from New York. You must stay at least 6 days, and not more than 60; your ticket must be bought at least 21 days before you leave.

There are surcharges of $20 on weekends (eastbound Friday 7 a.m. to Sunday 7 a.m., and westbound Saturday 7 a.m. to Sunday midnight), and $50 within seven days before Christmas and Passover. Stopovers can be made westbound only at an extra cost of $75. Cancellation and refund charges will be $50.

Economy 6-to-120-Day Individual Excursion Fare

For $1,156 basic season and $1,258 peak season, plus a minimum of $100 in ground arrangements (hotels, meals, etc.), with a minimum stay of 6 days, maximum of 120, you can make the roundtrip to Tel Aviv without the advance purchase requirement. You are entitled to one free stopover, plus one stopover at $75 extra on your westbound journey.

Economy 6-to-60-Day Group Fare

With 10 or more people traveling together, the group fare roundtrip is $842 basic season, $981 shoulder, and $1,050 peak. You must travel together, but can make independent stopover arrangements after commencement of travel, westbound at an extra charge of $75. All documentation—names, changes, additions, lists, and applications—must be submitted five days prior to departure, after which there will be a cancellation charge of $50.

Economy Budget Fare

This fare allows a one-way ticket at $612 basic season, $661 peak, with roundtrip at $1,224 and $1,322 respectively. You can stay up to 365 days, *but* the ticket can only be confirmed within seven days of departure. No stopovers allowed.

Economy Youth Individual 6-to-120-Day Excursion Fare

If you are aged between 12 and 23, and stay at least 6, but not more than 120 days, your roundtrip ticket will cost $919 in basic season and $969 in peak. A stopover is allowed at an additional cost of $75 westbound, but only $20 if it is made in Europe or the Middle East. This ticket can be extended for a further 365 days for another $100.

Economy Fare and First Class Fare

If the above are too restricting, the regular economy fare is $942 one way and $1,844 roundtrip. First class will cost you $1,478 and $2,956 respectively.

WHO FLIES TO ISRAEL: Fourteen international airlines fly from New York to Tel Aviv. But only on one of them, **El Al**, does your breakfast come with a witty little booklet called *El Al Looks into the Bagel,* a historical survey of the bagel's origins. But that's not the only difference among the airlines available to you. El Al, apart from giving you a book on bagels, has the only non-stop flights to Israel, and more frequently than the others. During the summer peak periods (and the spring Passover-Easter and winter Christmas-pilgrimage time), it offers 30 weekly flights to Israel—and the majority of the flights are non-stop (10¼ hours). El Al was also the pioneer of the longest non-stop westbound flight in its time in aviation history (12 hours).

Trailing directly behind El Al on transatlantic frequencies to Israel is **TWA,** with daily or multiple flights offered year round. And, for students and pilgrims, there is a plethora of charter possibilities from Europe to Israel.

Information of this sort is available from tour organizers and student organizations. A major charter springboard to Israel is Luxembourg.

El Al's Check-In Service

Passengers on El Al flights who are leaving from Jerusalem or Tel Aviv can avail themselves of El Al's in-city check-in service. The Jerusalem office, 12 Hillel St., opens especially for this purpose every evening (except Fridays and eves of holidays) from 6 p.m. to midnight, and on Saturday nights after the termination of the Sabbath. In Tel Aviv, El Al's main office on Ben Yehuda St. opens nightly from 7:30 to 11 p.m. (with the same Sabbath and holiday restrictions) for check-in.

Passengers using this service have their baggage sent directly to the plane, and they receive their stamped boarding cards on the spot. In addition, once they have checked in at either office, they need check in at the airport only one hour before flight time rather than the usual two hours.

Phone El Al at 02-233333 for further information.

Note: This service is not available to passengers on flights to Johannesburg or Nairobi.

FLY-NOW, PAY-LATER: Can't pay for your ticket all at once? There's one device available to you: an installment plan for purchasing your ticket. You're permitted to pay in monthly payments spread over a period of three to 36 months. To buy your ticket in that manner, you need only fill out a fairly simple form that's used for credit-checking purposes. If you have "steady earning power" (a steady job is steady earning power), then you're most likely to be approved. There is, of course, an interest charge assessed on this sort of purchase, but it adds up to very little in relation to the advantage of being able to pay off the cost of your trip over a period as long as 36 months.

2. Traveling Within Israel

Now that you have arrived, you face the problem of traveling through Israel. But this, you'll find, is a simple and quite economical task, thanks to a large, efficient network of buses and trains in Israel—and thanks, also, to the relative compactness of the country. The transportation possibilities involve (a) buses; (b) trains; (c) regular taxis and (d) special taxis, called *sheruts,* which supplement the bus runs for only about 10% more; (e) flying; and (f) drive-it-yourself cars. And if paying for transportation doesn't appeal to you at all, you can even consider the alternative of hitchhiking—a widespread practice (details in Chapter XI).

BUSES WITHIN ISRAEL: All city and intercity bus routes are operated by two cooperative shareholder companies, Dan and Egged. Their equipment varies widely. Depending on the whim of fortune, you'll take your intercity bus ride in either spanking new buses with red upholstery and efficient air conditioning, or in a run-down, torn-upholstered, dirty-windowed, breathlessly hot bus. There's no way to control it.

There is, however, one general rule to observe: Try not to make an intercity trip between 7 and 8 a.m. and 4 to 6 p.m. The bus stations are packed at that hour, especially in Tel Aviv, and Israelis are not noted for their politesse when it comes to standing in lines.

It might be of interest to note that Israeli bus drivers are often among the nation's upper-income bracket workers. Most of them have become drivers by buying into the cooperative. Also, most bus drivers are multilingual—and are even compelled to take language courses—so you won't have too much trouble being understood.

Here are some sample Egged bus fares (as of December, 1979), one way between various cities, stated in terms of Israeli shekel.

Tel Aviv–Jerusalem	6.90
Tel Aviv–Haifa	7.90
Tel Aviv–Beersheba	7.90
Tel Aviv–Eilat	25.70
Tel Aviv–Tiberias	10.10
Tel Aviv–Masada	15.40
Jerusalem–Haifa	13.10
Jerusalem–Beersheba	10.10
Jerusalem–Tiberias	11.10
Jerusalem–Sharm-el-Sheikh	55.60
Jerusalem–Masada	9.90
Jerusalem–Eilat	25.70
Eilat–Sharm-el-Sheikh	29.90

As you can see, these fares are quite reasonable, and you don't have to figure on spending much money for transportation in Israel. You can travel from Jerusalem to Tiberias, nearly half the length of the country, for less than $3.50.

The **Dan** bus company, at the Hadar Dafna Building, Sderot Shaul Hamelech, Tel Aviv, tel. 25-3411, offers a monthly ticket for 50 rides at a reduction of 25%. This ticket expires at the end of the month, but there are also tickets unrestricted in time—23 rides for the price of 20.

Dan also provides a worthwhile route map—but it's in Hebrew. Multiple ride tickets are available at 3 Hagalil St. (open from 7 a.m. to 2 p.m.) or from kiosks and stands located throughout Tel Aviv. They are obtainable on Dizengoff Rd. at numbers 280, 289; 26 Allenby Rd.; 16 Hacarmel St., and 1 Baalei Melacha St.

There is a reduction on return tickets on certain **Egged** lines, and for an additional SH.30 on your ticket to Jerusalem you can get a transfer for one local ride in the city from the terminal.

You can also buy a 14-day, 21-day or 30-day ticket for traveling anywhere throughout the country except Sinai. The tickets can be obtained from any Egged Tours office.

A 14-day ticket is $35, a 21-day ticket is $45, and a 30-day ticket is $55. Egged offices are generally open from 7 a.m. to 7 p.m., closing Friday at 2:45 p.m. The Tel Aviv office stays open until 8 p.m. except on Friday. Students are eligible for discounts.

Some Egged buses travel up to 8-9 p.m., others up to midnight. Buses start rolling at 5:40 a.m.

Egged has restaurants in 19 Central Bus Stations, where prices are considerably cheaper than restaurants with the same level of food and service elsewhere. They are strictly kosher. Don't miss the bus ride from Beersheba to Eilat; the views are spectacular.

A local joke is that El Al is one of Israel's largest bus operators—as a matter of fact it has five times the number of buses as airplanes. Every plane is met, and the 30-minute trip from airport to north Tel Aviv costs SH4 ($1.18) one way (half price for children). El Al buses from the terminal to the airport depart every hour on the half hour from 3:30 a.m. to 9 a.m., from 10 a.m. to 10 p.m., they leave every hour on the hour.

A good airport service from Jerusalem is **Nesher.** The sherut departs from King George St. and the tab is SH19 ($5.59) each way. Book your seat beforehand. There's also a regular Egged bus service from the capital to the airport. The one-way fare is SH4.30 ($1.26); from Haifa to the airport the fare is SH4.60 ($1.35).

TRAINS IN ISRAEL: Trains are even cheaper than buses, but they link only six cities—Jerusalem, Beersheba, Dimona, Tel Aviv, Haifa and Nahariya (with local stops made along the way). Though the vintage of some of the trains is rather ancient, they are usually roomy, and the railroad tracks run through some of central Israel's most beautiful areas. Just as you should experience the bus ride to Eilat, so too you really should make the trip from Tel Aviv to Jerusalem by train. The route is through the beautiful Judean Hills, a winding, mountain-clinging ride through a parched and rugged landscape.

By the way, when you're traveling by bus or sherut, you'll notice unused railroad tracks running seemingly to nowhere, in various parts of the country. These abandoned tracks are a throwback to the British Mandate times, when these railway lines connected Israel with Jordan, Egypt and Lebanon. Note: the International Student Identity Card holder obtains a 25% train discount.

Excepting the Sabbath and religious holidays, trains run daily. Operations close earlier on Friday and prior to holidays.

There are two train stations in Tel Aviv. The Central Depot, tel. 03-254271, and the Tel Aviv South station, tel. 03-822676. Some sample one-way train costs are Tel Aviv–Jerusalem SH4.50 ($1.32), Tel Aviv–Haifa SH6 ($1.76), Tel Aviv–Nahariya SH7.95 ($2.34), Jerusalem–Haifa SH8.80 ($2.59), Jerusalem–Nahariya SH10.75 ($3.16).

SHERUTS: These are jitney-type taxis, which charge slightly more than a bus. They supplement city and intercity bus routes and often go where the bus doesn't go. On Saturdays in many parts of the country, they are the only transportation available.

Figure a few percent more than the bus fare if you want to know how much the sherut will cost. All sherut fares are about 25% higher at night, by the way.

Special rates for children are available. There is no charge for a child under five traveling with an adult. Two children under five pay one adult fare. For each additional child under five, the full fare is required.

There's also a special sherut fare of SH19 ($5.59) for the journey from Ben-Gurion Airport to any destination in Jerusalem, or vice versa, with the exceptions of the Hadassah Hospital, Ein Kerem and Neve Ya'akov.

You'll be sure to recognize these taxis. Some are old De Sotos, those long, humped-back New York City limousine-taxis that were in fashion years ago. The Israelis saved them from death in an American junkyard, put in diesel motors, and now they're on their second quarter of a million miles. But lately the Mercedes-Benz has gained preeminence. Sheruts usually make regular stops, but by and large they'll let you off at any bus stop in or out of the city along their routes, and you can reserve your seat in advance on a long trip. (Israel also has regular taxis, so when you hail what looks like a cab, make sure you ask if it's a sherut before you get in—it is an expensive difference.)

FLIGHTS WITHIN ISRAEL: If you can afford it, and if traveling overland on hot days just isn't your cup of tea, then by all means use **Arkia,** Israel's inland air service. Arkia provides a safe and quick way to get around the country, and the service is being expanded wherever landing facilities permit. Arkia regularly flies turbo-prop Viscounts between the following cities (among others) at the following fares (in Israeli shekels, one way):

Tel Aviv–Jerusalem	56
Tel Aviv/Jerusalem–Eilat	189.50
Tel Aviv–Dead Sea	96.50
Tel Aviv/Jerusalem–Sharm-el-Sheikh	274.40
Tel Aviv–Beersheba	113.60
Tel Aviv/Jerusalem–Mt. Sinai	261.60
Tel Aviv–Haifa	82.30
Jerusalem–Haifa	95.60
Haifa–Eilat	232.70
Haifa–Beersheba	133.30

Students get a 10% reduction, children up to age 12 a 50% reduction. Arkia also offers "Vacation Plans" including hotels and rental cars (special reductions for honeymooners), and air tours which provide a swift and exciting (though not inexpensive) way to see less accessible areas of the country.

Arkia Offices

You can book tickets and check flight schedules at the following Arkia offices:

Tel Aviv	88 Ha'hasmonaim St., tel. 03-266161
	11 Frishman St., tel. 03-231735 or 226640
	Lod Airport, tel. 03-972551/2
Jerusalem	Bank Tfahot, Hamalka St. at Horkenus St., tel. 02-225888
Haifa	4 Ibn Sina St., tel. 04-667722/3
Netanya	7 Ha'atzmauth St., tel. 053-23644
Eilat	Beit Arkia, Mercaz Tayarut Hachadash, tel. 059-6102/3,
Rosh Pinna	Airport, tel. 067-37301/2
Safed	100 Jerusalem St., tel. 067-31128
Ophira (Sharm-el-Sheikh)	Airport, tel. 057-99227
Beersheba	31 Herzl St., tel. 057-73308

For information and reservations, you can also contact Arkia's New York office before you leave. It is located at 575 Lexington Ave., New York, New York 10022, tel. (212) 486-8835.

FROM ISRAEL TO EGYPT: The land border between Israel and Egypt officially opened at the end of January, 1980. If you would like to include Egypt in your itinerary, you must get a visa before leaving the States. This can be obtained by visiting or writing to the Egyptian mission nearest you: Egyptian Embassy, 2310 Decatur Pl. N.W., Washington, D.C. 20008, tel. (202) 234-3903; Egyptian Consulate, 1110 Second Ave., New York, N.Y. 10022, tel. (212)

759-7120; or Egyptian Consulate, 3001 Pacific Ave., San Francisco, California 94115.

If you make the trip in your own vehicle you must obtain a permit to take a vehicle into Egypt from the Consular Section, Ministry for Foreign Affairs, Hakirya, Romema, Jerusalem, tel. 02-235111. Driving time from the Neot Sinai border point to Cairo is about seven hours.

Egged operates a shuttle bus service between the Israeli and Egyptian terminals at the Neot Sinai border point; fare is SH2.30 (65¢).

Air service commenced March 3, 1980. El Al flights operate twice weekly between Tel Aviv and Cairo, a 45-minute flight priced at $170 round trip. In Egypt, Lotus Airways offers the same service.

Of course, an increasing number of tours are being developed. Make inquiries at tourist offices or tour operators in the U.S. or Israel.

Further details, as they become available, may be obtained from the Israel Government Tourist Offices in Atlanta, Chicago, Los Angeles, New York, and Toronto.

RENTING CARS: This is a desirable way to travel in Israel, if you can afford it. Rent-a-car agencies, both the international ones such as Avis and Hertz, as well as local agencies, rent small cars at about $16 a day, plus a 16¢ per kilometer charge, rates depending on the season and the size of the car. The lower rates are for such cars as Fiats and Autobianchis.

Driving is one of the best ways to see Israel. And should you feel that car-renting is too great a luxury for your budget, remember that with your new-found mobility you can stay at any of the camping-bungalow sites, and thus recoup in low hotel accommodations your car-rental splurge. (See Chapter XI for bungalow camp details.)

Hertz adheres to its international policy of rent-it-here/leave-it-there (except Eilat) at no extra charge. Hertz's head office is in Tel Aviv at 10 Carlebach St., tel. 03-264141. Another Tel Aviv office is in the Hilton Hotel, tel. 03-238588. In Jerusalem, offices are at 18 King David St., tel. 02-231351, and at Sinbad Tours, 27 Saladin St., East Jerusalem, tel. 02-283415. The Haifa office is at 8 Shabtai Levi St., tel. 04-666633. There is an office at Ben-Gurion Airport, tel. 03-971165, and one in Netanya at 1 Ha'atzmauth, tel. 053-28890.

Avis headquarters in Tel Aviv: Avis House, 80 Hamasger St., tel. 03-336363; and at the Park Hotel, 75 Hayarkon St., tel. 03-651093. Other Tel Aviv locations: Hilton Hotel, tel. 03-222045; Plaza Hotel, tel. 03-297567.

Additional Avis locations are as follows:

Ben-Gurion Airport, tel. 03-971080.

Netanya, 1 Ussishkin, tel. 053-31619.

Jerusalem, 210 Jaffa Rd., tel. 02-534464/525030; King David Hotel, tel. 02-222250; Hilton Hotel, tel. 02-533122.

Haifa, 20 Ha'atzmauth Rd., tel. 04-520347, 04-665491; Dan Carmel, tel. 04-84959.

Generally, gasoline is not included in rental rates, although most companies provide the first fill-up free. Maintenance and oil are included in the rates (refunds against receipts).

Taxes are waived if payment is by travelers checks or accepted foreign credit cards. A rental day covers 24 hours. Excess is paid by the hour.

Some of the smaller but equally reputable rent-a-car agencies, listed by city, are Tel Aviv: **Kopel**, 252 Hayarkon St. Netanya: **Sharet Tours and Transport**, 3 Ahad Ha'am St.; **Sverdlov Ltd.**, 54 Herzl St. Jerusalem: **Lucky Drive**, 8 Shamai St.; **Tip-Top Rent-a-Car**, 3 Shamai St. Haifa: **Auto Haifa**, 3

Tel Aviv St.; **Best Drive Yourself,** 5/10 May St.; **Heskerchev Ltd.,** 3 Tel Aviv St.; **Hi-Car,** 118 Derech Ha'atzmauth. Nahariya: **Rehov Atzmon Ltd.,** 57 Herzl St. Beersheba: **Khish Bazak,** 93 Hahistadrut St.

Note
Car Rental agencies demand a valid driver's license of at least one year's standing. Often the minimum age for renting a car is 25.

Caution
In renting cars, tourists are cautioned to deal only with reputable companies, not to sign a contract without reading it thoroughly in a language completely understood, and to make sure of proper and full insurance coverage.

To Calculate the Mileage Charges
Distances in Israel, by road, are:

	Kilometers	Miles
Jerusalem–Tel Aviv	61	38
Jerusalem–Haifa	150	93
Jerusalem–Beersheba	91	56
Tel Aviv–Haifa	97	60
Tel Aviv–Ashkelon	60	37
Tel Aviv–Beersheba	107	66
Tel Aviv–Eilat	342	212
Tel Aviv–Tiberias	134	83

DRIVING IN ISRAEL: Although Israel honors an American driver's license, they prefer you to have an International Driver's License, which should be obtained in advance in your home town. The local automobile club, called MEMSI, has its main office in Tel Aviv at 19 Derech Petach Tikva Rd. tel: 03-622961. It offers AAA members (1) information on touring, hotels, car hire, etc.; (2) emergency assistance on the roads, patrolled by radio-controlled yellow vans with MEMSI's name and emblem; (3) legal and technical advice; (4) guarantor of letters of credit issued by A.I.T. and F.I.A. clubs; (5) acceptance of members of affiliated clubs without paying registration fee.

Provided a tourist's foreign car registration is valid and he is in possession of a valid driving license, he may bring his car into Israel for a period of up to one year. No customs document or deposit of customs duty is required.

But before you decide to bring in a car or even drive in Israel, you should understand that this is a tough country for autos. Auxiliary roads are rarely wide and straight, and once you're off the main highways, you're faced with winding, narrow mountain roads—particularly in the Galilee and the Negev. Our recommendation is that unless you're familiar with this type of road, and unless you're confident you can handle it, you do not drive in Israel. Roads in Israel are being widened constantly, but even so, they are far from the turnpikes Americans are used to, excepting the major arteries—Haifa–Tel Aviv, Jerusalem–Tel Aviv.

Besides the roads themselves, there are many other problems confronting a driver in Israel. The main problem is the Israeli driver himself: brashness on the road is his national sport. The Israeli's driving habits, especially those of taxi drivers, directly reflect two main components of his personality: aggressiveness and impatience. You will see cars taking daredevil chances and overtaking regularly on blind curves and without any sensible regard for oncoming traffic, narrowly squeezing back into lane only by a hair's breadth. Such foolishness (or should we say fearlessness and recklessness?) has caused tragedy and death on Israel's roads to an extent way out of proportion to the number of cars in the country.

Other hazards? First, rains bring up loose gravel and dirt, and make for unstable, slippery conditions. Flash floods occur in the desert during the rainy season, often gutting low sections of the highway. The road to Eilat is well-banked but narrow, and many a truck, having the right of way, has forced a passenger car onto the sand by not getting over far enough at the point of passing. If you drive through the desert to Eilat at night, you're really living dangerously.

Gas stations are plentiful enough on the main roads, except that on Saturdays some of them are closed. And on Saturdays and Jewish holidays it's virtually impossible to have a flat tire repaired in the Jewish sections of Israel.

Whether you rent a car or drive your own, be sure to pick up a road map. Also, stop into any tourist office and request the pamphlet *Driving Rules for a Motoring Holiday in Israel.* It gives detailed speed limits and a list of international traffic signs.

3. Student Travel

ISSTA: **The Israeli National Student Travel Bureau (ISSTA)** is the travel department of the National Union of Israeli Students. It is a non-profit organization whose aim is to cater to the needs of the student traveler in Israel. ISSTA offices, which also provide the services of regular travel agencies, are located in Israel's three major cities:

Tel Aviv:	109 Ben Yehuda St., tel. 03-247164/5
Jerusalem:	Eliashar St., tel. 02-231418
Haifa:	Beit Hakranot, Herzl St., tel. 04-669139

ISSTA's staff is comprised of young people, specialists in the field of student and youth travel. Here the student is treated as a first-class client and is offered a wide variety of special services, planned and developed by people who fully understand the student's needs and problems. ISSTA accommodates students (bring proof) from the start to finish of their stay in Israel with:

1. Special inland tours at very inexpensive prices.
2. Volunteer work groups in kibbutzim (volunteers only accepted if they register abroad in advance).
3. Reservations in inexpensive hotels, university dormitories, and vacation centers for the youth/student.
4. Inexpensive inland flights and bus tickets.
5. Special student charter flights between Israel and almost any point in Europe, also the Far East and Africa. European flights are guaranteed by the operator.

Most of these services are operated throughout the year, the main ISSTA seasons being winter (December-January), spring (April-May), and summer (June-November).

Tours Within Israel

ISSTA operates tours within Israel ranging from two to nine days, with daily departures in season; they're open to individual as well as group booking.

The tour price includes full-board accommodations in three- to four-bedded rooms, entrance fees, a tour bus and a government-licensed guide. Prices range from $68 for two days in Jerusalem to $302 for a nine-day excursion covering the entire country, including the Red Sea Coast down to Sharm-el-Sheikh. There are a great variety of tours to choose from. Check it out.

Living on a Kibbutz

For the many students wishing to live and work on kibbutzim, ISSTA offers a special program throughout the year. For full information contact ISSTA offices in the U.S.

ISSTA does not accept volunteers for kibbutz stays during July and August, as all the settlements in Israel are overcrowded at this time.

Hotel Accommodations

ISSTA can book accommodations for students in modest hotels at student rates; accommodations at vacation centers are also possible. The price for one person in Tel Aviv, Eilat, or Jerusalem is about $11 to $16. Students holding reservations for Tel Aviv should apply to the above-mentioned ISSTA offices. Rates are for bed and breakfast, three and four in a room. They will advise about hostels too.

Inland Flights and Buses

Inland flights between Tel Aviv Haifa, and Jerusalem to or from Eilat or Sharm-el-Sheikh, are available to students at inexpensive prices. It is also possible to book an unlimited mileage two-, three- or four-week bus ticket through ISSTA.

Charter Flights from Europe

ISSTA operates, on a year-round basis, special charter flights between Europe and Israel for students and scholars. The seat you buy is confirmed— you are *not* a standby. These flights are jointly operated with various national student travel bureaus in Europe and form an extensive network of flights between Israel and Europe. All aircraft used are jets, and all flights are on non-IATA carriers such as BEA Airtours and Sterling Airways. These flights are priced specially for students and offer discounts of 40%-70% off the regular fare. From mid-April to mid-September, you can fly to Israel from London, Paris, Rome, Athens, Zurich, Amsterdam, Copenhagen, Madrid, Barcelona, Dublin, Stockholm, Helsinki, Oslo, Munich, Dusseldorf, the Far East, Africa and vice-versa, and can also time your flights in conjunction with flights to or from the U.S. The rest of the year you can fly from Athens, London, Zurich, and Copenhagen.

Members of students' families—husband or wife and children—are now allowed to fly to and from Israel on student charter flights, at the same rates and subject to the same conditions as the student in the family.

ISSTA's New York Office

ISSTA is represented in New York by **CIEE/SOFA Student Travel Services**, William Sloane House, 354 West 34th Street, New York, N.Y. 10001. They can book almost all the above-mentioned ISSTA services in advance, and they'll gladly provide any and all information concerning ISSTA.

Note: Be sure to ask for ISSTA's brochure *Student Travel to Israel,* which will fill you in on all the travel plans ISSTA makes available to students.

Chapter III

JERUSALEM, THE HOLY CITY

**1. On the Way
2. The City in a Word and at a Glance
3. West Jerusalem
4. East Jerusalem and the Old (Walled) City**

JERUSALEM CANNOT BE TERMED simply "a city." It is the stone-faced affirmation of man's continuing struggle to uplift himself. First mentioned in Genesis when Abraham visited the King of Salem, the name, Salem, or Shalom, means the "city of peace"—a fact which seems to have stopped no one from attacking, pillaging and razing the city's holy places during its 4,000 years of history.

Wise writers avoid hyperbole, but it is impossible to comment on the Israeli capital without calling it what it is—architecturally one of the world's most beautiful sites; spiritually the holiest location of Western man; historically the mortar and cohesiveness of the Jewish people and a key landmark for both Christianity and Islam; pragmatically a multilingual, multicultural outgrowth making it one of the most interesting enclaves to be found anywhere.

Jerusalem was David's city. Jerusalem cradled the temples. Jerusalem is the pulsebeat of the Bible and the heart of modern Israel.

United Jerusalem— *Yerushalayim Hashleyma*—officially came into existence June 29, 1967, barely three weeks after the start of the Six-Day War. Cleaved in half by the 1948 armistice, Israel's capital had been one of those phenomena of modern times: a divided city. When the barriers once dividing the city were finally removed, Jews and Arabs began to mingle freely, visiting and sightseeing throughout the city, renewing old acquaintances and forging the human bond that now welds together Jerusalem's citizens.

Jerusalem was taken away from the Jews, as Jeremiah prophesied, by a Babylonian invasion in 586 B.C., an event biblically viewed as God's punishment for the transgressions of the Jewish people. Jerusalem was the number-one goal of the Crusaders, who conquered the city and slaughtered its inhabitants in 1099. Jews returned here time and again, to live under a succession of rulers (Persians, Assyrians, Greeks, Romans, "pagans," Byzantines, Moslems, Turks, British), but not until June 7, 1967 was it theirs to rule again. On that day the Six-Day War brought to an end 2,000 years of foreign occupation, Defense Minister and Commander-in-Chief of the Israeli Defense Forces

Moshe Dayan spoke words which still echo in Israeli hearts and thoughts: "We have returned to our holy places, never to part from them again."

1. On the Way

Back in biblical times, it used to take many days for a pilgrim to travel from the Mediterranean coast to Jerusalem. Today, the ride requires an hour or, if you have a particularly aggressive sherut driver, around 45 minutes. Whatever the speed you travel, the last part of your gradually ascending ride will undoubtedly be one of the most dramatic and memorable phases of any journey you've ever made.

There are many ways to enter Jerusalem, or to "go up" to the city, as the Hebrew word, implying a physical and spiritual ascension, expresses. From the north, you can either take the Jordan Valley way passing through Tiberias, Beit Shean and Jericho and enter Jerusalem from the east, or an alternative, a beautiful way between mountains passing Jenin, Nablus and Ramallah. The third and longest way is via Afula, Hadera and the coastal plain to Tel Aviv, and reaching the city from the west. The southern entry is Beersheba through Hebron and Bethlehem.

A brand new road from Tel Aviv—officially opened on July 11th, 1979—cuts the journey between Tel Aviv and Jerusalem to 50 minutes. A 57-kilometer, four-lane highway, it passes by beautiful countryside and the Ben-Gurion Airport, en route to the Latrun area which bisects a wide natural pass between the Judean hills and the coastal region—an area that's known bloodshed since biblical days, when Joshua prayed for the sun to stand still over Gibeon and the moon to remain over this **Ajalon Valley** (Joshua 10:12). Locals know the Scriptures well, and mark with interest every square foot of ground that has biblical significance, but they are quicker to note that it was in this valley that over 1,000 Israelis died during the 1948 War of Independence, trying to take **Fortress Latrun** in what can only be described as human-wave assaults. Because of its crucial position on the approach to Jerusalem, Latrun became a battlefront once again in the 1967 war. The blood-saturated plain was cleared and planted with life-supporting crops, which, other than the pock-marked and deserted former police station (Fortress Latrun) and the romantic and peaceful **Latrun Monastery,** are all that you'll see today. (Though locals and tourists look searchingly at the still-haunting fortress, they seldom stop there. But often they enter the road to the Trappist monastery, where the monks have two distinctions: they've vowed not to speak, and they make—and sell—cheese and excellent wine. The vineyards surrounding the monastery are theirs, as is much of the land on both sides of the road.)

Directly past the monastery, the road forks to the left to Ramallah, then straight ahead to Jerusalem. From here on, you'll be climbing ever higher, through steep but lovely terraced hills.

The last leg of the trip is a steep ascent up a corridor strewn right and left with wrecked, rusted military vehicles, phantoms of a recent time. The smashed, overturned trucks and tanks, lying in the sun beside the road, are mute reminders of the men and equipment sacrificed in the 1948 war to keep this pass open. Were it not for that sacrifice—similar to the one at Latrun—the population of Jerusalem, cut off and under continuous bombardment, might have starved to death. Today, these silent and dead vehicles are a terribly telling war memorial, perhaps, in their stark appearance, the most convincing we have ever seen.

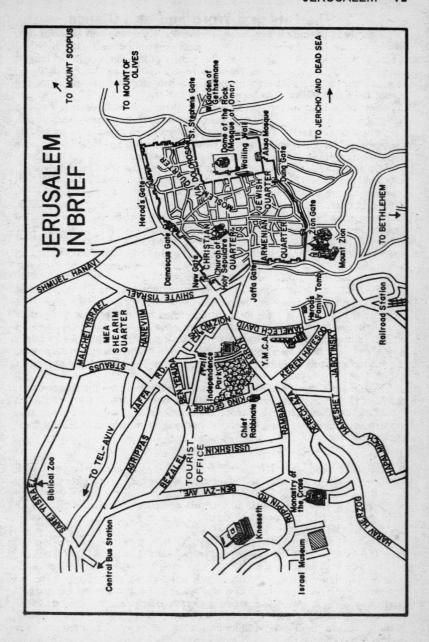

2. The City in a Word and at a Glance

Despite everything it's endured, Jerusalem is a serene and peaceful city, as old as time itself, with streets that seem to breathe an almost hypnotic lassitude. It ranks among the two or three cities of the world with the longest record of continual habitation. Needless to say, its citizens have seen everything, and there's a solidity about them and their city that has withstood the test of time and will obviously continue to endure.

Few cities have such a special mood to them as does Jerusalem. For one thing, it is the most exotic of Israel's three principal cities, partly because it is the holiest of the three. To many of the religious immigrants from Middle Eastern and North African countries (who now comprise over 50% of Israel's population), going to Israel means going to Jerusalem.

On Jerusalem's streets you'll recognize the long-bearded Hasidic element, in broad fur hats and black caftans. Perhaps less recognizable, but equally well represented, are Europeans, Asians, Americans—quite literally peoples from the world over. Along the eastern streets, outside shops and business areas, Arab men sit in the sunlight—heads usually covered with flowing scarves called *kefiyas*—drinking coffee. Arab women—often draped head to toe and wearing hand-embroidered dresses—scurry around, laden with bundles. Within the walls of the Old City, most people live as they have for some 2,000 years, in somnolence and a mixture of fragrances. If you've ever thought New York was a melting pot, wait until you see Jerusalem.

The city's old-time residents take an uncommon pride in living in Jerusalem—for a number of reasons. Some fought for the city during the war; some venerate the city for its religious meaning; some just regard it as the perfect place to live in Israel, with its cool, crisp evenings and sweet, clear days. Israelis who have lived in Jerusalem and moved to another part of the country somehow always return to Jerusalem to retrace the charming dignity of its streets, the aged grace of its neighborhoods, the memories of a youth spent among its golden-stoned byways.

While the western half is highly charged with a spirit of progressiveness, the eastern part is permeated with an easier, slower atmosphere. You'll see more "picturesquely biblical" houses in the east, as opposed to the many tall, modern and efficient-looking structures studding the west's architectural complex.

A QUICK ORIENTATION: United Jerusalem is a city easily navigated, with excellent hotels, restaurants and nightspots everywhere. We tackle the entity from three different angles for one reason only: to make it easier for you to organize your stay and sightseeing in this compact and intense city. Walk through the western area one day and the eastern part the next, saving another day for the Old City.

The easiest way to understand the layout of the city is to know how it grew. First there was a small city surrounded by huge walls (the Old City). Then the suburbs outside the walls grew to such an extent that they became an even greater city than the first. Finally, a war split the suburbs-city in half; the eastern side remained just about as it was before the war, while the western half continued to swell, with newer, more modern buildings and more active, 20th-century inhabitants. Since the 1967 war, the eastern half has experienced fantastic redevelopment, rebuilding and conservation of old structures, so it retains a predominantly Arab-Oriental flavor.

Your first stop should be the **Municipal Tourist Information Office**, 34 Jaffa Road, tel. 02-228844 (open 8 a.m. to 6 p.m. Sundays through Thursdays,

8 a.m. to 1:30 p.m. Fridays and eves of holidays), or one of the **Israel Government Tourist Information Offices**: 24 King George St. (west), tel. 02-241281/2 (open 8 a.m. to 6 p.m. Sundays through Thursdays, 8 a.m. to 3 p.m. Fridays and holiday eves; closed Saturdays); Jaffa Gate (east, just inside the Old City walls), tel. 02-282295/6 (open 8 a.m. to 6 p.m. Sundays through Thursdays, 10 a.m. to 2 p.m. Saturdays and holidays, 8 a.m. to 3 p.m. Fridays and holiday eves). At any of these places you can pick up a free detailed map of all Jerusalem. The central areas are easy enough to find your way around, but a map is essential for the older, more winding streets.

3. West Jerusalem

Generally speaking, the activity in West Jerusalem centers on a triangle formed by three streets: **Jaffa Road, King George Avenue** and **Ben Yehuda Street.** Jaffa Road, the western side's main street, is the continuation of the highway coming in from the coast.

HOTELS: Fortunately, many of the budget hotels in West Jerusalem are located inside the central triangle, clustered within the several-block area of **Kikar Zion** (Zion Square).

Jerusalem attracts a large number of tourists in the springtime, during the holiday seasons of Passover and Easter, and during Jewish High Holidays as well as at Christmas and New Year's. Jerusalem can be fairly cold in winter—it snows at least once every few years here—and you ought to be careful to inquire, before checking in, whether your room will be given an electric heater (if the hotel isn't centrally heated). In Israel's baking-hot summer, when the bulk of our readers will be visiting, the temperature of Jerusalem is the coolest of Israel's three main cities—and yet hotel prices remain moderate, as we'll now see:

Budget Hotels

The 15-room **Ron Hotel,** at 42A Jaffa Rd., tel. 02-223471, is well located, and a real study in graceful decline of sheer elegance. At the entrance, arched wrought-iron gates, heavy wooden doors with glass ovals, and tall pillars flanked by small potted palms; inside, marble floors, a two-story winding staircase, mirrors, vaulted ceilings. Rooms are heated and have private showers. The reception desk is at the top of the first landing. The rest of the hotel also shows signs of middle-aged elegance, but not quite so grandly. The dining room fronts directly on Zion Square, and while you're sipping your morning coffee, you can watch Jerusalem waking up for a new day—people running for buses, shopkeepers pulling up their shutters. Prices for all this: SH59.50 ($17.50) to SH68 ($20) single, SH51 ($15) per person double.

Around a corner, at 1 Ha'havatzelet St., is the ten-room **Hotel Kaplan,** tel. 02-224591. Small and very inexpensive, it is a typical bleak-but-clean walk-up—serving no meals—with shared baths and cold running water in rooms. Year-round rates are SH15 ($4.41) per bed for four in a room, SH17.50 ($5.15) for a double room.

The **Gefen Hotel,** 4 Frumkin St., tel. 02-224075, has 19 no-frills rooms, nine with private showers, all with H&C in the room and toilet facilities down the hall. The Gefen offers central heating in cold weather, fans in summer. Rates are SH44.20 ($13) single, SH34 ($10) double.

From the top of Ha'havatzelet St., a right turn onto Harkenus (a quiet sidestreet with little traffic) will lead you to the **Hotel Jerusalem,** at No. 7, tel.

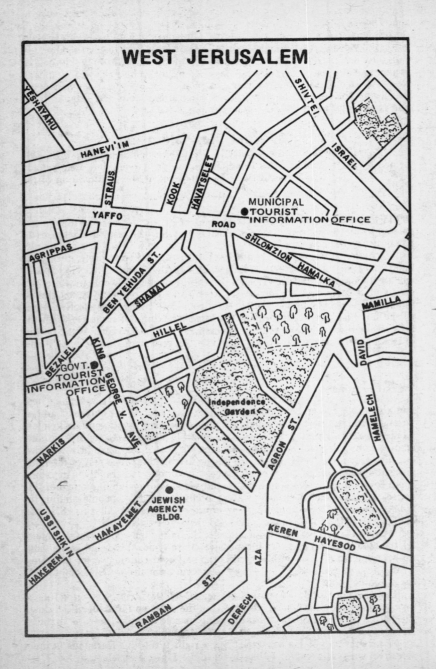

02-222757. Over the reception desk, a sign states: "Open until 12 o'clock by night, please be punctual!"—which should tell you something about the atmosphere of this hotel. It's operated by religious people, who keep all 28 rooms spotless. Each room has hot and cold running water, is simply decorated, and has low rates considering the quality. Singles are SH40.80 ($12), doubles SH68 ($20). Students receive a 10% discount on rooms.

Near the heart of the city, at 4 Luntz St., is the **Zion Hotel**, tel. 02-232367, which sits on a curve facing Ben Yehuda Street and overlooks a constant stream of traffic from sherut cars and minibuses. It's convenient to transportation, and since it's situated in something like a cul-de-sac, it somehow manages to be fairly quiet at night. It is a budget-style walk-up (three flights), with shared facilities. There's heating, but no air conditioning. It's recently been completely refurbished. Breakfast is available. Singles pay SH51 ($15) to SH68 ($20), doubles SH44.20 ($13) to SH51 ($15) per person. Students get a 10% reduction.

Two blocks down the hill from the easy-to-locate buzzing intersection of King George and Ben Yehuda, at 4 Agrippas St. (opposite the Eden Cinema), is the **Palatin,** tel. 02-231141. Enter at street level through glass doors, hike one flight up to the cozy lobby, then sign for a double room that'll run SH51 ($15) per person; singles are SH59.50 ($17.50) to SH68 ($20). The simple dining room serves strictly kosher food.

The **Pension Har Aviv** is seven minutes from town by bus 6, 18, 20, or 10, located on Beit Hakerem St. No. 16a, tel. 02-521515. All of the Har Aviv's 12 rooms have terraces, private toilets, and baths. Decorative throw rugs and printed curtains add charm: heating and air conditioning add comfort. Rates are: SH68 ($20) single, SH51 ($15) per person double. Students get a 20% to 25% reduction. Add SH22.95 ($6.75) for half-board, SH40.80 ($12) for full board.

Many advantages can be found in the cozy and cheerful atmosphere of the **Gidron House Rama Hotel**, 15 Ein Zurim Blvd., in the Talpioth section, tel. 02-37722. The 19 rooms are equipped with tubs or showers. There is a refrigerator on the ground floor and a full kitchen on the top floor, plus a covered terrace and bar where you have a view of the whole city. Every room has a bell to inform you of a phone call, and the sitting room has a TV for those who care to watch. It is a very quiet area far from the noise of traffic. Prices are SH47.60 ($14) single, SH44.20 ($13) per person double. Half-board is SH15.30 ($4.50). To get to Gidron House take bus 8.

One of the city's most majestic hotels is—believe it or not—the **YMCA,** 26 King David St., tel. 02-227111, directly opposite the big King David Hotel. You can't miss the Y building (called the *Imka* by Israelis), because its tall spire can be seen from almost any point in Jerusalem. Available to both men and women, rooms cost SH46.75 ($13.75) to SH68 ($20) single, SH51 ($15) double, including breakfast. Half-board is SH23.80 ($7), full board SH45.90 ($13.50). A look inside reveals a superbly elegant mixture of oriental lushness and medieval-like vastness and arches, plus all the modern comforts and conveniences. After you've checked in, go to the top of the building, via the elevator, and you'll have an extraordinary view of the entire city. The Imka also has an indoor swimming pool and tennis courts. As an added feature, lectures and entertainment are always scheduled for the Y's auditorium, so if you do take a room, be sure to consult the posted schedule in the lobby to see what's doing.

One block west of Jaffa Road, you'll find the 70-room **Orgil,** at 18 Hillel St., tel. 02-224261, where doubles with breakfast range from SH34 ($10) to SH47.60 ($14) per person, depending on the season and facilities.

Just a bit out of the way (about 20 minutes from the center of town) the **Neve Shoshana**, 5 Beit Hakerem St. (in Beit Hakerem), tel. 02-524294, is highly recommended. It's not really much of a hardship being a little out of town since buses 3, 6, 8, 10, 12, 16, 18, 20 and 27 service the hotel. And the 20 rooms here are clean, each with a tiny kitchenette wherein are a stove, refrigerator, sink, dishes, pots, pans, etc. What's more, the hotel is elevator-equipped, partially air-conditioned and has heating throughout. Rates are SH85 ($25) single, SH64.60 ($19) per person double, and if you choose to avoid the kitchenette at breakfast you can order that meal (kosher) for an additional cost.

Also in Beit Hakerem, and equally accessible by bus, is the **Tadmor-Jerusalem Hotel**, 1 Hagai St., tel. 02-523121. Here, however, you're in for a rather unique hotel experience. The Tadmor-Jerusalem is actually a training school for hotel personnel and chefs—all enthusiastically trying to prove their ability. Graded four stars, it's elevator-equipped, air-conditioned, fully heated, and pleasantly situated next to a park. Each of the rooms has a phone and private bath. A kosher, Israeli breakfast is served. There are only three single rooms priced at SH68 ($20); if these are full, singles are put in double rooms and pay SH81.60 ($24), two persons in a double room pay SH59.50 ($17.50) each. Off-season rates are a trifle lower.

Starvation Budget

If you're really watching your pennies, consider the hostels and hospices presented further on, and the following places, some of which are a short bus ride out of the center of things. Though students and young people frequent such places, working people on visits stay in them as well, and many older couples might really enjoy the uniqueness and simplicity found here.

If you're game, try the **Noga** first—just opposite the old Bezalel Museum, at 4 Bezalel St., tel. 02-224590. *Note:* you have to climb three flights to get there. The nice, elderly landlady, Leah Crystal, charges SH25 ($7.35) per person for, as the sign over a small desk says, "Resting for a Night." Off-season rates are lower. There are only ten beds, two rooms, one bathroom and a separate toilet in this simple place. Women are put up with women, men with men, or you can come with your own group. No food is served.

Still in town is the **Eretz Israel Hotel**, 51 King George St. (across the street from Heichal Shlomo), tel. 02-39071. You pay only SH27.20 ($8) for a bed, not including breakfast. It is an old building, but clean and homey when you get up to the second floor. Sinks in the rooms, showers in the hall.

The **Migdal Hotel**, 11 Histadruth St., corner Ben Yehuda St., tel. 02-224749, offers just six rooms, all with the barest necessary furnishings and terraces. There's a TV lounge; no heating or air conditioning. Some rooms have H&C. Singles pay SH18 ($5.30), doubles SH15 ($4.41) per person.

The **Klein Hotel**, 10 King George St., tel. 02-228988, offers four rooms at SH11 ($3.25) per person, SH13 ($3.80) in summer. It is four flights up, but allows use of refrigerator and stove (to make coffee or tea). Mrs. Klein also has an apartment which is simply furnished and equipped with a bathroom and kitchen. In summer, she charges SH40 ($11.75) double for this accommodation, SH30 ($8.80) the rest of the year.

Rooms and Apartments for Rent

Another choice you have in Jerusalem, as well as in most larger towns and cities, is to rent a room in a private home or boarding house. Should this appeal to you (it's a good way to get to know the "real" Israel), check the classified section of the daily *Jerusalem Post,* where you'll surely find several ads for rooms in or near Jerusalem. Then too, keep your eyes open for small signs tacked to store and shop windows—often seen, they're usually in rather bad English or French or German, and announce rooms to let by the week, or more, or less.

Dahaf, Ltd., 43 Jaffa Rd. tel. 02-233941 and 226335, provides a service for SH50 ($1.47) for two months which enables you to look through listings of rooms and flats for rent. Their office is open from 8 a.m. to 7 p.m.

Sheal, 7 Hillel St. tel. 02-226919, offers the same service and rates. Office hours: 8:30 a.m. to 1 p.m. and then again from 4 to 7 p.m., Friday till 12:45 p.m.

Room Renting, Ltd., P.O.B. 8035, tel. 02-633563, offers several standards of accommodation, all without meals. Length of stay can be anywhere from one night to a month or more. Lowest-rated rooms are SH35.70 ($10.50) single, SH51 ($15) double. Better rooms are SH40.80 ($12) single, SH57.80 ($17) double. All rooms offered by this firm have been approved by the Ministry of Tourism. Rates for longer stays are lower. You may request breakfast for an additional charge not exceeding SH5.10 ($1.50) a day.

If you are interested in an apartment and hotel arrangement, that too is available. One is called **Apartotel, Ltd.,** at the Nordau Towers, 214 Jaffa Rd., tel. 02-531221. Minimum stay is one week; prices will be given by the week, but monthly rates are cheaper. A small apartment with two beds is SH428.40 ($126) to SH642.60 ($189), a medium apartment with three beds is SH499.80 ($147) to SH761.60 ($224), and a large apartment with four beds is SH571.20 ($168) to SH880.60 ($259). Your apartment is cleaned twice weekly, linens changed once a week. The kitchenette is equipped for use and all utilities are included. For a small charge washing and drying machines are available, plus baby sitting and grocery delivery service. Reservations and deposits should be made in advance.

Youth Hostels

Whether you're 16 or 65, a member or not, you're welcome to stay at one of Israel's 31 youth hostels, where accommodations are about the cheapest you'll find anywhere. All provide clean and dependable shelter to anyone who wants to travel the land. Hostels are sometimes similar to summer camps, sometimes more like luxury hotels, depending on where they are and how new. Though each has a director, none has servants, and the overall accent is on "simplicity, self-help and mutual service." Usually well maintained, the rooms and furnishings are bright and fresh, and when meals are offered, they're nourishing, if sometimes plain. Separate dormitory facilities (usually double-decker beds with linen and blankets) are available for males and females. Most hostels have at least one kitchen where guests can cook and prepare their own meals, plus dining facilities, a common room, playgrounds and good sanitary facilities. In Israel, the youth hostels are scattered around in spots of natural beauty and high travel interest, from the Negev to the Galilee; they're usually as full as they are attractive, so make reservations in advance, if possible.

Should you want to join the International Youth Hostel Association, you can do so in Israel, or in the States before you leave. Full data can be had from the **Israel Youth Hostel Association,** P.O. Box 1075, 3 Dorot Rishonim St., Jerusalem, tel. 02-225925; from Israel Government Tourist Offices; and even from most offices of El Al Airlines. The membership card gets you reductions on already rock-bottom fees for overnight lodgings. See Chapter XI for details about youth hostels and a rundown of hostel choices in Jerusalem.

Christian Hospices

Originally for pilgrims of their particular sects, most Christian hospices today are flooded with students and tourists of all faiths and ages. The accommodations are always clean, but often spartan, and usually quite inexpensive. Many students take residence in these hospices for the school year, and many tourists like to stay in one simply for the adventure of it—so they're usually well filled. Please note: Most hospices lock up for the night between 10 and 11 p.m.—be sure to ask specifically about this when you register, to avoid misunderstanding.

Over in what is called the German colony is a German hospice, **St. Charles,** P.O.B. 28020, tel. 026-37737, which has ten single and 15 double rooms, and asks no questions about religion or mission. Living quarters are plain but immaculate. Bath and toilet facilities are shared. Rates for half board are SH27.50 ($8.10) single, SH22.50 ($6.60) per person double; with full board rates are SH35 ($10.30) single, SH33 ($9.70) per person double. Unfortunately, the St. Charles is usually filled, so write far in advance.

The **Sisters of the Rosary Hospice,** 14 Agron St., tel. 02-228529, charges just $10 per person per night B&B for accommodations with private toilet and shower. Housed in a large building, it offers 17 spotless rooms set off vast hallways. There are also four dormitories where the B&B rate is $6 a night. Lunch or dinner is $3. Take buses 4, 7, 8, or 10.

St. Andrews Hospice (Church of Scotland), Harakevet St., near the railway station and Khan Theatre, tel. 02-717701, is situated on a small hill and surrounded by a garden. The lobby is graced with an upright piano and a portrait of General Allenby, who laid the foundation for the church in 1930. Eighteen of the 20 rooms have running water, and five have private toilet and shower. Throw rugs add a warm touch to the rooms, as do electric heaters. B&B costs SH37.40 ($11) per person single or double, SH30.60 ($9) for a third occupant. A three-course dinner, by arrangement, is $4.50. Take bus no. 6.

Student Deals

The Jerusalem ISSTA office can be found at 5 Eliashar St., tel. 02-231418. If you are on a seminar program, you can obtain accommodation from them at the **Kiryat Shmuel** seminar dorms. And if you are a full-time student at the Hebrew University, ISSTA can direct you to the **Students Hostel,** Kiryat Ha'university, tel. 02-27581, where you can get centrally heated on-campus bathless doubles. Students who are just visiting can call the Students Hostel, too; they'll accommodate you if any of the rooms are free (unfortunately, there are seldom vacancies).

Inquire about the student program at the **Beit Hillel,** 4 Balfour St. (in back of the Terra Sancta Bldg.), which is used as a kind of student union by Israeli students. Their program of activities, concerts, lectures and such tends to drop off during the summer months though.

EATING PLACES: For purposes of organization, we've grouped the eateries of Western Jerusalem into four rather broad headings. What we called "restaurants" are a variety of sit-down-and-be-served places offering anything from familiar Western to vegetarian to not-so-familiar oriental fare. Next are "light snacks and 'quick counters,'" as varied in cuisine and atmosphere as the above, but not where you'd make an evening of it. Under "cafes" are honest-to-goodness cafes, plus coffee shops, ice cream and dairy parlors, cake shops and the like; some of these serve breakfast, and all, at other times, provide sustenance in a more social sense. Last comes "big splurge restaurants," a purely financial heading this time. These are special, different, even exclusive places that provide relaxation, service, luxury and menus that make the higher prices worthwhile.

Restaurants

Should you find yourself in Jerusalem at the end of your trip, your travelers checks giving out, take heart: one of the country's cheapest and best restaurants awaits you. It's called the Ta-ami, meaning "my taste," and you'll find it on the top of Shamai Street, at No. 3, a block from Ben Yehuda. This is a very small place, tiny even, but its reputation is solidly established among Jerusalemites—and you may have to wait a few minutes for one of the simple, small tables, even to share a table with others. But the wait will be worth it. House specialties are vegetarian-oriental foods, prepared in mouth-watering style. We recommend the stuffed koosa (zucchini), priced at SH2 (59¢). Also good here is bamia, a juicy Middle Eastern okra, also SH2 (59¢). Bean soup, Middle Eastern style (which means it bears no relation whatever to our American bean soup), costs SH1.80 (53¢). Another specialty of the house, filets of fish, costs SH2.80 (60¢). The classic humus and pitta is only SH1.80 (53¢) here. Closed Friday from 2 p.m. and all day Saturday.

The **Taj**, 27 Jaffa Rd., across the road from the Municipal Information Office, tel. 02-241515, is a kosher Persian restaurant. Entered via an alley, it's an attractive place, with Persian art on the walls, velvet-upholstered, high-backed chairs, and lots of plants and greenery. All dishes are served with dilled rice, Persian-style rice (chelo), or rice with carrots and raisins. You might begin your meal with an appetizer of stuffed vine leaves for SH5 ($1.50), and follow up with meat in tomato and eggplant sauce at SH15 ($4.40). A dessert of fresh fruit is SH5 ($1.50). Open Sunday to Thursday from noon to midnight.

An elegant choice that won't bust your budget is the **Ashafit Restaurant,** housed in the spacious balcony of the new Jerusalem Theatre, 20 Marcus St., tel. 02-630078. Luxuriously furnished with deep-red carpeting and handsome black leather chairs, this restaurant offers all the trappings of gracious dining—attentive waiters, a large menu, mood music, even petits fours and cigarettes gratis with your coffee. But it's got more than just ambience—the food is terrific and reasonably priced. You might begin your meal with a Waldorf cocktail, soup, or stuffed cabbage appetizer for SH4 ($1.20). For a main dish, perhaps grilled chicken at SH9 ($2.65) or roast veal with mushrooms at SH12 ($3.55). For dessert try the chocolate mousse SH5 ($1.45). Another option, however, is to order the SH12.50 ($3.70) fixed-price menu, which consists of an appetizer or soup, entree, dessert and coffee. Open 1 to 3 p.m., and 6 to 11 p.m., closed Fridays and Saturday afternoons. ISSTA card-carrying students get a 10% discount.

Deservedly popular is Leah and Ernest Brumer's **Europa**, 48 Jaffa Rd., tel. 02-228953, a Hungarian eatery situated on the first floor of a building overlooking Zion Square. It's fancier at dinner than lunch when paper place mats and napkins are replaced with white, orange, or purple cloths. A quarter stuffed chicken, priced at SH9 ($2.65) comes with a choice of rice, carrots, baked potato, spinach, or dumplings. Sweet-and-sour pot roast, a specialty, is SH2 ($3.55). Leave room for a dessert of palassinta at SH3 (90¢). There's often a line waiting to get in, but you can while away the time with a drink at the bar. Open Sunday to Thursday from noon to 10 p.m., Friday till 3 p.m.

At 4 Luntz St. is the **Rimon**, tel. 02-222772, a favorite of university folk in particular and Jerusalemites in general. Big, crowded and friendly, it has grilled meats for SH7.50 ($2.20), eggplant stuffed with meat for SH4 ($1.15), and roast lamb for SH13.50 ($3.95), not to mention a well-stocked bar and a pleasant Persian decor. Open 8 a.m. to midnight, Friday till about 3 p.m., and Saturday after sunset only.

In a large, round building aptly called the **Rondo Restaurant and Cafe,** 41 King George St., tel. 02-232223, you may enjoy a mushroom omelet for SH3.50 ($1.05) or a cheese and eggplant savory for SH4.50 ($1.30). Other light or more substantial choices are available, all served on a large terrace overlooking Independence Park. Hours: 10 a.m. to 1 a.m.; closed Friday and Saturday until sunset. For card-carrying students—a 10% reduction.

The **Restaurant Stark,** tel. 02-226757, another favorite of the locals, is located in the No. 21 building on King George Ave. So you won't miss it, the signs outside are in English and Hebrew, pointing to a door; at the front of the hallway a menu's posted, and other signs guide you to a right turn, then through a garden-lined passage and at last into the spanking-clean restaurant. The fare is a mixture of oriental/European/Hungarian cuisine, served up with smiles. Flowers adorn the cheery yellow tables. Goulash is a specialty, as is lecco—a unique egg and vegetable Hungarian dish. A good buy is the SH13 ($3.80) meal offered from noon to 4 p.m. and consisting of soup, a main course (perhaps roast chicken or turkey schnitzel), salad, two vegetables, bread, and compote. Open from noon to 9:30 p.m., till 2:30 p.m. on Friday, closed Saturday.

Also on King George Ave., at No. 12, is a tiny modern place named **Marvad Haksamin** (Magic Carpet), tel. 02-231460, which also has moderate prices: goulash and vegetables for SH8 ($2.35), salads and soups at SH2 (60¢), sausage and egg SH3.50 ($1), and fish filet à mere SH6 ($1.75). Perched on leather stool-like chairs, you'll dine on well-scrubbed tables. Open 10:30 a.m. to 11:30 p.m.

The **Sova,** 3 Histadrut St., tel. 02-222266, has both a self-service cafeteria and a dining room with waiter service. Basically, the prices here work out as follows: a three-course cafeteria meal will cost about SH8.50 ($2.50), while the same thing in the dining room will be SH12 ($3.50) (portions in dining room are larger, though, and you get four courses instead of three). Everyone who has ever eaten here has marveled at the jumbo portions served. There are many items to recommend; we personally like the "p'tscha," the calf's foot jelly. Keep in mind that the Sova is kosher and your Friday night and Saturday afternoon meal here must be paid for in advance. If you forget to pre-pay, you'll still be served—if you leave your watch or passport to ensure your return after sundown. Students get a 10% reduction here.

Walk to the bottom of Mamilla St., turn left onto King David St., cross the street, and you'll come to the **Sinaia,** 4 King David, which is possibly the cheapest place to purchase a filling meal in all Jerusalem. This bare little room is always crowded with soldiers and kibbutzniks, which vouches for its prices and generous portions. A main course with two vegetables costs SH5.50 ($4.55) to SH10 ($2.95), soup or humus SH2 (60¢). The turnover is so great here that the food is guaranteed always to be fresh. Open from 8 a.m. to 6 p.m.

Step down into the **Ma'adan,** 35 Jaffa Rd., tel. 02-225631, a white stucco-walled dining room with tables covered in red-and-white checkered cloths. Order up a hearty plate of goulash soup for SH4 ($1.20), almost a meal in itself. A veal roast or chicken schnitzel is SH9 ($2.65), and for dessert there's fresh fruit at SH3 (90¢). Open Sunday to Thursday from 11 a.m. to 11 p.m., closing Friday before sundown until after sunset on Saturday.

At 52 Jaffa Rd., right at a big intersection, you'll find the **Jerusalem Restaurant** (it's called **Trablous** by the locals, in case you're asking directions), tel. 02-222875. Before you go into the dining area, you'll see the menu (in English) posted on the wall to your left: you must place your order here and pay for it before choosing a table. A meal consisting of soup, two vegetables and a choice of meat dishes, plus dessert, runs SH8 ($2.35). Less expensive three-course meals are SH6.50 ($1.90) to SH7 ($2.05). Kosher; open Sunday to Thursday from 9 a.m. to 9 p.m., Friday until 8 p.m., Saturday from 7 to 10 p.m. (Sabbath or holiday lunch must be pre-ordered and pre-paid.) It has a wonderful traditional atmosphere.

The **Jerusalem Artists' House Restaurant and Club,** at 12 Shmuel Hanagid St., tel. 02-232920, next door to the Bezalel Art Academy, is open from 10 a.m. to 1 a.m. Sunday to Thursday, closed Friday, Saturday 11 a.m. to 3 p.m., then from 7 p.m. on. If you eat here, you can take in free painting and sculpture exhibitions, maybe even buy something from one of the 200 exhibiting members of the Association of Jerusalem Artists. And sometimes you can stay for an evening of jazz, chamber music, concerts, readings or lectures. A charming, intimate place, it has reasonable rates and good food: SH2 (60¢) for salads, SH8 ($2.35) for a meal featuring lamb or veal, SH2.50 (75¢) for soups.

You can dine under the trees in **Maskit's Garden Cafe,** 12 Harav Kook St., near Kikar Zion, a small outdoor eatery with rattan furnishings and colorful umbrellas. It's a pleasant place to partake of croissants with butter and jam (or a hot bagel with cream cheese) and a pot of tea or coffee for SH3.50 ($1). From noon to 4 p.m. a prix fixe meal, including cold soup, salad, main course and˙beverage, is SH7.50 ($2.20) to SH9.50 ($2.80). A mocha cooler—iced coffee and chocolate ice cream—for dessert is SH4 ($1.20). Open from May to the end of October, 9 a.m. to 6 p.m. The Cafe closes Friday at noon until Sunday morning.

The **Citadel,** in the Hutzoth Hayotzer Building at 14 Hativat Yerushalaim, tel. 02-288887, is actually three restaurants in one. Upstairs is the Cafe on the Terrace with umbrella tables, (open 8 a.m. to midnight) for light fare such as cheese toast at SH2.50 (75¢), homemade blintzes SH3.20 (95¢), or ice cream SH3.70 ($1.10). Downstairs is a meat restaurant where you might order meatballs, chicken, or roast beef for SH8 ($2.35); soup, salad, or dessert is an additional SH2.50 (75¢). And below this dining area is a Chinese eatery (open noon to 3 p.m. and 6:30 to 11 p.m.) offering the likes of sweet-and-sour pork or shrimp and other oriental dishes for SH11 ($3.25) to SH13.50 ($3.95).

For a change of pace, head for **Poire and Pomme,** 7 Ha'malot St., tel. 02-221975, a cute little crêperie with just seven brown-clothed tables, rattan furnishings, green-and-white-checkered curtains and dark green carpeting. Crêpes filled with vegetables, tuna, or dessert makings are SH3.80 ($1.10) to SH6 ($1.75). Open from noon to 11:30 p.m.; closed Friday from 2:30 p.m. until Saturday evening.

Sima Restaurant and Steakia, 82 Agrippas St., corner of Beit Yaacov St., is a small restaurant/grill with a counter and tables. Very popular, Sima is always packed with families, and frequently there's a line of people waiting for seats. Roast meat in a pitta is SH7.50 ($2.20), grilled steak, kebabs, shashlik, chicken livers, or mixed grill SH10 ($2.95). Open noon to midnight; closed all day Friday and Saturday until sunset.

Good grilled fare can also be had at **Abu Shaul Restaurant,** Mahaneh Yehuda Market, tel. 02-246198, with just seven tables covered in blue-and-white-checkered oilcloth. All food is grilled on charcoal. Open from noon to about 1 a.m., closed Friday, open Saturday after sunset.

Light Snacks and "Quick Counters"

Although many hotel eating places are terribly expensive (compared to the ones we list), *some* of them have more reasonable rates, and most have air conditioning and somewhat better than usual service. So if you're in the neighborhood of a hotel when hunger strikes, check its restaurant—and always its snack bar. The **Jerusalem Tower's Coffee Shop**, 23 Hillel St., is a case in point. Here salads, soups and desserts average SH2 (60¢). Top prices for main courses are SH9 ($2.65) for steak or beef. Open from 7 to 9:30 a.m., noon to 3 p.m. and 6:30 to 9 p.m. Cocktails are served from noon to midnight at the bar to soothing taped music.

The **King David Hotel**, 23 King David St., may be ultra-expensive for living or swimming, but it has, considering all, an almost moderate tab for food at the first-floor coffee shop. While you nibble you can catch some great scenery through the windows, or check out the celebrities sitting nearby (yes, really). For SH6.50 ($1.90) or less you can choose hot or cold beverages, soups, appetizers, yogurt, assorted pastries, an egg or cheese sandwich, potato latkes, omelets or cheese blintzes. The coffee shop is open daily from 10 a.m. to 11 p.m.

And don't overlook the cafe in the **YMCA**, just across the street. It is surprisingly low-priced, considering the fact that the YMCA rooms are surprisingly high-priced. The self-service fountain shop (closed Sundays) is entered from the lobby through a vaulted door, and at the fountain or tables milkshakes are SH1.50 (45¢), ice cream sodas SH1.20 (35¢), hamburgers SH2 (60¢). A full dinner in the dining room starts at SH11 ($3.25).

At 9 King George, near the Agrippas intersection, is the **Tuv Ta'am**, which translates to mean "good taste"—and the food here has exactly that. What's more, the folks are really friendly and give good service. Strictly kosher, the large, open and sunny restaurant serves an egg-less breakfast for SH3 (90¢), marvelous cakes for SH1.20 (35¢) to SH2.50 (75¢); omelets from SH1.50 (45¢). Fresh borscht, juices and drinks start at SH1.60 (47¢), and toasted sandwiches (cheese, lox, tuna, eggs, etc.) range upward from SH2 (60¢). Students receive a 20% discount. Open from 6:30 a.m. to 1 a.m.

Papi's Pizzeria, 9 Ben Hillel St. (another at the Central Bus Station on Jaffa Rd., and a third at Kiryat Hayovel Center) not only features 18 reasonably priced varieties of pizza (including Israeli variations like eggplant and spinach toppings); they also serve omelets from SH3.50 ($1.03) to SH7 ($2.05), meat meals, desserts, wines, and juices. Open 9 a.m. to 9 p.m., except on Friday when closing time is 1:30 p.m., and Saturday, when all branches open after sunset.

Also try **Pizzeria Rimini**, at 15 King George St., tel. 02-225609, and 43 Jaffa Rd., tel. 02-225534. Open 8 a.m. to midnight, closing Friday at 3 p.m. until 8 p.m. Saturday night. Seventeen varieties of pizza ranging in price from SH5 ($1.50) to SH9 ($2.65) a pie.

At 4 Luntz St. (a street crowded with waiting sheruts), you'll find the small, modern **Restaurant Heppner**, tel. 02-221703, which has counter service only. There's no ambience; this is a place to fill up on hearty fare. You can get a tasty bowl of chicken or vegetable soup for SH1.60 (50¢), salads like herring, egg, eggplant, chopped liver, tuna, or Waldorf for SH1.50 (45¢) to SH2.90 (85¢). Inexpensive sandwiches are another option, as is a prix fixe lunch or dinner for SH10.80 ($3.15). Open 10 a.m. to 8 p.m., till 9 p.m. in summer; closed Friday, Saturday, and Sunday until 3 p.m.

At 55 Jaffa Rd., corner of King George, is the **Strauss Milk Bar**, tel. 02-231955, where a mushroom omelet is SH6 ($1.75), and pancakes start at SH5.50 ($1.60), depending on what you want topping them. Cakes are SH2.20

(65¢), beverages SH1.50–1.70 (45–50¢). Open Sunday to Thursday 7:30 a.m. to midnight, closing Friday at 3 p.m. until after sunset on Saturday.

Contrary to what you'd think, **Uncle Sam,** 7 King George St., tel. 02-244228, is German-owned. The menu gives you 83 items to choose from, among them burgers, omelets, hot dogs, and steak sandwiches for SH3.50 ($1.02) to SH6.50 ($1.90), fish platters SH9 ($2.65), and schnitzels SH10 ($2.95) to SH12 ($3.50). It's open 9 a.m. to midnight, Friday till 3 p.m., Saturday from after sunset.

If you've been hitting the oriental eateries rather hard and want a change of pace, head for **Cafe Max,** 23 Ben Yehuda St. (where King George intersects, across from the big new Hamashbir Letzarchan department store), tel. 02-233722. Open daily from 7 a.m. to midnight (Friday till 3 p.m.), Max serves an SH5.50 ($1.60) Swedish plate, blintzes for the same price, omelets for SH3.50 ($1.02). Reasonably priced sandwiches, pastries, and cakes are also offered, as is an SH4 ($1.20) breakfast with rolls, salad, cheese, jam, and coffee. A friendly place.

At 21 Ben Yehuda St., the **Shemesh,** tel. 02-222418, offers a counter grill in addition to its posh restaurant (see "Big Splurge" selections below). Here you can get a meal of soup and moussaka, for SH4.5 ($1.30), chicken livers with onions, baked potato and salad for SH8.50 ($2.50), a pitta filled with humus, tchina, and eggplant for SH2.50 (75¢)—all at 10% less for students. Open noon to midnight; closed from before sunset on Friday till after sunset on Saturday.

About a 15-minute walk from the railroad station, at 5 Ein Rogel St., there's an excellent, air-conditioned self-service cafe in the **Abu Tor Observatory,** tel. 02-718668. The vegetarian food is well prepared and the prices are moderate. SH1 (30¢) buys either pudding or pastries; SH2 (60¢) soup, entree or a vegetable plate. SH12 ($3.50) is about top price for a full, big meal. Everything's spotless and clean. (This particular location, by the way, has been special since the first century, when Titus chose it as launching point for attacking Jerusalem. Today, one of the most interesting things to note from here is the contrast between sleepy, picturesque Arab house clusters and sleek, efficient new buildings.) Open 9 a.m. to 3 p.m. daily except Saturday.

The **Hen Restaurant,** just across from the main post office at 30 Jaffa Rd., tel. 02-227317, is a Kurdistan mom and pop establishment (she cooks, he serves). The ambience is pleasant, and there's air conditioning. Kurdish specialties are featured Tuesdays and Fridays; try the kharshuf—chopped meat rolled in artichoke leaves, fried, then cooked in sauce—for SH3.50 ($1.02). A serving of stuffed vegetables—grape leaves, zucchini, eggplant, and onions—is SH6.50 ($1.90). Open Sunday to Thursday 8:30 a.m. to 6:30 p.m., Friday till 3 p.m.

A window display of pastries and cakes will lure you into the **Cafe Navah,** 44 Jaffa Rd., tel. 02-222861, where a specialty is sugarless cake (sold by weight). A Swedish plate of hard-boiled egg, potato salad, lox, sardines, and bread and butter is SH5 ($1.50), two blintzes with sour cream SH4.30 ($1.25), a standard breakfast SH3.20 (95¢). You can get waitress service, but the counter is cheaper. Open 7 a.m. to 7 p.m.

Catering to a young and hip crowd, **Chocolate Soup,** 14 Rivlin St., is a tiny place, its walls hung with tapestries. Menu items have names like Pink Floyd—it's fresh strawberries and lemon juice—SH2.50 (75¢). Two crêpes with a milkshake cost SH5.30 ($1.55), SH5 ($1.50) with tea or coffee. And you *can* order chocolate soup, a rich pudding made of oats, fruit, cocoa and milk—yummy at SH2.40 (70¢). Open Sunday to Thursday from 10 a.m. to 2 p.m. and 5 p.m. to midnight, closing Friday from 2 p.m. until Saturday after sunset.

Another option is the do-it-yourself snack or meal—a picnic outside or even in your room. Jerusalem (and most of Israel) is swamped with delicatessens, small food shops, large supermarkets, bakeries and so forth, where you can buy all the fixings for considerably less than a restaurant would charge.

One of the best places for picnic fare is the **Picnic Grill**, 57 Jaffa Rd., tel. 02-224195, where you can also eat at the counter. But it's cheaper to take the food with you: SH3 (90¢) for a quarter grilled chicken, SH4.20 ($1.25) for a half. A nine-ounce portion of salad (there are 13 kinds) costs SH2 (60¢), rice-filled vegetables SH1.50 (45¢) apiece. Open 8 a.m. to 8 p.m., closed Friday from 3 p.m. until Sunday morning.

Cafes

At 7 Ben Yehuda St., the **Atara**, tel. 02-225008, is a bit pricey for many items. However, it has a good selection of cakes and pastries from SH1.30 (40¢) to SH2.70 (80¢), as well as our favorite drink, which can be enjoyed from a perch on the Atara's second-floor balcony—a coffee ice cream soda for SH4 ($1.20). A Swedish plate is SH7.50 ($2.20). Food eaten at the counter is cheaper. Open 6:30 a.m. to midnight; closed from Friday at 2:30 p.m. until after sunset on Saturday.

Also in this class, at 40 Jaffa Road, is the **Alaska** cafe, tel. 02-222989, roosting spot for newspaper-reading coffee-sippers. Coffee is SH2 (60¢), and nobody bothers you if you sit for an hour or two. Breakfast is served until 11 a.m.: two eggs, rolls, butter, cheese, jam, and tea or coffee for SH4.40 ($1.30). Fish and chips with salad and bread is SH6.50 ($1.90). Ice cream is a specialty. Open 7 a.m. to 8 p.m., till 10 p.m. in summer. Closed Friday from 3 p.m. until 8 p.m. Saturday, except in winter when the Alaska stays closed all day Saturday.

Pie House, 5 Horkenos St., next door to the Jerusalem Hotel, is a wood shack which opens onto a gravel-floored patio under the trees. The young owners offer a full meal and a glass of wine to any *good* musician who will play for them, and there's usually one on hand to entertain you while you dine; on Friday afternoons classical music is played. The patio has marble-topped tables; the interior is rustic with wooden furnishings and glasses of flowers on every table. Pies are filled with beef, vegetables, chicken, or fruit and cost between SH3 (90¢) and SH12 ($3.50). Since they're about seven inches in diameter, you might consider sharing. A Caesar salad for two is SH7 ($2.05). Tempting pie fillings include chicken with almonds and raisins, sweet-and-sour chicken, beef and olive, and traditional steak and kidney. Pie House is not kosher though it does close Friday at 6 p.m. and re-open Saturday at 7 p.m.; other days its open from noon to midnight.

Hauga Cafe, 2 Hasoreg St., opposite the Israel Bank on Jaffa Rd., tel. 02-244491, displays its scrumptious wares—cakes, eclairs, cookies, etc.—in glass cases. They cost SH1.50 (45¢) to SH3.50 ($1), but you can also order pizza for SH2 (60¢), sandwiches for about the same price, or, until 9:30 a.m., a complete SH4 ($1.20) breakfast. Everything is a bit cheaper if you take it out. Open 7 a.m. to 7 p.m.; closed Friday from 2 p.m. until Sunday morning.

Big Splurge Restaurants

The **Shemesh Restaurant**, behind the Shemesh grill-counter at 21 Ben Yehuda, tel. 02-222418, is a marvelous place for relaxing meals and interesting people. If you're lucky, you'll meet the owner, Yeheskel Shemesh, one of Jerusalem's better-known figures, who's often called "The Sun" (Shemesh in Hebrew). Aside from operating a great food place for many years, Shemesh is known for giving much time, and food, to wounded soldiers. After the war, he was visiting a hospital for some of the handicapped wounded, and, thinking it would be good therapy, invited a soldier to come in for dinner and bring his buddies. The soldier showed up, as did his buddies, and from that time on one night each week was set aside for handicapped soldiers—everything the boys could eat and drink, on the house. For this, and other such generous actions, Mr. Shemesh has received many commendations and medals—but what he values most are the many friendships. Take a look at the photos on the walls, and you'll recognize many of Israel's leaders.

House specialties—gourmet dishes—are baked lamb and steak à la Shemesh, at SH20 ($5.90) each (for the main course only). Every first course is SH2.50 (75¢), as is the meat, bean or chicken soup. There's a good selection of wines at around SH1.50 (45¢) a glass. Fresh fruits make a great dessert for SH2.50 (75¢). Open noon to midnight, it has soft lights and a restful atmosphere. Closed Friday night and Saturday until evening.

The number is 2 and the street is Queen Shlomzion, but you don't need either to find the **Mandarin Chinese Restaurant and Bar,** tel. 02-222890. From the Jaffa Road Jerusalem Municipality Building, just look diagonally across the street and you'll see a huge red sign bearing a dragon (naturally) and the restaurant's name in gold. Under the sign, an arched stone entrance opens to stairs that lead past hand-painted murals to the dining room and bar. It's a large room, yes, but you'll probably be struck more by the atmosphere of peaceful harmony. All is in order here, even the colors, with reds and blues softened by arched stained-glass windows and flowers offsetting each red- or lavender-clothed table. A main dish averages SH14.50 ($4.25) to SH16 ($4.70), and choices include duck, chow mein and a variety of sweet-and-sour specialties. Shrimp dishes are SH16.50 ($4.85), egg roll SH5 ($1.50), soups SH4 ($1.20) to SH6 ($1.80). The interesting and obviously old bar serves cocktails and hard drinks. Open from noon to 3 p.m. and 6:30 to 11:30 p.m.

The highly recommended **Georgia Restaurant,** 4 King David St., tel. 02-227577, features Russian cuisine, including Caucasian specialties. There is a popular-priced restaurant upstairs and a larger and more elegant dining room downstairs, each offering old favorites and new eating adventures. Upstairs you might try a piquant Georgian soup ("Hartsou") cooked with fresh vegetables and rice for SH2.80 (80¢), meat pancakes SH4 ($1.20), or stuffed cabbage SH5.50 ($1.60). Open noon to 4 p.m., till 5 p.m. in summer.

WHAT TO DO AT NIGHT: West Jerusalem is not exactly bursting with nightlife, but there are a few spots where you can enjoy yourself and see what appeals to the Jerusalem night people. You'll notice that Israelis are great movie-goers—and that usually takes care of their after-dinner entertainment, except for the young who frequent the discos.

The very contemporary **Jerusalem Theatre,** 20 David Marcus St., tel. 02-667167, opened its doors in 1975. Original Israeli plays, and Hebrew translations of foreign classics and modern plays, are performed in the theatre's main hall; visiting troupes also use the main hall for performances in foreign languages. The Auditorium is the home of the Jerusalem Symphony Orchestra and the Israel Chamber Ensemble. (The Israel Philharmonic Orchestra hold their concerts in the Binyanei Ha'Uma, off Jaffa Rd. facing the bus station.) On the top floor is the Ashafit Restaurant, highly recommended above.

A uniquely Israeli entertainment is offered at **Assaf's Cave,** on Mount Zion, near David's Tomb, tel. 02-716760. It's a unique kind of nightclub presenting a folkloric show of Hasidic music and dancing. All the performers are men. The entire audience joins in a hora before and after the show. Admis-

sion is SH34 ($10), including all the wine you can drink. Open 8:30 to 11:30
p.m. Tuesday and Saturday nights, nightly except Friday in summer.

Also check out the doings at the **Jerusalem Hilton,** tel. 02-536151—
bridge tournaments, theater nights, etc., open to the public as well as guests.

Big Splurge Evenings

The **Khan Club,** located diagonally opposite the railway station, is just
one part of the Khan complex, which was opened in 1968. The theater has seats
for 400 theater-goers, and the emphasis is on Israeli folklore. The Club is built
into a high-vaulted room that reflects the history of the Khan building. It
started out as a *caravanserai* (a sort of Turkish motel) in Ottoman times,
graduated to a beer garden serving the German Knights Templar in the 19th
century, was converted into an ammunition depot under the British Mandate,
and was, most recently, a carpenter shop. The atmosphere of the club—rough-
walled and candlelit—harkens back to the Turkish times, although the entertainment is strictly Israeli: lively traditional dances, Israeli folksongs and singers, plus a sing-along with the enthusiastic combo. Unfortunately, the
admission price is so high at SH34 ($10) that those with whom you will be
singing are more likely to be other American tourists than any local Israelis.
The admission includes the show and unlimited soft drinks or wine. There is
one show nightly at 10 p.m. Reservations are necessary: call 02-718283.

Also in the complex are: **The Khan Bar,** tel. 02-718283, for dancing to
taped music. Open nightly from 9 p.m. Drinks are SH5 ($1.50), SH7 ($2.05)
Friday nights. Then there are performances at the **Khan Theatre,** tel. 02-
718282, in Hebrew with tickets priced at SH10 ($2.95), SH7 ($2.05) for students; performances at 9 p.m. Even if you don't speak Hebrew, you can enjoy
the Sunday night chamber music concerts and Wednesday folklore evenings.
Also here, the **Khan Cafe and Restaurant** where you can have coffee and cake
or ice cream.

All the above are in one building in David Remez Square across from the
railroad station.

Folk songs and dances are the entertainment fare at the **Jerusalem of Gold
Nightclub,** housed on the bottom floor of the Abu Tor Observatory. The
admission price is a rather steep SH34 ($10), but for that you get all the wine
or soft drinks you can down. Open nightly except Friday 9 a.m. to midnight.

THE SIGHTS OF WEST JERUSALEM: From three high vantage points
in the city, you'll be able to obtain a picture of Jerusalem's general layout that
will be most helpful in your touring. It would be wise to include these three
sights among your first stops.

The first view is from **King George Avenue,** between the Jewish Agency
building (which consists of a large courtyard housing a trio of connected
administrative buildings) and the Hechal Shlomo, the domed, imposing Seat
of the Rabbinate. From here, you can look directly out over Independence Park
(Gan Ha'atzmauth), with its carefully gardened slopes and flower beds, clear
across the Old City wall, beyond which lie the Mount of Olives and the
Ascension Site (on the left). In the distance, the cream and orange stone of
Jerusalem's houses blends into the earth itself. On the right side, bordering the
park, is the American Consulate, with its tall flagpole; at the extreme right of
this panorama stands the oddly Victorian King David Hotel, a big rectangular
building; at its right, slightly in the foreground, is an impressive building, the
Jerusalem YMCA. Its tall tower, surrounded by domes, suggests some mam-

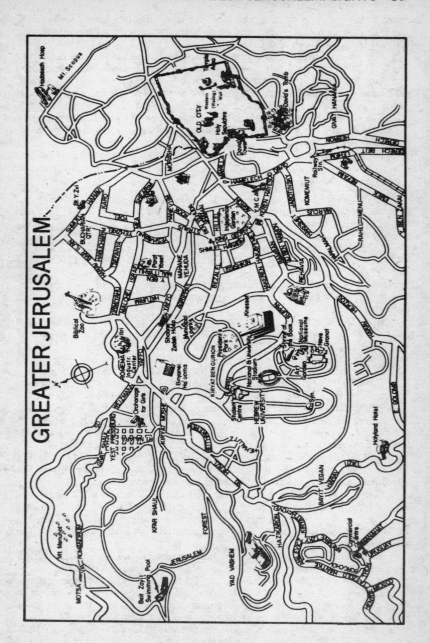

moth minaret and mosque, giving it an exotically Eastern flavor. Away off to the right, on a clear day, the landscape blurs into a maze of mountains, the biblical range of Moab and Gilead.

For an even broader panoramic view, take the elevator up to the top of the YMCA's 152-foot **Jesus' Tower.** Hours are from 9 a.m. to noon and tours run Monday through Saturday; tour price is 10 agorat if you climb yourself, 20 agorat if you opt for the elevator. Once at the top, the entire city spreads around you, and you are able to really see Jerusalem.

The third location from which to orient yourself to Jerusalem's geography is **Abu Tor,** a promontory near the railroad station (the Observatory is described below).

Now on to the sights of Jerusalem, one by one:

Mount Zion

This is an important location, the site of an impressive cluster of buildings, and can be easily spotted from almost any point in Jerusalem. The building to the left (with a tower) is the **Dormition Abbey,** and on the same site is **King David's Tomb** and the **Room of the Last Supper (Coenaculum)** above it.

Entrance to the grounds is a short walk after passing through Zion Gate, or from the foot of Kings St., the avenue which goes past the King David Hotel and YMCA building. You must wear a hat to set foot upon these sacred grounds, but there's a stand near the entrance that will loan you one in exchange for a returnable deposit. The grounds are open till sunset daily except Saturday, Friday till 2 p.m.

King David's Tomb is a rock-walled room lit by flickering candles and overseen by a devout couple who will light a candle for you and say a few prayers. Upstairs is the sacred **Last Supper Room.** In the cellar of the building next door is the **Chamber of Martyrs**—another eerie room lit by candles—dedicated to the memory of 6,000,000 Jews slain by the Nazis.

Close by, the graceful **Dormition Abbey** building stands, according to tradition, on the spot where Mary fell into eternal sleep. It was erected in 1906 on a plot of land presented to the German kaiser by the Turkish sultan. Inside the church are an elaborate golden mosaic, a crypt containing particularly interesting religious artwork, and a statue of Mary, around which are chapels donated by various countries: the Austrian Chapel is a memorial to its slain prime minister and the Hungarian chapel depicts famous saints and Hungarian kings. From the tower of the church there's a good panoramic view of the surrounding region. No visitors allowed between 1 and 3 p.m.

South of Mount Zion, across the valley called "Hinon" or "Gehenna," is an old section called **Mishkanoth Sha'ananim,** built by Sir Moses Montefiore in 1859. It was the first venture of settlers outside the city walls. Today, the building is used as a residence for visiting artists and official guests of the government.

Vis-à-vis Mount Zion road is a **peace memorial,** a slender pillar with a tangle of metal at the bottom. The inscribed legend is Isaiah's swords-into-ploughshares admonition, and the memorial itself is a gift from Abie Nathan, Israel's celebrated flying and sailing "peacenik." Nearby is a road winding to the right, clear up to the top. Jerusalemites call it the "Pope's Road," since it was built especially for the Pope's visit several years back. During its construction part of a ceramic aqueduct was uncovered. Believed to have been built during the Second Temple era, it runs through hills and valleys for 45 kilometers to Solomon's Pool. Parts can be seen today in the area of Hativat Yerushalayim St. south of Mount Zion.

Herod's Family Tomb

This burial cave, discovered in the late 19th century, is off King David St., just a few steps down from the King David Hotel. Used as an air-raid shelter during the 1948 war, it is believed to be the tomb of some member of Herod's family rather than his actual burial site (that's called Herodion and is in the mountains south of Bethlehem). Open 10 a.m.–1 p.m. Monday through Thursday; small entrance fee. Buses 6, 15 and 18 will take you there.

King David Hotel

This is the famous hotel blown up in July, 1946, by Israeli underground fighters—an act which hastened the departure of the Crown from Israel. The entire right wing of the building was subsequently rebuilt, and if you look closely, you can see the difference in the stone. (The bomb was hidden in a milk container in the basement, in what is now the Regence Grill.) The outdoor patio here is a lovely place for a drink, but the lobby of the hotel should be experienced just for its own sake. It is something out of a bygone era, and if you let your imagination go, you can visualize British ladies in long skirts, their gentlemen in white double-breasted panama suits, with Arab sheikhs in flowing gowns seated nearby. Kissinger has been a frequent guest at the King David, and it was the official World War II residence of Haile Selassie of Ethiopia. Incidentally, when the hotel was built, in 1934, the designers thought to give each public room an "ancient" influence. A poster in the lobby tells you how the lobby has a Hittite influence, the bar King Solomon's influence, the restaurant Hellenistic, and the Banquet Hall Phoenician. Buses: 6, 15 and 18.

An exact replica of the Liberty Bell in Philadelphia stands in the center of Jerusalem's **Liberty Bell Garden,** about 700 feet south of the King David Hotel. The seven-acre garden has a picnic area, and future plans include a large children's playground and an entertainment area.

Abu Tor Observatory

The Abu Tor Observatory opened in the summer of 1971—thanks to the dream of Mrs. Shoshanna Schwartz, a warm and lovely lady who has lived on this site since 1959. Before the 1967 war that united Jerusalem, her home was right on the border of No Man's Land, an easy target for Jordanian potshots. When the war broke out, Mrs. Schwartz stuck to her ground and kept her stove going to provide hot coffee, soup and such for weary soldiers. Afterward, her little lot drew crowds of locals and tourists alike, because it offered one of the most breathtaking views of all Jerusalem. With much imagination, plus a little help from friends and a partner, she transformed her crumbling Arab house into this three-story, top-quality welcoming station. Though she makes good money from the main-floor.(posh) gift shop, and the above-mentioned upstairs restaurant-cafeteria-nightclub, Mrs. Schwartz charges absolutely nothing for the view from the rooftop observation point (open from 9 a.m. to 6 p.m.). If you do decide to souvenir shop here, you'll find that the arts and crafts, jewelry, and paintings all express excellent taste, and that the quality is good. Should the view inspire an appetite, you'll find a selection of moderately inexpensive food.

As for that view: to the left you'll see the far side of Mount Zion. Beyond the walls of Jerusalem is the Mount of Olives. And in front of the Mount of Olives is one of the oldest and most sacred Jewish cemeteries in existence, part of which lies outside of, and part under, the Intercontinental Hotel. Also in view from this point is Gethsemane and the Mosque of Omar, site of Solomon's Temple.

Off to the left is the famous Mount Scopus, site of the first Hadassah Hospital and Hebrew University. Although Mount Scopus remained in Jordanian hands at the end of the 1948 war, access to the buildings was promised to the Israelis—a promise that was never kept. The Jordanians denied Israelis the right to use the buildings or any of the equipment—nothing could even be transferred out. Consequently, the libraries and laboratories and lecture halls collected dust for some 20 years.

Buses 6, 7, 8, and 30 stop at Abu Tor, but you can walk if you'd rather: just head for the railroad station and you'll find it. If you do get lost, most anyone can guide you to this well-known spot. (The official address is 5 Ein Rogel St., but many people won't know that.) If you're walking from Mt. Zion path, turn left at Kings St. and walk toward the railroad station, but make a left turn when you get there; then follow the road, keeping the view of Mt. Zion rampart directly on your left. The Observatory is built on a promontory at the end of this road.

The YMCA

One of the most outstanding landmarks of the city (when you get lost, look for its tower; you'll find that you're never really too far from it anywhere in Jerusalem) was built in 1928 from funds donated by a Montclair, New Jersey millionaire, James Jarvie. The top of its tower provides a view second only to the roof of the Jerusalem Hilton. (See above for specifics.) The YMCA has a swimming pool, tennis courts, lecture hall and gymnasium—not to mention an archeological museum, the **Herbert E. Clark Collection of Near Eastern Antiquities,** housing flint implements, Palestinian pottery from the Chalcolithic to the Middle Ages, clay and bronze figures, seals, scarabs, ancient glass, tools, weapons etc. The Y also holds organ concerts Saturday mornings at 11:30—on the largest pipe organ in the Middle East. And it is probably the only YMCA in the world where the clientele is consistently 95% Jewish! Buses 6, 15 and 18 stop here.

Jewish Agency Compound

The three connected buildings, around a big courtyard on King George Avenue, were the seat of the "secondary" government under the British Mandate. The Jewish Agency headquarters is here, as is the Jewish National Fund and Keren Hayesod (UJA buildings). The Jewish Agency structure was severely damaged just before the establishment of the State, when a booby-trapped car, driven by an Arab chauffeur on the American Embassy staff, exploded against the building's courtyard facade. All is well now, and the three giant institutions still play a major role in immigrant absorption and the reclamation of land. There are various displays—the Golden Book, recording donors' names, and the Zionist Archives. Free films about Israel are shown occasionally at noon. Buses 8, 9 and 10.

Heichal Shlomo

At 58 King George Ave., facing the large main park, Gan Ha'atzmauth, is the imposing **Seat of the Rabbinate** building, styled along the lines of King Solomon's Temple. Square at the bottom and round at the top, the lofty building offers quite a view from its uppermost balcony. It houses the country's highest religious offices and contains a synagogue. Free tours from 9 a.m. to

1 p.m. Sundays through Thursdays; till noon on Fridays. Weekly programs here—religious and folk songs, lectures and readings—mark *Melave Malka,* the end of the sabbath and the beginning of the new week. For times of these traditional festivities, check at Heichal Shlomo, your hotel or the Tourist Information Office. Buses 8, 9, and 19.

Rehavia

A right turn on King George Avenue, either at the Jewish Agency compound or at the Kings Hotel, will bring you into Jerusalem's handsomest residential section: Rehavia, with its middle- and upper-class, tree-lined, quiet streets. Main streets are Ramban Street, Usishkin, Abarbanel, Ben Maimon, Gaza, Alfasi. This is an area of character and charm, well worth a leisurely stroll.

Some sights along the way include the **Prime Minister's residence,** at the corner of Balfour and Smolenskin; **The Alfasi Grotto** (also called the Tomb of Jason), on Alfasi St., a frescoed and inscribed tomb discovered by builders while they were digging foundations (open 10 a.m.–4 p.m.); and the **Monastery of the Cross,** built by Gregorian monks in the 11th century and now maintained by the Greek Orthodox Church. According to tradition, the beautiful monastery is located on the spot where stood the tree from which the Cross was made. Its interior is splendidly medieval. If you don't want to walk down the rocky hillside from Rehavia to the monastery, take bus 9 or 16. South of Rehavia, in Kiryat Shmuel, is **Beit Hanassi,** the President's residence.

Post Office

Continue up Jaffa Road and you can't miss it. Here's where you mail your cables—a special 24-hour service—and, if you're staying around awhile (and shifting addresses frequently), obtain an address called: General Delivery, Jerusalem Post Office, Israel. This main office opens at 7 a.m. daily except Saturday. It closes at 7 p.m. daily, 2 p.m. Fridays and holidays. Other post offices are at 8 Keren Kayemet St.; Hadassah Hospital; Ein Kerem; Hordus (Old City); Mea Shearim 9; David's Tower; 94 Herzl St., Rehavia, and Beit Hakerem. Most post offices open at 8 a.m.

Russian Compound

Back down Jaffa Road a little is the incongruous-looking **Russian Church,** an edifice which looks as if it was lifted from the heart of Leningrad. The green-domed cathedral and surrounding land long remained the property of the Russian Church (the Israeli Government rented some of it for administrative offices). In 1965, Israel finally purchased the compound from Russia. Once this structure was the world's largest "hotel"; it could accommodate 10,000 Russian pilgrims at one time (that was in the 1920s, when the Russians were the most numerous pilgrims to Israel). A permanent exhibit stands in the **Hall of Heroism,** which once served as the Mandate's Jerusalem Central Prison (see the cells and execution chambers). It focuses on Jewish underground activities of the pre-1948 period. Open daily, 10 a.m. to 4 p.m.

Inside the compound, by the way—between the Cathedral and the Police Station—stands **Herod's Pillar** (circled by an iron fence), thought to have been intended, once upon a time, for Herod's Temple.

Buses 6, 13, 18, 20, and 23.

Windmill and Yemin Moshe

There's no confusing Jerusalem with Holland, but all the same, the windmill across from Mt. Zion has piqued many a tourist's curiosity. As it happened, Sir Moses Montefiore, the British philanthropist, visited Palestine a century and a half ago and was appalled by the ghetto conditions of the Jews in the Old City. He decided to build them a new residential section just outside the walls, and soon New Orleans philanthropist Judah Touro joined in the project, becoming the first American Jew to contribute to Israel. The new quarter was called Yemin Moshe, and the philanthropists even provided a windmill for the grinding of flour. Standing on the upper part of Yemin Moshe, facing the Old City ramparts, the windmill was an important observation point during the 1948 War of Independence. In fact, the entire Yemin Moshe quarter was under persistent siege during the war, taking the full brunt of the attack, hopelessly surrounded a dozen times but still managing to hold out. The windmill, now a museum dedicated to Montefiore, may be visited daily from 4 to 7 p.m. and from 10 a.m. to 1 p.m. on Saturdays. Tourists and residents alike swarm the area at all times, peering into the artists' galleries that have been fashioned out of the original homes. After the 1967 war, the Jerusalem Municipality offered help and grants to artists to reconstruct the houses and stables and convert the area into a small artists' colony. As the area became more and more desirable, and thus expensive, many artists could no longer afford to live there, and wealthy foreigners began buying up the property. Famous local poets, novelists and about a dozen artists live here now. If you're around in August, don't miss the special art fair centering around the square next to the windmill. Take buses 6 or 18.

Bezalel Academy of Arts and Design

Located behind the old Knesset building, at 10 Shmuel Hanagid St., the school was founded in 1906; many of Israel's artists have attended classes here at one time or another. The name Bezalel is that of the Old Testament's famous artist, Bezalel ben Ouri, "full of divine inspiration in the art of combining cloths, working gold, silver, copper, precious stones and woods" (Exodus 31:2-11); Bezalel built the Holy Tabernacle for the tribes of Israel while they were wandering in the desert on their way to the Promised Land. (The museum that used to be here is now part of the Israel Museum.) The Academy's five departments are: fine arts, environmental and industrial design, graphic design, ceramics, and gold- and silversmithing. Take buses 16 or 19.

Jerusalem Artists' House

Next door to Bezalel, at 12 Shmuel Hanagid St., tel. 02-223653, a flurry of cultural activities centers around exhibitions of the Jerusalem Artists' Association. Evenings of chamber music, concerts, readings, jazz and art lectures are scheduled each year (for specifics check with the Tourist Office or at the office here); there's a restaurant and a club, with moderate prices, where tourists are welcome—open daily 10 a.m. to midnight, closed Friday and open Saturday nights. On the main floor, paintings and sculpture of all 200 member artists are exhibited and sold (if you buy, they'll ship your purchases). Upstairs and throughout the building are general exhibitions in August and the spring; special exhibitions, featuring about three artists at a time, change every three weeks during the rest of the year. When you visit here, don't miss a close look at the beautifully carved outside doors, the crenellated roof and dome, and the garden sculpture. Open 10 a.m. to 1 p.m. and 4 p.m. to 7 p.m. daily, 10 a.m. to 1 p.m. Saturdays; free entrance. Restaurant and club tel. 02-232920.

Prophets Street

Called **Rehov Hanviim,** this is the "Christian Street" of Western Jerusalem, housing a variety of missionary societies and foreign churches. From Zion Square, in the heart of downtown Jerusalem, go right up any of the two or three narrow streets branching off up the hill.

On Prophets Street you'll find the **Swedish Theological Seminary,** the **Christian Missionary Alliance,** the **American Bible Institute** and, branching off at Abyssinian Street, the splendid **Abyssinian** (Ethiopian) **Church,** with a Lion of Judah carved on the gate above the courtyard. The reason for the Lion of Judah (emblem of the late King Haile Selassie of Ethiopia): the Ethiopians believe that the Queen of Sheba was an Ethiopian empress and that on her first visit to Jerusalem she received the Lion of Judah emblem from King Solomon. Haile Selassie himself traced his royal lineage to the meeting of King Solomon and the Queen of Sheba.

Mahane Yehuda

Just off Jaffa Road, before you reach the center of Jerusalem, is an old market quarter where the streets are named for fruits and the atmosphere is at its liveliest on Wednesdays and Thursdays, when the streets are jam-packed. Here, in a square off Mahane Yehuda and Jaffa Rd., stands a small war memorial commemorating the success of the Israelis' homemade secret weapon in the 1948 battle of Jerusalem. The gun, a **Davidka mortar,** was the major weapon used in the defense of Jerusalem. It threw a small shell, did a bit of damage, but made such an earsplitting roar that, as legend has it, it scared the devil out of the Arabs.

Binyanai Ha'ooma

This imposing auditorium on the northwestern part of Jaffa Road, just opposite the new central bus station, often has interesting exhibitions. King-size conventions take place on the premises, and it is the concert hall for the Israel Philharmonic Orchestra. The Tourist Office has a schedule of current doings.

Mea Shearim

A visit to this religious quarter is bound to be informative, and at the same time either fascinating or chilling, depending on your attitude. The stronghold of an extreme sect of Jewish orthodoxy since 1887, Mea Shearim derives its name from the account of Isaac, son of Abraham: "Then Isaac sowed in that land, and received in the same year a hundredfold [Mea Shearim] and the Lord blessed him" (Genesis 26:12).

Center of the mystical Hasidic religious sect, Mea Shearim, with its winding cobbled alleys, could have been taken from a classical picture of the Eastern European ghetto. The customs, clothing and language fill out the picture. Here you can see scribes painstakingly copying the Scriptures by hand. Long-bearded men in black gowns trudge the streets. On their heads they wear beaver-fur hats or sometimes more broad-brimmed black hats. Young boys with pale white faces wear bobbing side-curls (payot), short black pants and high black socks. The married women, according to strict Orthodox tradition, wear wigs and scarves over their shaved heads. Dozens of tiny shops sell religious ornaments and artifacts, and almost every other door is either a Talmudic school or a synagogue. Many residents speak only Yiddish in conversation, regarding Hebrew as too sacred a language for everyday use. These fiercely religious Russian and Polish Jews are fighting what they consider the blasphemous modern life of Israel. Some of them don't even recognize the laws of the Israeli government. One group, called the Guardians of the City (Neturei Karta), claim that no State of Israel can exist before the coming of the Messiah. The sect has frequently clashed with police in demonstrations protesting autopsies, driving on Saturday, and mixed swimming pools.

Long-sleeved dresses, lengthy skirts, and head coverings are *musts* for women visiting the synagogues; in fact, they are recommended for all women touring this area. Stretched across several streets are banners proclaiming: "Daughters of Israel, the Torah obligates you to dress with modesty. We do not tolerate immodestly dressed people on our streets." The alternative for an immodestly dressed woman is not made clear, but if these are the customs here, why ask for trouble?

And speaking of trouble, there's the matter of photography. Since photographs represent "graven images" to some residents here, and are considered just plain taboo by others, you're strongly advised to resist all temptation to snap pictures in this area.

In fringe areas around this Ashkenazi—or Eastern European—section are other religious neighborhoods, composed of Yemenite, Bukharian and Persian Jews.

Good buys can be found in the old market shops here, better than Jaffa Road.

Mea Shearim can be reached by turning on to Mea Shearim Street from Prophets Street (or take bus 11 from Zion Square).

Sanhedrian Tombs

Go up Shmuel Hanavy Street to northwest Jerusalem's beautiful public gardens of **Sanhedria** (or take bus 2). Called either the Tombs of Sanhedria or the Tombs of the Judges, this is where the judges of ancient Israel's "Supreme Court" (during the first and second centuries) lie buried. The three-story burial catacomb is carved out of rock, with many an intricate feature—some niches have rolling stone closures. The gardens are open every day from 9 a.m. to 4 or 5 p.m.; the tombs are closed Saturdays. (This is one of the Plant-a-Tree places, by the way.)

The Biblical Zoo

This is one of our favorite places in Jerusalem. (Near the corner of Yermiyahu and Brandeis streets ask directions from there to the "Gan Ha-cha-yot Ha-ta-nachi," because there's no longer a street name.) The zoo contains many of the birds and animals described in the Bible, with a plaque citing the chapter and verse in which each creature is mentioned. Signs are also in Arabic, since the zoo is a favorite excursion for East Jerusalem's Arab families.

Located in a natural animal haven, a glen shaded by tall fir and cypress trees, the Jerusalem Bible Zoo is undoubtedly one of the most unusual animal collections in the world. Here, Professor Aaron Shulov of the Hebrew University's Biology Department has gathered together almost all of the 100 animals and 30 birds mentioned in the Bible. Many of the animals in the zoo are still indigenous to Israel; even today you can find jackals, wild boar, wildcats, porcupines, wolves, gazelles, camels, eagles and vultures throughout the country. In front of the gazelle cage is a plaque reading: "I adjure you, O daughters of Jerusalem, by the gazelles and the hinds of the field" (Song of Solomon 2:7). In front of the lion's cage, the sign reads: "As a roaring lion and a greedy bear, so is a wicked ruler over an indigent people" (Proverbs 28:15).

Not all the animals and rare birds in the zoo still exist in their natural state in Israel, though. Certainly, the lion doesn't. Nor does the crocodile: "The great crocodile that lieth in the midst of his streams" (Ezekiel 29:3). Nor does the caged squirrel, an animal we wouldn't expect to see in captivity. Professor Shulov told us that the squirrels are *not* native to Israel; they were sent as a gift by some boys in Pennsylvania. They populated briskly and then some of them were set free. No sooner done than the university's biology department was besieged by calls from an agitated public who reported seeing strange little animals with funny tails running across their lawns. Squirrels, as we said, were not native to Israel . . . but they are now!

The zoo has managed to prove that Isaiah's prophecy depicting peaceful coexistence between deadly predators and their natural prey is not impossible. A wolf and a lamb, a leopard and a kid goat have been raised together for almost one year!

Price of admission here is SH3 (90¢) for adults, SH2.50 (75¢) for students and youths, SH1.50 (45¢) for children ages three to 13. Hours are 7:30 a.m. till dark. (Though the zoo is open Saturdays, no tickets are sold—so buy them beforehand at one of the ticket agencies or at the zoo.) Buses 7, 15, and 28; tel. 02-814822.

Major Christian Landmarks

Although many of the more important Christian monuments are located in the eastern section of Jerusalem, the western side has a number of historic churches and monasteries that you can visit.

Terra Sancta: Once the temporary quarters of the Hebrew University, the splendid-looking Franciscan Church in the garden, is on the corner of King George Ave. and Gaza Rd., opposite the Kings Hotel. Bus 4.

Notre Dame de France: From the roof here is a splendid view of the Old City of Jerusalem. Situated on Shivtei Israel St., this monastery was built by the Assumptionist Fathers in 1887 to serve as a pilgrim's hostel. The church, on the old border, was the scene of heavy fighting during the 1948 war. It is a hospital and hostel too. Buses 6, 15, 16 and 20.

Pontifical Jesuit Monastery: Around the corner from the King David Hotel, it has a large biblical library and archeological collection. Bus 6. Open 9 a.m.-12 p.m. except Sunday.

St. Vincent de Paul: Belonging to the order of the Sisters of Charity, this convent is at the end of Agron St., near the American Consulate. Bus 15.

San Rosaire: Also on Agron St., right next to the American Consulate, the convent belongs to the Order of the Sisters of the Holy Rosary. Bus 4 or 15.

St. Peter of Ratisbone Monastery: Next to the Yeshurun Synagogue, on Shmuel Hanagid St., this is one of the city's newer sanctuaries, founded in 1874. It belongs to the Fathers of Zion Order and has a boy's orphanage. Bus 4.

Church and Monastery of St. John: This fifth-century Franciscan sanctuary is located in Ein Kerem, built on the site said to be the birthplace of St. John the Baptist. Take bus 6/2.

Church of the Visitation: A Franciscan church, dedicated to the visit of Mary, mother of Jesus, and to Elizabeth, mother of St. John the Baptist, it's also located in Ein Kerem. Bus 6/2.

Monastery of St. John of the Desert: The grotto where St. John is believed to have spent his early years is the site of this Franciscan monastery, on a hillside some two miles outside of Ein Karem. Bus 6/2 and then a long walk.

Benedictine Monastery: Built over the site of a 12th-century Crusader's Church in Abu Ghosh, five miles outside Jerusalem on the main road to Tel Aviv. Bus to Abu Ghosh.

Church of Notre Dame of the Ark: Served by the Sisters of Saint Joseph, this is near a famous statue of the Virgin holding the infant Jesus in her arms which dominates the surrounding countryside. Bus to Abu Ghosh.

St. Andrew's Church of Scotland: Built by the people of Scotland, this Presbyterian Church is situated on a hilltop near Abu Tor and the railroad station. Buses 4, 6 and 7.

Monastery of the Cross: In a valley below the residential section of Rehavia, the monastery stands on the site where the tree was cut for the Cross. It has a beautiful garden and a medieval church with restored mosaics.

Greek Orthodox Monastery: Built over the foundations of a medieval church at Abu Tor, it is called the Church of Evil Counsel, and contains interesting catacombs and crypts. Buses 6 and 7.

Monastery of Saint Simeon: Part of the Greek Patriarch's summer residence, the monastery and church are on Katamon Ridge. Buses 4 and 15.

Russian Orthodox Cathedral: Just off Jaffa Rd., the green-domed edifice was originally constructed after the Crimean War for pilgrims of the Russian Orthodox faith. Buses 6, 20 and 19 from Old City.

Russian Church of St. John: Identified by its bright green steeple, this sanctuary is located in Ein Kerem. Bus 6/2.

Abyssinian Church: Off Prophets St., the elegant building with the Lion of Judah framing the entranceway is the spiritual home of the Coptic Ethiopian clergy. Buses 4 and 9 and then a short walk.

Hebrew University

Take bus 9, 24, or 28 for a ten-minute ride to the new **Givat Ram** campus, which, from a distance, looks like an architect's model—with clean functional lines for its modern buildings and fastidiously landscaped grounds. Located in the midst of rolling hills, the Hebrew University is one of Israel's most dramatic accomplishments, with 14,000 students on this and the Mount Scopus campus.

Mosaics adorn the entranceways to the various buildings on the campus. See especially the **Belgium House Faculty Club, La Maison de France,** the **Physics Building,** and the huge **National and Universal Library** (changing exhibits of Jewish bibliographical lore and data) at the far end of the promenade. And don't miss the mushroom-shaped synagogue behind the library. The 21st-century-looking gymnasium and the swimming pool are interesting structures on campus.

Free tours start daily except Saturday and Jewish holidays at 9 a.m. and at 11 a.m. from the Administration Bldg. You can stop for lunch (about $1.50 to $2) in the cafeteria of the Administration Bldg., or in the Jewish National and University Library where meals cost about $1. Tours of the Mount Scopus campus leave at 11 a.m. from the Martin Buber Building.

The older and original site of the Hebrew University and Hadassah Hospital on Mount Scopus (buses 9 and 28) are described later in this chapter.

Mount Herzl

Now, from the university, take bus 24 to Herzl Blvd., and soon you'll come to Mount Herzl, the resting place of Theodore Herzl, prophet and visionary, who predicted and worked for the founding of Israel 40 years prior to World War I. Mount Herzl is located at the end of the Beit Hakerem section. Down the road from the Herzl cemetery, inside an entrance made of slabs of orange Jerusalem stone, is a military cemetery where thousands of Israeli men and women who died in battle are interred. Particularly stirring is the memorial to the sailors who died at sea. Tablets on the floor at a pool of water quote Psalm 69: "I will bring my people from the depth of the sea."

In the **Mount Herzl Cemetery,** a black gravestone marks Herzl's interment. Herzl's wife and his parents are buried there too.

Facing Yad Vashem is the final resting place of Vladimar Jobotinsky and his wife. After years of controversy, the body of Jabotinsky, revisionist philosopher, was moved here from abroad.

There's a **museum** on the grounds, to which entrance is free (same for the park). April through October, the park is open from 8 a.m. to 7 p.m. daily; museum hours are 9 a.m. to 6:30 p.m. daily, Friday and Saturday 9 a.m. to 1 p.m. Closed Wednesday. The park and museum close at 5 p.m. during the winter. The museum has a replica of Herzl's Vienna study with his own library and furniture. Bus 6, 6/1, 6/2, 12, 18, 20, 21, 23, 26 or 27.

Yad Vashem Memorial

Down the road from Mount Herzl is a memorial ridge called **Har Hazikaron** (Hill of the Remembrance), dedicate to the six million Jews murdered by the Nazis. The **Avenue of the Righteous Gentiles,** lined with trees, leads into the Memorial, in tribute to those who helped save Jewish lives during the Nazi era.

In all the world, there is no more terrifying a memorial than the massive structure atop this hill. Here the Israelis have constructed a rectangular building whose lower walls are formed out of mammoth, uncut boulders. The heavy entrance gate by David Polombo is an abstract tapestry of jagged, twisted steel, an anguished, agonizing pattern of shapes. Inside is a huge stone room, like a crypt, where flames in the middle shed an eerie light over the plaques on the floor: Bergen-Belsen, Auschwitz, Dachau. . . . In here, there is no poetry or weeping or sermonizing. The almost hallucinatory mood captured in the design and architecture of the memorial is unbelieveably moving.

The building to the left has a permanent exhibition of photographs and effects relating to the slaughter of World War II, a period forever inscribed in history as the "holocaust." Across the hill is an **archive building,** probably the most complete library and permanent testimony to that awful time. From here came the piles of documentary evidence used in the trial of Adolf Eichmann. The memorial is open daily from 9 a.m. to 5 p.m., Friday till 1:45 p.m., closed Sáturday. Ceremonies can be held in the memorial shrine (**Ohel Yizkor)** and will include the rekindling of the mourning light.

Any of the following buses will bring you here: 6/1, 6/2, 12, 18, 20, 27.

Ein Kerem

From Herzl Boulevard, the route to the Hadassah Hospital, you'll have a beautiful view of this enchanting village, nestled on a hillside of tall cypress and olive groves and scattered through with monasteries and Christian holy places. Ein Kerem is the birthplace of John the Baptist, as well as the place where Mary visited Zachariah and Elizabeth before Jesus was born. A stone-age spring in the village is called **Mary's Well,** and most churches have displays of archeological finds. **The Church of St. John** and **The Church of the Visitation** are especially worth seeing.

Many of Jerusalem's professional people are now moving to Ein Kerem—away from apartments and into lovely homes with gardens, in a unique area just ten minutes or so from town. There are several good restaurants here, and an interesting art gallery (operated by an art colony) in an old Arab house. To find the latter, pass through the village then head right, down a hill. Bus 6/2 goes directly to Ein Kerem.

Hadassah Hospital

The largest medical center in the Middle East, the $30 million Hadassah Hebrew University Medical Center stands on a hilltop several miles from downtown Jerusalem. Take bus 19 from the Menora Club (in back of the former Knesset) or from King George Ave.

This project contains a medical school, nursing school, 550-bed hospital, dental and pharmacy schools and various laboratory buildings. Hadassah, the Women's Zionist Organization of America, was the sponsor here, and in the hospital's synagogue is displayed the organization's most important acquisition: Chagall's monumental stained-glass masterpiece depicting the 12 tribes of Israel. Daily tours to the complex and other local Hadassah projects leave at 8:30 a.m. from the **Hadassah Visitors' Club,** Strauss Health Center, 24 Strauss St., in Jerusalem. Free medical center tours, including a look at the Chagall windows, at 9, 10, 11 a.m., and noon. No tours on Fridays, Saturdays or holidays. Half-day tours of all projects cost $5 and are by reservation: tel. 02-416333 at least a day in advance.

To better accommodate the 50,000 annual visitors to the hospital, the **Kennedy Information Center** was opened in 1966. It has a cafeteria and provides all necessary information on hospital facilities, tours, etc.

Kennedy Memorial

About two miles from downtown Jerusalem, in the same general direction of Hadassah Hospital, **Yad Kennedy** is reached by following the winding mountain roads out past the Aminadav Moshav. Opened in May, 1966, the 60-foot-high poured-concrete memorial is designed in the shape of a cut tree trunk, symbolizing the president whose life was cut short in its prime. Inside it is virtually barren—an eternal flame in the center of the floor, a shaft of light from an opening in the roof illuminating a bust of the late president. Said to be visible on a clear day from Tel Aviv, 40 miles away, the mountaintop memorial is encircled by 51 columns, each bearing the emblem of a State of the Union, plus the District of Columbia. The city bus 21 stops quite a distance away. Be prepared to walk or take a cab and have the driver wait.

To the west is the village of **Batir,** site of a stronghold that witnessed the last Jewish revolt against the Romans, in 135 A.D., by Bar Kochba. The view from the parking lot is breathtaking—a never-ending succession of mountains and valleys. In one valley you can see the railroad tracks running from Jerusalem to Tel Aviv.

The monument, and adjoining picnic grounds, are part of the **John F. Kennedy Peace Forest.**

Model of Ancient Jerusalem

Next, take the road opposite Mount Herzl and follow the sign pointing to the Holyland Hotel. A short walk from the hotel's entrance brings you to a garden in which stands a painstakingly complete, perfectly scaled-down model of Jerusalem as it was in the time of the Second Temple. This is Herod's Jerusalem, a grand, opulent place of palaces, mammoth walls, and elegant towers. This impressive project is the result of years of collaboration by a team of architects, historians, archeologists and builders, led by Prof. M. Avi-Yonah. Open daily 8 a.m. to 4 p.m. in winter, to 6 p.m. in summer, Fridays to 4 or 5 p.m. Admission is minimal; Saturday and holiday tickets must be bought in advance from a ticket agency. Bus 6/1.

By the way, that cluster of hunched-together houses and minarets on the opposite hill, 200 yards away, is the Arab village of **Malcha.**

Government Quarter—Kiryat Ben-Gurion

Opposite the university, on Kaplan St. (halfway back to Jerusalem), is an assortment of buildings comprising most of the government quarter. Until a few years ago, such places as the Prime Minister's Office, the Ministry of Finance, the Ministry of Interior, and other important departments of state were scattered about town in rented office space—if not housed in temporary prefabricated bungalow-like structures.

Most impressive of the new government buildings is the **Parliament (Knesset).** A $7 million structure of peach-colored stone, this elegant landmark on Jerusalem's "Acropolis" has a 24-foot-high Chagall mosaic in the reception hall, and contains a synagogue, separate kitchens for meat and milk dishes (you can stop for a moderately priced meal in the cafeteria) and exhibition rooms. The entranceway, a grillwork of hammered metal, is the work of the Israeli sculptor Polombo, who did the dramatic doors at Yad Vashem.

The new Knesset is Israel's third Parliament building—and the first permanent one. Previous Parliaments were convened in a converted cinema in Tel Aviv and a converted bank (Beit Froumine) in downtown Jerusalem at the junction of King George and Ben Yehuda Sts., which now houses the Government Tourist offices. The Menorah that stood in the park next to that last Knesset is now positioned across from the entrance to the new one. Open for guided tours of the building on Sunday and Thursday from 8:30 a.m. to 2:30 p.m.; reached by bus 9. You can attend a session of Knesset Monday, Tuesday or Wednesday from 4 to 9 p.m. Bring your passport. Knesset recesses during Jewish holidays and summer.

Israel Museum

Opened in May, 1965 to great fanfare, the Museum complex lies on Ruppin St., near Hakirya (buses 9, 16, and 24). Israelis say it's the largest museum between Rome and Tokyo.

The complex is an outstanding example of modern Israeli architecture.

There are four main components: the **Bezalel Art Museum,** the **Samuel Bronfman Biblical and Archeological Museum, The Billy Rose Art Garden, The Shrine of the Book,** and the **Ruth Youth Wing.**

Collections of Jewish ceremonial artifacts, gleaned from Israel's many historic sites and going back thousands of years, form the bulk of the collection at the first two. On view here are decorative pages from centuries-old Torahs—from Iran, Italy and Singapore. In one room there are dozens of Hanukah lamps, silver Torah ornaments, serving trays, shofars, and an exhibit of costumes worn by Jewish women in Yemen on festival occasions. There are two reconstructed synagogues, one 17th-century Italian, the other 18th-century German. The art museum shows the work of Israeli contemporaries and also contains period rooms. The Bronfman-Bezalel complex, in the main building of adjoining wings, houses a gift shop well stocked with books, prints, and posters. Outside, to the right of the stairs, is the museum cafeteria (moderate prices).

Three important new pavilions have been added since the last edition of this book. One contains an impressive collection of pre-Columbian Central American art from 2000 B.C. to 1550 A.D.; another is a separate building housing ancient glass; and the third is the Walter and Charlotte Floersheimer Pavilion for Impressionist and Postimpressionist Art (referred to above) with works by Corot, Monet, Renoir, Degas, Gauguin, Matisse, etc.

Another recent addition is an **archeological garden** between the Shrine of the Book and the new Youth Wing complex. It contains classical Greco-Roman sculptures, sarcophagi, and mosaics, most of which were discovered and excavated in Israel.

Free guided tours of the museum are conducted in English Sunday, Wednesday, and Thursday at 11 a.m., and Tuesday at 4:30 p.m.

The Billy Rose Art Garden, on a 20-acre plot, has been impressively landscaped by the renowned Japanese-American artist, Isamu Noguchi. In the garden of semicircular earth-and-stone embankments is found a 100-piece sculpture collection, much of it donated by Mr. Rose.

The outdoor sculpture garden, on successive pebbled slopes, houses both classical and modern, European, American and Israeli works—Rodin, Zorach, Henry Moore, Picasso, Maillol and Channa Orloff.

Head toward the edge of the hill at the end of the sculpture park for a magnificent 180-degree panoramic view: from right to left, the Parliament and Government buildings, the university and the hills directly ahead; and to the left, the levels of cypress, golden and pink stone, rich brown slopes. All the hues of Jerusalem's stone are seen from here, a spectrum of browns, cream shades and whites.

Then there's the Shrine of the Book, with its distinctive onion-shaped top, contoured to resemble—in 275,000 glazed white bricks—the jar covers in which the Dead Sea Scrolls were discovered. In addition to housing the prized Dead Sea Scrolls and the Bar Kochba letters, the underground shrine is the exhibition site for many additional finds from Masada.

Specifically, The Shrine of the Book exhibits the scrolls and documents discovered at three sites at the Dead Sea: Qumran Cave (second century B.C. to 71 A.D.), the Nahal Hever Cave (post-135 A.D.) and Masada (second century B.C. to 73 A.D.). The Shrine is constructed inside like a series of underground caves; the entrance corridor displays letters in Aramaic telling of real estate leases 2,000 years back. There's also a marriage contract, dated April 5, 128 A.D. In the circular underground chamber are the shreds of parchments from Leviticus, Psalms, and Isaiah. The best-known exhibit here is the Dead Sea scroll, "The War of the Sons of Light Against the Sons of Darkness." Down the steps are rare finds from the Bar Kochba period, including a perfect large glass plate, nearly intact baskets, tools, utensils, vessels.

Museum hours are Sunday, Monday, Wednesday, and Thursday from 10 a.m. to 5 p.m. The main building is open on Tuesdays from 4 to 10 p.m. (nighttime, when the buildings are illuminated, is an excellent time to visit). The Billy Rose Garden and the Shrine of the Book are also open on Tuesdays from 10 a.m. to 10 p.m. Friday, Saturday, eve of holidays, and holidays, the Museum is open from 10 a.m. to 2 p.m.

Entrance fee is SH2.50 (75¢) for adults, SH.50 (15¢) for children, and SH1 (30¢) for students. If you go on a Saturday or holiday you have to buy your tickets ahead of time from the Museum, a local ticket agent, or your hotel. Bus 9, 16, or 24.

And More Museums

L.A. Mayer Memorial Institute for Islamic Art, 2 Hapalmach St., tel. 02-661291, is another Jerusalem museum worth visiting. The name explains the types of exhibitions. No entrance fee. Open Sunday, Monday, Tuesday and Thursday 10 a.m.-12:30 p.m. and 3:30 p.m.-6 p.m. The museum is also open from 3:30 p.m. to 9 p.m. on Wednesdays and from 10:30 a.m. to 1 p.m. on Saturdays. Adults pay SH1.50, children up to age 18 SH.70. Saturday tickets must be purchased in advance from the King David, Moriah, or Plaza Hotels.

Some other museums: The **Museum of Natural History,** 6 Mohilever St., displaying local flora and fauna. Take bus 4, 10 or 18; closed in August. **Dor Va-Dor Museum,** Heichal Shlomo, displaying religious artifacts. Bus 4, 7, 8, 9, 10 or 19. **The Jerusalem City Museum,** located in the Citadel (David's Tower). Bus 1, 13, 19, 20 or 23. **The Agricultural Museum,** Helena Hamalka St., displaying an exhibition of agricultural instruments (some older than 2,000 years). **The Musical Instrument Museum,** at the Rubin Academy of Music on Smolenskin St., displaying a collection of ancient and modern instruments from all over the world. **The Taxation Museum,** 1 Agron St., the second museum of its kind in the world devoted entirely to aspects of taxation and collection in ancient Israel, during the Diaspora and in Israel today. **Givat Hatachmoshet Memorial and Museum,** at the top of Givat Hatachmoshet (Ammunition Hill), between Sheikh Jarrakh and Ramot Eshkol, dedicated to the liberation of Jerusalem and the Six-Day War. Its setting is the scene of the fiercest fighting in the city. You can walk through bunkers and trenches, and five exhibition halls display weapons used in the war, maps, battle plans, and suchlike. Take buses 4, 9, 25, 28 or 40. Closed Friday afternoons and Saturdays. The **Pontifical Biblical Institute,** 3 Paul Botta St., tel. 02-222843, near the King David Hotel, houses a rich archeological collection, including an Egyptian mummy; by appointment only.

Ramat Rachel

In southeastern Jerusalem, on the road leading to Bethlehem, is Mizpe Rachel Guest House in Ramat Rachel, tel. 02-711919, a kibbutz which was right on the border, until the 1967 war. Along the way (take bus 7), if the weather is clear, you can see past the mountains of Moab to the Dead Sea. This kibbutz changed hands several times during the 1948 war and was a strategic military point—many of its settlers were killed and its buildings destroyed. You can see the after-effects of two wars on several walls peppered with machine-gun bullets. Before the 1967 war there was considerable difficulty in repopulating this settlement, because of its continuing vulnerability.

From a lookout platform atop the water tower there's a magnificent panoramic view of Bethlehem, the Judean wilderness, Herod's burial place, and Rachel's tomb. Recent archeological work in this area has uncovered a multitude of ancient fortifications and churches, including remains from the early Israelite period, plus others from times of Persian, Roman, Byzantine and Arabian rule.

SPECIAL TOURS OF JERUSALEM: You can do all these sights on your own, of course, but you might enjoy "joining up" for some of the following:

Walking Tours

Starting each Saturday at 10 a.m. from 34 Jaffa St. is a Hebrew and English tour of interesting places, conducted free by the Jerusalem Municipality.

You can also take a 3–3½-hour tour in English that begins with a 45-minute lecture on Jerusalem. It starts at 9:30 a.m. Tuesday and Sunday, 2 p.m. Thursday. Leaving from the Citadel courtyard (Tower of David) at Jaffa Gate, it takes in the Jewish Quarter, reconstructed synagogues, the Western Wall excavations, and other interesting sites. Tickets are $5.

Another tour, leaving from the same place, goes on Wednesdays at 9:30 a.m. and covers, on alternate weeks, the First Temple period and the Second Temple period. Tickets are $4.

The **Plaza Hotel,** King George St., tel. 02-228133, organizes free 1½-hour walking tours daily at 9 a.m. and 1:30 p.m. On Friday there's a morning tour only, and on Saturday the morning tour begins at 10 a.m. Weekday tours sometimes include a cab ride, in which case the fare is shared by occupants. You needn't be a hotel guest to participate.

During Pesach and Succoth there are free daily walking tours of the Old City. Inquire at the I.G.T.O.

Wall-Walking Tour

If you're not afraid of heights, and are a good walker, you can take a walk on top of the surrounding Wall of the Old City. The I.G.T.O. near Jaffa Gate can give you information.

Synagogue Tour

Guided walking tours of Jerusalem synagogues take place every Friday afternoon and have become quite a popular attraction. They start from Egged Tours on Kikar Zion. In winter they leave at 2 p.m. and in summer at 2:30 p.m.—it's best to arrive at least 15 minutes ahead of time. The fee for the tour is $4, and a partial list of the places you'll visit includes the new and "Western" **Yeshurun Synagogue** and **Heichal Shlomo Synagogue,** both on King George Ave.; the **Beit Yossef** synagogue of the extremist Hasidic sect called Guardians of the City, which doesn't recognize the national existence of Israel; the **Cabalistic Synagogue** on David St., where ten other synagogues also stand; the **Persian Synagogue,** where the services have maintained some Moslem characteristics, and the **Oriental Abrahamo Synagogue** in the Bukharian quarter.

Organizational Tours

Special tours are sponsored by several local, national and international organizations. A brief list of these groups follows, but for specifics of the tours themselves, check with the organization mentioned or with the I.G.T.O.:

WIZO (Women's Zionist Organization), Mapu St., tel 02-226060;

American Mizrahi Women's Organization, 19A Keren Hayesod St., tel. 02-232758;

Women's League for Israel, Beit Hahaluzot, 14 Ibn Gvirol St., tel. 02-639840;

Pioneer Women (Moetzet Hapoalot), 17 Strauss St., tel. 02-228203;

The General Israel Orphan's Home for Girls, in Kiryat Moshe, tel. 02-523291/2;

ORT (School of Engineering at the Hebrew University, Givat Ram), tel. 02-533141;

Shaare Zedek, tel. 02-555111;

Ezrat Nashim, Psychiatric Hospital in Givat Shaul, tel. 02-521191;

Akim, the Israel Association for the Rehabilitation of the Mentally Handicapped, 21 Radak St., tel. 02-631728;

Emunah—World Religious Zionist Women's Organization, 26 Ben Maimon St., tel. 02-630620, 811588;

Hadassah Hospital, tel. 02-416333 (see "Hadassah Hospital" above).

Those Who "Toured" Before You

In Jerusalem, as throughout most of Israel, if you give your imagination some rein, you can feel that peculiar identification with history, the kinship with thousands of travelers from myriad cultures who have passed this way over the past 4,000 years.

In biblical times, the Hebrew farmers trudged up this road on the agricultural holidays to bring their offerings to the Holy City. The Pharaoh's legions and Roman Centurions came this way, as did Crusader forces and armies of pilgrims, Christian, Jewish and Moslem.

Traveling to Jerusalem has always been colorful. In the 12th century, a tourist to Jerusalem had to hire mercenaries to protect him on the trip, since the area was rife with bands of robbers who made their living by preying on the pilgrims. The pilgrim caravans were supervised by guides equipped with maces and spears and shields. Then came the Arab occupants who charged enormous road taxes to the weary pilgrims for the right to use the pass. In the 19th century, Austrian Emperor Franz Josef made the trip, and he was the first man ever to use a carriage to do so. And then, during the Turkish Occupation in 1908, an American tourist came, bringing a motor car with him, and after the sensation he created, mechanized transport became the rule of thumb. The pilgrimage to Jerusalem forever lost some of its uniqueness, but now many more people can make the trip.

Great ones for keeping alive the biblical traditions of years gone by, the Israelis have instituted an **"Aliya le' Regel"** (walking pilgrimage) to Jerusalem, which takes place each year around Passover/Easter and Succoth time. Thousands participate, and during this three-day excursion period you can see them walking along this road just as their ancestors did—youngsters from the kibbutzim, columns of paratroopers, female soldiers, athletic middle-aged residents who've made the hike for years and footsore tourists who like the drama of the thing and become swept up in the fervor attached to this march. If you are in Israel in the spring around Passover time or in the autumn during Succoth, do catch this event. (Overseas visitors need pay no registration fee and are guests of the March Command for all meals, camp accommodations, and evening programs during the march. To register, contact: the Government Tourist Office.) And if walking up and down hills isn't your idea of fun, then be sure to catch the procession as it comes into Jerusalem. Pick out a spot along King George Ave. and watch them strut by.

AND NOW, A SWIM: You have a choice of many pools if you want to take a dip in Jerusalem on a summer's day. One of the cheapest (but most crowded) is the Jerusalem public pool, 43 Emek Rephaim St., tel. 02-632-042. Adults pay

SH.4 ($1.20), children SH3 (85¢). On Saturdays and holidays, when Israelis pack the pools, the price goes up to SH6 ($1.75) and SH4 ($1.20), respectively. Take bus 4, 10, or 18. Open 8 a.m. to 5 p.m.

More expensive (but more convenient) is the swanky **President Hotel** pool, tel. 02-631237, open to outsiders upon payment of SH6.50 adults ($1.90), SH5 ($1.45) children on weekdays, SH10 ($2.95) and SH8 ($2.35), respectively, on Friday and Saturday. It's just off King George Ave., toward the bottom of the hill. Open 9 a.m. to 5 p.m.

The **Beit Tailor,** on Zangwil St. in Kiryat Yovel, tel. 02-414362, charges SH4 ($1.20) for adults, SH2.50 (75¢) for children during the week, SH5 ($1.45) and SH4 ($1.20), respectively, on Saturday. Open 8 a.m. to 4:30 p.m. Take bus 18.

During the week you can use the pool at the **YMCA** on Nablus Rd., tel. 02-282375, for SH5 ($1.45) adults, SH3 (90¢) children, that payment allowing for a 45-minute swim.

Outside Jerusalem, in the Judean hills, **Kibbutz Shoresh,** tel. 02-533477, has built a pool high on a hilltop; it's endowed with such country-club amenities as lounge chairs, a lifeguard and a snack bar. From April 29 to October 10 the pool, called **Shoresh,** is open from 8 a.m. to 5 p.m.; entrance fee is SH5 ($1.45) for adults and SH4 ($1.20) for children weekdays, SH10 ($2.95) and SH8 ($2.35), respectively, on Saturdays and holidays. It's rarely crowded and the scenery is marvelous. Buses 65 and 401 leave from the central bus station. Check the schedule.

A handsomely situated pool is at **Kibbutz Ma'ale Hahamisha,** tel. 02-539872, out in the Judean Hills. It's in the middle of a pine forest and you can picnic in the shade of the tall trees. Admission is SH5.50 ($1.60) for adults, SH4.50 ($1.32) for children; on Saturdays and holidays it's for members only. Buses 63 and 403 from the central station.

Lastly, don't forget the pool at **Kibbutz Ramat Rachel,** tel. 02-715711. The SH7.50 ($2.20) admission for adults, SH6 ($1.75) for children, allows you to use both the pool and the tennis courts. Saturday fees are SH13 ($3.80) and SH10 ($2.95), respectively.

Note: admission charges at swimming pools are subject to change; and discounts sometimes are given to students.

The **Turkish Bath** (Ha'Hamam Ha'Turki), 36 Yekezkel, tel. 02-287542 (buses 4, 9, 25 27, 35, and 37), was built by the Bukharian Jews over 90 years ago as one of their first endeavors upon arriving in Jerusalem. It was designed according to the ideas of typical Roman Empire bath houses. You have a choice of hot, tepid, or cold pools, a steam room or the dry-heat sauna. One of the rooms has three slabs of marble, each a different temperature, and they are believed to be beneficial for many sorts of aches and pains. After you've tried them all, head for a "resting room," where you may relax upon colored cushions and sip coffee and imagine yourself in a harem of long ago. Entrance is SH8.50 ($2.50); a visit to the hairdresser or a massage are additional options; you can also get soap, or rent a robe, towels, or hair dryer. There's a snack bar on the premises. Open 11 a.m. to 10 p.m., Friday till 3 p.m.

4. East Jerusalem and the Old (Walled) City

Jerusalem, united, represents the guts of Israel. Immediately after the 1967 war, the local Arab population in the eastern sectors of the city was given the choice of assuming Israeli citizenship or remaining Jordanian subjects. A high percentage of the indigenous population voted for full Israeli membership. Since that time the standard of living has risen enormously, and better sanita-

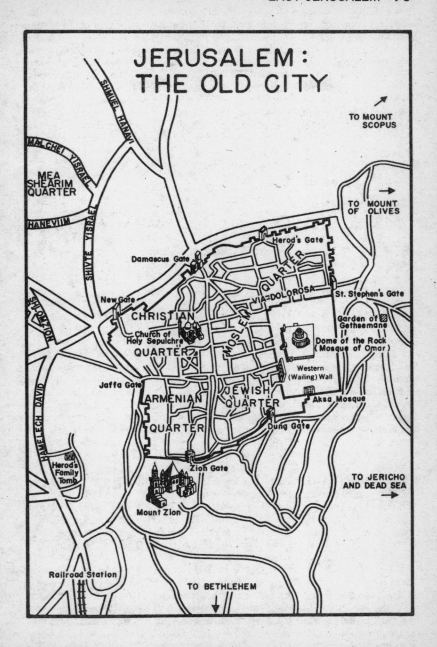

JERUSALEM:
THE OLD CITY

TO MOUNT
SCOPUS

SHMUEL HANAVI

MALCHEI YISRAEL

MEA
SHEARIM
QUARTER

HANEVIIM

SHIVTE YISRAEL

TO MOUNT
OF OLIVES

Herod's Gate

Damascus Gate

QUARTER

VIA DOLOROSA

St. Stephen's Gate

New Gate

Garden of
Gethsemane

CHRISTIAN

MOSLEM

Dome of the Rock
(Mosque of Omar)

Church of
Holy Sepulchre

QUARTER

Western
(Wailing) Wall

NEVIIM

HAMELECH DAVID

Jaffa Gate

JEWISH
QUARTER

ARMENIAN

Aksa Mosque

QUARTER

Dung Gate

Herod's
Family
Tomb

Zion Gate

TO JERICHO
AND DEAD SEA

Mount Zion

Railroad Station

TO BETHLEHEM

tion and clean, piped water was introduced. At the same time, under the administration of Mayor Teddy Kollek, the essential Arab flavor of the eastern section was preserved. Fundamental architectural changes were proscribed without specific permission from experts. Loans were provided to encourage the local populace to spruce up the area. The Jewish section was rebuilt along the specific lines that existed before it had been destroyed. The bazaar area was left intact. Over the past years, Jerusalem has become a living testament of the ability of Jews and Arabs to coexist in an ambience of mutual respect. While terror attempts proliferated elsewhere in the country, Jerusalem seemed to be almost immune to the phenomenon, above it all. And when there were several scattered incidents, both in the east and west, the populace of the city was stunned, shocked and outraged. Intense police investigations determined one thing—in *every* case the terrorists came from areas far from the city; in no case were the deeds perpetrated by local Arab citizens.

This is not to say that every Jerusalem Arab is happy with an Israeli regime; nor does it imply that some citizens still don't yearn for an Arab government in the city. It does mean, however, that Jerusalem is fundamentally a safe and comfortable city to be in. Our children travel there freely and we've never given a thought to possible dangers—uncontrolled traffic not withstanding. So before we embark into the eastern regions of the city, dispel any thoughts of ominous, lurking danger. It simply doesn't exist. One of the cornerstones of civilization, Jerusalem is a very civilized place indeed to visit.

THE HOLIEST SPOT ON EARTH: How does one begin to write about this part of Jerusalem? For ages it's been sacred to Jews, Christians and Moslems. The center of Jewish national dreams, Jerusalem has been remembered in the daily prayers of the Orthodox throughout the centuries of the dispersion. Some 3,000 years ago, David set an altar here, then built his capital city. Solomon's Temple stood here, and the city saw the trials and crucifixion of Christ. Also in Eastern Jerusalem are the Dome of the Rock sacred to Moslems, the Western (Wailing) Wall (remnant of the Temple and holiest of Jewish prayer sites), and countless other spots rich in religious significance . . . so you can see why these eastern slopes and the walled Old City well deserve being called the holiest spot on earth.

TRANSPORTATION: Since chances are quite good that you'll arrive in the western part of the city first, you might want to take one of the three buses that ply through the entire city, from west to east: bus 2 runs along Jaffa Road, passes close to Zion Square and ends at the Damascus Gate; bus 27 starts from the Convention Center, passes the Damascus Gate and stops finally at the Dung Gate, through which you can enter the Old City to reach the Western Wall; bus 12 follows a similar route.

If you're walking, either follow Jaffa Road directly to the Jaffa Gate, or (depending on your starting point) turn left off King George Ave. at the Kings Hotel, proceed down Agron Street past Independence Park, up Mamilla Street past the auto repair shops, and you will arrive at Jaffa Gate. By car, head down the same route, past Independence Park; after about 20 yards make a left, then a right onto Shlomo Hamelech and drive past Notre Dame. You will come over a hilltop and see the fortress walls on your right. This route leads to the Damascus Gate.

Jaffa Gate and **Damascus Gate** are the main portals to the walled city. Should you be in the Mea Shearim quarter, follow Shivtei Israel or Shmuel Hanavi and you will enter East Jerusalem around Nablus Road.

USEFUL INFORMATION: In this part of Jerusalem, it helps to keep some of the terminology straight: the **Old City (Ir Ha-atika)** refers to the section of bazaars and holy sites (Western Wall, Mosque of Omar, Holy Sepulchre) within the ancient fortress ramparts; **Ir Hakodesh** is The Holy City, within the walls; **Mount Scopus** and the **Mount of Olives** sit nestled among the hills to the northeast of the Old City.

Don't forget that the **Ministry of Tourism** has an office directly inside the Jaffa Gate to service visitors to the Old City. Unlike the office on the western side, this one is open on Saturday.

Shop Hours and such often depend on the management's religion. It might help to remember that Friday is the Moslem holy day, Saturday is the Jewish Sabbath, and Sunday is the Christian day of rest.

HOTELS: You'll find loads of hotels in East Jerusalem, in the downtown area, inside the walls and on the Mount of Olives—more than in West Jerusalem, in fact. United Jerusalem (Yerushalayim Hashleyma), a term one hears often, now offers the visitor well over 2,500 hotel rooms, with more being built every day, despite general economic problems in the country.

In East Jerusalem, there is a tradition of hotel service that is unequaled throughout most of the rest of Israel—which is understandable, since Old Jerusalem and its Holy Land sites have drawn more tourists than perhaps any other part of this small country, and the hotels there are thus more competitive.

Almost all two- and three-star East Jerusalem hotels (so graded by the Israeli Ministry of Tourism) contain, in each room, telephone, toilet, hot water shower/baths, and central heating. Maintenance is somewhat better too: bathroom appliances are modern and they work properly, plaster cracks are quickly patched up, furniture is in better shape, rooms are decorated with more taste and feeling for color. And the warmth of hospitality is very much in the Arabic tradition.

East Jerusalem's hotels are located in three main areas: downtown East Jerusalem, on or near Saladin Street; inside the Old City walls; on the way to, and on top of, the Mount of Olives.

The following recommended hotels are discussed more in order of location than by price, since in East Jerusalem you often find "budget" hotels side by side with moderately priced or "big splurge" hotels. At the end, we have included a small section for "starvation budget" travelers, along with a list of tourist-accepting Christian hospices on this side of the city. All prices include your room and breakfast, unless otherwise noted, and hold true throughout the year. Also, the majority of East Jerusalem hotels raise their prices by from 20% to 25% during the Christmas and Easter holidays. And while you're at it, keep in mind that all hotels charge a 10-15% service charge, over and above room rates. And once again, for ungraded hotels, we want to re-emphasize that the prices quoted were obtained near the end of 1979. Certain rises must be anticipated due to Israel's galloping inflation.

Budget-to-Moderate Hotels in Downtown East Jerusalem

The first thing you ought to get straight is that **Saladin Street**—the main thoroughfare, the Fifth Avenue of this part of town—is spelled Saladin, Salah Ed-Din, Salah Eddine, Salach A' Din, and Salah E-Din. It's all the same street.

Take a look at the map: Saladin Street begins opposite Herod's Gate and runs north for about half a mile. It roughly parallels Nablus Road, which begins at Herod's Gate and meets Saladin at the crest of a hill near the American Colony Hotel. The center of the downtown area is roughly a triangle formed by Saladin, **Port Said** and **Rasheed Street.** Port Said Street is frequently called **Azzahra Street** and Rasheed is sometimes called **Rachidya Street.**

As you come down the street from the New City, over the crest of a hill at the Notre Dame Hospice, you will continue parallel to the old fortress wall. The street you are on is **Sultan Suleiman.**

Just past Damascus Gate **(Sh'ar Shchem)** look across Sultan Suleiman Street and you'll see the big black letters of the **Pilgrim's Palace,** tel. 02-284831, staring you in the face. (It's almost opposite the Old City bus station—which means rooms on that side tend to be noisier.) The big limestone two-story, 95-room hotel has a wide reputation for cleanliness: its management boasts that a fly has never been seen in the dining room or lobby—quite a boast, since Jerusalem has its share of the world's fly population. The Palace is a comfortable, spacious and well-serviced three-star hotel. One flight up is the lobby, which has quite an array of stuffed chairs and sofas as well as a broad expanse of windows offering exciting day or night views of the Old City walls (across the street) and the busy folks bustling around them. It's not an opulent place, but it does have a corner bar (souvenir shop too). As for the rooms: spic and span, centrally heated and air-conditioned, with phones, toilets and shower/baths . . . the works! Singles start at SH73.40 ($21.60), doubles at SH57.10 ($16.80) per person. Lunch or dinner is SH23.80 ($7). Students get a 15% discount.

Saladin St. begins at the modern post office, and there, on the opposite side of the street, you'll see the 31-room **Rivoli Hotel,** tel. 02-284871. Rooms here are cheerful enough, with cream-colored walls and a bright wool blanket on each bed, and each has phone, central heating, wall-to-wall carpeting, shower/bath, and toilet. The Rivoli boasts an opulent lounge, two TV rooms, and air-conditioned public areas. The service is usually all you'd want it to be, in the rooms or in the restaurant. The price? SH52.70 ($15.50) single, SH42.50 ($12.50) each double, $6.50 for lunch or dinner.

Further up Saladin, at No. 6 (next to the Universal Library Book Store, biggest, best-stocked bookstore in this part of Jerusalem), is the five-story elevator-equipped **Metropole,** tel. 02-282507. All 30 rooms here have phones, central heating, and fully equipped bathrooms; the cost, SH44.20 ($13) to SH57.80 ($17) single, SH42.50 ($12.50) per person double; rates are slightly lower off-season. From the pleasant roof garden (where lunch and dinner are served in the summertime) you can view Mount Scopus, the Mount of Olives, and the Rockefeller Museum. The Metropole is, by the way, the traditional stopping place for Arab pilgrims, Moslem and Christian. Half or full board possible—add SH40.80 ($12) a day for lunch and dinner.

At 18 Saladin St., opposite the Capitol Hotel, is the 30-room **Lawrence Hotel,** tel. 02-282585. Central heating, and showers or baths in each room here, which you've come to expect in this part of Jerusalem, but what you don't expect is the elevator. In the spacious but a bit musty lobby, sedately furnished with glass-topped tables, is a well-equipped (tiny) gift shop. Carpeting in the rooms, but few frills outside of that—just the necessities. Rates are SH49.30

($14.50) to IL578 ($17) single, SH45.90 ($13.50) per person double. Lunch or dinner is SH15.70 ($5.50). Discounts for students.

Continue north past the movie theater, the St. George Hotel, and the large Ministry of Justice administrative building. Just at the top of Saladin St., look to the right and you'll see the clean and pleasant **Christmas Hotel,** tel. 02-282588. Here, the 20 rooms are each outfitted with splash wool blankets—in addition, of course, to the bathrooms and the central heating. A couple of larger, posher suites are practically the equivalent of Class A accommodations. There are two dining rooms: one indoors, with a red motif, and the Jerusalem Garden outdoors amid flowers and vines. Rates—SH68 ($20) to SH78.20 ($23) single and SH59.50 ($17.50) per person double—include a continental breakfast; add $2 for an Israeli breakfast.

Behind the Christmas Hotel, technically on American Colony St. (you'll have to circle the block), is the **New Orient House,** tel. 02-282437, opposite an orphanage school. The New Orient really looks like what it once was: the residence of high officials during the Turkish rule. Its dining room is straight out of that era—light blue walls, vaulted archways, massive hanging fans. Note the unique bar made from pounded copper. Rooms are adequate, if not as exciting as the public rooms, and they're outfitted with bathrooms, phones, and central heating. Singles are SH44.20 ($13) to SH51 ($15), doubles SH40.80 ($12) per person. Slight reductions off-season. Lunch or dinner is about SH20.40 ($6).

Just past the top of Azzahra St. (officially, it's Museum St.), practically behind the Rockefeller Museum, you'll find Doris and Farid Salman's **Jordan House,** 12 Nureldin St., tel. 02-283430, one of Jerusalem's most distinctive, intriguing hotels. Constructed from rough-cut local stone, it sits amid a grouping of pine trees, a panorama of the Mount of Olives behind it. The owners are dealers in antiquities and this accounts for the splendid Middle Eastern furnishings within. The Arabic decor begins in the lobby and hallway and continues into the rooms. Look again at those cushions, copper tables, old brass lamps and assorted objets d'art: they're the real thing, heavy and ornate, not the kind you find in some tourist shops hereabouts. In the older rooms (centrally heated) are magnificent oil lamps (now electrified, of course), highlighting the venerable old look. The bathrooms are brand-new, though—porcelain plumbing, tiling . . . all's agleam. Rooms at Jordan House go for SH69.70 ($20.50) to SH78.20 ($23) single, SH57.80 ($17) per person double.

Oriental in feeling, with beautiful gardens and an unforgettable atmosphere, the **American Colony,** once the home of a grand pasha, is practically in a class by itself. The hotel is within the walled courtyard just past the top of the hill where Saladin St. and Nablus Rd. meet. Some rooms here are outfitted with mother-of-pearl cocktail tables, copper trays, feenjons, and ornate gold and blue ceilings. You'll find an intriguing duality in these rooms: antique Arabic furnishings and modern tile bathrooms. In the cloister-like lobby above the garden, archeological finds are displayed in glass cases. The garden, ablaze with crimson and orange flowers, sends up a 20-foot palm tree. Potted plants and mosaic tables lend atmosphere to the sitting rooms and lounges. Only 13 of the 50 rooms here are in the museum-like old building; the rest are in newer buildings across the courtyard. Rates are SH66.30 ($19.50) single, from SH52.70 ($15.50) and up, per person double. Quite near what was the Mandelbaum Gate, the American Colony, tel. 02-282421, sustained damage in the 1967 war; today you'd hardly know it, unless you stick your nose up close to the blue mosaic in the lobby and spot the mortar bomb holes.

On Nablus Road, the **YMCA East** (Aeila Capitolina Hotel), tel. 02-282375, just past the American Consulate, is a perfect example of "contemporary Middle Eastern decor" (built in 1960). The imperial-looking lobby—with its brass lamps, great pillars, archways and low couches—resembles a sheikh's sitting room. Rooms in the four-floor hotel are clean and airy, each with phone, bathroom, and central heating. There's a swimming pool in the basement and squash and tennis courts outside. Beyond the lobby's grillwork, brass tables and mosaic fountain is a coffee bar. In the garden in front of the hotel stands a directional marker, noting that New York is 5,785 miles away, Baghdad 543 miles, London 2,290 miles and Cairo 256 miles away. Singles are SH56.10 ($16.50) to SH62.90 ($18.50), doubles SH49.30 ($14.50) per person. Lunch or dinner is about SH21.20 ($6.25).

There's a **YWCA** on Wadi el Jose in Sheikh Jarrah, tel. 02-282593. A big, solidly built, Jerusalem-stone structure, it is supported by round pillars. Shiny marble floors create a feeling of opulence. Bedrooms at the elevator-equipped Y have private baths, central heating, and throw rugs on the floors. There is a large dining room and a snack bar on the premises. Single occupancy is SH71.40 ($21), double occupancy SH61.20 ($18) per person; there's a 25% surcharge during Easter week.

Once you enter the lobby of the 100-room **Holy Land East** (or **Old City**), on Rasheed St., tel. 02-284841, you may have the feeling you're in a well-run, orderly hotel in America or in Europe—the careful arrangement of plumpish sort-of-modern chairs and tables is Western indeed. Rooms are tastefully furnished in the Western idiom, and most have balconies offering a fine view of the Mount of Olives. Telephones, bathrooms and central heating in all. Rates are SH73.10 ($21.50) to SH81.60 ($24) single, SH57.80 ($17) per person double.

A few additional selections in a slightly lower price range: **Az-Zahara Hotel**, 13 Azzahra St., tel. 02-282447, with 23 rooms, 12 of which have private baths, 10 private showers, one a sink only. It's heated, and there are phones in the rooms. B&B rates are SH40.80 ($12) to SH47.60 ($14) single, SH35.70 ($10.50) per person double. Lunch or dinner is $5.

Vienna East Hotel, 47 Wadi El-Joz St., Sheikh Jarrah, tel. 02-284826, elevator equipped and heated. Some of the bedrooms, which are painted in pastel colors and carpeted, have terraces; all have baths. Rates are SH53 ($15.60) single, SH38.80 ($11.40) per person double. Students get a 10% discount. Off-season rates are a bit lower. Full board is SH34 ($10).

Savoy Hotel, 5 Ibn Sina St., tel. 02-283366, is also elevator-equipped and heated. All of the 17 rooms have private bath or shower and toilet, but are basically of the no-frills variety. Rates are SH47.60 ($14) single, SH37.40 ($11) per person double. Students get a 15% discount, except during high season. Full board is SH40.80 ($12).

Starvation Budget

For travelers whose budget is on the lower end of the scale, there are a few hostels in the downtown area you might consider—if you don't mind roughing it. The first is the **New Raghadan,** tel. 02-282725, on Musrara St. opposite Damascus Gate. (Officially, the name of the street is Haneviim St., and that's what the street signs say. But the resident Arabs still call it Musrara, the Jordanian appellation.) The Raghadan is small (18 rooms) and very modest. Walk up one flight to the desk and lounge. Only doubles and triples here, all with stoves for wintertime heating and most with baths. For a double with bath, the per person charge is SH5 ($1.50); for a triple with hot showers, each person pays SH4 ($1.20). Breakfast, served in a coffee shop just downstairs, is extra.

Another very cheap place for young people to stay in Eastern Jerusalem is the **Jerusalem Student House,** on Musrara St., tel. 02-283733. Opened in 1968, the hotel is not, as it would seem, a students-only place, and neither a student nor hostel card is needed for admission—it simply caters to young people in the student age range. There are ten starkly furnished rooms, with cot-like beds (clean sheets and blankets). Each room holds from two to six beds, and 35 people can be accommodated in total. There are shower rooms at the end of the hallways; no breakfast is served, but in a small restaurant nearby, **Ali Baba,** you can get an inexpensive breakfast, lunch, or dinner, and coffee or tea until midnight. No evening curfew here. The price is SH10 ($2.95) per person in two-bedded rooms; SH5 ($1.50) in multi-bedded rooms.

There's another place by the name of **Jerusalem Student House,** but this one's neither hotel nor hostel—it's a service that helps students find rooms in town. Operated by Southern Baptists from the U.S., it's open during regular business hours on St. Paul St., near the YMCA East, tel. 02-283258; they will help you find a place to stay.

Inside the Walls

Within the fortress walls are an unbelievable number of small hotels—most for Arab visitors and monks on pilgrimage. These hotels are everywhere: in the bazaars, at the gate entrances, in the Moslem, Armenian and Christian quarters. Their rates may be rock-bottom but, in most cases, so are the beds and the breakfasts and the floors. We have, however, found four hotels to recommend within the Old City walls, each reasonably priced. One is located quite near New Gate; the other three are a short way inside Jaffa Gate.

Our own favorite here is the **Knights Palace Hotel,** tel. 02-282537, built in 1874 and called "palace" quite aptly. The huge old stone building, with steep stairs, very old heavily carved furniture, gothic-type arches and high ceilings, was orginally part of the Latin Patriarchate, later became a religious seminary, and eventually (1954) a pilgrimage hotel for Knights of the Holy Sepulchre. Now it welcomes any and all visitors to the Holy Land. When you first enter, through wrought-iron outer gates and heavy front doors, you encounter a large beautiful statue of the Madonna and Child. Miss Anholt, the spry little lady who runs the hotel, is one of the Sisters of Sion (though she doesn't dress the part). Fluent in many languages, she delights in showing guests the lovely view from the many windows, terraces, and the roof. She'll also show you downstairs to the lovely, high-ceilinged dining room where lunch or dinner will cost you SH20.40 ($6). Further down the hall is a spacious high-ceilinged bar. It's a one-star hotel despite all this seeming glamor and charges a minimum B&B rate of SH23.80 ($7) per person in a bathless double. You can drive right up to the front door here, via New Gate.

On the main courtyard just inside the Jaffa Gate, is the **New Imperial Hotel,** tel. 02-282261, its not-so-new sign easily spotted. Head through the archway and you'll find yourself in a high-ceilinged lobby. The walls of the large dining room are cream colored, and the bar is outfitted like a sheikh's tent, with red and black fabric-covered ceilings and walls, copper trays, low cushions, and camel saddles. Forty of the 52 rooms have been renovated; almost all of them have complete bathrooms, and central heating. Rooms overlooking the street have terraces. Rates, including breakfast, are SH35.70 ($10.50) to SH47.60 ($14) single, SH34 ($10) per person double; slightly lower rates off-season.

Twenty paces inside Jaffa Gate, turn left on Latin Patriarchate St. and you'll find the **Gloria Hotel,** tel. 02-282432. The entrance is up a flight of blue-carpeted stairs; up another floor (take the elevator) is the hotel desk, with a bevy of friendly folks to help you. Rooms here have bathrooms, central heating and phones, as well as decorative throw rugs and vividly colored woolen blankets. They cost SH68 ($20) to SH78.20 ($23) single, SH54.40 ($16) per person double. You can take your meals here if you wish—the dining room overlooks the citadel wall, the Tower of David, Western Jerusalem's King David Hotel, and the YMCA tower. Students get a 10% reduction in low season.

From the doorway of the Gloria, look left and across the street and you'll spot the **Lark House Hotel,** tel. 02-283620, where the standards are more spartan and hostel-like than at any of the others suggested here—but the rates are much lower. Each stucco-walled, high-ceilinged room has its own tiny toilet/shower facility. In high season, singles pay SH27.20 ($8), doubles SH23.80 ($7) per person. Low-season rates are $1 per person less. These prices include breakfast, which is served in the cave-like restaurant-bar downstairs. Crowded for lunch and dinner (Armenian cuisine), the bar's packed in the evenings, when tourists and some locals gather for music and drinks. Mostly frequented by the young crowd, the Lark has a smiling, friendly staff.

Mount of Olives Hotels

Up here the view is grand and biblical—churches and mosques every-where, among hillsides of golden stone and cypress trees. A good selection of $20-a-day hotels is available. One drawback worth noting, however, is that bus service to and from this area is not as regular or fast as one would like. Buses 42 and 75 run up from the bus station opposite the Damascus Gate, at well-spaced intervals, and only bus 75 operates on Saturdays. But despair not: you can call a sherut taxi from any hotel up here, and for a loadful (seven people) the cost will be quite reasonable.

On a quiet hillside off Mount of Olives Rd. are several good hotels. To reach them take bus 75 from the bus station at Herod's Gate. The first is the **Astoria,** tel. 02-284965, which has a nice outdoor terrace. The rooms here are decorated in the Western idiom, and each is fully equipped: bathroom (tub or shower), phone, and central heating. Singles are SH47.60 ($14) to SH62.90 ($18.50), doubles SH45.90 ($13.50) per person. Add SH37.40 ($11) for full board.

Up the hill on the same side is the 45-room **Commodore,** tel. 02-284845. This is an exceptionally tidy, well-groomed place, with a big, handsome lobby (look for the painting of Petra on the wall), an elevator and rooms with all the conveniences. Singles are SH62.90 ($18.50) to SH73.10 ($21.50), doubles SH49.30 ($14.50) per person. Lunch or dinner is SH25.50 ($7.50).

Back on the Mount of Olives Rd., you pass through the Arab village of E-Tur and continue past two hospitals. The steeple of the Russian church will be on your left and at a bend in the road you'll see the **Mount of Olives Hotel,** tel. 02-284877. The distinguishing features of this small hotel are its tent-like, red-cloth bar and its proximity to the Church of the Ascension, just next door. Rooms are simply furnished, all with bathtubs or showers, and central heating; some have phones. Singles are SH40.80 ($12) to SH47.60 ($14), doubles SH37.40 ($11) per person, including continental breakfast. Lunch or dinner is SH18.70 ($5.50).

Christian Hospices

Like their counterparts in Western Jerusalem, these hospices were built primarily to house pilgrims, but they do take in tourists; they always have clean, neat accommodations, often in dormitories, which range in both amenities and price from ascetic-monkish to two-star-hotel-ish. Brief listings follow:

The **Armenian Catholic Partriarchate,** Via Dolorosa Station 3, P.O.B. 190546, tel. 02-284262, has 76 bunks; showers and toilets are in a separate area. These are priced at just SH8.50 ($2.50) a night. For SH20.40 ($6) a night, you can get a bed in a bathless double, $1 more will get you a bed in a double with bath. The ambience is rather cheerless. No meals are served. Doors close at 10:30 p.m. until 6 a.m. the following morning.

Christ Church Hostel, Jaffa Gate, P.O.B. 14037, tel. 02-282082, is a highly recommended Anglican hospice. Located opposite David's Tower, it is situated around a flagstone plaza with trees and old garden furniture. Rooms with private toilets and showers cost SH49.30 ($14.50) for half board, SH56.10 ($16.50) for full board. Rooms with showers and sinks (toilets shared with adjoining room), are $2 a night less. And there are also dorm rooms where bed and breakfast is SH7.50 ($2.20) per person nightly. Dorms are closed between 10 a.m. and 4 p.m., and, at night, the front gate is locked from 11 p.m. until 6 a.m. The Christ Church offers a variety of reasonably priced tours.

Ecco Homo Convent, Via Dolorosa, P.O.B. 19056, tel. 02-282445 (Roman Catholic), is a friendly place where singles pay SH40.80 ($12) for B&B in a room with private bath, doubles pay SH34 ($10) per person; rooms with showers only are a few dollars less. There are two dormitories which are divided into cubicles, each with a bed, sink, closet, and mirror. Here the rate is SH23.80 ($7) per person for B&B. Add $3 for half board, $6 for full board. More primitive dorm facilities (for women only) are SH8.50 ($2.50) a night. The door closes at 10 p.m. till 5:45 a.m.

Franciscains de Marie ("White Sisters"), Shechem Rd., P.O.B. 19049, tel. 02-282633 (Roman Catholic), has dorms for women only. You pay SH6.80 ($2) per person without meals. Breakfast is an additional $2, lunch or dinner $3.

St. George's Hostel, Nablus Road/Saladin St., P.O.B. 19018, tel. 02-283302, is a 22-bed Anglican/Episcopal establishment charging SH68 ($20) a night for full board, SH57.80 ($17) for half board.

Lutheran House, St. Marks St., P.O.B. 14051, tel. 02-282120, is clean and lovely, with its own garden, fountain, and pool—even an outdoor bar with colored umbrellas offering shade from the sun. In the guest house (in double-bedded rooms, shared showers and toilets), bed and breakfast costs SH35.70 ($10.50) per person half board SH54 ($15.87) and full board SH68.50 ($20.15). Rates are $1–2 higher with shower and toilet in the room. There are also dorm facilities, where no meals are served, but there is a fully equipped kitchen for guests. To stay in a dorm, you must be between ages 16 and 32. Nightly rate for bed only is SH5 ($1.50), and there's an SH2 (60¢) deposit for use of the kitchen. Register in advance and get confirmation before arriving.

Casa Nova P.P. Franciscains, 10 Casa Nova St., P.O.B. 1321, tel. 02-282791, has 100 rooms. Both the lobby and dining room are impressive, with vaulted ceilings, and, in the former, massive marble pillars. Rooms are pleasant and equipped with shower and toilet; the building is centrally heated throughout. Half board is SH34 ($10), full board SH40.80 ($12). Doors close at 11 p.m. till 5 a.m. Highly recommended.

EATING PLACES: Inexpensive eateries abound in East Jerusalem, but the number of "budget finds" we recommend is a bit more limited than one might expect. The reason? It takes time to bring all the restaurants up to par. The Israeli health authorities and Ministry of Tourism are encouraging established places to raise their sanitary standards and new restaurants to open—so you can be assured of eating safely and well.

This is the area in Israel to get acquainted with authentic Arabic cuisine. Ask for *mazza* before your meal, and you will be served a large variety of small, spicy salads to scoop up with pitta, plus assorted hot and cold appetizers. In most Arab restaurants, mazza can often make up a meal in itself and is especially good with a cold beer after the movies at night. After your meal, try Turkish coffee with *haile,* pronounced "hell." It is cardamom that adds the pungent aroma to the thick, sweet coffee and is claimed by Arabs to have a wonderfully calming effect on an over-full stomach. Arab cookery concentrates heavily on lamb, served several ways, and rice, often topped with nuts. The English-speaking waiters in most Arab restaurants will be glad to recommend their restaurant's specialties and are unendingly patient about describing each dish in detail.

Inside the Walls

The first port of call is the area just inside the Jaffa Gate. Here, you'll find a number of restaurants catering to every conceivable type of pocketbook requirement. And, happily, they're all within easy walking distance of each other.

Budget Restaurants: Abu Seif & Sons is our first choice in this category. Modest-looking from the outside, it has two floors and is open from 8 a.m. to 7 or 8 p.m. every day except Sunday. On Saturdays, the management prepares many different dishes and the food is all fresh. Appetizers such as humus, tomato salad with tchina, eggplant salad, or soup, cost a uniform SH2 (60¢). In the more exotic department, you can purchase potatoes, grape leaves or marrow stuffed with meat for SH4 ($1.20). Felafel is SH2 (60¢), spinach with beef or lamb SH6 ($1.75), roast meat with rice SH12 ($3.50). Abu Seif also has a fish restaurant around the corner on Latin Patriarchate Rd.

Very nearby is the **Citadel Bar and Restaurant,** Omar Ibn el Khatab Square, tel. 02-282043. Just a few steps from the Christian Information Center, the restaurant is open every day in summer from 7 a.m. to 10:30 p.m. and from 7:30 a.m. to 7:30 p.m. in winter. A plate of soup is SH4 ($1.20), bacon and eggs or a ham and egg sandwich cost SH6.50 ($1.90), a toasted cheese sandwich in a pitta is SH5 ($1.45).

The above-mentioned **Lark House Hotel,** tel. 02-283620, has an Armenian restaurant that is open to the public. An order of ten meat- or rice-stuffed vine leaves costs SH3.90 ($1.15), tabbouleh—bulgur wheat with onion, tomato, parsley, and mint leaves—is SH1.80 (55¢), soup SH2.50 (75¢). Main courses are in the SH7.50 ($2.20) to SH15 ($4.40) range; they include stuffed eggplant and roast ground lamb. For dessert there's baklava for SH2 (60¢).

Located a few minutes' walk down David St., at No. 38-40 is the **Arches Restaurant and Patisserie,** tel. 02-284453. Open from early in the morning until 7 p.m. (9 p.m. in summer), it proffers a large selection of main courses for SH7.50 ($2.20) to SH9 ($2.65), all including rice or chips and salad. Among these: lamb chops and fried lamb brains. Less expensive are cubes of meat cooked with vegetables for SH5 ($1.50) or a cheese sandwich with salad for SH3 (90¢). Fruit desserts or sweets are SH2 (60¢). Do try an oriental drink called *sahlab* for SH2 (60¢); served hot in winter and cold in summer, it consists of milk, sugar, sahlab powder, rose water, coconut, nuts and cinnamon.

The Golden Jerusalem, located near the New Gate, tel. 02-282309, is a gaily decorated fish restaurant with plastic grapes, peppers, and plants suspended from the ceiling, and a bar cluttered with knickknacks. Grilled St. Peters fish with chips for SH8 ($2.35) is the specialty; for the same price you can have lamb shwarma, cutlets, steak or kabab with chips. Wash it down with a glass of beer for SH3 (90¢). Open daily except Sunday from 8 a.m. to 10 p.m.

Starvation Budget: Uncle Moustache's Restaurant and Tea Room may well be the ultimate budget eating spot in the world. It is certainly the only place we've ever seen with a hand-lettered sign in the window welcoming "Hippies, Beatnicks and Hikers"! But thereby hangs the tale. Uncle Moustache's is the simplest of storefront cafes, located about 20 yards inside Herod's Gate. Up until about ten years ago, it was probably undistinguishable from all the other tiny storefront cafes that line these broad courtyard steps. Then one day Uncle Moustache—a gentle, big-bellied man with a black handlebar moustache—invited a couple of long-haired young travelers in for a cup of tea. They declined, saying that they couldn't afford anything right now. He discovered that they were broke and hungry and invited them in for a full meal. They all got friendly and the young travelers took their meals for the next few days at Uncle Moustache's, promising that some day when they had it, they would send back the money in payment. About six months later, Uncle Moustache did receive the money, but from the day the young travelers left, he also received streams of long-haired youngsters who were passing along the information that there dwelt a saint inside Herod's Gate. Uncle Moustache developed the lowest of low-priced menus and sometimes, when a kid really couldn't pay him, would take the payment in services. The sign in the window was hand-lettered by a passing artist. One group left Uncle Moustache a large notebook and inscribed inside its front cover: "Donated by Uncle Moustache for sayings of wit, humour, profanity and for useful information to fellow travelers, hitchhikers, vagabonds and bums alike on economy places to eat and sleep. Jerusalem's answer to *Europe on $5 A Day.*" The book got filled quickly, and now there are four filled with such idealistic statements as: "If human relationships were as good as Uncle Moustache's humus, there would be no war in the world." Opinions differ on the quality of the cuisine, but appreciation of the hospitality is a central theme. And nobody complains about the prices: A cheese omelet with rice or chips, and salad is SH2 (60¢), humus and tchina with salad in a pitta just SH1.50 (45¢), and a main course of chicken, kabab, shashlik, liver or fish, all served with rice or chips, and salad SH3 (90¢). Open daily from 7 a.m. to 10 p.m., till midnight in summer.

Run by Uncle Moustache and his brother, the restaurant has been open every day for the past two decades. "Once," reminisced the proprieter (real name Ahmed), "I closed for the day. By 11 a.m., though, there were customers banging at my door at home. I dressed and opened the restaurant. I love the people and they love me and that is my secret."

You might have a bit of trouble finding **Abu Shukri,** Aqabat el-Khanqa St. in the Christian Section of the bazaar, and when you finally find the stall, with only a few tables inside, you might wonder why you made the effort. The answer is simple. Abu Shukri is the home of the freshest, the best, and the most tantalizing humus in the world. For exactly SH2.10 (60¢), you'll undergo a major culinary experience and, at the same time, be satisfying caloric needs until nighttime. That's the price of freshly made humus, served with *fooul* (a spicy bean paste) and an omelet in a fresh pitta. Open daily from 8 a.m. to 6 p.m. Closed during the month of Ramadan.

Highly recommended is the **Roman Inn Restaurant,** 4 Via Dolorosa, tel. 02-284417, housed in a 1500-year-old building that was originally a Roman inn.

It still evokes antiquity with high vaulted ceilings and arches, wrought-iron lamps, and stained-glass windows. The cuisine is oriental/European. For SH9 ($2.65) you can order fried beef-liver and onions, fried fish, or lamb chops; grilled or roast chicken is SH8 ($2.35). Desserts are SH2 (60¢) to SH3 (90¢), a glass of fresh orange or carrot juice SH2 (60¢). Open daily from 7 a.m. to 10 p.m.

Just inside Herod's Gate, a few doors away from the above-mentioned Uncle Moustache's, is the **City Restaurant,** tel. 02-284008, an immaculate, air-conditioned eatery serving fresh meats and fish. White lace curtains cover the glass door and windows, and fresh flowers grace the counter. If you start your meal with mazza, you have ten portions to choose from at SH1 (30¢) each. A choice of six salads are SH.20 (5¢) each, portions of stuffed vine leaves, artichoke, potatoes, or eggplant SH2 (60¢) each. Main courses are a very reasonable SH5.50 ($1.60) and include ground roast meat with tchina or tomatoes, lamb chops, stuffed roast chicken, and fish—all served with rice or fresh vegetables. For dessert try an Arab sweet at SH1 (30¢). Open daily except Sunday from 1 to 9 p.m.

Another reasonable restaurant in the Old City is the **Samara,** near the Jaffa Gate, which is totally unpretentious and sells sandwiches, soup, meat and salad plates.

Big Splurge: Although the prices are high, of all the Jaffa Gate restaurants, our favorite is the **Select,** tel. 02-283325. Hamdan Dahoud is the young smiling owner who swears that he tastes every dish before it's served. He was a cook in Europe for 13 years, and his second chef worked for Egypt's late King Farouk. The restaurant is elegant, with red pillars, red walls, red tablecloths, and a sleek red, black, and silver bar. Hamdan claims that given one day's notice, he'll cook you anything to order. ("Just try me," he dares.) An entree or salad is SH2 (60¢), two fried eggs with potatoes SH6 ($1.75), main courses like roast beef or roast veal SH12 ($3.50). Open every day 8 a.m.-midnight. The Select is packed on Saturdays, so reserve in advance.

The **Hahoma Restaurant,** situated a short walk from the Western Wall at 128 Hayehudim St., tel. 02-271332, enjoys a marvelous location. It serves strictly kosher, gourmet French and Moroccan fare in posh surroundings. Tables are elegantly set with copper wine and water goblets, flowers, and candlesticks. Go on Thursday night and enjoy a Moroccan feast of fried meat pastry, fish or chicken couscous, a honey-rich dessert, and mint tea for SH19 ($5.60). Students get a 15% reduction on all meals. Open Sunday to Thursday from 11 a.m. to 3 p.m. and from 6 to 11 p.m.; closed from early Friday afternoon till Saturday after sunset.

Fink's 2 Histadruth st at corner of King George Ave.

Downtown East Jerusalem

Kfir Restaurant, 25 Saladin St.; tel. 02-280555, is brand new, but chef Réne has 40 years of culinary expertise behind him. It's a festive-looking place with yellow and off-white walls, midnight blue ceilings and curtains, red and black wooden chairs with rope seats, wrought-iron lighting fixtures, and red-and-white tablecloths. The Kfir is so new that their menu is still in a state of flux. On our last visit they offered a mazza with ten salads for SH5 ($1.50), spaghetti for SH4 ($1.20), stuffed vegetable or vine leaves for SH4 ($1.20), and lamb cutlet at SH9 ($2.65), not to mention very good baklava for dessert at SH2.50 (75¢). Show a copy of this book, and you'll get a 10% discount. Open daily from noon to midnight.

Between the Lawrence and Capitol Hotels is the **Patisserie Suisse,** tel. 02-284377, perhaps the only Swiss tea shop in the world with both Swiss and

The Philadelphia- Azzahra st. opposite Al-Quds Cinema

Lebanese pastry chefs. The entrance looks like a Swiss chalet. You can enjoy your tea, coffee, or hot chocolate for SH1.50 (45¢), and luscious cakes SH1.50 (45¢), either on the main level, or upstairs on a balcony. Ham and cheese sandwiches and ice cream are also served here. Open daily from about 8 a.m. to 10 p.m.

Just across the street from the Ministry of Justice, on Saladin St., is the **Golden Chicken Restaurant,** tel. 02-284289. The street level is furnished with high-backed wooden chairs, and copper lamps are suspended from the ceiling. Upstairs, thick rugs cover the floors; the walls are upholstered seating arrangements, with low tables and poufs; woven pictures of Arab motif, beaded curtains, colored-glass windows, and Arab artifacts complete the exotic setting. For SH10 ($2.95) you can get sliced mutton with rice or chips, and vegetables, or cubed grilled lamb marinated in yogurt and served over rice. For dessert, the traditional baklava is SH1.50 (45¢). Open daily from 11 a.m. to 10:30 p.m.

Over on Rasheed St. is another exotic choice—the **Jerusalem Oriental Restaurant,** tel. 02-284397, lavishly decorated like a Bedouin tent with waiters in Bedouin dress. (Guests can have photographs of themselves taken in Bedouin dress, too.) Mazza with 13 different kinds of salad is SH10 ($2.95) to SH15 ($4.40); other choices for SH10 ($2.95) include lamb with yogurt sauce, fried ground beef simmered in tomato or tchina sauce, and chicken roasted on bread with spices and onions. Open daily 10 a.m. to 11 p.m.

Another plush-Arab-motif Rasheed St. restaurant, is **Hassan Effendi-al-Arabi,** tel. 02-283599. There's a uniformed doorman outside, and patrons are ushered upstairs to an ornate dining room, which is open daily from noon to 11 p.m. Main courses run the gamut from grilled pigeon SH13.60 ($4) to SH17 ($5) choices such as oriental meats and vegetables, lamb chops, and fried fish. A bottle of local red wine with your meal is SH13.60 ($4).

Lamb, and only lamb, bought from the kosher butcher "because it's the best," is served at the **Siam Restaurant,** tel. 02-282977, in the alleyway off Ibn Sina St., around the corner from the main post office, tel. 02-282977. It's a simple little place, oddly adorned with kitchen paraphernelia. Lamb dishes—kababs, chops, liver, kidney, etc.—are SH10 ($2.95) and served with fresh salads, humus, and tchina. A beer is SH2 (60¢) to SH3 (90¢); students can get lamb skewers for SH2.50 (75¢). Open daily from 10 a.m. to 10 p.m.

The **Ali Baba Restaurant,** 16 Hanviim St. (not far from Damascus Gate), tel. 02-282748, has two price levels, one for regular customers, the other for students. The lucky latter can get lunch or dinner here consisting of soup, meat or chicken, chips, salad and bread for SH4.20 ($1.25), and a big breakfast for SH2 (60¢). Regular prices are SH6.50 ($1.90) to SH8.50 ($2.50) for a main course—chicken in a basket—with chips and salad. Open 7:30 a.m. to midnight daily.

The **Al Americaine,** corner of Saladin and Azzahra Sts., tel. 02-284017, is small and unobtrusive, with just eight Formica tables, and blue walls decorated with small prints. It offers a 10% discount to students if they order a two-course meal. Soup or salad is SH2 (60¢), fried eggs SH2.50 (75¢), moussaka, steak, or roast chicken SH7.50 ($2.20). Open daily from 10 a.m. to 10 p.m.

La Gondola Tea Room, 8 Azzahra St., tel. 02-225944, serves tea and light fare on a beautifully carved wood balcony. Ice cream, tea or coffee, sandwiches, etc. are in the SH2.50 (75¢) range. Open daily from noon to 2:30 p.m. and 6:30 to 10 p.m.

Santo's Cafeteria, Dar el Awlad St., near the Ministry of Justice and the New Orient House Hotel, is a small place with an orange awning outside, just four yellow and white tables and chairs and a few hanging plants within. Help yourself to a plate of salads—SH5 ($1.50) for a large plate, SH3 (90¢) medium, and SH2 (60¢) small. A pizza or a hamburger in a pitta is SH2 (60¢), fresh-squeezed juice IL25 (75¢), fried chicken with french fries SH5 ($1.50). Open daily 9 a.m. to midnight. Under the same ownership is **Manex—King of Shwarma Cafeteria,** on 10 Azzahra St., tel. 02-272204, specializing, of course, in shwarma—made with beef and 15 kinds of spices and served in a pitta with salad, tchina, and pickles—for SH3 (90¢). Open 8 a.m. to midnight daily.

Al Salam Restaurant and Sweets, 10 Saladin St., tel. 02-281060, is down a flight of steps. The sweets factory is behind the restaurant which is a large room with pillars. It's being renovated at this writing, so there is no point in describing decor. Delicious Arab dishes are served. Try the mansaf, made with dried curdled milk, meat, and rice for SH7.50 ($2.20) or, for the same price, mousakhan—chicken fried with onions, saffron, cloves, and sumac in a pitta topped with pine nuts. Rice with chick-peas is SH2 (60¢), stuffed vegetables SH2 (60¢). And do leave room for those made-on-the-premises Arab pastries. Open daily from 7 a.m. to 10 p.m., till 6 p.m. only during Ramadan.

At **Quick Lunch,** 25 Azzahra St., tel. 02-284228, you can get a half grilled chicken for SH4 ($1.20), a salad of fresh vegetables and a pitta to go with it for an additional SH1.65 (50¢), and a beer for SH2 (60¢). That's practically the entire menu at this tiny seven-table eatery. Open daily except Monday from 9 a.m. to 7 p.m.

Finally, check out the restaurant that belongs to the somewhat splurgy **American Colony Hotel,** where the pleasures are not only gourmet, but atmospheric. To find the complex, you'll have to traverse all of Saladin St., then take a sharp right and proceed for two blocks. We've already described the hotel above. A full meal—soup, main course, dessert, and Turkish coffee—is about SH27.20 ($8) here. You have three seating options at the American Colony; you can choose from the garden, the grill room or the coffee bar for your dining.

SIGHTSEEING IN EAST JERUSALEM: Any understanding of the sights of East Jerusalem, apart from their sheer physical beauty, must first be based on an appreciation of the section's history, an evolution that shaped the destiny of the Western world.

What follows are the bare essentials of the city's remarkable history.

In Genesis 14, it is recorded that Abraham visited Melchizedek, "king of Salem"; this is the first known reference to Jerusalem. Not until 800 years later did the Jews settle in the city. Then, in 1000 B.C., King David captured Jerusalem, at the time a Jebusite city. David brought the ark to Jerusalem from his former capital, Hebron. On Mount Ophel, a hillock to the southeast of East Jerusalem, David built his city and declared that henceforth Jerusalem would be the capital. Under the reign of his son, Solomon, Jerusalem grew in importance. Solomon built the great temple (960 B.C.), and constructed a magnificent palace. Jerusalem, and Israel, prospered under Solomon's rule. After his death, the kingdom split in two, Israel to the north and Judea to the south, with Jerusalem becoming Judea's capital. After seeing a succession of kings, prophets and invaders, Jerusalem fell to the armies of Nebuchadnezzar, who in 586 B.C. destroyed the Temple, sacked the city, and carried off many thousands of Jerusalem's inhabitants into exile in Babylonia. But Babylonia soon fell to the Persians, and Cyrus, in 540 B.C., allowed the Jews to return to their homeland and rebuild the Temple. This was carried out under the prophets Zechariah, Ezra and Nehemiah.

Jerusalem fell under the domain of Alexander the Great in 331 B.C. The Hellenistic rule passed to the Selucids, and it was against their domination that

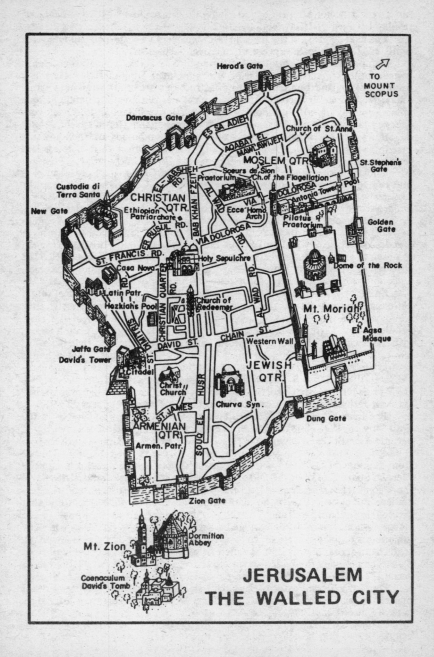

JERUSALEM
THE WALLED CITY

(under the Hasmonean priests and kings) the Maccabees staged their famous revolt—between 167 B.C. and 141 B.C.

The next 80 years of the Jewish Hasmonean era were the penultimate years (until 1967) that the Jews were to rule over Jerusalem.

Pompey claimed Jerusalem for Rome in 63 B.C., and in 37 B.C. Herod (whose father converted to Judaism) was appointed King of Judea. He was a frantic builder, and remnants of his constructions are seen throughout Israel today. Herod rebuilt Jerusalem, and in particular designed a palatial Temple area more magnificent than Solomon's. (Thus far, scholars and archeologists believe that the present Western Wall is a remnant of Herod's Temple, not Solomon's—but excavations down to the wall's foundations are shedding further light.) Herod died in 4 B.C. The city that he built, with its fortress and towers and aqueducts, was the Jerusalem that Christ knew.

Under Pontius Pilate, the Roman procurator, Christ lived, preached, was imprisoned, and crucified. According to certain Christian traditions, the Church of the Holy Sepulchre marks the site of the crucifixion, and the Via Dolorosa the way he trod, carrying the cross, from prison to Golgotha.

An unsuccessful rebellion against Roman rule brought Vespasian's armies to deal with the Jews. In 70 A.D. he starved out the population of Jerusalem and destroyed the city and its Temple. Bar Kochba's revolt returned Jerusalem to the Jews for three short years, but in 132 A.D. Emperor Hadrian leveled the city, rebuilt it with the name "Aelia Capitolina," erected statues of Roman gods, and decreed that henceforth Jews were forbidden entry to the city.

Emperor Constantine, a convert to Christianity, turned Jerusalem into a Christian city and opened the gates to Jewish and Christian pilgrims so they could visit the holy places. Constantine built the first Church of the Holy Sepulchre, and Justinian, 200 years later, rebuilt and enlarged it. Caliph Omar, in 639, began the Moslem occupation—and built the mosque that bears his name. After the first Crusader invasion in 1099, Jerusalem changed hands several times—between Crusader and Arab (most notably Saladin). Five centuries later, the Ottoman Turks, also Moslems, conquered Jerusalem. From 1517, the Turkish rule lasted exactly 400 years—until General Allenby marched through Jerusalem's Jaffa Gate at the head of a British regiment in 1917.

The British Mandate—a mixed blessing for both Arabs and Jews—lasted until May 15, 1948. The day the British left, Jerusalem, and all of Israel, again became a battlefield. Once again this city was besieged, almost entirely surrounded by Jordanian forces, and pinched off from the rest of Israel. Cut off from supplies of food and water, the Israeli section held out—although the "Jewish quarter" within the Old City walls was abandoned and destroyed. At the second truce, the Israelis held the western half of Jerusalem and the Jordanians the eastern half. A no-man's-land was marked out along a line that divided Jerusalem. On June 5, 1967, within minutes of the outbreak of the Egyptian-Israeli war, Jordanian shells began pounding West Jerusalem. The inhabitants of the city were taken by surprise; they had anticipated a few token shells from Jordan, but hadn't expected Hussein's country to launch a full-scale fight. The next day the Israelis returned the fire, went on the attack, and in 36 hours the entire city, East and West, was in Israeli hands. And here we are.

Don't try to see Eastern Jerusalem's sights in a day, or two days for that matter. In fact, anyone trying to "do" East Jerusalem in less than three days is guilty of criminal haste.

For the purposes of organization, since there is so much to see, our sightseeing section here is divided into three parts:

—Inside the Old City walls.

—Downtown East Jerusalem.

—Mount Scopus, Mount of Olives, Valley of Kidron.

But before you set out to any of these areas, remember that tourists can get a "combined ticket" to six Jerusalem sights which represents a 50% reduction on admission prices to such places as the Rockefeller Museum, Solomon's Quarries, the Citadel (David's Tower) and so forth. The discount book, which must be used during two weeks, costs SH8 ($2.35). Ask about it at I.G.T.O. or the Jerusalem Tourist Information Office, the latter at 34 Jaffa Road tel. 02-228844. The I.G.T.O. office in the Jaffa Gate and the Municipality Information Office are excellent sources of local information. Open daily 8 a.m. to 6 p.m.; Fridays 8 a.m. to 3 p.m.; Saturdays 10 a.m. to 2 p.m. Tel. 02-282295. The Municipality Office is open the same hours; except for Friday when it closes at 1:30 p.m. until Sunday morning.

The Old City

An uneven rectangle of 40-foot-high wall encloses the **Ir Hakodesh,** the holy city, the Old City. The wall is at least 400 years old (some portions, in fact, date back more than 2,000 years), built by Suleiman the Magnificent and repaired several times since. In their present form, the grandiose towers, battlements and sentry walks are quite handsome, with the new parks and gardens beneath them in full bloom. At night the walls are impressively illuminated by golden lights.

Main gates into the wall are **Jaffa Gate,** entered from Mamilla-Agron Street, and **Damascus Gate,** on the road paralleling the wall. Israelis call Damascus Gate **Sh'ar Shchem.** In the Six-Day War, the Israeli army breached the Old City wall at **Lion's Gate** (also called St. Stephen's Gate), just opposite the Garden of Gethsemane, on the eastern wall. It was the first time in the city's long history that an invading force succeeded in attacking from that direction. In all, there are eight gates in the Old City fortress-wall.

The Old City itself is divided into five sections—the **Christian Quarter,** the **Armenian Quarter,** the **Moslem Quarter,** the **Jewish Quarter** and **Temple Mount** (Mount Moriah), the latter housing the Western (Wailing) Wall, the Mosque of Omar (Dome of the Rock) and El Aksa Mosque.

Through Jaffa Gate: The citadel tower at the entrance is called the **Tower of David.** It marks the place where stood three towers built by Herod near his palace (it also marks a Jordanian mortar position at the start of the Six-Day War). Today there is a museum here showing ancient maps of Jerusalem. It also houses an exhibit of 66 dolls in ethnological dress of the diverse population of this region. It's open Sunday to Thursday and Saturday from 8:30 a.m. to 4:30 p.m., Friday and holiday eves until 2 p.m. Adults pay SH1.50 (45¢) for admission, students and children half price. For further information tel. 02-285770. The Tower of David is also the setting for a **Sound and Light** show (held nightly from March 15th to November 15th, except Fridays and holiday eves) the theme of which is the Old City's biblical history. Performances in English are at 8:45 p.m. Adults pay SH6 ($1.75), children and students SH4.50 ($1.35). Dress warmly, as evenings are chilly here even in summer.

Jaffa Gate is said to have been widened to its present size for the visit of Kaiser Wilhelm and his entourage in 1898. Here Allenby entered Jerusalem in 1917. The Balfour Declaration Ceremony, held soon thereafter, was held here as well.

As you come inside the courtyard, you'll see a road heading off to the right, past the moat. This route leads into the **Armenian Quarter,** a quiet residential area of small churches that parallels the wall; the road leads to the Western Wall and the Mosque of Omar (Dome of the Rock).

In the Armenian Quarter are many green courtyards and ancient buildings, including the splendid **St. James Cathedral,** the **Church of the Holy Archangels** (said to be from the Early Medieval period), the **Gulbenkian Public Library,** the **Library of Manuscripts,** and the **Helen and Edward Mardigian Museum of Armenian Art and History;** the latter is open daily except Tuesday from 10 a.m. to 5 p.m., admission SH1.20 (35¢) for adults, SH.30 (9¢) for children and students.

If you head straight across the courtyard into the bazaar (the *suq*), you'll enter **David St.,** bustling with shops vending bushels of mother-of-pearl and olive wood rosary beads, other religious crafts and souvenirs, maps and household items. If your first destination is the Church of the Holy Sepulchre, then take the first left off David Street to **Christian Quarter Rd.** This latter takes you right to Christianity's most hallowed shrine.

But if the Western Wall and Temple Mount is your first goal, then continue straight along David St. It changes its name halfway to **Chain St.** Follow the signs to "The Wall." On your first trip you may think you forgot to take a turn somewhere and that you're lost in a maze of narrow bazaar streets and noisy, crowded shops. The air grows heavy with spices and fragrances, the throughway fills with milling people and donkeys, and the archways blot out the sky from view. As the smell of spices becomes stronger, the little street shrinks further, and soon it is a teeming mob scene of shoulder-to-shoulder traffic. Stay with it. You're almost there.

The Western Wall: This is the **Ha'kotel Ha'ma'aravi.** It was formerly called "Wailing" because the Jews have traditionally come here to bewail the loss of their Temple. It is the holiest of Jewish sites, a remnant of the wall that once supported the Temple Mount. During the night and early in the morning, the large blocks of the wall are covered with dew, which tradition claims are the tears shed by the wall that weeps with its mourners. For over 2,000 years, at this place and wherever they have lived in the diaspora, Jews have bemoaned the loss of the Temple: "For the temple that is desolate, we sit in solitude and mourn." They prayed for forgiveness for their transgressions, and they prayed that God might one day give Jerusalem back to the chosen people. On June 14, 1967—Shavuoth—the way to the wall was opened for the first time. A quarter-million Israelis walked from Mount Zion through the Dung Gate to renew their contact with this symbol of Israel and its long past.

For centuries the Wall had stood 60-feet high and 91-feet long, towering over a narrow alley 12-feet wide which could accommodate a few hundred worshippers standing. To make room for the stream of pilgrims after the Old City was restored to Jewish hands in the Six-Day War, the Israelis bulldozed the Moors Quarter facing the Wall to create a plaza that could accommodate tens of thousands. They also made the Wall about 6½-feet higher by digging down and exposing two more tiers of ashlars from the Second Temple which had been underground for centuries. Apart from the traditional area which is still reserved for prayer and worship, archeologists have exposed an area down at the southern end and uncovered remains from various periods. At the prayer section of the Western Wall, grass grows out of the upper cracks. The lower cracks of the chalky, streaked, yellow-white blocks have been stuffed with bits of paper containing prayers. Black-robed Orthodox Jews are always seen standing at the wall, praying and chanting and swaying. If you care to go down to the wall, but are hatless, you can acquire a hat, at no cost, at the little stand at the top of the path. Women may borrow shawls and short skirt coverings.

There are usually some Hasids around who are dedicated to drawing assimilated Jews back to the faith, and will invite men to a nearby Yeshiva for a meal, a discussion, even a bed. Yeshivat Aish Hatorah, overlooking the

Western Wall, holds classes, in English for estranged Jews. Rebbetzin Denah Weinberg offers classes for women in her home. Inquire at the Yeshiva. Serious interest will be encouraged.

The area surrounding the wall and immediately to the west of it was for centuries the Jewish Quarter of the Old City. Over 50 synagogues and yeshivas (Talmudic schools) stood there—all systematically destroyed since the 1948 war. The separate section at the extreme right of the Western Wall is reserved for women, who are not allowed at the other section, in keeping with Orthodox Jewish tradition.

A tour of the **Temple Mount excavations,** which were done between 1967 and 1977, takes place every Wednesday afternoon at 2:30 p.m. It's run by the Society for the Protection of Nature in Israel, 13 Heleni Hamalka St., tel. 02-222357, and costs SH1.50 (45¢). Don't miss it. Remains of the First Temple built in 961 B.C. by King Solomon, and the Second Temple built in 515 B.C. by King Herod, as well as remnants of Byzantine and Moslem periods have been revealed.

Workmen are busily refurbishing the area adjacent to the wall (some distance away); already completed are expensive, modernized homes plus synagogues and yeshivas. A tunnel has been opened at the Western Wall, its roof consisting of a series of arches from the Herodian (1st century B.C. to 1st century A.D.) to the Crusader (11th to 13th centuries) periods. It leads from the plaza of the Western Wall to Hagai St. in the Old City.

Facilities at the wall area include water fountains and bathrooms. Nearby is a permanent first aid station.

The gate to the right is **Dung Gate.** Many stories surround the origin of this name. One story is that the name resulted from the debris from each consecutive destruction of Jerusalem that was pushed out into the valley below. Another is that the area above the wall extending to the gate region was, in fact, the Jerusalem garbage dump. Rubbish was heaped on the wall and in the gate area because, according to one story, the rulers of Jerusalem were cruel; yet another version has it that the rubbish dump kept the wall hidden so that, for the time being, no further harm would come to it. Take your pick.

Beyond Dung Gate is the Valley of Kidron and Mount Ophel, where David built his city.

If the Jewish Quarter is your first sightseeing goal, go through Jaffa Gate, and turn right after passing Suq el Husr in the Armenian Quarter. Many of the houses here have been rebuilt, and one of them, at 6 Old Yishuv Court, tel. 02-284636, is now a museum. It belongs to the Weingarten family, whose great-great-grandfather lived in it in the 18th century. Within, the displays reflect Ashkenazi and Sephardic lifestyles from the middle of the 19th century to the end of Turkish rule in 1917. The living quarters, kitchens, and several very important synagogues have been restored. The museum is open Sundays through Thursdays, 10 a.m. to 5 p.m.; adults pay SH1.50 (45¢), students SH.80 (23¢), children SH.40 (12¢).

Temple Mount—Dome of the Rock: Take the staircase to the right of the Western Wall to Temple Mount, **Mount Moriah.** This is the **Haram esh-Sharif,** the Noble Enclosure of the Moslems. When David first came to Jerusalem, he purchased the flat rock on Moriah from Orhan the Jebusite, who had used it as a threshing floor. II Chronicles 3 relates that "Solomon began to build the house of the Lord at Jerusalem on Mount Moriah." The Second Temple (Solomon's was destroyed by Nebuchadnezzar in 586 B.C.) was first built between 525 and 520 B.C., and later enlarged and beautified by Herod shortly before the time of Christ. The Temple Mount you see here is a stone-paved platform, about 30 acres in area. There is a small admission to the two mosques at the Mount. Visiting hours are 8:30-11 a.m., 12:15-3 p.m., and 4-5 p.m. Neither may be visited on Friday or Moslem holidays.

The **El Aksa Mosque** is the first shrine you come to. Leave your shoes outside, and enter a broad open hall hung with chandeliers. (You won't miss your shoes—the floors are covered with Oriental rugs.) Just to the left of the door as you enter is the site where King Abdullah was murdered by the Mufti's men in 1951. The mosque's lofty ceilings are embellished in Byzantine design. Stonework keeps the mosque's interior cool and comfortable in summertime. Up front, past rows of great marble pillars, is a wood-partitioned platform that had been reserved for King Hussein when he came here to pray. A separate woman's prayer chamber, in blue decor, is at the right.

Outside, to the right of the El Aksa Mosque, is a small door leading to what is presumed to be **Solomon's Stables,** an underground arena of enormous pillars and arches that housed Roman and Crusader horses as well as Solomon's.

Heading straight across the broad open temple deck, you'll pass **El-Kas,** the fountain where Moslems wash themselves before entering their holy places. It is equipped with a circular row of pink marble seats, each with a faucet.

The golden-domed **Dome of the Rock (Mosque of Omar)** is reached by heading straight across the platform under the Roman archway. The mosque's interior is every bit as fantastically ornate as the outside, a geometric display of blue, green, yellow and white tiles. Anyone intrigued by Byzantine art and architecture will go into ecstasies here. Inside, plush red and green carpets line the floor. There is not a piece of wall or ceiling space without some design on it. The marble is not white as it is at the Aksa; here it is striped gray and streaked purple. Stained-glass windows cap the ceiling at the top of the dome.

Everything in this beautiful Moslem sanctuary (built in 691 A.D.) centers on the rock, which occupies the middle of the shrine. Traditionally, this is the spot where Abraham, in 1800 B.C., prepared the sacrifice of his son Isaac at the Lord's command. On this rock, the Jewish religion was founded. Genesis 22 relates how Abraham followed God's instructions to go to Moriah and sacrifice Isaac, his only son. Isaac, puzzled, said to his father: "Behold the fire and the wood: but where is the lamb for a burnt offering?" Abraham built the altar and bound his son, but an angel intervened and told him to lower his knife. God told Abraham that because he did not withhold his only son, he would be blessed: "Thy seed will multiply as the stars of Heaven and the sand which is upon the seashore . . . because thou hast obeyed my voice." Later, around this rock, the Temple of Solomon was built.

To Moslems, the rock is equally holy ("the third most important shrine in Islam, after Mecca and Medina"), not only because of Abraham's near-sacrifice, but because from this rock Mohammed ascended to heaven. (Mohammed said that one prayer at this rock is worth a thousand anywhere else.) Footprints of Mohammed are pointed out on the rock—which is about 30 feet by 30 feet, rising six feet above the floor.

Next to the rock, a few strands of Mohammed's hair are kept in a lattice-work wooden cabinet. A stairway leads under the rock to a cave-like chamber where glass partitions have been built so that pilgrims will stop eroding the sacred rock: for centuries it has been chipped away at by the faithful who want to bring home a memento.

From the flat courtyard surrounding the two mosques you have a wonderful view. There's usually a gusty wind blowing across the flat expanse. To the south, the Valley of Jehosophat (Valley of Kidron) and the hilltop, tree-bordered U.N. Government House (Mount of Contempt). To the east, the lower slopes of the Mount of Olives, the Russian Magdalene Church, the Tomb of the Virgin and, on top of the Mount of Olives, the Intercontinental Hotel (also called "Seven Arches") and the high-steepled Russian Monastery.

Head down the steps, past the **Antonia,** the remnants of Herod's fortress-castle, and through Bab en-Nazir to reach the Via Dolorosa. From here it is just a short walk, crossing Al Wad Road, to the Holy Sepulchre.

Via Dolorosa: This is the Way of the Cross, the route followed by Christ from the Praetorium, the Roman Judgment Hall, to Calvary, scene of the crucifixion. Over the centuries, millions of pilgrims have come here to walk the way that Christ took to his death. Each Friday at 3 p.m. priests lead a ceremony for pilgrims along Via Dolorosa (starting just inside St. Stephen's Gate at the tower of Antonia), and prayers are said at each of the 14 Stations of the Cross.

It must be noted that the Stations are not well marked, and that they're not easy to follow consecutively. Only an unobtrusive sign on a door informs you that it is a Station point, and there is no indication of how far away the next one is. In some cases movie posters slapped up on the wall obscure the sign completely. Should you find the Station door closed, knock: chances are the nun or monk within will let you in for a look.

Station One: Jesus is condemned to death (Sisters of Zion girl's school, now closed). Station Two: Jesus receives the cross (at the foot of the Antonia). Station Three: Jesus falls for the first time (Polish biblical-archeological museum). Station Four: Jesus meets his mother. Station Five: Simon the Cyrene helps Jesus carry the cross. Station Six: Veronica wipes Jesus' face. Station Seven: Jesus falls the second time (at bazaar crossroads). Station Eight: Jesus consoles the women of Jerusalem. Station Nine: Jesus falls the third time (Coptic Monastery).

The five remaining Stations of the Cross are inside the Church of the Holy Sepulchre. Station Ten: Jesus is stripped of his garments. Station Eleven: Jesus is nailed to the cross. Station Twelve: Jesus dies on the cross. Station Thirteen: Jesus is taken down from the cross and given over to Mary. Station Fourteen: Jesus is laid in the chamber of the Sepulchre and from here is resurrected.

Church of the Holy Sepulchre at Golgotha: It doesn't look like Christendom's most sacred shrine—perhaps because of the scaffolding and workmen that have cluttered the outside and inside for years. The repair work is designed to buttress the church against earthquakes (a bad one hit it in 1927) and to reconstruct it along cleaner lines. But the repairs go on at snail's pace—between services and the daily visits of hundreds of pilgrims. A feeling of clutter and compartmentalization reigns within, for the church itself is cared for by five different sects—Roman Catholic, Armenian Orthodox, Greek Orthodox, Abyssinian Coptic and Syrian Orthodox. Each denomination has its own traditions, and its own ownership of space—right down to lines drawn down the middle of floors and pillars. The decor, partitioned and changed every few feet, is a mixture of Byzantine and Frankish styles. To say there is no overall church plan is an understatement.

Monks and nuns show you the various Stations inside the church—the marble slab as you enter, the Stone of Unction, where Jesus was anointed, the site of Calvary on the second floor, the glass-enclosed marble tomb in the sepulchre. Candles light the way to reveal a piece of the true cross (in Armenian territory).

The church evolved thusly: After Constantine had converted to Christianity, his mother, Queen Helena, came on pilgrimage to the Holy Land. She searched out the area of the crucifixion and found part of the wood thought to be from the true cross. Over this spot, Constantine built the first church, and, two centuries later, Justinian enlarged it. Fire, earthquake, and the Persians destroyed the church, but the Crusaders rebuilt it in the 12th century.

If you're in Jerusalem during Easter week, you can attend many of the fascinating services, based on ancient Eastern Church traditions, that are held at the Church of the Holy Sepulchre—most notably the Service of the Holy Fire, and the dramatic pageant called The Washing of the Feet.

Other Christian Sights in the Old City: Just inside St. Stephen's Gate, on the right, is the **Church of St. Anne,** a particularly beautiful 12th-century Crusader Church erected in honor of Mary's birthplace. It is built over the **Pool of Bethesda,** the site where Jesus is believed to have healed the cripple. The seminary gardens here are attractive and conducive to meditation. Just three minutes up the street is the **Church of the Sisters of Zion,** in the cellar of which exploration has uncovered part of Pilate's Judgment Hall, where Jesus was condemned to death. The **Ecce Homo** arch stands outside the school.

Through Damascus Gate: Everyone says this is the handsomest and showiest of the gates. Maybe so, but it won't by any means dazzle you. The walls here are just a bit more ornate than those at the other gates. Inside, all is as oriental as can be. Cafes line a wide entrance street; Arabs sit inside and out smoking water pipes and watching you as you watch them. The game they're playing is *shaish-baish,* a sort of backgammon; when the shaish-baish boards are busy, they play dominos. Music emanates from these coffee houses, and occasionally a donkey joins in, protesting at the crowds which block his way. Whether you take **El Wad Road** or **Bab Khan El-zeit,** the way becomes very narrow and all is mobbed, surging confusion. You'll see stalls of spices, silversmiths, craft shops, pastries, blanket shops, mosaic-tile barber chairs, shoe stores, fruit and vegetable stands.

Turn down the **Street of the Spices:** You wouldn't believe there were so many spices and nuts. Decked out in open sacks, you'll see (and smell) curry, cocoa, sesame, pepper and all kinds of beans. For a bazaar street you won't soon forget, turn down **Suq El-Lahhamin** (Butcher Street); it's to the left of the Holy Sepulchre, at the junction with Dabbaga Road. The narrow bazaar manages to get even more narrow, the light grows more scarce, and the slabs of fresh meat hanging out in front give you pause. There are no tourist shops in here, just repair shops and heaven knows what else. The smells become thicker and sweeter, punctuated by an occasional pungent odor. The chief attraction about this particular suq is its anything-can-happen air.

You can't really get lost here. If you just continue on, you're bound to get where you want to go after another five minutes. The area, incidentally, is well patrolled by Israeli policemen, some of whom are actually ex-Jordanian policemen.

Notice that the shops nearer the gates are uncovered to the sky. Notice also the meticulous attention to arrangement in certain shops—thousands of pieces of fruit piled in perfectly symmetrical stacks, kitchen gadgets and household appliances in conspicuously well-arranged patterns of yellow baskets, purple hangers and green sponges.

The Local Populace: It is really impossible to generalize about the people of East Jerusalem. They run the gamut from Christian to traditionalist Moslem to the bearded rabbi to a mob of kibbutz youngsters sharing the tourist sights with you. The two dominating themes of the area, however, are religion and tourism. Both these factors are evidenced everywhere.

You move from the sanctity of a church to the tumult of the bazaar. You're etched in the cool, melancholy shadows of the Western Wall one moment and then you're suddenly accosted by a swirling, noisy band of Arab youngsters. You stare at a shop window and, before 60 seconds pass, you're not only drinking hot coffee with the owner, but perilously close to purchasing brassware that you'd never dreamed of acquiring. It's reverence and fun all mixed together, and neither of these components will ever be forgotten. And, despite the fact that the city is united and part and parcel of Israel proper, the dominating motif of this part of the capital is Arab. The food is Arabic. The language is Arabic. The customs are Eastern. Bartering for goods is a way of life. Unlike the rest of Israel, children will ask for handouts. You'll also be approached by a plethora of would-be guides, offering cut-rate expertise. As a general rule of thumb, if you're going to be guided—and it's not a bad idea— make certain that your mentor is officially licensed by the Ministry of Tourism.

A Note About Islam: You will have discovered, inside the Old City, that Moslems venerate many of the shrines sacred as well to Jews or Christians. To the Moslem, the patriarchs were holy men and Jesus was a prophet, though not the final one. Islam, in fact, is closer to Judaism than to Christianity, closer to the nomadic-type culture of the patriarchs than to the Trinity of Christianity. The Moslem is dedicatedly monotheistic: there is but one God, Allah, and the only way is to submit to his will. A Moslem's principal beliefs center on monotheism, praying five times a day, observing the Ramadan month, making a pilgrimage to Mecca, and giving alms. Friday is the Moslem Sabbath. Like Jews, Moslems are enjoined from eating pork. Gambling and drinking alcohol are also prohibited to the Moslems, and they may not make paintings or sculptures of human beings or animals. The men may marry up to four wives— but only the very rich can afford this. As a result of the many restrictions imposed on them by their religion, the Moslems you see in Jerusalem hold dear their three "vices": smoking (bubble pipes, cigarettes, anything that burns), consuming tremendous amounts of coffee . . . and movie-going.

Downtown East Jerusalem

The modern part of East Jerusalem is not a very large area, and you can probably cover its major sights in half a day. Start at the **Rockefeller Museum,** on Sultan Suleiman Rd. near Herod's Gate. Visiting hours are 10 a.m. to 5 p.m. Sunday, Tuesday, and Thursday; 10 a.m. to 2 p.m. Saturday. Admission is SH1.50 (45¢) for an adult, SH1 (30¢) for a student, SH.50 (15¢) for children aged five to ten. A combined Israel Museum and Rockefeller Museum ticket is SH3 (90¢). Tickets must be bought in advance at the museum for Saturday and holiday admission.

Architecturally, this is a handsome place, with a castle-like rotunda and cloister gardens in the middle. The top of the Moorish castle-turret was badly shot up during the Six-Day War and in fact, the entire museum is pock-marked from shells and machine-gun fire. But the damage to the displays was scant; and, reportedly, there was no damage at all to the Dead Sea Scrolls, which were wrapped up and tucked away in the basement.

The northern and southern galleries contain one of the most extensive archeological collections in this part of the world. Much of the treasure here was excavated in the areas of Acre and the Galilee by American and English archeologists in the 1930s. Pottery, tools, and household effects are arranged by periods—Iron Age, Persian, Hellenistic, Roman, Byzantine. In the south gallery's Paleolithic section are displayed the bones of Mount Carmel Man, "an extinct race combining the characteristics of Neanderthal and Modern Man which lived in Israel about 100,000 years ago."

Head back down along the walls until you are just across from the Old City bus station (between Herod's and Damascus Gates). Here you'll see an entrance leading down under the walls into **Solomon's Quarries,** which tradition calls the source of the stones for Solomon's Temple. To Masons the spot is considered the origin of their group, the builders of Solomon's Temple. Jewish and Moslem legends claim that tunnels in those caves extended to the Sinai Desert and Jericho. The quarries are also called **Zedekiah's Caves,** since in 587 B.C. King Zedekiah was supposed to have fled from the Babylonians through these tunnels, to be captured subsequently near Jericho. You can enter the caves, for a fee of SH.60 (17¢), half price for children or students, from 8:30 a.m. to 4:30 p.m., Friday till 2:30 p.m. On Saturday tickets are sold at the grocery nearby. An illuminated path leads you far back into the caves and under the Old City.

Head up Nablus Road now, opposite Damascus Gate. On your right, through a courtyard, is the **Garden Tomb.** General Gordon, of Khartoum fame, did some archeological work here in the mid-19th century and made a case for the claim that Christ's tomb is located at this serene garden spot. John 19:41, mentioning an unused sepulchre in a garden, gave Gordon the clue to this location. Open Monday through Saturday from 8 a.m. to 1 p.m. and 3 to 5:30 p.m. Except for an English service at 9 a.m., it's closed Sunday.

Just across the street you'll see a small makeshift monument, made of piles of stone, a gun stock, a helmet and a mass of pine twigs. Next to the number "6/6/67" on a rock are the names of several young men of a paratrooper unit who died on this street during the Six-Day War. Just another block up, on the same side of the street, you'll see another such memorial (Israelis call them **Gal-Ed**), on the road heading toward the Mandelbaum Gate. This one is opposite the American Consulate building, which occupies the facing corner.

At the crest of Nablus Road, on the right, are the striking towers of **St. George Cathedral,** Holy Land headquarters of the Anglican Church. The **Mandelbaum Gate**—which, like Paris' Bastille, no longer exists—is (was) on your left. Take a right at the top of the street. The section up here is called alternately Sheikh Jarrah and the American Colony. Just as you head for the top of Saladin Street, you'll confront the **Tomb of the Kings.** Fifteen or 20 feet down a stone stairway, you'll see a hollowed-out courtyard, in which are several small cave openings. Inside one of them, four sarcophagi, covered with carvings of fruit and vines, rest in a crypt-like chamber. It's been over 100 years since scholars discovered that, in fact, no kings are buried here (rather, the family of Queen Helena of Adiabene, who converted to Judaism in Jerusalem around 50 A.D.)—but what's in a name?

Coming down Saladin Street, in the direction of the Old City walls, you'll pass the **Ministry of Justice.** Further down, across the street, is the **Albright Institute of Archeological Research.** Just after it, on the left, you'll find Azzahra Street, a modern thoroughfare of bookshops, restaurants, and hotels, leading to the Rockefeller Museum. If you continue down Saladin Street to the wall, you'll be on the block known as East Jerusalem's "Fifth Avenue" because of its smart shops.

Mount Scopus, Mount of Olives, Valley of Kidron

You reach Mount of Olives Road either by heading north up Saladin Street or by taking a left turn at the wall, just past the Rockefeller Museum. If you want to go by bus, go to the bus station and take the one that goes to the village of E-Tur.

From Sheikh Jarrah (on Shchem Rd.), the road heads up past the Mount Scopus Hotel and proceeds, gradually curving, past Shepherd's Hotel. Now you're on Mt. Scopus Road, and at a bend in the road, to your left, you'll see the **Jerusalem War Cemetery,** resting place for British World War I dead. To the left—past tombstones identifying soldiers of the Royal Welsh Fusiliers, Black Watch, and Devonshire Regiment—are several gravestones of Jewish Legion soldiers who died along with the British in World War I. You are now on Mount Scopus—**Har Hatsofim,** which means "Mt. Observation."

About a hundred yards farther along the ridge is the checkpost through which passed the fortnightly convoy of Jewish police that tended to the Mt. Scopus university complex for 19 years. The Mt. Scopus **Hadassah Hospital** is on your left. Lining both sides of the roads are university buildings, the result of a fast and furious building program that was launched to place these units back in operation as part of the Hebrew University complex. Today you'll see dorms housing 3,000 students, and the construction continues. From the Truman Research Institute (a pink stone building) there's a fine panoramic view: the Seat of the Rabbinate, Mt. Zion, the Mosque of Omar.

A view of a different nature can be had from the outdoor **amphitheater** across the road: here, on April 1, 1925, the Hebrew University was opened in a ceremony attended by such notables as Lord Arthur Balfour, Sir Herbert Samuel (then High Commissioner for Palestine), Chaim Weizmann, Haim Nahman Bialik (the foremost Hebrew poet of the day), and Rabbi Kook, then Chief Rabbi of Palestine. The Mount Scopus university buildings were in Israeli hands during the first ceasefire of the 1948 war, and although the enclave was surrounded by Arab-held territory, it received a "demilitarized" status. Police and civilian caretakers, in two-week shifts, looked after the buildings over the succeeding 19 years—while another hospital and university compound was built in Givat Ram, West Jerusalem.

In July, 1967, Leonard Bernstein conducted the Israeli Philharmonic at the amphitheater, which is the easternmost limit of modern Jerusalem; the view to the east is magnificent—the parched, tawny Judean Hills falling in endless small waves down to the Dead Sea.

During the Six-Day War, the university compound held out against great odds. It was defended by the 120 "policemen" who were there on duty. Over the years they had smuggled up an impressive cache of small arms and light artillery—piece by piece—and when the occasion arose, as many Israelis suspected it one day would, the weapons were put to good use. At the far edge of the university complex, an Arab Legion army barracks stands (mostly in ruins), and you can see the positions of trenches and fortification.

The Best View in Jerusalem: The road skirting the ridge proceeds past the high-towered **Augusta Victoria Hospital,** an Arab Legion bastion during the Six-Day War (its steeple is peppered with bullet holes) and the Arab village of E-Tur, the Mount of Olives, the Jewish Cemetery, and the Intercontinental Hotel. From the Hebrew University on Mt. Scopus, and the Intercontinental Hotel, you have absolutely the most exciting views that Jerusalem has to offer. Come here early in the morning and see all of Jerusalem below in a soft, pinkish hue of limestone white. Return in the late afternoon and you will see why the city is called Jerusalem the Golden.

Mount of Olives: Here you'll find a half-dozen churches—and the oldest Jewish Cemetery in the world. It was this cemetery that religious Jews had in mind when they came to die in the Holy Land, and many legends have emerged to surround it throughout its long, long history (start down the path on the right and you'll come to the **Tomb of the Prophets,** believed to be the burial place of Haggai, Malachi and Zacharia). Many Jews have believed, perhaps still do, that from here the route to heaven is the shortest, since God's presence is always hovering over Jerusalem; others have held that here, on the Mount of Olives, the resurrection of the dead will occur—so you can imagine the anguish many Jews felt when the Intercontinental Hotel was built over the easternmost perimeters of the old cemetery, and when the Jordanians used some of the tombstones in the construction of army barracks.

Further back up the road, on the southern fringe of E-Tur, stands the **Mosque of the Ascension,** marking the spot where Jesus ascended to heaven. Interestingly enough, this Christian shrine is under Moslem control. Moslems revere Jesus as a prophet and believe in the doctrine of the ascension. Jesus, they believe, will raise Mohammed on Resurrection Day. From the roof, there is a magnificent 360-degree view—the city below, Mount Scopus, the Dead Sea and Judean Hills, the Hill of Evil Counsel (housing the U.N. Government House, scene of early fighting in the June, 1967 war).

Just a few steps away is the **Church of the Pater Noster,** built on the traditional spot where Christ instructed his disciples on the Lord's Prayer. Tiles along the walls of the church are inscribed with the Lord's Prayer—in 44 languages. **The Carmelite Convent** and **Basilica of the Sacred Heart** are on the adjoining hill.

From up here you can see a cluster of churches on the lower slopes of the Mount of Olives. All can be reached either from here or from the road paralleling the fortress wall, diagonally opposite St. Stephen's Gate (Lion's Gate).

If you head down the path to the right of the Tomb of the Prophets, you'll come to the only church in this area built along contemporary architectural lines. It is **Dominus Flevit,** a Franciscan Church marking the spot where Jesus wept over Jerusalem. The Russian Orthodox **Church of Mary Magdalene,** topped off strikingly with onion-shaped spires, is next (no precise tariff); it was built in 1888 by Czar Alexander III. The Roman Catholic **Garden of Gethsemane Church** adjoins the **Basilica of Agony (Church of All Nations),** containing a piece of the rock at which Jesus is said to have prayed the night before he entered Jerusalem for the Passover supper. The mosaic facade of the church is impressive: it shows God looking down from heaven over Jesus and the peoples of the world (16 nations worth of "peoples" contributed to the building of this church in 1924). Next door, past beautifully tended gardens of ancient olive trees and bougainvillea, is the **Tomb of the Virgin,** a deep underground chamber housing the tombs of Mary and Joseph.

Valley of Kidron: This is the depression between the foot of the Mount of Olives and the Old City walls. It runs south, between Mt. Ophel (where David built his city) and the Mount of Contempt. Just under the wall here, roughly in front of the El Aksa Mosque, are two tombs: **Absalom's Pillar** and the **Tomb of Zechariah.** At one time religious Jews would throw stones at Absalom's Pillar **(Yad Av-Shalom),** in condemnation of Absalom, who rebelled against his father, King David. A hand (the *yad*) is used to top the conical monument.

The Valley of Kidron is also known as the **Valley of Jehoshaphat.** The Book of Joel, 3:2, 12, records that here the judgments will be rendered on Resurrection Day: "Let the heathen be awakened, and come up to the Valley of Jehoshaphat, for there will I sit to judge all the heathen round about." Moslems hold to a similar belief. They believe Mohammed will sit astride a pillar under the wall of the Mosque of Omar. A wire will be stretched from the pillar to the Mount of Olives, opposite, where Christ will be seated. All mankind will walk across the wire on its way to eternity. The righteous and faithful will reach the other side safely; the rest will drop down in the Valley of Jehoshaphat and perish.

About 200 yards down the valley is the **Fountain of the Virgin,** at the Arab village of **Silwan.** This spring is the **Gihon,** whose waters anointed Solomon king and served as the only water source for ancient Jerusalem. During the Assyrian and Babylonian attacks (eighth century B.C.), King Hezekiah constructed an aqueduct through which the waters could flow into the city. **Hezekiah's Aqueduct** is still there (underneath the church commemorating the spot where Mary once drew water to wash the clothes of Jesus), and its interesting expanse, ending up at the **Pool of Siloam,** can be negotiated—but not too easily. It's about 1600-feet long, and the depth of the water is ten to 16 inches. The walk takes about 40 minutes; best to have a flashlight with you. You can walk through from Sunday to Thursday between 8:30 a.m. and 3 p.m., Fridays and holidays eves till 1 p.m. Entrance is free.

Chapter IV

THE WEST BANK

1. Jericho, the Dead Sea, and Qumran
2. Bethlehem
3. Hebron
4. Ramallah, Shechem, Nablus, and Samaria

JERUSALEM IS THE BEST jumping-off point for visits to the majority of West Bank sites described here. Most of them are within an hour's drive of the capital city. Consequently, you will find few hotels described in this chapter —mainly places to visit, among them the sites which are holiest and most meaningful to Judaism and Christianity. We would recommend that you take a Bible with you on these outings, for in few other places on your trip to Israel will the mountains and cities described in both the Old and New Testaments come alive with such drama. Christ was born in Bethlehem, Abraham entered the land of Canaan in Samaria, the patriarchs are buried at Hebron, and Mount Gerizim at Shechem looks much the same today as when Joshua described it.

THE WEST BANK TODAY: Many changes have taken place since the Israelis first occupied the West Bank, now designated by Israelis as Judea and Samaria (Biblical names). For the first six months after the Six-Day War, all visitors to this area needed military permits, soldiers were everywhere to be seen, hotels were not functioning, and a nighttime curfew was in effect. Now life has become normal again. Tourists can come and go without permits; the only soldiers you'll see are those at checkpoints or those guarding shrines. The Israeli Government is in the midst of a program of improvements. The Ministry of Tourism has encouraged Arab hotel owners to repair damaged hotels—often with the help of loans—and to reopen them to the public. Hotels are operating in Bethlehem and in the crossroads town of Ramallah; more restaurants have opened in the area. There are Ministry of Tourism offices in Bethlehem and Ramallah. Green and white signposts in English guide you to all the major points of interest.

It is still wise, however, to stick to the main roads—the routes are marked clearly—and not wander off by yourself through the hills around Hebron and Nablus. Around Jericho, which is close to the border, be sure to observe carefully the round red sign crossed by a horizontal white bar. That means "No Entry" and broaches no arguments. Don't pass that sign or you may find yourself an unwelcome guest in a military zone or headed on your way to Jordan.

If there are any changes affecting travel in these parts, you can get details from the tourist offices in Israel. If you have questions or concerns while in the area, stop in any local police station, where you will be courteously and efficiently assisted. Another word of caution: Leave politics alone. Despite material improvements, the local population still considers itself occupied. The future is unclear and the less political the verbiage, the better.

VIA SHERUT: You might be interested in knowing what the sherut taxi services cost between various West Bank points. So here goes: Allenby Bridge–Jerusalem, SH5.50 ($1.60); Allenby Bridge–Hebron SH8 ($2.35); Allenby Bridge–Ramallah, SH6.50 ($1.90); Allenby Bridge–Bethlehem, SH6.50 ($1.90); Allenby Bridge–Gaza, SH13 ($3.80); Damiya Bridge–Nablus, SH5.50 ($1.60); Damiya Bridge–Jenin, SH8 ($2.35); Damiya Bridge–Tulkarm, SH7 ($2.05); Damiya Bridge–Qalqilya, SH8 ($2.35); Bethlehem–Jerusalem, SH1.10 (35¢); Ramallah–Jerusalem, SH1.10 (35¢); Nablus–Jerusalem, SH5.50 ($1.60); Jericho–Jerusalem, SH3 (90¢); Hebron–Jerusalem, SH3 (90¢); Nablus–Tulkarm, SH2 (60¢); Nablus–Jenin, SH3.50 ($1.02); Nablus–Qalqilya, SH2.50 (75¢).

SIGHTS TO EXPECT: The character of this part of the country is different from that of all other parts of Israel—make no mistake about it. The landscape is more biblical, the atmosphere more primitive. Everywhere you drive you will see Arab women walking by the roadside balancing great loads on their heads. Donkeys, urged on by old men or little boys, groan under their burden of olive wood twigs, the main fuel in these parts. In sharp contrast, the most common car you'll see driven by Arabs in the West Bank is a Mercedes Benz sedan. The reason: the car is assembled locally. From Bethlehem to Hebron and from Ramallah to Nablus, you'll see men in headdress riding in these Mercedes cruisers. Many more women wear the veil in these parts, a custom the Christian Arab women in Nazareth and the Galilee seem to have discarded. And you will notice at the entrance of towns that there is often an arched, metal gateway. Before the war, a king's crown sat at the pinnacle of these metal arches. Now only the archways remain—crownless.

1. Jericho, the Dead Sea, and Qumran

ON THE ROAD TO JERICHO: A car trip from Jerusalem to Jericho and the Dead Sea is only a 45-minute drive. You'll soon notice the difference in elevation between Jerusalem's 2,700 feet *above* sea level and Jericho's 1,300 feet *below* sea level. Happily, the road is one of the best in this part of the world, wide and beautifully graded.

The Jericho road passes through **Bethany**—the Arabs call the village **El 'Azariya** ("from Lazarus"). It is just three miles outside Jerusalem, and it is here that Jesus performed the miracle of resurrecting Lazarus from the dead. A tomb marks the site, and nearby is a large modern white limestone church, the **Church of St. Lazarus,** run by Franciscans. (The Lazarus story is the stock-in-trade of the village's inhabitants, and if you want to look around you have to put up with the usual commercial exploitations which attend so many religious shrines hereabouts.)

Take a good look at the hills around Bethany—the arrangement of houses on orange and limestone slopes, the pine groves, the sheep grazing on the hillocks. It is as serene, pastoral, and biblical a landscape as you'll see anywhere in the Holy Land. Just outside Bethany are a few houses where some Bedouins

AN HISTORICAL
MAP OF
ISRAEL

TYRE
UPPER
GALILEE
HAZOR
SAFED
ACRE LOWER
GALILEE
HAIFA TZIPPORI
CARMEL
Mt. Tabor
NAZARETH
LAKE
KINNERET
TIBERIAS

MEGIDDO
CAESAREA
BETH SHEAN

SHARON

SAMARIA

TEL AVIV
JAFFA
LOD
RAMLAH
GEZER
ASHDOD BETH SHEMESH
ASHKELON
LACHISH
GAZA
BETHEL
Judea
JERICHO
JERUSALEM
BETHLEHEM QUMRAN
HEBRON
EIN GEDI
MASADA

JORDAN RIVER
JORDAN VALLEY
DEAD SEA

MISH

BEERSHEBA

SODOM

N E G E V

SINAI

EILAT

have settled. Here you may see Arabs riding camels or donkeys or Bedouin women and children walking beside heavily laden donkeys.

A turn in the road here reveals an excellent view of Jerusalem—you'll recognize the Mount of Olives, the Russian Church, Mt. Scopus, the Augusta Victoria Tower. Then, abruptly, as the turn in the road ends, you're in the wilderness of Judea. The sky here is pale blue; the land sandy and chalky, with patches of sunburnt green scrub and scattered trees. Many Bedouin live here, and though you'll seldom see their tents, you often see the Bedouin with their sheep, goats and donkeys. The sight of a black-clad Bedouin woman surrounded by a flock of black goats, in sharp contrast with the stark whiteness of the landscape, is startling and timelessly beautiful. Startling, too, are the strange rock patterns wrought by centuries of erosion. One of the loveliest sights to look for: the eternal shepherd leading his flock.

As the road continues, you'll find yourself surrounded by mountains, but not really the same as the saw-toothed mountains of the Negev. Note the artistry with which road workers have carved passes in the mountains. The walls have been specially contoured to expose the interesting color gradations to best advantage: you see pastel-toned streaks of rose, pink, orange, and soft greens in the rock walls bordering the highway. About halfway along this route a very distinctive pointed mountain appears. As you get closer you'll notice something different about its crest: on it stand the ruins of an old Crusader fortress. Here you'll see signs pointing to side roads on the right and left. To the right, within sight of the main road, is what is known as the **Inn of the Good Samaritan,** supposedly the site where Jesus' parable of the Good Samaritan took place. What is definitely known is that this site has always been an important roadmark. A Roman road once passed here, as did others even before that, including an ancient caravan route. The present inn is of Turkish construction, some 400 years old, with a large entranceway and huge rooms leading off on either side of it. Each room has arched windows and wall niches (supposedly for fires). The entranceway opens into a huge central courtyard. In the middle of the courtyard is a large circular stone cooking area, and a well so deep the bottom of it can't be seen. There are also stone troughs. Much of what is found in the courtyard is said to date from Roman times, when the site was a military stronghold.

Back on the main road, follow the sign pointing left to the **St. George Monastery (Khoziba),** where monks live near a spring named **Wadi Kelt,** whose waters have quenched the thirst of centuries; it once ran through the aqueducts of Herod's time and today continues to irrigate part of Jericho. On the banks of Wadi Kelt are the remains of winter palaces of the Hasmonean and Herodian periods. Much of interest has been uncovered here during archeological digs.

Now the main road curves down more steeply, and you soon come upon a Jordanian encampment that was used during the Six-Day War. Within the encampment are several ancient buildings on a site called **Nebi Musa**—according to Moslem belief, the "Tomb of Moses" (the Bible cites Mt. Nebo as Moses' burial place). A right turn off the road here (there are signs pointing to it) will take you to this abandoned city-like cluster of buildings—abandoned that is, by all but the dead, for all devout Moslems wish to be buried here. The cemetery here is a fascinating holy site.

As the drive takes up again, you'll descend into the Jordan Valley, from which you'll make a left off the main highway to go to Jericho. As you travel toward Jericho, you'll notice hundreds of mud huts, once occupied by refugees. Today they are empty, but when occupied after the war, these Jericho camps formed the largest refugee village in Jordan. These desolate camps are quite a contrast to Jericho, which is a blooming, sweet-smelling oasis, so fertile and lush that it seems a miracle in this dry, sun-baked countryside. Underground streams feed the soil here, and the combination of heat, low altitude and fresh water makes the many tropical plants and fruits grow all year. This year-round paradise is a spot sun-worshippers and vacationers have been coming to for some 4,000 winters.

IN JERICHO: Jericho is one of the world's oldest cities—some claim it's the oldest. Archeologists have discovered habitations, in several different strata, of civilizations that date back 9,000-12,000 years. This is the Jericho Joshua conquered, and parts of the walls that came tumbling down are still here. Jericho was the first city captured by the Israelites after their 40 years in the wilderness. The tribes approached it from the other side of the Jordan River, sent in spies and, to the blasts of trumpets blown by priests, the city was attacked and captured. To the east of Jericho is the place where the Israelites crossed the Jordan into the Promised Land.

Lunch in Jericho

Jericho has several cafes, with sign names in Arabic and Hebrew, where you can get refreshments or full meals at lunchtime. The cost is low, and the meals are strictly local. We found that the most enjoyable way to lunch hereabouts is to take a walk around the **Municipality** (it looks like Jericho's version of Courthouse Square, U.S.A.), stopping in at the shops lining its sides. There are loads of fresh vegetables and fruits for sale here, as are inedible but fun-to-look-at items such as cooking utensils, shoes, sacks of dried tobacco, and soaps. At an indoor/outdoor bakery you can get two enormous round rolls—like big bagels with sesame seeds—which you can take to a nearby merchant, who will sell you a Coke and let you sit on his low stools while you munch and sip. The entire transaction will cost you about a dollar.

If you have worked up a somewhat larger hunger and yearn for a full meal, walk up Ein El Sultan St. till you see the **Al Gandoul** and **Al Khayyam** restaurants, which face each other on that street. At either of these garden restaurants you can have a substantial, reasonably priced meal. The most pleasant is Al Gandoul, tel. 02-922349, where half a roast chicken goes for SH6 ($1.75), steak is SH10 ($2.95), and humus with meat SH7 ($2.05). Open daily from 7:30 a.m. to 9–10 p.m. At Al Khayyam, tel. 02-922477, you might opt for mazza at SH15 ($4.40), grilled chicken, fried liver, or kababs at SH10 ($2.95). Open daily 7:30 a.m. to 10–11 p.m. Yet a third choice is the **Green Valley Park Restaurant and Bar,** tel. 02-922349, where main courses like mousakhan and humus with meat are SH8 ($2.35). Open 7 a.m. to midnight daily. Tourist groups often stop at the **Moghrabi Cafeteria,** on the same street, for pitta sandwiches and fresh-squeezed juices; open 7 a.m. to 8–9 p.m. Another clean little Ein El Sultan St. cafeteria is the **Maxim,** tel. 02-922410, open 7 a.m. to 11 p.m.

In the Jericho area, please note, it's best to drink water only where *signs say* the water is for drinking. Also, avoid meats in summer months, unless you're sure the cafe or restaurant has refrigeration.

The Sights

Continue along the main road past the two above-mentioned restaurants and look for signs to the **Old Walls** at **Tel es Sultan** (there is no entrance fee). The walls really aren't much as walls go—just mounds of rock and some trenches—and perhaps you won't find them too exciting unless you're a Bible buff or an archaeologist. But remember what they once meant. On a hill in this area, you can look down at the archeological excavations of a stone tower from the Neolithic period, ancient walls and gates, with their arches standing out clearly. Here's where you may realize it's hard work being a tourist—the ground is sandy and rocky, and the walking is steep. You'll be only too glad, we think, after the jaunt back to the road, to see the **Old Jericho Rest House** directly opposite. A clean, colorful, shady place, the House offers chairs and tables and cool drinks to refresh weary tourists. While you drink and rest, you can take in the tastefully painted walls and chat with the hospitable, knowledgeable owner. Nearby is **Elisha's Fountain,** where the Prophet Elisha found polluted waters and threw salts in them to make them pure. Arab legend has it that barren women who drink these waters will become fruitful and multiply. The dozens of Arab women seen at the well are not all faced with the same problem: most are simply filling tins and pitchers with the well's cool, sweet water for ordinary household use. (These waters are eminently drinkable.)

A road to the west leads to the fortress-like monastery you see on the hill, the **Greek Monastery of the Forty Days,** dedicated to Christ's temptations with Satan following his 40-day fast. You can't drive all the way, but the climb is worth the effort, because the view from the top is magnificent—the mountains of Moab, the Jordan Valley, Mt. Hermon far in the distance.

A small road heading northeasterly from Elisha's Fountain leads to two interesting historical sites. First, a mile on, is a sultan's palace—the **Caliph Hisham's Palace.** Archeologists place this in the Omayyad Dynasty of the seventh and eighth centuries, and inscriptions show it was built in 724 A.D. as a winter resort. Unfortunately, it was destroyed soon after by an earthquake, but today is worth seeing for the many well-preserved bathhouse structures, heating systems, pools and sauna-like chambers. The pillars and stone carvings are elegant, and one magnificent mosaic depicts two gazelles feeding under a pomegranate tree, while a lion feeds on a third gazelle. Admission to the site, which is now under the jurisdiction of the National Parks Authority, is SH3 (85¢) for adults, SH1 (30¢) for children and students. Outside the Palace, you can buy cool drinks; inside, near the museum area, fresh, but not particularly cool, water is available in large pottery urns.

TO THE DEAD SEA AND QUMRAN: Now head back through Jericho to the main road and continue the southeasterly descent, following the signs to the Qumran Caves. En route is a row of dark trees along the Jordan River. The building in front of them is the Abyssinian-style **Monastery of John the Baptist,** built on the spot where John the Baptist is said to have baptized Jesus.

You're now in the Jordan Valley, and here the land is flat, with sprinklings of shrubbery and interesting erosion formations. To the left, you'll pass a slumbering racetrack, where before the war both camels and horses raced, and wealthy sheikhs came to bet their fortunes on their favorite steeds. As you drive toward the Dead Sea you'll come across a building complex called the **Lido,** where tourists can stop for a snack, a meal and a "float" on the Dead Sea. The Lido has been privately operated since the war, and though some say the owner has no authorization to do so, nobody feels like quarreling with him, so he continues to collect a $1 entrance fee from folks who flock here.

If you swim here, or elsewhere in the Dead Sea, please be kind to yourself —wear shoes to protect your feet from the sharp stones that cover the beach and shore; do not let the water get in your eyes because the salt will really smart. If you have any scrapes, insect bites or recently shaved areas, expect them to tingle in the salty water, but remember that it's healing rather than harmful. When you get out, hot showers are available to wash off the thin residue of minerals and oils from your body. Local folk, by the way, don't bathe till bedtime in order to get all possible benefits from the water's richness. Also, make certain to rinse your bathing suit in fresh water.

Since temperatures are high here, you'll probably welcome a cold drink at the Lido. Drinks are sold in the large building, as are lots of souvenirs; you can take your drink out to the courtyard and sip in the shade at small tables.

After leaving the Lido and turning onto the road running along the Dead Sea in the direction of the Qumran area, you'll see buildings scattered between the road and sea; these were once Jordanian military encampments and now are used as homes by people who settled here soon after the 1967 war. This, and other settlements in new areas, are the work of **Nahal** ("Pioneering Fighting Youth"), who concentrate on agricultural projects. In the fields they've created along the side of the road are melons, eggplants, tomatoes, and similar crops that thrive in this region.

As you drive by you'll of course notice how extremely still the Dead Sea is. It's like this most of the year, but when there's a storm, especially one with a south wind, the sea becomes wild and very dangerous. The mountains along this stretch are sand-colored with black-hued, fierce-looking peaks. When the mountains turn to a reddish hue, you're near the **Qumran Caves** area. A side road leads up to the **Qumran Village,** where the Dead Sea Scrolls were found in a cave in 1947 by a Bedouin shepherd boy.

Qumran

Archeological finds have indicated that this area was first settled in the eighth century B.C. and that those who wrote the scrolls lived here around the end of the second century B.C. It appears the place was deserted during Herod's reign (37 to 4 B.C.), but resettled soon afterward by members of the same sect, usually called the Essenes. The Romans conquered the area during the 66 to 70 A.D. wars, and it's been largely deserted since then. Today, though, many people visit the area for various reasons. Kibbutzniks love to bring their children here to show them "the world's oldest kibbutz" (so-called because here the Essenes evidently lived a collective community life). It's said that the historian Josephus Flauvius lived in the area for three years. It's also been speculated that the idea of monastic celibacy originated here with a certain group of Essenes who believed in devoting their entire lives to divine study and work.

The excavated Qumran Village is a rather small-scale outdoor museum of trenches, pottery sheds, step-down baths, cisterns, bakery sites, and cemetery plots. You can see all the excavations from the top of the village tower. Near the village ruins are the caves where the first scrolls were found. High above, in the mountains, are more caves, as yet mostly unexplored. If you care to check them out yourself (and it's almost impossible to get lost around here), you're welcome to do it. Just let one of the three permanent watchmen know where you'll be. You'll find the going extra-hard in sandals, so wear rubber-soled shoes. Be sure to keep a hat on your head at all times, and wear sunglasses. If you're a real explorer, you might want to do the hands-and-knees-walk along an ancient aqueduct. Cut through one of the mountains, the aqueduct is a small passage, about 50 meters long, 60 centimeters high, but it's safe. Since you'll never find it by yourself, you might talk about it to Abed-Al-Rhman, one of the three watchmen. If he feels like it, he'll guide you (no charge unless you just want to give him something), and you could hardly find a better guide—

he's been working around these caves and mountains since the first excavations in 1947.

Near the parking lot are a couple of large sun-shelter constructions with thatched roofs. One has long picnic tables and benches and is often used for tour lectures as well as for eating. This is a good spot from which to search the mountainsides for caves while you're resting or snacking. If you look across the gorge and to the right, you'll see a white-painted rock; above it is a cave where more scrolls were found. Admission is SH4 ($1.20) for adults SH1.40 (40¢) for children and students. Restrooms near the entrance.

Ein Feshcha

Three miles further on, parallel to the Dead Sea (heading south), lies Ein Feshcha. **Feshcha Springs** is now spruced up, and if you go on a Saturday you'll have to fight half of Israel and three quarters of Jerusalem for elbow room. But on a weekday the place receives much less traffic. There are three pools for children only. By noon, the pools can be murky, and you may find an occasional fish or two joining you. So if the pools find little favor in your eyes, walk on to the sandy, clean beach nearby, where you can dip in the Dead Sea. Admission fee to the area includes the cost of a shower after your swim and a storage bag for your clothes. On the beach you'll also find shady shelters and a bungalow clinic. It may surprise you to learn that enough people get ill around here to justify this clinic, which is staffed by two nurses. The problems almost always come from overexposure to the sun. So be smart and protect yourself—drink as much as you can, keep your head covered, and don't stay in the sun too long! Also, try to avoid all pools, and the area in general, between 12 and 3 p.m. The heat is murderous during those hours all year long, although it's far worse in summer.

Recently, the Nature Reserves Authority has outfitted the springs with dressing rooms, restrooms, and a buffet eatery that also sells postcards and souvenirs. Ein Feshcha is open 8 a.m. to 3 p.m. in the winter, to 4 p.m. in the summer. Entrance to the whole area costs SH2.50 (75¢) for adults, SH1.20 (35¢) for children.

From here, it's only 51 kilometers to Masada, with Ein Gedi en route, along the sea-skirting road. From there, you could travel on to Sodom and the fast highway to Eilat, or to Arad and Beersheba and then on to the central, but slower, highway to Eilat. See the Negev chapter for details.

2. Bethlehem

ON THE ROAD TO BETHLEHEM: To reach Bethlehem, which is only seven miles south of Jerusalem, you can take the Arab bus 22, or Egged buses 34 or 44; or take a 20-minute drive in a sherut (both leaving from Damascus Gate); or drive out in your rented car. Then, too, you can walk it, as pilgrims do yearly on Christmas. If you have the time, the latter course is very interesting. It should take between two and 2½ hours. Head out past the Jerusalem railway station at Abu Tor, and simply keep going straight on the main road near the Talpiot section, past the remaining few buildings of the Allenby Barracks on your left, past Jerusalem's new industrial area on your right. When you pass some handsome new projects, you will have crossed the former border point. From there on the landscape changes, becoming ancient and Arabic. Small boys ride past you on donkeys, and farmers work in the fields on either side of the road. Eventually the road passes the Greek Monastery of Elias, then past an old two-story building on the right that once was a hospital. From here, take a look left to the tallest mountain, the one with a flat top—that's Herodion. The road takes a sharp turn here; olive trees line the right now, and the low hills beyond the trees host the Arab village of Bet Jallah (biblical Gelo), birthplace of the prophet Nathan. Now you're at the northern edge of Bethlehem (the biblical name of this road is Bethlehem Efrata).

An alternate road, for drivers, totaling 11 miles from Jerusalem to Bethlehem, is even more fascinating than the walk. This road starts from the Mount of Olives, cuts through Surbacher, and winds its way in hilly curves down into the Hebron Valley. As the road descends, notice the caves on the hillside around you. They are inhabited—and have been for centuries. Some cave entrances are covered by flapping blankets, some by arrangements of bramble bushes, others by a door. Apart from farmers, Christian hermits and monks have lived in these caves down through the centuries. The road leads up to the U.N. headquarters, atop the Hill of the Evil Counsel, then joins another road at Mar Elias and continues on to Rachel's Tomb.

Rachel's Tomb

This unprepossessing little shrine, just past a bus stop, is a low rectangular building with clean Turkish lines and dome, built in 1860 by Moses Montefiore. Rachel, wife of Jacob and mother of Joseph, is revered by Moslems, Jews and Christians. (Men need a head covering to enter the shrine, by the way.) The outer room is empty; the inner room, the cupola, contains the tomb of Rachel, where dozens of women are usually seen praying and weeping.

Across the street from the Tomb are several shops for souvenirs, crafts, arts, rugs and religious items. Just past the Tomb, you'll see an open courtyard circled by a low wall with a few olive trees and a few small houses rising behind another wall. Take a long look at the latter, almost unnoticeable in this ramshackle area. The stones there are part of a water pipe made 3,000 years ago by King Solomon. Inside, the wall is hollow, and once conducted water from King Solomon's Pools (not far from here) to Jerusalem.

Back on the road, take the left-hand fork just ahead and continue past olive groves and vineyards—another 1½ miles and you are in Bethlehem.

IN BETHLEHEM: Bethlehem is the birthplace of Christ. Pilgrims have been coming here to see the traditional cave and manger of Jesus' birth for 16 centuries. In the Old Testament, Bethlehem is mentioned several times, first in connection with Rachel, who died there after giving birth to Benjamin, her second and Jacob's twelfth son. Bethlehem was also the place where Ruth, the Moabite girl, married Boaz in one of history's most famous love stories. Joseph visited Bethlehem. David, a descendent of Ruth and Boaz, was born in Bethlehem and tended his sheep in the hills of Judea. From Bethlehem he went out to fight Goliath; later he was summoned from Bethlehem by Samuel to become King of Judah.

To Israelis, Bethlehem is **Beit Lechem,** house of bread; to Arabs **Beit Lahm,** house of meat.

Church of the Nativity

This is the principal shrine of Bethlehem, a fortress-like structure facing the paved expanse of Manger Square. On Manger Square, by the way, you'll find official guides, working in rotation, who will offer their services for a fee of about a dollar. Hire one if you wish to see the shrine in every detail.

You enter the famed church—the oldest in the country—through a doorway so low that you have to bend over to go through it. Legend has it that the doorway was made that small to prevent the unbelievers from riding into the church on horseback. It does make you pause for a moment to bow and show reverence . . . perhaps another motive.

The basilica of the church is divided into five naves by four rows of pinkish Corinthian pillars. As the Church stands on its disciples, so the building is supported by its pillars, and every pillar bears the picture of an apostle. Several dozen gilded lamp fixtures hang from the rafter-like oaken ceiling. The floor is stone and wood, with occasional trap-door openings that reveal the original mosaic floor beneath. Up front, beyond a magnificent silver and gold chandelier, is the Altar of the Nativity, equally ornate with gold and silver decoration. The Greek Orthodox occupy the area to the right of the altar, the Armenian denomination the area to the left. Armenian, Greek and Franciscan priests are responsible for the care and preservation of the church.

On either side of the altar, narrow stone staircases lead underneath to the manger, scene of Christ's birth. Simply lit by hanging lights, the grotto is in the wall of the cave, marked by a silver star.

Back upstairs, leave the church via the courtyards of cloisters and convents. Notice the difference in dress of the various priests who administer the church—the Greeks in long black robes, bearded, and with their long hair tied into a bun; the Armenians in purple- and cream-colored long robes, and the Franciscans in simple brown.

The construction of the church goes back to the time of the mother of Constantine the Great, Queen Helena, who made a pilgrimage to the Holy Land in the early part of the fourth century. She searched out the grotto of Christ's birth, and then Constantine built a church over the spot. The Emperor Justinian, 200 years later, found the original church destroyed (probably by an earthquake), and built a new church on the old site. The present church is a restoration of both early churches—carried out by the Crusaders, which explains its fortress-like appearance.

Other Bethlehem Sights

The conscientious visitor will want to visit the **Milk Grotto,** run by the Franciscans. This is the place where Mary, in nursing the infant Jesus, dropped some milk which, according to certain traditions, promptly turned the rocks of the cavern chalky white. Visits made here by nursing mothers are supposed to help their lactation. Round cakes made from the powdered stone are sold as souvenirs.

Bethlehem is that kind of a wildly commercial place. Seemingly everyone has something to sell you—from religious crafts to pencils and ballpoint pens made in The People's Republic of China. The bazaar streets are busy, noisy and colorful, similar to the atmosphere of Jerusalem's walled Old City.

Bethlehem at Christmas

There are special telephone booths for tourists to phone Christmas greetings home with the bells of Bethlehem pealing in the background. . . . Restaurants and coffee houses stay open all night during Christmas season, and some banks operated until midnight. . . . Rates in Bethlehem, Nazareth, and even some Jerusalem hotels, go up during the holiday period. Be sure of your accommodations before you arrive. . . . Weather gets very cold, especially at night—it might even snow. . . . *Most important:* admission to Bethlehem on

Christmas Eve is restricted to tourists holding special tickets; these can be obtained free from the I.G.T.O. offices in Jerusalem, Tel Aviv, and Haifa, or, on December 24th, from the Ben-Gurion Airport.

Hotels and Restaurants

Set in a garden to one side of Manger Square is the 25-room **Palace Hotel,** tel. 02-742798, which provides excellent modern accommodations for the price. So close to the church that you can reach it in two minutes, and surrounded by the sounds of tolling bells, the Palace was built by the Greek Orthodox Committee. It has a large dining room, a colorful sitting room with a view of the city from its bar, and many attractive rooms, all with private bathrooms and many with balconies looking out toward the Judean Hills. The doubles are equipped with wide twin beds; there are only two single rooms. All are accented with bright Persian throw rugs and have central heating. Yet the price is a low SH51 ($15) single, SH40.80 ($12) per person double, for bed and breakfast; add SH20.40 ($6) for half-board and SH40.80 ($12) for full board, per person.

The **Al Andalus Hotel,** Manger Square, in the New Tourists Shopping Center Building, tel. 02-743519, has ten rooms with private shower, toilet, and phone. There's central heating, but no air conditioning. B&B rates are SH51 ($15) double; students receive a 10% reduction.

Half-board rates are slightly higher, but you can get truly first-class accommodations at the **Handal Hotel** on Dehaisheh Street, just off Paul VI Street, which runs directly into Manger Square, tel. 02-742494. Here there are 40 double rooms, all with private baths or showers, wall heaters, electric coolers, telephones and balconies. The rooms are spacious and well maintained, with speckled floors and brilliantly striped bedspreads. There's a fully-staffed dining room, gift shop and all first-class hotel services. The location, by the way, is the very best in Bethlehem, with stunning villas all around. From March 1 to October 31 bed with breakfast costs SH35.70 ($10.50) per person double half-board SH17 ($5), and full board SH34 ($10) per person. Add 10% service and a surcharge of 25% during Christmas and Easter weeks. Rates are a bit lower off season. Continental breakfast is included. Both the Palace and Handal are managed by gentle, helpful people who are more than glad to go out of their way to make you feel comfortable.

There are several restaurants close to Manger Square that are clean and cheap. The closest is right on the square, in the **New Tourists Shopping Center,** opened in 1971. The Center's a neat two-story building packed with shops, a bank and the **Granada Grill Bar,** which is where we're heading. The Granada is a small, modern, place, where music is always playing. There's counter service downstairs—and speaking of the counter, take a look at the wooden sign above it: "Patience, Passion, Penitence, Prudence, Penalty." Upstairs you'll find tables and chairs, and a service charge. Hot meals, snacks and drinks are served on both levels. Phone number is 02-742810, and sample fare and prices run the following gamut: Nearly all the appetizers, including humus, tchina, eggplant or oriental salad cost SH2 (60¢); mixed grill, lamb chops or shashlik run about SH10 ($2.95), hamburger with potatoes and salad goes for SH6.50 ($1.90); for the exotic-minded, grilled pigeon is tagged at SH10 ($2.95); and a plate of kubbeh (lamb or beef meat balls served with a condiment of cedar-tree seeds) costs SH8.50 ($2.50). Beer runs SH2 (60¢) to SH3 (90¢), and most cocktails can be obtained for twice that price.

In the same building, the **Al Andalus Restaurant,** tel. 02-743519, caters to tourist groups with an SH13.60 ($4) set meal consisting of soup or grapefruit (depending on the season), salad, and a main course of roast beef, chicken,

kabab, or veal cutlet with vegetable and potatoes, and fruit. You can also order
à la carte here—e.g. kufta (ground beef in spices) baked in tomato or tchina
sauce with potatoes or rice for SH8 ($2.35). Open daily 8 a.m. to midnight.

For sandwiches and light fare, the very clean and pleasant little **Tel Star
Cafeteria,** a few paces up from the Mosque on Manger Square, tel. 02-742744,
is highly recommended. It's open daily from 7 a.m. to 9 p.m.

If you want something more substantial try the **St. George Restaurant** in
the Municipality Building, next door to the Government Tourist Office, tel.
02-743780. Out front are umbrella tables for al fresco dining; within, the
cream-colored walls are adorned with murals of Bethlehem, and tables are
covered with red cloths and graced with flowers; background music further
enhances the ambience. Try the roast pigeon stuffed with rice, meat, and
almonds for SH12 ($3.55), or a platter of six different kinds of vegetables for
SH6 ($1.75). Open daily from 11:30 a.m. to about 11 p.m. or midnight.

Another good restaurant, on Paul VI St., is the two-level **Horse Shoe,** tel.
02-742287. All the cooking is supervised by the owners, and the modern, stylish
eatery is located within a five-minute walk of Manger Square. The meals are
inexpensive and really good. An order of chicken with salad and potatoes will
set you back SH8 ($2.35). Save room for homemade ice cream at SH2.50 (75¢)
to SH4 ($1.20). Open daily 10 a.m. to 10 p.m.

On Milk Grotto St., to the right of Manger Square as you face the church,
is the **Vienna Restaurant and Bar,** tel. 02-742783. Walk through the front room
and courtyard into the back room, where an entire wall of windows overlooks
the hills and valleys of Bethlehem. That wonderfully aromatic Arabic coffee
with haile costs only SH7 (30¢). If you are ready for a meal, you might start
with *fooul,* a great favorite. It is that versatile bean, cooked, mashed and
served hot with spices and olive oil. What comes on top is a personal choice,
sometimes raw onions or hot peppers. It is a very filling beginning for SH2
(60¢). Among the SH10 ($2.95) main course options are shashlik, meat with
humus, and kabab. Beer and liquor are available, as well as soft drinks. Open
daily from 7 a.m. to midnight.

3. Hebron

ON THE WAY: The distance is only 20 miles, the road wide and in good
repair, and you should figure on a 30-minute drive over the twisting southward
route. Beautiful villas line part of the road on the outskirts of Bethlehem; the
road then dips close to the picturesque village of **Bet Jalla,** to the right in the
nearby hills. Further along come rich fields, more villas and new homes. Soon
you pass a big archway (on the right) spanning a road leading to the nearby
villages of **Husan** and **Nahhalim.** The archway honors St. George, depicted on
horseback in the arch's center. This is the road David took from Bethlehem
to carry his brother's food to the battle area in the Valley of Elah, where he
subsequently met up with Goliath.

Beyond here, turn left to **Solomon's Pools.** If you haven't eaten, this is a
good place for lunch—either a picnic or a sit-down meal at **King Solomon's
Gardens,** a small cafe opposite the first of the three large rectangular pools. Tall
pine trees and flowery shrubs make this a shady, restful spot.

There's been some quibbling about the exact origin of the pools. Some hold
that they're really the work of Herod, who brought the water here by aqueduct
from springs near Hebron. Others argue vociferously that these pools were
indeed built by Solomon as part of his grand scheme for supplying Jerusalem

with water. Some say part of the water is from three nearby wells that belonged to Solomon's good—and wealthy—friend, Itam. And many claim the pools' origin can be found in the Book of Ecclesiastes: "I made me pools of water, to water therewith the wood that bringeth forth trees." An adjoining spring, **Ein Salah,** is considered the one referred to by Solomon in the Song of Songs: "A garden enclosed my sister, my spouse, a spring shut up, a fountain sealed."

Meanwhile, back on the road: houses become fewer, and terraced slopes reach almost to the highway. The vines and trees are heavy with grapes, apples, peaches, figs, and plums. This is a fertile area—the best land in this whole rich region.

Where the road takes a sharp left, look on the facing mountainside for three ancient wells. Two of them are marked by window-like holes in the rock walls; the third is marked by a tall structure with built-in arches. These are **Itam's Wells,** which fed Solomon's Pools and which are still in use today. As the highway levels out now, you pass more fields—often divided by low rock walls—and occasional side roads leading to nearby villages. Halfway between Bethlehem and Hebron a green road sign points to a right fork leading to **Kfar Ezyon** or **Etzion.** At Etzion, a settlement has been reactivated (after being completely destroyed in the 1948 war), and you'll find the new **Etzion Youth Hostel** with its adjoining popular-priced restaurant.

The Etzion region is a graphic example of recent Middle East history. It was originally settled by fervent religious Zionist farmers. Not only were the complex and its inhabitants wiped out in the convolutions resulting from the declaration of a Jewish State, but every trace of the settlements was eliminated. By 1949, it was as if there had never been a Jewish presence in Hebron.

After the Six-Day War, tremendous local pressures were exerted on the Israeli government for the settlement of the captured West Bank. At least one out of every two Israelis (including not only the right-wing Likud, but the powerful religious parties represented in the government) believes that the area is historically a part of the rest of the country and that there has been a significant Jewish imprint in the region for well over 3,000 years. Because of international pressures, the Israeli government was cautious about approving the establishment of new Jewish settlements. The West Bank was not like the Golan Heights (virtually deserted after the war) nor the coastal strip of Sinai (with only a small, indigenous Bedouin population). The West Bank was highly populated, well settled, and highly developed. In the case of Hebron, however, the pressures were irresistible. A new Etzion Bloc was established and the volunteers were the very sons and daughters of the original settlers.

Again, back to the road.

Nearing the large village of **Halhool,** construction and donkey traffic increase noticeably. Farmers operate roadside stands and rich fields often are stripped with plastic to protect them from birds and insects. Entering the village, note the ancient well and stone cave-like structure looming on the left. A road here leads off to the **Tombs of Nathan and Gad.** In the center of "town"—a few buildings lining the main road—there's the bustle of local people shopping for daily needs, or smoking and sipping coffee in the cafe. Though there's nothing to warrant stopping here, it's a colorful area, with many people and lovely houses further on dotting the roadsides and surrounding hills.

Once past town, a left turn will take you to **Ramat Al Khaled,** where you'll find **Abraham's Oak,** supposedly on the site where Abraham pitched his tent and met the three angels who announced that Sarah would bear Isaac. Here's where he built an altar, and where David was anointed king. The oak, although very old, is hardly 3,000 years old—perhaps 500-600 years. Another biblical legend surrounds the dust of the Hebron fields, out of which God, some speculate, created Adam. Adam and Eve are also considered by some to be buried in the **Cave of Machpelah.** A little further north is the **Valley of Eshkol,** from whence Moses' spies returned carrying clusters of grapes, symbol of the fertility of the Promised Land. (This picture—two men in robes carrying bunches of grapes on a long stick—has been adopted as the official tourist emblem of Israel.) Another left, further along the highway, leads to **Kiryat Arba,** a new Israeli town near Hebron. Ahead the highway splits: Beersheba is to the right, and Hebron, our destination, is immediately beyond the left fork.

IN HEBRON: Artifacts provide a useful message about the past, but human beings are a preview of the future. So even if Hebron had nothing more to offer than its contemporary history, we would find the city fascinating. Israel calls the region the West Bank, Jordan sees the city as an integral part of the Hashemite Kingdom, the Hebronites regard themselves as Palestinians.

Certainly, the people of Hebron have had their ups and downs with the Jews, and vice versa. In 1929 and 1948, there was bloodshed sufficient to decimate the local Jewish population, for which the Hebronites expected comparable retribution when Israeli forces moved into the area in 1967. There was none—no excesses, no punishment, no ironclad Israeli posture. Instead, Israel adopted a low-profile approach and it worked. Visiting Hebron today, you will find it difficult to believe that this is a conquered area. Total local autonomy exists. Israeli soldiers are hardly in evidence. Jews and Arabs cooperate—not because they love each other, but because it is to their mutual advantage. So keep all this in mind when visiting the area. An exciting evolution is taking place and the Hebronites are right in the middle of it. You'll be dealing with a proud and cultured people, so don't patronize them. In a maelstrom of politics and war, they are trying to find their own identity.

Taking the main road through Hebron, you'll first pass lovely villas and a few shops and grocery stores. At one point, islands of trees, flowers and greenery divide the highway lanes, after which the archeological **Museum of Hebron** will be on your left (nearby are several places for cool drinks). On the right is the **Israel Government House;** when you see a glass factory, a pottery factory, and a woodwork factory side by side in a huge three-story building on your left, you'll be in the shopping district (photo shops, tailors, tiny clothing stores, shoe stores, grocery stores, etc.). In this area you'll see a roadside pillar pointing to **Abraham's Tomb;** when the road forks, bear left toward the Tombs. Shortly there's another sign, a red one, pointing out the **Jewish Cemetery.** Dating back 3,700 years, this cemetery was almost entirely destroyed during the 1929 slaughter, but people still come here to pray and stand in awe. Hereabouts the road narrows until it is just barely two lanes and leads by shops of shoemakers, carpenters, leather workers and saddle makers (who outfit camels and donkeys). Some of the most interesting shops in this area, exhibiting great imagination and enterprise, are those that collect old rubber tires and convert them into shoes, carryalls, water bags and so forth—very popular among the Arabs. Coming into the vegetable area, the road widens and the **Moslem Cemetery** is to the right.

And now there's an open expanse and a sign guiding you left to Abraham's Tomb.

Tomb of the Patriarchs

Enclosing the **Cave of Machpelah,** the Tomb is what gives Hebron its designation as one of Israel's four "Holy Cities"—the others being Jerusalem, Tiberias and Safed.

To religious Jews who now can worship at the sacred Tomb of the Patriarchs, the holy experience is second only to worshipping at the Western (Wailing) Wall in Jerusalem. Genesis tells how Abraham bought his family burial cave from Ephron for 400 silver shekels. Tradition has it that Hebron is thus one of the three places in Israel that Jews can claim by virtue of having purchased the property, the same claim is made for the Jerusalem Temple and the Tomb of Joseph.

The tombs of Abraham, Isaac, and Jacob (and their wives) are housed in a fortress built by Herod. The walls range from 40 to 60 feet high. You may visit the Tombs between 7:30 and 11:30 a.m. and 1:30 to 3 p.m. (till 4 or 5 p.m. in summer). From 11:30 a.m. to 1:30 p.m. devout Moslems worship inside, and no visitors are allowed. No visitors are permitted on Fridays, the Moslem Sabbath, or on Moslem holidays.

Inside the walls, the Moslems built a mosque around the tombs. The square main basilica is richly decorated with inlaid wood and ornate mosaic work reminiscent of the Mosque of Omar. Inscriptions from the Koran run along the walls and, in one corner, a tape recorder plays Moslem prayers. In the main section you will see the tombs of Isaac and Rebecca, red and white stone "huts" with green roofs. Looking inside, you'll see the richly embroidered drapes covering the cenotaphs. ("Cenotaph," according to Webster, means "an empty tomb in honor of a person buried elsewhere." The real tombs are supposed to be underground, beneath the cenotaphs.) In an adjoining courtyard are the gold-embroidered tapestries covering the cenotaphs of Abraham and Sarah—behind a silver grating. Just opposite is the tomb of Jacob and Leah, with a 700-year-old stained-glass window. A shrine to Joseph is right next door, but the authentic tomb of Joseph is generally thought to be at Nablus.

Restaurants

If you've worked up a full-blown hunger in Hebron, head to the market area, where you'll find the **Mitnahalim Kosher Snackbar,** owned and run by settlers from Kiryat Arba, the new Jewish settlement outside Hebron.

4. Ramallah, Shechem, Nablus, and Samaria

ON THE ROAD: This route takes you into biblical Samaria, the land of Canaan that Abraham first saw over 4,000 years ago, the scene of great events involving Jacob, Joseph, Joshua and the rulers of the northern kingdom.

Note: There have been incidents of violence in Shechem and Nablus, and we cannot guarantee the safety of those areas. Much depends on current events at the time of your visit. It's not a bad idea to check with the I.G.T.O.

From Jerusalem, you climb above Mount Scopus, following the signs to Ramallah. The road passes **Shu'afat,** biblical Gibeah, Saul's capital when he became the first king of Israel. This is a prosperous region. About seven miles out of Jerusalem you'll find yourself in the "better" suburban quarter of what was Jordanian Jerusalem: new development areas of high-rise apartments give way to posh private villas. The mountains reveal themselves off to the left, as does a particularly distinguishable building with a high tower. This is the **Tomb of the Prophet Samuel,** and it rises above the scattered buildings of more new suburban projects. (A left turn a bit further on leads you through the valley to the Tomb site.)

One of the most prominent buildings you'll pass on the main road, on the right, is the **Semaris Hotel.** Used now as a lecture hall, it once was considered the best hotel by tourists in Jordan. After passing it, note the Ramallah Arak factory to the left—it's small, but produces a well-known quality brew, arak (which, by the way, is the licorice-scented favorite Arab liquor; an absinthe derivative, it's powerful but slow-acting stuff—so if you're not used to it, drink carefully). Ramallah is around the next bend of the road. And the closer you get, the more television aerials you see on the horizon.

RAMALLAH — Arabic for "the Heights of the Lord"—is a cool, high town, once the most popular summer resort in Jordan ("Switzerland of Jordan"). You will see elegant villas on hillsides green with pine groves. At 2,900 feet, Ramallah sits some 300 feet higher than Jerusalem. A Christian and Moslem town, Ramallah is quite well off, with many good restaurants, hotels and shops. Interestingly, about 25% of the population are U.S. citizens, and another 15,000 are native Americans who are or hope to become Israeli citizens. On Saturdays, many Israelis flock here to take advantage of the bargain shopping, especially the furniture buys. It's a truly Arab place, Ramallah, chock full of the "local color" many people go halfway around the world to see. The average man on the street is an Arab dressed in traditional gear. You'll see the men sitting around the coffee houses, the merchants trading with veiled women in a bustling commercial area.

Should you stop for a while in Ramallah, make sure to see the town's large, beautiful park, which contains a well-equipped children's playground. You might also want to see **King Hussein's former palace,** a pleasant, but unostentatious building. If you'd like to stay the night consider the **Grand Hotel,** tel. 02-952505, a stately lodging with large high-ceilinged rooms that rent from SH51 ($15) single SH95.20 ($28) double a night; breakfast included. A large garden with pine trees and flower beds is a plus here. Alternatively, the **Miami Hotel,** Jaffa Rd., tel. 02-952808 charges SH30 ($8.80) a night for a single or double room with private shower; no meals.

If you'd just like to dine in Ramallah, head for the lovely **Na'oum's Restaurant and Bar,** tel. 02-952894. Located near Midan Center on Mughtaribeen Square, and open 8 a.m. to midnight. Na'oum's is the place to try mazza—the Arab answer to rijsttafel, consisting of over 30 different dishes for SH30 ($8.80). A less costly specialty here is mousakhan—half a grilled chicken with onions for SH6 ($1.75).

Save dessert for **Damascus Sweets,** across the street from Cinema Dunia, where baklava and other sweets made with tissue-thin pastry, pistachio nuts, coconut, and honey are SH.50 (15¢) and up (sold by weight). Delicious. Open daily from 7 a.m. to 9 p.m.

El Bira, the town adjoining Ramallah, is considered to have been the first caravan stop on the ancient Jerusalem–Galilee route. Neither Ramallah nor El Bira has any biblical sights to see these days, though.

Once past Ramallah, a road on your left will take you on a shortcut to Jericho (34 kilometers), via the Arab village of **Taiybah.** You'll see a large compound on your right as you continue; it was once a Jordanian hospital, and in the hills further on is what was once a Jordanian training camp. The buildings are still in use . . . by the Israelis. At this point you'll begin to notice an occasional shepherd with his flock—it might take you back to biblical days, when this was the area of the Tribe of Benjamin.

Two miles further on is the Arab village of **Beitin**—biblical Bethel, "House of God." This is one of the key places mentioned in Genesis 12. "I will make thee a great nation and I will bless thee, and make thy name great." Abraham passed into Canaan at Shechem, "And he removed from thence unto a mountain on the east of Bethel, and pitched his tent . . . and there he builded an altar unto the Lord." (Gen. 12:1-8) It was also to Bethel that Abraham and Lot returned from Egypt, "with their flocks and herds and tents." Later, as described in Genesis 28, the Lord appeared to Jacob in a dream: ". . . and behold a ladder set up on the earth, and the top of it reached to heaven: and behold the angels of God ascending and descending it. And, behold, the Lord stood above it, and said, I am the Lord God of Abraham thy father, and the God of Isaac: the land whereon thou liest, to thee will I give it, and unto thy seed." Jacob was in awe, and because his home was visited by God, he named it "House of God," Bethel, and set up a stone pillar at the spot marking the ladder. The hill today is called **Jacob's Ladder,** but unless you have a guide to point it out, you'll never find it.

After a bit of countryside, a few large buildings are seen on either side of the road, and a smaller paved road leads left and down into a small valley. The buildings are schools, new since the Six-Day War, built for the children of the village below. Part of this lovely village is also a refugee camp, but it's hard to tell which part, as the entire village looks so well kept and pretty, with most houses painted blue and lavender. Here you'll see a mosque with a difference—it's the only mosque tower with glass windows. When the meuzzin calls villagers to prayer in this extremely windy village, he simply opens one or more of the windows and closes them immediately afterwards to guard against the chill wind. The people here work mostly at agricultural tasks, and they tend trees bearing almonds, figs, apples, peaches, and olives—you'll note large groves lining the road and nearby hills.

The next village you'll see is **Bir Zeit,** which means "the Oil Well," and a bit further along is the village of **Ein Sinya,** with its cluster of old and new buildings on the left, some dating back to Turkish times when the family of the late Israeli Prime Minister Moshe Sharet settled here to build up the land. When tension mounted between Arab and Jew before 1948, the Sharet family (then called Shartok) escaped. Further along, high in the hills, is the town of **Sinjil,** the Arab name for the settlement of the French monk St. Giles, who was less fortunate than the Shartoks and lost his life here.

Now the road twists and turns through low hills covered by groves of olive trees. Soon you'll see a five-foot stone pillar pointing to the ruins of ancient **Shiloh** on the left: Shiloh is where the Tabernacle and the Ark of the Covenant were once housed. It is also the place where the men of Benjamin's tribe, short of women, carried away the daughters of Shiloh who were innocently dancing in their vineyards.

But to get back to modern times . . . there are some excellent shopping buys in and around Shiloh.

Valley of Dotan

As you pass Shiloh, note the natural Canaanite agricultural terraces still being worked in the hills. The steep winding road here was constructed originally by the British. It snakes down toward the village of **Lubban,** and the rich fields in the Valley of Dotan. Pull over before you descend and take in the magnificent view of the valley and Lubban. You have to look carefully at first to find the village, as it blends in so perfectly with the slopes. This area, in biblical times, was famous for myrrh and other incense. This industry still exists and tobacco is also grown here. Between Shiloh and here is the area where Saul met the Philistines, and Eli prophesied doom for Shiloh, then capital of the land. The territory from Shiloh northward belonged to the tribe of Manasseh. Entering the valley, you'll see houses begun in Turkish times and repaired and refurbished throughout the years. Many were, and still are, called *khans* and once served as wayside inns for travelers, housing both animals and men within their walls. To the left, at a sharp curve, is a roadside house with chairs and tables on patios front and side. A young Arab sells warm soda and juice here; no food. He does sell bags of almonds and walnuts, though, which make for good munching and are welcome gifts for friends who have never eaten fruits or nuts from the Holy Land.

As you continue on, keep an eye out for the small villages which dot the surrounding hills. And along the roadside, depending on the season, you'll see boys and men selling fruits, fresh or dried figs and such. The earth of the valley is plowed to show its rich redness, in sharp contrast to the chalky sand color of the hills. A bit of history: The Valley of Dotan was where Joseph was sold into slavery. One of the Via Maris roads ran through here, and the area was part of a caravan route traveled over by many, including the Maccabees.

SHECHEM: Just before you reach Nablus, the largest town of the West Bank, you'll want to stop on its southern outskirts for **Jacob's Well, Joseph's Tomb** and biblical **Shechem.** At Shechem, Abraham first entered the land of Canaan. The town was built much earlier by Shechem, Hamor's father. Jacob lived here, built an altar and dug a well. Joshua also built an altar at Shechem and summoned the tribes together, "half of them against Mount Gerizim and half of them over against Mount Ebal" (which are on either side of Shechem). Joshua united the tribes in a covenant ceremony which is considered the beginning of the Israeli nation. (Josh. 8:30-35.) Joseph, who was sold into slavery in the Valley of Dotan, was buried here. Archeological remains of ancient Shechem show that it was a large city; some of the finds are displayed in the Rockefeller Museum in East Jerusalem. Archeologists have long puzzled over why Shechem, if it was such an important place, was situated in such a vulnerable place—in a pass between two mountains, Ebal and Gerizim.

Mount Gerizim became very holy to the Samaritans, who today believe it to be the authentic Mount Sinai as well as the site of **Abraham's Altar,** where he prepared to sacrifice his son Isaac. The present-day Samaritans will show it to you, between the rocks at the summit of Gerizim. (Others believe the near-sacrifice took place on Mount Moriah in Jerusalem.) The Samaritans, who celebrate many of the traditional Jewish holidays, will be glad to point out altars built by Adam and Noah on Gerizim. (Moses and Joshua also attached great significance to Mount Gerizim. See Deut. 6, Josh. 8.) About 275 Samaritans live here these days, calling themselves the children of the Tribes of Manasseh, Aaron and Efraim. Other remnants of that proud tribe are to be found south of Tel Aviv in Holon.

Originally descended from the tribes of Israel, the Samaritans are those who remained behind when the Babylonians carried off the population of Israel in the sixth century B.C. When Cyrus released the Jews and they returned to Israel after a 60-year absence, the Samaritans wanted to help them reconstruct the Temple. The Jews refused their help, declaring that the Samaritans were no longer Jews, that they had intermarried with the Assyrians and Babylonians and adopted pagan customs. The factions split and remained split down through the centuries, the Samaritans claiming that they and only they have continuously inhabited Israel and kept the traditions pure. They also claim themselves to be the keepers of a Pentateuch (the first five books of Moses) which they say came to them from Aaron, Moses' brother. If this is the case, it's the oldest biblical scroll in existence; you can see it in the Samaritan synagogue in Shechem.

On Passover, the Samaritans of Shechem are joined by those from Holon; together they sacrifice a lamb on the site of Abraham's Altar, observing, they say, the tradition begun by their forebears 25 centuries ago.

In Shechem too is the **Convent of Jacob's Well.** You'll recognize it by its two large metal doors painted bright blue. Ring the electric buzzer to notify the convent's sole monk that you'd like to enter the locked gate. As the doors open, you see a beautiful cluster of well-tended small gardens. To the right is a tiny station for prayer, housing a picture of Jesus and the Woman of the Well, another name for this convent. Directly ahead are two blue pillars, mounted with ancient Roman capitol stones that support a new ceramic arch leading to the shrine and the huge unfinished church. In 1912, the Russian Orthodox Church began building this enormous basilica, but work stopped with the onset of the First World War. Later, this and all other Russian Orthodox holy places were turned over to the Greek Orthodox Church, which still maintains them.

The outside walls were part of a Byzantine church which once stood on this site. Walk around the back to the northeast corner of the newer structure for a look at what remains of the Byzantine mosaic floors, with stones of red, blue, green, black and cream. Here you can also see where old Roman columns were used in the foundation work of the newer church. Inside the basilica area, with its three separate nave sections, the larger and central section is sheltered with tent-like fabrics and contains a cross atop a broken Roman pillar. Here is held the Feast of the Samaritan Woman. Two painted cement buildings, looking much like guard stations, cover and secure two 18-step passages leading down to the chapel and well. Although the small, beautiful chapel looks older, it was built in 1910, on the site of the earlier chapel, which was built in the times of Queen Helena, mother of Constantine. Rich and intimate, the chapel is hung with shining incense burners and paved with painted tiles; its walls are covered with old paintings and icons, most depicting Jesus and the Woman at the Well. In the center is **Jacob's Well,** with wrought-iron fixtures and a metal pail—a bit incongruous amid so much elegance.

The well itself is 115 feet deep (89 feet before you reach water level). The topmost structure is Greek; beneath it, lining the interior of the well for about 13 feet, is stonework dating back to Byzantine, Roman and Marmaluke times. The balance is believed to be original well stone from Jacob's day. The water, besides being cold and sweet, is supposed to have special properties; indeed, old-timers here will tell you of the days, 70 or 80 years ago, when Russian Orthodox pilgrims came by thousands to this shrine. In those days several monks were needed to aid the pilgrims and maintain the shrine; today's lone vigil is kept by young Father Kelladion. You may buy religious souvenirs here and you can come away with small brown bottles of the well water for whatever donation you care to leave.

From here it's a hundred yards north to the traditional site of **Joseph's Tomb,** in a little white, domed house, similar in appearance to Rachel's Tomb. Since this was the land parceled out by the Lord to the Patriarchs, the Israelites brought Joseph's bones back from Egypt and placed them in Shechem, "in a parcel of ground which Jacob bought of the sons of Hamor, the father of Shechem, for a hundred pieces of silver: and it became the inheritance of the children of Joseph" (Josh. 25:32). This is one of the three places—along with the Jerusalem Temple and the Patriarch's Tomb in Hebron—that religious Jews claim is historically theirs by right of documented purchase.

NABLUS: The largest West Bank town, with houses piled up like white chalky soap bubbles on the hillsides, Nablus is somewhat modern and business-like compared to, say, Hebron, which has nearly the same population but which looks hundreds of years older . . . and drearier. Nablus is in fact a business center, home of the local soap-making industry and equally known for the sweet, sticky baklava pastries made here. The name Nablus is the Arabic contraction of the Greco-Roman city built here, Neapolis. It was founded by Titus who named it Flavia Neopolis in honor of his father, Flavius Vespasian.

We'll quickly pass through the town, noting what's around: the large complex to the right is an old Arab-British prison, still being used, and further on are beautiful villas and a lovely small mosque with a huge blue-green dome and stained-glass windows. Past here, to the left, the Casbah area starts—this is the older quarter and strictly off-limits to tourists. Within it is the dome of another mosque, and above it, on the hillside, is the Samaritan quarter, opposite a Moslem cemetery. The streets are filled with black-veiled Moslem women and head-scarfed men, and the outskirts are scattered with more beautiful villas that almost touch the next small village. The road winds on through small villages between low hills and mountains and eventually forks: right to Samaria; left is a shortcut to Netanya.

Samaria

The road to Samaria curves downward, and, by paying attention, you'll note the many caves in the area and small houses built into the hillsides. Women sit in front of their houses near the road working with stitchery or wool and you may see a group of them working together to sift or grind grain beside the road. On the hill to the right is Samaria (**Sebastia** today), and as you climb the Israeli road watch for niches in the mountainside. These were discovered when the road was being built—they're burial caves, many of which were found filled with ancient sarcophagi dating back to around 800 B.C. Today, this is a tiny Samaritan village, its winding narrow streets topping ruins from the days of Ahab, the Romans, Byzantines, and Crusaders. The small, poor houses often are made or propped up with bits of stone and pillars from past eras. The main square, if we may call it that, has an outdoor cafe where you can get cold drinks.

The entire region of Samaria was occupied by the tribes of Ephraim and Manasseh, the children of Joseph, in biblical times. Samaria was once the capital of the Kingdom of Israel. Inside the village a mosque has been built within an old Crusader cathedral. Beneath it, reputedly, is the tomb of Elisha, the prophet, and also the head of John the Baptist, brought here by Herod Antipas at the request of Salome. The hills bear witness to the Roman city that once stood here: ruins of a hippodrome, columns, towers, a theater, palace walls.

At an earlier time, however (around 876 B.C.), Omri founded the capital of the Kingdom of Israel here. His son Arab married Jezebel, daughter of a Phoenician king. She brought Baal and other idolatrous pagan gods to the people of Israel. The prophets fought her, particularly Elijah, who challenged the priests of Baal in the famous cliffside battle on Mount Carmel. Samaria remained the capital under Jeru and Jeroboam, but the Old Testament recounts bad times of transgression, corruption, vice and drunkenness. In 725 B.C., the Assyrians plundered Samaria, ending the Kingdom of Israel, and carried off 25,000 of its inhabitants.

To Jenin, Nazareth, and the Jordan Valley

The road moves on past **Dotan,** traditionally the city where Joseph was sold into slavery by his brothers, to Jenin. Take a left at the square in the middle of this little town and follow the road north. From here you can head north to Afula and thence to Nazareth and Haifa, or east to the Jordan Valley and the Sea of Galilee.

TEL AVIV

COMPARED WITH JERUSALEM, Israel's largest metropolis is a gawky, incoherent mass of undistinguished architecture and frantic commotion. Highlighted against Haifa, Tel Aviv is unkempt, noisy, and hopelessly uncoordinated. The city doesn't have the saving grace of Beersheba—the wide expanse of lapping wilderness and desert. Nor does it compare favorably with the Red Sea coral empire of Eilat. It isn't cleanly fashioned like Arad, and its questionable beauty is a lightyear removed from the pious serenity of Safed.

And yet Tel Aviv is where the action is. It is the brash, polyglot microcosm of all of Israel. It is a city that never sleeps, and it is also the largest completely (or nearly completely) Jewish metropolis in the world.

Only 70 years ago, the area on which modern Tel Aviv stands was a dismal landscape of sand dunes. Jackals howled in the evening at sites where you now hear the roar of diesel engines. Snakes and lizards slithered around Dizengoff Square, where actors and writers now sip their drinks at crowded outdoor cafes. Bedouins camped in black tents on the sand flats above the sea, in the exact spot where the Dan, Hilton, Plaza, Ramada, and many more plush hotels are fast converting Tel Aviv's seafront into a Middle Eastern Miami Beach.

As Israel's most cosmopolitan city (population 348,500), Tel Aviv is unique, a perfect product of the 20th century—bold, crowded and impolite, lacking the mannered graces of an earlier time, and indifferent to the aesthetics of architecture. It has pizza parlors, nightclubs, and acres and acres of modern apartment buildings. To an idealistic kibbutznik, the mere mention of its name conjures up an image of Gomorrah in its worst depravity.

But for all that, Tel Aviv is the cultural, business and entertainment center of Israel. The newspapers are published here (excepting the Jerusalem Post), the books are published here, the concerts are given here, and the theaters thrive here. Say what you want, this is the commercial and fun capital of Israel—a city born of necessity, growing up too fast to worry about its style or appearance.

1. The City

A BIT OF HISTORY: Back in 1906, the Jews of Jaffa (the old port of Tel Aviv) decided that they were tired of their cramped and noisy quarters in that

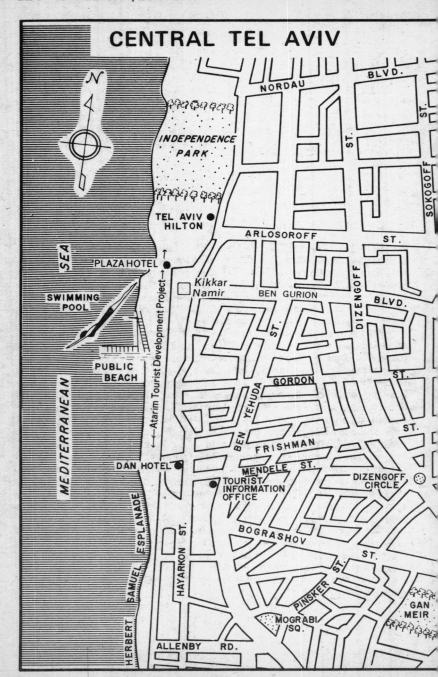

CENTRAL TEL AVIV

Arab city. With a boost from the Jewish National Fund, a group of them decided to build their own city on Jaffa's northern outskirts. In 1909, they bought 32 acres, and under the leadership of Meir Dizengoff, 60 families (about 250 people) staked out their claims. A famous photograph of these people, who had sufficient sense of history to pose for the occasion, recalls the moment. You'll probably see this picture at one time or another at some exhibition in Israel: the 60 posed families, stuffed into their fluffy Victorian clothes. Dizengoff, in his invocation address prophesied a town of 25,000; his hopes have been exceeded 20 times over.

Most of the pioneers' wealth went into the building of a fine school, the famous Herzilia Gymnasium (Palestine's first high school), which was modeled after an ancient drawing of Solomon's Temple but emerged resembling a Turkish fortress. Later, they turned their tents into cottages and named their first thoroughfare Herzl Street. They argued with the encamped Arabs over their rights to the land, persevered, and, by the time World War I began, the city's population had grown to 3,000.

During the war, the Turks dispossessed the residents of Tel Aviv, but they all came back when General Allenby's British Army dispossessed the Turks. Subsequently, the Balfour Declaration launched a wave of immigration, and, by 1921, Tel Aviv had blossomed into a separate town from Jaffa, elected Dizengoff mayor, and become home to 15,000 residents.

The city's motto, "I shall build thee and thou shalt be built," inspired many of the immigrants who came into Israel from Jaffa port to stay right in Tel Aviv and do their building—instead of pioneering in the malarial swamps of the agricultural settlements. Sporadic fighting with Arab neighbors in Jaffa accompanied Tel Aviv's early history.

By the outbreak of World War II, Tel Aviv was a small metropolis of 100,000 people, and in that capacity, the city played host to 2,000,000 Allied soldiers who passed through Tel Aviv during the war. Although most of Israel escaped the ravages of that war, Tel Aviv was bombed by Italian and Vichy French planes.

After the war, Tel Aviv became a center of Israeli dissatisfaction with the British Mandate policy that prevented Jewish DP's from entering Israel. Once, in 1946, 20,000 British soldiers placed the entire city under rigid curfew while a search was conducted for underground members. After interrogating almost the entire population of 110,000 residents, the British made two arrests. In 1948, just as the British were pulling out of Israel, the Israelis launched an attack against Jaffa, headquarters for Arab guerrillas and snipers: Jaffa's Arab population, dispersed to Arab-controlled areas, thereupon fell from 50,000 to 5,000.

Once the British were gone, Tel Aviv really began to mushroom. The city's suburbs spread out in three directions. Between the establishment of Israel in 1948 and the present time, the population of the greater Tel Aviv region has more than quadrupled.

ACCOMMODATIONS: Naturally, Tel Aviv has Israel's largest collection of good budget hotels. But a warning—which can make a big difference in your stay—should precede our discussion of them.

If one word could describe Tel Aviv's hotel situation, that word would be "noisy." Ninety percent of these establishments are built directly on the main streets—**Ben Yehuda, Allenby** and **Hayarkon.** And for sheer diesel roar and motorscooter cough, Tel Aviv is unsurpassed in all the world. We once stayed in a conveniently located hotel on a busy corner, facing on the street, and soon discovered that not only was an afternoon nap impossible, but the sound and fury outside the window didn't abate till well after midnight.

Therefore, more than any other commodity—the bathroom; the shower, the plaster job on the ceiling—make sure you value the location of your Tel Aviv room. Don't take a room facing on the main street, unless of course it has air conditioning and sound-proofed windows . . . and very few do. Get off the heavily trafficked streets or take a room in the back. Sightseeing is a tiring business and you need your rest. (Strangely enough, Tel Aviv hoteliers don't seem to realize that rooms in back, away from the noise are highly desirable; they charge precisely the same for front and back rooms.)

Before entering into specific details, we want once again to emphasize the following postulates: rates in Tel Aviv (as elsewhere in the country) are seasonal; nearly all hotels add a service charge; inflationary trends and devaluations require a certain amount of mental gymnastics—perhaps as much as 15% over the prices quoted.

And now one final note before we begin searching out hotel bargains. There was very little substantial planning involved with Tel Aviv—it grew because of pressures and needs. Even after it became apparent that tourism was going to become one of the major industries of the country, hotel construction and tourist facilities rose in answer to immediate demands and not as an integral component of an overall scheme.

In 1968, a company called **Kikar Namir** was created, representing both the municipality of Tel Aviv–Jaffa and the Ministry of Tourism. The purpose of the body was to reconstitute the beachfront area running along the coast of those once separate entities. And despite adversity, war, and economic recession, the plan has been splendidly executed. Today Kikar Namir is a three-story complex encompassing, among other things, the Marina Hotel, restaurants, open-air cafes, shops, a swimming pool, and a Municipal Information Office. There is an additional tourist office at 42 Frishman St., corner of Dizengoff Rd., tel. 03-223692. We'll be mentioning Kikar Namir's hotels and restaurants further down.

Budget Hotels

In this category we have included the very best bargains in Tel Aviv. What is a "bargain"? It could mean the best combination of amenities (private shower, balcony, breakfast) at the most reasonable price, all considered. Or it could mean a roof over your head at the lowest possible price. We suggest you read through this section completely before making a choice. You're sure to find the kind of bargain *you* are looking for. Don't forget the youth hostels (details in Chapter XI).

The **Nes Ziona,** 10 Nes Ziona St., off Ben Yehuda and one block from Allenby, tel. 03-656587. This gray-faced hotel of three stories is on a quiet street two blocks from the sea. Of its 21 rooms, 17 have showers and four have sinks only. It is very simple and clean; the highlight is the lounge-lobby wherein paintings of local artists are displayed. Per person rate for one or two people is SH25.50 ($7.50) a night. Three in a room will be cheaper. No meals.

On the second floor of 9 Allenby is the **Hotel Galim,** tel. 03-655703. It is an old-fashioned Israeli hotel and was the setting of the film "The Joker." These days it's pretty run down, and definitely not a choice for the overly fastidious, but rates are low: SH20 ($5.85) to SH30 ($8.85) single or double, not including breakfast; your room will have a private shower, but no toilet.

Off 56 Allenby, on Hillel Hazaken St., through a passageway loaded with pictures, real and plastic flowers, is the **Hagalil Hotel,** tel. 03-655036. The owner takes great pride in his hotel and is much appreciated by his guests. We advise that you write well in advance to reserve your accommodations. All rooms have hot water, though showers and toilets are shared; a good Israeli breakfast is included. Singles are SH23.80 ($7), doubles SH25.20 ($7.40) per person. Highly recommended.

The **Riviera Hotel,** 52 Hayarkon St., corner 7 Allenby, tel. 03-656870, caters to younger tourists, offering a 15% discount to under-35s. There are 30 rooms, most with private shower, some with toilets, all with heaters, and a few with air conditioning as well. A cafeteria on the premises offers snack fare from 4 p.m. to about midnight, and a full breakfast is included in your rates. Rates are SH34 ($10) to SH51 ($15) single, SH25.50 ($7.50) to SH39.10 ($11.50) per person in a double room. Three people sharing a room pay SH15.30 ($4.50) to SH20.40 ($6) each; four or five in a room pay SH15.30 ($4.50) each.

The **Hostel,** 60 Ben Yehuda St., diagonally across from Mendele corner, tel. 03-287088 or 281500, is found up 80 steps on the fourth floor of the building. It has no connection to the recommended hostels of the Israel Youth Hostels Association. Singles or doubles pay SH16 ($4.70) per person nightly; triples or quadruples are SH12 ($3.50) per person; dormitory accommodations are SH9 ($2.65) each. You get bed linens, which are changed daily, and there are hot showers in each room. If you pay six days in advance, you get one day free. There is a refrigerator and a gas stove, the latter for heating and not cooking. No meals are served. Guests can occupy dorms or rooms from 5 p.m. to 9 a.m. only. Students get a 10% reduction.

The **Ambassador,** 2 Allenby Rd., tel. 02-55118, is a three-star hotel; its 50 rooms are all equipped with phones, heating, air conditioning, and private bath or shower. One side of the hotel faces the sea, the other side Allenby Rd. Rates, including and Israeli breakfast, are SH62.90 ($18.50) to SH66.30 ($19.50) per person. Students get a 10% discount.

Where Allenby meets the sea at No. 4, and opposite the Opera House, is the **Monopol Hotel,** tel. 03-55906. It has 26 rooms on three very high-ceilinged floors. Six rooms have toilets, seven have air conditioning, all have heating, 20 have balconies facing the sea. Singles are SH37.40 ($11), doubles are SH40.80 ($12) per person, including a self-service Israeli breakfast. The same people also own the **Imperial** at 66 Hayarkon.

The **Europa,** 42 Allenby Rd., tel. 03-657913, is an older hotel with 16 rooms, all with private shower; toilets are shared. B&B rates are SH35.70 ($10.50) single, SH37.40 ($11) per person double.

On Ben Yehuda at No. 35, across the street from the El Al Building, is the **Ora,** tel. 03-650941. An elevator services its five floors (54 rooms), there's a carpeted bar, and each guest room comes with such extras as air conditioning, a radio and a sitzbath. The hotel's entrance is near the KLM office. Double rooms are SH45.90 ($13.50) to SH51 ($15) per person, including an Israeli breakfast. Students get a 10% reduction.

The **Migdal David Hotel,** 8 Allenby, tel. 03-656392, is in a large building on a street of inexpensive hotels, bars and restaurants. It has 20 double and triple rooms on the second and third floors. All rooms have running water, and most have showers. You can help yourself to tea and coffee free all day in the dining room. Prices include breakfast; a single is SH51 ($15), a double SH40.80 ($12) per person; students get a small discount.

At the three-story **Eilat Hotel,** 58 Hayarkon St., tel. 03-655368, all rooms offer heating, air conditioning, private baths and toilets; a phone is conveniently placed on each floor. There's a TV lounge and dining room. Singles pay SH51 ($15) a night, a double room is SH42.50 ($12.50) per person. Discounts available for students.

At the **Imperial Hotel**, 69 Hayarkon St., tel. 03-657002, you can help yourself to tea all day long, courtesy of the management. All rooms have bathroom facilities, most have balconies, and prices include Israeli breakfast and tax. Singles are SH56.10 ($16.50) to SH68 ($20) doubles SH47.60 ($14) per person; rooms in the back are slightly cheaper. Prices about 10% less in low season.

The **Excelsior**, 88 Hayarkon St., tel. 03-655486, is at the corner of Bograshov. Here front rooms face the sea and back rooms have balconies. All rooms have showers and toilets, some have baths and air conditioning (heaters are available). B&B rates are SH59.50 ($17.50) to SH68 ($20) single, SH53.70 ($15.80) per person double; less in low season or for long stays. Reductions for students.

The **Hotel Commodore**, 2 Zamenhoff St., corner Dizengoff Circle; tel. 03-296181/5, is the only hotel at Dizengoff Circle, just about the busiest part of town. Here you'll be a stone's throw from fancy shops, banks, a post office, a supermarket, cafes, restaurants, everything. It is an excellent location in terms of transportation, for there is a virtual army of buses on Dizengoff to take you practically anywhere in town. The hotel itself, with balconies in front overlooking the action on Dizengoff Circle, has an "Olde English-style" lobby. Double occupancy rate is SH54.40 ($16) per person, singles pay SH78.20 ($23).

If you are interested in staying in a family pension in the center of town, try the **Sidonie Frankenstein**, 22 King George St., tel. 03-232901. A single is SH54.40 ($16), a double SH51 ($15) per person, including a big breakfast, afternoon coffee and cake, and fruit in the evening. It is very clean and pleasant, as attested to by the many thank you letters received by the lovely Viennese lady who owns the pension. (Note the artistic mending she does.)

A cozy hotel decorated with subdued colors is the **Adiv**, 5 Mendele St., tel. 03-229141/4. It has a popular self-service restaurant and milk bar, La Pergola. Rooms have baths, radios, carpeting, heating, and air conditioning. Rates are SH81.60 ($24) single, SH57.80 ($17) per person in a double room.

A newer hotel within walking distance of the sea is the family-run **Star Hotel**, 9 Trumpeldor St., tel. 03-652127/8. It has a large, bright lobby and lounge, and the inviting bar serves alcoholic drinks, tea and coffee. It has parking facilities, phones, air conditioning, heating and an elevator. The colorful rooms go for SH55.40 ($16.30) per person double, including breakfast.

Also fairly new, the **Moss Hotel**, 6 Nes Ziona St., tel 03-651655, is large and very tastefully appointed. The manager, Albert H. Goldman, is an artist in his own right and you may see his paintings throughout the hotel. Carpeting, air conditioning, heating, a colorful bath, telephone and a radio come with each room, and the hotel has a small parking lot; you can rent a TV by the day. Rates, including Israeli breakfast, are SH68 ($20) single, SH47.60 ($14) per person double; contact ISSTA to obtain student rates. An agreeable place, in all.

On Hayarkon St., out near the Tel Aviv Hilton, is the three-star **Shalom Hotel**, at No. 216, tel. 03-243277, 243037, 243278, 249444. It is a modern, five-story structure housing 42 rooms, 30 with bath and 12 with shower. All the front rooms have balconies providing fine views of the Mediterranean and Independence Park. Done up in understated contemporary hotel fashion, the rooms come complete with air conditioning, central heating, and telephones, and cost SH54.40 ($16) to SH59.50 ($17.50) per person double during the summer, about $1 less off-season. Students receive a 10% discount. Breakfast, included in the room rate, is served in the ground floor self-service restaurant, which offers all meals (see "Meals," below).

A Country Club

The **Country Club Hotel,** tel. 03-415261, is on the grounds of the **Tel Aviv Country Club,** located on the Haifa Road between Tel Aviv and Herzlia, easily accessible by bus. It's a posh place that rents rooms for far above our budget.

The reason we mention it is that non-members can use the facilities here for a fee of SH14 ($4.10), SH19 ($5.60) on Saturdays and holidays (closed Mondays). These include tennis courts, a gymnasium, sauna and Olympic-size pool. You can also participate in classes in fencing, karate, yoga, jazz dancing, etc.; call 03-418181 for a schedule of classes. So you can stay at the cheapest budget hotel, and still occasionally treat yourself to the country club lifestyle.

Private Rooms and Apartments

If you plan to stay in Tel Aviv awhile and prefer renting a private room or apartment, contact **Paradise Tours,** 43 Ben Yehuda St. at the corner of Mendele St., tel. 03-240942. Ask to speak to Mrs. Lily Don-Yechiya, daily between 10 a.m. and 1 p.m. She will help you find a suitable room in a private apartment, with breakfast included, or an apartment of your own, furnished, for short or long-lease periods. The room-with-breakfast rate usually starts at around $8 to $10 per person, with a minimum of five days rental. A studio apartment, with weekly maid and linen service, starts in the neighborhood of $15 to $20 for two on a seven- to ten-day basis. If you prefer a two-room apartment, figure on no less than $18 to $25 a day. If interested, be sure to write ahead to the agency, explaining which accommodation you'd prefer and the length of your stay. Allow plenty of time for an answer before you arrive; then plan on staying one or two nights in a hotel while you check out the choices offered you. If you are arriving with children, be sure to mention how many and their ages.

MEALS: In Israel's most cosmopolitan city, you can find a wide variety of cuisines. Of course, typical Israeli cuisine is the most widespread and popular, and prices for native food are certainly going to be lower than for the imitated foreign dishes.

To keep your food costs low in Tel Aviv, here are a few tips to follow: Breakfast is usually provided by your hotel, so you have only lunch and dinner to consider. You might make one a heavy three- or four-course meal at the many restaurants that advertise reasonably priced fixed menus. Several such restaurants are recommended below, but you can find many more—often with sandwich boards outside advertising their prices—along Allenby, Ben Yehuda and Dizengoff Sts., and at the Central Bus Station. You might make the other meal a lighter one, consisting of a pitta stuffed with steak or shwarma and salad, plus a fruit drink, at the open stands that line either side of Dizengoff and that can be found readily enough on Allenby Street. Even cheaper is a felafel-stuffed pitta, with salad.

As elsewhere in Israel, the least expensive restaurants in Tel Aviv are the small, family-owned vegetarian spots and those serving oriental fare. For the latter, the cheapest and tastiest food in the entire city is served up in the Yemenite quarter of town, in the maze of streets that surround the Carmel Market, off Allenby Street.

And now for specific suggestions.

Budget Restaurants

As the majority of modest restaurants in Tel Aviv are more utilitarian than aesthetic, and since the food is of similar robust quality almost anywhere you go, it is better to choose a place in the vicinity of where you happen to be when you're hungry, rather than walk too far out of your way to go to one particular place. Except, that is, in the case of several exceptional spots—recommended by location below.

On Ben Yehuda Street: One of the best lunchtime bargains in all Tel Aviv is found at the **Restaurant Vienna,** 48a Ben Yehuda, tucked back in an alley-way close to the corner of Bograshov. This tiny gold-walled restaurant, with tables covered in checkered cloths, is open daily from 11:30 a.m. to 3:30 p.m. A three-course lunch is SH9 ($2.65) to SH10 ($2.95). A la carte, you might order goulash for SH7.50 ($2.20) or wiener schnitzel for SH8 ($2.35). Don't be surprised if you have to wait on line for a table or be asked to share your table with others—the Vienna has been in business for a long time and is deservedly popular.

At the **Grill Center,** 2 Ben Yehuda, tel. 03-296894, next to the Mograbi Cinema, right off Allenby St., is a large self-service restaurant. The restaurant, identified by the chicken rotisserie up front, offers chicken with chips and pitta for SH7.70 ($2.95). Other choices: schnitzel in pitta for SH1.25 (35¢), a hamburger for SH4.10 ($1.20), and kishke for SH3.70 ($1.10). Open Sunday to Thursday from 7:30 a.m. to 10 p.m., closing Friday at 3 p.m. until after sunset on Saturday.

In the Ben Yehuda vicinity, **Nes Ziona,** 8A Nes Ziona St., tel. 03-652855, is well known for its authentic and delicious Hungarian fare. It's a homey place with walls covered in imitation wood and wallpaper, and curtained windows. For SH17 ($5) you can get a full meal beginning with an appetizer of chopped liver, soup, or gefilte fish, proceeding to a main course of goulash, chicken, schnitzel, or roast beef—all served with two side dishes, and winding up with a dessert of apple compote, blintzes, or strudel. Open from noon to 10 p.m.; till 3 p.m. on Fridays, closed Saturdays.

Checkered red and white tablecloths greet you at the **Napoli Restaurant,** 9 Ben Yehuda St., tel. 03-650694. Steak pizzaiola (with tomato, garlic and mushroom sauce) served with rice or spaghetti costs SH8 ($2.35) as do many other meat main dishes. For SH7 ($2.05), you can enjoy fresh fish accompanied by spaghetti, rice or potatoes or a crisp salad. Ravioli and spaghetti come to SH3.50 ($1.02) to SH5 ($1.45), and minestrone, onion, mushroom or bean soup is SH2.50 (75¢). Any tourist carrying this book and ordering a meal at the Napoli will be served a glass of wine—on the house. Open daily except Saturday from 11 a.m. to 4 p.m. and 6 to 9 p.m.

A good breakfast can be had at **Hamozeg,** 21 Ben Yehuda, corner of Shalom Aleichem, tel. 03-658527. It opens at 6:30 a.m., so you can get an early start, and you can fuel up with a SH4.40 ($1.30) breakfast. Lunch and dinner are also served. Hungarian goulash is SH10.50 ($3.10), chicken with side dishes is SH6.50 ($1.90). Wash it down with cold draft beer—SH1.50 (45¢) for a small glass and SH3 (90¢) for a large mug. If you prefer a more genteel atmosphere at dinnertime, be seated in the dining room instead of the cafeteria. The latter has brown-carpeted floors, air conditioning, and tables covered in red cloths. Open daily until midnight.

The Burger Ranch, 21a Ben Yehuda, tel. 03-657365, is open Sunday to Thursday 10 a.m. to 10:30 p.m., Saturday from 5 p.m. to midnight, and closes Friday at 3 p.m. The menu reflects the decor: branded on wood with a real branding iron. It is an easygoing place, with Americanesque fare. A hamburger on a bun is SH3.30 (95¢), SH3.70 ($1.10) topped with cheese, pineapple, or onion. A quartered chicken with chips is SH7.40 ($2.17). There is a counter inside and tables and chairs outside. Eat in or take out.

Another place for an early start is the **Hollenberg**, 98 Ben Yehuda. As early as 6 a.m., you can fill up on two rolls, butter or margarine, two eggs, white cheese, jam and coffee for SH4.50 ($1.35). The restaurant is open until 4 p.m. (3 p.m. Friday, closed Saturday), and all main courses are served with three cooked vegetables and a salad. For SH10 ($2.95) you can order fish or meatballs with the above, SH11 ($3.25) will get you roast meat, schnitzel, or chicken.

At 113 Ben Yehuda St. you'll find the corner restaurant **Nitzan**, tel. 03-226422, serving good European food plus many Jewish specialties in a homey atmosphere. Soups, including borscht and fruit soup, are SH2 (60¢); gefilte fish or kishke SH3 (90¢), cheese blintzes SH2 (60¢) each. Main courses—boiled fish, boiled chicken, meatballs, liver schnitzel, chicken livers—range in price from about SH6.50 ($1.90) to SH8 ($2.35). The decor runs largely to orange with orange tablecloths, orange and black wallpaper, and orange curtains. Open Sunday to Thursday from 10 a.m. to 6 p.m., Friday to 4 p.m., closed Saturday.

In the Allenby Area: Along the entire length of Allenby St., especially among the budget hotels in the two blocks closest to the seafront, you'll find cafes and snack bars serving the common Israeli cuisine. Most of these charge modest prices and have little to differentiate them one from another.

For a low-cost restaurant, look for the **Nahariya**, 44 Geula St., at the corner of Allenby. A small place with just eight tables, and strictly kosher, it's so quiet we've actually seen people whispering to each other over dinner. Meat or chicken with potatoes and salad is SH7.50 ($2.20). An appetizer of chopped liver SH2.50 (75¢), cooked or fried fish SH3 (90¢). For SH2 (60¢) you can get a dessert of noodle pudding. Open 11 a.m. to 4 p.m.; closed Saturdays.

The **Hamashbir Latzarchan Department Store**, 115 Allenby, has a pleasant kosher eatery on the basement level. Open daily except Saturday from 8:30 a.m. to 7 p.m., Friday till 3 p.m., it offers blintzes or a cheese omelet for SH3.50 ($1), schnitzel, roast chicken, goulash, or shashlik for SH10.50 ($3.10).

A long-time popular place is **Bikovsky Restaurant**, 63 Allenby Road (open 10 a.m. to 7 p.m., Friday till 3, closed Saturday). Prices are appealingly low—just SH2.50 (75¢) for the likes of chopped liver or gefilte fish, SH8 ($2.35) for goulash, roast meat, schnitzel, or chicken with two vegetables. And it's even cheaper if you take food out.

"Weight Watchers" will appreciate knowing that the **Atara Cafe and Self-Service Restaurant** at No. 54 Allenby, tel. 03-656653, is where their Israeli counterparts meet and try not to overeat. They serve hot and cold vegetable dishes from 6 a.m. to 11 p.m. daily, Saturday evening to midnight, Friday until 5 p.m. There are two prices for everything, depending whether you help yourself at the counter or are served at your table. Gefilte fish is SH3 (90¢) when you help yourself, SH3.50 ($1) served at the table. A low-calorie meal of grilled fish and salad with two vegetables can be had for SH8.50 ($2.50) self-service. A cheese sandwich and a glass of juice is SH3.20 (95¢) at the self-service counter. A standard breakfast of two rolls, cottage cheese, butter, jam, coffee or tea—table service only—is priced at SH3.50 ($1).

The musical-sounding **Li-La-Lo Restaurant**, 15 Allenby, tel: 03-659058, is a large, inviting place specializing in Romanian cookery. Open from noon to midnight (except on Fridays when it's closed), Li-La-Lo dishes up the likes of stuffed cabbage for SH7.90 ($2.30), Viennese schnitzel for SH9 ($2.65), and goulash for SH7.50 ($2.20). If you eat at the counter you save 10%, however, the best ambience is on the large patio where the ceiling is covered in red floral fabric.

The **Ambassador Hotel,** 2 Allenby, has a very pleasant cafeteria with a basically blue and white decor. You might make a meal of a bowl of soup for SH2.60 (75¢), meat blintzes for SH6.50 ($1.90), and coffee at SH1.80 (50¢). Roast beef or goulash with vegetables is SH10 ($2.95). Open daily from 7 to 9 a.m., noon to 2 p.m., and 6 to 9 p.m.

Highly recommended is the **Strauss Milk Bar,** 111 Allenby, tel. 03-613335, a small eatery with a counter and just a few tables. A big pitta with felafel is SH2.40 (70¢), and you can get a half portion for half price. Fried fish is SH4 ($1.15), SH3.20 ($1) if served in a pitta. Fried meatballs in a pitta are SH2.80 (85¢), chicken SH5.50 ($1.60). All of the above come with selections from the salad bar—over 20 salads. Open Sunday to Thursday from about 9:30–10 a.m. to 6:30–7 p.m., closed Friday afternoon until Sunday morning. Another location at 143 Dizengoff, open 7:30 a.m. to 1 a.m., Friday and Saturday till 2 a.m.

TIV Self-Service, 130 Allenby, corner of Yehuda Halevi St., tel. 03-642125, is a simply furnished eatery offering hearty portions of gefilte fish for SH3 (90¢), steak, schnitzel, or chicken with vegetables for SH8 ($2.35); a plate of vegetables for SH4.50 ($1.35). Open Sunday to Thursday from 10:30 a.m. to 5:30 p.m., Friday till 3 p.m., closed Saturday.

In the Yemenite Quarter: Budget eateries will be found in the blocks that branch off Allenby just above Geula St., between Geula and the Carmel Market. This is the Yemenite Quarter, a section of squat houses and shops, exotic by day, dimly lit and shadowy at night. Don't let the neighborhood's appearance rattle you. The people here are honest and respectable, if a bit boisterous, and it's a perfectly safe area to traverse. This is one of the first parts of Tel Aviv built in 1909 when the Jews decided to leave Arab Jaffa and start an all-Jewish city.

Before deciding on a restaurant in the Yemenite Quarter, do check out **Shaul's Inn**—see "Big Splurges" below.

The tangled streets of the Yemenite Quarter—which, by the way, is not too easy to find your way around in; if confused, don't hesitate to ask—harbor masses of tiny inexpensive restaurants serving the tastiest oriental food in all Tel Aviv and some of the best in the country. A notably good example is **Halev Harachav** (The Open Heart), at 10 Rabbi Akiva St., at the corner of Beit Yosef St. This tiny place can barely squeeze 40 people into its small inside room and street patio, but Israelis come from miles around for the food and the service "with a sense of humor." Charcoal-broiled meat is the specialty. Dark meat, heart and liver of turkey grilled on a skewer costs SH3.50 ($1). Before you get your skewer, you can enjoy tchina and something the place calls *s'choog*—a mixture of a hot herb and spice sauce that's usually served in a small red dish, and a red tomato-base mixture served in a small oblong dish. A package deal of two skewers, tchina, two pittas, and a soda drink costs SH10 ($2.95). Open from 6 till after midnight.

Pninat Hakerem, 38 Hakovshim St., tel. 03-658779, is the domain of owner Gamliel, whose specialties are different kinds of meat- and rice-filled vegetables at SH4 ($1.15) a serving. This is an especially attractive place, with an interior terrace, lots of greenery, an aquarium, and splashing fountains. If you feel brave, try some of the regional specialties—pigeon spleens or beef lungs for SH6 ($1.75). But less adventurous diners needn't worry. They can order lamb shashlik or kabab for SH10 ($3.25). Save room for an SH3 (90¢) dessert of Bavarian cream. Open Sunday to Thursday from noon to 12:30 a.m., closed all day Friday until Saturday evening.

Owner Oda Nagi takes great pride in his **Ali-Esh Oriental Restaurant** at 22 Gedera St., behind the Allenby Cinema. A pleasant place, it is adorned with pictures of planes and helicopters, autographed photos, letters of thanks and assorted other mementos. If you don't want the pickles and pittas placed on your table automatically, have them taken away or you will be charged SH1 (30¢) for them. Try the goulash soup for SH3.50 ($1). A main course of kabab, shwarma, steak, or liver (not to mention spleen, kidneys, lungs, or lamb testicles) is SH8 ($2.35). A platter of five cooked vegetables is SH10 ($2.95). Open in winter from 8 a.m. to 7:30 p.m. Sunday to Thursday, closed Friday from 3 p.m. until Sunday morning. Open till 10 p.m. in summer.

At 26 Rabbi Meir St., just where Najara St. ends, bright red and blue neon signs announce the **Maganda Restaurant.** If the weather's good, you'll find about ten tables outside on the street, in addition to the others inside this bright, clean and cheery place. Inside are counters displaying assorted foods and meats; and on the ceilings and walls, huge photos of paratroopers and skydivers—all put up by Zadok Maganda, one of the four brothers who own the restaurant. Though you can get standard fare at excellent prices here—baked lamb, grilled shashlik, grilled beef for SH9 ($2.65), all with salad or chips—you can also get some rare dishes. For SH12 ($3.50) you can make a meal of beef testicles, and SH4 ($1.20) buys an appetizer of intestines (kishke). If all this makes you a little queasy, please remember that to many these dishes are considered hard-to-find gourmet treats. Regular vegetables or humus are SH2 (60¢), stuffed peppers only SH2.50 (75¢). Open from 11 a.m. till midnight, and sometimes later. This is truly an excellent place to eat.

Another spot for those who like their food tangy and flavorful is the **Chirbe,** at 2 Najara St., on the corner of Rabbi Meir. A one-room restaurant with glass and wrought-iron doors, stucco walls and archways, the Chirbe dishes out shashlik with chips for SH7 ($2.05) and will even sell a half-portion. Other fare includes eggplant salad for SH2 (60¢), steak with salad and chips for SH8. Open from noon to midnight daily; on Saturday from nightfall, closed Friday.

The **Zion,** at 28 Peduyim St., tel. 03-657323, serves authentic Yemenite dishes, and kicks in a bit of atmosphere, too. You walk down several stairs into the center room of the restaurant, which is plain and over-lighted. Off the main room are several small anterooms, with flagstone floors, stained-glass doors and romantic dim lights. Slip into one of the anterooms ("Zion Exclusive") for dinner, but keep in mind that prices are much higher in this section, and that the hours differ. The cheaper section is open from noon to 11 p.m. Friday until 3 p.m., the "Zion Exclusive," closed all day Friday and Saturday until sundown, is open from noon to 3:30 p.m. and 6:30 p.m. to midnight.

As for the food at the Zion, it is uniformly excellent. Try one of the spicy soups at SH4 ($1.20) to SH6 ($2.35); a salad appetizer is SH2.50 (75¢), and you'll pay SH9 ($2.65) for a kabab main course, with delicious vegetables or chips on the side. Such a feast will be accompanied by pitta, olives and peppers for SH1 (30¢). Try experimenting with choices on the menu and ask the English-speaking waiter to be your guide.

On Dizengoff Street: On Dizengoff Street, steak-and-pitta, shwarma and hamburger stands abound, especially around Dizengoff Circle, where the street takes on the aspect of both Times Square and the Via Veneto. These are quick-service places, with a grill in the middle and possibly a rotisserie for the shwarma. Frankly, we find the shwarma far tastier than the steaks, which are frozen and then quickly defrosted over the flaming grill, and all the spicy salad stuffed around the steak can't change the often low quality of the meat. Heading around Dizengoff Circle, you'll find at No. 12, the **Bar-B-Que Chicken House,**

tel. 03-231467. The advertised "Kingy" is a large hamburger with cole slaw and chips in a pitta for SH3.50 ($1). Other pitta fillings include stuffed peppers for SH2 (60¢), two kabab skewers for SH4 ($1.20), and three hot dogs for SH3.50 ($1). Open Sunday to Thursday from 10 a.m. to midnight. All food is kosher.

At No. 6 is the **Steak House** (Poondock Hastekim), offering counter service or tables and chairs on the sidewalk. Open 10 a.m. to midnight daily, closed Friday at 4 p.m. until Saturday sundown. In your pitta you may have shwarma or hamburger for SH4 ($1.20), steak or liver for SH6 ($2.35), all with salad and pickle. Cold drinks from SH1.50 (45¢).

Food like mother used to make can be found at the **Naknikiya Hakikar,** 4 Dizengoff Circle, tel. 03-280939. In this small and simple place you can enjoy gefilte fish (slightly sweet), chopped liver or kreplach in chicken soup or sauce for SH2.50 (75¢), and those stick-to-the-ribs foods like tcholent and kishke for SH5.50 ($1.60). Chicken or goulash with vegetables is SH7 ($2.05). Open Sunday to Thursday from 8 a.m. to 10 p.m., closed Friday afternoon until Saturday evning.

Oriental and European fare is served at the sedate **Finjan Restaurant,** 94 Dizengoff St., tel. 03-233466. Try an appetizer of baked eggplant or stuffed vegetables for SH3.50 ($1), a main course of turkey steak, turkey schnitzel, rump steak, shashlik, kabab, or roast chicken for SH8.50 ($2.50). For dessert we love the baked apple filled with nuts and sauce for SH3 (90¢). Open daily from noon to midnight. The street level of the **Camp David Restaurant,** Dizengoff Circle, tel. 03-221967, offers inexpensive oriental fare in modernistic surroundings. It's decorated with blue and silver mirrors. Chopped chicken breasts with humus is SH8 ($2.35), two skewers of kababs SH9 ($2.65), and two skewers of shashlik SH10 ($2.95); all are served with rice. A side order of dilled stringbeans is SH4 ($1.20). Open 8:30 a.m. to midnight, closed Friday from 3 p.m. till Saturday after sunset.

The **Shelly Coffee Shop,** 67 Dizengoff St., near the entrance to the Hamashbir Lazarchan Department Store, tel. 03-290369, is a kosher cafeteria offering such American-style fare as a hero sandwich for SH5 ($1.45), hot dog SH1.70 (50¢), and tuna salad on French bread SH4.50 ($1.35). It's fairly authentic since the owner spent five years in the U.S. He also serves Israeli fare. A large assortment of salads (from a choice of 16) on a plate is SH2.70 (80¢) to SH4.80 ($1.40). Open Sunday to Thursday from 8 a.m. to 8 p.m., Friday till 3 p.m.

The **Commodore Self-Service Restaurant,** Dizengoff Circle, corner of Zamenhoff St., tel. 03-296181, is a large corner cafeteria offering the usual falafel, schnitzel, meatballs, etc., in a pitta or on a platter, at low prices. Open daily from 10 a.m. to midnight.

Also on the circle is the **Halav Udvash Cafeteria** at No. 13, tel. 03-221156, open daily from 7 a.m. (Saturday from 10 a.m.) until midnight. You can sit at orange tables outside or brown ones inside and breakfast on two rolls, butter, jam and a hot drink for SH3.50 ($1); another SH1.50 (45¢) will add a pair of eggs to the meal. You can breakfast any time of the day here. Owner Yaacov Lazar recommends his pancakes with syrup at SH3.50 ($1), up to SH6 ($1.75) if a fancy topping of nuts, pineapple or ice cream tempts you. You're perfectly welcome just to cafe-sit with a beer, which costs SH3 (90¢), and watch the world go by.

A cafeteria called the **Numero Uno,** 89 Dizengoff St., tel. 03-225978, offers an array of Italian foods. Spaghetti (of course), cannelloni with mushrooms, lots of things in tomato sauce with cheese on top, are all SH4 ($1.20). And there's pizza at SH6 ($1.75), a cheese omelet at SH4 ($1.20). A dessert specialty is a crêpe made with apples, pineapple, cheese or strawberries (in season), whipped cream, nuts and chocolate syrup, SH4.50 ($1.35). Closed from Friday at 4 p.m. to Saturday at 7 p.m.; hours are 8 a.m. to 1 a.m. other days.

Students get a 10% reduction at **Pundak 91,** 91 Dizengoff St., tel. 03-225941, an oriental/European eatery with mirrored walls inside and green chairs at yellow tables on the sidewalk out front. You can choose from about 17 kinds of salad—SH4 ($1.20) for a small plate, double that for a large. Kabab in a pitta is SH5 ($1.45), shwarma is SH4 ($1.20). Open daily from 8 a.m. to 1 a.m.

Thirteen varieties of pizza are offered at **Pizzeria Rimini,** 93 Dizengoff, tel. 03-221681, ranging in price from SH7 ($2.05) to SH11 ($3.25). Pasta, meat dishes, wine, and liquor are also available. Pizzeria Rimini is at five other centrally located addresses: 4 Kikar Malchei Israel, tel. 03-263987; 24 Ibn Gvirol, tel. 03-266177; 3 Ahuzat Bait St., tel. 03-253287; Kikar Namir, tel. 03-288800; and 262 Ben Yehuda St., tel. 03-457050. All are open daily from 11 a.m. to 1 a.m.

The Almagor, 97 Dizengoff, tel. 03-232207, open from 9 a.m. to 1 a.m. but closed Friday afternoon till Saturday evening, offers a large choice in or out of pitta. In pitta, shashlik or steak is SH6 ($1.75), on a plate with extras, SH8 ($2.35). Choose from hot dogs, shwarma, chicken livers, hearts, or kabab.

The **Rowal,** 111 Dizengoff, tel. 03-225838, has much to offer. It is a cafe, self-service or restaurant. It has a vegetarian section, an indoor area and a very large outdoor area. Salads are SH2.50 (75¢) to SH3 (90¢), cheese omelet or gefilte fish SH4 ($1.20). It is a favorite Tel Aviv place to see and be seen, and has been for years. Open 8 a.m. to midnight; closes at 3 p.m. Fridays, and Saturdays until evening.

At 197 Dizengoff St. is **Batya,** where they have been serving Russian-Jewish cuisine for years. Three kreplach in soup are SH3 (90¢), or perhaps gefilte fish will start you off at SH2.70 (80¢), on to fried fish, chicken, meatballs, osso bucco, tongue, liver or other main dishes for SH7 ($2.05) to SH11 ($3.25), with extras. Open from 6 a.m. to 10 p.m.

The **Banana Natural Foods Restaurant,** 334 Dizengoff, tel. 03-457491, offers strictly vegetarian fare in a fittingly natural setting. The window is filled with plants, chairs and tables are unfinished wood, and the ceiling has wooden beams. Only fresh, natural foods are served. Juices and soups are SH3 (90¢), a salad of beets, cabbage, carrots, pecans, and mint leaves SH5 ($1.45), steamed veggies and brown rice SH7.50 ($2.20), and homemade healthy cakes SH2.50 (75¢) and up. Open Sunday to Thursday from noon to midnight, Saturday 1 p.m. to midnight.

Hayarkon and vicinity: Over toward the sea and around Hayarkon St. you have a large choice for light or more serious eating. The **Adiv Hotel,** cafeteria, called **La Pergola,** air-conditioned or heated as demanded by the season, offers a four-course meal for SH14.50 ($4.25), sandwiches from SH2.10 (60¢). Open from 10 to 10; address is 5 Mendele, tel. 03-229141/4.

The **Taste of Honey** (Zapihit Bidvash), 14 Frishman, is exclusively for you vegetarians out there. The owner is from California. He offers salads from SH2.50 (75¢) to SH3.50 ($1). No meat, but you can get a sardine and lox plate for SH5.50 ($1.60); other choices include stuffed cabbage, moussaka, or souffle for IL70, two blintzes with sour cream for SH5 ($1.45). Portions are large— they try hard to please. Hours: 7:30 a.m. to 11:30 p.m.; closed Friday afternoon till Saturday at 8 p.m.

The Pub, 10 Frishman St., not far from the Dan Hotel, has a charming cottage-like ambience with sturdy wooden chairs and tables, red wall-to-wall carpeting, and green-and-white checkered curtains on the windows. Light fare is featured: pancakes with syrup and jam for SH3.50 ($1), a cheeseburger or bacon and eggs for SH5.50 ($1.60), a tuna salad plate for SH6 ($1.75), etc. Open daily from 8 a.m. to midnight.

Tel Aviv's most highly recommended Hungarian restaurant is **Budapest,** 9 Hayarden St., corner of Hayarkon, tel. 03-658412. It's an immaculate little place, the tables covered with white cloths, walls adorned with flowered ceramic tiles; the front window has green glass panes. For SH4 ($1.20) you can begin your meal with chopped liver, herring, eggplant salad, or chicken soup. A main course of goulash or stuffed cabbage is SH9 ($2.65). Open daily from noon to 10 p.m.

MacDavid, 39 Frishman St., corner of Dizengoff St., tel. 03-220826, is a self-service eatery specializing in hamburgers. A plain burger in a bun (with or without hot sauce) is SH3.70 ($1.10), SH4 ($1.20) if you add cheese or mushrooms. You can also fill your bun with roast beef or tongue for SH5 ($1.45). A side of french fries is SH2 (60¢), and ice cream for dessert SH1.50 (45¢). Open Sunday to Thursday from 9:30 a.m. to 1 a.m., Friday 9 a.m. to 3 p.m. and 7 p.m. to 2 a.m., Saturday 10:30 a.m. to 1 a.m.

Midway between the municipal Gordon Swimming Pool and the public beach in front of the PAL Hotel is the **Shalom Hotel Self-Service Restaurant,** 216 Hayarkon, tel. 03-243277. The Shalom serves a complete SH8 ($2.35) Israeli breakfast, a hearty roast beef sandwich for SH6 ($1.75), and a good selection of reasonably priced salads, sandwiches, and omelets. Open daily from 7 a.m. to 11 p.m.

If you get hunger pangs at weird hours, there's the **Baba Restaurant,** 1 Yeshayahu St., tel. 03-447929, dishing out oriental and European specialties almost around the clock (6 a.m. to 2 a.m. Monday to Thursday, Friday morning to Sunday at 2 a.m. without closing). Everything from moussaka for SH4 ($1.20) to osso buco for SH10 ($2.95), and Bavarian cream for dessert at SH3 (90¢).

Kikar Namir Restaurants: As we mentioned earlier, Kikar Namir is a beachfront complex—Tel Aviv's answer to Ghirardelli Square, complete with cafes, ice cream parlors, restaurants, and shops of every variety. There are plenty of small food stands where you can buy food to go; in this category you might try a strawberry whip for SH2.70 (80¢) from **Fruit House.** For sit-down meals, however, the two most interesting possibilities are: **The Safari,** wherein lots of jungle ambience—African masks, zebra skins, bamboo furnishings, etc. The food is typically Israeli though, with shwarma in a pitta for SH12 ($3.50), that price includes chips, baked potato, or rice, plus all you want from a very well-stocked salad bar. And the newly opened **Crêperie** offers crêpes filled with cheese, salami, and egg for SH6 ($1.75), blintzes for SH6.50 ($1.90), banana and Grand Marnier for SH7.50 ($2.20).

Around the Central Bus Terminal: The whole area is much trafficked and gives a very grubby appearance. (It is slated to be replaced by a modern, new complex.) There are many eating places, more often than not in keeping with the general atmosphere. Don't let this turn you off completely, as some small restaurants are run by husband and wife teams and serve genuine home cooking.

There are many restaurants on Salomon Street, which is a main thoroughfare. At No. 2 is the **Mercaz Ha'steak;** No. 10 is **Biki's;** No. 16 is **Atara's;** No. 8 is **Leon Cohen,** to name a few. All have an unending supply of felafel. They all will grill meat and offer chips, salads and lots of relishes (including the spicy ones) stuffed into pitta. A large assortment of soft, hard and hot drinks are there for the thirsty, and you can sit or stand. Some of these places are open into the evening, others to the wee hours; all open early but are closed Friday afternoon until sundown on Saturday.

Ibn Gvirol Street: Here you'll also find a large variety of eateries. **Ba-Li Miznon Eliahu,** 8 Ibn Gvirol, tel. 03-255661, has both indoor and outdoor seating and offers a rather wide range of choices. A Turkish or Greek salad is SH2 (60¢), pastries filled with cheese, or onions and mushrooms are SH5.50 ($1.60), lasagne is SH8 ($2.35), and two blintzes with nuts SH3.60 ($1.05). Students get a 10% discount. Open Sunday to Thursday from 7 a.m. to midnight, Friday till 2 p.m., Saturday after sunset.

For a change of pace try **Taco Taco,** 23 Ibn Gvirol, a strictly kosher Mexican restaurant run by an Israeli who lived in California for 25 years. Tacos are SH3.90 ($1.15), enchiladas SH8.90 ($2.60), burritos SH4.50 ($1.35), and all come with salad. The decor is attractively rustic, with chili peppers and ears of corn hanging from wooden beams overhead. You can enjoy tequila with your meal for SH4 ($1.20). Open 11 a.m. to midnight; closed Friday and Saturday until after sunset. Another Taco Taco at Kikar Malchei Israel at the corner of Ben-Gurion Blvd.

Pundak Ministore, also at 30 Ibn Gvirol, tel. 03-265373, is a corner eatery with orange chairs and olive green Formica-topped tables. Salads are featured —35 varieties of them including Waldorf, asparagus, eggplant, tuna, and mushroom. When served in a pitta, these cost between about SH2 (60¢) and SH3 (90¢). A plate of 12 salads is SH8 ($2.35). Meats—e.g. chicken livers and mushrooms—served in a pitta are SH5 ($1.45). Open daily from 9 a.m. to midnight.

For a slightly splurgy, but delicious and filling lunch, try the **Madeleine Restaurant,** 49 Ibn Gvirol, tel. 03-261546. For SH13.50 ($3.95) they offer a four-course meal consisting of a plate with three or four salads, soup, a main course—perhaps meat-filled artichokes or steak in Spanish sauce, and dessert— fresh fruit salad or mousse. A la carte listings are beyond our budget. The Madeleine has a well-stocked bar, behind which are tacked menus from all over the world. The ambience is rather elegant, the tables set with green tablecloths, sparkling glassware and vases of flowers. Open from noon to 4:30 p.m. for lunch daily except Friday.

Drive-In, 54 Ibn Gvirol, two blocks from Municipality Square, tel. 03-264682, is not actually a drive-in; it's just called that, perhaps in an attempt at "Americanization." It has a cheerful red, yellow, and white decor. Typical fare: hamburger served in a roll with ketchup and salad for SH3.50 ($1), SH4 ($1.20) with cheese, SH2 (60¢) for a side order of chips, and SH4.50 ($1.35) for a dessert of banana split. Open Sunday to Thursday from 10 a.m. to 1 a.m., Friday and Saturday nights till 2 a.m.

If "strictly kosher" is a concern of yours, head for **Beit Ha'ochel Hamuchan,** 59 Ibn Gvirol, tel. 03-266799, a tiny, no-frills restaurant offering gefilte fish for SH2.70 (80¢), stuffed cabbage or peppers for SH2.50 (75¢), goulash for SH9.50 ($2.80), and schnitzel in a pitta with salad for SH4.50 ($1.35). Open Sunday to Thursday from 9:30 a.m. to 4 p.m., closed from 4 p.m. on Friday until Sunday morning.

Burger Ranch, 67 Ibn Gvirol, tel. 03-256813, with several branches around town, is a cheerful two-level eatery. Of course, burgers are featured, plain for SH3.30 (95¢), SH3.70 ($1.10) with pineapple, onion, or cheese toppings. You can also get chicken with chips and salad for SH7.40 ($2.20), fish filet, also with chips and salad, for SH6.30 ($1.85), or a couple of hot dogs in a roll for SH3 (90¢). Drink it down with a milkshake for SH2.30 (65¢). Open daily from 10 a.m. to 1 a.m.

And Elsewhere: At # 10 Kikar Malchei Israel, **Carambul's** offers glasses of whipped fruit for SH3 (90¢), cheese blintzes for SH4 ($1.20), and a scrumptious waffle topped with fruit, syrup, fresh whipped cream, and nuts for SH10

($2.95). Students with an ISSTA card get 15% off; readers carrying this book get a discount of SH1 on the blintzes and SH2 on the waffle. There's seating outside as well as within. Open Sunday to Thursday from 8 a.m. to midnight, Saturday from 2 p.m., closed Friday.

Beit Liesin, 32 Weizman St., tel. 03-252595, is open from noon till 3:30 p.m. (closes a bit earlier on Friday, all day Saturday and holidays) and serves lunch only. You can have a four-course meal starting off with bureka (meat-filled flaky pastry), gefilte fish, omelet or stuffed vegetable. Soup, a meat main dish and dessert follow, and the price for all is SH12 ($3.50). Coffee or tea is SH1.50 (45¢) extra. It is kosher. The air conditioning is a blessing. A service charge will be added if you desire a special amenity like a tablecloth. All the following buses will take you there: 12, 20, 21, 22, 25, 26, 28, 55, 61, 62, 64, 66, 89 and the United Tours bus to Herzlia.

Mis'adat Yitzhak, 48 Montefiore St., is a tiny Hungarian restaurant, where red-bearded owner Gingi offers traditional specialties like gefilte fish, chopped liver, or kishke for SH2.70 (80¢), main courses such as roast meat, chicken livers, or grilled chicken for SH9 ($2.65). Strictly kosher, this restaurant is open Sunday to Friday from noon to 2:30 p.m.

Big Splurge

Shaul's Inn is probably the most expensive restaurant in the Yemenite Quarter, but it is without doubt the very best. Address is Kehilat Aden St., corner Elyashiv, tel. 03-653303. Nicely atmospheric, with heavy wooden chairs, flagstone floors and a large photo-mural of a Yemenite wedding on one wall, this restaurant can get packed out to the street on Saturday nights. Stick to the main room on the ground floor; downstairs, where there is an intimate restaurant and bar, the prices go up by over 100%. English is spoken here, and the waiters will help you choose from the oriental specialties. The "Specialty of the Inn" is the lamb's breast stuffed with rice and pine nuts—deliciously tasty at SH15 ($4.40). Have a Turkish or Greek salad (scoop it up on pitta) for SH3 (90¢), or a gorgeous stuffed eggplant, cabbage or pepper for SH3.50 ($1). At Shaul's, you can eat very reasonably by choosing from such dishes as shashlik or kabab for SH9 ($2.65) to SH10 ($2.95). Ask Shaul to show you his kitchen—he takes great pride in its cleanliness and totally modern equipment and is always happy to show it off. Hours: noon till midnight, Friday till 3 p.m., Saturday after sundown.

Cafe Life

Tel Aviv's sidewalk coffee shops enjoy a far-flung reputation. Nothing delights an Israeli more than to sit out at night surrounded by friends and watch the evening walkers stream by. Two areas are traditionally popular for this pastime: Dizengoff Street and the Herbert Samuel Esplanade—**Ha'Boardwalk**—which runs along the sandy beach (women take note: it's best to walk or sit in pairs in this second area, particularly at night). Before you pick out a seat for yourself at one of these cafes, however, make sure you understand that you will have to pay up to three times as much here for coffee as you would anywhere else. But no one will force you to order more than a single cup. If you're cafe-ing by day, and it's hot, cool off with a coffee ice cream soda, one of the most popular Israeli drinks, or apple cider, very refreshing and tasty. And if you want to conserve your pennies, order tea, Tempo (like Seven-Up), Crystal (plain soda water), or Orangeade, all of which are fairly cheap.

On Dizengoff Street: Outdoor cafe life here starts near Dizengoff Circle, and works northwards. The "scene" is pretty packed most nights, but its real crescendo is reached on Saturday nights after the movies let out. Before you settle on one cafe, it's fun to take a stroll from one end of the area to the other, checking out the different types of places and crowds, and keeping in mind that you can sit and eat a meal as well as simply have coffee or dessert. As you stroll, you'll note many places that we've suggested in the restaurant section.

NIGHTLIFE IN TEL AVIV: Along with the sidewalk cafes, Tel Aviv is rife with discos. They're not the screaming, thunder-and-lighting hallucinogenic types. Rather, they're more like the kind that flourished in France years ago— just a tape recorder or phonograph, a Bohemian atmosphere, and dancing.

Piano bars are the "in" thing at present. Nightclubs are still around in the usual way, or the same establishment might be all three depending on which night of the week you are there. Their prices vary. Some are on rather tacky-looking streets, but that's no indication they'll be cheap; the atmosphere can be very different inside. Check the prices carefully before you start downing the drinks.

For Students Especially

Up at **Tel Aviv University,** the students' club is called **Barminan.** The discotheque here is open all year, Friday evenings from 9:30 p.m. to 1 a.m.; entrance fee is SH5 ($1.45). Saturday nights there's folk dancing from 9 to 11 p.m., disco dancing from 11 p.m. to 1 a.m.; entrance is SH2.50 (75¢). More folk dancing Mondays and Wednesdays—beginners 7:30–9 p.m., advanced 9:30 p.m. to midnight; entrance is SH1.20 (35¢). Other activities at the University include film evenings and concerts; you can also use the swimming pool and play tennis here. Reductions are granted on all events to holders of the International Student Card. Buses 13, 24, 25, 27, 45, 74, 79, and 80 go to the University; for further information on events here call the Student Organization at 03-420591.

At the Hotels

A singer and a pianist appear nightly at the **Dan's Bar.** . . . At the **Hilton,** you'll find the **Coral Piano Bar.** . . . The **Plaza** has the **Marina Bar.** . . . At the **Ramada Continental** there's a pianist nightly at the **Europa Bar.** . . . The **Basel** has a very pleasant bar. . . . And best of all, the **Beach Bar** at the **Grand Beach,** where there's dancing nightly at the pool (you can also take a moonlight swim), and dining at the rooftop Barbecue Bar.

Around Town

A young, arty crowd patronizes **Hamakom Hehadash,** 47 Yirmiyahu St., tel. 03-444003. During the week there's no entrance fee, but on Friday nights, when there's entertainment (electric guitar) and dancing, a couple pays SH30 ($8.85) admission, including first drinks for each. Open nightly from about 9:30 p.m. till 4 a.m.

Darts and films are among the attractions at the **Video Pub,** 171 Ben Yehuda St., tel. 03-241431. The walls are adorned with flags of many countries, and many English-speaking customers patronize this relaxed hangout. A burger or liver with chips costs SH10 ($2.95); alcoholic beverages are SH7 ($2.05). Open daily from 4 p.m. to 2–3 a.m., in summer from noon.

Owned by a former American, **Bernie's Bottle Club (BBC)**, 231 Ben Yehuda St., at Dizengoff St., tel. 03-451629, is a favorite with foreign embassy staffs, UN personnel, and American and Canadian tourists. Currency notes from all over the world are suspended from the ceiling. You can order reasonably priced light food—e.g. bacon and eggs, sandwiches, burgers, etc.—and the bar is well stocked. Beer begins at SH3 (90¢), mixed drinks at SH4.50 ($1.35). Open daily from 8 a.m. to 1 a.m.

Another lively spot is the **Bodega Piano Bar and Bodegatron Jazz Club**, 30 Ibn Gvirol St., tel. 03-264594. There's no admission in the dimly lit piano bar; beer is SH3 (90¢), whiskey SH6 ($1.75). The basement jazz club charges SH8 ($2.35) during the week, SH10 ($2.95) Friday and Saturday nights; both of those prices include a first drink. After that, you'll pay a minimum of SH4 ($1.20) per libation. Entertainment begins at 10:30 p.m. and sometimes includes country music as well as jazz. Both the piano bar and jazz club are open nightly till 2 a.m.

Right near City Hall, at 19 Kikar Malchei Israel, is the **Prince of Wales Pub**, tel. 03-249947, where after a few drinks you'll almost think you're in London. Sandwiches from SH2.50 (75¢) to SH5 ($1.45), draft beer SH3 (90¢), spirits SH5 ($1.45) and up. Open daily from 11 a.m. to 2 a.m.

Budget Nights in Tel Aviv

One of the least expensive forms of nighttime entertainment in Tel Aviv is to stroll around and people-watch. You might even take a romantic stroll to a lovely little park which juts out on a promontory 100 feet above the rolling surf. It's called **Gan Ha'atzmauth,** and it's located north of the Hilton Hotel, on upper Hayarkon Street. Also, see our notes under "Cafe Life" in the restaurant section above.

Then there are the movies. Tel Aviv has at least two dozen cinema houses, and they don't dub the English or American films. You can enjoy first-run shows for SH6 ($1.75) to SH7.50 ($2.20). Also enjoyable is the rare experience of seeing what, to the Israeli, is a foreign film, and watching others crane their necks to read the Hebrew subtitles, while you sit back and enjoy the English sound track.

SWIMMING IN TEL AVIV: Tel Aviv's seashore is within walking distance of Dizengoff Circle. This extraordinary tourist asset has been neglected for many years, and is only now beginning to be properly developed. Beaches are being widened, and breakwaters are being constructed to make swimming safer. A promenade is in the works which will eventually cross the entire length of the beach. The cleanest beach in the city is Clore Park. Most beaches have free facilities for changing clothes and showers.

There's a swimming pool open year round at Gordon St., tel. 03-233241, on the beach facing Namir Square. Entrance fee is SH6 ($1.50) for adults, SH5 ($1.45) for children, SH7 more for everyone on Saturdays. The pool is open from 4 a.m. to 5 p.m., till 6–7 p.m. in summer.

In a slightly more remote location, the **Bat Yam Beach,** three miles south of Jaffa, is wide and sandy, and gets crowded only on hot Saturdays in summer. From Mograbi Square, you can get a sherut going there. Also bus 10, which begins its run at the City Hall.

There is a good beach at **Herzlia.** United buses to Herzlia leave regularly from 3 Allenby Road.

Facing Kikar Namir and the Hilton is the **Hof Hadarim** (Orange Beach), more generally known as the Hilton Beach. Entrance and use of changing rooms are free; you can rent lockers and deck chairs. A snack bar and restaurant are also on the premises. Finally, there is the pool at Kikar Namir open from 4 a.m. to 5–6 p.m. Adults pay SH4.50 ($1.35), children SH3.50 ($1), SH.50 extra for everyone on Saturdays. Check our "Golden Coast" chapter for other beaches.

A word of caution: Swimming at Israeli beaches can be dangerous. Every summer, the local papers report an all-too-high number of drownings. The problem is an unpredictable undertow that can be hazardous even for a strong swimmer. It's entirely safe, however, to swim at beaches where guards are stationed. Elsewhere it's risky, and you shouldn't do it; but if you have to be defiant—don't go swimming alone. In any case, it is best to pay attention to the safety symbols, in the form of small flags, along Israeli beaches. The color of the flag tells the story: *black* means *absolutely no swimming* in the area; *red* warns you to be especially *cautious; white* indicates that *the water's fine,* so jump right in.

STUDENT AID: ISSTA headquarters for all of Israel is in Tel Aviv at 109 Ben Yehuda St., tel. 03-247164/5. For further details check "Especially for Students," Chapter I.

SIGHTSEEING IN TEL AVIV: There's much to see and do during the daytime, and all of it is either free or very inexpensive. We've set forth the places you'll want to visit, grouped according to the general areas in which they're found: (1) near or along Allenby St.; (2) along Rothschild Blvd.; (3) along or near Dizengoff St.; (4) near Hayarkon Street and the Yarkon River, and (5) elsewhere.

Allenby Street

This long street, which begins at the seaside, was named after the British general who took Palestine from the Turks in 1917. It is a street of furniture stores, bakeries, book stores, kiosks, jammed sidewalks, and screeching buses. Allenby St. is what non-Tel Avivians mean when they speak about "one of those typical Tel Aviv streets—if you know what I mean."

A few blocks down from the top of Allenby, at No. 110, is the domed **Great Synagogue,** quite handsome since extensive exterior renovations were completed a few years ago. (Work is still in progress inside.) It is the largest synagogue in Tel Aviv.

Go around the corner to Ahad Ha'am Street; one block down is the **Shalom Tower** (Migdal Shalom). Its 34 floors make it the tallest building not only in Tel Aviv, but throughout the entire Middle East. It is an outstanding commercial shopping center, housing a large department store, shops and offices. The view from the **Observatory** can be magnificent, by the naked eye or by the telescopes set out for that purpose. Take the glass elevator to the top. There is a cafe up top, too—but all this is hardly half of what goes on at Shalom Tower. There is **Mayerland,** an amusement park with many kinds of rides, arts and crafts booths, and the typical goodies that go with such installations, such as cotton candy, ice cream and popcorn. Entrance is free; each ride is SH1 (30¢) to SH2 (60¢). **The Wax Museum** depicts events in Israeli history, personalities and in some cases sensational news items.

The amusement park, Observatory and Wax museum are open Sunday–Thursday from 9 a.m. to 7 p.m., Fridays and holiday eves till 2 p.m. Entrance to both is SH8 ($2.35) adults, SH6.50 ($1.90) for a child or student. Separate tickets to each are SH5 ($1.45) and SH4 ($1.20), respectively.

The department store, called **Shalom Stores,** tel. 03-652131, can sell you everything from shoe laces to furniture; you can have your hair done, be photographed, eat in one of the many restaurants, even mail a letter in the post office. Open daily 9 a.m. to 7 p.m., till 3 p.m. Friday. 1, 4, 12, 25, 30, 33 or 43.

Before you leave the building, you might want to check out the **Israel Export Institute's** displays of fashion, arts and crafts.

Back now to Allenby. At No. 115 is **Hamashbir Latzarchan,** another department store, this one and part of a chain throughout the country. Open from 8:30 a.m. to 7 p.m. daily, but only till 2–3 p.m. on Friday. It too offers a huge assortment of merchandise, from the basement with kitchenware, a milk bar and a supermarket, on up through its escalated levels.

Carmel Market: Going uptown, where Allenby Road approaches Magen David Square, a six-sided intersection, you'll find a colorful market area, an open-air affair of vegetables, fragrant fruit and shining kitchenware. There are vendors selling everything from food to clothing on open tables down the main street. Many have their own songs, which tell you all about the price and quality of what is being sold. Sometimes one vendor sings against another in a competitive duet. The market runs into side streets, large and small, one side favoring dry goods, and the other side dried beans, fruit, nuts and spices in all colors and fragrances, sold from sacks. Opposite the market, at the King George Street intersection, is where free-lance housepainters gather, simply hanging around and waiting for a floor to scrub or a wall to paint.

Kerem Hateimanim (the **Yemenite Quarter**) is near the Carmel Market and if you are eager for a meal, you are near the source of some of the best oriental dishes you can find anywhere (see "Meals"). It is a network of narrow lanes and alleys and despite its exotic quality, it's a perfectly safe place to be. If you get a bit lost, just ask—people will be helpful.

At Allenby St. near the sea you can pick up Hayarkon Street, the hotel, cafe and embassy row; and Herbert Samuel Esplanade for Tel Aviv strolling.

Rothschild Boulevard

The center of Tel Aviv's cultural life is at the end of tree-lined Rothschild Boulevard. Clustered here together are the Habimah Theatre; a youth museum, the big Mann Auditorium, home of the Israel Philharmonic (IPO), and lovely Gan Yaacov Park. Further south along Rothschild, in the center of the island at Nachlat Benyamin Street, is the impressive **Founder's Monument,** depicting the three phases of Tel Aviv's history. The bottom of the bas-relief tier shows the workers of 1909 digging and planting, while snakes and animals form a lower border. The middle level shows the Herzlia Gymnasium (which was demolished in 1959 and rebuilt in the northern part of the city); the uppermost section is modern Tel Aviv, with the Habimah Theatre, Bialik's home and many modern houses.

Habimah National Theatre, tel. 03-283742, is the nation's first and best-known repertory theater. Founded in Moscow in 1918 by the renowned Stanislavsky, it moved to Palestine in 1928. The great Russian artist inspired the group and it went on to achieve a fantastic reputation, both in Palestine and at other great theaters throughout the world (best remembered are their performances of *The Golem* and *The Dybbuk,* which played to hundreds of thousands of people; they also presented the first Hebrew translations of plays by Shakespeare, Molière, Shaw and O'Neill). All performances are in Hebrew.

Around the corner is the **Helena Rubinstein Art Pavilion,** tel. 03-287196, where exhibits of the works of guest artists, Israeli and foreign, change every couple of weeks. Open most days 10 a.m. to 5 p.m., until 2 p.m. on Friday. Tuesday 10 a.m. to 1 p.m. and then again from 4 to 10 p.m. Saturday night from 7 to 11 p.m. Bus 5, 11, 12, 19, 63 or 92.

The **Mann Auditorium,** tel. 03-295092, which can seat 3,000 concert-goers, is the permanent home of the Israel Philharmonic Orchestra. Bronislaw Huberman founded the orchestra in 1936 by bringing together many renowned European musicians who had become refugees in Israel. Since then, some of the world's leading conductors and soloists have appeared with the Israel Philharmonic: Arturo Toscanini, Serge Koussevitzky, Leonard Bernstein, Arthur Rubinstein, Isaac Stern, Jascha Heifetz, Yehudi Menuhin and Zubin Mehta (Music Director since 1969). Yet even now that the magnificent concert hall has been built, the orchestra continues to give performances in other towns, carrying on a tradition that began during the War of Independence, when they played just behind the lines for the troops near Jerusalem and Beersheba. The orchestra is on vacation during August and September.

At **Beit Tanach** (Bible House), 16 Rothschild Blvd., tel. 03-657760, you can see an exhibition on the Bible, in print and art. Hours are from 9:30 a.m. to 1 p.m. Sunday through Friday. Meir Dizengoff, the first mayor of Tel Aviv lived here, and it was in this same historic house that the independence of Israel was declared in 1948. Adults pay SH1 (30¢), half price for students and children.

Haganah Museum: This is a fascinating place, well worth a two-hour visit. It's at 23 Rothschild Blvd., tel. 03-623624, site of a former Haganah general's home. The museum records the history of the Israeli military from the time of the farmfield watchmen at the beginning of the century down through the Yom Kippur War. Here are interesting photos, documents, uniforms, scale models and weapons. On the third floor, you see the various ways the Israelis hid arms inside farm machinery to escape British detection, and how they stealthily manufactured hand grenades and Sten guns in clandestine kibbutz workshops. There's one homemade grenade with the letters USA stamped on it—so that, had a Haganah soldier been caught with the bomb, the British wouldn't have suspected that it had been made locally. But the joke here was that "USA" were the first letters of three Yiddish words meaning "Our piece of work." Other items relate to the Arab riots of 1937, the World War II Jewish Brigade that fought with the British throughout the Mediterranean and Middle East, and the bizarre authorization papers printed during the Exodus affair.

Almost all of the explanatory captions in this four-story museum are in Hebrew—but never fear, the museum has stationed a group of English-speaking young women to act as interpreters and guides.

Entrance to the museum costs SH.50 (15¢) for adults, SH.20 (5¢) for children and students; hours are 9 a.m. to 3 p.m., till 12:30 p.m. on Fridays, closed Saturdays; take bus 1 or 4.

Dizengoff Square

Dizengoff Square comes to life at night. Lights flash from overhead advertisements, a cinema marquee calls to you in no uncertain terms, motorcycles roar by, and wide-eyed provincials gape in astonishment. Here you can have a hot dog, pizza, hamburger or ice cream soda—but try the exotic Israeli fare (felafel and tchina) first: cheaper, yes, and also better prepared.

Just down the street from the circle is Dizengoff St.'s famous stretch of sidewalk cafes, peopled with Tel Aviv's brand of bohemia and cafe society. Beards and long hair are always in fashion here. You'll see that there is a definite "in" set of artists and actors congregating at the cafes, as well as a good many refugees from both Greenwich Village and the kibbutz.

Paralleling Dizengoff St., several blocks closer to the sea, is **Ben Yehuda St.**, a commercial thoroughfare. Several of our top-recommended budget restaurants are located on this thoroughfare.

Just off Ben Yehuda St., at 7 Mendele St., is the **Israel Government Tourist Office**—in case you need maps, tour suggestions, or a booklet on what's happening in town the week you're there.

If you take a right off Ben Yehuda St. at Trumpeldor St. (just north of Allenby), you'll come to the **Old Cemetery,** resting place of early Israel's most outstanding figures. Here you'll find the grave of the father of Tel Aviv, Meir Dizengoff, as well as the burial places of Max Nordau, Ahad Ha'am, Haim Arlosoroff and the writers H. N. Bialik and S. Tchernihovsky.

Hayarkon Street and the Yarkon River

Hayarkon Street, which parallels the seafront, is the thoroughfare of most of Tel Aviv's hotels. Like two other main streets—Dizengoff and Ben Yehuda—it terminates at the Yarkon River.

Traditionally, the Yarkon was the scene of picnicking and rowboat excursions along its serpentine, tree-canopied waters. But the Yarkon River Diversion Plan, which pipes off water to the Negev, substantially depleted this river—which never was much more than a large stream in the first place.

Today, the area has been revitalized by landscape architect Moshe Ekron, and is well worth a visit. Ekron planted a vast area with trees and lawns, set up playgrounds for children, picnic areas, a rose garden and an exotic tropical garden. There's now a park with a concert shell, in the middle of an artificial lake, a kiddie train, and a roller-skating rink for children. Plans call for an Olympic-size swimming pool, sports facilities, riding facilities, art galleries and showrooms, restaurants, cafes, shops and parking lots.

Though not the same as punting on the Thames, boat rides on the Yarkon River are definitely a nice diversion. Bus 24 or 26 to the end of Ibn Gvirol will bring you to the Yarkon River; bus 1, 4 or 5 takes you to within easy walking distance. Boats can be rented from 9 a.m. until midnight (except when it rains). One firm is called **Tikvah-Dagon,** tel. 03-412921. Rate for a small boat is SH2 (30¢) for a couple per hour; for a larger boat holding up to six people, it's SH4 ($1.20) per hour; a canoe, catamaran, or kayak for two is SH3 (90¢) per hour. Ice cream and soft drinks are on sale here too. There is a second operator, **Irgun Hayarkon,** whose office is near Yirmiyahu Street, tel. 03-448422. They offer the same equipment plus a motorboat ride.

There have been free outdoor concerts in the Yarkon Park for the past number of summers. Check the newspapers or the Government Tourist Office for dates.

Beyond Power Station Reading IV is **Sde Dov** airport for domestic service, a secondary terminal for **Arkia,** Israel's inland passenger and freight airline. East of the airport, on the Abba Hillel Road, is the country's "Yankee Stadium," a sports arena that seats 30,000 soccer-mad spectators.

The Ha'aretz Museum Complex, tel. 03-415244. Just across the Yarkon Bridge, west of the stadium and north of the Yarkon River, in Ramat Aviv, is a grouping which includes the: **Ha'aretz Glass Museum, Kadman Numismatic Museum, Museum of Ethnography and Folklore (Judaica), Museum of**

Science and Technology, the **Lasky Planetarium** and the **Museum of Ceramics.** The museums are grouped near a site called **Tel Qasile,** where archeologists have uncovered relics from Philistine, ancient Hebrew and Roman periods. The buildings display these findings among others. The Ha'aretz Museum of Ancient Glass, a circular green building on the hilltop next to the Tel, is highly unusual. Opened several years ago, it specializes in ancient glassware, and many of its exhibits are unique in this line. The other museums concentrate on ceramics, coins, antique pottery and ethnographic exhibits. The newest addition is **The Alphabet Museum.** The entire collection was presented by Prof. Diringer, formerly of the University of Florence and now a lecturer at Cambridge. It is the history and development of writing and alphabets, and represents his life's work.

A ticket to enter all the museums is SH2.50 (75¢) for an adult, SH1 (30¢) for students and children. The Planetarium costs another SH2.50 and SH1, respectively. Admission is free to all museums, except the Planetarium, on Saturdays and holidays. Museums are open daily from 9 a.m. to 4 p.m.; till 1 p.m. on Fridays; Saturdays and holidays from 10 a.m. to 2 p.m. Planetarium shows daily at 10 and 11 a.m., and noon, and on the first Tuesday of every month at 7:15 p.m. Take buses 13, 24, 25, 27, 74, or 79.

If you continue on these same buses, you will come to **Tel Aviv University,** tel. 03-420111. It has a handsome, multi-faceted campus and an extensive library. Thirty-five buildings house the widest spectrum of studies of any university in Israel and its enrollment of 18,000 students is the largest as well. The faculties encompass fine arts, the humanities, history, Jewish studies, law, medicine, the sciences, engineering, business administration, and there are special colleges research institutes. Courses for English-speaking students are given here.

Be sure to visit the fascinating **Beth Hatefutsot** (Nahum Goldmann Museum of the Jewish Diaspora), on the campus of Tel Aviv University, tel. 03-425161. Through ingenious technological devices, models, films, slides, etc., the museum displays Jewish life outside the national homeland throughout history. Attractions include a model of a 13th-century Jewish community peopled by over 100 tiny figurines of men, women, and children clad in period dress and engaged in their various occupations; films showing the traditional shtetl life in Eastern Europe, Greece, and Morocco; scale models of famous synagogues, including one in China in 1653. For SH1 (30¢) you can get a computer print-out on any of 3,000 Jewish communities—perhaps the home of your ancestors. You can pick up a headset and listen to a dialogue (in English) between a 13th-century monk, Pablo Christiani, and a Jewish scholar, Nachmanides, about whether or not Jesus was the Messiah. There's a dairy cafeteria on the premises. Admission is SH4 ($1.20) for adults, SH3 (90¢) for students or children. The museum is open Sunday, Monday, and Thursday from 10 a.m. to 5 p.m., Tuesday and Wednesday from 3 to 10 p.m.; Saturday admission is free, and the hours are 10 a.m. to 2 p.m.

Elsewhere

The **Tel Aviv Art Museum,** 27 Shaul Hamelech Blvd., tel. 03-257361, houses temporary as well as permanent exhibitions—paintings, drawings, prints, sculpture, photography, etc., of both Israeli and foreign artists from the 16th century to the present. Films, concerts and lectures are also offered to the public. It's open Sunday to Thursday from 10 a.m. to 10 p.m., Saturday 10 a.m. to 2 p.m. and 10 to 11 p.m., closed Friday. Fees are SH4 ($1.20) for an adult, SH1 (30¢) for a child.

Beit Bialik Museum, 22 Bialik St., tel. 03-651530, was the home of the great Hebrew writer Haim Nachman Bialik, and it remains for all to see just as it was when he died. His 94 books, with translations in 28 languages, are there, as are articles, correspondence, paintings, photographs and an archive of hundreds of his manuscripts. Moshe Ungerfeld, who manages the museum, was a great friend of Bialik's, and if you know Hebrew or Yiddish he will tell you many interesting stories about him. It is a favorite visiting place of school classes. Open daily 9 a.m. to 7 p.m., till 1 p.m. on Friday. Closed on Saturday.

Just up the street is the **Museum of the History of Tel Aviv,** at No. 27, tel. 03-653052. Photographs and documents tell the story of the city's founding and early history. Open Sunday through Thursday from 9 a.m. to 3 or 4 p.m., until 1 p.m. on Friday. Entrance fee is minimal, free on Saturdays when they're open from 10 a.m. to 2 p.m.

A new museum is the **Israel Theatre Museum,** 3 Melchet St., tel. 03-292686, housing historic memorabilia and documents of the Jewish theater. Open Sundays to Thursdays, 9 a.m. to 2 p.m. Buses 4 and 5.

The Tel Aviv **home of David Ben-Gurion** is open to the public. It stands on Ben-Gurion Blvd., tel. 03-221010. The personal items belonged to Paula and David Ben-Gurion and are shown as they were when they lived here. The library comprises some 20,000 books and was bequeathed by Ben-Gurion himself. Open from Sunday to Friday from 8 a.m. to 1 p.m. Afternoon hours from 5 to 7 p.m. on Monday and Thursday. Open Saturdays 10 a.m. to 1 p.m. from December to April.

The **Jabotinsky Institute,** 38 King George St., in Metzudat Zeev, tel. 03-248261, is an historical research organization devoted to the study of the activist trend in the Jewish Resistance Movement. Here, archives are preserved connected with the activities of Nili, the Jewish Legion in World War I, the Revisionist Movement, Betar, Irgun Zevai Leumi, Fighters for the Freedom of Israel (Lehi), etc. Jabotinsky was a poet, writer, journalist, soldier, and founder, during World War I, of the Jewish Legion, which helped liberate Eretz Israel from Turkish rule under Field Marshal Allenby. He called into being many of the above-mentioned groups and movements as well. Attached to the Institute is a museum devoted to his life and activities—a collection that sheds a very interesting light on Israel's dramatic history. Open Sunday, Tuesday and Thursday from 8 a.m. to 3 p.m., Monday and Wednesday 8 a.m. to 1 p.m. and 6 to 8 p.m., Friday 8 a.m. to 1 p.m. Adults pay 20 agorat, students 10 agorat. Take bus 13, 24, 25, 26 or 61.

In the northern part of the city, overlooking the beach at the intersection of Dizengoff and Nordau Streets, is a handsome park with an impressive memorial—a slender eagle on a pedestal—commemorating the downed Israeli pilots of the 1948 war.

The **Tel Aviv Zoo,** tel 03-24361, is at the end of Ben-Gurion Boulevard, a street which branches off Dizengoff. It's a ten-minute walk along tree-shaded Ben-Gurion Blvd. to reach the zoo, and there you'll find a wonderful variety of animals, including giraffes, lions and leopards, splendid tropical birds, cages of monkeys, baboons, and a snake house. The zoo is now specializing in animals in danger of extinction; the Cyprus wild sheep, orangutans, Syrian bears, ibexes, black Celebes apes, black rhinoceroses, Cereopsis geese, gorillas, Swinhoe pheasants, Aldabras tortoises and wild mountain goats are now in residence in pairs. Admission is SH2 (60¢) for adults, SH1.80 (50¢) for students and children, SH1.50 (45¢) for children under eight. The zoo stays open from 8 a.m. to sunset daily, closing two hours earlier Friday. Closed Saturdays and holidays.

Safari Park is out of town at Ramat Gan, but it's really just a short bus ride from anywhere in Tel Aviv. The park is a wide-open plain (250 acres) where African animals roam free. For obvious reasons, visitors must remain in closed vehicles while traversing the five-mile trail. Admission is SH4 ($1.20) for an adult and SH3 (90¢) for a child. Private motorists can drive around as much as they want for their admission fee. You will have the opportunity to see the mighty lion, massive elephant and rhino, towering giraffe, swift gazelle, gnu, eland, impala and zebra, and the feathered ostrich, flamingo and stork. These and many more will make your visit memorable. Phone 03-762586 or 03-744981. Open daily from 9 a.m. until 3–4 p.m., until 6 p.m. in summer, until 2 p.m. on Fridays. Take bus 30 or 35 from Central Bus Station, bus 55 (which requires a bit of a walk) or bus 67.

The ZOA House (Zionist Organization of America), 1 Daniel Frish St., corner Ibn Gvirol, tel. 03-259341, always has a large choice of activities. Oneg Shabbat is held on Friday night at 9 p.m. SH3 (90¢). Its theme is Israeli folklore, which could mean singing, dancing, quizzes or anything else. Admission is SH6 ($1.75). Lectures are held in English on Thursday nights at 8 p.m.; admission SH2.50 (75¢). Plays are read (in English) the second Monday of every month; entrance fee is SH2 (60¢). Phone for information or check the newspaper for additional events.

The Tel Aviv Sailing Club P.O. Box 16285, tel. 03-224079, can be found at the marina in front of Namir (Atarim) Square near the Hilton Hotel. You can rent a sailboat here for SH13.60 ($4) an hour, a skipper for SH20.40 ($6) an hour. The marina is open from 9 a.m. to 5 p.m. daily, and there's a store called **Yamit-Sahar** there, tel. 03-229372, that sells any equipment and accessories you might desire. An alternative is merely looking—and it is a pretty sight too, seeing those white, bright and striped sails out on the waves.

FREE CONDUCTED SIGHTSEEING: If you're affiliated with some of the organized Zionist movements, you can take several free tours in the Tel Aviv area to the specific projects that have been assisted by foreign support. Every day (except Saturday), for example, **WIZO** (Women's International Zionist Organization) sponsors free escorted tours to various WIZO institutions around the city. Tours leave in the morning from 116 Hayarkon St. Phone 03-232939 the day before for reservations and schedules. For tours outside the city there is a nominal charge; afternoon tours are by previous arrangement only. . . . Right down the street is the **Hadassah Tourism Department in Israel,** Sheraton Hotel, Room 304, tel. 03-289784, which sponsors free tours to the local Youth Aliya Villages. . . . **The National Religious Women's Organizations,** 166 Ibn Gvirol St., tel. 03-440316 or 03-788942, takes members and other interested parties on tours of vocational high schools and such. Call a day or two in advance to make arrangements. . . . Likewise, the **Moetzet Hapoalot Pioneer Women,** located in the Histadrut Building, 93 Arlosoroff St., tel. 03-261111, ext. 290, will take tourists and members on a survey of its occupational, vocational and agricultural schools. Tours are not held every day, so call in advance for information and reservations. . . . The **American Mizrachi Women's Organization** leads tours daily (except Saturday) to its teen villages; apply to 16 Dov Hos St., tel. 03-220187 and 03-243106. Once again, make arrangements in advance. . . . **ORT Israel,** 39 Sderot David Hamelech, tel. 03-233231 will show you vocational training.

There are several free tours available to all tourists, simply by contacting the Tourist Office at 7 Mendele St. Also, guided tours are given of **Bar-Ilan University.** Call 03-757461 or 718506 for information and to arrange transportation. Tours of the Ramat Aviv campus of **Tel Aviv University** can be arranged by phoning 03-420945 or 413516; phone 03-422741 from 10 a.m. to noon. If you want to be taken through **Tel Aviv City Hall,** contact the I.G.T.O. or the Municipality Office for details.

MISCELLANY: If you're near a radio, try to catch the English language **Jerusalem Calling** program from 2 to 2:30 p.m. It frequently posts visitors on special events of interest to them. There's an English news broadcast at 7 a.m. and another 8–8:15 p.m. . . . You may see advertisements for a program called **An Evening of Israel Folklore and Dance.** It is held at various hotels in Tel Aviv and Haifa and at the Artists' House in Jerusalem. . . . With all of Haifa's bookstores and all of Jerusalem's professors, Tel Aviv nevertheless has more streets named after writers than those two cities. Among the many Tel Aviv streets honoring the scribes are Ben Yehuda, Shalom Aleichem, Yehuda Halevi, Bialik, Ahad Ha'am, Peretz, Mendele, Rambam, and even Emile Zola, a non-Jew who espoused a famous Jewish cause when he proclaimed the innocence of Alfred Dreyfus. . . . At **Beit HaHayal,** the Soldier's House, corner Weizmann and Pinsker, tourists are welcome in the afternoon or evening for concerts, art shows, snacks and so forth; chamber ensembles perform there, as do avant-garde musical groups—producing what's been called by some "the best music in Israel". . . . And speaking of embassies, keep in mind that each has a library open to the public, with newspapers and magazines as well as books and films. . . . If you're a country club joiner, check out foreign memberships at the **Tel Aviv Country Club** on the northern outskirts of town, with huge tennis courts and so forth. Non-members may pay to use the facilities. See the "Accommodations" section above for more information. . . . Opera buffs might find the **Israel Opera,** 1 Allenby Rd., tel. 03-657227, interesting, even if the audiences don't beg encores and shout bravos. . . . And dance enthusiasts should check around for tickets to the **Bat Dor Dance Theater,** 30 Ibn Gvirol, tel. 03-263178, and the much-proclaimed **Bat Sheva Ballet,** 9 Hahaskala Blvd., tel. 03-335597. . . . **Weight Watcher Society** members might check out the Tel Aviv meetings, held at 23 Arlosoroff on Sunday, Tuesday and Thursday at 7 p.m. Phone 03-222131. . . . Weight lifters or others who like to work out in gyms can investigate the **Mercaz Maccabi,** 58 Ibn Gvirol, fourth floor, tel. 03-264238. Perhaps you can use one of their gyms (if not, they'll refer you to the right place). Hours: 8 a.m. to 6 p.m., until 1 p.m. on Friday. . . . Bicycling buffs should contact the **Israel Bicycle Touring Club,** 20 Ben Yehuda St., tel. 03-297353 and 293996. . . . If you would like to buy the work of kibbutz artists in a variety of decorative arts, go to **Kibbutz Arts & Crafts,** 19 Frishman St., tel. 03-229426. Open 9 a.m. to 8 p.m. daily, 9–11 a.m. on Friday. . . . **MEMSI,** the automobile club of Israel, is headquartered in Tel Aviv, at 19 Petach Tikva Rd.; tel. 03-622961—this is the same number to call for all MEMSI emergency road service throughout Israel.

Municipal Libraries: Central Library in Jaffa, 45 Jerusalem Blvd. (for some odd reason it is registered as Hatchiya St. corner Hatkuma as well), tel. 03-820419; Sha'ar Zion Library, 25 Shaul Hamelech Blvd., tel. 03-251719; Beit Bialik, 22 Bialik St., tel. 03-651530; A.M.L.I. Music Library, 26 Bialik St., tel. 03-658106; Ariel Library, 32 Ben Yehuda, tel. 03-298320; Migdal Shalom Library, 5 Hashahar St., tel. 03-651165.

Ticket Offices: Hakartis, 31 Allenby, tel. 03-297665; Kanaf, 83 Allenby, tel. 03-295566; Kohav, 113 Allenby, tel. 03-623925; Rokoko, 93 Dizengoff, tel. 03-223663; Yoki, 14 Kikar Dizengoff, tel. 03-222445, second floor; Union, 118 Dizengoff, tel. 03-248518.

2. The Suburbs

Within a half-hour of Tel Aviv are some eight or so suburban residential communities, many of which were born when Tel Aviv ran out of elbow room. Before we go into the somewhat brief particulars, please note that for detailed data on accommodations in Herzlia, Bat Yam and other nearby coastal areas, see our "Golden Coast" chapter.

BAT YAM: Meaning "Daughter of the Sea," Bat Yam is 3½ miles south of Tel Aviv, right on the beach. It is a summer resort community, with fine wide beaches. Population: 130,000.

HOLON: A half-mile southeast of Bat Yam, Holon was founded in 1933 by settlers who eventually transformed the shifting sand dunes into an aggressively industrial city. (Present population: 120,000, most of whom work in textiles, metalworking, leather goods and nylon products.) Yet despite all this industrialism, Holon is a garden community of parks and tree-lined streets. In the town is a handsome old-age home—a collection of modest bungalows, pretty gardens, a library and community dining hall. There's also a Samaritan Colony here.

RAMAT GAN: "Garden Heights" is what this one means, and it's located, gardens and all, two miles east of Tel Aviv. Also an industrial community, Ramat Gan is the upper-middle class suburbia of Tel Aviv, with many private houses, flourishing gardens, and a population of 150,000. In the large garden opposite the police station stands a striking monument to the heroism of an Irgun fighter, Dov Gruner, who was captured when his group raided a British police station, and later hanged, in 1947, in Acre prison. The statue, a small struggling lion wrestling with a big powerful lion, symbolizes the clash between the young Lion of Judah and the great Lion of England. Inscribed are the words: "A few against many."

In Ramat Gan, the "village" of **Kfar Hamaccabia**—which looks like a group of college dormitories—was built by sports enthusiasts to accommodate the international athletes who participate in the Maccabee Games. But since the games are held once every four years, and in order not to let the investment go to waste, the rooms are rented out between games, the swimming pool remains in use, and the dining room offers first-class service and kosher meals.

A nice thing about this hotel-like village is that it offers accommodations in differing price categories, from single rooms to 12-bed dormitories. Large, clean and attractive, the rooms go for SH71.40 ($21) to SH85 ($25) single, SH44.20 ($13) to SH51 ($15) per person double—including the use of the big swimming pool. Dormitory beds (three or more to a room) go for as little as SH27.20 ($8), also including swimming, and they're perfect for younger travelers. Bus 30 and 35 from the Central Station in Tel Aviv takes you out here, a mere 20-minute ride. Telephone 03-749711. It is a five-minute walk from Safari Park.

Also in Ramat Gan is **Bar Ilan University** which emphasizes Judaic studies in conjunction with major academic subjects. The campus accommodates 8,000 students, of whom 1,000 are from abroad. The faculties include humanities, Judaic studies, languages and literature, social sciences, natural sciences, and mathematics, and there are professional schools of education, social work, and law. Tours are conducted on weekday mornings, and they visit the computer center, the central library and the scientific laboratories, among other things. For further information, call 03-757461 or 718506. Guests may dine in the cafeteria and have a three-course meal for as little as SH9 ($2.65). Take bus 45, 64, 68, 69 or 70 from Tel Aviv. The University has a month-long summer course (Ulpan) which visiting students can take for SH210 ($62), and other courses for which students can get credits. Apply to Bar Ilan's U.S. office at 641 Lexington Ave., New York, N.Y. 10022

BNEI BRAK: This one's an Orthodox Jewish community founded in 1924, located one mile east of Ramat Gan. The town houses a cluster of yeshivas and other religious institutions.

PETACH TIKVA: Meaning "Gate of Hope," Petach Tikva was begun as a moshava in 1878, built with the help of Baron Benjamin Edmond de Rothschild. A stone archway commemorates Rothschild's influence on this town of 115,000. The Petach Tikva synagogue was the first to be built in a Jewish village in modern times. Seven miles east of Tel Aviv and highly industrial, Petach Tikva is nevertheless surrounded by about 1,500 acres of orange groves.

SAVYON: Organized by a South African group, Savyon is a posh community, eight miles southeast of Tel Aviv. Many expensive villa-type houses are found here—also a tennis club, swimming pool and gardens of iris, tulip and gladioli.

ZAHALA: Zahala is a pleasant garden suburb which started out as a community for the families of career army personnel.

HERZLIA: Ten miles north of Tel Aviv, Herzlia was founded in 1924 as an agricultural community. Later it made the switch to industry, and now it earns much of its income from a spate of luxury hotels on the seafront (see Chapter VII).

3. Jaffa

Jaffa, now an integrated component in the sprawling Tel Aviv–Jaffa complex has a long and colorful history, dating back to biblical times. It was the principal port area of Palestine prior to the British decision to create a new harbor in Haifa. The old oriental town of bazaars, peeling buildings and narrow cul de sacs is rich in history and legend. The old Arab site was noisy, dirty, sleepy, and indigenous to a different age. Many of the earliest Zionist settlers opted for Jaffa before Tel Aviv began to emerge out of the northern sand dunes. Crusaders, pilgrims, and occasional merchants considered the city the "port of Jerusalem," although alighting meant trudging several yards through the water or riding the back of an Arab porter, and cargo was physically manhandled from rowboats by chains of men.

Jaffa and Tel Aviv were like two trees planted too closely together. In the beginning, Tel Aviv fell under the austere shadow of the Arab enclave. Afterward, the trend was reversed. The old section of the city has become the starlit patio of Tel Aviv, providing an exceptional view, fine restaurants, the best artists' section in the country, refurbished streets and shops. The beachfront is being claimed for luxurious new hotels, the largest edifice being the Laromme.

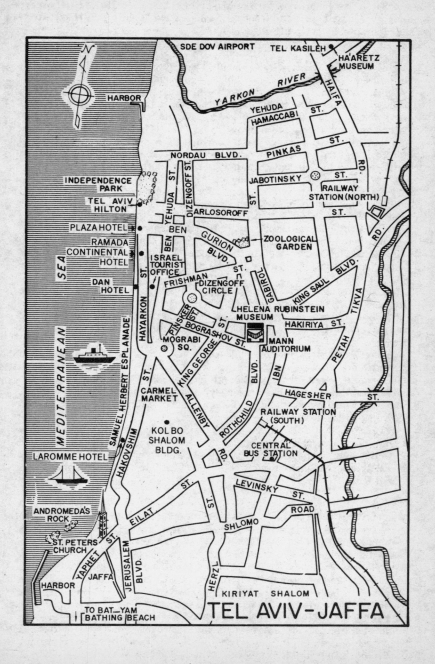

TEL AVIV-JAFFA

To get to Jaffa from Tel Aviv, take bus 8, 10, 18, 25 or 26. If you're walking, simply head south from the Shalom Tower building on Herzl Street, which eventually runs into Jaffa.

A BIT OF HISTORY: Why the name? One legend has it that Jaffa was built just after the flood by Noah's son Japhet—and hence the city's name. Another explanation is that the word "Yafah," which means "beautiful," is the town's namesake. At any rate, this is the port, the Bible tells us, where Hiram landed the Lebanon cedars for King Solomon's Temple; and from here Jonah embarked for his fabulous adventure with the whale. The Greeks were here, too, and they fostered the legend that a poor maiden named Andromeda, chained to a rock and on the verge of being sacrificed to a sea monster, was rescued by Perseus on his winged white horse. Today tourists are shown this rock. (Things haven't changed much: one historian notes that as far back as 58 B.C., and continuing into the Middle Ages, tourists were being shown the alleged broken chains that bound Andromeda and the skeleton of the fabulous marine monster that nearly did her in.)

The Crusaders came this way, of course. Richard the Lion-Hearted built a citadel here, which was promptly snatched away by Saladin's brother, who slaughtered 20,000 Christians in the process. A few hundred years or so later Napoleon passed through, a few Jewish settlers came in the 1890s, and Allenby routed the Turks from the port in 1917.

Countless ships have sunk in Jaffa port, although none so tragically as the fleet back in the second century B.C., when, persecuted by Jaffa's Greek rulers, the Hebrew citizens were lured aboard ships, taken out to the high seas, and cast overboard. This was a major factor in the subsequent revolt of the Maccabees.

Of capsized ships, one Jewish legend notes that all the sunken treasure in the world flows toward Jaffa, and that in King Solomon's day the sea offered him this rich bounty, thereby accounting for the king's wealth. According to the legend, the treasure has once again been accumulating since Solomon's time—to be distributed by the Messiah on the Day of the Coming "to each man according to his merits."

Today, Jaffa still shows traces of its romantic and mysterious past. The city is built into a kind of amphitheater on the side of a hill, thereby doubling the protection afforded by the bay, enclosed as it is by a natural promontory. The imaginative development project on the top of the hill is rapidly altering Jaffa's overall face.

SIGHTSEEING IN JAFFA: The streets from Tel Aviv run into Jaffa's Jerusalem Avenue and Tarshish Street, where a great stone tower and a Turkish Mosque remind you of the city's former occupants.

Although the 1948 war reduced Jaffa's Arab population to 5,000, the city, as you'll plainly see, has retained an oriental character, and indeed, most of the 100,000 Jewish population here is from the North African and Middle Eastern countries. In Jaffa's shops, you'll hear mainly Arabic and French, with some Rumanian, Hungarian and Yiddish thrown in for good measure. On the streets, Jaffa's children yell in Hebrew. Jaffa's oriental flavor is captured most definitely in the **Flea Market**, off Jerusalem Avenue near Olei Zion. Combing through these stalls and shops (open every day but Saturday) will produce everything from antique Bulgarian costumes to contemporary junk.

To the right through the city, up the hill, is the section called Old Jaffa.

Old Jaffa

The reclamation of Old Jaffa—only a short time ago a slum-like area of war ruins and crumbling Turkish palaces—has proven one of the most imaginative of such projects in all Israel. Atop the hill and running down in a maze of descending streets to the sea are artists' studios and galleries, outdoor cafes, fairly expensive restaurants and magnificent gift shops, all artfully arranged among the reconstructed ruins. Climb to the top of the hill and wander through the lanes (named for signs of the zodiac) at will; often an artist will invite you into his studio for a chat. At the summit is the Franciscan **Monastery of St. Peter,** which was built above a medieval citadel. You can visit the church for prayers on Sunday. Opposite the church is an excavation area, surrounded by a fence, where you can inspect remnants of a third-century B.C. catacomb. Facing the catacomb is a hilltop garden, atop which, surrounded by trees, is a white monument depicting scenes from the Bible.

Past the church gardens, on the sea side of the hill, is a small and charming cafe. Wander through the elaborately decorated and lit dome-roofed room and out onto the deck, from which the all-encompassing view of Tel Aviv and the Mediterranean coastline is superb. Incidentally, Andromeda's rock is the most prominent of those blackened stones jutting up from the floor of the bay. The view is the most brilliant in the morning sunlight. At night it takes on more of a fairytale aura, with the Tel Aviv lights glittering on the curved coastline, especially when viewed from the gardens behind and below.

Do make it a point to visit a gallery or two up here: some of Israel's top artists are now working in Jaffa. You can see some exceptionally fine exhibitions. Note the Yemenite-designed and contemporary jewelry. Unfortunately, seeing is just about all a budget traveler can do in Old Jaffa, as the price tabs reflect the unquestionable quality.

Jaffa's Port

Frank Carpenter, that venerable travel writer of the '20s solemnly declared that the harbor of Jaffa is one of the worst in the world. In his 1926 *Holy Land* book, he recounted how the small boat that took him from his liner to the port bobbed up and down so much that his luggage was soaked. Worse yet, he reported, was the treatment accorded to passengers of steerage and third class, who came into this port. They "were hung over the sides of the deck of the steamer by the arms, and dropped into the boats, twelve or more feet below. Some of the women screamed as they fell, making the rocks re-echo with their cries, as though the beautiful Andromeda were still chained there."

Old-timers in Israel recall similar experiences during the days when they landed at Jaffa port. Several people who immigrated in the '20s have told us it was the custom to be transported ashore on the shoulders of Arab porters who waded through the water.

Today, replaced by the modern harbor at Haifa and the newest port, at Ashdod, Jaffa port basks only in former glories.

Simon's House

Christian tradition places the house of Simon the Tanner next to the lighthouse of the port, at the site of a small mosque. Acts 10 recalls St. Peter's visit to Simon's house in "Joppa."

Museum of Antiquities

The Museum building was a Turkish administrative and detention center during the previous century. Care has been taken to preserve its vaulted ceilings and archways. Displays in the five halls are of objects and finds that have been concealed beneath Jaffa for hundreds to thousands of years and were excavated from 30 sites within the city. They cover a time span from the fifth millennium B.C. ending with the Arab period. Located at 10 Mifratz Shlomo, tel. 03-825375, on a hill facing the sea, it is open between 9 a.m. and 4 p.m. daily, until 1 p.m. on Friday. Tickets are SH1 (30¢) for adults, half price for children and students. On Saturday and holidays admission is free, and the hours are 10 a.m. to 2 p.m. Take bus 10, 18 or 46.

The Flea Market

Tradition has it that you can get the best buy here early Sunday morning. If you are the first customer on the first day of the week, the seller hopes a quick sale will bring him luck through the week. The market is a tight group of alleys east of the Clock Tower. It is roofed, which makes it good for all seasons, and you can weave your way in and out sorting through a mixed array of treasures and junk. The kinds of merchandise change from time to time, but copper, brass and jewelry are always to be found. Bargaining is the order of the day and expected. In the end it really comes to how much the item is worth to you, but feel free to indulge in lengthy haggling. Even if there is a little language problem, you can get a lot understood with your hands. It's great fun even if you don't buy anything.

RESTAURANTS: Eating places abound in Jaffa. Seafood is plentiful, some restaurants specialize in spicy Mediterranean dishes, and there is the haute cuisine of the elegant and high-priced restaurants.

For those who have been seeing Jaffa by day, there is the **Milk Bar,** Kedumim Square in the Old City. It is a large, attractive place facing into the square, with outdoor service as well. The interior has a medieval look, with high arched ceilings, leather-backed chairs, brown-tiled tables, and dark marble floors. An order of blintzes with sour cream is SH5.50 ($1.60) for two, waffles topped with nuts and maple syrup are SH5 ($1.45), egg and cheese toast is SH3.50 ($1). Open daily from 10:30 a.m. until midnight.

A favorite year in and year out is **Yunis Restaurant** Street 60 (some know it as Kedem Street), which is famous in Tel Aviv for serving some of the best-prepared Arab food in all Israel at exceptionally reasonable prices. It's almost impossible to tell you how to find the restaurant—walk down the hill from Kedumim Square passing the Old Jaffa port; just keep asking and don't give up. When you get there, you'll find a plain cafe-style entrance and tables set up in two tree-shaded courtyards out back. There are 15 salads to choose from and enjoy with pitta, olives and sharp peppers. Three lamb chops or three skewers of lamb with salad and rice cooked with lentils are SH9 ($2.65). They grill fish crisp on the outside and juicy inside here (price according to size), and you have your choice of mullet, grouper, drum, or St. Peter's fish. Perhaps you'd like to try the fooul (ground hot broad beans done in a special way), siniyah (baked ground beef in a tomato or tchina sauce) or another of the numerous exotic dishes. Coffee is on the house—except on Saturdays and Jewish holidays, when they are too busy feeding hungry people to make coffee at all. There is no service charge so do tip. Closed on Moslem holidays. Open daily otherwise from 6 a.m. to after midnight.

The Tripoli, 27 Raziel St., is a family-run restaurant that specializes in couscous for SH9 ($2.65); other choices are charami—a fish in piquant sauce for SH6.50 ($1.90), mafrum—potatoes stuffed with meat in a sauce for SH6.50 ($1.90), and green peas with meat and a stuffed vegetable for SH8 ($2.35). Chips and salad are served with all the above. The Tripoli is open 8 a.m. to 1 a.m., closing Friday at 4 p.m. until Saturday at 7 p.m.

Out by the Blumfield Stadium, first choice for dining after a soccer game, is the **Ha' Nemala Restaurant,** 44 Hatkuma St., tel. 03-829175. The name means "the ant," and it refers not to the available fare, but to the slow and ponderous ant-like work the Syrian-Yemenite owners put into building the place. You can order ten different kinds of meat, including ham, for SH9 ($2.65), a choice of about a dozen salads at SH1.50 (45¢) each, stuffed vegetables for SH2 (60¢). For dessert there's a rich chocolate souffle or Bavarian cream at SH2.50 (75¢). Coffee and tea are gratis. Students get a 10% reduction. Open daily from noon to 1 a.m.

NIGHTLIFE: Between them, Tel Aviv and Jaffa are the nightlife centers of Israel. Their clubs have been the breeding ground for almost every Israeli singer who has gone on to international popularity. But the real center of things—Israel's Montmartre—is located in Old Jaffa, on the side of the hill that slopes down toward Tel Aviv, where creative minds have taken wrecked Turkish baths and once-grand palaces and wrought several different and very esoteric clubs. They are, however, almost all wildly expensive and should be prudently saved for that one "big splurge" evening out of your Israeli vacation.

A very exotic club is the **Omar Khayam,** 5 Netiv Hamazaloth, tel. 03-825865, a huge room in an old Arab mansion, with lofty vaulted ceilings and stone walls. Omar Khayam abounds with atmosphere—fish netting strung about, soft candles on every table. Top Israeli singers and pianists appear nightly. Open at 9:30 p.m. until 1:30 a.m. The show starts at 10:45 p.m., but come earlier to get good seats. The show is in Hebrew and English. Admission, including one drink, is SH18.50 ($5.45) Sunday to Thursday nights, SH20 ($5.85) Friday and Saturday nights. A second drink is IL50. Upstairs is the studio of artist Schlomo Zafrir, whose works are sold internationally and are exhibited in many museums.

Glowing among the trees up the hillside behind the Antiquity Museum is the **Caravan Night Club,** 10 Mifratz Shlomo, tel. 03-828255, whose high-arched windows offer a magnificent view of the Tel Aviv–Jaffa area. (Framed by two mosques and the tall Jaffa minaret in the foreground, and bounded by the Mediterranean breakers on the west, the Tel Aviv coastline gracefully curls northward in a busy, crowded, serpentine panorama.) The club opens at 8 p.m. There is dancing until 10:30 p.m., when there is a show of international artists (including striptease). Dancing is resumed after the show. Cover charge is SH5 ($1.45) on weekdays, SH11 ($3.25) on Fridays, when a light drink is included. Saturday night entrance is SH6 ($1.75), not including a drink; Saturday afternoon you can see the same show at 5 p.m. for SH5 ($1.45). Alcoholic drinks begin at SH3.50 ($1). Closing time is about 2 a.m.; closed entirely on Sundays.

One of the most popular clubs in Jaffa, **The Cave,** 14 Kikar Kedumim, tel. 03-829018, is housed in an 800-year-old building that was once a Turkish bath. The cavernous nightclub is down a flight of stairs, and it's usually packed. The rollicking show features a four-piece combo, pantomimists, singers, dancers, and comedians. Entrance fee is a steep SH30.60 ($9), which includes a glass of champagne; a second drink will cost you SH10.20 ($3), half that for a soft drink. Down another flight of steps is the **Little Cave,** catering to a younger—

early 20s—crowd. Here the entertainment consists of a pianist, singer, and disco, and the entrance fee is SH8.50 ($2.50), about a dollar more on Friday nights; one drink is included. Action at the upstairs club begins about 10:45 p.m., a bit earlier at the Little Cave.

HAIFA

1. The City
2. Half-Day Excursions
3. Suggestions for Tours from Your Haifa Base

MOST HAIFA RESIDENTS feel sorry for anyone who doesn't live there. After visiting Haifa, you may well agree. Some compare the town, beautifully situated on a hill overlooking a broad bay, to San Francisco and Naples . . . and it's hard to be more complimentary than that.

Israel's third-largest city (population 250,000; 30% are Christians and Moslems), and the capital of the north, Haifa is like a triple-decker sandwich—the raucous port area being the first tier; the clean and efficient business district (**Hadar**), higher up, being the second; the enchanting **Carmel** district, nestled even higher on the upper pine slopes, constituting the third.

A QUICK HISTORY: Almost every square foot of Israel has been populated since earliest ages, and Haifa is no exception. The prophet Elijah knew this territory well—from the top of Mt. Carmel, he won a major victory over 450 priests of Baal (I Kings 18:19-40) during the reign of King Ahab and his notorious wife Jezebel. Also in biblical times, the Phoenician harbor center Zalemona thrived here, with predominantly Greek settlers, and the Jewish agricultural village of Sycaminos (sometimes called Shikmona) clung to the northwestern peak of Mt. Carmel (third-century Talmudic literature mentions both towns).

The Crusaders called the area Caife, Cayphe and sometimes Caiphas—which suggests the modern town's name might stem from Caiaphas, the name of Jerusalem's high priest during the days of Jesus.

Once a center of glass and cochineal-purple industries, Haifa was destroyed when the Arabs reconquered the area, and it virtually slept until the late 19th century when Jewish idealists moved into the area. Even with a population of 10,000 at the beginning of the 20th century, the city as we know it today scarcely existed: the huge port area was still a tangled marsh, with Bedouins encamped on nearby sand dunes. In the Carmel hills above the city, shepherds brought their flocks to graze.

Haifa got its first shot in the arm in 1905, when the Haifa–Damascus Railway was built. The Balfour Declaration and British occupation boosted it some more, as did a 1919 railway link to Egypt. But the real kick-off came when the British built its modern harbor—an arduous enterprise begun in 1929 and completed in 1934. Thereupon Haifa began its transformation into the vital trading and communications center it is today, taking on major importance as a shipping base, naval center and terminal point for oil pipelines. For some reason, the ancient engineers of Caesarea, Athlit, Achziv and Acre—the most historic ports along Israel's coast—had never foreseen the advantages of building a major harbor at this point on the Mediterranean coast, naturally sheltered by the Carmel mountains.

One visionary, however, did realize the future role of Haifa. In 1898, when he sailed past the spot that was to become modern Haifa, he foresaw that "huge liners rode at anchor" and at "the top of the mountain there were thousands of white homes and the mountain itself was crowned with imposing villas. . . . A beautiful city had been built close to the deep blue sea. . . ." He saw "a serpentine road to Mount Carmel." The visionary was Theodor Herzl, father of Zionism, who recorded these prophesies in his book, *Old New Land.* Miraculously, the city developed precisely along the lines he predicted.

The vision of the Zionist leader was a reality for hundreds of thousands of immigrants, whose first glimpse of the Promised Land came as they crowded the rails, their ships drawing through the morning haze, with Haifa looming up on the Carmel hills before them. The port below, the Baha'i dome shining in the lower hills, and the mountain clustered with forests and houses, was like the sight of heaven for the tides of homeless, scarred refugees who fled here after the war.

On April 21, 1948, Haifa became the first major city controlled by Jews after the end of the British Mandate and the U.N. Partition decision in 1947. Although Haifa's previous growth had already spurred development of residential areas such as Bat Galim, Hadar Hacarmel, Neveh-Shaanan and even Herzlia, the new wave of immigration (more than 100,000) gave rise to others: Ramot Ramez, Kiryat Elizer, Neveh Yosef and Kiryat Shprinzak. Haifa Bay, east of the port, became the "backbone" of the country's heavy industries, with oil refineries and associated industries, foundries, glass factories, fertilizer and chemical industries, cement works, textile manufacturing and yards for shipbuilding and repair in preponderance. Plans are now in progress to convert the areas southwest of the port into Israel's own "Riviera." (The beaches are already excellent.)

1. The City

Israelis say that Tel Aviv is the place for fun, Jerusalem for learning and Haifa for work. Haifa does have a brisk workingman's flavor about it, although the residents bristle when one implies that the town is just a "bourgeois workers' village"—a favorite taunt of Tel Avivians.

Of all its graces, Haifa is richest in panoramic views. It is also a marvelously clean city, perhaps because of the strong German-Jewish influence in the city.

For purposes of orientation, you might think of Haifa as already described —a city built on three levels. Whether you come by ship, bus or train, you will arrive on the first or the **port** level of the city. The second level, **Hadar Ha'Carmel**, meaning "Glory of the Carmel," is referred to simply as the **Hadar.** This is the central business section, with the majority of restaurants, hotels and shops. At the top of the hills is the **Carmel** district, primarily a residential neighborhood but with several superbly situated hotels.

TRANSPORTATION: The Carmelit (the subway) is a fast and efficient means of getting up and down Haifa's various levels. Its terminal station is located on Jaffa Road, a few blocks north of the port entrance and not far from the central (Mercaz) railway station. If you have trouble finding it, just ask

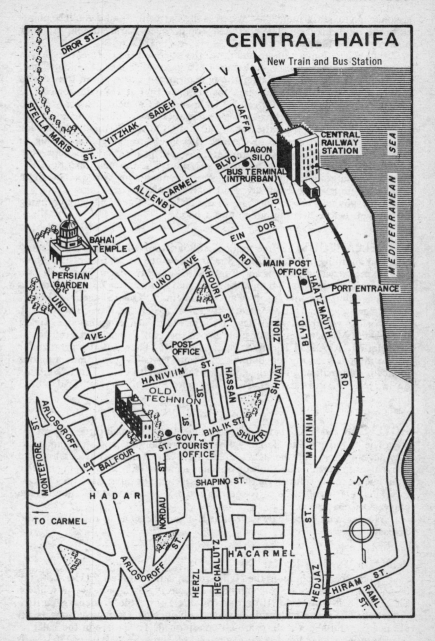

CENTRAL HAIFA

New Train and Bus Station

CENTRAL
RAILWAY
STATION

MEDITERRANEAN SEA

DROR ST.

STELLA MARIS ST.

YITZHAK

SADEH ST.

JAFFA BLVD.

DAGON SILO

BUS TERMINAL (INTRURBAN)

ALLENBY

CARMEL

EIN DOR RD.

RD.

BAHA'I TEMPLE

PERSIAN GARDEN

UNO

UNO AVE.

AVE.

KHOURI ST.

MAIN POST OFFICE

HAATZMAUTH

PORT ENTRANCE

POST OFFICE

HANIVIIM

OLD TECHNION

ST.

ST.

ST.

HASSAN

ST.

BIALIK ST.

SHUKRI

SHIVAT ZION

BLVD.

RD.

MAGINIM

ARLOSOROFF ST.

MONTEFIORE ST.

BALFOUR

GOVT. TOURIST OFFICE

ST.

NORDAU ST.

SHAPINO ST.

HADAR

TO CARMEL

ARLOSOROFF ST.

HERZL

HECHALUTZ

HACARMEL

ST.

HEDJAZ ST.

HIRAM ST.

RAML ST.

anyone, "Ayfo ha'Carmelit?"—"Where is the Carmelit?"—and you'll be pointed in the right direction. The port area stop is called **Paris Station,** in honor of its French builders.

Pulled on a long chain up and down the steep hill the Carmelit resembles a sort of scale-model Metro, with only 1,800 yards of tunnel. It's picturesque, yes—and it also happens to offer the best means of getting from the port to Hadar and Carmel. There are six stops in all. Get off at **Hanviim** for central Hadar and at **Gan Ha'em** for central Carmel. The Carmelit costs only SH.06 (15¢) and is much quicker than a bus or sherut (trains run every ten minutes).

It is a long walk from the bus or rail station to the Carmelit, so take bus 10 or 12 to Hadar, bus 22 to Carmel. Bus fares are charged according to destination. In Haifa, buses run on Saturday, except for the hours between 6 p.m. Friday night and 9 a.m. Saturday morning. The Carmelit operates daily from 5:30 a.m. to midnight and does not run from an hour before sundown on Friday to sundown on Saturday. And taxis can always be found.

Note: you may check your bags in Bat Galim at Egged's baggage checking department before heading out to find a hotel.

MISCELLANEOUS: A free guided **walking tour** of Haifa departs every Saturday morning at 10 a.m. from Sha'ar Halevanon St., corner of Panorama St. Commentary is in Hebrew and English. . . . Monday afternoons at 5:30 p.m. and Saturday evenings at 8 p.m. during July and August, free **open-air concerts** and other entertainments are given at Gan Ha'em. . . . **Oneg Shabbat**—a Friday evening get-together with songs and stories—is free at the Dan Carmel Hotel. . . . A visitor who spends three days in the city is given a **complimentary ticket** to all Haifa Municipal museums; inquire at the **Haifa Tourism Development Association,** 10 Achad Ha'am St., tel. 04-665645. They can also arrange for you to meet Israelis in their homes. . . . Phone 04-640840 any time of day or night for information, in English, about **Haifa activities.** . . . The **I.G.T.O.** is on 18 Herzl St., in Hadar, tel. 04-666521; open 8 a.m. to 6 p.m., Friday till 3 p.m.

HOTELS IN HAIFA: There are good budget lodgings in all three areas of the city. The majority are in Hadar—close to the restaurants and shops and with easy accessibility to all the sights. There are a few in the port area, which are convenient to the bus and train stations, and a cluster of hotels, ranging in price from budget to big splurge, on the hills of Carmel. The latter have the choicest locations in terms of rustic surroundings and magnificent views—and often the choicest of tariffs, too.

The seasonal price scale for rooms is about the same as in Tel Aviv and Jerusalem.

From the Port to Hadar

An inexpensive hotel in the Hadar region is the **Nesher,** 53 Herzl St., tel. 04-640644. The two-star, 15-room hotel charges high-season prices as follows: SH29.60 ($8.70) to SH34 ($10) per person single or double. Students get a 10% reduction. The pastel-painted rooms have running water, ten have showers, all are heated, and about a third are air-conditioned. Toilets are in the hall.

Another Hadar hotel is the **Talpioth,** 61 Herzl St., tel. 04-662753, with 24 rooms, all heated (nine air-conditioned), over half with private shower, and two with bath and toilet facilities. Students receive a 15% reduction from

November to February. Rates are SH34 ($10) to SH40.80 ($12) single, SH27.20 ($8) to SH30.60 ($9) per person in a double room.

On Carmel

If you'd prefer a room in the quieter and more expensive part of the city, you'll be pleased to know that, while most of the "rooms at the top" are decidedly in the higher purse range, there are at least a few pensions suited to less extravagant spenders. One is the **Pension and Hotel Lea**, 14 Habroshim Ave., tel. 04-81567, a guest house surrounded by shady gardens with benches. There are nine bright and homey rooms, all with cold water and shared facilities. The dining room faces the garden. Cost of a single room is SH36 ($10.60) to SH50.30 ($14.80), SH39.40 ($11.60) per person for a double room. Breakfast is SH10.20 ($3) extra, lunch or dinner SH21.70 ($6.40).

The **Wohlman Hotel**, 16 Sea Rd., tel. 04-81884, is a two-story white house perched on a hill and containing five rooms for rent. Rates are SH68 ($20) single, SH51 ($15) per person double. Every room comes with a private bath or shower, toilet, and telephone, is brightly decorated, and has a terrace. There is a small TV lounge. Breakfasts are included.

The **Dvir Hotel**, Panorama Rd., tel. 04-83717, 82777, has a fantastic view of the city. The hotel is managed by the Dan Hotel Corp., which operates a hotel school on the premises. Amenities are appropriate to the Dan image, but prices are quite reasonable. A single room costs SH54.40 ($16) to SH78.20 ($23) double occupancy SH47.60 ($14) apiece. The low-season rates for the same accommodations are a few dollars less. Breakfasts are wholesome and Israeli. Highly recommended.

At the three-star **Ben Yehuda Hotel** there's an outdoor swimming pool, and every room is provided with bath and balcony. It is in a slightly out-of-the-way location on western Carmel—154 and 179 Sea Rd., tel. 04-80023/28—but buses 3 and 5 pass every ten minutes from 5:30 a.m. to 9 p.m., after which bus 35 takes over until 11:30 p.m. All of the 59 rooms have private toilet, bath or shower, phone, air conditioning, heating, and terraces. They're nicely decorated with throw rugs on the floor and floral-design curtains. Facilities include a swimming pool and a kosher dining room. Rates are SH45.90 ($13.50) to SH62.90 ($18.50) single, SH37.40 ($11) to SH45.90 ($13.50) per person double; full board is SH37.40 ($11) extra.

Beth Shalom Carmel, 110 Hanassi Blvd., tel. 04-80481, is a Protestant guesthouse, open to all comers, with 34 rooms. All are clean and airy, and equipped with phones, heating, private bath or shower, and toilet. The rate for double occupancy is $12 per person; meals are an additional SH5 ($1.50) each.

Hospices

The **Bethel Hostel** (Protestant), 40 Hagefen St., tel. 04-521110, has seven clean, colorful rooms with double- and triple-decker bunks which cost SH7.50 ($2.20) per night. Rooms have heaters, and showers are on the premises. No meals are served, except on the Sabbath, when you can get hot cereal, eggs, toast with jam, and tea or coffee for SH2 (60¢); a grocery store is nearby. There's a recreation room with table tennis. Curfew is 10 p.m., and guests must be out by 8:30 a.m. each morning. Maximum stay is three days.

RESTAURANTS: Haifa can cater to every culinary taste and pocketbook. The eateries are everywhere, escalating in price and geographic levels from the felafel stands adjacent to the port area to the Dan Carmel Grill Room overlooking the Mediterranean from one of Israel's most scenic spots. There are a couple of expensive Chinese restaurants and a plethora of more modest establishments where tourist and citizen can feast for the equivalent of about four dollars.

Around the Port

Right in the bus/train station is **Egged's Restaurant,** not the most romantic place to dine but very cheap. There's a full menu for SH13.50 ($3.95)—soup, chicken or meat course, vegetables and dessert—and filling à la carte dishes are in the SH7 ($2.05) range. Open from 7 a.m. to 4 p.m., closed Saturdays.

Olamei Hod, in the Bat Galim Railway Station, opened in 1979. An SH6.80 ($2) breakfast here consists of an egg, cheese, salad, bread and margarine, and tea or coffee. For SH13.60 ($4) you can have a complete lunch—soup, roast chicken, cole slaw, potatoes, salad, bread, and pudding or fresh fruit compote. It's a cheerful air-conditioned restaurant, with tables covered in colorful prints and adorned with flowers. Open Sunday to Thursday from 6:30 a.m. to 8 p.m., Friday till 4 p.m., closed Saturday.

The Abu Yusuf Restaurant, 29 Al Zisu St., near the new railway station, tel. 04-527583, provides a good assortment of Arab food. Shashlik made from pork costs SH8 ($2.35), same price for fried fish, or meat with humus in a pitta. Homemade Arab yogurt costs SH1.20 (35¢), and the locally produced sahlab pudding sells for SH1 (30¢). Open Saturday to Thursday from 7:30 a.m. to 10 p.m., Friday till 6 p.m.

The **U.N.O. Restaurant,** 10 Hatzionoot Ave. (Zionism Ave.), tel. 04-531046, offers tasty Arab fare in pleasant surroundings. Tables are covered with red cloths and enhanced by vases of flowers. There are 30 salads to choose from at SH3 (90¢) a portion. Humus with pine nuts for SH3 (90¢) is a delicious appetizer; main courses include moussaka for SH5 ($1.45), lamb chops SH11 ($3.25), and kabab SH8 ($2.35). Open Saturday to Thursday from 11 a.m. to 2 a.m., Friday till 3 or 4 a.m.

The award-winning Italian fare at the **Popolo Restaurant,** 17 Ben-Gurion Blvd., tel. 04-522093, is generally above our budget, but you might consider one of their prix-fixe dinners. For SH12 ($3.55), for instance, you can have a meal of eggplant salad, canneloni, fruit salad, and coffee. A la carte you might consider pizza, priced from SH5.40 ($1.60) to SH9.90 ($2.90), or pasta dishes in the SH6 ($1.75) to SH9 ($2.65) range.

President Sadat's daughter dined at the **Pninat Hamizrah Restaurant,** 35 Ben-Gurion Blvd., tel. 04-512528, when she visited Haifa, and reportedly was delighted with the kubeh (chopped lamb with pine nuts and cracked wheat) in tchina sauce. You can try it for SH3 (90¢). Other choices include shashlik for SH8.50 ($2.50), lamb chops for SH10 ($2.95), and humus with meat for SH8 ($2.35). Open Saturday to Thursday from 7:30 a.m. to midnight, Friday till 5:30 p.m.

Located in the Haifa Mercaz Railway Station, **Miznon Harakevet,** tel. 04-662632, is both clean and cheap. There's both counter and table seating, and some tables are even outside on the platform facing the tracks. An SH10 ($2.95) fixed-price lunch menu offers vegetable soup, meatball with chips, cooked vegetable or salad, a roll, and a soft drink. A la carte you might order an omelet for SH1.50 (45¢), a roll with cheese and salami for SH1.10 (32¢), or goulash with two vegetables for SH6.50 ($1.90). Alcoholic beverages are available. Open 5:15 a.m. to 5:30 p.m., closed Friday from 2 p.m. to Sunday morning.

For dessert or afternoon tea, try the **Exodus Conditoria,** 31 Ha'atzmauth Rd., tel. 04-669072, where scores of delicious croissants, chocolate cakes, French pastries, strudels, cream cakes, etc., are displayed. Most are under SH2

(60¢), and tea or coffee is SH1.20 (35¢). Open from 7 a.m. to 6 p.m., closed Friday from 3 p.m. to Sunday morning.

In the center of the fruit market is the **Restaurant Shichmona,** at 3 Nahum Dovrin St., tel. 04-666253. It's a bit hard to find, tucked in as it is behind stalls that line one side of the narrow street. It's worth looking for, though, as much for the food—some of the best Oriental fare in the port area—as for the fascinating venture through the market. The unadorned Shichmona is frequented by a curious mixture of Haifa's businessmen, clerks and laborers. The last time we were there, we had a vegetable plate priced at SH4 ($1.20); lamb and beef dishes were in the SH7 ($2.05) to SH9 ($2.65) range. Shichmona opens Sunday through Thursday at noon and closes at 3 p.m.; on Friday it closes at 2 p.m. and remains closed till Sunday morning.

Larger, better-known, and equally excellent for oriental cuisine, is the **Iskander Restaurant,** 3 Hatzionoot Ave., tel. 04-524407. Owner Iskander Migdalani's family came here from Lebanon in 1882. He has had the restaurant since 1948, when he provided food for the Haganah; and he has many an enthralling tale to tell of those days. Half a chicken stuffed with rice, lamb, pine nuts and almonds, served with pitta and pickles, is SH9 ($2.65); humus with pine nuts and cubed meat is the same price; a salad plate (select from 35 different kinds of salad) is SH6 ($1.75). Open daily from 7 a.m. to midnight–1 a.m.

Near the entrance to the Carmelit, **Zvi Cafe-Restaurant,** on Paris Square, tel. 04-668596, offers chicken with rice and salad for SH9 ($2.65), pork chops for SH10 ($2.95), stuffed marrow or pepper for SH4 ($1.20), and Bavarian cream for dessert at SH3 (90¢). Open daily from 11 a.m. to midnight, later on Friday nights.

In the same area, **Abed's,** 1 Kikar Paris, tel. 04-663723, caters to local Arab and Druze workmen with dishes like lamb cutlets for SH11 ($3.25) and kabab for SH8 ($2.35). Also very good here, shashlik for SH9 ($2.65). All dishes come with chips, rice, or salad. Open 7 a.m. to midnight.

Naim's Restaurant, 6 Eliya St., tel. 04-604309, opposite the Carmelit, provides a steaming bowl of vegetable soup for SH2.50 (75¢), meat with okra for SH8 ($2.35), roast lamb or veal for SH8.50 ($2.50), and duck with rice for SH9 ($2.65). Heart, kidneys, and lamb testicles, should you so desire, are SH7.50 ($2.20). Open from 6:30 a.m. to 5 p.m., closing Friday at 2 p.m. until Sunday morning. Naim means "pleasant" in Hebrew and that is exactly the atmosphere.

Yet a fourth eatery near the Carmelit entrance, **Saleh Bros. Restaurant,** Kikar Paris, tel. 04-640763, is the best of this group. It's clean and spacious, with vaulted ceilings, an arched door, plant-filled front windows, Spanish-style lighting fixtures, and red-clothed tables. Try the fried eggplant appetizer for SH3 (90¢), followed by goulash or chicken for SH7 ($2.05). A salad plate is SH3 (90¢). Students get a 10% reduction. Open daily from 8:30 a.m. to midnight, later on Friday.

Shmulik and Dany Restaurant, 7 Habankim St., tel. 04-514411, is deservedly popular for first-class cuisine. The walls display awards for excellence, and glowing reviews, along with Shmulik's collection of Israeli art. Stuffed duck is SH9 ($2.65), fried chicken with vegetables SH8 ($2.35), stuffed vegetables SH3.50 ($1). Open 11:30 a.m. to 4 p.m., closed Friday from 2:30 p.m. until Sunday morning.

In Hadar

For Oriental fare, two good choices are **Diab Bros. Restaurant,** 6 Herzlia St., tel. 04-660342, offering chicken, kabab, or shashlik with rice for SH8.50 ($2.50), open 7 a.m. to 11:30 p.m., Saturday 9 a.m. to midnight; and the **Ahlan-Wesahlan Restaurant,** also at 6 Herzlia St. (open 10 a.m. to 11:30– midnight, Saturday from noon), offering a 10% reduction for students, and entrees like kabab with chips for SH8.50 ($2.50), chicken livers with chips for SH9 ($2.65), and a variety of soups and salads.

Though a bit more expensive than some of the other restaurants in the area, the clean and pleasant atmosphere at **Gan Armon Restaurant & Cafe,** 16 Hanviim St., tel. 04-664111, makes spending a few extra shekels worthwhile. An SH13 ($3.80) business lunch might consist of chopped liver, schnitzel with chips and salad, ice cream, and coffee. A la carte a cheese omelet with potatoes is SH8.50 ($2.50), sandwiches SH1.50 (45¢) to SH3 (90¢). Open Sunday to Thursday from 8 a.m. to midnight, Friday till 4 p.m., Saturday 9 a.m. to midnight.

Beit Hasandwich, 20 Hanviim St., Masaryk Square, tel. 04-642162, dispenses sandwiches only, on roll or pitta, garnished with a choice of vegetable, eggplant, mayonnaise salad, or sharp sauce. SH3 (90¢) will get you pastrami or turkey, SH2.50 (75¢) tuna fish, SH1.50 (45¢) egg or cheese. Fresh fruit juice is SH1.20 (35¢). Open Sunday to Thursday from 9 a.m. to 10 p.m., Friday till 2 p.m., Saturday from sunset to midnight.

For kosher take-out meals, picnic fare, and such, try **Salama & Sons,** 3 Hechalutz St., tel. 04-538628, where 3½ ounces of salad—tchina, humus, eggplant, tuna, etc.—will cost you SH1 (30¢) to SH2 (60¢); SH1.20 (35¢) will get 3½ ounces of smoked fish, SH2.50 (75¢) 3½ ounces of turkey breast. Open 7 a.m. to 7 p.m., Closed Friday from 2 p.m. to Sunday morning.

The **Coffee Shop Vegetarian Restaurant,** near the Zion Hotel at 21 Hechalutz St., sports a cheerful yellow and orange decor. Fish is served, but no meat. A platter of five veggies is SH4 ($1.20), a cheese or mushroom omelet SH3 (90¢), gefilte fish SH2.50 (75¢), blintzes SH3 (90¢), compote or pudding for dessert SH1.60 (47¢). Open 7:30 a.m. to 9 p.m., closed from before sunset on Friday until Sunday morning.

The restaurant on the third floor of the new **Hamashbir Latzarchan Department Store,** 1 Yona St., near Hanviim St., is clean and pleasant. You might have gefilte fish or spaghetti for SH3 (90¢), cheese blintzes for SH2.20 (65¢), or a sandwich for SH1.50 (45¢). Open Sunday to Thursday from 8:30 a.m. to 7 p.m., closing from Friday at 2:30 or 3 p.m. until Sunday morning.

Across the street (6 Yona) is a very good vegetarian eatery, the **Hamasbia Self-Service Restaurant,** tel. 04-666195. An SH6.80 ($2) breakfast gives you one of a choice of 20 salads, two eggs any style, cheese, bread and butter, cream or leben, and tea or coffee. For SH10.20 ($3) at lunch you can have soup or salad, a fish and vegetable main course, bread, and dessert (fresh fruit or ice cream). You can also order à la carte. Open 7:30 a.m. to 8 p.m., closed Friday from 2 p.m. until Sunday morning.

Hearty home cooking—also vegetarian only—is featured at **Haim Tzimhonia,** 30 Herzl St., a functional-looking restaurant that is always jam-packed with hungry locals at lunch. For SH6.10 ($1.80) you can have a soup, fish, and vegetable lunch; add SH1.50 (45¢) if you want dessert. A la carte, a Swedish plate (cold salads) or cooked vegetable plate is SH3 (90¢). Open 8 a.m. to 9 p.m., closed Friday from 2 p.m. until Sunday morning.

The clean and shiny **Tivoli Milk Bar,** 32 Herzl St., offers a pleasant ambience. Tables are set with flowered place mats and vases with a single flower, there's background music, and the front counter is piled high with oranges, apples, and grapefruits. You can order two blintzes for SH4.20 ($1.25), pizza or omelets for SH3.50 ($1) to SH5.20 ($1.55). Open daily from 7 a.m. to midnight.

Small and old-fashioned in decor, the **Auerbach Restaurant & Sausage Shop**, 36 Herzl St., tel. 04-662786, has been dishing up homemade kosher fare to Haifa residents for almost 50 years. A large portion of roast beef or chicken with side dishes is SH6 ($1.75), sausages SH5 ($1.50); an appetizer of stuffed derma or stuffed cabbage is SH1.50 (45¢). Open 11:30 a.m. to 8 p.m., closed from Friday at 2 p.m. until Sunday morning.

For afternoon tea or a light meal, try the **Ritz Self-Service Conditoria**, 5 Haim St. near Nordau St., tel. 04-662520. An Old World sort of place, the Ritz attends to your visual as well as gustatory pleasures—there are magazines and newspapers in full supply, and there is an art gallery on the premises. The food is excellent. Breakfast consists of coffee, two rolls, butter and jam and costs less than a dollar. Sandwiches of egg or cheese sell for SH1.70 (50¢). Cold snacks such as Russian eggs are priced at IL30 (90¢), and ice cream will run you SH2.20 (65¢). Homemade cakes, strudels, tortes, etc., are in the SH1.30 (40¢) to SH2 (60¢) range. Open 7:30 a.m. to 11 p.m., closed Friday from 3 p.m. until Sunday morning.

The Balfour Restaurant, 3 Balfour St., tel. 04-662219, is a three-in-one place: a budget eatery, a bar and a big splurge restaurant—all kosher. In the budget category is the Milk Corner, a large room with a counter to one side, which offers a daily special menu. Stuffed pepper or eggplant sells for SH3 (90¢), boiled filet of fish and one side dish SH4.50 ($1.30), soups SH1.30 (40¢). The actual restaurant, which consists of two wood-beamed dining rooms, is attractive. Top price on the meat menu is about SH25 ($7.35) for veal goulash, but you can eat for a lot less. Those with a taste for authentic East-European Jewish cooking should try the main dish of kishke and tcholent for SH7 ($2.05). Part of the Balfour is air-conditioned. The Milk Corner is open noon to midnight, closed Friday at 3 p.m. until after sunset on Saturday; the regular meat restaurant closes at 10 p.m.

The air-conditioned **Beiteinu**, 29 Jerusalem Rd., tel. 04-668059, is open from noon until 9 p.m., Friday till 2 p.m. Self-service is the order of the day. Salads, goulash, moussaka, gefilte fish, or stuffed vegetables are SH3.50 ($1); schnitzel, roast beef, or liver—all served with mashed potatoes and salad—are SH7 ($2.05) to SH7.50 ($2.20).

The non-kosher **Quick Restaurant**, 15 Nordau St., offers such exotica as Hawaiian schnitzel for SH11 ($3.25) and pork chops (exotic only in Israel) for SH8.50 ($2.50). More in the usual tradition are borscht for SH1.50 (45¢) and eggplant salad for SH2.50 (75¢). Open noon to 5 p.m., closed Friday from 2:30 p.m. until noon on Sunday.

Finally, one last Arab eatery with the romantic name of **Restaurant 1001 Nights**, 3 Daniel St., off Hanviim St., tel. 04-663704. Try the dish called *siniya* —ground meat baked in the oven with tchina sauce and topped with pine nuts—for SH9 ($2.65); other good choices are meat-filled eggplant for SH5 ($1.45) and shashlik with chips and vegetables for SH10 ($2.95). Open Sunday to Thursday from 7:45 a.m. to 10–11 p.m., Friday till 3 p.m., Saturday from 11 a.m. to midnight

Big Splurge: Peer Amram Brothers, 1 Atlit St., corner Hanviim, tel. 04-665707, is a delightful place, gaily decorated with hanging plants, brightly colored tablecloths and napkins. And the food is as good as the ambience is festive. An SH20.40 ($6) dinner consists of soup, salad, chicken or meat with chips or rice, dessert, and a soft drink or coffee. A la carte you can order lamb kabab for SH9 ($2.65), shashlik for SH10 ($2.95); Bavarian cream for dessert is SH3.50 ($1). Open daily from 7 a.m. to midnight.

On Carmel

The aroma of fresh-baked cakes and pastries will lure you into the tiny **Mul Hayam Cafeteria,** 6 Sha'ar Halevanon St., tel. 04-86184. There are only a few tables inside, a few more out on the sidewalk. An omelet and salad is SH2.50 (75¢), eggplant, vegetable, or humus salad SH1.50 (45¢), a knish SH2 (60¢). Be sure to sample the apple pie or chocolate cake for SH3 (90¢). Students get a 20% reduction. Open 8 a.m. to midnight, closed Friday from 3:30 p.m. until after sunset Saturday.

The **Cafe Restaurant Carmel,** 125 Hanassi Blvd., opposite the Supersol Supermarket, tel. 04-81082, can accommodate up to 400 people at one sitting. The establishment has tables outside on the sidewalk as well as inside. A large orange awning helps identify the place. European food is the specialty here. An English breakfast, consisting of egg, two rolls, butter, jam, and coffee or tea, costs SH6 ($1.75). Other options are three potato latkes or a mushroom omelet for SH6 ($1.75), two blintzes for SH8 ($2.35), and pancakes with maple syrup for SH4 ($1.20). Open from 8 a.m. to midnight daily, 7 a.m. to 1 a.m. in summer.

Nearby the **Peer Cafe and Restaurant,** 130 Hanassi Blvd., tel. 04-82333, which is open from 6 a.m. to midnight, serves European and oriental cuisine. It has an outdoor terrace open to the sky in summer, and has many plants inside. An order of fish and chips is SH7.50 ($2.20), Russian egg SH3.50 ($1), a vegetable platter or mushroom omelet with bread, salad, and chips SH7 ($2.05). There's a snack bar on the premises where prices are lower.

The **Cafe Rothschild,** 142 Hanassi Blvd., seats 80 diners inside and another 120 on the adjacent patio. There's self-service up to 4 p.m., when prices rise 20%. For SH7 ($2.05) you can order a plate of gefilte fish with eggplant salad, carrot salad, and other vegetables; a blintz is SH2 (60¢), pizza SH2.50 (75¢). Open from 9 a.m. to midnight, closed Friday from 3 p.m. until 4 p.m. on Saturday; in summer open Friday from 9 a.m. to 2 p.m. and 7:30 p.m. to midnight. The cuisine here is strictly vegetarian/dairy.

The **Zvika Milk Bar,** on the corner of Wedgwood and Hanassi Blvds., tel. 04-85293, offers students a 10% discount on its light-meal fare, which consists of pizza for SH2 (60¢), two blintzes for SH3.50 ($1), and the like. Open 8 a.m. to 1 a.m., Friday till 2 a.m.

One of the very nicest places for an afternoon meal—and a sun and a swim—is the **Dan Carmel Hotel,** tel. 04-86211, without doubt Haifa's poshest hotel. Surprisingly, you can do all this relatively economically; a whole day at the swimming pool is just SH7 ($2.05) for an adult, SH5 ($1.45) for a child (more on Saturday), and that includes hot showers, private deck chairs, sporting facilities, access to the adjoining gardens and, of course, the pool. As for food, the poolside coffee shop serves fish and dairy dishes, salads, cakes and soft drinks. Prices are fair, but still geared to five-star-hotel standards; you are paying not only for the food, but for the spectacular scenery and luxury services. Buses 22 and 23 will take you to the Dan Carmel.

If you just want a light meal at the Dan Carmel, then try the very nice **Sabra** coffee shop here. The sandwiches served here come with so many garnishes that they're just about a full meal in themselves. But again, the prices are high.

For an exceptionally low-cost meal—in exceptional surroundings—take bus 21/37 from Central Carmel to the campus of the **University of Haifa.** The bus ride will cost about SH.04, but the view from the campus—situated as one person said, "at the top of the world"—is worth a million. On the campus you can have lunch, dinner or a snack in the restaurant or *menza* located inside the "Multi-Purpose" building. You don't have to be a student—guests of all ages are welcome—but you do pay student prices: three-course meals for SH3.50 ($1) to SH4.50 ($1.35), and they're generous ones (soup, chicken, beef or shashlik, vegetables and dessert). These three-course menus are served from 11:30 a.m. till 2:30 p.m. There are also several snack bars on campus serving sandwiches on rolls, cakes and coffee, ice cream, juice and other such fare at prices that are comfortably within our economic guidelines.

In Bat Galim

If you find yourself in the suburb of Bat Galim, just outside Haifa on the way to Tel Aviv, try the **Pagoda Chinese Restaurant,** 1 Bat Galim Ave., tel. 04-524585. It's one of the attractions of a new promenade along Haifa's southern shore area (now under construction), which will, when completed, feature fishing areas, gardens, motels, restaurants, nightclubs, and a boardwalk made of colored cement tile. The Pagoda is an attractive place with Chinese lamps, flowers and cloths on the tables, and red-painted woodwork. The Szechuan menu lists shredded chicken with spicy sauce for SH5.40 ($1.60), Chinese salad for SH3 (90¢), cabbage in sweet and sour sauce for SH8 ($2.35), and 11 fish and shrimp dishes for SH12 ($3.50) to SH15 ($4.40). Some items are a bit above our budget, but as a welcome change from tchina and shashlik, it's worth it. Open daily from noon to 3 p.m. and 6:30 p.m. to midnight.

NIGHTLIFE IN HAIFA: Not too much in this category—which may explain why Haifa has so many movie theaters.

Frequently there's evening entertainment and dancing at the **Beit Rothschild** in the Merkaz section. And there's a **cinematique** in the building (that's an Israeli movie theater featuring art and experimental films).

Variety shows geared mostly to tourists take place nightly except Sundays at the **Theatre Club,** 50 Pevzner St., tel. 04-640956. Before the show there's a dance band. Admission is SH17.50 ($5.15) per person, SH19 ($5.60) Friday and Saturday nights; students pay SH1.50 less.

Our favorite place to hang out of an evening is the **Tea House,** 120 George Eliot St., tel. 04-82979. You can lounge about here on low couches covered with throw rugs, sipping tea and enjoying the performance (a singer) along with a superb view. Open from 9 p.m. to the wee hours, the Tea House charges SH5 ($1.50) admission during the week, SH6 ($1.75) per person on weekends, those prices including one drink.

The **Technion Students' Association,** tel. 04-234148, has entertainment of one kind or another—folk dancing, movies, dances of the 60s, live entertainment, etc.—every night except Monday. Admission price ranges from SH4.50 ($1.30) to SH8 ($2.35), depending on what's happening. Men must show student cards, women can get in without them. Call for details.

At **Haifa University,** you'll find the **I.Q. Club,** offering dancing, films, art exhibits and buffets Friday and Saturday nights from October to June, 8 p.m. to 2 a.m. You don't need to reveal yours to get in; you don't even have to say something smart. You do have to flash your student card (one card per couple is adequate) and pay an entrance fee of SH2.50 (75¢). There is also a **Student Club** offering coffee, music, and exhibitions, open Sunday to Friday from 10 a.m. to 4 p.m.; admission free; no card necessary.

SPORTS IN HAIFA: Hapoel and **Maccabi** are two sports leagues in Israel. By contacting either of these—or the Haifa Municipality or the local I.G.T.O. —you'll get the latest data on where you can play tennis, do gym exercises and workouts, or take in sports events as a spectator.

Haifa is well stocked in the water-sports department, and you'll have many excellent swimming areas from which to choose: the **Carmel Beach,** reached by bus 3 or 45 from Shapiro Street, charges SH1.90 (55¢) for adults, SH1.20 (35¢) for children, more on Saturdays. . . . **Hof Shaket,** in the harbor area of Bat Galim, reached via bus 40, 41 or 42, charges SH2 (60¢) for adults, SH1.30 (40¢) for children. . . . **Bat Galim** swimming pool and sea beach on the opposite side of the small Bat Galim promontory. Admission fees to the Olympic-size swimming pool and beach are SH2.50 (75¢) for adults, SH1.50 (45¢) for children. There are also tennis courts here, and adjoining the beach, a sandy stretch known as the **Municipal Beach,** and this—budgeteers note—is free to all comers. . . . In the central Carmel section you'll find the **Maccabi** swimming pool, adults SH3 (90¢), children SH2 (60¢), more on Saturday, serviced by bus 21, 22 or 23 and by the Carmelit (rates double in winter). . . . Open the usual May–October season, the **Hapoel** swimming pool, on Hapoel Street, charges adults SH2.50 (75¢), children SH1.60 (47¢). . . . There's also a public beach at Kiryat Haim, a Haifa suburb; take bus 51. . . . And don't forget the pool at the **Dan Carmel Hotel,** where SH7 ($2.05) will get you a whole day's worth of pool, shower and sporting privileges (for details, see the Restaurant section above). Finally, you'll find several wonderful swimming areas outside Haifa, at **Achziv, Tantura** and **Caesarea**—all described in the next chapter.

There's a **Municipal Sauna and Bath House,** tel. 04-640552, at the corner of Arlosoroff and Bezalel Streets, where tourists can undo the side effects of heavy sightseeing. For women, it's open Wednesday from 9 a.m. to 12:30 p.m.; Sunday and Tuesday from 2:30 to 9 p.m. Entrance fee is SH3.50 ($1) to SH5 ($1.45). Men are welcome on Sunday, Monday, and Wednesday from 2:30 p.m. to 9 p.m., Thursday from 1 to 9 p.m., Friday from 8 a.m. to 2 p.m.

STUDENTS IN HAIFA: The **Israel Students Tourist Association (ISSTA)** has an office smack in the center of town, in the big building called Beit Hakranoth, at 20 Herzl Street, Room 245, tel. 04-669139. It's open Sunday through Thursday from 9 a.m. to noon, then from 3 to 6 p.m., except Wednesday and Friday when it's open from 9 a.m. to 1 p.m. This should definitely be a stopping point for any traveling student who needs information on budget student deals in Haifa.

SIGHTSEEING IN HAIFA: We'll group the major sights according to the three main sections of the city. But before setting out, you would be well advised to check with the Haifa Municipality Information Offices for additional information. They can be found at the Municipal Building, 14 Hassan Shukri, tel. 04-645359; the Egged Bus Terminal, 170 Jaffa Road, tel. 04-512208; Central Carmel, near the Carmelit station, tel. 04-83683; and at 25 Hanviim St., tel. 04-663056.

In the Port

Just as you wouldn't judge a book by its cover, don't judge countries by their ports. Haifa's port is marred by a badly dated, dusty and chaotic customs shed, which is scheduled to be demolished and replaced as soon as enough shekels are gathered.

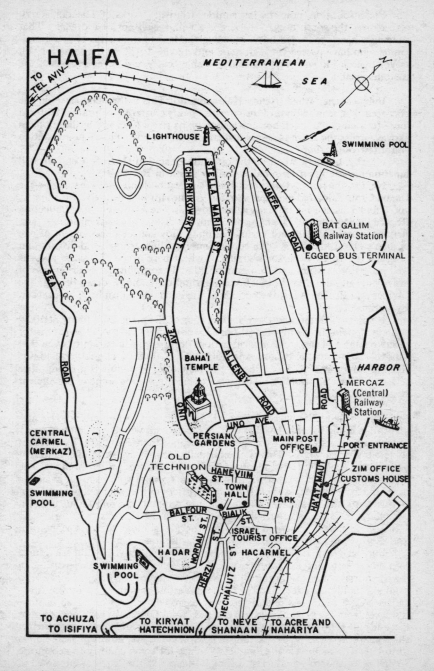

HAIFA

MEDITERRANEAN SEA

TO TEL AVIV

LIGHTHOUSE

SWIMMING POOL

CHERNIKOWSKY ST.

STELLA MARIS ST.

JAFFA ROAD

BAT GALIM
Railway Station

EGGED BUS TERMINAL

SEA ROAD

UNO AVE.

ALLENBY ROAD

BAHA'I
TEMPLE

HARBOR

MERCAZ
(Central)
Railway
Station

UNO AVE.

PERSIAN
GARDENS

MAIN POST
OFFICE

PORT ENTRANCE

CENTRAL
CARMEL
(MERKAZ)

OLD
TECHNION

HANEVIIM
ST.

TOWN
HALL

PARK

ROAD

HAATZMAUT

ZIM OFFICE
CUSTOMS HOUSE

SWIMMING
POOL

BALFOUR
ST.

BIALIK
ST.

ISRAEL
TOURIST OFFICE

HACARMEL

HADAR

HERZL ST.

NORDAU ST.

HECHALUTZ ST.

SWIMMING
POOL

TO ACHUZA
TO ISIFIYA

TO KIRYAT
HATECHNION

TO NEVE
SHANAAN

TO ACRE AND
NAHARIYA

For inspiration, note the inscriptions from the works of Theodor Herzl, placed over the south door: "If there is a will, it will not be a dream." That statement has encouraged lofty visions in the tens of thousands of new immigrants who have passed through here, and maybe it will do the same for you as you search for your luggage and grumble that you'll never get out of the customs shed.

Independence Road (Rehov Ha'atzmauth): This is the main street in the port area. The seaward side of the street is thickly clustered with rather battered four-story buildings, each housing a shop on its street level and business offices above. Across the street is an assortment of cafes, a post office, a police station and a few other shops.

Nearby, on Jaffa Road, is the old railway station (Mercaz Central), still functioning; the main terminal is further south in Bat Galim.

Next to the railroad station is Haifa's tallest building—215 feet high—the **Dagon Grain Silo,** and a unique silo it is. At the entrance facing Kikar Plumer, you'll find a fascinating little museum known as **The Archaeological Collection Regarding Storage and Handling of Grain.** On display are earthen storage jars, striking mosaic murals and various exhibits showing the development of one of man's oldest industries—the cultivation, handling, storage and distribution of grain. There are even some grains of wheat here over 4,000 years old—as well as fertility statues and flint grain sickles. The exhibit traces the course of history in this land from 12,000 B.C., the Middle Stone Age, down through the Copper and Bronze Ages, the periods of the Patriarchs, Prophets, Maccabees, Byzantines, etc.

It's a free exhibit, and there's a free tour of the plant itself (daily at 10:30 a.m., by appointment only; tel. 04-664221 for reservations). Also, every visitor receives a table of the archeological periods of history, which reminds you that Moses lived during the Bronze Age, 1300 B.C.–1200 B.C., and that David was King of Israel in 1000 B.C., during the Iron Age. The table is a handy little reference, especially valuable when you go poking around some of the ancient sites in the Galilee and Negev.

Jaffa Road: The street behind Independence Avenue (Rehov Ha'atzmauth), running roughly parallel to it, is Jaffa Road, where you can buy many of your souvenirs at prices considerably cheaper than elsewhere. But it takes some window shopping. This is an unusually inexpensive area, off the tourist path, where you'll see the residents of the lower town doing their shopping. The finjan coffee sets and brass trays, as well as the oriental-style earrings available here, undercut by several shekels the going prices in the fancier-looking shops.

At the southernmost end, Independence Avenue runs into Jaffa Road. On your left, you'll see the Ford showroom. Across the street is the World War I British Military Cemetery. Just after the gas station there's a right turn leading to Rambam Hospital and to the Bat Galim beach.

Further along Jaffa Road, in the direction of Tel Aviv, you'll see a huge ship on the left-hand side of the road. The vessel, **Af-Al-Pi** ("Nevertheless"), is a memorial commemorating all the ships that defied the British blockade to smuggle immigrants into Israel. This clandestine immigration movement—called "Aliya Beth"—is one of the most harrowing phases of Israeli history. Refugees from the Nazi plague and escapees from DP camps were packed onto these illegal ships, and many succeeded in making it undetected past British ships guarding Israel's Mediterranean coastline. Others, however, were not so fortunate. The *Struma* waited endlessly at sea for some country to accept the 765 refugees aboard until at last it sank. Others, like the *Patria,* went down in

Haifa harbor, with hundreds killed; still others, like the *Exodus,* ran the British blockade only to have its passengers shipped to a Cyprus detention camp, or, pathetically enough, returned to a detention area in Germany, the nightmare from which the survivors had just come. A historical museum dealing with these days is now open here. Nearby, on Allenby Road, is the Maritime Museum (see below for details).

Elijah's Cave: From the Af-Al-Pi, it's just a short walk up to Elijah's Cave, tel. 04-527430, nestled at the base of steep Cape Carmel, below the Stella Maris lighthouse and the Carmelite Monastery. Tradition has it that Elijah hid here when fleeing the wrath of King Ahab and his wife Jezebel. Holy to Jews, Christians and Moslems, the cave is the setting for huge dramatic ceremonies each year. This same site is also believed by some to have sheltered the Holy Family when they returned from Egypt. Elijah's Cave is open daily from 8 a.m. to 5 p.m., Friday till 1 p.m., and admission is free. Convenient buses are 43, 44 and 45.

In Hadar

As we've noted before, Hadar Ha'Carmel is the central business section of Haifa, located halfway between the lower town and the Carmel residential section. If you come up by bus or taxi from the port, you'll probably travel via Sderot Carmel, a wide, tree-lined street leading to the steep hill with the magnificent Baha'i Temple on top. Or you can take a bus (10 or 12) from the port to the foot of Hadar's main street, Herzl Street, which is where you'll also emerge from the underground, if you come up via the Carmelit.

Herzl Street—Main Street of Haifa: You'll want to stroll here just to catch the bustling flavor of this busy shopping street. All manner of things are available for refreshment on Herzl St. During the season, entrepreneurs set up big vats of boiling water and sell you fresh ears of corn wrapped in their husks. Other exotica for your palate: felafel, carrot juice, watermelons, inexpensive fruit punch, and plain soda (gazoz)—a wide choice of snacks to sustain yourself while window shopping.

At 18 Herzl St. you'll find the **Israel Government Tourist Office,** a storehouse of information on hotels, tour possibilities, and special events. They also publish a pamphlet telling you what's doing the week you're in Israel. Take one, and you may discover some special concert or art exhibit that you hadn't heard about. Also be sure to ask about new sights and sites, data and entertainment in and around the Haifa area. I.G.T.O. is open from 8 a.m. to 6 p.m. daily except Friday, when it closes at 2 p.m. In winter months, it closes daily at 5 p.m. Closed on Saturday, of course.

Old Technion: Continue up Herzl Street, turn right on Balfour, and you'll find the entrance to the Old Technion campus still very much in use. (The new, modern Technion campus, in Carmel, will be discussed later.) This old campus has 10% of the Technion's 8,000 students. Both old and new Technion comprise Israel's equivalent of M.I.T., offering courses in all phases of engineering —chemical, industrial, agricultural, electrical, mechanical, civil—as well as in architecture, town planning, nuclear science, aeronautics, electronics, and metallurgy. The faculty at both locations totals in excess of 1,500 persons.

In Hadar, the original Technion building looks like an ancient Turkish palace, and there's a very good reason for that. In 1913, a group of German benefactors, non-Zionist Jews who were running schools in Palestine, decided to establish a training ground for Jewish engineers who would work for the sultan of Turkey, then ruler of Palestine. (The Germans built all sorts of things for the Turks in the Middle East—hospitals, roads, mosques, factories—and when countries were choosing up sides in the First World War, Turkey naturally sided with Germany, the architects and engineers of the Ottoman Empire. But Turkey picked the losing side, and lost the entire Middle East, when the League of Nations gave England the Mandate for the previously Turkish-occupied Palestine.) The handsome Arabian Nights palace, now the Technion building, was constructed—but never put to use by the German group.

What happened was a language problem. The German donors insisted that German, the classic language of science and technology, be the language of instruction. But the Jewish engineering students, ardent Zionists, insisted that Hebrew be the language of instruction. As a result, the students refused to attend classes, and the staff walked out: a complete stalemate—and then the war came. The abandoned Technion became first a delousing station, then a meat slaughterhouse, a hospital and a target for artillery shells. In 1925, the school was renovated, and more buildings were constructed; ultimately the eight acres of midtown campus became hemmed in by Haifa's growing business and residential district, which didn't permit the campus to expand any further in Hadar. Hence, the "new" Technion City in Carmel.

Baha'i Temple: Haifa's most impressive sightseeing attraction is the splendid **Baha'i Shrine and Gardens,** tel. 04-528221, reached from United Nations Ave. (take bus 22 from the port, or bus 23 or 25 from Hadar). Haifa is international headquarters for the Baha'i faith, which began in Persia in the mid-19th century in a bloodbath of persecution.

The Baha'i leaders were exiled to Palestine in the latter part of the last century, and much of the Baha'i doctrine was then formulated in the Holy Land. The immaculate, majestic Baha'i gardens—with their stone peacocks and eagles, and delicately manicured cypress trees—are a restful, aesthetic memorial to the founders of this faith. Baha'i leaders claim some 3,000,000 adherents all over the world, with fast-growing numbers in newly developed countries. In the States, there's a white-domed nine-sided Baha'i Temple on the shores of Lake Michigan, at Wilmette, just outside Chicago.

Baha'is believe in the brotherhood of all men, a common world language, and the unity of all religions. They see the leaders of the different religions—Christ, Buddha, Mohammed, Moses—as messengers of God, sent at different times in history with doctrines varying to fit changing social needs, but all preaching substantially the same message. The most recent of these heavenly teachers, according to the Baha'is, was Bahaullah. He was exiled by Moslem and Turkish authorities to Acre, wrote his doctrines there, and died a peaceful death in the Baha'i House (which you should visit) just outside Acre.

In the Haifa Gardens, the huge domed Shrine entombs the remains of The Bab, the Bahaulla's herald. It is open to visitors from 9 a.m. to noon daily; you must remove your shoes before entering. The tomb is a sight to see—with ornamental goldwork and flowers in almost every nook and cranny. The Bab's remains, incidentally, were hidden for years after he died a martyr's death in front of a firing squad. Eventually, however, his followers secretly carried his remains to the Holy Land. The Gardens are open until 5 p.m. Admission is free.

On a higher hilltop stands the Corinthian-styled archives building, the library of Baha'i history. All the beautiful grounds that you see were planned by Shoghi Effendi, the late Guardian of the Faith. In addition to curious tourists, you'll see pilgrims who have come from all parts of the world to pay homage to the first leaders of this universal faith. (Incidentally, at the entrance to the shrine you will be given a pamphlet providing further details on Baha'i history and doctrine.)

Before you reach the Baha'i Gardens you'll come across **Mitzpoor Hashalom,** a lovely sculpture garden at 135 Zionism Ave. that opened in 1979. Amidst trees, flowers, and sloping lawns are 18 bronze sculptures of men, women, children, and animals at play by Ursula Malbin. Entrance is free.

On Carmel

Carmel means "Vineyard of the Lord"—from the two Hebrew words, "Kerem-El"—and this merging of the religious and agricultural is most appropriate in view of the fact that a great religious trial once took place on this fertile hilltop chain: the confrontation of the vengeful prophet Elijah with the idolators of Baal.

You'd never know there was ever anything but utter tranquility up here, because the range is an area of gentle breezes and wooded ravines, its sloping hills dotted with white homes. Each of Carmel's houses has a spritely little garden, and almost every one of them has a view of the Mediterranean. To Carmel residents, the sight of a flaming orange sun dipping into the sea at six o'clock is almost commonplace. The pace here is leisurely, the air clear, the skies blue and sunny, the view magnificent. You can readily see why the citizens of Carmel are so chauvinistic about their neighborhood.

Haifa also boasts Israel's largest national park—25,000 acres of pine, eucalyptus and cypress forest. It encompasses a large area of the Carmel mountain range, and contains many points of interest that are well marked and easily reachable. And, of course, it also has picnic areas, playgrounds, a restaurant, etc. Take bus 37 to get to it.

Technion City: This 300-acre campus in the Carmel hills is one of Israel's major showplaces. Begun in 1954, it now consists of 50 buildings, including 12 dormitories, a wind tunnel laboratory, and the Churchill Auditorium. All in all, it's a most impressive university complex, and the view of the city, the bay, the coastline clear to Lebanon and the snow-topped Syrian mountains is simply superb. Most important, the reputation of the school has grown so rapidly that, like many of the world's leading scientific institutions, it attracts students from many foreign countries—you'll see them strolling on the campus. A visitor center is open from 9 a.m. to 2 p.m. daily except Saturday and until 1 p.m. on Friday. To reach the Technion, take bus 31 from central Carmel, or bus 19 from Daniel St., next to the Armon Cinema.

University of Haifa: On the road from Haifa to the nearby Druze village of Daliat-el-Carmel you'll see the buildings and tower of the University of Haifa, a sprawling, somewhat sensational educational center now nearing completion. Designed by world-famous architect Niemeier, the University began operation in 1963, under the joint auspices of the City of Haifa and the Hebrew University. At that time, the students numbered 650, now 6,500, and today the University offers Bachelor of Arts programs in some 29 departments as well as Masters of Arts, Ph.D.'s, and other graduate programs. They also offer a ten-week Hebrew "Ulpan" for visiting students. For information write to **American Friends of the University,** 60 E. 42nd St., Suite 1656, New York, N.Y. 10017. Covering fully 200 acres, the campus is well worth a visit: The view is magnificent, as is the architecture. The snack shop and restaurant are described earlier in this chapter. Regular bus (21/37, 37, 24, 18/36) and sherut service. Free tours daily except Saturday, Sunday through Thursday from 9 a.m. to 2 p.m., Friday till noon.

Carmelite Monastery: A lower Carmel road descends to a French Carmelite monastery and hospice. Situated on Stella Maris Rd., with a magnificent view of the sea, the Monastery, served as a hospital for Napoleon's soldiers during his unsuccessful siege of Acre in 1799. On the grounds are an impressive church, a small collection of antiquities, and the Pilgrims Hostel—Stella Maris Hospice. Nearby is a cave associated with the prophets Elijah and Elisha. The church and antiquities can be seen daily except Sunday from 8:30 a.m. to 1:30 p.m. and from 3 to 6 p.m. Entrance is free, tel. 04-523460. When the hospice is open, individual visitors may be accommodated if there's room.

Residential Districts: Most of Haifa's middle- and upper-middle-class residents live in five main areas of Carmel: Neve Shanaan Ramat Ramez, the Merkaz section, Ahuza, French Carmel, and Danya.

Neve Shanaan is a typical Israeli *shikun,* a housing project, complete with stereotyped apartments, play areas for children and a small shopping center. The living quarters in these buildings are fairly small, but very light and airy, with a balcony patio for each one of them. You reach Neve Shanaan by winding around the Carmel granite quarries, with their cliffside caves, climbing in the direction of the new Technion. The road is serpentine, and foot by foot you'll find yourself mounting higher and higher over the city of Haifa. (Buses 15, 16, 17, 18 or 19.)

Merkaz is the central portion of Carmel, last stop on the Carmelit. It's the smallest of the three large shopping areas in Haifa, and you'll find here banks and shops, a supermarket and outdoor cafe, a zoo, a Rothschild community house, and a main square with a road branching off into four different directions on Carmel. (All the 20 buses, 30, 31, 37, 91, and 92.)

Ahuza is the last stop on the Haifa bus line (21, 22, 23, 24, 28, 37), and it's the swanky, northernmost part of town. Many homes here are villa-sized, each strategically built on the side of a hill with a view.

French Carmel is a middle-class residential area above the lighthouse and Carmelite Monastery. (Buses 25, 30, 31.)

Danya is a relatively new, exclusive neighborhood skirting the top of Carmel. New buildings rising all the time here, some architecturally startling. (Bus 24 or 37.)

An Arabic community is also located on Carmel—**Kababir,** with about 700 people and a very fine view. (Bus 30.)

Museums, Institutes, Galleries and So Forth

The following three museums are housed in new quarters in the Haifa Museum complex at 26 Shabtai Levi St., tel. 04-523255.

The Museum of Ancient Art displays archeological collections of Mediterranean cultures from the beginning of history until the Islamic conquest in the seventh century. Outstanding collections of Greco-Roman culture, Coptic art, painted portraits from Faiyum, coins of Caesarea and Acre, terra-cottas of all periods, and finds from the Haifa area. **The Museum of Modern Art** has a collection of paintings and sculptures by Israeli artists as well as prints by Israeli and foreign artists. A library and slide collection is open to the public. Lectures, art films, and slide presentations are held in the evenings. The visiting hours for both museums are Tuesday to Thursday and Sunday from 10 a.m. to 5 p.m., Monday 10 a.m. to 1 p.m. and 5 to 10 p.m., Saturday 10 a.m. to 1 p.m., closed Friday. **The Ethnological Museum and Folklore Archives** (not yet open at this writing) will display items of ancient Jewish origin plus African, Asian and American Indian tribal art. The Folktale Archives will contain about 10,000 tales, most in Hebrew but with English summaries. It will be open the same hours as the above museums.

The **Haifa Music Museum and Amli Library,** 23 Arlosorov St., tel. 04-644485, has a collection including musical instruments, reconstructions of musical instruments according to archeological finds, manuscripts, autographs, coins, and medals. There is a lending library of books, records, and musical scores, as well as a listening corner. Open Sunday to Friday from 10 a.m. to 1 p.m., Sunday and Wednesday afternoons from 4 to 7 p.m., closed on Saturday.

The **Tikotin Museum of Japanese Art,** 89 Hanassi Blvd., tel. 04-83554, has examples of almost all kinds of Japanese art and crafts, along with a library of 2,000 books. Hours on Saturday and holidays 10 a.m. to 2 p.m.; Sunday through Thursday 10 a.m. to 1 p.m. and 4 to 7 p.m.; closed on Fridays.

Grouped together at 124 Hatishbi St. are **The Prehistoric Museum "M. Stekelis,"** the **Natural History Museum,** the **Zoo** and the **Biological Institute.** The first of these maintains a permanent exhibit of fossils and artifacts from the Carmel Region. Each of the others, in its own way, features the animal life of the country, with particular attention paid the fish indigenous to Israel's waters and the fauna of the Carmel region. Visiting hours are 8 a.m. to 4 p.m. Sunday through Thursday; 8 a.m. to 1 p.m. Friday; 9 a.m. to 4 p.m. Saturday. In July and August, they open from 8 a.m. to 6 p.m. Sunday through Thursday, Friday and Saturday as above. Tel. 04-85833.

The **National Maritime Museum,** 198 Allenby Rd., tel. 04-536622, encompasses 5,000 years of seafaring along the coasts of Israel (the Mediterranean and the Red Sea). Hours: Monday through Thursday 10 a.m. to 5 p.m.; Saturday and holidays 10 a.m. to 2 p.m.; Friday 9 a.m. to 1 p.m.

The **Illegal Immigration and Naval Museum,** 204 Allenby Rd., tel. 04-536249 (next door to the Maritime Museum and opposite Elijah's Cave) details the story of illegal immigration during the British mandatory period. The Af-Al-Pi is on the grounds here. Open Sunday to Thursday from 10 a.m. to 3 p.m., Friday to 1 p.m., closed Saturday.

The **Mane Katz Museum,** 89 Yafe Nof St., tel. 04-83482, houses his works and collection—drawings, aquarelles, gouaches, oil paintings, sculpture, and Judaica. Open daily except Sunday from 10 a.m. to 1 p.m. and 4 to 6 p.m., Friday to noon only, Saturday to 1 p.m.

The **Chagall Artist's House,** 24 Zionut Ave. (at Herzl), exhibits the works of contemporary Israeli artists. Open 10 a.m. to 1 p.m. and 4 to 7 p.m. Sunday through Thursday; 10 a.m. to 2 p.m. Saturday, closed Friday.

For a change of pace, visit the **Haifa Trade and Exhibition Center** on Histadruth St., the diamonds they deal in will dazzle your eyes. Buy or just gape.

And then there is the **Rothschild Community House,** 142 Hanassi Blvd., tel. 04-82749 or 83424, which always has something of interest for tourists. Call to see what's up. Interesting too are the lectures at the **Institute for Relations Between Arabs and Jews,** on Ha'gefen St. at Beit Hagefen (opposite the Chagall Artist's House).

The **Dany Sharon Institute of Urbanology,** 92 Hanassi Blvd., tel. 04-89254, promotes familiarization with environmental problems. The library contains all manner of printed material pertaining to towns, their inhabitants and history. Wooden replicas of various cities in Israel and Europe can be seen as well. Open daily from 9 a.m. to 1 p.m. and on Tuesday also from 4–7 p.m.

The **Grain Silo and Dagon Archaeological Museum,** tel. 04-664221, offers free tours daily at 10:30 a.m. (except Saturday). It's at Kikar Plumer; bus 10, 12, or 22.

Costs involved in visiting any of the above-mentioned museums are so low they're not worth mentioning. And those museums which are open on Saturday mornings are free to the public on that day.

SHOPPING NOTES: Though there is a flea market in Haifa, it does not generate much interest. You may find some bargains along Jaffa Road and Hechalutz Road, as shops are numerous and prices competitive. The souvenir/ religious book/antique store at 38 Jaffa Rd. is worth a stop. There is no sign outside; Mr. L. Kania, the owner, says he's so well known customers find him. He proudly states he has sold items to museums throughout the world including the Metropolitan Museum in New York. He will show you photographs of valuable items in his possession as well as antiques, silver, and bronze items in his very packed shop. His phone number (at home) is 04-660139. Open from 8 a.m. to 5 p.m., Friday to 2 p.m.

Open Markets

You will find a most delightful market called the **Shuk Harumanim** by walking up to the Star Restaurant on 19 Hamaginim St. (near the Carmelit). Across the street, under corrugated roofs and down a stairway, are stalls piled high with spices, sacks of vegetables, pastas of all shapes—a fragrant change from the organized modern supermarkets. Continuing along you will come to the **Shuk Haturkim.** This market abounds in wholesale and retail fruit and vegetables, but clothing, housewares, shoes, and gifts can be purchased too. This market can be entered from Jaffa Rd. and Ha'atzmauth St. The **Shuk Talpioth** on Sirkin St. is the largest of Haifa's open markets and spills into the street in a frenzy of activity. There's another market in the lower city on Wadi Nisnas St., yet another on the corner of Hechalutz and Yoel Sts. Prices are rarely marked, so for serious shopping you should do your homework and know the going rates.

HELP! The **U.S. Consulate General** and **U.S. Culture Center** offices in Haifa are conveniently located in a huge building in the port area, across from the Korngold Restaurant. The local Consular Agent is at your service for any matters concerning credentials, visas, passports and all kinds of problems. The telephone number is 04-669042; in case of emergency 04-241395.

2. Half-Day Excursions

Many of the villages outside Haifa are among the most interesting attractions in Israel. We'll visit three of them: **Daliat-el-Carmel, Isfiya,** and **Muhraka.**

DALIAT-EL-CARMEL AND ISFIYA: These sister Druze villages are located 15 minutes from the Ahuza section of Carmel. If you're driving, just ask for the road to Daliat-el-Carmel ("Ayfo ha'derech l'Dalia?"). By bus (92 or 93), the trip takes a half-hour from the central station, and it's a splendid drive along the uppermost rim of Carmel. The Mediterranean is way down below you, and so is the entire city, the port, and the industrial area. Bring your camera.

As mentioned, these villages are inhabited in the main by Druze, Arabic-speaking (and appearing) people who are, however, not Moslems. Theirs is a rather secretive religion; they draw heavily on the Bible and venerate such personages as Jethro (father-in-law of Moses). The Druze were loyal to Israel during the 1948 war, and several of their brigades are highly respected detachments in the Israeli army. There are three Druze in the current Knesset. The Druze gravitate toward big swarthy mustaches, and due to "genetic influence" (Romans, Crusaders, and British) several centuries back, many of them are blond. Druze children and young women are well known for their beauty.

Unlike the Arab men, who often prefer to sit and supervise while their women do the agricultural work, the Druze husband allows his wife more freedom, and the girls go to school. They are an industrious people, and you'll see that their terraced hillsides are meticulously cared for and, as a result, very fertile. The houses are also square and box-like in the Arabic style—but many are new, built by Druze construction experts. Outside their own villages, the Druze find employment on kibbutzim as paid electricians, builders, carpenters, and mechanics; in the extreme north and south of the country, many Druze are border policemen—and you'll never find a tougher, more uncompromising lot when it comes to that kind of work. Their hospitality, though, is legendary.

In both villages, you can buy quite extraordinary souvenirs and handcrafted items, new or antique, at moderate prices. See Chapter XIII for details.

There are several cafes in both villages well worth stopping into for a drink, just to observe the local citizenry. As you'll soon see, the conservative Eastern European Jew and his boisterous sabra son aren't the only ones in Israel to be affected by the generation gap, Israeli style: in these Druze villages, you'll see only older men in flowing gowns and headdresses, while the younger men wear Western-style clothes.

But family codes and ancient biblical social customs are still strictly observed here. If a man discovers that his daughter has compromised herself with a young man, he may avenge the stain on the family's name by killing both his daughter and the young man. It has happened in these villages, as well as in Arab towns and in some of the Yemenite settlements in Israel.

Should you become friendly with a Druze while you're in Israel, try to get yourself invited into the village when there's a wedding. It's a happy, spectacular, all-day affair, marked by intriguing customs and foods that you'll never forget.

Isfiya is the first village you'll reach from Haifa; Daliat-el-Carmel is a very short ride further.

A 3½-hour tour of both villages, Muhraka, and the Menashe Forest is offered on Sundays and Tuesdays at 9:30 a.m. by **Mitzpa Tours**, 1 Nordau St., in Haifa, tel. 04-666898. Book at least one day in advance. It costs $8.

You can also go to the villages on your own. There's a sherut service which leaves Haifa during the evening from 6 p.m. to 6 a.m., departing from the Hadar at the corner of Shmaryahu Levin and Herzl Sts. Between 6 a.m. and 6 p.m. the sherut service is downtown at the corner of Ha'atzmauth Road and Eliahu Hanavi Street, near Kikar Paris. The sherut takes 25 minutes to reach Daliat-el-Carmel.

Overnight in Isfiya? The **Stella Carmel Hospice**, tel. 04-222692, charges $11 B&B per person for simple but pleasant accommodations. Lunch and dinner are available.

MUHRAKA: A half-mile south of Daliat-el-Carmel is a road on the left side of the main road. Its destination is not posted, but it meanders and climbs to the monastery at Muhraka, where Elijah defeated the prophets of Baal. (Interurban bus 92.) The monastery is open 8 a.m. to 5 p.m. in winter (to 6 p.m. in summer). The view from here is unsurpassed. A minimal entrance fee is charged.

3. Suggestions for Tours from Your Haifa Base

Haifa proves to be an excellent place to park your bags while scouting out other attractions around Israel, for in Israel nothing's really that far away. And while Haifa's not exactly in the middle of the country, it does happen to be quite close to some of the more popular sights. The nearer places include Ein Hod, Caesarea, Acre and other locations described in the following chapter. It's also quite a simple matter to cover the Galilee and the Golan Heights from Haifa. There's excellent and inexpensive transportation to all points, including buses, sheruts, trains, and planes (Arkia flies from Haifa's bay-area airport on regularly scheduled inland tours of points including the Negev and Sinai, Jerusalem and the West Bank). For specifics about transportation and prices, your best bet is to visit the I.G.T.O., which can help you plan the next leg of your trip and will even help arrange for self-drive or chauffeured rental cars.

Aside from I.G.T.O., the following companies have all sorts of tour plans for your consideration: **Egged Tours,** 4 Nordau St., tel. 04-643131; **United Tours,** 5 Nordau St., tel. 04-668886; **Carmel Touring,** 126 Hanassi Blvd., tel. 04-82277; **Mitzpa Tours,** 1 Nordau St., tel. 04-666898.

THE GOLDEN COAST

THROUGHOUT ITS LONG, long history, the land now called Israel has played host to pilgrims seeking solace, penance, union, communion with the deity or deities they most fervently believed in. Today these pilgrims still come, but there's a new kind among them, with a different but equally fervent kind of an old worship: sun worship. What they seek is a rich golden tan, and for this they flock to their own particular mecca—the long, unbroken strip of Israel's eastern Mediterranean shoreline, where they bask in the sunshine and sea.

These pilgrims are of every class and nationality. Some move bag and baggage into first-class resorts; others drop their backpacks on the sands and dig in for a fortnight. In between, there are pleasant accommodations for everyone.

Like the rest of the country, the shore strip combines the old and the new in uniquely Israeli juxtaposition. There's neon and chrome side by side with biblical and even pre-biblical ruins. And there's much to do: beaches of sand, pebbles or rocks with fascinations on, in or under the waters. Sports enthusiasts can swim, fish, dive, boat, ski or surf. Good sightseeing here, and good relaxation.

1. Ashkelon

Though the beach winds much further south, the southernmost tourist accommodations are found in a thriving community that's grown up over the ruins of civilizations buried in its sands for 25 centuries. One of the five Philistine city-states (the others were Gath, Gaza, Ekron and Ashdod, all within today's Israel), Ashkelon was an important caravan stop. Here's where Delilah snipped Samson's hair and strength, where Herod was born, where Romans and Crusaders rallied. Today, the territory called the Sands of Ashkelon includes **Migdal** and **Givat Zion,** the oldest of the contemporary areas;

Afridar, built in 1952 by a South African development company; **Samson District;** and **Barnea.**

Ashkelon has several hotels (most—but not all—being expensive establishments) and a marvelous beach which stretches for miles in each direction along the Mediterranean.

Some Israelis think that Ashkelon has the perfect climate, blessed by cool breezes from the sea, but modified by the dryness of desert winds. It definitely does have good weather and on a summer night, you'll appreciate those breezes.

The city can be reached by bus from Tel Aviv in one hour and 15 minutes.

ACCOMMODATIONS: You should know, first, that Ashkelon's hotel prices operate under a special framework. This fast-growing beach town charges its highest rates from mid-July till the end of August, and during Passover and the September holidays. This all has to do with Ashkelon's weather, a commodity that local residents discuss with fanatic possessiveness, not unlike the Miami Beach taxi drivers who always talk as if they own the weather. All the hotels below offer rain insurance: for every day it rains, beginning on the second day of your stay, you get to stay a day free—breakfast included!

The **Ashkelon Hotel,** 7 South Africa Blvd., tel. 051-34188, is only 15 minutes away from the beach by foot. It has 24 rooms, eight with bath and the balance with shower. Single occupancy is SH31.40 ($9.25), doubles cost SH22.40 ($6.60) per person. While here take a look at the huge surrealistic mural depicting the 300 foxes caught by Samson.

King Shaul Hotel, 23 Harakefet St., tel. 051-24124, includes 18 bungalows, two of them connecting, in its 110-room count. Among its numerous amenities are air conditioning and heating, an exercise hall, two swimming pools (one for children), a sauna—and a nightclub, which features entertainment (with cover charge) on Friday and Saturday nights, dancing to records on other nights. Nightly rates are SH74.80 ($22) single, SH57.80 ($17) per person double; add 20% during July, August, and Jewish holidays. Breakfast is included in rates; half-board is SH23.80 ($7), full board SH44.20 ($13).

Samson's Gardens, 38 Sonnebend St., tel. 051-34666, has 22 rooms, all with bath or shower. And as the name suggests, it's situated in a garden; all rooms have terraces overlooking it. Guests can use the pool at the nearby King Shaul Hotel at reduced rates. Kosher meals are available. Single occupancy is SH45.90 ($13.50), double occupancy SH42.50 ($12.50) per person; half-board is SH22.10 ($6.50), full board SH45.90 ($13.50).

An inexpensive alternative to hotels is to stay in a private home. Generally, this costs SH12 ($3.50) to SH15 ($4.40) a night. To find out about home accommodations contact the Government and Municipal Tourist Office, Afridar Center, tel. 051-32412.

Camping

Ashkelon has a beautiful and extensive camping ground—a 15-acre swath of lawns dotted with trees and marble pillars, located inside the seaside **National Antiquities Park.** Tents, caravans and bungalows are available for hire year round. There are three to four beds in each bungalow, two to four beds per tent; the large caravans (trailers) can accommodate six, the smaller ones four. Three shower and toilet areas contain ample facilities. For food, there are a grocery store and a restaurant, or you may purchase bottled cooking gas for your own equipment. Entrance to the park is SH2.50 (75¢) for an adult, SH.50 (15¢) for child or student.

For further information, you may write to the campsite at P.O.B. 5052, tel. 051-25228. Or contact the Israel Camping Union, P.O.B. 53, Nahariya, tel. 04-923366. Members of the Israel or International Camping Union will receive a 5-10% discount on certain items.

BUDGET MEALS: The **Ma'adan Cafe,** in the center of town, opposite the Municipal Tourist Office, tel. 051-31925, has both indoor and outdoor seating. You might order a dairy plate here with cheeses, hard-boiled egg, and salad for SH8.50 ($2.50), a platter of four appetizers for SH7.50 ($2.20), a fish meal or cold cuts and salad for SH10 ($2.95). Open 9 a.m. to 8 p.m., till 11 p.m. in summer.

Little ambience but low prices are what you get at the **Egged Self-Service Restaurant** at the bus station, open from 5:30 a.m. to 3:30 p.m. daily.

The **Hanitzahon Restaurant,** 149 Herzl St., in the old city, serves oriental and European fare ranging from grilled beef or pork for SH6 ($1.75) to SH8 ($2.35) to gefilte fish for SH2.50 (75¢), and chicken livers or shashlik for SH6 ($1.75). Open daily except Friday from 10 a.m. to 11 p.m.

WHAT TO DO IN ASHKELON: Ashkelon offers a wide variety of activities. The main source of information on all the goings-on is the Government and Municipal Tourist Information Office, Afridar Center, tel. 051-32412. It's open in summer from 9 a.m. to 1 p.m. and 3 to 7 p.m., Fridays from 9 a.m. to 3 p.m. In winter afternoon hours change from 2 to 6 p.m. You can obtain up-to-date information on everything from picnicking in the National Park to seasonal events, such as the Arts and Crafts Fair in July or August.

A Little Archeology

Exactly what happened at Ashkelon over the last 4,000 years is a chapter of history still waiting to be written. What Ashkelon really needs is a rich archeological expedition, for only occasional pokes and gropes have thus far been made into the sand-covered cities of antiquity that lie within its boundaries. At one point along the shore, you'll see where some scientists have made a tentative longitudinal slice into the cliff, revealing a network of pillars and caves several strata deep that seem like a mysterious royal basement from Ashkelon's past.

It's a virtual certainty that further excavations will reveal important historical treasures, because the Bible mentions Ashkelon frequently. When King Saul was killed by the Philistines, David lamented: "Tell it not in Gath, publish it not in the streets of Ashkelon, lest the daughters of the Philistines rejoice."

Some scholars of Greek legend claim that Ashkelon—and not Crete—may have been the original home of Aphrodite, goddess of love. Here, too, Herod built great works of marble and granite, and the Arab settlers who came later called Ashkelon "the bride of the east."

When the Crusaders and Moslems fought over the city, Ashkelon, like so many other Israeli locations, fell into utter ruin. The Arabs then stripped Ashkelon of Roman staircases, Hellenistic pillars, and Crusader stonemasonry, and used all these materials for building houses around Jaffa and Acre.

National Antiquities Park

As you'd expect, the main sights are archeological in nature. For example, take a walk along the sea in a southerly direction, and you'll see bits and pieces of pillar and column poking through the sand, just waiting for that excavating team we've been hoping for. Toward the end of the public beach section, you'll then come to a staircase leading into a park. Proceed through the park, and you'll soon come upon the sunken arena (the "Sculpture Corner") that houses Ashkelon's handful of finds: a headless Winged Victory supported on the shoulders of a childlike Atlas, Isis and child, and grouped pieces of colonnade from Herod's collection of carved capitals, "Stoa of a Hundred Columns."

There's also a refreshment stand here—in case you're weary from the walk through the park. Entrance is SH2.50 (75¢) for adults, SH.50 (15¢) for children.

The Painted Tomb

Practically hidden in the sand dunes, this dome pokes upward just enough so that you can see it when you leave the main road and enter the beach. This Roman burial cave is the work of an artist who had a happy and secure vision of the afterlife. Romance and eternal springtime abide in the paintings here—reclining nymphs and their pitchers of water, marsh birds nesting in a stream thick with fish. On the ceiling are nude children playing, greyhounds and gazelles, birds and clusters of grapes. The gods Apollo and Demeter look down from between some vines, assuring the entombed man, whoever he was, that things in the afterlife are really pretty good. Open daily from 9 a.m. to 3 p.m.

Public Beaches

Ashkelon has several public beaches. Swim only if there is a lifeguard present, since the water tends to have tricky currents. They are all free and seldom crowded.

2. Ashdod and Environs

Another of those five Philistine city-states, Ashdod today is smaller and newer than Ashkelon, and also of a different nature. It is said that this will be Israel's largest commercial and trading sea gateway, and, in fact, the town's prize possession is its modern, fully-equipped harbor, where the Israeli Navy's Nautical School is located. From the Observation Post here, you can see big ships cruising and loading and also get a view of this rapidly developing town with its nearby industrial area.

Ashdod is growing wildly: Everywhere you go the ground is being readied for more factories or plants, new high-rise apartments or schools, more shops or hotels. One of Israel's "planned" cities, it's all built on sand dunes which accounts for its lack of grass lawns and such except in specially nurtured areas. If you want a garden here the first thing you have to come up with is soil, but somehow that doesn't seem to discourage the 70,000 folk who live here (about 60% Sephardic Jews, plus many from India) and carefully tend their greenery.

Ashdod has three shopping centers, and the largest is nearest the hotels and beach areas. From its large courtyard you can see an attractive modern building with a tile wall mural facing the main street; it's the local absorption center where many new immigrants live for several months and study Hebrew. In the shopping center you'll find cinemas, department stores, shops, and banks, plus a pharmacy, deli shop, newsstand, and bookstore.

WHERE TO EAT: Ashdod has a number of inexpensive eating places both in the center of the small city and in the port area. They feature the typical oriental and European fare. As for recommendations, it's catch-as-catch-can; you'll find that variety, quality and price are all on a par at whatever place you find. The town also has its share of felafel stands, and for pizza during the hours of 9 a.m. and midnight (Fridays till 3 p.m., Saturdays from 6 p.m.), there's **Pizza Don Pedro** in Mercaz Mischari Alef (Commercial Center A), with pies hot from the oven beginning at SH1.20 (35¢).

IN THE ENVIRONS: There are two ways of heading north from Ashdod. The easier and faster way is along the coastal road, which intentionally misses several of the population centers in the region. The inner road, however, connecting with Gedera—once the northern tip of the Negev until Israeli farmers pushed the desert back beyond Beersheba—is well worth the extra effort and time.

Rehovot and the Weizmann Institute

Without returning to the coastal highway, you can reach Rehovot from Gedera; there's also a road directly off the coastal highway. Either way, it's a short drive to Israel's foremost scientific establishment—the **Weizmann Institute of Science**, tel. 054-82111. You enter through a gateway on Rehovot's main street, and as soon as you're inside the grounds you'll feel as if you've stepped into another world. This is a beautiful compound of futuristic buildings, lawns of the deepest golf-course green, lily ponds, and colorful gardens—all, apparently, for the spiritual satisfaction of the hundreds of scientists at work here.

Dedicated in 1949 in honor of Israel's first president (himself an important chemist), the institute grew out of the Daniel Sieff Research Institute, established in 1934. Conducting both fundamental and applied research, the Weizmann Institute also has a graduate school where about 500 students work for their doctorates. The majestic buildings, in a pastoral, tranquil setting, have been a drawing card for scientists from all over the world.

On the grounds are the Wix Library, where there is an exhibition on Dr. Weizmann's life; the Wix Auditorium where films on the Institute's activities are shown at 11 a.m. and 3 p.m. daily (except Friday when they are shown at 11 a.m. only); and the residence of the late Dr. and Mrs. Weizmann, built in the 1930s. The residence is open daily except Saturday and Jewish holidays from 9 a.m. to 3:30 p.m., admission about 50¢. Near the residence is a simple tomb marking the Weizmanns' resting place and a Memorial Plaza dominated by a Holocaust Memorial depicting the Torah being snatched from flames. A restaurant on the premises serves light dairy meals.

Rishon-le-Zion

Should it be an unusually hot and thirsty day, you'll be well advised to stop off in nearby Rishon-le-Zion, home of Israel's wine industry. Here you can catch a free tour of the wine cellars, refreshingly concluded with samples of the local stock (no tours, however, late Friday afternoon or Saturday).

Free wine shouldn't be your only object here, though, because this is an important historic site—one of the first Jewish settlements in Israel. Started in 1882 by a group of idealistic Russian Jews escaping Czarist persecution, Rishon-le-Zion nearly didn't make it. Things went from bad to worse for the settlers, who suffered not only from inexperience with agricultural techniques, but from Arab marauders, malaria, squalid living conditions, and a rapidly degenerating morale. Finally, they sent an emissary to see Baron Rothschild in Paris. The financier and philanthropist aided the cause by dispatching agricultural experts to help the settlers find water and transplant young French vines. (This was the benefactor's first enterprise in Israel.) The vines from Beaujolais, Bordeaux and Burgundy took hold, and in 1887 the Israeli wine industry was born, under the name **Carmel Oriental.** Today, these wines are generously exported and can be found in almost all liquor stores throughout the world. (Zichron-Yaakov, south of Haifa, is also a leading wine center.)

History was again made in Rishon-le-Zion, which means "First in Zion," when Naftali Imber wrote "Hatikva," Israel's national anthem, in this very village.

3. Bat Yam

Though there are numerous public beaches between Ashdod and Tel Aviv, Bat Yam ("Daughter of the Sea") is one of the most pleasant. On the southern fringes of Tel Aviv–Jaffa, and boasting an ever-growing population of 130,000 inhabitants, Bat Yam is a popular resort area and, fortunately for us, has some relatively inexpensive tourist accommodations.

The **Municipal Tourist Information Bureau,** Ben-Gurion Ave., tel. 03-889776, is open on Sunday to Thursday 8 a.m. to 6:30 p.m., on Fridays 8 a.m. to 1 p.m. In winter they close between 1:30 and 4 p.m. on Monday and Wednesday.

ACCOMMODATIONS: The three-star **Armon Yam Hotel,** 95 Ben-Gurion Ave., tel. 03-882424, has 66 rooms, all with phone, radio, bath, and air conditioning. High-season rates are SH81.60 ($24) single, SH57.80 ($17) per person double occupancy. The corresponding off-season rates are SH57.80 ($17) and SH51 ($15). Students up to the age of 26 receive a 15% reduction off season.

The **Palm Beach Hotel,** 41 Ben-Gurion Ave., tel. 03-879131/2/3, charges SH54.40 ($16) single, SH40.80 ($12) per person double. Off-season rates are a trifle lower. Palm Beach has a bar and dining room. Reductions are available to students and to tourists who book reservations through a travel agency.

The **Panorama Hotel,** Ben-Gurion Ave., tel. 03-861141, has 44 rooms with white furnishings offset by dark blue curtains. Single occupancy in high season is SH68 ($20), SH47.60 ($14) per person double, SH27.20 ($8) for a third person in a room. Low-season rates are a few dollars less. Meals available. Half of the rooms have a sea view; some have air conditioning or heating.

Security buffs will like the highly recommended **Sarita Hotel,** 127 Ben-Gurion Ave., tel. 03-889183; there's actually a safe for storing valuables in every room. Rooms also have private bath, heating, air conditioning, phone, and radio, and there's a restaurant on the premises offering light meals. Rates are SH57.80 ($17) single, SH37.40 ($11) per person double, SH30.60 ($9) per person triple. Students get a 15% reduction.

Bat Yam Hotel, 53 Ben-Gurion Ave., tel. 03-864373, has 20 tastefully furnished rooms, each equipped with bath or shower, heating and air conditioning as needed, and phones. Rates, including breakfast, are SH68 ($20) single, SH47.60 ($14) per person double, 10% reduction for students, 50% for children up to age 12. Rates are a few dollars lower off season.

RESTAURANTS: At **Mifgash Jo,** 93 Ben-Gurion Ave., a cheerfully decorated eatery with pastel green walls, blue-green curtains, and red tablecloths, you can get a salad entree for SH3.50 ($1), a main course from SH5 ($1.45) to SH7 ($2.05); follow it up with a piece of cake for SH2 (60¢); tea and coffee are on the house. The restaurant is open daily April through the end of September from 10 a.m. to midnight.

The **Phantom Cafe and Restaurant,** 61 Ben-Gurion Ave., offers sidewalk-cafe seating and fresh-baked cheese- or potato-filled burekas for SH1 (30¢) each, American waffles for SH6 ($1.75), and salads—vegetables, humus, tchina, tuna, etc.—for SH1.50 (45¢). Open from 8 a.m. to 11–midnight daily.

Kontiki, 1 Rothschild St., corner of Ben-Gurion Ave., tel. 03-860171, is really three restaurants in one. The largest section serves French and Moroccan fare: couscous with meat and vegetables for SH10 ($2.95), SH10.20 ($3) for char-grilled chicken with baked potato and salad (add another $1 and you get soup and dessert with it). In the Milk Bar section you can have pancakes for SH3.50 ($1), waffles for SH7 ($2.05); and in the third part, a pizzeria (open June to September only), try the ravioli, pizza, or lasagne for SH4 ($1.20). Open daily from 10 a.m. to 2 a.m.

The unusual little **Korso Restaurant,** 43 Ben-Gurion Ave., has just four tables and is open Monday to Saturday from noon to 4 p.m. and Sunday from 7 p.m. to midnight June to September. The rest of the year hours are noon to 4 p.m. Monday to Saturday. The chef takes great care in preparing each meal. For SH10.20 ($3) you can get a lunch of soup, three skewers of kabab, and chips; SH20.40 ($6) will buy a more elaborate lunch—soup or caviar salad, steak with potatoes, and a sumptuous dessert like Bavarian cream or crêpes.

4. Herzlia

Herzlia, ten miles north of Tel Aviv, is one of Israel's most famous beach resorts. It was founded in 1924 as an agricultural center, but the years have changed its face and purpose. Perhaps, for accuracy's sake, we ought to admit that the real twist in the village's fortunes came about as the result of the unexpected growth of Tel Aviv. As the large Israeli metropolis grew northward, the beaches of Herzlia suddenly became much more accessible and a good deal more desirable. Today, when you're talking about Herzlia, you're talking about luxury. The entire waterfront area is studded with fine hotels, none of which fall within the budget of this book. Fine restaurants abound in Herzlia, as do some of the country's most expensive villas. A disproportionate number of foreign diplomats reside in Herzlia; their neighbors are airline captains and other high earners.

An Egged bus ride from Tel Aviv to Herzlia takes about 45 minutes; a special bus service run by United Tours connects the Herzlia hotels with downtown and north Tel Aviv. From Herzlia you take another bus to the beach.

The Herzlia beach is lovely, but expensive by Israeli standards. Best beaches are the **Zebulun,** near the Daniel Hotel; the **Sharon,** next to the Sharon Hotel; and the **Accadia,** between the Accadia and Daniel Hotels. One additional word about the beach: A dangerous undertow exists and bathing is strictly prohibited when a lifeguard is not on duty.

ACCOMMODATIONS: While hotels abound in the area, most of them are just too expensive for the budget-conscious. There are a few bargains, however, one such being the **Cymberg Hotel,** 29 Ma'agshim St., tel. 03-932179. Graded two stars, it contains 12 rooms (all with bath or shower and refrigerator) and is a five-minute walk from the beach. The Cymberg's new owners are Ruth and Willy Feinberg from the Bronx, and they have displayed works of art and sculpture throughout the hotel and garden. Single occupancy is SH51 ($15) to

SH68 ($20) year round, breakfast included; doubles pay SH40.80 ($12) to SH61.20 ($18) per person. A three-bedroom family apartment costs SH170 ($50) a day for up to five people.

The **Tadmor Hotel**, 38 Basle St., tel. 03-938321, is a sort of Israeli institution. Hotel staffs from all over the country train there, and chefs are assiduously cultivated and launched from the Tadmor. There is a radio in each of the 68 air-conditioned rooms; large gardens and a fine park with a children's playground are additional highlights. A single room costs SH64.60 ($19) to SH71.40 ($21), a double SH44.20 ($13) to SH51 ($15) per person.

A good deal is offered at the **New Hod**, 89 Hanassi St., tel. 03-938621. Formerly an old-age home, it now functions as a hotel with 28 air-conditioned and heated rooms, almost all with terraces. Though it's a bit far from the sea, it is across the street from a large park. B&B rates are SH44.20 ($13) single, SH3.40 ($10) per person double. A large lunch is available for SH10 ($2.95), a light dinner for SH6 ($1.75).

One novel solution to the problem of accommodations is provided by **Herzlia Heights**, fully serviced apartments at 4 El Al St., tel. 03-930251. You must book for at least one week; daily rates, depending on the season, are SH85 ($25) to SH119 ($35) double. When you consider what you'll be getting for the money, the prices won't sound quite so high: a furnished apartment with one bedroom, a living room/dining area, a kitchen, a bathroom, switchboard service, and air conditioning. The location is five minutes (by car) from the sea.

RESTAURANTS: At Sharon Beach is the **Ginat Whitman Milk Bar,** a large blue and orange tent, where you can get waffles for SH8 ($2.35), an ice cream soda or milkshake for SH4 ($1.20), cheese toast for SH2 (60¢), and other light fare. Open daily from 9 a.m. to about midnight.

In the Zebulun Beach area is the very nice **Hof Zebulun Restaurant**, tel. 03-930046, with a window wall overlooking the sea and outdoor patio seating. You can get grilled hamburgers for SH6 ($1.75), a steak for SH9 ($2.65), lamb chops for SH12 ($3.50), all served with chips and salad. Open daily from 9 a.m. to 4 p.m. and 7:30 p.m. to midnight.

Facing a large square called **Kikar de Shalit** is a shopping area with quite a few places to eat. For ice cream concoctions and other desserts, as well as light snack fare, try the **House of Ice Cream** (20 flavors), **the Ice Cream Nest,** or **Glidaria.**

5. Netanya

Located about 21 miles from Tel Aviv and a third of the way up to Haifa, Netanya is regarded as the capital of the Sharon Plain, the rich and fertile citrus-grove area stretching from the outskirts of Tel Aviv to Caesarea. Perched on verdant cliffs overlooking the Mediterranean, it is also the center of Israel's diamond industry. Founded in 1929 as a citrus center, the seaside town has for many years been a popular flocking place among Israelis. Lately, however, tourists have been joining them, for they've discovered Netanya to be quiet and convenient, charming and hospitable, geared to service and in easy reach of several areas, including Tel Aviv and Caesarea. It's a sizable town, with all sorts of cafes, hotels, and shops—but the real appeal remains the sunny beach and quiet.

A handsome park parallels the beach—and the coast itself has achieved great popularity with Scandinavian visitors who take dips in December and

January. Most everybody else waits until April or May, when the weather at the attractive beach in this pleasant garden town is near perfect.

The city of 100,000 is easily accessible from everywhere in Israel. Several express buses ply the route between Netanya and Jerusalem. Connections are available from Haifa, and there is regular bus and train service from Tel Aviv. Sherut service is most frequent, followed by bus and then train; also the train station is some distance from the center of the city. Netanya buses leave Tel Aviv at an average of about every 15 minutes during most of the day. Buses from Tel Aviv to Netanya operate until 11:30 p.m. The last bus to Tel Aviv departs at 11 p.m.

HOTELS: You'll find several inexpensive hotels at your disposal—if you remember one rule of thumb: the further inland you go, the less you spend. So start looking at least two blocks from the cliff overhanging the beach. If you absolutely must have a place smack on the cliff, be prepared to spend more for the privilege. And remember that just because a hotel isn't overlooking the sea doesn't mean it isn't a pleasant place to stay. Low season is mid-November to the end of February.

The nine-story **Topaz Hotel,** 25 King David St., tel. 053-91229, has 64 rooms and all the usual big-splurge amenities, including showers, baths, air conditioning and heating. Bed-and-breakfast rate is SH80.10 ($23.55) single, SH53.40 ($15.70) per person double. Off-season rates are SH69.70 ($20.50) single, SH46.40 ($13.65) per person in a double. Breakfasts are Israeli, and for an additional per day charge you can rent one of the hotel's 32 units with refrigerator, stove, and cooking and eating utensils.

The **Atzmauth Hotel,** 2 Ussishkin St., tel. 053-22562, is a two-star hotel located on the fourth and fifth floors of an elevator building that's about a five-minute walk from the beach. The 20 rooms are very simple, all with showers and eight with toilets; others use toilets in the hall. Many of the guests are French and Scandinavian. The kitchen is kosher. Students get a whopping 40% reduction off season (September through June, excluding the High Holidays). Year-round rates are SH40.80 ($12) for a single, SH32.30 ($9.50) per person for a double. Lunch or dinner is SH20.40 ($6).

The ultra-Orthodox **Sara Pension,** 7 Kikar Ha'atzmauth, tel. 053-23066, has three very plain three-room apartments. No air conditioning, but there is heating. In July, August, and during holidays rates must include full board which comes to SH50 ($14.70) per person. Bed-and-breakfast off season is SH25 ($7.35) per person, full board SH35 ($10.30).

The **Metropol Hotel,** 18 Rishon LeZion St., tel. 053-38038, is near the seashore and has 27 rooms, all with bath or shower. The accommodations are large and clean, and meals are provided at the adjacent Grand Metropol, where guests can also enjoy the swimming pool and piano bar. Singles pay SH47.60 ($14), doubles SH40.80 ($12) per person. Off-season rates are a few dollars lower, and students are given a 20% discount on rates off-season.

Nearby is the highly recommended **Winkelsberg Hotel,** 22 Rishon LeZion St., tel. 053-22769. Here ten large, airy rooms cost SH51 ($15) single and SH34 ($10) per person double. The hotel serves a good Israeli breakfast.

Down the street at 29 Rishon LeZion St., is the very simply furnished one-star **Daphna Hotel,** tel. 053-23655. Rooms have showers and toilets, but otherwise are distinctly of the no-frills variety. Rates are SH34 ($10) to SH51 ($15) single, SH25.50 ($7.50) per person for double occupancy.

The **Margoa Hotel,** near the seashore at 9 Gad Machness St., tel. 053-34434, has 36 rooms, all with air conditioning, private bath or shower, and toilet; most have terraces. There's an attractively furnished modern dining room and bar, plus an outdoor terrace with chairs, tables, and even a hammock. Meals are kosher. A single room is SH52.70 ($15.50) to SH57.80 ($17), doubles SH39.10 ($11.50) to SH44.20 ($13) per person.

Near the sea, the **Yahalom Hotel**, 11 Gad Machness St., tel. 053-35345, has three stars and 48 clean, pleasant rooms, all with bath or shower. Year-round room rates, including Israeli breakfasts, are SH81.60 ($24) for a single, SH54.40 ($16) per person for double occupancy. Meals are served at the nearby Grand Yahalom Hotel, where guests can also use the swimming pool.

Another three-star enterprise is the **Palace Hotel**, 33 Gad Machness St., tel. 053-37631, five minutes walk from the beach though it overlooks the sea. Walk-in closets and comfortable armchairs are among the amenities in the 71 rooms. Rates are SH71.40 ($21) single, SH51 ($15) per person for a double occupancy. Off-season rates drop by $3 per person. A nice hotel—but take a look at the bedrooms to see if they're what you want.

The 40-room **Grinstein Hotel**, 47 Dizengoff St., tel. 053-22026, is graded two stars. A short walk from the beach, it has a large terrace with chairs and colored umbrellas. The 40 rooms are painted in pastel colors, and all have private bath or shower, terraces, and electric heaters; some have air conditioning. The dining room is pleasant and airy. A single room is SH46.20 ($13.60), a double SH36 ($10.60) per person; rates are a trifle lower off-season.

The three-story (no elevator) **Gal Yam Hotel**, 46 Dizengoff St., tel. 053-22603, recently added a new wing, bringing its room count to 22, all with bath or shower, electric heaters, and tiny terraces. Year-round rate for a single room is SH42.50 ($12.50) to SH47.60 ($14), SH37.40 ($11) per person for a double.

Close to the sea, the **Ast Hotel**, 6 Harav Kook St., near Herzl St., tel. 053-22157 has 29 rooms, 15 of them air-conditioned, and all with bath or shower. The dining room is rustic, and the lobby sports an aquarium. Students get a 25% discount on rates off-season.

The **Gan Hamelech Hotel**, 10 King David St., tel. 053-39341, has 50 rooms, occupies four stories, provides baths, air conditioning and heating. The tariff is SH52.70 ($15.50) per person for double occupancy, SH73.10 ($21.50) for a single. Low-season rates are several dollars lower. There is a 10% reduction for students and youths off-season. The hotel also has suites and cottages for groups of four to six. Pension arrangements available.

The **Ginot Yam Hotel**, 9 King David St., tel. 053-23007, faces the sea. All of the 34 rooms have showers, terraces, and electric heaters; 15 have air conditioning. There's a rattan-furnished piano bar on the premises, and a TV set in the lobby; outside is a large terrace with garden furnishings. Singles pay SH47.60 ($14), doubles SH37.40 ($11) per person; lower rates off-season.

Rooms at the **Hof Hotel**, 7 Kikar Ha'atzmauth, tel. 053-22825, are well equipped with phones, air conditioning, heating, and private baths or showers. There's an elevator, a pleasant dining room, and a comfortable bar. A single room is SH72.90 ($21.45) a night, a double SH54.20 ($15.95) per person. Off-season rates are a few dollars less.

The strictly kosher **Galei Ruth Hotel**, 11 King David St., tel. 053-22647, actually has a synagogue on the premises. It's conveniently located across from the sea, and the 18 rooms all have bath or shower, small terraces, and heating; half are air-conditioned. Singles pay SH40.80 ($12) a night for B&B, doubles pay SH32.30 ($9.50) each; during July, August, and holidays rates go up about $1.50 per person. Lunch and dinner are available for SH20.40 ($6) per meal in the cheerful yellow and orange dining room.

Also try the five-story, elevator-equipped **Mitzpe Yam Hotel**, 4 Karlebach St., tel. 053-23730, where the 28 rooms are equipped with fans, private showers, and central heating. In addition to the dining room (breakfast only is served), there's a small bar adjoining the lobby. It's just five minutes from the sea. Singles pay SH57.80 ($17) a night, doubles SH47.60 ($14) per person; a 10% reduction is offered to students.

Situated in a lovely residential area, away from the center of town, the three-star **Feldman Hotel**, 9 Hashivah St., tel. 053-22193, is surrounded by palm trees and gardens. The 22 rooms have attractive furnishings, private kitchenettes, baths or showers, and wall-to-wall carpeting. The redwood-paneled dining room is also very nicely decorated, and fresh flowers grace every table. Throughout the year, students are given a 15% reduction. Singles pay SH68 ($20), doubles SH51 ($15) per person. Off-season rates are about $3 per person lower. Highly recommended.

The much-recommended **Orit**, 21 Hen Blvd., tel. 053-23465, is a small, quiet family-run hotel with just seven rooms, each with private shower, toilet, and a small terrace. It's set in a lovely garden with chairs under the trees. B&B rates are SH45.90 ($13.50) single, SH35.70 ($10.50) per person double.

Just five minutes from the beach, the **Talmor Hotel**, 25 Ussishkin St., tel. 053-23107, has 27 rooms with bath or shower. The kitchen is kosher. Year-round rates are SH45.90 ($13.50) single, SH40.80 ($12) per person double.

A Resort at Budget Prices

South of the city is the **Green Beach Holiday Village**, P.O.B. 230, tel. 053-38141, which is far more than just a hotel. It has a full range of recreational facilities, including a fine swimming pool and horseback-riding. As for the rooms, there are 165 in all, two-thirds of them air-conditioned, all heated. Rates are SH60.70 ($17.85) for single occupancy, SH45 ($13.25) per person double. Off-season, the rates are SH56.10 ($16.50) and SH41.60 ($12.25), respectively. The **Green Beach Night Club**, on the premises, is open from 9:30 p.m. to 2 a.m. on Fridays.

Private Rooms and Apartments

One of the best ways to save money on accommodations, particularly if you plan to stay in Netanya for some time, is to rent a private room or apartment. Consult the Municipal Tourist Information Office, Kikar Ha'atzmauth, tel. 053-27286 for listings. The office is open from 8:30 a.m. to 2 p.m. and 3 to 7 p.m. April through October, 8:30 a.m. to 2 p.m. November through March. The actual rental arrangements will generally be handled by local agents. And you'll have to pay an agent's fee, which is a flat 10% of the total rental (no extra charge if meal arrangements are made, fortunately).

Room rentals are available for at least three to four days, apartments for a week or more. Most of them are within walking distance of the sea.

Rooms in private homes come with sheets and blankets, and guests may use the refrigerator and stove. The cost without meals is SH17 ($5) to SH20.40 ($6) per person.

In an apartment, you are provided with basic furniture requirements. The place is cleaned up before you arrive, but the onus of upkeep is on you for the length of your stay. What is known as a two-room flat (living room, one bedroom, kitchen, bath, balconies) costs SH1020 ($300) per couple per month. A three-room flat (two bedrooms plus) costs SH1360 ($400) to SH1700 ($500) per month. A four-room flat (three bedrooms plus) costs SH2040 ($600) for the same period. Considering that the larger apartments can accommodate six to eight persons, the daily average cost per bed is really quite low.

If you plan on taking a room or an apartment during the high season (July–September), you should make arrangements in April or May.

Send a deposit (the usual deposit is about a third of the monthly rental)—which you'll probably lose if you cancel close to arrival time. You definitely won't get back the agent's fee. In return you'll receive a contract and exact information about what you'll be renting.

Two local agencies handling apartment rentals on a monthly basis are the **Anglo-Saxon Real Estate Agency,** 7 Kikar Ha'atzmauth, tel. 053-28290; and **Signal,** Kikar Zion, tel. 053-23198.

RESTAURANTS: Easiest to spot is **Pancake House,** Kikar Ha'atzmauth, with its red, yellow, and blue striped awning visible from afar. In addition to pancakes with maple syrup for SH2.50 (75¢), this eatery features blintzes with sour cream at SH2 (60¢) each, and fried fish with chips, pitta, and salad for SH10 ($2.95). Open from 9 a.m. until the last of the hungry are fed.

The **Renaissance Restaurant,** 6 Kikar Ha'atzmauth, tel. 053-28653, offers Israeli fare with a slight French accent. The decor is attractive and modernistic, with tables both inside and out under the flowered awning. An order of kabab or hamburger topped with egg, either served with salad and chips, is SH8 ($2.35). Open daily from 8 a.m. to 1 a.m.

Another place offering indoor and outdoor dining is the **Exodus Cafe and Restaurant,** 1 Herzl St., tel. 053-35916. Inside the white walls are adorned with paintings, and the tables are covered with colorful cloths. The bill of fare lists grilled chicken or a cheese omelet with salad for SH4 ($1.20); goulash, steak, or shashlik are SH7.90 ($2.30), fish with chips and salad SH10 ($2.95). Hours vary a bit; basically the Exodus is open daily from early morning to late at night.

Nearby, at 1 Herzl St., the **Hasharon,** tel. 053-22311, is a large but unpretentious restaurant, with tables covered in floral-design plastic cloths and adorned with flowers in Sabra liqueur bottles. There's additional seating outside under an orange and blue awning. Grilled or fried trout with salad and potatoes is a house specialty at SH10 ($2.95); other choices include roast goose with all the trimmings for SH9 ($2.65), blintzes for SH3 (90¢), and a platter of four vegetables for SH4 ($1.20). For dessert there's Bavarian cream at SH1.50 (45¢). Open daily from 7 a.m. to midnight.

The **"Hanassi" President Restaurant and Cafe Bar,** 5 Herzl St., tel. 053-22952, is open daily 7 a.m.–midnight, Friday until 4 p.m., Saturday from sundown to midnight–1:30 a.m. Cuisine is Hungarian/oriental, and main courses include stuffed cabbage for SH4 ($1.20) and veal escalope with rice and salad for SH7.50 ($2.20). You can order a complete meal for SH15 ($4.40) on the Sabbath, payable in advance, that will include an appetizer of gefilte fish or chopped liver, soup, a main course—perhaps goulash with potatoes and a vegetable, wine for kiddush, and fruit compote for dessert.

The **Sara Pension,** 7 Kikar Ha'atzmauth, tel. 053-23066, mentioned above in "Hotels," serves strictly kosher Hungarian meals—SH10 ($2.95) for a dairy supper, SH16 ($4.70) for a meat lunch or dinner.

The **Egged Bus Station Restaurant** here as elsewhere offers some of the least expensive food in town. It's a self-service place, and you can get a three-course meal for about SH13.60 ($4). Open from early morning to 9 p.m., closed for the Sabbath.

The **"Baiza" Grill Bar,** 5 Herzl St., dishes out strictly kosher grilled meats, all with chips, salads, pickles and pitta, priced at SH4 ($1.20); another choice is couscous with meat for SH9 ($2.65). Open 11:30 a.m. to 1 a.m., closed from 2 p.m. Friday until after sunset on Saturday.

As for pizza, they're lining up for it at **Don Pedro,** 7 Herzl St., where pizza goes for SH1.20 (35¢) to SH1.40 (40¢). Open from 10 a.m. to 2 p.m. and 4 to 10–11 p.m., closed from Friday at 2 p.m. until Saturday at 4 p.m. .

WHAT TO DO, DAY AND NIGHT: During the 90% of the year when the sun is in full bloom, you bake under the Mediterranean sun, swim in protected areas, fish, boat, stroll, and while away the hours in a sidewalk cafe. In other words, you relax and enjoy yourself.

Winter or summer, Netanya is alive at night. There are movie houses everywhere and you have to fight for leg room along the city's main drag. There is commotion and pandemonium and there is also culture.

In July, there is a one-week **art exhibit** on Ha'atzmauth Square (Sunday through Thursday from 5:30 to 11 p.m.; closed Friday; Saturday from 8:30 p.m. to midnight). . . . The **Netanya Orchestra** provides free music at the square every Tuesday evening from July through September. It is all gloriously free and the conductor is England's Sam Lewis. . . . For SH7.50 ($2.20), which includes a drink, there is an **Israeli Folklore Evening** twice a month. The tourist office, Kikar Ha'atzmaut, tel. 053-27286, will provide precise information. . . . For the more cerebral, a **chess tournament** is held in the city yearly during May and June. The location varies. The event is a big draw, and every two years there's a match for international contestants. The games start at 3:30 p.m. and last until 10 p.m. For further information, contact the Tourist Information Office or the Israel Chess Federation, 6 Frisch St., Tel Aviv, tel. 03-258102.

If you'd like to meet an Israeli citizen, apply three days in advance at the tourist office and you'll soon find yourself invited to a home for a friendly chat and a cup of coffee.

As for sports, there's **mini-golf**—18 holes—near the Four Seasons Hotel on Nice Blvd.; **tennis** at the Elizur Sports Center on Radak St.; **horseback riding** at the Green Beach Ranch near the Green Beach Holiday Village mentioned above.

Many discos in town, but they tend to get a bit rowdy sometimes. If you're not up for quite that much action, join the folk dancing every Saturday beginning at 8:30 p.m., May to October, in Ha'atzmaut Square. It's free.

EN ROUTE TO CAESAREA: On the coastal highway just north of Netanya, in Kfar Vitkin, there's a large gas station, **Paznon,** with a great snack restaurant that's open from 7 a.m. to 1 a.m. daily, and a gift shop flanking it. While you have the car tanked up, you can fill up on the specialty of this American-owned place: pancakes. Two of them with maple syrup will cost you SH3 (90¢). More exotic varieties—with salami, apple sauce, coconuts, cherries, lemons, raisins, cheese or an egg—cost more. Many other choices are available, ranging from humus or tchina in a pitta for SH2.50 (75¢) to grilled chicken with chips for SH9.50 ($2.80).

6. Caesarea and Vicinity

This is one of our favorite places in Israel. Among Caesarea's beautiful excavations you get an inspired feeling for the tide of history that has washed Israel's shores.

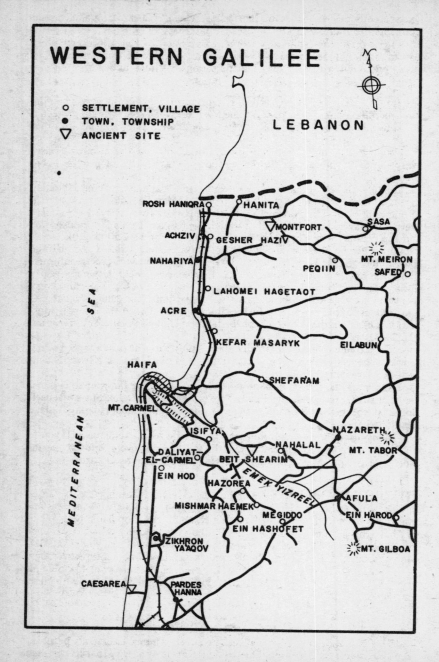

WESTERN GALILEE

○ SETTLEMENT, VILLAGE
● TOWN, TOWNSHIP
▽ ANCIENT SITE

LEBANON

ROSH HANIQRA   HANITA
ACHZIV   GESHER HAZIV   MONTFORT   SASA
NAHARIYA
PEQIIN   MT. MEIRON
SAFED
LAHOMEI HAGETAOT
ACRE
KEFAR MASARYK   EILABUN
HAIFA
SHEFARAM
MT. CARMEL
ISIFYA   NAZARETH
NAHALAL   MT. TABOR
DALIYAT-EL-CARMEL   BEIT SHEARIM
EIN HOD
HAZOREA   EMEK YIZREEL
MISHMAR HAEMEK   AFULA
MEGIDDO   EIN HAROD
EIN HASHOFET
ZIKHRON YA'AQOV   MT. GILBOA
CAESAREA   PARDES HANNA

SEA

MEDITERRANEAN

Located about a third of the way from Tel Aviv to Haifa, behind an immigrant's village and a cluster of banana groves, Caesarea has recently been the scene of considerable activity and development—archeological digs, concerts, a golf course and country club.

Caesarea is the spectacular city of Herod the Great, built when Jesus was a carpenter in Nazareth. Herod set out to construct a port to equal Athens, and judging from scientific reconstructions, he probably succeeded. The magnificent harbor town was dedicated to Augustus Caesar, Emperor of Rome from 27 B.C. to 14 A.D. It later became the largest city in Judea, the chief port, the governor's residence and the home of Pontius Pilate. Despite its splendor, it was also a cruel Roman city, and within its gates hundreds of Jews and Christians were thrown to the lions following the revolt of 66 A.D.

Ancient Caesarea was a diplomat's city, a merchant's city, and a sportsman's city—a cosmopolitan delight for the sophisticates of the time. Its grandeur lasted for about 300 years, but ultimately the Arabs took the town from the Byzantines in the seventh century.

Four hundred years later, the Frank Crusaders reconquered Caesarea, and among the treasures they recovered was the famous Holy Grail, the green crystal vessel from the Last Supper, which figured in so many of the Arthurian romances. Saint Louis later built a fort here, portions of which still remain. The Moslems recaptured it in 1291, when they killed the last of the Crusaders in the Holy Land.

LIFE ON A KIBBUTZ: The **Caesarea Shore Resort,** tel. 063-61161, sounds like one of those posh places for internationals. Well, people from all over the world do frequent it, but it's not all posh. It is pleasant, casual and beautiful in its own way. And the people who operate it, Sdot Yam kibbutzniks, are friendly, warm and conscientious. It's also known as **Kayit V'shayit Ltd.,** and road signs will direct you until you arrive in the large parking lot facing a small snack bar that fronts the main dining room. If you want to stop just for a meal or snack, you're better off in the dining room. Many of the folks working here, by the way, are part of the Kibbutz's Ulpan, a six-month work/study program for people from all over the world.

If you'd like to stay overnight or longer, there's a range of facilities that includes a **Guest House,** where SH49.30 ($14.50) per person covers bed and breakfast in a double with private shower/bath. Or you could stay in the cleverly designed prefabricated (insulated wood) **double-bungalow huts** that dot the sand dunes—a bit cheaper. Finally, there's full camping regalia here—with showers and guards, the works. A children's playpool stands near the restaurant, and in the distance, a lifeguard surveys happy bathers on the private beach. Without staying over, you can enjoy beach fun, tennis courts, and showers for a modest charge. Those who sleep here have nightly entertainment to boot. The resort is open from May 1 to November 1, and, while there is no actual off-season discount, in May and October they don't take the 10% service charge that is added throughout the midsummer months. Should you decide to stay here, you'll not only have relaxing delight, you'll also get an inside look at kibbutz personalities and enterprise.

THE SIGHTS OF CAESAREA: That's what we're here for, and we'll take them one by one:

Golf Course

Entering Caesarea from the main road, you will first see the country's only golf club on your left. It has already accumulated about 2,000 overseas members, much to the chagrin of the local kibbutzniks who argue that the water cultivating the greens for the rich man's folly could better be used on the scrubby farmlands of their settlements. Non-members can use the facilities, equipment can be rented, and even lessons are available. Call 063-88174 for further information.

Statues

Past the golf course, on your left, you'll see a large dug-out trench of columns and statues. This area was accidentally discovered by Sdot Yam kibbutzniks while they were ploughing one day. Uncovered was a Byzantine forum with two headless statues: one red-stoned and toga-draped, and the other on a gray porphyry throne, with its toga cut from marble. Archeologists believe the statues to be of second- to fourth-century Roman emperors, pillaged and used for decorative purposes by the Byzantines around the fifth or sixth century. (The area's souvenir shop is located here.)

Fort and Port

At a glance, you'll see vestiges of three civilizations here: the steps leading to St. Louis' Crusader fortress, the crumbled Roman columns jutting out of the sea, and a minaret from the 19th-century Turkish occupation. Climb the steps to the top of the fort and you'll have a magnificent view of the Caesarea enclave—from the swimmers in the green harbor below you to the Roman race course, or hippodrome, which encircles the entire area. Experts claim some 20,000 spectators could have watched the races. Between the beach and the hippodrome, archeologists have recently been busy digging down into buried Crusader and Roman towns.

There's a lot to see at Caesarea, and if the sun gets too strong for you, there's a picturesque cafe, the **Straton,** refreshingly situated right in the harbor walls.

Amphitheater

South of the harbor, on a hill facing the sea, is a beautifully preserved Roman amphitheater, uncovered only within the last decade. It actually looks like a miniature of the Roman Coliseum. A hundred yards long and sixty yards wide, it was used for the first time in 1,700 years when Pablo Casals played here in the summer of 1961.

Above the amphitheater note the strewn columns, each painted with a number, waiting to be joined together. The amphitheater, incidentally, is probably one of the places where prisoners and gladiators fought with lions to entertain the local populace. Today's populace is also entertained here—by everyone from jazz to classical artists—each summer, during the Israel Festival. Completely renovated and restored, the amphitheater now boasts a large stage, sound systems, and an acoustical "umbrella."

Mosaic Floor and Aqueduct

Backtracking along the road to the golf course make a left turn, and on a nearby hill you'll find a Byzantine mosaic floor. It is made of interlaced circles, each containing a different bird or animal from this area, circa fifth century. A Roman aqueduct is further along on the same road, built in the second century to carry water from the hills down to Caesarea.

LOCAL ENTERTAINMENT: Into those crumbling vaults in the port/ancient city area, imaginative planners have installed a **Disco** complete with go-go dancers. With the lights playing on the minaret and breakers, this is a wonderfully romantic place at night.

If you want to see how the other half lives, stop in for a look around the **Dan Caesarea Hotel,** which was built originally by and for Baron Rothschild and later ceded temporarily to the Club Méditerranée. Stop in for a drink at the bar, should you be in the neighborhood. Maybe you'll rub shoulders with some of the international crowd which seems to make the Dan Caesarea its home when in Israel: movie stars, politicians, tycoons, playboys, playgirls. In all the Caesarea is an unusually handsome place.

IN THE VICINITY: Heading northward from Caesarea, we come across Zichron Yaakov, Tantura, Athlit and Ein Hod.

Zichron Yaakov

In the hills north of Caesarea, Zichron Yaakov has the distinction of being one of the first towns to be settled in Israel, founded in 1882. Of interest here are the wine cellars (they'll give you a tour and some wine afterward), and the **Rothschild Family Tomb** set in handsome gardens. And right near the wine cellar, stop in to see the **Aaronson Museum;** it commemorates the days during World War I when the Aaronson family worked at an experimental farm at Athlit and supplied the British with intelligence information.

Opposite Zichron Yaakov is **Kibbutz Maagan Michael,** whose beautiful carp ponds at the edge of the sea also serve as a bird sanctuary. Depending on the season, bird-watchers can find herons, cranes, and storks. This kibbutz is also a livestock center with herds of Brahmin-type cows and in-residence Israeli cowboys.

Tantura

On the highway skirting the beach, road signs announce **Nahsholim,** a kibbutz located on one of Israel's most beautiful bathing beaches: Tantura. A wide expanse of sandy beach, it is beautified by natural lagoons and a backdrop of Arab ruins. It is the site of the ancient city of Dor—a port and famous Tyrian dye-making center. Here Israeli archeologists partly excavated a Roman theater facing the sea. All the way to the right at Tantura is a picturesque area of caves eroded by the sea to form a natural tunnel at the water's edge.

Here, too, is another kibbutz-operated vacation village, **Hof Dor,** Mobile Post Hacarmel, tel. 063-99121. About an hour's drive from Tel Aviv, and easily reached via local buses or sheruts, it's a great place to spend the day, or several days. The islets around the beach make for sheltered and warm swimming, even during the winter or storm seasons, and the recreation facilities cover almost everything you can think of. There are antiquities around this recreation village, and it's a good base for sightseeing tours. Meals are available in the air-conditioned dining room.

Aside from the usual camping facilities and fees (see Caesarea Shore Resort, above), Hof Dor provides picturesque huts (they call them "igloos") grouped together in a way that allows for privacy. The "igloos" are air-conditioned and equipped with showers, gas burners, refrigerators, and toilets. They accommodate four and rent for SH187 ($55) a day. This is a very popular place for families and young people, who appreciate the informality as much as the reasonable rates. There are several other kinds of accommodation here.

Just a short drive further north is a camping site, **Neve Yam,** with the same rates and similar facilities. Tel. 04-942240 for further information. The campgrounds are open all year, but provisions are only attainable from May to October.

Athlit

A short drive northward along the coast brings you to the ruins of a castle from Crusader times—the last Crusader fortress, in fact, to fall to the Arabs, in 1291 A.D. In the ruins, archeologists have also discovered relics and pottery from the Persian-Hellenistic and Phoenician periods. They might have been able to find more, but the earthquake in 1837 caused the Turkish ruler, Ibrahim Pasha, to remove much of Athlit's crumbled masonry and send it to Acre and Jaffa for reconstructing damaged buildings. The Turks and the Arabs were notorious for chopping up lovely Corinthian columns and dispatching them as ordinary building materials. Unfortunately, you can't go into the Athlit castle for a closer look, because it's smack in the heart of a security zone of the Israeli navy. (The military base you see at Athlit was originally built by the British as an internment camp for immigrants who illegally entered the country.)

Ein Hod

Inland, and almost directly across from Athlit, is the artists' village of Ein Hod. Road signs will point the way for drivers, and from 10 a.m. to 5:30 p.m. there's Egged bus service all the way up the mountainside to this famous colony. You can also take bus 921 to the Ein Hod roadway that intersects with the older, more inland Tel Aviv–Haifa highway, and hitchhike up the mountainside from there. (True hikers will find the ten-minute, half-mile trek a simple one.) Regardless of how you get up there, do make the trip.

Built over an abandoned Arab village, Ein Hod ("Well of Beauty") is the world-famous Israeli artists' colony, operated along certain cooperative lines: The village members have their own council of elders; the handyman is employed by the entire community; the gallery takes a much smaller percentage on sales than do other galleries; the workshops are shared, and the proceeds from the amphitheater's shows (summer weekends only) are used for the welfare of the village.

Under the guidance of the village's former Mukhtar (headman), Marcel Yanko, the sculptors, painters, and potters rebuilt an old village according to their own specifications in 1953. They sawed, hammered and plastered, planted gardens, patched leaky ceilings, installed plumbing, and turned a mosque and storehouse into a cafe and workshop. With help from the Tourist Office, the Haifa Municipality, and private donations, they now have a large gallery, several workshops, and an outdoor theater.

It's a picturesque place, tranquil and rugged-looking, with a view of sloping olive groves and the broad Mediterranean that can inspire even the nonartistic. Crumbling archways and Moorish vaults are left as relics of the past.

Ein Hod's restaurant, tel. 04-942016, displays brightly covered murals by some of its artist-members in an otherwise simple but roomy place. Moderately priced, it offers typical Israeli fare. A reduction of 25% is available to students.

The restaurant is particularly popular on Friday nights, when it serves a traditional Sabbath meal, including homemade gefilte fish and tcholent.

The Ein Hod gallery, tel. 04-942029, carries a good selection of the village's work—silver jewelry, lots of ceramics, lithographs, etchings, oil paintings, water colors, tapestries and shawls, sculpture and woodwork. Most of Ein Hod's 200 full-time residents are craftspeople. They'll box your purchases and mail them to you wherever you live.

Admission to the gallery is an SH.30 (10¢) donation for adults. Its hours are 9:30 a.m. to 5:30 p.m. every day of the week, but it's closed Yom Kippur and Israeli Independence Day.

A three-hour tour to Ein Hod takes place three times a week: Mondays at 3 p.m., Thursdays at 9 a.m., and Saturdays at 9:30 a.m. It includes a drive through the Carmel mountain range, and visits to art galleries, artist's studios, etc. Contact **Mitzpe Tours,** 1 Nordau St., Haifa, tel. 04-666898; tour price: SH20.40 ($6).

Continue driving along the road that runs through Ein Hod, and you'll reach the delightful resort of **Nir Etzion.** It's run by the kibbutz of the same name. The kibbutz offers rooms, kosher meals conducted in a religious, warm, friendly atmosphere, and transportation to nearby Tantura Beach. It's also near Mount Carmel woods. The address is Nir Etzion, Mount Carmel; tel. 04-942542.

ON TO ACRE: Not far from Athlit, you enter the outskirts of Haifa, and you'll notice signs for the lovely **Carmel Beach** (Hof HaCarmel), where for a small fee you can sun and shower afterwards. But if you happen to be broke, backtrack half a kilometer to the **Municipal Beach,** which is free, including shower. The **Bat Galim Beach,** in the same vicinity, is free too.

Independence Road in Haifa port runs northward out of the city past a heavily industrial area. At a crossroads called the "checkpost" bear left over the railroad tracks and you'll be on the northern coastal road to Acre and Nahariya. This latter road is also heavy with industry, and it's an industry you won't miss, because the smell of a sprawling chemical and fertilizer company overpowers the entire area.

The road to Acre and Nahariya passes through the Haifa suburbs of **Kiryat Motzkin** and **Kiryat Bialik,** both German-Jewish settlements. Kiryat Bialik is famous for its "Yekkes," the word Israelis affectionately give to German-Jewish settlers. In fact, Kiryat Bialik is so German-Jewish that the mother of a friend of ours, who has lived there for over 25 years, only recently began taking beginner's Hebrew lessons.

Kiryat Bialik is also famous for an ambush the Haganah staged there in March of 1948, when an Arab munitions convoy blew up and nearly took Kiryat Bialik with it. The ambush averted the invasion of Haifa.

7. Acre

Acre, with its romantic minarets and palm trees framed against the sea, has a long, startlingly eventful history. It figured in wars during the time of Jonathan, the Hasmonean. It was a leading Phoenician port. Caesar camped here in 48–47 B.C. Roman sailors discovered that the local sand made superior glass. In 1104, the Crusaders made Acre the principal port of the Holy Land. Saladin took it in 1187, and Richard the Lion-Hearted reclaimed it for Christianity four years later. In the last few centuries it has been the landing point for pilgrims to the Holy Land, and in the 19th century the Turks made it their capital in Palestine. In 1799, Napoleon's thrust into the East was decisively stopped here by a combined English and Turkish defense. The notorious ruler at the time, Ahmed Jezzar Pasha, who earned a considerable reputation for cruelty, built the town's splendid mosque and luxurious steam baths. Students of modern Israeli history will recall that the Pasha's mosque and baths figured prominently in the daring escape from Acre prison during the British Mandate.

HOTELS AND RESTAURANTS: There are two widely divergent possibilities for those wishing to stay in Acre itself. On one side of the spectrum is the **Argaman Motel**, tel. 04-913755, a holiday village with 75 air-conditioned rooms, a spectacular view, a splendid beach and per person prices of SH56.10 ($16.50) to SH71.40 ($21), including Israeli breakfast. Students get a 10% discount. All rooms have bath and shower, toilet, radio, and phone. On the other side of the scale (and on the other side of the town) is the **youth hostel**, with accommodations for 120 people, no age limit, and regular youth hostel prices (see Chapter XI). The hostel is in the building that was once the palace of the local Ottoman governors.

There are a number of good restaurants in this ancient city. The **Migdal Or**, 11/325 Haganah St., tel. 04-911957, in the Old City, is open daily from 9:30 a.m. to midnight dishing up shashlik for SH6 ($1.75), steak or fish with chips for SH8 ($2.35), etc. An unusual choice is a pair of grilled pigeons filled with rice and pine nuts for SH10 ($2.95). Some tables offer a view of the sea. If you show a copy of this book you'll get a 10% reduction on your dinner bill; students, with or without the book, get a 15% reduction.

A good choice is the exceptionally clean and pleasant **Oudeh Brothers Restaurant**, in the Old City market area, tel. 04-912013, with three large, airy dining rooms. Open daily from 9 a.m. to midnight, it offers a ten-salad mazza for SH6 ($1.75), lamb shashlik with rice and salad for SH8.50 ($2.50), meat with humus, pickles, and pitta for SH5 ($1.45). Turkish coffee is on the house if you've ordered a meal.

One of Acre's best-known eateries is **Abu Christo**, near the Old Port, tel. 04-910065, where your meal is enhanced by a waterfront view. It's particularly nice in good weather, when you can sit out on the terrace. Choices include steak with chips for SH6 ($1.75), fish with chips for SH8 ($2.35), and shrimps with tartar sauce for SH10 ($2.95). Open daily from 9 a.m. to midnight.

A sea view is also one of the attractions at **Ptolemais Restaurant**, in the fisherman's quay, tel. 04-912600. Open daily from 8 a.m. to midnight, it dishes up terrific fish entrees at SH8 ($2.35), and meat meals like beef with humus at SH6 ($1.75). Watermelon, for SH2 (60¢), makes a refreshing dessert. Students get a 10% reduction.

Highly recommended is the **Palm Beach Self-Service Restaurant** on Acre Beach, tel. 04-910888, part of the four-star Palm Beach Hotel. There's a meat section where you can order the likes of stuffed cabbage for SH7.50 ($2.20) and goulash or schnitzel with latkes for SH10 ($2.95), and a milk section where blintzes can be had for SH4 ($1.20). You can dine in the large dining room or outside on the patio. Open daily from 8:30 a.m. to 6 p.m., till midnight in summer.

Also very good is the self-service restaurant of the **Argaman Motel**, Acre Beach, tel. 04-913755, where items like Hungarian goulash and braised beef are SH9 ($2.65), side dishes SH2 (60¢) to SH3 (90¢) extra.

WHAT TO DO AND SEE: If you want a **motorboat ride** around the walls of the Old City to the Argaman Beach and back, look for Kamel and Mouner Sa'adi on the dock at the harbor. The Sa'adis have a boat that they call the *"Joan d'Arc,"* which accommodates 50 people and sails from 9:30 a.m. to 6 p.m., June 15–Oct. 1.

By land, little in the town's outward appearance reveals its infamous past: The streets are narrow and smelly, the rampart along the sea is in disuse, the new quarter of the city is very ordinary looking. Acre does have a lot to offer the more discerning sightseer, however, and you must give yourself some time to capture the Eastern rhythms in the teeming bazaar and to see the curious relics of the past in the citadel and prison.

Into the Citadel

The main road through new Acre curves parallel to the sea wall. Opposite the wall is the Turkish-built prison used as the nation's central prison by the British during the Mandate. On public view is the English hanging-room, where members of the Israeli underground forces were put to death; inscriptions in this dungeon commemorate the names of those unfortunate fighters. Called Museum Hagvurah, it's not a prison any more; it's been converted to a mental institution.

Mosque of El Jezzar

This is a large and most splendid mosque, tel. 04-910078. You reach it by going around the sea wall and past the lighthouse, entering the main street of the Old City. The square you'll pass is a Turkish caravanserai (known as the Khan, described further on) dominated by a tall tower. These odd-looking buildings, a series of galleries on a quadrangle, were once used as lodging places for caravan merchants who had trekked hundreds of miles to do their trading in Acre. Continue through the square and you'll come out at the mosque.

The mosque itself, styled along exotic Arabian Nights lines, was built in 1781. It has been spruced up and made even more splendid with a courtyard patio and graceful palm trees in a garden outside, all rounded out by a sun dial and fountain. Inside, it's a bit disappointing, but Moslem mosques are usually cavernous and empty. The tomb of El Jezzar is decorated with various arabesques, vaults, and oriental carpets.

Back outside, down a flight of stairs, is the Pasha's Turkish bath, **Hammam el-Pasha.** It has since been converted into a museum, tel. 04-910251, filled with common objects of the oriental world that once were used in Acre.

Next to the mosque and the museum is one of Acre's most important Crusader sites. A subterranean city, it was the rectory of the Knights Hospitallers of St. John. Recent excavations have opened a fine vaulted Gothic hall, styled with sculptured decorations on the arches and columns. Check to see if they've opened the underground passage to the **Posta,** once an infirmary for wounded knights and later a Turkish post office, hence its name. Open daily from 8:30 a.m. to 4:30 p.m., Friday till 1 p.m. Entrance fee is minimal.

The Khan

Acre is the only Crusader town that remains "alive" today. Not every house is intact, but people still live in the same rooms Crusaders occupied. Many of those rooms are in the Khan, which was an inn (or caravanserai) for 2,000 years. The maze of rooms and stalls branching off from the courtyard were stables, and the knights and their friends, as well as passing tourists and businessmen, slept crowded (20 to 30) together on the usually bare floors of the rooms upstairs—rooms reached by narrow and slick stone stairs, which lead to a balcony that overlooks the enormous courtyard. Today the Ministry of Tourism and the Acre Development Corporation are joining forces to reconstruct and resurrect the Old City of Acre, with prime focus on reconverting the Khan into what it once was—a place to accommodate visitors. But before the actual renovation can get underway, the rooms must be vacated, so the Ministry and the A.D.C. are trying to buy these historical rooms and move the residents into nearby modern housing. The new hotel may even be underway by the time you arrive. If it isn't, you can still peek at the rooms, because that stairway leads up to the roof and tower, from which there's a terrific view of the city and harbor. It's a good place to gain some perspective on how this confusing maze of streets is laid out.

In the vast courtyard, where caravans once stopped, tourists can now browse, buy, and eat in street-level shops that were stables for camels, donkeys, and horses before their recent facelift.

Acre Market

The winding, noisy bazaar—the "suq"—still exudes the sights and smells of Arabia.

You can find the following for exceptionally low prices: army surplus sweaters, paratroopers' boots, brass and copper coffee table trays, Arab pottery, handmade jewelry, and picture postcards—to give you some idea of the variety. And if you're looking for something in particular, don't give up easily if you can't initially find it. It's here, somewhere, amid the teeming jumble of languages, beggars, tiny shops, and swarms of flies. From now on, when someone speaks of a bazaar with that exotic Arabic flavor, you'll know exactly what is meant.

ON THE ROAD TO NAHARIYA: Paralleling the road, on the east, is a handsome **aqueduct** built by Jezzar over one the Romans left. The aqueduct originally supplied Acre with water from the Galilee's springs. Its ruins are beautifully picturesque, with many archways framing sabra plants. . . . A lovely Baha'i garden, called **Bahje House** (meaning "garden" in Turkish), lies one mile north of Acre, on the left of the road. This is the place where the sect's leader, Bahaulla, was placed by the Turks in nominal freedom. His remains are entombed in the main house, which is at once oriental and Victorian-looking. The grounds here comprise lovely velvet-green carpets of grass, bronze peacocks adorning the pathways, and slender cypress trees. . . . Two miles along is another memorial, although much less serene. This one is in **Kibbutz Lohame Ha'geta'ot** ("Fighters of the Ghettos"), founded by fighters and survivors of ghettos in Poland, Germany, and Lithuania, and it displays an exhibit of relics from ghettos and concentration camps similar to the one at Yad Vashem in Jerusalem. The most telling and grotesque exhibit here, so far as we're concerned, is in the library room. Here are gathered recent newspapers and magazines that tell of Gestapo squad reunions in Germany, the recent commercial successes of the former crematorium manufacturers, and the German schoolchildren's history books that casually refer to the murder of six-million Jews. There is also an extremely moving exhibition of paintings and drawings done by the children of the camps—bits of realistic, fantasy-world horror tales set down on scraps of paper, recording the life of a child in a concentration camp. Admission to the memorial is free. Open daily from 9 a.m. to 4 p.m.

8. From Nahariya to the Border

NAHARIYA: Founded by German Jews in the mid-1930s, Nahariya is a popular summer resort with Israelis, but foreigners are catching on. On the Lag b'Omer holiday in the spring, which is the only day a Jew can marry during the six weeks between the Passover and Shavouth holidays, Nahariya is packed with honeymooners. Maybe there's a connection between Nahariya's honeymoon attractions and the fact that on its beach archeologists dug up a Canaanite fertility goddess. And maybe not.

This holiday town has an unusual main street: A stream runs down the middle of it. Horsecarts clop-clop along the thoroughfare and will take you around town; settle on a price before you start out.

Hotels

Like Netanya, Nahariya ranks as a favorite resort area among Israelis and foreign visitors. There are many hotels to choose from, also rooms in private homes. The local I.G.T.O., in the Egged Bus Station Building, has an up-to-date list of these. The prices are fixed, but the kind of accommodations vary greatly, so better check before registering. Also, be aware that a surcharge of $2 or $3 is added to hotel rates during July and August and on Jewish holidays.

As far as hotels are concerned, there are quite a number that fit into our price structure. **The Kalman Hotel,** 26/7 Jabotinsky St., tel. 04-920355, has two stars, 20 rooms with bath and shower, air conditioning, and heating. The owner, who has been in the hotel business over 50 years, is the president of the Hotel Association of Nahariya. A single room in season costs SH47.60 ($14), double occupancy is SH39.10 ($11.50) per person, and a third party obtains a 20% discount; students get a 15% discount year round. Kosher Israeli breakfasts are served.

Just a few steps from the entrance to the Galei-Galil bathing beach is the three-story (no elevator) **Nof Yam Hotel,** 14 Hama'apilim St., tel. 04-920059. All rooms have bath or shower, heating, and air conditioning; most have terraces and sea views. They're painted in pastel colors with flowered curtains on the windows. There's a TV set in the lobby-lounge and an outdoor terrace with umbrella tables and chairs. Students get a 20% reduction on rates year round; during high season a 20% surcharge is added to your bill. The kosher kitchen offers lunch for SH17 ($5) and dinner for SH15.30 ($4.50).

A sauna bath, billiard table, and rooftop sundeck offering views of Rosh Hanikra and Haifa, are among the attractions at the **Pallas Athene Hotel,** 28 Hama'apalim St., tel. 04-922381, a 53-room, three-star establishment. You'll pay SH61.20 ($18) for a single here, SH47.60 ($14) per person for a double, and SH51 ($15) for full board.

Set in a garden, and housed in a two-story blue and white stucco building, the **Panorama,** 6 Hama'apalim St., tel. 04-920555, has five single and 20 double rooms, all nicely decorated with wall-to-wall carpeting, orange blankets, and print-curtained windows. All rooms have toilet, and bath or shower, and most face the sea. Rates are SH40.80 ($12) single, SH37.40 ($11) per person in a double, breakfast included. Add about $2 per person during high season. Lunch or dinner is an additional SH23.80 ($7), full board SH37.40 ($11). Students get a 10% reduction on rates.

Three stars belong to the **Astar Hotel,** 27 Ga'aton Blvd., tel. 04-923431. Singles pay SH54.40 ($16) to SH64.60 ($19), doubles are SH47.60 ($14) per person. Add $2 July, August, and Jewish holidays. Some noteworthy pluses here: proximity to the bus station, a very helpful, friendly owner, and air conditioning, baths, and phones in every room. Only breakfast is served.

Just a three-minute walk from the beach, **Laufer Hotel**, 31 Hameyasdim, tel. 04-920130, offers modest accommodations—all with showers or baths, and toilets—but does have a dining room and a garden patio. Out on the lawn are a Ping-Pong table and hammock. The tariff is SH42.50 ($12.50) to SH47.60 ($14) single, SH37.40 ($11) per person double. Full board is SH37.40 ($11).

The Frank Hotel, 4 Aliyah St., tel. 04-920278, is a three-star place with all the amenities and a pleasant, warm atmosphere. All rooms are air-conditioned and equipped with bath or shower. Singles pay SH61.20 ($18) to SH78.20 ($23), doubles SH51 ($15) per person. There's an off-season reduction of 10% for students. Full board is SH51 ($15).

The **Rosenblatt Hotel**, 59 Weizmann St., tel. 04-923469, is in the center of town, just a five minute walk from the beach. The 34 rooms are on three floors (no elevator); all have private showers and toilets, air conditioning, and heating, but little in the way of charm. Both lunch and dinner are available, either meal costing SH17 ($5). Students get a 10% discount on room rate here; there's a surcharge of about $2 in high season. At other times you'll pay SH40.80 ($12) single, SH34 ($10) per person double.

The small, family-run **Gan Shoshanim Hotel** is situated in a quiet resident area at 43 Weizmann St., tel. 04-921088. All rooms have showers and toilets, air conditioning, and gaily colored curtains on the windows. Out front is a garden with deck chairs. Bed and breakfast is SH23.80 ($7) per person; add SH6.80 ($2) during July, August, and holidays.

The one-star **Beit Erna Hotel**, 29 Jabotinsky St., tel. 04-920170, has 11 simply furnished, air-conditioned rooms, all with showers and eight with toilets as well. Not many frills. Singles pay SH39 ($11.20), doubles SH33 ($9.70) per person. Students get a 15% reduction off-season when rates are also a few dollars less.

Rooms in private homes are also an option. **Beit Milgram**, 36 Balfour St., tel. 04-924331, is close to both town and the beach, and the owners are an extremely-pleasant couple. All nine rooms have showers and toilets, and four have kitchenettes with stoves and refrigerators. In July, August, and holidays, a two-bedded room will cost SH51 ($15) a night, SH64.60 ($19) for a three-bedded room, SH78.20 ($23) for a four-bedded room, off-season rates are lower.

For more private homes that take in guests check with the Tourist Office.

Restaurants

As in other cities, the eatery at the **Egged Bus Station** is recommended for low-priced fare.

For the yummiest cakes and pastries in town, check out the **Conditoria Har'el**, 20 Ha'gaaton Blvd., tel. 04-927655. Here you can watch the passing scene from a sidewalk cafe with umbrella tables or sit cozily within while enjoying rich cream cakes, fruit tortes, almond pies, etc., for SH1.60 (47¢) and espresso for SH1.20 (35¢). Open from 8 a.m. to 9 p.m. (6:45 a.m. to midnight in summer) daily, closed Friday from 4 p.m. until after sunset on Saturday.

There's indoor/outdoor seating, too, at **Cafe Li La Lo**, 21 Ha'gaaton Blvd., tel. 04-921876, where a variety of sandwiches can be had for SH2 (60¢) and under. Open 10 a.m. to midnight daily except Friday when it opens from 10 a.m. to 2 p.m. and 8 p.m. to midnight.

At **Pizzeria Rimini**, 31 Ha'gaaton Blvd., tel. 04-920027, you can have pizza, priced from SH4.20 ($1.25) to SH7.90 ($2.30), or pasta, priced from SH3.50 ($1) to SH6 ($1.75), or a full SH4.80 ($1.35) breakfast of egg, salad, sour cream, juice, sausage or cheese, rolls with butter and jam, and coffee. Open daily from 8 a.m. to midnight.

Frozen yogurt is sold at the **Penguin Yoghurt Cafe,** 33 Ha'gaaton Blvd., for SH1.60 (47¢) a portion; ice cream is also available.

And finally, **Wimpy,** Kikar Ha'Iriya, tel. 04-921209, is a red- and white-painted place where you might order beef stroganoff with chips for SH8.50 ($2.50), humus and pitta for SH2.30 (70¢), or, on Friday only, gefilte fish with horseradish and challah for SH1.70 (50¢). Open Sunday to Thursday from 9:30 a.m. to midnight, Friday from 8 a.m. to 3:30 p.m. and 9 p.m. to 1 a.m., Saturday from 6 p.m. to 1 a.m.

WHAT TO SEE AND DO: One of the best possibilities is to get married here on Lag b'Omer, and stay over for at least three days so that you can be entertained every day by the municipality and enjoy a discount on facilities and services. If you're already married, you're out of luck, because bigamy in Israel is considered a major crime—though even married folks do get some discounts at this time of year.

The main beach, **Galei-Galil,** has won prizes for cleanliness and safety. It offers (in addition, of course, to the Mediterranean Sea) an Olympic-size outdoor pool, a heated, glass-enclosed indoor pool, a children's pool, dressing rooms, playgrounds for children, and restaurants. A marina is being completed at this writing; basketball and volleyball courts are planned. Entrance fee to the private beach and pool is SH2.50 (75¢) for an adult, SH7 (30¢) for a student or child under 14. Entry to the indoor heated pool is a steep SH12.50 ($3.70).

If you're interested in meeting the locals, contact Mr. Sasson Levy, Director of Tourism of the Municipality, tel. 04-922121; he can arrange it.

In the **Municipality Building** is a museum of archeological finds from the area dating from 100,000 B.C. through the Natufian Culture (10,000 to 8,000 B.C.). Also in the building is a malacological (that means shells) museum. Both are open from 10 a.m. to noon daily, Sundays and Wednesdays from 4 to 6 p.m. as well, closed Saturdays; entrance is free.

You might want to visit **Nes Amin,** tel. 04-922566, an international Christian rural cooperative village in the Galilee, just south of Nahariya. The members of this unique settlement have dedicated themselves to the task of righting the wrongs done to the Jews through the ages by the Church. They demonstrate their solidarity with Israel by helping to build the state. On the premises are some 4,000 meters of greenhouses where roses are cultivated. You can have a reasonably priced breakfast, lunch or dinner here.

THE ACHZIVS: North along the main road out of Nahariya are the several "Achzivs": the Club Méditerranée, a public beach, a camping site, a kibbutz called Gesher Haziv, a small museum, and a memorial. A new swimming area has been formed at the Achziv Beach; a breakwater has been erected enclosing a natural bay, and a new continental/oriental restaurant has sprung up.

Achziv Bridge

A little further along, on the righthand side of the road, is a memorial to a mysterious espionage operation. In 1946, Israeli underground fighters wanted to make a show of strength by blowing up all the important bridges in the country during the dead of night. Fourteen young men took part in the Achziv attempt to foul British communications. The bridge was actually blown up on schedule, but no trace of the 14 men was ever found. Whether they were ambushed by Arabs or dispatched by the British has remained a puzzle. The monument here, in poetically spine-chilling language, recalls the famous incident.

Gesher Haziv

This settlement, named after the incident at the bridge, was founded in 1949 by a group of Americans and Israelis. They began with tents, upset kibbutz tradition by keeping the children in the parents' home, and now have a handsome settlement on a hill overlooking their fertile fields by the sea. They also have an excellent kibbutz **restaurant, guest house**—see Chapter XII for details—and down below there is a **youth hostel** and **camping site** where equipment can be rented.

ROSH HANIQRA: This is a location on the border with Lebanon, astride a tall cliff overlooking the sea. On a clear day, standing atop the cliff, you can see the coastline as far as Haifa. Beneath the cliffs are grottoes carved out by the sea, reachable via cable car. Operating from 8 a.m. to 4 p.m. (till 5 p.m. in summer), the cable car ride costs SH2.50 (75¢) for adults, SH2 (60¢) for children and students. You can walk out into the caves and passages and see the pools of water lapping the rocks.

To reach Rosh Haniqra take the bus from Nahariya; during the summer the bus reaches Rosh Haniqra, but the rest of the year you have a half-hour walk uphill from the Shlomi junction.

You can dine at a reasonably priced self-service restaurant on top of the cliff called **Mitzpe Rosh Haniqra.** The view is terrific. Open 9 a.m. to 4 p.m., till 5 p.m. in summer.

THE GALILEE

ROUGHLY SPEAKING, everything to the north and east of Haifa is known as "the Galilee"—Israel's lushest region. Every springtime the residents of Haifa pour out into the Galilee to experience anew that sense of wonder at the return of foliage to the valleys and slopes, and to marvel again at the pioneer perseverance of the old-time settlers of the Galilee farm communities (kibbutzim) who lived in tents, risked malaria, and fought off Arab attacks to cultivate this land.

Beginning in March a vast blanket of green covers the Galilee and seems almost to inundate the watchtowers, settlements, and stone Arab villages of the region. One Haifa Galilee-lover told us: "In March the Galilee is so green that it hurts your eyes." Everywhere you see farms whose fields are carefully tilled patterns of orange groves, rich vegetation, vineyards, and fruit orchards.

In biblical times, according to Josephus, some 204 towns in these hills supported about 15,000 residents each, giving the Galilee a dense 3,000,000 population. Today this fertile countryside is the site of the majority of Israel's collective farms, but it is also home for most of Israel's long-time Arab residents, and it is in their sleepy little villages that you can still witness the classical rhythm and character of biblical days. Veiled women draw water from a well and slowly walk alongside a road with large jugs on their heads, ragged shepherd boys herd flocks of black goats onto the hillsides where they graze, and long-gowned Arabs sit atop sleepy donkeys. Sometimes it seems that the character of Arab life up here has been untouched by the past 2,000 years . . . except that today the fellow on top of the donkey often has a transistor radio plugged into his ear.

It was only natural, of course, that this fertile region should have been the first in Israel to have been developed. Initially it was to the shores of the Sea of Galilee, in the Jordan Valley and around the Emek Yizreel (Valley of Jezreel, usually just called the Emek) that the early Zionist pioneers came with their dreams of a socialistic utopia, founded on principles of agricultural toil. Then, in the '20s and '30s, they took their bucolic Marxism into the Galilee's plains and forests. They established Israel's front line of defense, sweating out malaria attacks and returning the fire of Arab snipers. They considered it a luxury when they changed from tents to modest little houses, but as they prospered so did Israel itself grow. Babies born in these settlements grew into hardy young farmers, their playfields not the ghettos of Russia and Poland that their parents had known, but rather the grassy meadows and fruit fields of their settlement. During the War of Independence in 1948 several Galilee settlements shook under the fury of invading Arab armies, but most held out, farming and fighting at the same time. In at least one case, the tenacity of the settlers under fire prevented a massive breakthrough that could have caused the fall of Haifa. War memorials throughout the Galilee tell you about these times.

Aside from the Galilee–Jerusalem road skirting the Jordan, there are two good central routes for entering the Galilee: one is from Haifa to Acre and east to Safed, then down to the Sea of Galilee. The other is due east from Haifa to Nazareth and straight across to Tiberias. We'll follow one route and then the other—and then a third, an offshoot of the Haifa–Nazareth road which will detour down through the Jordan Valley and land us south of the Sea of Galilee. (For additional information on the more remote Galilee sightseeing spots— Peqiin, Montfort, Yechiam, Hula Preserve—consult Chapter XI.)

1. Safed

A bus from Haifa's central station or a sherut will take you to Safed, via the northern coast road that parallels the Mediterranean until Acre, where a right turn leads directly into the lower Galilee hills. Bus 361 operates from 5:15 a.m. to 9 p.m.

ON THE WAY: We'll take our time getting to Safed, for the terrain is magnificent, and there's a town or two worth seeing along the way.

Beit Hakerem

Initially you drive into a valley called Beit Hakerem, the southern limit of the upper Galilee. The valley's rich red earth is extremely fertile due to the fact that it has one of Israel's highest annual rainfalls—about 43 inches.

You begin climbing upward, and soon you encounter an almost unending panorama of hills with beautifully manicured terracing. This area is predominantly Arabic, and the slopes glisten with the silver leaves from the olive trees they cultivate.

Rama

Rama is a large village of Arabs and Druze entirely surrounded by olive plantations. It has kept its Arabic name, Rama, which, like the Hebrew word "ramat," means height.

To the left of the main road past Rama are crypts and caves that the Arabs have carved out of the side of the mountains. To the right are inaccessible hills where army camps lie hidden and where many of the Galilee Bedouins dwell.

Meiron

Five miles before Safed you come to the town of Meiron, a holy place for religious Jews for 1,700 years. Like Safed, Meiron is an extremely religious town, having had a continuously Jewish population for nearly 18 centuries. When Jerusalem fell to the Romans in the second century, the Israeli tribes took to the high grounds near here, settling in isolated areas too remote for their persecutors' vigilance. One early Meiron inhabitant, a second-century Talmudist named Shimon Bar Yochai, continued to defy the Romans and was ultimately forced to hide in a cave at Peqiin, outside Meiron. There, according to legend, he wrote the Zohar, the *Book of Splendor,* which is the bible of the mystical Cabalist sect.

Meiron is the scene of considerable pageantry during the holiday of Lag b'Omer, which occurs in the spring just three-and-a-half weeks after Passover. Thousands of Orthodox Jews pour into Safed from all over the country. There follows a torchlight parade with singing and dancing as the column of black-gowned zealots hike to Meiron. There they burn candles on top of **Rabbi Shimon's tomb** and light a great bonfire into which some, overcome by emotion, throw their clothes. The festivities go on all night. In the morning three-year-old boys are given their first haircuts, and the cut hair is thrown into the fire.

In this devoutly religious town there still exists an ancient **synagogue** from the second century, as well as Rabbi Shimon's tomb, and a rock called the **Messiah's Chair.** Reputedly, on the day the Messiah arrives, He will sit right here while Elijah blows the trumpet to announce His coming.

Picnic tables are scattered along the roadside between here and Safed—bring a sandwich. An excellent base for seeing the Galilee is the **Moshav Meiron Guest House,** tel. 067-39361, a 12-minute drive from Safed. It is a complex of individual, steep-roofed, multi-colored cottages which provide family facilities and sleeping accommodations for six—two on the ground floor and four in an attic room. Total cost is about $30 per day and this includes cooking facilities, bedding, kitchenware, etc. The moshav itself was founded in 1949 and is home to Hungarian and Rumanian immigrants. A good place to visit and truly inexpensive when you're sharing costs.

SAFED, YESTERDAY AND TODAY: Skirting the Jermak, Israel's lofty mountain range (3,000 feet), you finally climb up into Safed, Israel's highest town with an elevation of 2,790 feet. This quiet city is built on three slopes and looks down onto a beautiful panorama of white Arab villages and tiered hillsides.

Safed dozed until the 16th century, when the persecuted Sephardic Jews from Spain came here. Having escaped the horrors of the Inquisition, these Jewish intellectuals launched into a complex and quiet mystical interpretation of the Old Testament called Cabala. The town became a great center of learning, with a score of synagogues and universities. During this period of intellectual mysticism the first printing press in the east was introduced here, and in 1578 the first Hebrew book was printed, a commentary on the scroll of Esther. The back streets of the city, winding and cobbled, and resounding with the chant of prayers, are still frankly medieval.

But two developments have recently occurred to interrupt Safed's tranquility. First, it has become a resort town with many hotels, and second, it now plays host to an artists' colony which flourishes right down the street from the row of synagogues. Perhaps it was Safed's mysticism, coupled with its picturesque lanes and scenic location, that prompted that substantial flock of painters, sculptors, and ceramicists to settle here. However, there is no mystery about Safed's magnificent location, its high and cool atmosphere, and its dramatic landscape. The city, not very mystically, is also a favorite summer resort for Israelis who yearn to escape from the heat of the plains to the crispness of the Galilee's heights.

ACCOMMODATIONS IN SAFED: Unfortunately, the hotel situation here, although not entirely discouraging, is tricky for the budget tourist. During July, August, and holidays, rates go up 15-20%. That situation stems from the fact that Safed receives tourists mostly in the summer months when its mountain air is a refreshing change from the baking temperatures of the plains. In the winter, however, it's one of the coldest locations in Israel. Consequently the Safed hoteliers feel they must earn their year's income in the summer. Many Safed hotels require full board during the peak period, and even some of the shoddier third-class establishments may charge ridiculously high rates. Don't be deterred—come off-season. The hotels are heated, and, with the crowds gone, you get extra attention.

Budget Hotels

Next to the municipal swimming pool at 2 Jerusalem Rd., the **Hadar Hotel,** tel. 067-30068, has 20 air-conditioned rooms, all with private shower and toilet. It's a well-run family operation, with care taken over details. Rates are SH61.20 ($18) single, SH51 ($15) per person double; off-season rates drop a few dollars. Full board is SH37.40 ($11).

The **Central Hotel,** 37 Jerusalem Rd., tel. 067-30015, has 55 rooms, two stars, and some fine examples of local art. Rooms have air conditioning and heating, and they're equipped with phones, toilets, and baths or showers. A single room is SH63.60 ($18.70), a double SH52.40 ($15.40) per person. Add SH20.40 ($6) for half-board, SH39.10 ($11.50) for full board.

The **Zion Hotel,** 36 Jerusalem Rd., tel. 067-31629, has 11 very simply furnished rooms, all with hot and cold running water (sinks), but only four with showers. In July and August B&B rate is SH15 ($4.40) per person; it's a little less than that (without breakfast) the rest of the year.

The **Gil Hotel,** 39 Jerusalem Rd., tel. 067-30530, has 20 air-conditioned rooms, all with showers and sinks, eight with toilets as well. It's simply furnished. Singles pay SH30 ($8.80), doubles SH20 ($5.90) each.

At 59 Jerusalem Rd. is the **Yair Hotel,** tel. 067-30245, has 35 rooms, all with heating and bath or shower. They're priced at SH49.80 ($14.65) to SH58.50 ($17.20) single, SH40.80 ($12) to SH45.90 ($13.50) per person double. There's a 10% discount for students.

The nearby **Hotel Friedman,** Israel Bek St., tel. 067-30036, has two stars and very clean rooms. A large terrace provides an unforgettable view of the surroundings. A single costs SH32.30 ($9.50) to SH39.10 ($11.50), a double SH24.30 ($7.15) to SH30.90 ($9.10) per person. Add SH88.40 ($2.60) for breakfast. There's a 10-15% reduction for students except in the summer.

Another three-star establishment is the **Nof Hagalil Hotel,** Canaan, tel. 067-31595. Rates begin at SH64.60 ($19) per person in a double ($1 less off-season), with a 10% reduction for the third person in the room. There are 36 rooms with heating, phones, baths, and toilets; a warm, family atmosphere prevails. Students who book rooms through ISSTA get a 15% reduction.

You might also check with the local tourist authorities about the possibility of renting a room in a private home (minimum stay two nights). Prices range from SH15 ($4.40) upward in season, no meals.

RESTAURANTS: Safed doesn't have a large selection of good eating places, but, since you'll most likely take your meals at your hotel, that shouldn't be much of a concern. If you do eat out, try **Hamifgash** (which means "meeting place" in Hebrew), right on the main street in the center of town, at 75

Jerusalem Rd., tel. 067-30510. Expertly operated by Shlomo Reouveni, Hamifgash has a fine reputation all over Israel, and food and service to match. The kitchen here is spotless and sends out marvelous aromas to fill the restaurant, which is fitted tightly with tables and chairs, plus a counter where a great variety of appetizers, salads and such are displayed for your approval. Moussaka, one of the specialties, will run SH3.50 ($1), and can be followed by main dishes that range from SH6.50 ($1.90) to SH8 ($2.35). SH12 ($3.50) will get you a full meal of soup, bread, meat with chips, and compote. A la carte you might consider baked chicken with eggplant and pitta for SH7.50 ($2.20). Hamifgash opens at noon and remains open until quite late during tourist season (which seems to expand each year). (They do take a break between 4 and 6 p.m.) Since it is strictly kosher, there's no smoking here on Saturday, though it stays open to feed the hungry with previously prepared food. Students pay the same price as soldiers—in other words, a big discount.

A view of mountains in the distance is one of the assets of the **Mool Ha'har Cafe,** 70 Jerusalem Rd., tel. 067-30404, a dairy eatery that also serves espresso and alcoholic beverages. Sandwiches or a blintz cost SH1.50 (45¢). Open Sunday to Friday from 6 a.m. to 11 p.m., Saturday from sunset until 11 p.m.–midnight, till 1 a.m. Fridays during summer.

In addition to the above, Safed has a profusion of kiosks and cheap snack bars where the normal bill of fare is felafel and cold drinks.

By far the best buy in town is the **Egged Restaurant** in the bus terminal, where a three-course meal can be acquired for SH13.50 ($4), a huge breakfast for SH5.50 ($1.60).

NIGHTLIFE: There really isn't too much organized activity. The most fun is simply mingling with the artists, almost all of whom speak English and are quite willing to discourse on any subject—from Picasso to Freud.

SIGHTSEEING IN SAFED: Jerusalem Rd. winds and twists from the bottom of the town up the three tiers on which the city is built. Along this main traffic artery is the police station, which is badly pockmarked by machine gun bullets from the heavy fighting that took place here when Safed was cut off and overrun by Arabs in May of 1948. Another of those noisy Davidka mortars, like the one in a Jerusalem square, sits across from the police station.

There are five basic sights to see in Safed:

Artists' Colony

Just off the main street, at the top of town where a stone bridge spans the street, you'll spot a curve to the right. Some additional locomotion will bring you into the center of an enclave of outdoor art, picturesque houses, and manicured flower gardens.

The colony has a general exhibition, conducted in the Old Mosque, in the winter from 9 a.m. to 5 p.m.

This is also a good place to acquire inexpensive local gifts. Many of the artists have postcard-size reproductions of their work. The prices vary, but they're fairly inexpensive and an interesting reminder of Safed.

Synagogues

It's not easy to say exactly where these Cabalist synagogues are, because the religious quarter has few street names, and the streets are really a collection of alleyways and courtyards. Ask for "kiryat batei knesset," the synagogue section. A good starting point is from the Hotel Herzlia on the main road, taking the first descending street on your left. It heads into a square and then a labyrinth of narrow alleys, staircases, and arches.

The first synagogue you should see is the **Ha'ari,** a stronghold of the local Ashkenazim named after Rabbi Isaac Louria, a guiding light in 16th-century Cabalism. From then on you'll just have to get lost a little by yourself: The synagogues are all hidden in the maze of alleys and squeezed between the houses—synagogues of Rabbi Isaac Aboad, Rabbi Moses Alshek, Rabbi Yosef Habanai the Stonemason, Rabbi Mendel of Vitebsk, and the Ha'ari Synagogue of the Sephardim, also dedicated to Rabbi Isaac Louria.

Cemetery

At the end of the synagogue area is a cemetery containing the tombs of many famous Cabala leaders. Here, too, is a military cemetery containing the resting places of soldiers who fell in in all the wars, and nearby is yet a third cemetery containing the graves of Israelis who served with the underground Stern Gang and Irgun forces. Buried here are members of these groups executed by the British in Acre prison, including Dov Gruner, one of the best-known of the outlawed fighters.

Citadel

At the top of the hill, past the hospital and rest home, are the ruins of a Crusader fortress from which you can enjoy a fine view of Mt. Meiron, Mt. Tabor, the Sea of Galilee, and a scattering of Arab hill villages and settlements. This site, the highest in Safed, was once the scene of a first-century Galilean stronghold and a 12th-century Crusaders' lookout post. Here again, the Israelis had to push the Arabs back from the heights—sustaining heavy losses—and a war memorial commemorates the event.

Museums

On the way to the Citadel you'll pass the Town Hall and Safed's **Beit Glicenstein Museum,** which houses a permanent Glicenstein sculpture exhibition and the Bernard Chapiro collection of French paintings. The building is open 9 a.m. to noon and 5 to 7 p.m. (closing at 1 p.m. on Fridays) during the summer months. There is a small entrance fee (well worth paying).

The Zvi Assaf Printing Museum in the Artists' Quarter has exhibitions on Jewish folklore, art and printing. The building is open all year from 10 a.m. to noon and from 4 to 6 p.m. (Friday and Saturday from 10 a.m. to noon); there is no entrance fee. The exhibitions are changed three times yearly.

MUSICAL EVENTS: Safed plays host to about eight chamber music concerts throughout the year as well as a musical summer workshop. The concerts are held at the **Wolfson Community Center,** on Palmach St. near the market. They begin at 8:30 p.m.

TOURS: Safed is an ideal site for roaming the Galilee, and the following tours are available:

Daily Galilee tours operate during the summer, with special tourist cars leaving at 8:30 a.m. and returning at 1:30 p.m. For information and registration contact hotels or Hagalil Tours, 18 Jerusalem Rd., tel. 067-30039. **Egged Tours**

cover the same route with air-conditioned buses leaving a half-hour earlier than the tourist cars. The hotels or Egged, tel. 067-31122, will provide the requisite information.

PLANT A TREE AND TAKE A SWIM: Just outside the highway entrance to Safed there's a **Keren Kayemet Center** where you can plant a tree with your own hands (it costs about $5). If this appeals to you—and it is a beautiful spot for your very own tree—check with the local I.G.T.O.

And, as you turn into town, in a hollow to the right of the road is **Emek Hatchelet Swimming Pool,** which has been around since 1959. It will cost SH2.50 (75¢) for adults and SH7 (30¢) for youngsters to enter the pool area, but it is one of the best recreation places around town. The area is beautifully landscaped, with small gardens and a tiny bridge flanked by lounge chairs, tables, and big colorful umbrellas. There are two pools here (one for children), game tables under thatched sun shelters, a completely equipped children's playground, plus a mini-golf course. Aside from showers and dressing rooms, facilities include a restaurant serving everything from ice cream to a full steak-and-chips meal.

2. Nazareth

Now we'll follow the other route into the Galilee, driving due east from Haifa to Nazareth, and eventually across to Tiberias.

ON THE WAY: The ride from Haifa to Nazareth takes just an hour (it's 25 miles), leaving the port city via Ha'atzmauth St. and then heading inland over the four-lane highway that runs along the foot of the Carmel range. On the left is the **Valley of Zebulon,** hidden behind the likes of oil refineries, soap factories and cement works.

After the industrial zone, the landscape undergoes a change in character. You begin to see farm settlements, the most important of which are **Yagur** and **Allonim.** Yagur, which now has 1,600 members, is one of the country's oldest kibbutzim, founded in 1922. You then start climbing into the foothills of the Lower Galilee, and soon, about 35-40 minutes out of Haifa, you'll see an observation signpost on your right. Be sure to stop, because this is one of the loveliest views in Israel.

The Emek

From this point, the **Yizreel Valley** (commonly called the Emek) spreads out below. The largest and most fertile valley in Israel, the Emek lies between the Galilee mountains to the north and the Samaria range to the south, and it houses some of Israel's oldest and best known settlements—**Mishmar Ha'e-mek, Hazorea, Givat Oz, Ginegar,** and the giant moshav, **Nahalal.** From the height on the Nazareth road, the valley has the appearance of being the most cultivated, fertile place in all the world. The rich, dark soil is crisscrossed in checker-board patterns of fruit trees, vineyards, and green vegetable fields. It is a breathtaking quilt of colors, some blocks golden with wheat, some black with heavy cultivation, others orange with brilliant flowers.

But it wasn't always this way. Fifty-five years ago, this was a breeding swamp of malaria. In the early 1920s, the Keren Kayemet (Jewish National Fund) launched its biggest land reclamation project; slowly but surely, each and every square foot of swampland was drained and every mosquito killed.

Russian, German, and Polish settlers filled the new settlements. The cultivation of the Emek soon became one of Israel's heroic, adventurous tales, rhapsodized in dozens of romantic songs in which the tilling of soil and the smell of roses are common lyrics.

But as you look at this splendid fertility, remember also that this was one of the bloodiest battlefields in history. Here the Egyptians shed blood 4,000 years ago, as did the Canaanites, the Mongols, the Greeks, the Romans, and the Crusaders in later centuries. From Mount Tabor, overlooking the Emek's northeast corner, the prophetess Deborah launched her famous attack against the Canaanite armies. And several years later, Gideon's forces swooped down from Mt. Gilboa on the Midianites and slaughtered the plundering Bedouin tribe.

But it was also on this fertile plain that the Israelite tribe suffered one of its most calamitous national defeats—when King Saul and his sons, including Jonathan, died during a clash with the Philistines. It is with regard to this battle that the Book of Samuel records David's immortal lament:

> The beauty of Israel is slain upon the high places:
> How are the mighty fallen!
> Tell it not in Gath,
> Publish it not in the streets of Ashkelon:
> Lest the daughters of the Philistines rejoice,
> Lest the daughters of the uncircumcised triumph.
>
> Ye mountains of Gilboa,
> Let there be no dew, neither let there be rain, upon you, nor fields of
>   offerings:
> For there the shield of the mighty is vilely cast away,
> The shield of Saul, as though he had not been annointed with oil.
> From the blood of the slain, from the fat of the mighty,
> The bow of Jonathan turned not back,
> And the sword of Saul returned not empty.
>
> Saul and Jonathan were lovely and pleasant in their lives,
> And in their death they were not divided:
> They were swifter than eagles,
> They were stronger than lions.
> Yet daughters of Israel, weep over Saul,
> Who clothed you in scarlet, with other delights,
> Who put on ornaments of gold upon your apparel.
> How are the mighty fallen,
> And the weapons of war perished! (II Samuel 1)

In post-biblical years the Turks fought here, and Napoleon battled at its edges. In 1918 General Allenby defeated the Turkish forces on the Emek, and here, too, Israel's armies in 1948 overwhelmed the Arabs.

It is an irony of history that the Emek region, which has known every conceivable type of war and human misery, today flourishes in such splendor.

NAZARETH, PAST AND PRESENT: The last leg of the journey to Nazareth consists of hairpin turns up through the **King George V Forest,** planted by Keren Kayemet and now, over 40 years later, lush and shady. You top the hill, and Nazareth is suddenly spread around you. At this point you can navigate in several directions. A right will take you to **Nazareth Elit,** which means "High City" but is better known as the New City or Upper Nazareth. This is the newer part of town, with a population of about 25,000 Jewish inhabitants and its own mayor. This area prospers with industry, and many Arabs commute here daily to work alongside their Jewish counterparts. All is shiny and modern, and you ought definitely to take a look at what goes on up here, but you'll probably prefer to spend most of your time in **Old Nazareth,** and for this you take the left turn.

This biblical town, where Jesus grew up, clings to the inside of a vast bowl, its mud and limestone houses tiered like the seats of an amphitheater. Today the city houses Israel's largest Arab community outside Jerusalem—some 40,000, about half of them Christian—and shares with Jerusalem its position as headquarters of the Christian mission movement in Israel, with over 40 churches, convents, monasteries, orphanages, and private parochial schools. In fact, Nazareth's very name is used by Arabs and Israelis to designate Christians, just as Jesus was also known as the Nazarene. In Arabic, Christians are called "Nasara," and in Hebrew "Notzrim."

Despite the fact that Jesus grew up here, Nazareth was only a tiny hamlet in biblical times, scarcely recorded on maps or mentioned in historical works. The legion of churches and monasteries came after Christ, of course. For the real flavor of what the village must have been like, turn into the narrow alleys which wind up and back into the terraced limestone ridges, and wander through the old **Arab Market** with its narrow cobbled streets. Here farmers patiently goad on their donkeys laden with stacks, men haggle over the fruit and vegetable stands, and dignified sheikhs in clean white kefiyas and gowns hold serious discussions.

An important thing to keep in mind is that Nazareth is virtually locked solid on Sunday, wide open on Saturday.

ACCOMMODATIONS IN NAZARETH:
There are three three-star hotels, one double-starred hotel and a surfeit of Christian hospices in Nazareth, and some in each category are suitable for our pocketbooks. As for the hospices, some of which we list below, we suggest you stop in at **Abu-Nassar's Cafe** on the main street for the moment-to-moment picture. He is a travel agent for the local hospices and he can always make arrangements for you. Most of the hospices charge about $5 for simple, bed-only accommodations.

Hotel Galilee, on Paul VI St. (the main road) and close to the center of town, tel. 065-71311, has 90 rooms, all with running water and showers. There's a large gift shop on the premises. Rates, including continental breakfast, are SH57.80 ($17) single, SH44.20 ($13) per person double. Lunch and dinner are available.

The Nazareth Hotel, tel. 065-72045, is a three-star hotel that's extremely well located—on Paul VI St. just past the turn to Haifa. It has 88 rooms, all with balconies, private baths and toilets, and phones. Facilities include an oriental bar and restaurant on the main floor, a TV lounge, and parking in front of the hotel. Per person rate is SH50 ($14.70) single or double.

The three-star, 90-room **Grand New Hotel,** St. Joseph St., tel. 065-73020, is a modern establishment with accommodations that offer good views. Rooms have air conditioning, heating, toilets, phones, and baths or showers. Guests pay SH71.40 ($21) single, SH52.70 ($15.50) per person double; rates drop a few dollars off-season. Lunch or dinner is SH22.10 ($6.50).

The Casa Nova Pilgrims House, tel. 065-71367, is located in the vicinity of the Basilica of the Annunciation. It has 43 rooms and charges SH27.20 ($8) for bed and breakfast. Add SH6.80 ($2) for half-board and SH13.60 ($4) for full board. Non-guests who come to lunch or dinner pay SH13.60 ($4) for each. It's a pleasant place, much sought after by pilgrims. The hotel is a favorite of Franciscans and is highly recommended.

The **Sisters of Nazareth,** off Casa Nova St., tel. 065-54304, provide 50 beds in immaculate dormitories, separate for men and women. Facilities include showers and a kitchen where you can prepare meals. You pay SH6.80 ($2) a night for a bed. Be aware that there's no heating in the winter.

RESTAURANTS: While you're checking on the room situation at **Abu-Nassar's Cafe,** you might as well stop for a meal here. The most popular and best-priced eating place in town, it serves from 150 to 200 people daily, its clientele running the gamut from diplomats to students. The food is excellent, but it's the service "with a smile from the heart" that Paul Abu-Nassar stresses. It comes naturally for him, so no wonder he won one of the coveted "Service With a Smile" awards during the *Jerusalem Post* national contest. Situated at the foot of the market on Casa Nova St., near the tourist office and the Basilica of the Annunciation, the restaurant holds forth in the family-owned building that's at least 200 years old—and that's about how long the Abu-Nassar family has been influential in this area. Though they're Arabs, the family has for ages been strictly orthodox Roman Catholic. The fare is oriental and European, but emphasis is on the former. For SH3 (90¢) you can opt for one of several delicious soups, or humus or tchina. A meal of shish kabab, chips, and salad goes for SH7 ($2.05). The enormous four-course meal of the day consists of appetizer, soup, meat and vegetables, salad, and fruit compote or other dessert. It costs SH13.60 ($4) and is one of the reasons why so many Israelis flock there. The owner not only loves good food, he enjoys company, so if you want to chat while you're eating, you've found the right place. Like most of the other facilities in Nazareth, the restaurant is closed on Sunday, open otherwise 7:30 a.m. to 6 p.m.

Should it be too packed at Abu-Nassar's, or if you want something slightly different, try the **Israel Restaurant,** a few doors down the same street. The food is distinctly oriental, main courses running SH6 ($1.75) to SH8 ($2.35), appetizers and soups costing SH2.50 (75¢). The original owner won the "Queen of the Kitchen" contest but has since emigrated to Miami Beach. Now her brother-in-law runs the restaurant.

The **Astoria Restaurant,** on Casa Nova St., is open daily—including Sunday—from 8:30 a.m. to 9 p.m. Once again, reasonably priced oriental fare is featured. Ditto the **Hatekva Restaurant,** on Paul VI St. at the foot of Casa Nova St.

A bit fancier is the **Diana Restaurant,** opposite the Cinema Diana, tel. 065-72919, offering such niceties as air conditioning, upholstered leather chairs, and tablecloths. Try the oriental version of pizza—bread filled with meat and pine nuts—for SH3.50 ($1); a Greek salad is SH2.50 (75¢), liver with vegetables SH77 ($3.25). Open daily from 8 a.m. to midnight.

And to satisfy your sweet tooth head for **Mamtakim Mahroom,** on Casa Nova St. near the Government Tourist Office. Here you can indulge in such delicacies as baklava, esh el bulbul—a pastry made from nuts in the form of a bird's nest, burma—a sugar, honey, and nut-filled pastry that looks like shredded wheat, etc., all fresh-baked and all under SH2 (60¢). Open daily from 7 a.m. to 9 p.m.

SIGHTS AND SITES OF NAZARETH: There are three occupations for tourists in Nazareth: shopping in the market, visiting the holy Christian shrines and taking a glance at the new Jewish quarter.

The Market

The market streets, entered via Casa Nova, are narrow, crowded and highly "scented." But they are also lively and interesting, and they afford some excellent bargains. Remember that the deeper you get into the market, the smaller the shops become and the lower prices. One of the first things to note is the trench running dead center of the street, and one of the first precautions is to stay out of it as much as possible—it's the donkey trail. Snaking upward, the narrow roadway is lined with tin-roofed shops that give you a good idea where the expression "hole-in-the-wall" originated. In these shops, you'll see everything from plows and ram horns, to cakes, leather goods, chandeliers, plastic buckets, and fine jewelry. Daily necessities are displayed side by side with antiques from Persian times that sell for hundreds of shekels. You can buy a finjan coffee set here or, if you want to play Lawrence of Arabia, a kefiya, the Arab headdress. One shop, deep in the market, carries narghilis (bubble pipes) at prices from SH20 ($5.90) for the plain glass bowl variety. One reliable shop is the **Mazzawi Bazaar.** If you're a coin collector, try the tiny shop of **Amin,** where you'll find quite an assortment of coins and prices. Whatever you buy, be sure to shop around, and whatever you do, bargain over everything.

Religious Edifices

One of Christianity's holiest shrines, the **Basilica of the Annunciation** is located on Casa Nova St. in Nazareth and it probably draws more religious pilgrims in Israel than any site outside of Jerusalem. It stands on the spot where, according to Christian tradition, the angel Gabriel appeared before Mary, saying: "Hail Mary, full of grace, the Lord is with thee, blessed art thou among women. . . . Behold, thou shalt conceive in thy womb, and bring forth a son, and shall call his name Jesus" (Luke 1). The present Basilica of the Annunciation, recently remodeled, was built over earlier structures dating from 1730 to 1877.

The **Church of St. Joseph** is 100 yards away, constructed on the site thought to be occupied by Joseph's carpentry workshop.

Nearby is the **Synagogue Church** which Jesus frequented: "And He came to Nazareth, where He had been brought up; and, as His custom was, He went into the synagogue on the Sabbath day" (Luke 4:16). Further along the road is the **Franciscan Mensa Christi Church,** believed to occupy the spot where Christ dined with his disciples after the resurrection.

Mary's Well, with its source inside the Greek Orthodox Church of St. Gabriel, is another holy site for Christians visiting Nazareth. The church is off the main square on the road to Tiberias. Although the well now has a faucet, it is still picturesque, with its arched wall and women carrying jugs on their heads, much as they did in biblical times.

The **Church of Jesus the Adolescent,** maintained by the French Salesian Order, is one of the handsomest churches in Nazareth, located on a high hill commanding a beautiful vista of the town.

Our Lady of Fright Chapel, sometimes called the Tremore, is built on a lofty wooded hill opposite the Galilee Hotel. It is in a quietly rustic location, built on the spot where Mary watched while the people of Nazareth attempted to throw Jesus over a cliff—the Precipice, or Lord's Leap rock, a quarter of a mile away.

Nazareth is a Christian city, but we would be remiss if we overlooked two very worthwhile Moslem structures. The beautiful and modern **Al-Salam Mosque** is in the eastern quarter of town. Started in 1960, it was completed five years later. Its platform resembles the Taj Mahal in India. In the southern part of the city is the new **Al-Huda Mosque.** It's well worth visiting.

And finally, a little over six miles southeast of Nazareth, **Mount Tabor** (at 1,800 feet above sea level the tallest of the Lower Galilee Mountains) merits a visit. At the summit stands the Basilica of the Transfiguration, which, according to Christian tradition, marks where Jesus was transfigured in the presence of three of his disciples. Also on the Mount is the Church of Elias, built in 1911 by the Greek Orthodox community. On a clear day, you can see the Sea of Galilee, Mount Hermon, the Mediterranean Sea, and the Emek from here. Mount Tabor is accessible from Nazareth by Egged bus or taxi.

The Israeli Quarter

Nazareth's 25,000 or so Jewish residents live in Upper Nazareth, a new part of town on a ridge to the northeast of the city. Construction was begun here in 1957, largely in connection with the establishment of several factories in the area, including a huge textile plant, an auto plant, and light industries producing biscuits, chocolate, and rugs.

3. The Jordan Valley

Now we take yet another trip into the Galilee from Haifa. Just after the Nesher Cement Works, the main road from Haifa forks: The right fork goes to Nazareth, the left towards the Jordan Valley, south of the Sea of Galilee.

ON THE WAY: Here are the leading sights on the southeasterly excursion, presented in the order in which you'll pass them.

Beit Shearim

Somewhat reminiscent of the Sanhedrian Tombs in Jerusalem, the **Beit Shearim Burial Caves** are located about 12 miles from Haifa, on the main road that heads toward Afula (which is the main town of the Jordan Valley).

In second-century Israel Beit Shearim was the home of Israel's Supreme Court, the Sanhedrin, as well as headquarters of the famous Rabbi Yehudi Ha'nassi, compiler of the Mishna. Many learned and famous Jews were laid to rest in the cemetery of the town, a tranquil grove of cypress and olive trees. Over the centuries, however, the tombs were destroyed and the caves looted. Earth and rock covered the catacombs as if they had never existed. But finally they were unearthed, first in 1936, and then fully explored after the War of Independence.

The entire site here is particularly well tended: parking lot, washroom facilities, and outdoor cafe.

All the burial caves are pretty much the same, entered through an opening in the rock or a stone door. Inside the cool chambers are sarcophagi carved with rams' horns and lions' heads, or a menorah, in some ancient time. Catacomb 20 is the most formidable unearthed so far from the point of view of legible inscriptions, carvings, and interesting relics, but archeologists claim that only a fraction of the original effects remain; over the centuries tomb robbers have looted the almost 200 sarcophagi.

The excavations and museum are open daily April through September from 8 a.m. to 5 p.m., Friday until 3 p.m.; October to March hours are 8 a.m. to 4 p.m., Friday until 3 p.m. For information tel. 04-931643.

Megiddo

Back on the road, you pass **Hazorea** and **Mishmar Ha'emek,** two old and large kibbutzim, and then you come to Megiddo, the leading fortress overlooking the Emek, and the site of countless past battles. Reached via a narrow and steep path, the site is presently being more fully excavated; archeologists have thus far uncovered layers from 25 distinct periods—towns and fortifications dating from 4,000 B.C. to 400 B.C.

The area presently visible is King Solomon's tenth century B.C. "chariot city," where he housed a sizable force of his stables and chariots. Most of Megiddo, however, has been removed to the Jerusalem Antiquities Museum and the Rockefeller Museum. General Allenby launched his attack against the Turks from the Megiddo Pass in 1917, and the Israeli forces in 1948 also used this fortress as a base of operation against the entrenched Arab armies.

In Hebrew, Megiddo is *Har Megiddon,* and in the Bible the name is used as the symbol of war. Thus, the Book of Revelation refers to Megiddo as the place where the last great battle will be fought when the forces of good triumph over the forces of evil. "They go forth unto the kings of the earth and the whole world to gather them to the battle of the great Day of God Almighty. And he gathered them together into a place called in the Hebrew tongue Armageddon" (Rev. 16:16).

Afula

After leaving Megiddo, the road swings across the Emek to Afula, a town in the center of the valley that serves as the administrative and commercial headquarters of the Emek. The road to Afula follows an historic route, although road signs announce only communal settlements. Through the centuries flocks of pilgrims have traveled along this path on mules, horses, and camels to reach the waters of the River Jordan.

Afula itself, though, is a fairly recent phenomenon. It was settled in about 1920, mostly by American Jews. Today the palm trees they planted back then tower over Afula's main street, a boulevard which leads to the circular flowering park that's more or less the center of town. The large yellow concrete building, straight ahead and slightly to the right was the British Mandate Police Headquarters.

You can get a good meal at the **San Remo Coffee Restaurant,** Kikar Ha'atzmauth, tel. 065-22458, an air-conditioned and very clean eatery. A full three-course meal is SH15 ($4.40); à la carte you might order chicken for SH9 ($2.65). Alcoholic beverages are served. Open 7:30 a.m. to 7 p.m., closed from Friday at 3 p.m. until Sunday morning.

Continuing Onward

The road next crosses the eastern end of the Emek, leaving the valley of **Kibbutz Yizreel.** Once an ancient Arab town, Yizreel was described by Edward Wilson in an 1889 travel account in the *Century Illustrated Magazine:* "It's location is central, and its position as a military stronghold admirable. The Arabs call their town Zerin [Yizreel]. Their houses are dreadfully humble and comfortless, and all the wealth of the town seems to have been used for the preservation of the ancient tower, which stands among the houses."

The road then skirts the slopes of Mt. Gilboa, where the tragedy of Saul (described previously) occurred. A new farm collective, recently started on Gilboa's slopes, presently defies the curse Samuel put upon this land. There is also a new Keren Kayemet road running right to the top of the mountain, where there is a view of everything—the Galilee mountains, the Emek, the Mediterranean, Jordan.

On the left of the road is a string of communal settlements—**Ein Harod, Tel Yosef, Beit Hashita.** A large, well-developed settlement, founded in 1921, Ein Harod has a population of nearly 2,000 settlers. It boasts a hostel, amphitheater, a culture hall where many ideological conferences are held, an archeological and natural history museum, and an art gallery which has had exhibitions of Chagall, Channa Orloff, Milich, and the American artist Selma Gubin.

Interesting enough, several years ago Ein Harod suffered from an ideological schism in the kibbutz world, and the settlement was actually divided into two camps with barbed wire separating one group from the other. This kibbutz was also the base of operations for the commando and self-defense lessons provided by Orde Wingate to the fledgling Haganah soldiers during the Arab revolt period of 1937 and 1938.

The Approach to the Valley

Just after Ein Harod, the road sign points to **Heftziba** and **Beit Alpha,** both communal settlements. Kibbutz Beit Alpha was one of the early Jordan Valley settlements, founded in 1922 by pioneers from Poland and Galicia who cleared the swamps and pummeled the poisonous scorpions into submission. During one of their swamp-draining operations, a remnant of a synagogue was uncovered, and experts from the Hebrew University attested it was a sixth-century B.C. find. Financed by Temple Emmanuel of New York City, excavation produced what is one of the most impressive ancient synagogues uncovered in Israel. Highly ornamental and somewhat oriental in motif, the **Beit Alpha Synagogue** has an elaborate mosaic floor divided into three panels: the first depicting Abraham's sacrifice of Isaac, the second a Zodiac wheel, and the third a pastiche of religious ornaments. Admission is SH1.50 (45¢) for adults, SH.80 (25¢) for students and children.

Sachne, Israel's largest natural swimming pool, lies in a cool scenic nook just beyond Beit Alpha Kibbutz. With its waterfall and splendid framework of tall trees and distant mountains, it is a favorite picnic site for Israeli families.

Right down the road is **Kibbutz Nir David** and its new **Museum of the Mediterranean,** an interesting exhibition that attempts to place ancient Palestine within the framework of Mediterranean civilization. Statuary, pottery, metal work, jewelry, and coins displayed here range from Mycenean to the Hellenistic eras, the finds themselves being products of Corinth, Cyprus, Persia, and elsewhere, from the Pillars of Hercules to the Jordan River.

Beit Shean

The weather grows a bit warmer as you approach the pass at Beit Shean, and the altitude, or lack of it, plummets to 300 feet below sea level. The rocky hillsides are harsh, and aglow with a burnt-orange color; indeed, in the dry seasons, the slopes seem almost feverish in their hot desolation. But don't be deceived. This is a highly fertile area, despite the low rainfall (12 inches annually). Springs and streams flowing down from Mt. Gilboa have been directed toward the Jordan Valley's fields, and the fertile soil here supports thousands of acres of wheat, vegetables, banana groves, and cotton fields.

Beit Shean is another pass which, like Megiddo, has had a long succession of militaristic rulers, situated as it is on the great caravan route from Damascus to Egypt. On a high hill in back of the recently uncovered amphitheater, archeologists have cut into layer upon layer of civilization, every 20 feet representing a culture and a few hundred years.

All the way down they uncovered five separate strata of Canaanite and Egyptian civilizations, with altars and ruins of the Ramses II period. From 1,200 B.C. they discovered Hebrew ceramics, the type used around the time King Saul's body was hung by the Philistines on the Beit Shean wall. Then came a Scythian period when the Greeks named the town Scythopolis, and in a higher slice, the layers of dirt and rock revealed fragments from Roman times. Seventy feet into the "tel" (Hebrew for an archeological kind of hill), parties dug up a seventh-century Byzantine town with a sizable quantity of mosaics and delicate columns. Closer to the top they uncovered the remains of Crusader castles from the Middle Ages. And still higher up, the jugs and farm tools of the Arab and Turkish settlers of the last five centuries.

If you have the energy you can climb to the top of the hill where trenches reveal an old fortification. On your way up (and the going is slow), you'll come upon all manner of chippings from jugs, ceramicware, and fractured pottery. Most of what you'll find on the surface is from the last 100 years. But if you want to have some fun, take a few pieces into the **Beit Shean Museum** and match your finds against the pieces on exhibition, comparing the circular ridges which, barring the authenticity of carbon tests, are usually the giveaway to defining the right period. The Beit Shean Museum, containing an interesting collection from this area, is open every weekday; admission is SH4 ($1.20) for an adult, SH1.40 (40¢) for a child.

Elsewhere at Beit Shean you'll see the **Roman Theater,** which strongly resembles the beautifully preserved Roman theater uncovered at Caesarea. This playhouse has 15 tiers of white limestone in nearly perfect condition, and several more tiers of crumbling black basalt. Nine exit tunnels cut through the upper gallery, giving it that baseball stadium appearance; these are also intact. And scattered on the floor—like a mammoth jigsaw puzzle—is a collection of broken columns and fragments of statues, all waiting to be fitted together. Estimates are that 8,000 people can be seated here.

The Jordan Valley

Once you leave Beit Shean, you are solidly in the Jordan Valley. The fertile abundance of the land becomes immediately apparent. You see the emerald-green splashes of farm settlements in the distance, and soon you come to them, with their straight, carefully planted rows of beautiful fruit trees. That slick, luxuriant vegetation is particularly apparent in the Beit Shean Valley, entrance to the Jordan Valley. One ancient sage has written: "If Israel is Paradise, then the Beit Shean Valley is the gate to Paradise."

You are now in subtropical country—notice the profusion of date palm trees, banana groves, and orchards of pomegranate. Colorful mango trees and grapefruit orchards are also a dominant theme, interrupted only by neat blue rectangles of carp-breeding ponds. But this area, for all its richly fertile appearance now, took a heavy toll on the lives of the early settlers. At all these Jordan Valley settlements—**Moaz Haim, Neve Eitan, Avuka** and **Kfar Ruppin**—the settlers fought an unhealthy, malarial climate, painstakingly draining swamps and pulling shrubs, under the almost constant fire of Arab bands. The frontier kibbutz ethic of a plough in your hand and rifle over your shoulder was a daily reality here.

Incidentally, if you're looking for the River Jordan and can't seem to find it, don't be discouraged. The reason it's hard to locate is that it often dwindles down to a mere trickling stream, winding capriciously inside a great rift in the earth. There are only a few places where it looks like it's supposed to—lush and green, with myrtle and reeds. Note: One good place to bathe in the Jordan is where the river comes out of the Sea of Galilee, opposite **Kibbutz Degania.** But its depth and swift current make it a dangerous spot, so exercise caution.

4. The Sea of Galilee

Five main roads lead to Tiberias and the Sea of Galilee: from Safed, from the Jordan Valley, via Mount Tabor and from Nazareth. Then too there's the shortcut from Afula to Tiberias. But the usual favorite is the road from Nazareth, if only for that dip in the road and that sudden unfolding of the mountains when the Sea of Galilee is suddenly spread below you—truly one of Israel's most enchanting and rewarding spectacles.

It happens best on a clear day, about five miles from Tiberias. You have been on winding mountain roads, going up and down from dale to dell. Half-ruined Arab villages are sprawled on the hillsides, their mud and stone houses packed onto the slopes, their ruined arches and crumbling walls dotting the landscape. You'll also have passed the famous sabra cactuses, thickly clustered at the road's edge, those monstrous prickly pear plants with their dangerous spiked arms and little orange fruits.

Then you round a bend and there it is—the Sea of Galilee, a tranquil lake in a pastoral valley almost too lovely to believe. As you get closer, you see how alive the landscape around the lake becomes, how the descending slopes are carpeted with green, with the almost make-believe white settlements nestled comfortably along the grassy hills that roll down to the lake. There is a smell of heaven in this lovely scene, and you can almost hear the shepherd's flute.

This is the lake where the miracles of the New Testament occurred. On its shores, Christ preached to the crowds and fed them by multiplying the bread and fish. Here he restored the sick and maimed to health. Today, on the waters where Christ once walked, speedboats zoom past in utter disregard of the sea's old-time magic, and water-skiers skim effortlessly along the surface of the lake.

Don't be startled by the number of names given to this body of water. In olden times, the Arabic and Aramaic poets called it The Bride, the Handmaiden of the Hills, and the Silver Woman. The ancient Hebrews called it the Lute in honor of the soothing harp-like sounds of its waves, and because of the form of the lake which is roughly lute-shaped. Today, Israelis still call the Sea of Galilee "lute"—in Hebrew "Kinnor," or **Kinneret,** as it is popularly known. According to one lexicographer, an ancient sage has written: "God created the seven seas, but the Kinneret is His pride and joy."

Seven hundred feet below sea level, the Sea of Galilee is only 13 miles long, from the place where the Jordan flows in at the north to where it empties out in the south. Its entire breadth and length is within Israeli territory, except that at some points along its northern and eastern reaches, the shoreline was, before the 1967 war, Syrian territory and is now within the Israeli-occupied Golan Heights. Defying the United Nations Armistice Lines, the Syrians continually harassed Israeli fishermen by either firing at the fishing boats or cutting the carefully laid nets.

Abundant in fish, Kinneret's waters are a vast reservoir of sardine, mullet, catfish, and the unusual combfish. They are the same fish once caught by the Disciples, and they are hauled in on nets today in the same manner. However, the boats have changed, the white-sailed fishing vessels of biblical times giving way to the kibbutzniks' diesel-powered craft, equipped with sonar devices for hunting out shoals of fish.

Many of the sights along the Sea of Galilee will be dealt with in the Tiberias section to follow, since most of you will be basing in Tiberias. Please note that we have included most of our accommodation recommendations in the entire area within the Tiberias section—but never fear, in this region nothing's ever that far away.

5. Tiberias

This ancient town, built in 18 A.D. by Herod Antipas (son of Herod the Great) in honor of the Roman Emperor Tiberias, is today one of Israel's leading winter resorts. That doesn't mean, however, that its shorefront architecture resembles the plush and palatial pleasure domes of the Riviera. On the contrary. Though the waterfront at Tiberias has large, beautiful hotels, and modern bathing beaches, there are also the Arabesque domes of the mineral water bathhouses, the scars of archeological digs, and the tombs of the great rabbinical sages.

After the Temple of Jerusalem was destroyed, Tiberias became the great Jewish center in the Holy Land. It was here the famous Mishna was completed in 209 A.D. at the direction of Rabbi Yehuda Ha'Nassi, "Judah the Prince." The Jerusalem Talmud was compiled in this town in 400 A.D., and the vowel and punctuation grammar was introduced into the Hebrew language by the learned men of Tiberias. Mystics, academicians, and men with supposedly magic powers populated Tiberias, breathing into the city a power and knowledge still held in reverence by many throughout Israel and the world today.

This towering scholarship, unfortunately, declined in the years that followed, due to the many battles fought here by the Arabs, Crusaders, and Turks. Tiberias must have reached a low ebb during the Middle Ages, because an Arab historian, El Makdase, recorded around 1000 A.D. that residents of the town languidly and wastefully passed each year by doing nothing more than dancing, feasting, playing the flute, running about naked, and swatting flies. So heavy were the flies, and so famous a reputation had Tiberias acquired, that one sage wrote: "Beelzebub, the Lord of the Flies, holds his court in Tiberias."

Efforts were made by pashas and scholars in the 18th and 19th centuries to restore some of the city's former potency, but such plans were doomed in 1837 by an earthquake, which reduced much of Tiberias to rubble. This year in Tiberias you can still see a few remains of those early times during your sightseeing. But you'll have to hunt out these old sights in Tiberias, because to most people the town is simply a resort and a good base of operations for excursions around the Sea of Galilee.

ACCOMMODATIONS: Although Tiberias is only an hour's drive from Safed, the hotel tariff system here is different—there's just one rate throughout the year. This lakefront town enjoys the mild breezes of a subtropical climate at a time when most of Israel is shivering under damp skies. Because of this Tiberias seems to be flooded with tourists all year long nowadays.

Many of the hotels are in the new part of town, right on the main street— Ohel Jacob—a five-minute bus ride from downtown Tiberias. The custom in some Tiberias hotels is to require that you take half-board (breakfast and dinner) at the hotel, mainly because there are so few decent restaurants in town, and also because the hoteliers know that most tourists stay away the entire day on their sightseeing excursions around the lake and into the Galilee.

The **Polonia Hotel,** 17 Hagalil St., tel. 067-90007, opposite the luxury Galei Kinneret Hotel, is our first port of call. It has 24 rooms, a 100-year-old facade, and charges SH40.80 ($12) to SH47.60 ($14) single, SH34 ($10) per person double; add SH8.50 ($2.50) for breakfast. Rooms are air-conditioned, and have showers and toilets. Quite pleasant.

In the same building as the Polonia, **Ha'emek Hotel,** tel. 067-20308, has a dozen simply furnished rooms that are done up in a cozy way with gaily colored curtains and bedspreads. Rooms are air-conditioned and have running water; showers and toilets are in the hall. Single occupancy is SH34 ($10), double occupancy SH61.20 ($18), triples SH85 ($25); those rates include a full Israeli breakfast.

The **Panorama Hotel,** next door to the above at 19 Hagalil St., tel. 067-22526, has 35 rooms with private shower and toilet, 14 of them air-conditioned. Not many frills here, but the rates are good: SH30 ($8.80) for a single, SH50 ($14.70) for doubles, SH65 ($19.10) for triples, those prices including breakfast; rates without breakfast are SH5 ($1.45) per person lower.

The **Continental Hotel,** 2 Nazareth St., tel. 067-90018, is near the new Municipality building. New owners, Russian immigrants named Bilenkin, have transformed this once-dilapidated hostelry into a recommended one. They've installed a lovely bar and a TV room where hot coffee is always brewing in a samovar. Bed and breakfast rates are SH51 ($15) to SH54.40 ($16) single, SH42.50 ($12.50) per person double. All rooms have showers and toilets. Students get reduced rates. Meals are SH20.40 ($6) each.

The **Eshel Hotel,** Tabur Ha'aretz St., tel. 067-90562, has 18 rooms, one star, and is strictly kosher. Singles pay SH51 ($15) to SH62.90 ($18.50), doubles SH45.90 ($13.50) each. Bedrooms are bright and pleasant and the terrace overlooks the lake and the Golan Heights. All rooms have shower or bath and toilet, air conditioning, and heating. Israeli breakfast is served.

The **Eden Hotel,** 4 Ohel Yaacov St., Kiryat Shmuel, tel. 067-90070, is a spacious, well-run establishment with 52 rooms, all with private toilet, bath or shower, air conditioning, heating, radio, and telephone. There's a kosher kitchen, and a large, attractive dining room. Rates are SH51 ($15) to SH59.50 ($17.50) single, SH47.60 ($14) per person double, SH37.40 ($11) per person triple; students get a $1 reduction per night. Rooms at the back are quieter. Lunch or dinner is SH20.40 ($6).

The **Astoria Hotel,** 13 Ohel Yaacov St., tel. 067-22351, is a three-star hostelry with 57 air-conditioned rooms. All have phone, private bath or shower, and toilet. Singles pay SH66.30 ($19.50), doubles SH52.70 ($15.50) per person, breakfast included. Half board is SH24.65 ($7.25), double that for full board.

There are two strictly kosher hotels on Herzl Blvd., near the municipality. The first is the somewhat run-down, one-star **Florida Hotel,** at No. 8, tel. 067-20047. All of the 13 rooms are air-conditioned and heated, and all have toilets and baths or showers. Singles pay SH44.20 ($13) to SH51 ($15), doubles SH37.40 ($11) per person, Israeli breakfast included. Half board is SH20.40 ($6), full board SH40.80 ($12). Closed during summer.

Much superior to the Florida, but more expensive, is the **Ariston Hotel,** 19 Herzl Blvd., tel. 067-22002. Currently, the Ariston offers 33 rooms, all air-conditioned and heated, with private toilets, and baths or showers. Another 28 rooms are being completed at this writing, and phones are being installed throughout. There's a synagogue on the premises. Owners are friendly and helpful, and the hotel is within walking distance of the center of town. Rates: SH51 ($15) single, SH37.40 ($11) per person double. Add SH20.40 ($6) for lunch or dinner.

The Heller Hotel, 10 Yehuda Hanassi St., tel. 067-22577, has 15 large, clean rooms, each comfortably furnished with a sofa, armchair, and table. It's a strictly kosher place, and the atmosphere is homey. All facilities are in the hall. Rates, including Israeli breakfast, are SH44.20 ($13) single, SH34 ($10) per person double.

If you're traveling with kids, consider the **Hotel Sarah,** 7 Zeidel St., tel. 067-20826, located across the street from a public park and playground. It's a pleasant, well-run hotel, its 19 rooms equipped with private toilets and showers, air conditioning, and heating. The kitchen is kosher. Students receive a 10% discount on rates, which are SH47.60 ($14) single, SH35.70 ($10.50) per person double. Meals are SH13.60 ($4) each.

The air-conditioned, three-star **Daphna Hotel,** Ussishkin St., Kiryat Shmuel, tel. 067-22261, has 75 air-conditioned rooms, all with bath or shower, private toilet, phone, and radio. The kitchen is kosher. Singles are SH68 ($20) to SH78.20 ($23), doubles SH56.10 ($16.50) per person. Lunch or dinner is SH25.50 ($7.50).

Dani Motel, 28 Hashomer St., Kiryat Shmuel, tel. 067-20181, offers 22 pastel-colored bedrooms with private bath or shower, toilet, wall-to-wall carpeting, and air conditioning. Singles pay SH47.60 ($14), doubles SH34 ($10) each, those rates including buffet breakfast.

Ganei Menora Hotel, at the southern shore of Tiberias, tel. 067-92770, has 60 air-conditioned rooms, all with toilet, and bath or shower, and many with terraces. The kitchen is kosher. A single room is SH52.70 ($15.50) to SH61.20 ($18), a double SH45.90 ($13.50) per person; lower rates off-season.

Starvation Budget

Castle-on-the-Lake Hostel, on the seafront near the museum, tel. 067-21175, is not a youth hostel. It has ten dormitory rooms with 90 beds. You can use the refrigerator and cook your own meals at no extra charge; hot showers are available; doors close at 12:30 a.m. Summer bed rate is SH8.50 ($2.50) a day, plus SH2 (60¢) for linens if you need them. The rest of the year rates rise to SH10.50 ($3.10) a day, same price as in summer for linens. Students pay summer rates year round.

Bungalows at the beach at **Hof Ilanot,** north of Tiberias, near Migdal, tel. 067-22925, accommodate four people and rent for SH40 ($11.75) per day, SH50 ($14.70) if used on Friday or Saturday. There are also air-conditioned seven-bedded rooms with kitchenettes (refrigerator, two-burner stove, and sink, no dishes or pots) priced at SH105 ($30.90) for full occupancy. Prices are lower off-season. There's a restaurant and barbecue grills on the premises; provisions can be obtained nearby. You can also rent boats here.

At **Sironit Beach,** near the municipal beach, tel. 067-21449, are cabins for two or four persons. Showers and toilets are nearby, and there's a restaurant on the premises. The whole place is clean and well cared for. Highly recommended. Rates are SH20 ($5.90) single, SH40 ($11.75) for two, less off-season.

Guy Beach, near Sironit Beach, tel. 067-20257, has 25 two-bedded cabins priced at SH20 ($5.90) per person. Breakfast here is SH7 ($2.05) and consists of two eggs, pitta, butter, salad or cheese, olives, jam, and a beverage. Both Sironit Beach and Guy Beach give discounts to students.

For further Starvation Budget suggestions check out the hostels and camping grounds in Chapter XI.

Rooms in Apartments

As in many parts of Israel, people rent out rooms in their homes and apartments. The closest of these to the center of town is **Beit Habler,** 16 Rachel St., Kiryat Shmuel, tel. 067-21746. Rooms are clean but very simply furnished, no bath in room, but you do have hot and cold running water; there's a TV room and two kitchens for guests. Per person rate, not including meals—none served here—is SH15 ($4.40) for one or two people; room rate is SH40 ($11.75) for triple occupancy. (Off-season rates are less.) Bring your own soap and towel.

A little further out, but highly recommended, **Beit Berger,** 27 Naiberg St., Kiryat Shmuel, tel. 067-20850, has pretty and clean rooms, all with private shower and heating. There's a TV room downstairs, and fully-equipped kitchens on each floor for guest use. Some of the bedrooms have terraces. Single occupancy is SH30 ($8.85), doubles pay SH20 ($5.90), per person, a room for three costs SH52 ($15.30).

Christian Hospices

An excellent possibility for low-cost accommodations in Tiberias are the Christian hospices, which accept both tourists and pilgrims: **Mount of the Beatitudes,** tel. 067-20878; **Peniel-by-Galilee,** tel. 067-20685; and the **Church of Scotland Centre,** tel. 067-20144. All of these are located in magnificent rustic surroundings near the holy sites, but their limited accommodations are much in demand by religious groups and you'll have to write well in advance to obtain a room in summer.

One of the most beautiful locations is occupied by **Peniel-by-Galilee** (Peniel means "Face of God"), which is nestled among date palm trees directly on the shores of the Sea of Galilee. Three miles north of Tiberias, and a ten-minute bus ride away, this hospice was built as a residence by the late Dr. Harte, who did missionary work in this area and was affiliated with the YMCA in Jerusalem (you can make reservations through them at P.O.B. 294). It's a widely known pilgrimage meeting place, and the simple stylistic chapel on the water is a moving monument to the Christian faith. The accommodations are simple. Half-board rates range from SH78.20 ($23) per night for one person to SH23.80 ($70) for five.

A few miles further south, on a high hill stands the **Mount Beatitudes Hospice,** run by Italian nuns who keep 24 rooms spotlessly clean, almost hospital-like. Your room will have running water, but other facilities are shared. The rate is SH34 ($10) per person, breakfast included; SH40.80 ($12) for half board, SH51 ($15) for full board. The location, where Christ preached the Sermon on the Mount, is splendid. From the far side of the chapel, you have a view of the entire area, a picture as simple and biblical as anything you'll see in Israel. The gentle descending hillocks, the date palm trees above, the shimmering Sea of Galilee in the distance—it all conjures up the days when the prophets and their flocks walked these very lands.

Also magnificently set by the sea is the **Church of Scotland Centre,** Safad Rd., where B&B rates are SH40.80 ($12) per person, half board is SH57.80 ($17), full board SH71.40 ($21). Students get a 33% reduction, children 50%. Rooms with full private facilities are available for a few shekels extra. While here, you may want to stop at the **Scottish Hospice Book Shop,** where a rather astonishing number of Bibles, in 26 languages, are on sale.

Kibbutzim

Probably your best values and facilities can be found in a kibbutz guest house, and the nearest one to Tiberias—only a six-minute ride from downtown —is the **Nof Ginossar Guest House,** Post Ginossar, tel. 067-22163. There is regular bus service, but for someone with a rented car, this is the perfect place to stay in Tiberias. Prices are very splurgy for us, but it is rated four stars, is right next to the sea, and has its own beach and gardens. The atmosphere is quiet, bucolic and unhurried. The second-floor dining room (kosher) has a fine view of the Sea of Galilee, as do the rooms. There are 106 rooms in all, with either private bath or shower, air conditioning, and central heating. The guest house conducts a regular series of lectures with slides of kibbutz life. Year-round rates for bed and breakfast are SH91.80 ($27) single, SH61.20 ($18) per person double.

If you don't mind commuting, the Upper Galilee region has several other fine motels maintained by kibbutzim, and you will find details in Chapter XII. They are all located in scenic, quiet regions, blessed with wonderful natural amenities (how about a morning swim in the source of the River Jordan?), and at all of them you'll find swimming pools, air-conditioned rooms, and good cooks. Within an hour's drive north of Tiberias are: **Ayelet Hashachar,** tel. 067-37364; **Hagoshrim,** tel. 067-40138; **Kfar Blum,** tel. 067-40468; and **Kfar Giladi,** tel. 067-41414—all doing a brisk business with their kibbutz motels.

West of Tiberias, in what is known as Lower Galilee, is the **Lavi Guest House** (tel. 067-21477). Buses travel to Lavi direct from Tiberias and the ride takes only 15 minutes. This is a religious kibbutz with a great swimming pool and comfortable accommodations plus lectures on kibbutz life. B&B rates— once again on the splurgy side for us—begin at SH71.40 ($21) single, SH95.20 ($28) double. There is a minimum weekend rate of one full board plus one half-board, and Holy Day prices are considerably higher. There is a central tureen, incidentally, where guests can serve themselves coffee or tea 24 hours a day.

All the kibbutz guest houses are, as a general rule, worthwhile places to visit. Food is always good and wholesome, the grounds are manicured, and the atmosphere is informal and unpretentious. One of our own favorites is **Ayelet Hashachar,** a superb jumping-off point for the Golan Heights. Rates are exactly the same as at Nof Ginossar, and the two managers of the guest house are almost legendary hoteliers who have really pioneered the kibbutz expansion into the area of tourism.

RESTAURANTS: The specialty in Tiberias is the St. Peter's fish, so-called because it is the very fish that swam the Sea of Galilee when Christ called Peter away from his nets to follow Him and become a "fisher of men." It's a white fish that is indigenous to the Sea of Galilee and its taste resembles bass. (The Waldorf Astoria has been importing it for some years, because of its subtle, very special taste.)

A good place to try it is at **Galei Gil,** on the seashore promenade, tel. 067-20699, a large and highly recommended restaurant with flower-bedecked tables both inside and out on the boardwalk and a terrace. St. Peter's fish with chips or salad is priced by weight, substitute chicken for the fish and the price of your meal is SH11 ($3.25). You get a 5% discount if you show a copy of this book. Open daily from 10 a.m. till midnight.

For Italian fare try **Beit Hapri** (Pizza and Fruit House), at the New Shekem Centre near the Meyouhas Youth Hostel, tel. 067-20362. Pizza is priced at SH4.50 ($1.30) to SH6.50 ($1.90), spaghetti at SH4.50 ($1.30). Other options are pancakes for SH4.50 ($1.30) to SH8 ($2.35), and ice cream from SH3.50 ($1). Open Sunday to Thursday from 10:30 a.m. to midnight, Friday and Saturday from 10:30 a.m. to noon and 6:30 p.m. to 3 a.m.

The splurgy **Ron Beach Hotel Restaurant,** tel. 067-21418, overlooks the lake, and has a tree-shaded garden and outside tables. Its snack bar is open from 9 a.m. to 7 p.m.; the restaurant is open lunchtime between noon and 2:30 p.m. You can get a full meal of an appetizer, main course (St. Peter's fish, goulash, chicken, schnitzel, or liver), salad, and dessert for SH27.20 ($8). You can swim here, too, and there is a large gift shop. They are kosher and have won a coveted I.G.T.O. award.

The large and centrally located **Hamercaz Restaurant,** 18 Hagalil St., tel. 067-20420, offers a 10% reduction to students. The fare is oriental and kosher: grilled fish is SH7.50 ($2.20) to SH8.50 ($2.50), shashlik or chicken SH6.50 ($1.90), kabab SH6 ($1.75); side dishes—rice, vegetables, etc.—are SH2 (60¢). Open 6:30 a.m. to midnight, closed Friday from 4:30 p.m. until Saturday evening.

At **Sironit Beach,** tel. 067-21449, you can get a complete SH20.40 ($6) meal consisting of a vegetable pastry, two salads, St. Peter's fish or chicken schnitzel with rice, beans, or potatoes, and a dessert of fresh fruit. The restaurant is clean and attractive. Open daily from 8 a.m. to 5 p.m.

The **Erez Restaurant,** Yohanan Ben Zakai St., tel. 067-21311, gives students a 10% rake-off on oriental fare such as ground meat with tchina, normally priced at SH7 ($2.05). Chicken with chips and salad costs the same, grilled fish (14 ounces) with chips and salad goes for SH9 ($2.65). Open daily from 8 a.m. to midnight.

The **Bar Ha'Omanim** (Artists Bar & Restaurant), 7 Naiberg St., tel. 067-22484, offers an intimate setting, an air-conditioned bar, and items like steak, liver, schnitzel, kabab, or shashlik with the usual side dishes for SH9 ($2.65). Open 4 p.m. (noon in summer) to midnight, closing Friday at 4:30 p.m. until after sunset on Saturday.

And for a change of pace, opt for Chinese cuisine at **The House,** across the road from Lido-Kinneret Beach, tel. 067-20226. Chinese paper lanterns and rattan furnishings create the proper ambience. The Chinese preparation of St. Peter's fish is SH12.50 ($3.65), sweet-and-sour chicken or pork SH10 ($2.95), fried banana for dessert SH4.50 ($1.30). A complete dinner for two is SH20 ($5.90). Open daily 5 p.m. to midnight.

Some other possibilities: **Milk Bar Tal,** in the New Shekem Centre, for reasonably priced dairy dishes like blintzes and pancakes. . . . Hot-from-the-oven pastries and cakes at **Golan Bakery,** Yarden St., mostly priced under SH1.50 (45¢). . . . **Pizza Rimini,** Nazareth Rd., open daily from 11 a.m. to midnight for 13 varieties of pizza priced from SH4.20. . . . And, as always, the **Egged Restaurant** in the main bus station for good prices and clean surroundings.

NIGHTLIFE: There is no shortage of nightlife in Tiberias. A good place for a quiet drink is the **Galei Kinneret bar.** While you're imbibing, glance at the exhibition of books that have mentioned the hotel. You'll find the works of Leon Uris, James D. McDonald, Taylor Caldwell, and Edwin Samuel. There are folklore events at the respective hotels as well. Check with the I.G.T.O. for specific information.

You can dine and dance for the price of a meal at **Minus 206,** Gdud Barak Rd., tel. 067-91765, a restaurant designed to look like a boat. Open nightly till 2 a.m. it offers steak in pitta for SH8 ($2.35), St. Peter's fish with chips and salad for SH14 ($4.10), grilled meat with chips and salad for SH12 ($3.50). Admission is free, and there's no minimum.

Folk dancing is taught and enthusiastically done Monday, Wednesday, Friday, and Saturday nights from 8 p.m. to 1 a.m. (nightly in summer) at **Blue Beach,** Gdud Barak Rd., tel. 067-20105; admission is SH5 ($1.45).

The nearby **Quiet Beach,** Gdud Barak Rd., tel. 067-21441, is anything but quiet. Before you even see the club, you'll hear the blare of music and the roar of motorcycles and cars fighting for space in the small off-road parking lot. The music of popular recording stars nightly keeps about 500 brightly clad people jumping about on the upstairs deck of this building. Though 800 can be accommodated, real full-house crowds appear usually during July and August. Open from 8 a.m. till after midnight nightly in summer, from 9 p.m. to midnight Monday, Tuesday, Friday, and Saturday the rest of the year. Entrance is SH6 ($1.75).

Then there is the **Castle Inn Restaurant Bar,** near the Plaza Hotel, tel. 067-21175. Winter hours are from 8 p.m. to midnight daily except Friday, when the place closes at 2 a.m. In summer they're open Friday and Saturday nights only. There are two large rooms with arched ceilings and colored glass doors, background music and bronze decorations. Entrance fee is SH6 ($1.75), alcoholic drinks begin at SH3 (90¢). The bar seats 100 people, and winter heating is provided by charcoal braziers. The Tirat Ha'agam Hostel is in the same building.

WHAT TO SEE AND DO: Tiberias is a small town, but it offers a great number of sights and activities.

Main Street, Tiberias

Galilee Street, which is impossible to miss since there's but one main thoroughfare in the town, runs outside the old wall. You can see the remains of the former rampart that enclosed the city, as well as a few old mosques in ruins at the wall's edge. Walk along the street running perpendicular to Galilee St. down toward the sea; on your left is a small war memorial, and on your right, the Bank Leumi, with a sculptured frieze on its outer wall.

Tours

A variety of reasonably priced half-day and day-long tours to the nearby Christian landmarks, Upper Galilee sights, and the Golan Heights are available through **Egged Tours** at the central station on Hayarden Street (tel. 067-91081). Ask your hotel or call for the latest tour schedule.

One tour that we can heartily recommend is the one-day No. 101, which takes you to the Upper Galilee and the Golan Heights on Tuesdays, Thursdays, and Saturdays at a cost of SH54.40 ($16), fare only. Pickup is 8-8:30 a.m. at your hotel. Tour No. 102 will take you around the Sea of Galilee. The price is SH34 ($10). Keep in mind that the Central bus terminal has a good and inexpensive restaurant.

View from the Water's Edge

Down from the artists' galleries, in front of a large outdoor cafe, you'll find the most popular gathering spot in Tiberias, with a magnificent view across the lake. If you arrive in summer, chances are there will be children here leaping off the rampart into the water, and then climbing back up the old steps for another foray. Off on the left, a hundred yards away, are the huge, castle-like remains of a **Crusader fort** (now the Castle Inn), jutting up in basalt stone from the water. Directly across the lake is a green patch, Kibbutz Ein Gev, and a few other brave settlements which for years endured periodic shelling from the Syrian heights. To the left is towering **Mount Hermon,** which perpetually wears a snow-laced peak. From the foothills pour the waters which form the sources of the Jordan River. The mountains in the distance, opposite you, are part of the **Golan Heights,** pink and desolate. (See the end of this chapter for description of a Golan trip.)

Tombs of the Rabbis

Located near the end of Rehov Galilee and opposite the bus station is **Maimonides' Tomb,** one of the principal reminders that Tiberias was once the central congregating spot of the learned. Rabbi Moses Ben Maimon, known as Maimonides, or Rambam, was the greatest Jewish theologian of the Middle Ages. A Sephardic Jew, born in Cordova, Spain, he was an Aristotelian philosopher, a humanistic physician, and a leading scientist and astronomer. His principal work was *The Guide for the Perplexed.* The famous philosopher, who died in 1204 A.D., is now honored by a fairly decrepit white tomb, framed by a pile of rubble and guarded by aged sentinels who automatically recite a prayer when you enter. Nearby is the tomb of **Rabbi Yochanon Ben Zakkai,** founder of the Yavne Academy, and on a hillside just north of town, on the outskirts of Kiryat Shmuel (about a 15-minute walk), is the memorial to **Rabbi Akiva.** this great sage compiled the commentaries of the Mishna before the Romans tortured him to death at Caesarea in 150 A.D. for his role in aiding the Bar Kochba revolt. The tomb of **Rabbi Meir,** located on the hill above the mineral baths, is considered one of Israel's holiest sites. Rabbi Meir, called the "Miracle-Worker" and the "Light-Giver," is remembered in a white building that has two tombs—one venerated by the Ashkenazim and the other by the Sephardim. Huge bonfires are lit at his tomb by the Orthodox four days before the Lag b'Omer holiday in the spring.

The Hot Springs of Tiberias

Famous for their curative powers for over 3,000 years, the thermal baths of Tiberias are heavily frequented by visitors and Israelis. Pharmacies in Israel keep weel-stocked supplies of mineral salts from these Tiberias springs, and many an Israeli swears by their therapeutic effects.

The hot waters contain high amounts of sulphuric, muriatic and calcium salts, and over the centuries they've reportedly cured such ailments as rheumatism, arthritis, and gynecological disorders. They are probably the earliest known thermal baths in the world, noted by Josephus, Pliny, church historians, and many Arabic writers. Some biblical commentators have surmised that at these baths Christ cured the sick and maimed, and others place their origin at the time of Noah, when the insides of the earth were turned upward by The Flood. In Israel, there's a legend that Solomon entered into a conspiracy with demons to heal his kingdom's ailing people at this site.

Some of the baths look like swimming pools, others like Turkish baths, complete with domes, vaulted ceilings, and marble columns. The largest is the **Ibrahim Pasha** pool, where inside a huge stone lion guards the clientele. Arabic legend says that a barren woman need only sit on this lion after bathing and her wish for conception will come true.

All of the springs, at the seafront, are operated by **Tiberias Hot Springs Company, Ltd.,** tel. 067-91967, which offers baths and treatments in both old and new buildings. Cost of treatment differs from old to new building. See Chapter XI for details. Bring a bathrobe or be prepared to rent one for SH3.50 ($1). There's an inexpensive restaurant on the premises. Egged bus #5 passes the Springs.

Cultural Events

The sleepy quality of Tiberias is really deceptive, because there's much going on—and we're not merely alluding to thermal cures or rock 'n' roll along the shore. Here are some examples:

The **Ein Gev Music Festival** takes place in spring during Passover week.

Israeli folkdance and song festivals organized along the waterfront; the I.G.T.O. will supply particulars.

The Succoth Swimathon across the Kinneret (three miles). Everyone is welcome to join, but bring a medical certificate attesting to the fact that you are not overly drownable. Contact the Jordan Valley Regional Council, Mobile Post, or the Hapoel Sports Organization, 8 Ha'arba'ah St., Tel Aviv, tel. 03-26018.

There are summertime shows and performances at the **Samakh Amphitheater** on the southern tip of the Sea of Galilee by local and foreign entertainers.

Special activities are organized for groups and include lectures and slide shows on the geographical, historical, and archeological aspects of the region. These shows are given, usually upon request, by the I.G.T.O. regional director.

Beaches

The **Blue Beach** charges SH5 ($1.45) for the use of its lake facilities. The price includes a beach chair.

The **Quiet Beach** fees of SH5 ($1.45) per adult, SH3–4 (85¢–$1.20) for a student or child, includes all the swimming facilities. Open 8 a.m. to 6 or 7 p.m.

The **Ganei Hamat Swimming Beach,** opposite the Ganei Hamat Hotel, near the Tiberias Hot Springs, is open daily from 9 a.m. to 5 p.m. and charges SH5 ($1.45) admission for an adult, SH4 ($1.20) for a child. It offers deck chairs, showers, and a snack kiosk.

The **Guy Beach** near the Galie Kinneret Hotel, tel. 067-20257, has a fine waterfront and all the requisite facilities. There's also a nearby Wimpy and the Guy Beach Restaurant. Guy Beach charges SH5 ($1.45) for entrance and use of facilities May to September, the rest of the year it's free.

Sironit Beach is open from 8 a.m. to 5 p.m., April through October; SH4 ($1.20) for adults, SH3 (90¢) for a child or student. And to round it all out, you have a municipal beach south of Sironit Beach, open 9 a.m. to 5 p.m. Adults pay SH1.50 (45¢), children SH1 (30¢).

MAJOR SIGHTS ALONG THE SEA OF GALILEE: It's time to take a tour around the Sea of Galilee, heading north to begin a circle which will bring us back to Tiberias—and then we'll head on into the Upper Galilee region.

Migdal

First, two miles north of Tiberias along the road paralleling the lake, you'll come to the old village of Migdal, called Magdala in the Bible, birthplace of

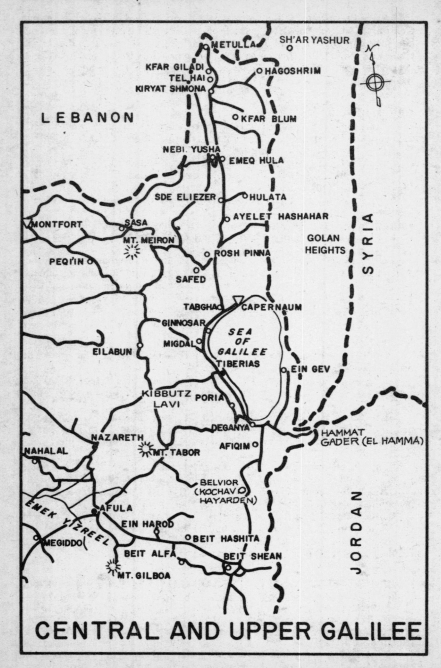

CENTRAL AND UPPER GALILEE

Mary Magdalene. The ride here is especially lovely, the tall eucalyptus trees and thick vegetation abundantly beautiful.

Tabgha

Getting to Tabgha, where Christ miraculously multiplied the loaves and fishes, you proceed northward along the shoreline from Migdal, passing **Minya,** a seventh-century Arabian palace that is one of the Moslem world's most ancient and holy prayer sites. At Tabgha, you'll find the Benedictine monastery and the **Church of the Multiplication of the Loaves and Fish,** tel. 067-21061, whose basilica floor is one of the best-preserved mosaic representations in all of Israel. In one scene it depicts a basket filled with loaves of bread, with two fishes standing upright. The larger mosaic, however, is a vivid and colorful tapestry of all the birds that once thrived in this area: swans, cranes, ducks, wild geese, and storks.

Mount of the Beatitudes

Just beyond Tabgha, on a high hill, is the famous Mount of the Beatitudes, now the site of an Italian convent and hospice. Here, Jesus preached the Sermon on the Mount.

There are many good views of the Sea of Galilee and its surroundings, but the vista from here is probably the best. One odd fact about this church is the inscription on the sanctuary, which informs you that the entire project was built by Mussolini in the 15th year of his rule in 1937. Exactly why the dictator chose this holiest of sites to express his benevolence has always been a great mystery to us.

Capernaum (Kfar Nahum)

"And they went into Capernaum; and straightaway on the sabbath day, He entered into the synagogue, and taught" (Mark 1:21). On this site where Christ preached are now an excavated synagogue and a Franciscan monastery. But the synagogue uncovered here was not the actual one in which Christ preached, since archeologists place its style of construction at around the second century A.D.

Capernaum's synagogue is a splendid Roman-like affair, with tall columns, marble steps, and shattered statuary, and numerous symbols from those times: carved seven-branched candelabras, stars of David, palm branches, and rams' horns. The rubble of basalt stone in the garden leads down towards the sea, where you can still glimpse the remains of a small boat basin with steps leading to the water. There is a small admission fee; the site is open daily from 8:30 a.m. to 4 p.m.

Ein Gev

Nestled between the hills of Golan and the lakefront, Ein Gev was founded in 1937 by German and Czechoslovakian pioneers. These days Ein Gev boasts a 5,000-seat amphitheater, which in recent years has presented some of the world's greatest musicians at its twice-yearly music festivals; Pablo Casals, Rudolf Serkin, Isaac Stern, and many other virtuosos have appeared here. On the hillsides around the amphitheater are tiers of vineyards, and elsewhere on the grounds are a banana plantation and date groves. Fishing is another flourishing industry here.

Not far from the amphitheater, in a handsome garden, is a bronze statue by Channa Orloff depicting a woman holding a child aloft. The inscription is from Nehemiah: "For the builders, every one had his sword girded by his side, and so builded."

This settlement bore the brunt of heavy attacks in the 1948 war, and its tempting position at the foothills, below heavy Arab military emplacements, made it a perennial target for Syrians. Rarely, however, was anyone here injured from those harassments, perhaps as a result of an endless maze of slit trenches throughout the grounds, as well as concrete shelters dug into the earth. Today the Ein Gev settlers no longer have to look over their shoulders as they farm their fields.

You can get to Ein Gev by bus, car or by ferry from Tiberias; the ferry leaves the quay at 10:30 a.m.

Degania

From Ein Gev, following the road as it winds around the lake toward Tiberias, you'll pass the settlements of Ha'on and Ma'agan on your way to Degania, itself just a 15-minute ride south of Tiberias (there's a bus from Tiberias). Degania is the country's very first kibbutz, founded in 1909 by Russian pioneers. Without any real experience in farming, this handful of self-made peasants left city jobs to fight malarial swamps and Arab bands.

Much of the philosophical basis of kibbutz life was first formulated in this Jordan Valley settlement by its leader, A. D. Gordon, a salt-of-the-earth thinker who was one of the most influential men in Israel's modern history. Gordon believed that a return to the soil and the honesty of manual work were the ingredients for creating a new spirit in man. He wielded a pick himself right till the day of his death at the age of 74—although he never, because of some abstruse matter of principle, joined the kibbutz as a member. On Degania's grounds a natural history museum, **Beit Gordon,** tel. 067-50040, contains a rich library and exhibition of the area's flora and fauna.

Degania grew so quickly that its citizens soon branched out to other settlements. The father of Moshe Dayan, famous patched-eye commander of the Sinai Campaign, left Degania to help establish **Nahalal,** Israel's largest moshav settlement. Eventually, too, some of the younger Degania settlers established their own kibbutz right next door, and called it simply **Degania B.**

If you get confused as to which is which, **Degania A** is the settlement with the tank at the gate—a reminder of the battle the settlers waged against Syrian tanks in 1948 (the members fought them off with Molotov cocktails). It also has a fairly ancient look about it—compared with the youthful fresh appearance of most kibbutzim. In contrast to some of Degania A's old yellow stucco buildings, Degania B exudes a fresh, just-built flavor.

Degania A and B have about 450 settlers each, and both settlements are prosperous, successful ventures, their beauty enhanced by subtropical plants and towering palm trees.

After you pass Degania on your way to Tiberias, you will come to the point where the Sea of Galilee flows into the River Jordan. This is where groups of pilgrims baptize themselves in the holy water of the Jordan. You can reach this spot from Tiberias by taking the bus that goes to Ein Gev or Emek Hayarden.

6. The Upper Galilee

From Tiberias, you can catch a bus going northward as far as **Metulla,** Israel's most northerly town—and you'll find that the ride passes fascinating sights. (Depending on the season, you might have to change buses at Kiryat Shmona.)

The trip begins along the western shore of the lake, goes through the valley of **Ginossar** and past Capernaum. Alongside the names of Kinneret, Galilee and Tiberias, Ginossar must also take its place as a biblical name for the Sea of Galilee.

Soon you'll pass the turn-off for **Rosh Pinna,** an undistinguished-looking place, but nevertheless the oldest modern town in the entire Galilee, founded in 1882. Just outside Rosh Pinna is the only memorial in the country to a member of the underground extremist army. Dedicated to Shmuel Ben Yosef, the first Jew hanged by the British in Palestine, this simple but striking monument looks from a distance like an arm thrust upwards at the sky, its fist shaking in defiance at the heavens.

Further along the main road is the turn-off to **Mishmar Ha'Yarden,** the Galilee's oldest moshav, established around the turn of the century, and one of the few settlements overrun and destroyed by the Arabs during the 1948 siege. Beyond the settlement, crossing the Jordan into Golan, is the bridge called **Benot Yaakov,** "Daughters of Jacob," believed to be the place where Jacob crossed the river upon his return from Mesopotamia. The bridge is also on the ancient caravan route from Damascus to Egypt, part of the Via Maris. It is the place where the infrequent Syrian-Israeli prisoner exchanges occurred.

A brand-new guest house has opened in **Moshav Sh'ar Yashuv,** called **Hotel Gan,** Mobile Post, Upper Galilee, tel. 067-41768. It is near Kiryat Shmona, perfectly situated for trips to the Golan and Banyas, and only one kilometer from Hurshat Tal, a beautiful national park. Bed and breakfast for a single occupant in double room costs $12, for a double $10 per person during low season. High-season rates are $14.50 and $12.50 respectively. During high season add $5 for dinner; $4.50 during off season. Lunch is not served. Add 10% to these rates during Pessah, Independence Day, Shavuoth, Rosh Hashanna, Succoth and Hanukka. Students get a 10% reduction. Singles are SH44.20 ($13), doubles SH35.70 ($10.50) per person, including Israeli breakfast. Dinner is SH17 ($5). There is both heating and air conditioning and it is a very lovely place.

Note: for those of you who love horsing around and would like staying in an Israeli dude ranch, be sure to check Chapter XI for information about **Vered HaGalil** and other Galilee exotica.

THE HULA VALLEY: The best view of this beautiful reclaimed swampland is from the **Nebi Yusha** fortress just off the main road, on the **Hill of the Twenty-Eight.** A memorial in front of the British Taggart Fort recalls the time when these Haganah soldiers climbed the hill from the Hula in the dead of night and fought to gain this strategic point. The odds were against them as they weathered a rain of machine-gun fire and grenades from the windows of the fort. When efforts to dynamite the building failed, because of the concrete-enforced base, the group's commander plunged into a suicidal mission. He strapped the dynamite to his back, ignited it, and threw himself at a weak point in the wall, sacrificing himself for the objective. In all, 28 fighters died in taking this hilltop strongpoint, and today birds nest in the many shell holes on the walls of the fort.

Beyond the memorial plaques is an observation point where the view of the Hula Valley down below is nothing short of magnificent.

This breathtaking area, which stretches in both directions as far as the eye can see, was once a vast marshland teeming with wildlife. It was considered the smallest of the three lakes fed by the Jordan, the Sea of Galilee and the Dead Sea being the other two. To Israelis who remember it in its marshland state, the Hula was a lovely place—a home for water buffalo and wild boar, a place abundant in exotic birds and wildflowers. Species of cranes and storks would migrate here, coming and going from as far away as Russia, Scandinavia, and India. To those who knew its thickets of papyrus, its dragonflies and kingfishers, and its tropical water lilies (some claim it looked a little like the shores of the Nile), the Hula was a bit of paradise. The Arabs had legends about the Hula's charms, where spirits walked in the evening mist luring young people into the mysterious marsh.

After years of wrangling with neighboring governments—as well as with the French and British—the Israelis got the chance to drain the Hula marshes after they achieved independence. The country needed every drop of water and every square foot of fertile land. So bulldozers and dredges changed the Hula, reclaiming its wild beauty into a mammoth checkerboard of rich fields. But in one small section, a wildlife preserve lingered, a vestige of the Hula's past.

The project took seven years, from 1950 to 1957. Control over the Hula's waters was also a necessary phase of the Lowdermilk and other Jordan River diversion plans, which brings water to the barren southern reaches of Israel.

However, the project cost the area in terms of an upset ecosystem, and, in 1970, a reconstruction project was launched. Today the Hula is again alive with grey herons, cormorants, ducks, wild boar, jamoos (water buffalo), and other former inhabitants that died or went elsewhere when the swamps were drained. Entrance fee to the Hula Valley is SH2.60 (75¢) for adults, SH1.20 (35¢) for children. Open daily from 8 a.m. to 4 p.m., Fridays till 3 p.m. Free guided tours take place Saturday, Sunday, Tuesday, and Thursday from 9:30 a.m. to 1 p.m.

TEL HAI AND TRUMPELDOR: Passing **Kiryat Shmona**, with its spanking new immigrant quarters, you might now begin thinking about Joseph Trumpeldor, in whose memory this town was founded. Kiryat Shmona means "Town of the Eight" and that refers to Trumpeldor's group of six men and two women who died at nearby **Tel Hai** defending their settlement from Arab attackers in 1920. It was also the scene of one of the worst terrorist attacks.

In another few miles, you come to the monument of Trumpeldor at Tel Hai, a statue of a lion at the edge of a cliff, his head thrown back and mouth open, bellowing his strength at the skies. Rarely do foreign visitors know about Trumpeldor, and to an Israeli this is shocking. For Trumpeldor is the Israeli Nathan Hale, a model of courage and heroism who continues to fire the spirit of the nation's youth. He was born in Russia in 1880, served in the Czar's army, lost an arm, and was decorated for gallantry by the Empress of Russia. Then, as an ambitious Zionist leader, he came to Palestine in 1912, and, with his self-styled Zion Mule Corps, fought with the British in the disastrous Gallipoli campaign. After the war he became a leader of Russia's pioneer agricultural youth movement and settled at the Tel Hai kibbutz. It was here that Trumpeldor fought off maurauding Arab bands with the other settlers, until one day when a particularly heavy attack came and the one-armed Trumpeldor refused to leave the settlement. In a furious last-ditch stand he and seven comrades were killed on the kibbutz grounds.

The grave of this national hero, beneath the roaring lion, is inscribed with his last words: "It is good to die for our country." The Jews got their own "country" 28 years after he uttered those words.

HATZOR MUSEUM: At the entrance to **Kibbutz Ayelet Hashachar,** tel. 067-37313, you'll see the new Hatzor Museum. It has exhibits from 21 different archeological strata spanning 2,500 years, from the early Bronze Age to the Hellenistic period in the second century B.C. (By the way, the kibbutz is one of Israel's handsomest—same goes for its guest house. See Chapter XII for complete descriptions.)

METULLA: This is as far north as you can go in Israel proper. Founded in 1896 by a Rothschild grant, the town has never really prospered, although farming, fruit-growing, and the cultivating of bees are vigorously pursued by the residents of this village at the Lebanese border. During the rainy season, you can see an Israeli waterfall in action here, cascading down from the Tanur pass into the Iyon River.

A quiet little town, with a lot of soldiers and considerable military action because of its proximity to the Lebanese border, Metulla does boast an old and elegant hotel and restaurant, the **Arazim,** tel. 067-40616, where everything gleams with love and polish, and the food, service, and accommodations are old-worldish in style and quality. It has 31 rooms, all with toilet, bath and/or shower, plus a bar, gift shop, private swimming pool, and tennis courts. The food's kosher and there's central heating. Bed-and-breakfast rates are SH54.40 ($16) per person double, SH68 ($20) single. Add SH20.40 ($6) for half-board, double that for full board. Students get a 10% reduction except during July and August and on Saturdays or holidays.

There's also the **Hamavri Hotel,** tel. 067-40150, with 18 rooms, all with shower and toilet. Singles are SH62.90 ($18.50), doubles SH49.30 ($14.50) per person. Add SH18.70 ($5.50) for half board, SH34 ($10) for full board. Students get a 10% reduction except on holidays and during the month of August.

An excellent choice is the **Sheleg Halevanon Hotel,** tel. 067-41315, with 35 rooms, all equipped with phones, private baths and showers, toilets, and clock radios. You can rent a TV for SH5 ($1.45) a day, though there's a color set in the lounge. Tennis courts, two swimming pools (one for children), a handsome bar/dining room, and a garden patio are other amenities. Rates are the same as at the above-mentioned Hamavri, however, students get a 15% discount.

At Metulla, and throughout the Golan Heights (see below), you can have a close view of "The Green Line." This is a nickname for Israel's borders (old and new), because there's such a marked difference between Israeli land and the Arab territory bounding it: One is green or gold with grass and crops, well irrigated, totally reclaimed; the other is barren, stony, parched, and full of weeds.

TO THE COAST ALONG THE LEBANESE BORDER: From Metulla, the road drops south and then heads west, following the ins and outs of the border with Lebanon. Small settlements dot the boulder-strewn landscape, and you'll be seeing many signs warning: "Halt, Frontier Ahead." Where there are no signs, the border is marked by pyramids of white stones which, in some sections, are right beside the road. Along the border, you'll see settlers working in tractors on fields where suddenly the green stops short; across, maybe 20 yards away, the earth is coarse and rubble-strewn, and Lebanese peasants work with donkeys and wooden ploughs at the tough soil. It's a beautiful artery, but we suggest you avoid it, or at least travel with a competent, local guide.

Sasa and the Biram Synagogue

On the northern foothills of Mount Meiron is Kibbutz Sasa, a settlement started by a group of Americans and Canadians in 1949 in a deliberately chosen region where the pioneers hoped to test their convictions. This settlement has more than its share of artists and university degree-holders, who built their settlement atop a hill 3,000 feet high and persevered despite many problems, including a polio epidemic which tragically took many lives and threatened to break the morale of the settlers. Sasa is called an "American" kibbutz, and consequently VIP guests are often brought here by the government to be shown what one group of American expatriates accomplished in Israel.

Just two miles away is Biram, the oldest and best-preserved synagogue in Israel, its grounds housing—according to legend—the grave of Queen Esther.

If you're interested in visiting Crusader castles (**Montfort** and **Yechiam**), see Chapter XI. The fortresses are well worth a visit, and both lie only a few miles off the main road leading down to the coast.

7. The Golan Heights

Throughout the writing of this book we've tried to provide a reasonable and honest appreciation of the local security situation. When we were in Jerusalem we emphasized, and we do so again, that despite occasional incidents the capital is one of the safer major cities of the world to visit. The same is true of most of the rest of the country, including the entire south—and this most certainly includes Sinai.

The northern region is more problematic, however. We introduced a few cautious commentaries about travel through the Metulla region and particularly along the open road between Lebanon and Israel. Tens of thousands of Israelis travel through this area every year and nothing happens to them. School children take picnics up there and return with nothing worse than sun blisters. But an element of danger does exist. There are katyusha rockets landing in the region. There are attempts at infiltration. There is occasional sniping. We wouldn't think of cautioning you not to visit the area, but tourists should be careful.

The same applies to the Golan Heights. There have been virtually no incidents in the area—not even attempts at sabotage—since the end of the Yom Kippur War. And yet the possibility of danger is a fact of hard reality. The relation between Syria and Israel is also unsettled, and the situation in the Middle East is still volatile. So by all means travel to the area—we wouldn't miss it for anything in the world—but take a few precautions.

Try not to travel into the area alone. If you drive up in a private car, take someone with you who is familiar with the area. Don't travel into the area if the political situation is restive. Even if the situation is quiet, it takes only a few seconds to lob a mortar. Never travel in the region at night. Not only is it not recommended, in the Golan Heights it is illegal. Opt when possible for the organized tours. You'll be in the hands of experts, you'll see more and do more, and there will be very little of a security problem.

And now that we've scared you, let's drive up and have a look around.

RECENT HISTORY: A trip through the Golan Heights is a lesson in contemporary history. This is where the June 1967 war really started, when two months earlier, on April 7, the Syrians bombarded Ein Gev from their positions on the hills above the eastern shore of the Sea of Galilee.

For perhaps the thousandth time in the history of these kibbutzim on the plains around the Sea of Galilee, settlers were wounded, livestock killed, buildings destroyed, and fields of produce set afire. Israel served notice on Syria that it would stand for no more, that Syria must be prepared to face the consequences. Syria appealed to Egypt and Iraq, claiming that an Israeli invasion was imminent. Egypt called for war, turned out the U.N. from Gaza and the Straits of Tiran, and massed its armies on the Israeli border.

What happened that May—the torturous waiting, the failure of diplomacy —is familiar to everyone interested in Israel. Equally familiar is the morning of June 5, when the Israeli Air Force destroyed the combined air forces of three Arab countries. All that week, however, Syria continued to rain fire on the settlements around the Sea of Galilee. Israeli planes, tanks, and paratroopers were spread thin fighting on the Egyptian, West Bank, and Jerusalem fronts.

Syria did not attack—only a probe here and there, at Tel Dan, at Sh'ar Yashuv—and continued shelling the farms and fields . . . until Friday, June 9. On that day, the Israeli army could spare the armor and men necessary; elsewhere, the job had been completed. Only the Golan remained. First, an aerial bombardment seared the mountain with napalm and pounded the bunkers with heavy bombs. Artillery joined in, shaking the hills and trenches with a ten-hour barrage. Spearheaded by the Golani Brigade, considered the toughest fighters in the Israeli army, infantry and tank columns launched a frontal attack on the Maginot Line of the Middle East. Concrete bunkers, some 30 feet deep, were unshaken by the airplane bombardments. Tanks could hardly move through the minefields. Anti-personnel mines and rolls of barbed wire took their toll of the advancing infantry. The lines of Syrian trenches and fortifications were five deep, ten deep. Armor-led infantry would take bunkers at great cost, only to find that ten more such entrenched hills waited behind them. So deep and well-constructed were the positions that they had to be taken, finally, by foot soldiers in trench-to-trench, bunker-to-bunker fighting. Infantry losses ran high. But soon the Syrian morale cracked. Widespread desertion of secondary positions followed, and the Arab Golan armies withdrew in a rout.

When you see these Golan hills—and the bunkers and gun emplacements still there—you will wonder how any army could ever be dislodged from them. Taking the Golan hills was a military feat equal in magnitude to the knockout punch that destroyed the Arab air forces. The Golan victory cost the lives of 115 Israeli soldiers.

After the Six-Day War, Israel embarked on a careful and selective policy of settling the Golan with kibbutzim and moshavim. Then, in 1973, the Yom Kippur War broke out, and the surprise Syrian attack nearly drove the Israeli forces back behind the original armistice line. Settlement after settlement fell as the initial onslaught caught Israel completely unprepared. It took about a week for Israel to enter into the offensive again, and the Syrian forces were not only pushed out of the region, but a salient (later returned) was cut into Syria itself. After the fighting, Kuneitra, the ruined principal city of the area, was returned to Syria.

GOLAN TRAVEL TIPS: The tour buses of Egged, United, Galilee, and Dan Tours make frequent one- to two-day trips through the Golan Heights. Prices vary with the starting point: Jerusalem, Tel Aviv, Haifa, Tiberias, or an Upper Galilee kibbutz guest house. Many such bus tour plans are available—to fit all pocketbooks.

If you go by rented car, get a new map, from a bookstore or gas station, that includes the Golan area (Carta's Holyland Touring Map will do). The size of the Golan region is roughly 35–40 miles from north to south, and 15 miles from west to east at the widest point—easily covered in a day. At present, you need no travel permit for the Golan trip, but there are night curfews.

As you enter the Golan Heights you will find signs mapping out those roads that are open. The roads here have been improved and paved since the Six-Day War; roadwork goes on constantly in this area and you'll marvel at the modern roadways.

Figure a whole day for your journey, and take a picnic lunch. There are cold drink stands near the major tourist attractions and you can obtain snacks at the Baniyas pools and at a cafe at Kibbutz Merom Hagolan. Otherwise, there is nothing much by way of foodstuff available. Start early, as soon after sunrise as possible, and with a full tank of gas.

There are also, as yet, no overnight accommodations in the Golan Heights. Your best base for touring the Golan, therefore, is one of the camping or vacation villages by the sea (most operated by kibbutzim), or a youth hostel. See Chapters XI and XII for details.

Snow in the Golan

The latest excitement for Israelis—accustomed as they are to the availability of year-round beach holidays—is the winter ski season on Mount Hermon. A variety of skiing services has been established under the aegis of the **Mount Hermon Ski Center;** phone 067-31103 for up-to-the-minute data on ski conditions.

The snow season begins in December/January and lasts until mid-April. The depth of the snow ranges from two to three meters on the high slopes to one meter at the base lodge. Equipment can be hired by adults for SH8.50 ($2.50) a day, SH5.50 ($1.60) for children; private lessons at the ski school cost SH4 ($1.20) for adults, SH2.50 (75¢) for children per hour.

A variety of tours and nearby accommodations are available—weeklong, weekend, one day. More information in Chapter XI.

One Last Warning

When touring the Golan area, do not go exploring for shell fragments or souvenirs in the hills near the bunkers. Estimates range from 100,000 to 1,000,000 for the number of mines Syria planted in this area over the last 20 years. It may be ten or 20 years before the Israeli Army finishes mine-sweeping the area. It must be done inch by inch, and, since many of the mines are the plastic kind not detectable by metal-seeking devices, laboriously slow probes and earth-turning machines must be used. En route you will see a couple of places where the tour buses stop to give visitors a look at the bunkers. Two million visitors (mostly Israeli) have been there before you—so you can be sure it's safe. The barbed wire fences that line much of the road, and the triangular yellow-and-red Hebrew signs on them, all mean the same thing: mine field.

BANYAS AND BIRKAT RAM: Head north on the road that connects Rosh Pinna and Kiryat Shmona. Make your right past Kiryat Shmona, and head toward Hagoshrim, Dan, and Dafna. A big green sign points the way. Just after Tel Dan you will cross into what was, till June 10, 1967, the impregnable fortress—Golan. This is a new road, with an abundance of signs pointing out just how close you are to Kuneitra and the Syrian border from here.

First stop is the **Banyas Waterfall,** less than a mile inside the new zone. Beyond the parking lot and cold-drink vendors, you'll see the biggest waterfall in these parts. (There's an equally big one at Metulla, but it cascades only in winter.) The Banyas is one of the principal sources of the Jordan River. Head down to the stream for a look at the waters rushing along clear and cold through an area of deep green growth. You should remember that these clear, fast-running waters have begun several hundred feet higher on the Hermon slopes, and that the destination, after dropping into the Jordan River, is the Sea of Galilee. Jordan ("yared Dan") means "descending from Dan," and the river, whose origins are right here, picks up again south of the Sea of Galilee for a twisting, turning run of 70 miles before emptying into the Dead Sea and becoming a stagnant, oily mixture.

Walk back above the cleft to the right of the parking lot, and you'll see a memorial to a suicidal, heroic mission: the jeep that has been pushed over the side to a permanent resting position. On June 10, 1967, the jeep's lieutenant took it on himself to race the car over a mine field in order to clear the way for a unit of tanks whose advance had been slowed down.

As you face the jeep, look at the hills about 45 degrees to the right. You'll see a cluster of rubble about two hillocks back: **Tel Faher,** considered the worst single fortification on the Syrian Heights. Thirty Israelis died taking Tel Faher in the Six-Day War. Directly behind the jeep, high up on the crest of the mountain, is **Nimrod Castle.**

Take a left driving out and head through the wrecked **Banyas Village,** once the headquarters of the Syrian Army in this area. The pink house at the entrance to the village was formerly the Syrian Officers Club; it is now a restaurant.

At the **Banyas Pools,** Druze farmers are selling their produce, and there is a self-service restaurant called **Ma'ayanoth Habanyas.** Behind the pools you'll see caves and temple remnants from the Hellenistic period. The deep caves have been the source of many old legends, some dating as far back as the Greek time when a temple to Pan was here. Apparently, only the Greeks would say Pan with a P, and the name of the city, Panias, became transformed to Banyas. It is also believed that at the time of Herod, Banyas was the northern capital known as Caesarea Philippi.

Next stop—just follow the signs—is **Birkat Ram,** "Pool of the Height." This is an odd geological formation, an improbable-looking lake. Dry, puckered brown hills rise up on all sides, and the lake sits way down at the bottom of a deep "soup bowl."

Restaurant Birkat Ram caused quite a sensation when it opened in 1971. Not because of the food, but because its owned half and half by Druze and Jew—a precedent everyone hopes will be followed often. Located near the extinct volcano between Kuneitra and Mount Hermon, it serves full meals for moderate prices and also has a shop for gifts and souvenirs.

In case you missed the Druze fruit vendors at Banyas, you've got another chance at Birkat Ram. These Druze are the only local citizens of the Golan who continued living here after the war. Of the former 80,000 inhabitants of the Golan, only these 5,000–6,000 Druze farmers remain. The Druze in these hills have suffered persecution at Moslem hands for centuries. During the Yom Kippur War the villages were singled out for intense Syrian air attack. Many Druze civilians died.

Hard-working farmers who have lived here for generations, the Druze have been the only local inhabitants to work the Golan lands. The stretches of barren, unworked fields up this way reveal that the Syrians who had been living here for 20 years could not have been terribly interested in farming; fortifications and the positioning of hundreds of cannons and mortars were of prime interest. An Israeli newspaper once reported a conversation with a Druze mukhtar (chieftain or mayor). "What will you do if the Israelis remain here permanently?" he was asked. "I will stay here. It is my land," he said. "And what if there is a settlement and the Syrians come back?" the reporter asked. "We will be here," came the answer.

NIMROD CASTLE: Follow the road signs to **Kalaat Namrud,** Nimrod Castle. It's worth going out of your way to see Nimrod for two reasons. First, it offers a spectacular view, and second, it's the biggest, best-preserved Crusader castle in these parts, in much better shape than those at Montfort and Belvoir.

As you come around under the wall of the castle you'll see the narrow vertical slits in the wall where archers were once stationed. From the high ground within the castle your eyes have a feast. To the left is the zigzagging cleft of Banyas rift. In a lush, green pocket further on you see Tel Dan kibbutz, then a series of carp ponds, Kiryat Shmona on the hills beyond, and the rectangles of brown and green of the Hula Valley extending southward for miles and miles.

Behind the castle to the north sits **Mount Hermon,** white-maned in winter months, snow-streaked in the spring and summer. This slope and pinnacles of Mount Hermon, 6,500 feet, are within Israel's borders, and ski holidays are already being sponsored in the area. (For details, consult the travel tips at the opening of this section and Chapter XI.)

Inside Nimrod you'll see many deep holes, water-filled cisterns 30 feet deep. Very little was damaged here during the Six-Day War, although its position dominating the area made it a strategic spot, and indeed a Syrian observation post/mortar position was attacked here. One version has it that only one 500-pound bomb was dropped on Nimrod—no one wanted to wreck such a pretty castle. Strafing attacks routed the Syrians, and the Israelis turned it into an artillery-spotter post of their own. As you can see from up here, whoever controlled Nimrod, in by-gone days as well as today, controlled the traffic from Lebanon to Tiberias and the Jordan Valley.

TOWARD THE BORDER: After the slow, bouncing ride back from Nimrod to the main road, the way becomes clear, flat, and well-paved. Heading toward Kuneitra and the Syrian emplacements, you pass villages of a type you haven't seen before, in which houses are made of the monotonous black basalt rock of this region. Where the roofs are tiled red on these black homes, the villages are Circassian ("Cheer-khasi" in Hebrew). The Circassians reached this part of the world via southern Russia, the Caucasus, and Iran.

A new road circumvents Kuneitra. There's a mound though, near the United Nations base, which is worth visiting. You can look out into the ruined city and across into the wide, barren plain that leads to Damascus.

Nearby is **Kibbutz Merom Hagolan,** a commune of youngsters tending fields and orchards and representing countries from all over the world. We once went out with an irrigating team consisting of five people: One was from Holland, another from Tel Aviv, a third was born in Detroit, the fourth had come from Morocco when he was two, and the fifth was a German volunteer.

There are similar settlements all over the Heights, and they are really worth visiting, spanning the spectrum from religion to irreligion and from socialism to quasi-free enterprise. The two denominators they all have in common are dedication and youth. If you're over 30 on the Golan, you're going to feel very old indeed.

Most of the kibbutzim and moshavin don't mind visitors, but they are really not equipped to entertain, and the members are frequently too busy to interrupt their labors. Still, if you need a helping hand, you'll get one. And restroom facilities are clean.

One thing you'll immediately notice: Wherever you find a new Israeli settlement, there is a great change in the landscape. Rubble and rock have been cleared away and intensive cultivation is in evidence. Add this veneer to the work already performed by the Druze and you have an approximate picture of what the Golan Heights might one day become.

KFAR HOREB AND THE SEA OF GALILEE: Coming down out of the hills, and heading closer to the Sea of Galilee, you'll reach Kfar Horeb, three miles past Fik. From this smashed-to-rubble Syrian village you'll appreciate what the Syrians saw from these heights. Load your camera, because from the western cliffs of Kfar Horeb you can see the entire Sea of Galilee, from Capernaum in the north to Degania in the south, an almost unbearably beautiful panorama. Chances are, if you've done your touring assiduously, you'll get here late in the afternoon after the peculiar local bluish haze has started to descend. It's a sight you won't soon forget. Directly below, you'll see Ein Gev. From Kfar Horeb it was a favorite Syrian trick to turn a giant searchlight onto Ein Gev in the middle of the night. Eucalyptus trees provide scant cover for the road that runs along the highway below, all within easy range of the Syrian positions that were dug in here.

On the very height of the mountain here, the road passes heavy fortifications on each side. To the left is a captured Syrian tank, sitting in a desolate area where today's tour buses stop. And young people and tourists are climbing around and on the tank, and walking across the roadway to the old bunkers and new monument, where they poke around and sit calmly eating picnic lunches. Times have changed.

Come down the new road to **El Hamma,** tel. 067-51039; the hot sulphur springs and baths. They operate under the same principle as the mineral baths near Tiberias, only the *hamamim* here are far more oriental in appearance. Don't take your eyes off the twisted, sharply dropping road for long, but do notice the dams and conduits of the Yarmuk River project. Like the Iraq-Lebanon pipeline, this also exists today by courtesy of Israel hospitality. A park opened here in 1977. Surrounded by ancient olive and fig trees, it has four springs. More modern medical spa facilities are planned for the future, but today visitors can bathe in natural open-air or covered mineral pools. At the edge of the park is a hill which covers the ancient town of Hammat Gader (El Hamma). The remains of a Roman amphitheater and the mosaic floor of a sixth-century synagogue can be seen, and archeological digs are being conducted on the site. Entrance to the pools is SH6 ($1.75) for adults, SH4 ($1.20) for children 12 and under. Open daily from 8:30 a.m. to 4 p.m., till 3 p.m. on Friday. Egged offers tours to El Hamma; check with them for details. Finally, having twisted your way down a dozen hairpin turns, you burst across the old frontier, from a good new road to a bad old road—from dry, parched hills to richly planted groves. These are the fields of **Tel Katzir**—you are back in Israel proper.

Chapter IX

THE NEGEV

**1. Beersheba
2. Arad
3. The Dead Sea: Ein Bokek,
Masada, Ein Gedi, and Sodom
4. The Roads to Eilat
5. Eilat**

IF YOU HAVE the usual preconception of what a desert is like—sand, nothing but sand—you're in for a surprise. The Negev is not a desert in that sense at all. In Hebrew the word for Israel's southern region is *midbar,* meaning wilderness, which is precisely what the Negev is. There are expanses of sand in the Arava region just north of Eilat, but for the most part the Negev is a great triangular swath of boulders, pebbles, wind-sculpted mountains, eroded landscape, Bedouin encampments, and brave, lonely settlements. The people of the region are different—they have to be. The Negev could easily be regarded as a sort of Israeli Siberia, and yet the contrary is true. The taming of the desert is the prime challenge of the idealistic, and perhaps the greatest single achievement of the people of Israel.

Just a few decades ago, the mighty Negev reached high into the north and lapped at the settlements of Rishon LeZion and Gedera. Now the Negev has been pummeled and forced backward. Traveling down south you'll see no desert traces at all until reaching Beersheba, and then, to your amazement, you'll discern that the formidable wilderness has been rolled back even beyond that city. Where vultures and scorpions once reigned, winter crops and early vegetables are grown. Inch by inch a dead land is being reclaimed, and if there is ever peace in the region, the most arid of lands will be taught to bloom again.

In Chapter XI, titled "Israeli Adventures," we dwell on the desert trips pioneered by Neot Hakikar. The founder of that company was a man named Amiram Ovrotsky, whose achievements represent far more to Israel than the expansion of tourism. Like so many Israeli youngsters, Ovrotsky fell in love with the desert at an early age. During his army service he spent long months in the Negev, checking out biblical references in the region, learning the secrets of Bedouin survivability, and classifying flora and fauna.

After the army he joined the Ministry of Agriculture and became obsessed by a single idea—proving that the most inhospitable of all Negev regions, the area around Sodom, could be made to sustain human life again. He extracted a parcel of salt-choked land from the Ministry for his private experiments, and labored at night to wash out the chemicals, working with his hands because he had no tools. After months of arduous effort, he proved a point. He began to scratch life out of the bleached, somnolent land.

Every previous study of the region, most conducted by the British, had indicated that the salinity in the soil was such that no successful farming could be embarked upon. Ovrotsky's achievement was therefore regarded as a fluke by his colleagues, and the experiment was deemed completed. So he quit the Ministry, bought a tent and proceeded to work the land by himself. The sun almost killed him. Lack of water was a constant peril. The only real food he obtained was the scraps and leftovers that the nearby Dead Sea Works employees left for him. It was an uphill struggle, but slowly he began to change the face of the soil. The dominant color became green.

Youngsters began appearing from all over the country. Somehow they'd heard about his work. They would simply arrive, unfurl sleeping bags, and begin working. No questions were asked. Payment was impossible. Some came for a month. Others stayed for years.

Sleep was at a premium because of the constant vigil necessary against Arab marauders from across the hills in Jordan. A gun was like a third arm. And despite all the difficulties, the landscape continued to change. Winter vegetables were produced in abundance. Onions and tomatoes were successfully grown on land once certified as dead. Cattle were imported from Africa.

Ovrotsky no longer has anything to do with the settlement he founded and called Neot Hakikar, but the living testament to his belief exists in the form of a neat moshav located in one of the Negev's most desolate regions.

Most people arrive in Israel with limited itineraries. There's so much to see, and so little time to do it all. A strong tendency exists to scrap the Negev in favor of the more conventional sites. We can only say that it is a pity to do so. The Negev is as much Israel as is Tel Aviv. The historical artifacts of the wilderness are as intrinsic to Jewish history as the more settled regions in the far north. Flying over the area, on the way to Eilat or Sharm-el-Sheikh, will give you a general appreciation of the region, but to really understand what Israel is about you have to smell the desert, wipe the sand out of your eyes, and tread the paths of the Hebrew nomads.

GETTING THERE: You can go to Beersheba not only by air but also by train, bus, or sherut from Jerusalem or Tel Aviv. The buses and sheruts run several times per hour. Bus fare from Tel Aviv is SH7.90 ($2.30), SH10.10 ($2.97) from Jerusalem. Sherut fare is SH8.80 ($2.60) from Tel Aviv, SH9.70 ($2.85) from Jerusalem. By any means of transportation the trip takes about two hours. The sherut service is operated by Yael Daroma whose terminals are at 44 Yavne St., Tel Aviv, tel. 03-622555, and 2 Lunz St., Jerusalem, tel. 02-226985.

The company also has a service to Eilat (a five-and-a-half hour trip) four times a day (three times on Fridays). The fare is SH27 ($7.95) from Tel Aviv or Jerusalem. Seats should be booked in advance. The same journey by bus is SH25.70 ($7.55) from Tel Aviv or Jerusalem. There is one bus a day from Eilat to Sharm-el-Sheikh. The fare is SH29.90 ($8.80) and the ride four hours.

By plane from Ben-Gurion Airport to Eilat the fare is SH189.50 ($55.75) and to Sharm-el-Sheikh SH274.40 ($80.70). If you can afford it, a one-way flight and return by road is strongly recommended. If you sit on the left side of the plane flying southward you will see Israel, Jordan, and then Saudi Arabia; if you sit on the right you will see the Mediterranean Sea and the Sinai Peninsula.

SOME PRACTICAL ADVICE ON DESERT TRAVELING: A preliminary caution: between April and October the desert is awfully hot. You'll discover this when you get to Beersheba, and if you think it's warm there, wait till you see what the areas of the Dead Sea and Eilat have for you in the way of dry air that feels as if it had been pumped in from a blast furnace.

Be prepared for the heat, but don't let it scare you off. During the six or seven really hot desert months, simply follow these rules:

Always wear a hat when out in the sun.

Drink plenty of liquids—as much and as often as possible. You needn't bring your own; the supply is plentiful.

Get an early start on your day.

Stay out of the sun between noon and 3 p.m.

Don't cram your schedule. Go slow.

Eat sparingly—of fruit, dairy, and seafood.

Dress as comfortably and lightly as possible.

Take salt pills, if you find they help you.

Be judicious about sunbathing (sun poisoning here is Israel's major tourist malady).

Bring insect repellent.

1. Beersheba

Beersheba is our jumping-off point. From here it's only an hour to Sodom and the Dead Sea, 45 minutes by plane to Eilat (or four hours by bus). Increasingly, tourists use this ancient biblical town as their base of operations for excursions into the desert.

Only a few years ago, this town of 130,000 was the "Dodge City" of Israel. It had an unruly wild west flavor about it, and only the toughest and most adventurous types came here to work and live. Today the town is growing up, and that old spirit is dwindling somewhat in the face of housing developments and municipal buildings in the new part of town. It is the capital of the Negev.

Still, when your car or bus is an hour out of Tel Aviv on the way to Beersheba, you'll know you're entering a different kind of Israel. The face of the countryside changes; hills disappear and green fields turn dustier and drier; housing projects give way to occasional black tents in the fields near the side of the road; the metal of the car burns you as you rest your arm on the window.

Beersheba is another of those ancient cities of Judah. Here Abraham dug a well and planted a tamarisk tree 4,000 years ago. But Beersheba has also been a watering place and trading post for thousands of post-biblical years. It was always a center of desert traffic, located as it is on the northern fringe of the Negev. It has been—and still is—the refueling and supply terminus for those hardy souls who venture into the desert.

THE BEDOUIN MARKET: Be sure to arrive in Beersheba on a Thursday—unequivocally, Thursday. That's market day for the Bedouin tribes who come in from the desert to buy and sell in the colorful marketplace. Walk straight through the center of town and take a left at the end of the main street in the old city. You can't miss what's happening. Lean, sun-seared Arabs in long gowns are bartering over sacks of flour and coffee, holding conferences on the exchange for handwoven rugs and baskets.

Besides watching the Bedouins go through their endless ritual of arguing and haggling, you can yourself pick up some (sometimes questionable) bargains on Thursday—in particular, clothes, spices, sheared wool in sacks, copper and brass coffee sets with shining, decorated trays, those lethal-looking long knives, wood carvings, fancy Arabian saddles, bubble pipes, and all manner of rugs and baskets. If the mood hits you, you can also climb aboard a camel in this market and be photographed atop him. Don't be perturbed, incidentally, by his protesting spits and snorts. It's not his resentment of tourists that he's emitting, but simply his own accompanying music for standing up and sitting down.

By the way, most of the marketeering here goes on between 6 a.m. and noon in an area set aside for this purpose.

ACCOMMODATIONS: As we've said, Beersheba has spruced itself up considerably, offering tourists a variety of clean, air-conditioned accommodations. In the budget category, the best bets are the following:

Budget Hotels

First there's the **Arava Hotel,** tel. 057-78792, at 37 Histadrut St., centrally located just one block from the police station. A tiny TV room behind the lobby is fixed up comfortably with chairs, a table, and a sofa. The Arava has simply furnished 27 rooms, two with private bath, the rest with private shower, and all are air-conditioned. Singles cost SH45.90 ($13.50) to SH51 ($15), doubles SH37.40 ($11) per person, breakfast included. By the way, the reception desk and hotel are one flight up.

Once no less than a sheikh's harem, the **HaNegev,** 26 Ha'atzmauth St., tel. 057-77026, is now a kosher and air-conditioned hotel. The old building is about 200 years old and has nine large rooms. The new building has 21 rooms, all with showers and air conditioners. Room rates here: singles SH45.90 ($13.50) to SH51 ($15), doubles SH37.40 ($11) per person. An Israeli breakfast is served and there is a TV in the dining room.

The **Rol,** 29 Hapalmach St., corner of Mordei Hagetaot St., tel. 057-77461, has 28 air-conditioned rooms. In the heart of the old city and the market, this one has a cozy bar and lounge as well as a small dining room with TV. Double rooms cost SH15 ($4.40) per person and singles go for SH25 ($7.35), those rates not including breakfast, which is SH5 ($1.45) extra. Every two to three rooms shares a toilet; some rooms have terraces. Two Hungarian brothers own this place, as well as some cinemas in Eilat. One of them, Mordekai Zaiger, a friendly, conversational man, is usually around the Rol.

One block away, at 48 Mordei Hagetaot, is the **Hotel Aviv,** tel. 057-78059, which has cactuses all over its tasteful modern lobby. Twenty-three pleasant rooms here, all air-conditioned/heated and supplied with either bath or shower, and toilet. Rates are SH45.90 ($13.50) to SH51 ($15), single, IL374 ($11) per person double. An Israeli breakfast is included.

Near the University you'll find the **Zohar,** tel. 057-77335, a three-star establishment well worth the outlay: it compares favorably with many first-class hotels in service and amenities. It's on Zalman Shazar Blvd. in Beersheba's new quarter, and it offers 66 rooms, 63 with bath, three with shower, most with telephones, all air-conditioned. The town swimming pool (as well as the municipal building) is just across the street. Prices are moderate: single room rate is SH57.80 ($17) to SH68 ($20), SH49.60 ($14.60) each for two in a room. Israeli breakfast is served. Some of the amenities: shoe polishing and drink machines, a bar, and a small gift counter.

The **Beit Yatziv Guest House,** Ha'atzmauth St., tel. 057-77444, has simply furnished 76 rooms with private shower and toilet, heating, and desert-cooler air conditioning. B&B rates are SH40.80 ($12) single, SH289 ($8.50) per person double, SH238 ($7) per person triple. A meat meal is SH13.60 ($4), a dairy meal SH10.20 ($3), both served in the cheerful and airy dining room. A youth hostel shares the premises; details in Chapter XI.

RESTAURANTS: As always you'll find a clean and reasonably priced restaurant in the **Egged Bus Station,** tel. 057-76604, a cafeteria-style operation that is always mobbed at lunch. In the meat section (open 5 a.m. to 9 p.m., closed Friday at 3 p.m. until sunset on Saturday) a main course of chicken, beef, schnitzel, or fish with two side dishes is SH6.50 ($1.90). The dairy section stays open from 5 a.m. to 11 p.m. and 5 to 9 p.m.

Another Beersheba favorite is the **Midnight Inn,** better known as **Pundak Hatzot,** 131 Keren Kayemet St., tel. 057-78510, which is, to say the least, avant-garde. Packed nightly with soldiers and locals, it consists of two sections. One part is a grill bar, with a counter that circles most of the huge grill; the other has tables and waiter service. At the grill bar you can have hamburgers for SH2 (60¢), kababs for SH3 (90¢). The restaurant specializes in kuskus (couscous to you) cooked with meat and vegetables and sold here for SH10 ($2.95). The grill section is open Sunday to Thursday from 10 a.m. to midnight, closing Friday shortly before sunset until after sunset on Saturday; the restaurant stays open from 11 a.m. to 10 p.m. with the same Sabbath exceptions.

Pizzas with abundant toppings are offered at **Pizza Scala,** 179 Keren Kayemet St., tel. 057-72122. A slice costs SH1.60 (47¢), an entire family-size pie SH12 ($3.80). Open 7 a.m. to 10 p.m., closed Friday at 3 p.m., open Saturday from 6 to 11 p.m. only.

The **Patio de Santos Self-Service Restaurant,** 41 Hadassah St., tel. 057-32300, offers large portions of highly spiced and low-priced kosher food. Wrought-iron on the colored glass windows and a mosaic depicting bullfighting supply the Spanish motif. You can have a four-course meat or chicken dinner for SH7.90 ($2.32); à la carte stuffed vegetables are SH1.80 (52¢), a meat or chicken main course SH3.90 ($1.15) to SH6.50 ($1.90). Open Sunday to Thursday from noon to 9:30 p.m., closed from Friday at 3 p.m. until noon on Sunday. Highly recommended.

Yet another favorite hereabouts is the **Milk Bar Whitman,** 97 Herzl St., tel. 057-72333. It's cool, modern and attractive throughout. Seated in a comfortable booth, you can order breakfast until noon. They're big on ice cream here, SH3 (90¢) and up; as well as cheese toast, for SH1.50 (45¢), and cheese blintzes, two for SH3.50 ($1). Open from 6 a.m. to 2 a.m. daily.

Keren Kayemet runs down the center of town, and on it you'll find several places for quick snacks and such.

NIGHTLIFE: At **Mandy's Discotheque,** 57 Hadassah St., tel. 057-35609, the entrance fee of SH30 ($8.80) per couple includes one drink each; every subsequent drink is SH6 ($1.75), and olives and cheese are on the house. Generally, you dance to recorded music, but occasionally there's live entertainment. Students get a discount of SH4 ($1.20) per couple. Open nightly from 9 p.m. to 3 a.m.

Musicians tend to congregate at **Shva Tea House,** 29 Smilansky St., tel. 057-71454, an Argentinian-owned club where anyone who can play can pick up one of the instruments hanging on the wall and join in the nightly musical entertainment. It's a pleasant setting. Inside, three rattan-furnished rooms are connected by archways, and walls are cluttered with old pictures, pots and pans, helmets, ice prongs, and other weird paraphernelia. There are lace curtains on the windows, and the tabletops have beautiful batik designs worked into the wood. There's additional seating outside in a lovely garden. When there's no live music classical and Spanish tapes are played. You can order sangria for SH6 ($1.75), spaghetti for the same price, omelets for SH5 ($1.45), two blintzes for SH4.50 ($1.30). Open nightly from 7 p.m. to 1 a.m.

Milk Bar Whitman's Night Club, 97 Herzl St., tel. 057-72333, is a lively disco nightly except Wednesday when folkloric entertainment is offered. Friday and Saturday admission is SH15 ($4.40), SH7.50 ($2.20) the rest of the week. Any night the price of admission includes your first drink, the second drink costs SH7 ($2.05), soft drinks SH3.50 ($1). Light fare—cheese, bagels, etc.—is on the house. Students get a 10% discount.

Beersheba is justifiably proud of its **Chamber Orchestra.** Tickets are by subscription—but you might be lucky enough to buy a ticket before the performance at the box office or from someone who is unable to go. The concerts start promptly at 8:30 p.m. when the doors shut tight. Ask at your hotel when the next concert will be held. Concerts are also given at the **S. Rubin Music Conservatory.** The **Beersheba Theater** performs at Beit Ha'am, tel. 057-73478. Check *This Week in the South* for current programs.

In Beersheba you can visit art galleries at night, and the I.G.T.O. can direct you to many of them. Of special note, however, is the **Liraz Art Gallery,** 25 Smilansky St., tel. 057-76747, situated in a turn-of-the-century colonnaded Turkish house surrounded by a high stone wall. Changing exhibits of Israeli art are shown along with permanent antique exhibits. Open 9 a.m. to 1 p.m. and 5 p.m. to midnight.

Meeting the Israelis can be arranged at the **Government Tourist Office,** 120 Herzl St., tel. 057-36001.

SEEING THE SIGHTS: We've already told you about the city's Bedouin marketplace, and after you've immersed yourself in the profusion of exotic sights and smells in that area, the second place to go in Beersheba is the **Negev Museum** in the Mosque, located on Ha'atzmaut St., tel. 057-39105, in a pleasant little park in the center of the old city.

The Mosque was built by the Turks (although designed by a German architect) in 1907. The museum exhibits deal with 5,000 years of Beersheba's history, including Bedouin folklore. There are some really classic photos in this collection—mustachioed Pashas, the British and Arabic soldiers entering Beersheba during World War I, the victorious Israeli army taking the city in 1948. Other sections display findings from excavations in the area. Admission fee is minimal. Open Sunday to Thursday from 8 a.m. to 12 p.m., Wednesday 4 to 7 p.m., Friday from 8 a.m. to 1 p.m., and Saturday from 10 a.m. to 1 p.m.

Climb the steps up the curling staircase and you'll have a dramatic panoramic view of this entire area. From up here you can understand why people call Beersheba a frontier town. Looking due south, you'll see where the green of the town abruptly ends and the desert formally begins, the paved highway twisting like black tape over the sand hills into the haze of dust on the horizon. You'll also see the old town with its yellow stone houses clustered together, as well as spanking-new modern buildings.

Monument to the Negev Fighters

Of all war memorials, this one—completed in 1969—is possibly the most original, certainly the most evocative, that we have ever seen. It is located on the northeastern edge of the city, just off the road that leads to Hebron, and commemorates the brigade that captured the Negev during the 1948 War of Independence. The memorial, consisting of 18 symbolic sections, flows like a fantastic cement garden over the summit of raw and windy hill. Here the entire Negev campaign has been reduced to its essentials: a concrete tent wall, a bunker, a hill crisscrossed by communications trenches, a pipeline, nine war maps engraved in the floor of the square. Over, through, and around these structures you can climb and walk, thus becoming part of the desert action. You can climb to the top of the tall cement tower—representing the watch and water towers that were shelled on the Negev settlements—and look out across the desert's vast sandy expanse; you can file singly through the inclined walls of The Pass that lead into the Memorial Dome, and enter the symbolic Bunker. The memorial is well worth seeing; there is no admission charge.

And Elsewhere

If you have the time, there are several other spots to see in Beersheba. There is, for example, the **Research and Development Authority of the Ben-Gurion University of the Negev**, in the new town, which is a unique establishment and altogether necessary in Israel. It investigates such matters as artificial rainmaking, the exploitation of solar energy, desalination of water, and the general chemical and biological conditions relating to the growth and maintenance of life in the desert climate. . . . The **cemetery** on Ha'atzmaut Rd. at the entrance to the town is for the British soldiers who died taking Beersheba from the Turks in 1917. Beersheba, incidentally, was the first city in Palestine to fall to the British in that war. . . . The old **railway station** on Tuviyahu St. is worth a look. It was along the Beersheba line that ran to Egypt that Lawrence of Arabia played his train-blowing tricks. Of course, that was the Turkish line dismantled by General Allenby. It ran along the western side of town. The current line is Israeli, built on the town's eastern side. In the future, this line will link up with Eilat. (Today you can travel by rail to and from Beersheba and Lod, and link with Dimona, Jerusalem and Haifa.) . . . Outside town on the Hebron Road is the place purported to be **Abraham's Well** of biblical fame.

Not to be missed is the **Ben-Gurion University of the Negev.** Its faculties include the humanities, social, technical, natural and health sciences, and a medical school. Many of the more than two-dozen departments emphasize the development of the Negev. The imaginative architecture combines the awareness of climatic conditions and the practical needs of the students and teachers. Tours can be arranged in advance through the Public Relations Department, tel. 057-39943. Visiting students might want to try the **Gimmel** discotheque, open nightly except Friday when the action moves to the Library Building on the new campus. Foreign students can also take an Ulpan here for credit.

Also worth a visit is **Tel Sheba**. It is a village of homes constructed for the usually nomadic Bedouin. Some keep tents nearby, perhaps in case four walls become a bit too much, but those who have chosen to live there seem to like it. Much thought indeed went into the feasibility of this project—on the part of builders and future residents alike.

The digs of many seasons have unearthed an ancient Israelite city at **Tel Beer Sheba**, in fact, many layers of civilization. The city walls and gates have been uncovered. A dominant feature of the city is a circular street with rows of buildings on both sides. A deep well was found right outside the city gates and the city's central canalization project was discovered. A huge ashlar four-horned altar was found and reconstructed. It is now exhibited in the Negev Museum, mentioned above. It is most definitely worth a visit.

Sightseeing Tours

It is possible, while in Beersheba, to visit a **Bedouin encampment** and to join in a Bedouin-style dinner. Group tours to the encampment are organized by **Mr. A. Zakai** in his tour office at 75 Hechalutz Street, tel. 057-77477. Drop in or phone ahead and see if you can hitch along with one of these groups. If so, the cost will be anywhere from about $2.50 for the "short visit," which consists of a chat with the sheikh over coffee or tea, a camel ride, and Bedouin music, to about $13 for the full "sunset visit" with Bedouin dinner, which includes the above, and a typical rice, mutton, and fruit meal, eaten with the fingers or on pitta. These prices include transportation to and from Beersheba, and can be higher if there are less than 25 people in the group. It might be wise to phone ahead before reaching Beersheba to find out when the next group is going out.

The **American Mizrahi Women's Organization**, Hameshahrerrim St., tel. 057-78171, offers free tours of the Beit Zeiroth Mizrahi School.

SWIMMING: This you'll definitely want to do here—we guarantee it. There's a public swimming pool in the new part of town, near the municipal buildings and the Hotel Zohar. It's open from May 1 to the end of September. There is a pool for youths near an area called **Shechunat Aleph;** open from 8 a.m. to 6 p.m. Bus 3 passes it. Another pool is near the University. Use bus 4 or 5. Both are open from May to September. Entrance fees at all three pools are reasonable.

In addition, there are two pools at the **Country Club,** one for children and the other for adults. A roof is under construction for winter use. Open from 7 a.m. to 6 p.m. from May to September for the uncovered pools. Friday afternoons and Saturdays are reserved for members only. The club also has tennis courts. Take a bus from the Central Bus Station.

2. Arad

The modern desert town of Arad is not a mirage, but rather a well-planned metropolis located on the site of an ancient Israelite settlement—a concrete testimonial to the continuity of Jewish history. Located about 30 miles east of Beersheba, it is regularly served by buses and sheruts. Of course, you can rent a car and drive there yourself.

ON THE ROAD: As soon as you leave Beersheba, you'll see clusters of Bedouin tents and flocks—and houses, for today the Bedouins are settling down more and more (perhaps because the government of Israel is making sure they have a fixed water supply, so they need no longer roam the land in search of it).

At the first major intersection not far from Beersheba you're presented with a choice: Shall it be straight on to Hebron, or a right turn for Arad and the Dead Sea? Since we've been to Hebron already (Chapter IV), we'll take the turn and watch the Bedouins, who work and live near the highway. One of the initial buildings on the right is the very first Bedouin grocery store in history, an indication that the now almost stationary Bedouins are establishing a new economy. Other stores appear as you travel; they're not for tourist shopping as they sell only Bedouin staples like coffee, sugar and such, but they are interesting to see—pieced together as they are from whatever materials are lying about. A bit further on you'll begin to see Bedouin villages—the Abu-Rabiya tribe has four such settlements between Beersheba and Arad, all fairly

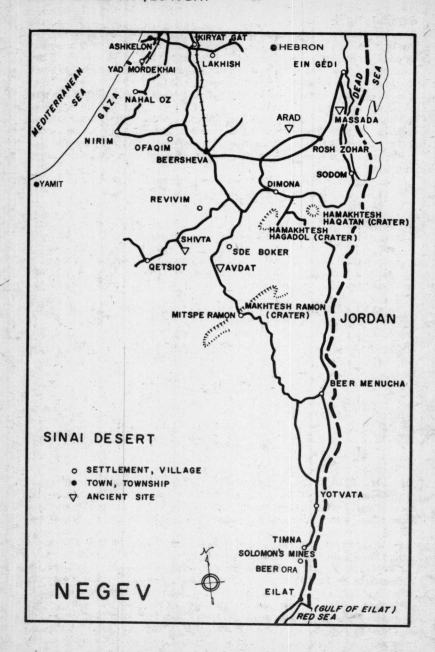

close together. Some of the villages consist of shacks, others of tents; some are quite large, others may be nothing more than three houses and five tents. Another thing to note is that the Bedouins here do a lot of farming, growing mostly wheat, but also other grains, and fruits and vegetables, most of which they sell in the Beersheba markets. And while you're busy noting things, note that there is a great deal of experimental agricultural work being done along this road: Sisal is grown without irrigation; tamarisk, eucalyptus, and other trees are planted in small areas, their growth watched carefully by scientists who are planning to cultivate even more of Israel's desert. As you ride along you'll see a cluster of spacious modern buildings—they're schools for Bedouin children, boys and girls (it's revolutionary for Bedouin girls to be educated). If you're passing by when school lets out, notice that very few of the kids walk home: Some hop on donkeys or bicycles, some wait for the bus—and others are picked up by taxicabs or posh limousines!

THE TOWN: When the road starts snaking around tight curves, you'll know you're just about in Arad. Driving into Arad is like entering almost any small American city: There are wide highways with overhanging lights, highrise apartments everywhere, and a busy shopping mall (they call it *merkaz* here).

One of the interesting things about Arad is that it's a planned city, begun in 1961, and mapped out for efficiency to meet the rigid desert restrictions in the most comfortable manner. It's some 2,000 feet above sea level and its ultra-dry climate is considered a blessing to sufferers of asthma and similar troubles. Each year it grows more popular as a vacation place for singles, couples, and families; by staying here, a tourist can get quite a realistic picture of Israeli life.

A clean, attractive town, Arad has several hotels, most of them just outside the city in a special hotel district. It's built on a rise that has a great observation point for viewing the wilderness down to the Dead Sea (about 17 miles away). Many people who stay here visit the Dead Sea daily.

ACCOMMODATIONS: There are several places to stay in this blooming desert citadel, but for the purposes of our budget, we strongly suggest the local youth hostel: **Beit Blau-Weiss,** tel. 057-97150, which we detail in Chapter XI.

Another comfortable place is the two-star **Arad Hotel,** 6 Hapalmach St., near the center of town next to the municipality, tel. 057-97040. Singles are SH51 ($15), doubles SH37.40 ($11) per person. The hotel has a tiny "pocket garden" full of roses and cactuses, not to mention a rather astounding sculpture of a bearded sage cut from a six-foot driftwood branch which is planted like a tree. This is not a luxury hotel, but it is clean and comfortable. Students, incidentally, get a discount simply by not paying the 15% service charge. The dining room is pleasant and not expensive. A four-course lunch or dinner costs about SH17 ($5). Of the 51 rooms, 35 are air-conditioned, all are heated and equipped with private shower and toilet.

One of the better buys in the Negev is the 20-room **Korré Bamidbar Motel,** 13 Ben Yair St., tel. 057-97364, near the shopping center. Rates are SH22.10 ($6.50) to SH23.80 ($7) per person, not including breakfast. The establishment has fully equipped kitchens for the use of guests, each well supplied with utensils, pots, pans, dishes, stoves and refrigerators. The motel is actually converted apartments and is especially clean and pleasant, though rooms do not have private facilities. Students get a 10% reduction; rates rise 20% during High Holidays.

The Nof Arad Hotel, tel 057-97056, has three stars and 101 rooms, 40 in cabins and 61 in the hotel itself. The cabins are cement structures containing four rooms, each with air conditioning, telephones, showers and toilets. Off-season rates (mid-November to the end of February) are SH49.30 ($14.50) to SH61.20 ($18) per person; high-season rates are about $5.50 higher. There is a swimming pool here, and the self-service breakfasts are good, particularly the fresh, hotel-baked rolls. Recommended.

Across the street from the Nof Arad is another three-star hotel, the **Margoa,** tel. 057-97014/5. It has 107 rooms and two different price scales—one for the hotel itself and the other for the semi-detached cottages. Single occupancy is SH71.10 ($20.90) to SH78.50 ($23.10), double occupancy SH52.70 ($15.50) to SH59.80 ($17.60). There's a large swimming pool here, open from the spring (Passover) to the late fall (Succoth). Entertainment is sometimes available during that same interval.

It is also possible to rent a room in a private home. Folks are very friendly in Arad; you can ask most anyone on the street, and if they can't help you, they'll probably have a friend who will. And since Arad is such a friendly place, it's a good spot to **Meet the Israeli.** Ask at the Tourist Information Office in the Magen David Building or call 057-97911.

RESTAURANTS: If you're looking for a gourmet experience, Arad is not the place. But wholesome food is available, and we'll cite a few eateries that we discovered in the town.

The Polish-owned **Galit Restaurant,** 37/7 Ben Yair St., tel. 057-90793, in the Commercial Center, has just six tables covered with red and white cloths. You might begin your meal with a bowl of borscht for SH1.50 (45¢), salad for SH2.50 (75¢), or gefilte fish for SH4 ($1.20). Among the main courses are goulash at SH8 ($2.35), roast chicken at SH7.50 ($2.20), and roast duck at SH9 ($2.65). Open Sunday to Thursday from noon to 4 p.m. and 6 to 9 p.m., Friday noon to 3 p.m., and Saturday noon to 4 p.m.

A pleasant place is **Dekel,** 27 Hen St., where music is always playing and ex-New Yorker Izhak Jalowski is dishing out eight-inch pizzas for SH3.20 (95¢) and up, shashlik with chips and garlic bread for SH7.50 ($2.20), and spaghetti for SH4 ($1.20). Open daily except Friday from 6 p.m. to 1 a.m.

Finally, there's the ubiquitous **Wimpy,** in the Commercial Center, offering the usual burgers, along with goulash, kabab, etc. in plate or pitta—all for $3 or less. Open Sunday to Thursday from 7:30 a.m. to 10 p.m., closed Friday from 3 p.m. until Saturday evening.

ARAD ACTIVITIES: Shopping has been centralized to a great degree in Arad and most everything can be found at the **Shopping Center.** Food, clothing, cosmetics, stationery, banks, a hairdresser, pharmacy, even a photography store.

The **Abir Riding School** can be found in the Industrial Area. Tel. 057-94147 for details.

Many activities take place at the **Matnas Cultural Center** opposite the Tourist Information Office. Youngsters meet on Friday night, the Chess Club and Melave Malka meet on Saturday night, the Bridge Club meets on Monday night, and there's folk dancing Tuesday night.

For other Arad activities, check with the **Government Tourist Information Office** in the Commercial Center. It's open Sunday to Thursday from 8 a.m. to noon and 4 to 7 p.m., Friday from 8 a.m. to noon only.

Tel Arad

Some four miles west of Arad is Tel Arad, a partially reconstructed 5000-year-old Canaanite town with a 3000-year-old Israeli fort. It's open Sunday to Thursday from 8 a.m. to 4 p.m. October to March; until 5 p.m. the rest of the year, closing an hour earlier, respectively, Fridays and holiday eves. Entrance fee is minimal.

3. The Dead Sea: Ein Bokek, Masada, Ein Gedi, and Sodom

If you're traveling during Israel's seven dry months, be sure to get an early start. The atmosphere becomes hot and sultry by noon, and a weird kind of languid breathless heat, in which nothing stirs, settles over the entire area.

ON THE ROAD: The ride from Arad to the Dead Sea (just 45 minutes) is almost all downhill, and the word "steep" is hardly adequate. From Arad's heights, where the land is all a chalky sandy color, the wilderness to the west turns increasingly darker, changing to tans and then deeper shades of brown. During the 17-mile trip, the scenery will doubtless hold your attention. You'll pass through the **Rosh Zohar** fields of large underground reservoirs of natural gas. Don't miss an observation point to the left, **Mezad Zohar;** you won't know its uniqueness till you're out of the car, leaning against the rail of the sun-shelter and looking out and down. Here are remains of a Roman fortress, down in the valley that served as the major roadway from the Dead Sea up until the day the superhighway you've been plying was opened. (These desert valleys, or wadis, were carved out over the centuries by the fast fierce floods of sudden rains.) A second observation point is a bit further down, this with a huge map so that you can identify what you're looking at. Then the road really swings down and you finally have before you a vista of the Dead Sea and part of the Judean wilderness beyond it.

Should you be coming directly from Beersheba (by bus, sherut, or private car), you'll drive just over an hour, and you can take the road through another of those desert development towns, **Dimona.** The most famous of Israel's hastily constructed boom towns, Dimona was the subject of considerable controversy, because at one time many thought it was inhuman and impossible to expect people to live and work in such a climate. However, the handful of tents which started the town in 1955 soon became a thriving community of 22,500 people living in stone houses—a town complete with movies, cultural centers, textile and phosphate plants, even an atomic reactor.

Three miles further, on the right, is a deserted stone blockhouse, a former police station on a high hill which stands on the site of an ancient Byzantine town (**Mamphis**). Nearby, in a deep gorge, are three dams dating from the sixth century A.D., in which ancient engineers were able to store enough water to keep the residents supplied even during the dry season.

Mamphis is one of the many ancient desert cities under close scrutiny by Israel's modern scientists, who are convinced that many of these classical methods of desert-living are still applicable in today's planning for cities in the Negev.

Beyond a Roman fort called **Tamar** (12 miles further on), the road starts to descend rapidly. Abruptly, around a turn, you are confronted with one of Israel's most amazing sights—and certainly the most bizarre—the Dead Sea. It lies there, 3000 feet below you, in a heavy haze. Around it the mountains of Moab and Edom are lifeless and parched.

Soon you pass the sea-level sign, all the time descending lower and lower through the Arava plain, passing potash and bromide factories along the way. Signs commemorate the workers who were ambushed constructing this road in 1951, and the actual opening of the road to Sodom in 1953. Then, with the dust churning up behind you, the car pulls to a stop: You are at the edge of the Dead Sea, the lowest point on earth, 1,300 feet below sea level. (Death Valley in California, America's lowest point, is only 282 feet below sea level.)

Half of the 48-mile Dead Sea is in Israel's territory (about 100 square miles of it), but even working with that little area the technicians find that they can scarcely deal fast enough with the vast reservoir of chemicals being constantly removed from the sea. This water is 25% solids of which 7% is salt, and that's the saltiest water on earth, six times as salty as the water in the ocean. Each day, tons of chlorides, bromides, and sulphides are removed for processing and export. No fish can live in these miles of mineral-rich liquid.

EIN BOKEK AND VICINITY: From Arad to the Dead Sea, as we said, is about a 45-minute ride. The main highway intersects a road paralleling the coast. Turn right for Sodom and the Dead Sea Works, and for the superhighway to Eilat. We'll take the left turn to Ein Bokek, Masada, and Ein Gedi (this road goes all the way to Jerusalem).

Just before the intersection, you can fill up on gasoline and such at a large modern filling station on your left, and from here you can catch sight of the **Neveh-Zohar Camping Site,** tel. 057-90906, on the hillside. Trees shade the area. There are kitchens with stoves, a place to buy food, a restaurant with moderate prices, a first-aid station, petrol pump, picnic area, post box, hot showers, parking lot, bus station . . . everything!

Also at Neveh Zohar you will find the **Beit Hayotzer** museum, which houses an exhibition of the Dead Sea Industries. It is free and open daily from 9 a.m. to 12:30 p.m. and again from 1:30 to 5 p.m.

Just across the road from the Camping Site is an excellent place to take your dip in the Dead Sea, an experience that will prove difficult to forget. But first listen to a few words of caution: Wear sandals and a hat—the sandals protect your feet against sharp stones, and the hat prevents the head from sizzling; and be sure to keep the water out of your eyes—it burns! The water has a very bitter, oily taste should you accidentally get a mouthful, but it's almost impossible to accidentally go under; you float on the Dead Sea even if you don't know how to float, so high is the water's density. Afterward you may opt to rinse off with a shower (some say the waters of the Dead Sea give them an "unpleasantly creepy feeling"; others love it), or leave the film of mineral residue on your body till bedtime, as the Israelis do. They say it's healthy and good for the skin. They go equally wild over the black mud scooped from the sea bed, smearing it all over themselves, especially any place that hurts or stings. It's supposed to be good for muscle and joint problems, and many physicians do in fact recommend Dead Sea soaks.

Israelis (Europeans too) also go for mineral water baths in a big way. If you want to give this sort of thing a try, go up the road to **Zohar Springs** (*Hamei Zohar*), and immerse yourself in the naturally hot waters that have even more minerals per gram than the Dead Sea. It's fun—see Chapter XI for details. If you're not so hot on this activity, stop by anyway, if only for a snack at the restaurant next door and a superb view of the Dead Sea and the surrounding wilderness mountains.

There are three covered sulphur pools here for the treatment of rheumatic ailments and 16 private sulphur baths for rheumatic and skin diseases. Prices vary according to treatment. Full information can be obtained by phoning 057-86013 between 7 a.m. and 3 p.m.

Accommodations and Meals

The Dead Sea area is fast becoming an important tourist resort; the following is worth checking into.

The already-mentioned **Neveh Zohar Camping Site and Restaurant** looks fine and is inexpensive. Bungalows sleep two people. The restaurant is very reasonably priced, but if you care to do your own cooking the adjoining grocery is well stocked. The camping ground facilities are open all year. Highest recommendation.

The **Lido** and **Ein Feshcha**, along the northern part of the Dead Sea, offer good eating and good swimming—see Chapter IV for details.

MASADA: Every Israeli school child has made the climb to Masada. It is a national tradition to have made the ascent at least once—for Masada is the scene of one of the most heroic and tragic incidents in Jewish history. Here a small garrison defied the might of the powerful Roman army. The story, as Flavius Josephus recorded it, is worth retelling. Few people ever hear of it before they come to Israel.

The fabulous King Herod had built a magnificent palace and fortress atop this mountain sometime around 40 A.D. He furnished the luxurious palace with every known comfort and laid in storehouses of food and arms, protecting the entire establishment with an impregnable fortress. In succeeding years, a small Roman garrison occupied the mount. However, during the Jewish revolt against the Romans in 66 A.D., an army of Jewish fighters suddenly attacked the garrison and took over the fortress. They lived off the vast storehouses of food and had more than enough arms with which to defend themselves. The weapons were even put to use in guerrilla raids and lightning attacks on Jerusalem.

Finally, in 70 A.D., two years after the fall of Jerusalem, the Romans became so incensed with the Masada situation that they decided to lay siege to the rebellious base of operations and put an end to all Jewish resistance. After a year's worth of siege engines, flaming torches, rock bombardments, and battering rams, the Masada fortress was still in Jewish hands. But with 10,000 Roman troops camped on the hillside and daily bombardments smashing at the walls, it became only a question of time until the 900 heroic defenders would succumb.

One brutal attack spelled the end: The flaming torches at the fort's wall were whipped by a wind into the midst of the defenders, and the garrison's ramparts came crashing down. The Romans, seeing that Masada was practically defenseless now, decided to wait until dawn before they would conquer it triumphantly in their own good time.

But that night the 900 men, women, and children who inhabited Masada held a strange meeting. Their leader, Eliezer ben Yair, persuaded them to accept death bravely, on their own terms, and not to die as slaves of the Romans, or be butchered by them. So that evening nearly 2,000 years ago, one of history's greatest mass suicides occurred. Ten men were chosen executioners, and they carried out their distasteful mission on the families who willingly lay down together. Then one man killed the other nine and ran himself through on his own sword. Two women and five children survived, hiding in one of the caves. The Romans, who had expected to fight their way in, were doubly astonished at the lack of resistance and at the "calm courage of their resolution . . . and utter contempt of death." So, Flavius Josephus wrote, ended the Jewish resistance in Palestine.

The Excavation Site

Masada excavations have unearthed perhaps the most exciting ruins in the entire country. Indeed, much of the historical information about the Masada episode is now authenticated as a result. Climbing paths from both the Dead Sea side and the Arad side can bring the visitor up to the top of the Masada mountain, which remains a symbol of courage, and one that has long moved scholars, laymen, and soldiers to make the ascent. (Traditionally, Israeli Armored Corps recruits swear the oath of allegiance on Masada's heights after climbing the difficult Snake Path.)

Professor Yadin, who led the exploration, finds it difficult to say which were the most important finds among the walls, houses, straw bags, plaits of hair, pottery shards, stone vessels, cosmetic items, cooking utensils, the synagogue, the scrolls—all invaluable for providing information about the Second Temple Period. But among the most intriguing finds are the ritual baths (mikves), the ostraca that might have been the very lots cast by the defenders in their final moments, and the Roman siege engines.

It is interesting to note that the enormous area of excavation here is the work of thousands of volunteer workers. Amateur archeologists from 23 countries answered newspaper ads to come and work on Masada. There were Danish nurses, French taxi drivers, English artists, students, models, pathologists, lawyers, waiters, librarians, housewives, actors, pharmacists, students, advertising men, dentists, and chambermaids. At any given time 300 volunteers were working with the handful of professionals digging out ancient Masada. Each considered it an honor to be a part of the dig.

Getting Up There

You've got two choices—climb or ride. If you climb, especially in the summer months, be sure to start literally at the crack of dawn. The gathering heat reaches murderously enervating proportions by the middle of the day. Climbers are frantically urged by the National Parks Authority to please—please—wear a good shade hat and drink as much as you can hold before starting up (again, for those who didn't catch it previously, this is because your head will fry without a hat, and you lose much more body moisture than you'd ever believe in this heat that evaporates it before it's noticeable).

Climbers have two choices of where they'll begin their ascent of this great high mountain: the route from the Dead Sea side, or the one from the mountain side. The route from where you are now, the Dead Sea side, is fondly called the **Snake Path**. Why? Well, the path does indeed snake up the mountain in steep, hairpin curves. As for actual snakes—we suppose it's easier for a reptile to get up the mountain via this path than it is for a biped, but we've never seen any trying. Depending on your age and vitality, your surefootedness, stamina, wind, and general muscle tone and fitness, the trip up will require from a half-hour to two hours. (We cannot imagine even a scared goat making it in half an hour, but many Israelis do it!) Getting down takes every bit as long and is equally awkward. The path's so steep one must lean backwards and continuously apply extreme braking pressure on one's own body—a difficult and unusual strain. Snake Path opens at 7:30 a.m. and closes at 3:30 p.m., and you must start down by then just to get to the bottom before dark. The same hours apply to the path up the other side. The mountain-side path is called **The Battery,** after a battery the Romans built there. Getting to the top via that route takes only 15 to 30 minutes, and many little old ladies do it frequently, not to mention younger folk.

In our opinion, tourists should get a reward for scaling Masada—but just the opposite is true—it costs money! The opportunity to brave Snake Path costs SH4 ($1.75) for adults, SH1.40 (40¢) for students or children up to age 18. Buses stop at both places, operating regularly between Masada and key cities.

Now be honest—isn't it worth the SH10.80 ($3.20), round trip, to ride up via cable car and be deposited about 75 steps from the fortress top? One way is SH6.70 ($1.95). Students and youngsters go both ways for SH5 ($1.45), one way for SH3.20 (65¢). Each bright yellow car holds 40 people and delivers them, via wire and electricity, in three minutes flat—hardly time to say, "My, what a lovely view." The cable-car launching structure is large and modern, built by a Swiss firm with lots of mountain-sidling experience. Cable cars operate from 8 a.m. to 4 p.m.; Fridays and eves of holidays from 8 a.m.–2 p.m. (also operates on Saturdays).

Meals and Accommodations

There's a moderately priced cafe here, called **Rakebel Miznon,** for light snacks, with ten to 12 tables, plus a souvenir stand. Beside the entrance gate is one of the eight reconstructed ruins in this area of Roman camps. And all this is situated quite a ways from the main road, overlooking the restaurant, guest House, and the youth hostel and its various facilities.

The **55 Guest House,** at the foot of Masada near the cable car, tel. 057-90802, has eight air-conditioned rooms with sink only; toilets and showers are shared. Guests are served coffee and cake in the morning and evening. Single occupancy is SH47.60 ($14) a night, double occupancy SH68 ($20). There's a very large, kosher, self-service restaurant on the premises where you can get a complete breakfast—roll, margarine, egg, cheeses, jam, and coffee for SH4.60 ($1.35), a chicken or meat dinner for SH9.50 ($2.80) to SH11.50 ($3.40). There's also a bar serving alcoholic beverages and soft drinks. Open daily from 8:15 a.m. to 4 p.m.

Miznon Camping, at the foot of Masada on the Dead Sea side, tel. 057-90802, is another option for light meals; it's open from 3 a.m. to 11 p.m. during July, August, and holidays, 7 a.m. to 9 p.m. the rest of the year. Humus in a pitta is SH2 (60¢), cheese toast or pizza SH1.50 (45¢). Show a copy of this book and you'll get reductions on certain items.

The **Isaac H. Taylor Youth Hostel** at Masada has 160 beds in a dormitory configuration. For further information see Chapter XI.

EIN GEDI: A few miles from Masada, on the north end of the Dead Sea, is the fertile kibbutz of Ein Gedi. Nearby are waterfalls (about which more below), a phenomenon that you would hardly expect in the midst of a desert. There are sulphur springs and ruins; it is, in all, a rich and rewarding area.

The kibbutz has a **Guest House,** and buses arrive from all the principal cities on regular schedules. The office is open from 8 a.m. to 4 p.m., tel. 057-90874, and the kiosk opens twice daily. Each day the kibbutz provides transportation to and from the sulphur springs establishment, as well as the nearby beach area. Room and full board costs SH98.60 ($29) to SH125.80 ($37) per person—a bit splurgy, but it does include three meals, snacks, movies, slides and lectures, the sulphur baths, and transportation to them and the beach daily.

Guests clean their own rooms, however. All the rooms are air-conditioned and have showers and TV; because of high occupancy, it's a good idea to book well in advance.

There's also a self-service restaurant called **Pundak Ein Gedi** at the **Ein Gedi Camping Site.** Air-conditioned, it seats 140 persons and serves breakfast, lunch and very early dinner, from 8:15 a.m. to 4:30 p.m. Prices are quite reasonable, with main courses from SH6 ($1.75) to SH7.50 ($2.20), desserts SH1.70 (50¢).

Another eating place in the vicinity is buffet at the **Ein Gedi Sulphur Springs,** open from 7 a.m. to 5 p.m. You can get light refreshments inexpensively here.

The buffet and Sulphur Springs entrance are in the same building. A ticket to the springs costs SH6 ($1.75), and this includes all the therapeutic mud on the beach that you can use. Beach chairs and showers are also available.

Next to the Ein Gedi Camping Site and Pundak Ein Gedi is the free **Ha'ashalim Camping Ground** with showers and drinking water.

Hiking, incidentally, is extremely popular around here, for it's one of the best ways to experience the extraordinary beauty of the area. Trips are timed for the early morning and late afternoon hours because of the high noonday temperatures. Good walking shoes, a canteen (or two), a hat, and sunglasses are essential. More about hiking in Chapter XI.

A 200-bed youth hostel, **Beit Sara,** Mobile Post Dead Sea, tel. 057-90871, is located just off the main road, about one mile north of the kibbutz. Very clean and well run, Beit Sara offers a fantastic view of the sea and mountains. Highly recommended. Details in Chapter XI.

Ein Gedi has been an oasis in the desert for thousands of years. The Song of Solomon rhapsodized it thus: "My beloved is unto me as a cluster of camphire from the vineyards of Ein Gedi." A place of fertility, Ein Gedi was settled in 1949 by a group of pioneers who planted it with cotton, grapes, vegetables, and flowers. The kibbutz planners built their houses where there was absolutely nothing. With seeming magic, they created beautiful locations affording them stunning views of the entire dramatic area and the wild, foaming **Ein David Gorge,** where the water drops from a height of nearly 300 feet.

You can reach **David's Spring** (the Ein Gedi waterfall and natural pools) from the kibbutz grounds, but it's a more direct route if you enter from the main road across from the free **Ha'ashalim Camping Ground.**

You'll spot a large parking lot, at the back of which is a small kiosk equipped, even in this arid wilderness, with a gleaming espresso machine, plus cold drinks, and snacks, of course. It's open daily from 9 a.m. to 4–5 p.m. From here you simply follow the trail and the signposts, winding through tall pines and palm trees up and into the desert hills. You proceed between slits in the rock formations, under canopies of papyrus reeds, and, after about ten minutes of steady climbing, you'll hear the wonderful sound of rushing water. In another five minutes, your appetite whetted, you arrive at what is surely one of the wonders of the world—the Ein Gedi waterfalls, hidden in an oasis of luxuriant green vegetation that hangs clustered around in a canyon wall. Tumbling down out of the heights, the falls represent the happiest sight you'll see in this blistering-hot region. Nature has conveniently etched pools at the foot of the falls, with water so cool you'll never want to leave.

The falls are within the **Ein Gedi Nature Reserve,** open from 8 a.m. to 3:30–4 p.m.; entrance is SH2.60 (76¢) for adults, SH1.20 (35¢) for children. No food is allowed within the grounds—conservation and ecology are of prime importance here.

Near Ein Gedi are the ruins of ancient Ein Gedi, one of Israel's most important archeological sites. A mosaic synagogue floor from the second or third century has been excavated, along with remains of a small pool and ancient buildings. Byzantine remains have also been found here, and on a nearby cliff is part of a sanctuary dating from about 4000 B.C.

Across the Dead Sea to the far left are the Moab Mountains, where Moses was buried, and Gad, Ruben and half the Mannasseh Tribe settled after helping Joshua claim the rest of the Promised Land. To the right, it seems the sea ends, but it's simply a strip of peninsula from the Jordanian side, and this is about the middle of the Dead Sea. It's called Haloshon (The Tongue). The water here is over 1,000 feet deep, but from the other side of the peninsula to Sodom it's only about 15 feet deep.

SODOM: Retrace your drive along the shore, back to whichever highway (Arad or Beersheba) brought you to the sea-hugging road. Only don't turn there, just keep going and you'll be in Sodom in no time. Bear in mind that today's Sodom is no real town as such, just factories and equipment. Once there was a cafe, a youth hostel, a pension-like hostel. Once it was possible to cool off in the famous Sodom cave, with its twisting labyrinth of shining salt walls, gleaming stalactites, and the broad chamber with a funneled chimney-like opening at the top. But that's been closed as a safety precaution. Today about all you can do here is look around at one of the most tortured-looking areas you're ever likely to see. Nearby, however, is **Moshav Neot Hakikar**—proof that even the most arid and desolate desert land can be reclaimed.

The calm, oily sea is on your right, bizarre, agonizing mountain slopes on your left. Clumps of white foam, a solid brine, cling to the dried shrubs and clumps of whitened stone. There is a noxious smell of sulphur in the air, and some of the trees next to the sea are petrified, with crystals of gypsum and bitumen hanging from them in weird shapes.

The wicked city of Sodom is no more. The famous citadel of degeneracy is now one big hot potash concession. Here the road that runs along the Dead Sea shore is bordered on the left by a wall of solid salt. (Taste it if you don't believe us.) Reportedly, one of the pillars along the bordering wall is of the curious woman who looked back. The legendary pillar—which does suggest such a shape—stands above the entrance to the Sodom cave. According to the Biblical story, angels were going to save Mr. and Mrs. Lot and family, and, in telling them to run for it, they also admonished them not to look back. Mrs. Lot's curiosity is mummified in perpetuity in the pillar of salt.

The fire and brimstone which hit Sodom and Gomorrah was probably a tertiary-era volcano that shattered this area, according to scientific evidence. In any event, a recent proposal for constructing a desert-like gambling casino here—along Las Vegas lines—drew a wrathful protest from religious leaders. Their objection? The city was destroyed once for its wickedness; don't tempt history to repeat itself.

On the road through the area of Sodom, you'll spot a post office which will stamp your mail "Lowest Point on Earth." If you go in for this offbeat sort of stuff—like people who make special trips to Scandinavia just to get a Hell, Norway, postage mark—it may even be worth the entire trip and all the heat.

4. The Roads to Eilat

Now you've got a choice. You can head toward the Jordanian border and take the superhighway from Sodom to Eilat; it's much faster, but there's only stark, indigenous scenery to see. Or you can go to Beersheba, and take the older and much slower road through the heart of the Negev to reach the Port of Eilat on the Red Sea. If you choose the latter, there are four major points of interest along this fascinating road: the Sde Boker settlement, Bedouin tribes, Mitspe Ramon, and the scenery, as well as a number of archeological sites and digs, the best known being Avdat.

SDE BOKER: Several miles outside Beersheba, where the only things you see are sand and parched mountains in every direction, you suddenly come to a farm settlement. Green orchards and blossoming vegetable fields seem to have miraculously sprung from the desert soil here. This is the famous Ben-Gurion kibbutz, **Sde Boker.** The settlement was begun just after the 1948 war, at the Prime Minister's instigation, when the country was first encouraging settlers to populate the Negev. His words, "If the State does not put an end to the desert, the desert may put an end to the State," provided an inspiration. He provided an example, for when he went into retirement he became a member of this commune. He and his wife Paula are buried here, and many of his books and papers may be seen in the **Paula and David Ben-Gurion Hut.** Visiting hours are Sunday to Thursday from 8:30 a.m. to 3:30 p.m.; on Friday, Saturday, holidays and holiday eves from 9 a.m. to 1 p.m. Groups are asked to phone 057-85124 in advance.

Over the years Sde Boker began to thrive, as did several other young settlements in the Negev peopled by a hardy and tough desert breed of Israeli. At present a campus of the Ben-Gurion University of the Negev is being established at Sde Boker. A modern library, housing the **Ben-Gurion Institute and Archives,** and containing 750,000 documents associated with Israel's first Chief of State, is already located here. The Institute will also serve as a center for the study of the founding and development of the Jewish State.

BEDOUIN TRIBES: After leaving Sde Boker, you are *really* in the desert. The black-tented Bedouin camps grow sparser as you proceed farther south; whatever the natural growth of grass and fruit in the Negev, it is all in the northern part, so even the perennial wanderers do most of their wandering in the northern desert regions.

Roughly 32,000 Bedouins roam Israel's deserts and hills, an estimated 27,000 in the Negev, 5,000 in the Galilee mountains. Until recently, they haven't respected border lines very much—as is their inherited prerogative—but Israel has been campaigning to entice them with the benefits of civilization in the modern land of the Bible. Clinics and hospitals give their babies free service, the government has provided them with land to till and develop, and some have settled down to become desert construction workers. A few years ago, the first ever Bedouin doctor graduated from the Hebrew University.

VIEW OF THE NEGEV: The Talmudic scholars say that Negev means "dry," and Old Testament experts claim it means "south." Both are correct—in literal terms. A vast wasteland of almost 4,000 square miles, this desert is Israel's future—for population expansion, for chemical industries, for farming. Studies have proved that one-fifth of the desert area can be used for some form of agriculture or other, and looking at the bleak, dry landscape, even this seems a high figure.

Some deserts can be boring, just hot and dry. Not the Negev. This region is a constantly varying landscape of red, black, and yellow, accented by valleys, deep craters and burnt-brown mountains.

Craggy limestone walls, mounds of sandstone, red and even green dunes of sand are everywhere strewn with great blocks of black volcanic silex. Saw-toothed mountain ridges, abruptly hollowed out by the wild gorges left from the Great Middle Eastern Earthquake, starkly point back to the day when these mountains just fell down and this desert opened its granite jaws to everything living on top of it—truly awesome.

MITSPE RAMON: At Mitspe Ramon, a clay-mining town where you'll pause for a drink, you'll find a view that will make you rub your eyes in disbelief. It's a combination of the Grand Canyon and the surface of the moon—a fantasy of orange and black patterns, in shapes at once flat, twisting and massive—that defies description. Should you get a late start on your trip south—and it's not advisable to drive this narrow road by night—your one solace is seeing this view by sunset. Then the enormous panorama, which resembles our notion of what the earth's surface looked like 50,000,000 years ago, becomes drenched with a reddish pastel hue.

Just in case you'd like to stay overnight, there's the modern, clean **Bet Noam Youth Hostel,** with 160 beds, family accommodations, hot showers, cooking facilities, and a cafe and supply store.

Incidentally, the region is now accessible by plane as well. Arkia has regular air service to Mitspe Ramon.

INSIDE THE NEGEV: This petrified desert world, with temperatures ranging from 125 degrees during the day to 50 degrees in the winter dawn, has been somewhat tamed by the 140-mile road, well-banked but a bit narrow, running from Beersheba to Eilat on the Red Sea. Unseen from this main road are the majority of the desert's agricultural settlements and mining works, as well as Nahal (Noar Halootzi Lo'hem or Pioneering Fighting Youth) military pioneering villages.

If you're going by sherut or driving by yourself, stop the car at some uninhabited spot and listen to the almost frightening stillness of a world where nothing seems to stir.

Equally mysterious in the Negev are the secondary roads leading off the main route—cryptic paths winding their way into the flatlands and beyond the dunes, seemingly without purpose, but actually ending up in an agricultural collective. Also unseen, except for an occasionally patrolled pumping station, is the vast network of cement water conduits based in part on the Jordan River diversion project, which brings life to these desert outposts.

At the end of the road: the port of Eilat on the Red Sea.

5. Eilat

This city at the southern tip of the Negev vies with Tiberias as the country's leading winter tourist resort. Eilat's chief claims to fame for the tourist are fine beaches and sunshine about 360 days out of the year. But with 20,000 inhabitants who have an average age of 26 years, Eilat is actually a combination military outpost-vacation center-shipping port. The city's first-class hotel area is less than a mile from the Jordanian border. Easily viewed across the bay, dazzling in a haze of desert sand, and partly shaded by rings of date palm trees, is the Jordanian port city of Aqaba, population 20,000. Twenty kilometers south of Aqaba begins Saudi Arabia. To the west are the mountains of Sinai.

IN KING SOLOMON'S TIME: It was from the port of Eilat that Solomon sent and received his ships from the land of Ophir, laden with gold, wood, and ivory. Israeli shipping rights on the Red Sea, opened by virtue of the Sinai campaign, and again during the Six-Day War, make the port of Eilat a bustling place which employs a large number of the residents. Although the harbor doesn't look like much, it is one of the most classical ports in all history. "And King Solomon built a navy of ships in Ezion-geber, which is beside Eloth on the shore of the Red Sea" (I Kings 9:26). Hiram, Solomon's famous admiral friend (he was King of Tyre), brought to Eilat his spices and gold from the land of Ophir, and it is even thought by some that the Queen of Sheba landed at Eilat when she came to Jerusalem to see Solomon and "commune with him all that was in her heart."

THE SPECIAL PEOPLE OF EILAT: Here you'll find all kinds of folks, from young men who are grimy, tough, and ready for anything, to young housewives wheeling the many baby carriages you see in this town. But Eilat definitely has a youthful, adventurous flavor, a rare freedom of spirit that seems to move the entire population. The cocky, happy-go-lucky attitude of Eilat's population is really a very necessary factor. Without it, they probably couldn't persevere over the indescribably hot summertime days. Israelis who had begun to find the north too confining and cramped have moved down here for the challenge; so, too, have a few who practice yoga, pluck guitar strings, and who, in general, were displeased with "the people up north"—for whom they have little hope. This is an individualist's town, and it's also a town for making money.

ORIENTATION: There are three easily distinguishable areas in Eilat: the town itself, built on gentle hills rolling down towards the sea; **Coral Beach,** about 2½ miles from town on the western shore of the harbor; and **Lagoon Beach,** a 20-minute walk from the center of town on the eastern shore of the harbor. This latter is where the major beach activity is concentrated, where you'll find the best accommodations, and where the public beach is located. This is also the site of an elaborate marina system which started with the building of a horseshoe-shaped lagoon, cutting several hundred yards inland in back of the "hotel row" section. Around this lagoon, in which you can swim, are hotels, motels, and a caravan camp. It's a masterful plan, worked out by teams of marine surveyors and architects; as a result of it, more and more tourists can enjoy Eilat—the languid days, the bountiful sun, the red-tinted green waters, the calm of the midday sloth, the dusty hills, the cool desert breezes of night.

The best way to pilot yourself around Eilat is to step into the Tourist Information Office, tel. 059-2268, in the Commercial Center, directly across from the Egged Bus Station and pick up a free English-language map on which everything is clearly marked out for you.

TRANSPORTATION: Several daily Arkia flights, tel. 059-6102, link Eilat with points north and south, and sheruts and Egged buses ply the route from Eilat to Beersheba, Sodom, Tel Aviv, and Jerusalem each day. To get around Eilat, there are local buses and taxis. All hotels have bus schedules (in Hebrew).

Hitchhiking is common and Eilat people tend to stop and ask if you need a ride, even if you're not thumbing.

If you arrive by bus, you will be planted squarely in the center of town on the main street—**Hatmarim Boulevard.** From there, any hotel in town is within walking distance, as are the North Beach hotels if your luggage is light. Better take a taxi if you're heading out to Coral Beach. You can also leave your luggage at the bus station while you go in search of accommodations. If you arrive at the airport, you will be just down the hill from the town and bus station and on the road to the Lagoon Beach.

KEEPING COOL IN EILAT: This is tricky, but it can definitely be done if you don't overbake, cover your body and head, and drink great quantities of liquid.

The winter is another and far better story. The thick dusty heat is gone, and the air is cool and dry, the sun out continuously, the water warm enough for swimming every day.

In the summer, most service establishments in town—hotels, motels, and the moderately priced restaurants—are air-conditioned. In some of the older homes you will still see the Eilat version of air conditioners, which are called "desert coolers." Based on the simple idea of injecting droplets of water in front of a fan, instead of dehumidifying (with an air conditioner) an already dehumidified place, the desert coolers keep indoor Eilat at a comfortable temperature.

During summer, the outdoor afternoon heat exceeds 110 degrees—they call it 45 degrees Centigrade, if that makes it seem better—and it's best to stay in the shade for the three hours between noon and 3 p.m. Severe cases of sun-poisoning are the comeuppance for those who don't heed the precaution. The warm breezes abate at night. Increasingly, Israelis are opting for summer vacations in Eilat. No reason why you shouldn't.

Once again, drink lots and lots of liquids here—you'll find yourself consuming six bottles of soda pop a day. There's nothing wrong with that in this climate.

By the way, you can now drink the water in Eilat—thanks to the large desalination plant. Prior to 1965 many a sightseer had his stay in Eilat ruined by a bad case of "tourist trots" caused largely by the heavy amounts of magnesium in Eilat's water. Tennis courts, discos, and now purified drinking water— civilization has come to Eilat.

ACCOMMODATIONS: Hotel prices at this Red Sea resort are lowest during the summer when Eilat is at its hottest. They increase by about 10% in the October to May period when Israelis escape to Eilat's warm climate and enjoy a respite from the cool dampness of the northern winter.

Despite the heat, Eilat is a wonderful sea resort even during the summer— if you observe the basic precautions about desert traveling. The Red Sea water is cool and refreshing during the hot part of the summer, when the Mediterranean is about the temperature of a lukewarm bathtub. The sea is calm, too, and you can get in some water-skiing.

Like magic every year a few more hotels blossom in Eilat—in all price ranges. We'll start our hotel exploration at the **Caravan Sun Club Hotel,** tel. 059-2776, across from Coral Beach and next to the luxury Laromme Hotel. Graded two stars, it has 108 rooms, all with toilets and baths or showers. A single is SH63.60 ($18.70) to SH71.70 ($21.10), a double is SH49.30 ($14.50) to SH57.10 ($16.80) per person. High season rates are about $3 extra per person. Students get a 10% discount. The hotel has a good bar (the Aladin), a volleyball court, swimming pool, playground, wind-surfing school, diving facilities, tennis courts, mini-market, and a disco.

The **Snapeer Hotel**, Hatmarim Blvd., P.O.B. 156, tel. 059-3188, charges SH59.50 ($17.50) to SH91.80 ($27) per person single or double. Only breakfast is served. The place is very simply furnished. Rooms have showers and toilets, phones, and air conditioning. It's only about 60 yards from the airport.

The **Etzion Hotel** is on the same street, but across from the Egged Bus Station, tel. 059-4131/2. It has two stars, dairy and meat restaurants, swimming pools for adults and children, and a nightclub. Rates are SH61.20 ($18) per person for double occupancy. Rooms have bath or shower, and toilet. There's a 10% reduction for students. Half-board is $6, full board $11.

The **Red Sea Hotel**, tel. 059-2171, is on that same central street, next to the Bank Discount. There are 42 rooms, all with toilet, bath or shower, telephone intercom, and wall to wall carpeting. The hotel is being refurbished at this writing, and 38 new rooms are being added. Singles pay SH74.80 ($22), doubles SH54.40 ($16) per person, triples SH37.40 ($11) apiece. Students get a 10% discount.

The air-conditioned **Eilat Center Hotel** is on the same Hatmarim Blvd., opposite the bus station, tel. 059-3334, is highly recommended. It has three stars and slightly over ten times that number of rooms. Each room has wall-to-wall carpeting, sofas, kitchenette, small refrigerator, cutlery (pots and pans are limited to first come, first grab), private toilet, bath, and shower. There's also a grill bar and a TV room. Including breakfast, single room price is SH84.10 ($24.75), double occupancy SH61.20 ($18) per person, SH30.60 ($9) for each additional person. Students get a 10% reduction.

A very pleasant hotel, set in a garden, is **Dekel Hotel**, Hativat Hanegev Blvd., tel. 059-3191. Accommodations are modest but clean and air-conditioned. There's running water (cold only) in your room, showers and toilets in the hall. B&B rates are SH49.30 ($14.50) single, SH40.80 ($12) per person double, SH92.50 ($27.20) for three.

The **Dalia Hotel**, near the elegant Neptune, tel. 059-5171, has 32 air-conditioned rooms, all with toilet and private bath or shower. Another 20 rooms are in construction at this writing. Off-season rates are SH56.10 ($16.50) single, SH44.90 ($13.20) per person double, SH37.40 ($11) for an additional person, those rates including an Israeli breakfast. Rates are a few dollars higher the rest of the year. Students get a 10% discount. Lunch or dinner is SH22.40 ($6.60).

The **Bel Hotel**, tel 059-6121/2/3, P.O.B. 897, opposite the Moriah Hotel, two stars, 84 rooms, and a pleasant ambience. It's a three-minute walk from the sea. All rooms have private bath, toilet, air-conditioning, phone, and a terrace. There's a dining room and bar on the premises. B&B rates, including an Israeli breakfast, are SH78.20 ($23) single, SH60.50 ($17.80) per person double; lunch or dinner is SH23.80 ($7).

The **Blue Sky Caravan Motel**, tel. 059-3953/4, is located on Eilat's north shore, near the Club Méditerranée and the Jordanian border. A single room is SH51 ($15), a double SH40.80 ($12) per person. There's a reasonably priced restaurant on the premises, and the air-conditioned caravans all have cooking facilities. Lunch or dinner is SH20.40 ($6).

Nearby is the **Sun Bay Camping and Holiday Village**, North Beach, tel. 059-2362. About two-thirds of the 100 bungalows are air-conditioned and equipped with toilets and showers. Rates SH62.90 ($18.50) single, SH27.20 ($8) to SH42.50 ($12.50) per person double. Students get a discount. You can also rent camping sites for SH7.60 ($2.25) per person, but you must provide your own tent. A restaurant and food store are on the premises. The bungalows at Sun Bay have colored curtains and bedspreads, facilities throughout are quite good, and the beach is especially beautiful.

The **Yerushalayim Hotel,** corner of Yerushalayim and Barnea Sts., tel. 059-2373, has 22 simply furnished rooms painted in flashy colors, all with shower, and many with toilet. No meals are served. Single or double occupancy is SH25 ($7.35) a night, triples pay SH34 ($10), four in a room SH45 ($13.25).

Hostels

In addition to the **Youth Hostel** (details in Chapter XI), there are three other places billing themselves as hostels in Eilat.

The **Nophit Hostel,** near the regular Youth Hostel and the Red Rock Hotel, tel. 059-2207, currently offers beds for SH10 ($2.95) a night in air-conditioned dorm rooms. However, at this writing, they're converting to two-bedded rooms with private facilities at a cost of SH30 ($8.85) a night for two. Unlike youth hostels, guests can stay on the grounds during the day. Students get a 10% reduction on rates. Israeli breakfast is SH6 ($1.75). Take buses 1, 2, or 5.

Beit Eshel Hostel is situated on Barnea St., near Lindi St., tel. 059-2737. The 24 two- and four-bedded rooms are air-conditioned but rather spartan. Every three rooms shares a gas burner, refrigerator, shower, and toilet. No meals are served. Single or double occupancy is SH25 ($7.35) a night, three in a room pay SH34 ($10), four pay SH45 ($13.25).

Finally, there's the 132-room **Eilat Hostel,** 685 Faran St., tel. 059-2862. Once again furnishings are on the spartan side. Kitchen facilities include a sink and refrigerator, but no stove. The price of a bed for a night is SH16 ($4.70), SH14.50 ($4.25) for students. A large but pricey breakfast is SH8.40 ($2.50), dinner SH8.96 ($2.65). There's a snack bar on the premises.

Rooms and Apartments

Another option in Eilat is to rent a room in someone's home, or, if you prefer, a whole apartment. Three agencies for these accommodations are recommended by the I.G.T.O., and be warned that there have been many complaints from tourists using other sources.

Hanan, in the bus terminal building, tel. 059-5815, has beds in a double room for SH15 ($4.40) a night; SH110 ($32.35) a night for a three-room apartment. Also try **Johnny,** whose office is in the Commercial Center, tel. 059-6777, and **Joe,** in the Etzion Hotel building on Hatmarim Blvd., tel. 059-3655.

All rentals include linens and air conditioning. Rates vary a bit with seasons and facilities; do look at the room before signing up.

RESTAURANTS: Eilat abounds with worthwhile eateries, hence we've a very long list of choices for a rather small city.

Nelson's Village, about ten kilometers south of the city and right on the beach, tel. 059-3922, is a place that we heartily recommend for a day of leisure, fun, and food. This is the domain of bearded bohemian ex-journalist Rafi Nelson, one of those legendary characters who provide Eilat with that extra modicum of spice. In keeping with his sense of humor, he has a statue of a golden calf perched on a nearby hill and is reputed to be the first Israeli ever to locate his bathtub in a fenceless garden in Eilat. Rafi has all the equipment necessary for diving, snorkeling, surfboarding, or water-skiing. There's even a tiny zoo on the premises. Taped classical and folk music is played all day. As for the food, you can get kabab or chicken with salads, pitta, and fruit for SH10 ($2.95). There's an entrance fee to the Village of SH4, which includes a drink. Open daily except Monday from 9:30 a.m. to 5 p.m.

French and Italian specialties are featured nightly from 8:30 to 11 p.m. at **Napoli Restaurant,** near the Eilat Center Hotel in Mercaz Center. Candlelit tables are covered with checkered cloths, and the walls are plastered with postcards from diners praising the restaurant. If you show a copy of this book you can have a $5 meal consisting of soup, a main course and two vegetables, dessert, and a soft drink.

The dairy cafeteria of the **Moon Valley Hotel,** tel. 059-5111, is open from 10 a.m. to 11 p.m. for blintzes at SH3.70 ($1.10), yogurt at SH1.30 (40¢), and the like. A dairy plate with tuna and vegetable salads, an omelette, olives, and cheese is SH9.30 ($2.75).

The **Ben-Harush Cafe,** on the beach across from the Caravan Hotel, tel. 059-3468, serves steak and salad in a pitta for SH7 ($2.05), cheese or sausage sandwiches for SH2 (60¢), a hamburger and salad plate with chips for SH8 ($2.35). You can also rent deck chairs, snorkeling equipment, kayaks, and water bicycles here. Open daily from 8 a.m. to 5 p.m.

The **Neve Eilat Restaurant,** 103 Hatarim Blvd., corner of Hativat Golani St., tel. 059-2074, serves European and Algerian fare. A traditional North African couscous is SH7.50 ($2.20); other dishes served with rice and salad include shashlik or kabab for SH6 ($1.75), goulash for SH5 ($1.45), and chicken with olives for SH6.50 ($1.90). There are also many salads available in the SH2 (60¢) to SH3.50 ($1) range. Open Sunday to Thursday from 6 a.m. to about midnight, closed from Friday at 4 p.m. until Saturday after sunset.

Yemenite specialties are served at **Hakerem Restaurant,** Eilat St., tel. 059-4577, which has both a terrace and interior dining room. Meatballs with chips, salad, or rice cost SH6.50 ($1.90), same price for the likes of cow stomach or lungs. Open Saturday to Thursday from 9 a.m. to 11 p.m., closing Friday at 4 p.m.

The sparsely furnished **Halleluja Restaurant,** 1 New Tourist Center, offers chicken with olives and rice for SH6.50 ($1.90), same price for shashlik or kabab with side dishes. Couscous for SH9 ($2.65) is served every Sunday. Salads are SH2 (60¢). Open noon to midnight Sunday to Friday, from after sunset on Saturday. On Friday you must pay for your meal before the Sabbath begins.

Petra Restaurant, in the New Tourist Center, has a patio for dining al fresco, offers background music while you eat, and grills meats over charcoal. SH6.50 ($1.90) will get you kabab, sausages, shwarma, hamburger, or beef liver with side dishes. A mixed salad plate—from a choice of 25 salads—is SH8 ($2.35), and pizzas are SH4.50 ($1.35) to SH8 ($2.35) depending on the toppings. Open daily from 6 p.m. to 1 a.m.

Also in the New Tourist Center is the **Ta'aman Delicatessen** for American-style sandwiches like ham and cheese at SH3 (90¢), bacon and eggs, at SH4.50 ($1.35), etc. Open Sunday to Thursday from 8 a.m. to 2 p.m. and 5 to 10 p.m., closed Friday from 3 p.m. until after sunset on Saturday.

The **Arkia Terminal Buffet** in the airport is open from 6 a.m. to 8 p.m. and provides cheese, egg, or salami sandwiches for SH1 (30¢). Cakes cost SH1.30 (38¢), coffee SH1.20 (35¢).

The **Arizona Restaurant,** offers kosher fare: chicken, goulash, turkey schnitzel, or meatballs with two side dishes for SH9 ($2.65), stuffed vegetables or gefilte fish for SH2.50 (75¢), 25 different salads at SH2.50 (75¢) a portion. Open 10 a.m. to 10 p.m., till 4 p.m. on Friday, closed Saturday.

The **Oasis Restaurant,** across from the Queen of Sheba Hotel, tel. 059-2414, is decorated with fish nets and hanging fish on wood-beamed walls; a terrace faces a lagoon. Grilled chicken, shashlik, kabab, or Viennese schnitzel cost SH8 ($2.35), and come with a choice of salads (potato, Greek, Turkish, or cole slaw) and chips. Students get a 10% reduction. Open daily from 1 p.m. to about midnight.

We've already mentioned some of the cluster of restaurants along and adjacent to Hatmarim Blvd. **Milk Bar Strauss,** 1 Hatmarim Blvd., tel. 059-2223, is another, open 7 a.m. to midnight daily, serving a large SH7 ($2.05) breakfast, a huge steak with salad in pitta for SH7.50 ($2.20), as well as kababs, shashlik, and dairy dishes.

Another milk bar, the **Capricho,** 133 Harmarim Blvd., specializes in crêpes—with banana, peach, fruit cocktail, and nuts—for SH6 ($1.75), pancakes with ice cream, syrup, and whipped cream for SH5.50 ($1.60), and homemade Italian ice cream for SH3.50 ($1) to SH6 ($1.75). Open Sunday to Friday from 8:30 a.m. to midnight, Saturday from 2 p.m. to midnight.

At the **Hotel Etzion's Dairy Cafeteria and Snack Bar,** Hatmarim Blvd., tel. 059-2457, you can get stuffed vegetables for SH3 (90¢), lasagne for SH3.50 ($1), two blintzes for SH5 ($1.45), and fried sole for SH6 ($1.75). Open Sunday to Thursday from 8 a.m. to 9 p.m., closed Friday from 3 p.m. until Saturday at 2 p.m.

Naturally there is an **Egged Bus Station Restaurant** in Eilat, tel. 059-4477, and naturally we recommend it. Breakfast costs SH5.50 ($1.60), soups and salads SH2 (60¢), lunch with a meat main course SH11.20 ($3.30). Open Sunday to Thursday from 7 a.m. to 3:45 p.m., Friday till 3 p.m., closed Saturday.

A good place for light fare is the cafeteria of the **Red Sea Hotel,** Hatmarim Blvd., tel. 059-2171. A hearty breakfast here will set you back SH6.50 ($1.90). Pancakes are SH3.50 ($1) with maple syrup, SH6 with ice cream, nuts, and cream; blintzes are SH5 ($1.45) and up. Open daily from 6 a.m. to 1 a.m. Students get a 10% discount.

Pubs

There are several pubs in Eilat, all in the Tourist Center.

The **Tavern Pub,** tel. 059-3406, has indoor and outdoor seating. The wood-beamed interior is decorated with wine and beer labels and postcards. Most mixed drinks are SH6.50 ($1.90), draft beer is SH3 (90¢). Light snacks are also served. Open nightly from 7 p.m. to about 2–3 a.m.

The **Picadilly Pub,** tel. 059-6425, is dimly lit, intimate, and woody in ambience, with dark paneled walls and brown leather chairs. Drinks at the bar cost SH6 ($1.75) to SH7.50 ($2.20), SH.50 more at a table. A cheese plate with your drink is SH3 (90¢); bagels and olives are free. Open nightly from 8 p.m. till 4–5 a.m.

TOURS AND SIGHTS: Eilat offers a wealth of activities to investigate before you go plummeting into the wide expanses of Sinai. If you wish to join up with a tour, consult the Sinai chapter for most of the required information—Sinai and Eilat are usually considered one great tour arena, and nearly all the major operators cited either include Eilat in their itineraries or use the city as the jumping-off point. If you want to combine Masada and Eilat on one tour, head for Egged, which offers a three-day tour by bus for SH506.60 ($149), another by bus and by plane for SH642.60 ($189).

Reasonably priced tours are also offered by **YaAlat Tours,** in the Tourist Center, tel. 059-2974; and **Johnny Desert Tours** in the Commercial Center, tel. 059-6777.

Boat Cruises, Boats for Hire, Etc.

In addition to the places we mentioned to hire boats in the restaurant section above, you can hire boats 24 hours a day at the Lagoon—there are boats for water-skiing, rowboats, kayaks, and motorboats available.

And in the etc. category, there's **Raffi Pipson's** place on the shore across from the Laromme and Caravan Sun Club Hotels, tel. 059-2909. Here you can loll on the beach, skindive, snack, shower, surf, sunbathe, and swim. Raffi is a licensed underwater and desert guide. For non-swimmers he provides air mattresses, snorkels, masks and fins to explore the wonders of Coral Beach— SH25 ($7.35) for the works. Swimmers can rent the equipment without the mattress for SH10 ($2.95). He also rents kayaks and flatboats for SH10 ($2.95) an hour. Open 7–8 a.m. to sunset.

Check the cruise offerings and sea tours at **Garry's Sea Service,** at the southern end of Lagoon Beach, tel. 059-6333; they also sell water sports equipment.

And **Venezia,** in a log cabin on the boardwalk, tel. 059-3817, rents all kinds of small seacraft—rowboats, canoes, equipped fishing boats, sailboats, etc., sells yacht tour tickets, operates a snack bar, and is open 24 hours a day.

Glass-Bottom Boats

Leaving from the jetty at Coral Beach, these boats offer a wonderful view of a fairytale marine world. You putt-putt out into the bay, and through the glass below you see the beginnings of tall mounds of coral on the fluted, pale green sandy floor. Then the waters turn a deeper green, the mounds of coral grow higher and thicker, and soon clusters of rainbow-colored fish are darting under your eyes—brilliantly blue fish, long-finned purple fish, pink blowfish, yellow and red striped fish. It's like looking into a giant, complex aquarium in Technicolor and Cinemascope, and the sight you see is that of a new world of mountains and soft plains, of sea creatures darting this way and that, slithering into crevices to escape marauding sand sharks and frolicking on the slopes of coral mountains. You can't help being hypnotized by this silent, dreamlike world. Cost is SH10 ($2.95), for adults, half price for children; hours of departure are 9:10, 10:10, and 11:10 a.m., 2:10 and 3:10 p.m. (last boat on Friday is at 2 p.m.).

Coral World Underwater Observatory and Aquarium

Located at Coral Beach and within ten minutes of the airport, this new tourist attraction is genuinely fascinating. The project consists of three one-story buildings on the beach with distinctive rounded roofs, and the observatory, which has been sunk into position 100 meters out to sea in that part of the coral reef known as the Japanese Gardens. A pier binds the observatory to the coast. Of the three buildings, two are the Maritime Museum and Aquarium, tel. 059-6666, and the third a cafeteria. The tower of the observatory rises out of the sea to a height of 20 feet; inside, a spiral staircase of 42 steps leads down to the observatory itself. Since the water in the gulf is generally crystal clear, observation of the magnificent fish and coral life is unparalleled.

The best time to visit the observatory is between noon and 3 p.m. Admission for an adult is SH5 ($1.45), half price for children ages five to 12. There's a bus every half-hour from town.

King Solomon's Pillars

There is a daily tour to King Solomon's Pillars, leaving from the hotels at 9:30 a.m. The five pillars of Solomon's mines are one of the mammoth wonders of nature—constructed, as one man put it, "by the same Architect who built the Grand Canyon." Reddish purple, stained with glints of black and green, they are regally evocative of a once-fabulous era. It was from the copper caves near these pillars that Solomon extracted the green gold which provided the foundation for his kingdom's wealth.

Modern Art Museum

Located near the Philip Murray Cultural Center, the museum has regular exhibitions from its own collection and other sources. Open Sunday, Tuesday, Wednesday, and Thursday from 5 to 7 p.m., Monday and Wednesday from 10 a.m. to noon; closed on Fridays and eves of holidays. Entrance is free.

Hai Bar Wildlife Reserve

The Hai Bar National Biblical Wildlife Reserve, all 8,000 acres' worth, is 40 kilometers north of Eilat. Its purpose is to save rare and endangered desert animals mentioned in the Bible, as well as other rare desert animals of Western Asia and Northern Africa. Among the 450 animals found here are the Nubian ibex, the Dorcas gazelle, the Persian onager, the scimitar-horned oryx, the addax antelope, and the Arabian gazelle. You can ride around the reserve in your car (closed vehicles only) and observe the animals at close range. Open from 6 a.m. to before sunset daily; entrance fee is SH4.30 ($1.25) for adults, SH2.60 (75¢) for children. The tour takes about two hours, and it's best to avoid the hot afternoon in summer. If you have no car, take a guided tour from town.

SWIMMING IN THE RED SEA: You have a choice of swimming spots in Eilat: either use the sand beach in front of the Moriah Hotel as far as the Sun Bay Caravan on one side, or Coral Beach, which is a short drive around the curve of the bay. The beach near the Moriah Hotel rents waterskis and boats, but make sure you know where you're going, because you don't have to ski very far to get into both Jordanian and hot water. Our preference, though, is Coral Beach. It's quiet, inundated with coral and fish, and always less crowded. And at Coral Beach you can swim underwater (by all means get a snorkel) and see the shimmering emerald waters and the bed of red coral stone. Hundreds of underwater prowlers have picked the floor of the sea clean around here, but if you're lucky, you may still find some interesting shells. At both beach areas there are cafes and shaded structures designed to keep you cool.

There are numerous specialists in diving and such here. Largest enterprise is **The Aqua Sport,** on Coral Beach, tel. 059-2788. Here you can rent a variety of equipment at low costs. There's a "scuba-christening" dive, accompanied by an instructor, lasting one hour. They offer a six-day diving course, in English, after which you must remain five days to carry out ten dives—that is if you want your certificate. They also offer seminars in underwater photography (credits non-transferable). Farther down the beach, you'll find **Nelson's Village,** which we mentioned earlier under "Restaurants." As a matter of fact, no matter where you walk, you'll discover diving clubs, snorkel-renting facilities, and diving schools. One local dream is to transform Eilat into the underwater diving capital of the world.

Although the waters around Eilat are safe, always take the elementary precautions of not going too far out alone, keeping in mind that depth is deceptive where the water is so clear, and understanding that the numerous sharks sharing the sea with you are not particularly hungry for you. You'd better know, too, that the corals and shells are protected by law; it is strictly forbidden to remove them from the water and to collect them from the beaches.

EILAT MISCELLANY: There is a new **Field School** in Eilat. You can obtain more information from the Society for the Protection of Nature in Tel Aviv. . . . Eilat citizens plant a new tree for each child born in the city, no mean feat in that arid environment. . . . Bicycles can be rented at **Rent-a-Bike** at the Caravan Sun Club Hotel. . . . To reiterate: Keep out of the noonday sun, drink vast quantities of liquids, and cover your head.

Chapter X

THE SINAI

1. The Sights and Sites of Sinai
2. Transportation and Tours
3. Meals and Accommodations

PERSONALLY, we would be suspicious of any travel writer who claimed to know Sinai. Sinai—that vast, triangular, nearly barren peninsula that is 3½ times larger than pre-1967 Israel and which has an indigenous population that would fit into the small corners of any of Israel's major cities—is simply too strange to grasp. A wretched acacia tree, by virtue of its even more wretched surroundings, becomes a thing of wonderment. The harsh, stone cliffs in the center of the region are awesome, but the long coastal strip is soft and undulatory. The bogs east of the Suez Canal transform the striking reflections of the sun into a perpetual mirage of blue water. Armies come and go, but only the Bedouin remain rooted to the area.

"We have known many strangers," a sheikh from the el-Muzzeina tribe once told us. "There were the Turks and the English, the Egyptians and the Israelis. They are like the sand. The wind blows them into a monument. And then the wind destroys them. Only the Bedouin remains."

RECENT HISTORY: Sinai was vacated by the Turks after their World War I defeat at the hands of England. Under British occupation the region was politically joined with Egypt to the west. During the 1948 War of Liberation, Israeli forces penetrated the area, but withdrew immediately after an armistice was signed in 1949. Then, in 1956, the Suez Campaign erupted, the Egyptian forces were pulverized, and the entire peninsula was occupied until American pressures forced a quick and reluctant Israeli retreat. The same story repeated itself in 1967, but the Israeli army remained this time. A road was paved from Eilat to Sharm-el-Sheikh, excursions were introduced into the area, tours were conducted to the lonely, majestic Santa Katarina Monastery in the mountainous center of the region, and a strong Israeli imprint was embossed on the desert. The Yom Kippur War produced new convulsions, and Israel withdrew from the entire area adjacent to the canal and from the oil fields of Abu Rhodeis.

The remainder of Sinai is being restored to Egypt in stages, in accordance with the terms of the peace treaty. The area west of the El Arish-Ras Muhammad line has already been returned; the rest of the territory, including the coastal tourist sites, will remain in Israeli hands until 1982. For purposes of this book, probably for the last time, we're treating the area as an integral part of the Israeli tourist hinterland.

TRAVEL TIPS: There are a few basic axioms to understand before embarking on a desert trip. If you travel by car then you will be treated to a fine, modern highway which runs all along the Red Sea coast. There are two gas stations on the way. Camping and picnicking sites are abundant, and more formal surroundings are available. Negotiating the wadis and camel trails into the heart of the region, however, absolutely requires four-wheeled vehicles. And once you leave the main road, there are not many signposts. Fortunately, there are regular jeep, command car, and bus tours to all the interesting sites in the region. If you're on your own, you must stick to the more civilized areas along the coast.

The climate is extreme and varies from coast to mountains. Coastal temperatures in the summer soar to over 110 degrees Fahrenheit during the day, cooling off pleasantly in the evening. It's a bit cooler in the mountains during the day, and even the summer evenings can be cool. Winters are another proposition, though. Along the coast, days can be warm enough for January bathing and nights mild enough to take a sleeping bag out to the beach. The mountains, however, can be bitterly cold at night. The winds are savage, and we've seen more than one stream turn into ice. So whatever you do, and whenever you do it, dress accordingly, keeping in mind that a warm sweater and a bathing suit are not mutually contradictory in Sinai.

The geography of the region is inhospitable, but the people are not. The Bedouins can be marvelously friendly, and the local Israeli citizenry are tanned, robust, amiable, and proud of their achievements.

As for security in the region, no problems. Terrorist penetrations into the area are virtually unknown, sabotage unheard of. Sticking to the coast and mountain areas, you'll discern that the Israeli military presence keeps an extremely low profile. There are no problems whatsoever between Eilat and Sharm-el-Shiekh. Visiting military areas in the region is a fairly tricky proposition, not recommended and usually not permitted. If you're motivated along these lines, however, then you absolutely should check with the Army Spokesman's Office, 9 Ittamar Ben Avi St., Tel Aviv.

Caution

We don't know how many of you have ever experienced a flash flood in the desert, but it's an awesome sight—and a dangerous phenomenon. If you're wadi-hiking in the winter and you hear a thunderous rumble, scramble for the high ground as quickly as possible. The water rushes down from the mountains, carrying with it everything in its path, and then vanishes as quickly as it appeared.

1. The Sights and Sites of Sinai

There are a variety of ways of seeing Sinai, by organized tour, by rental car, by air—and then there is always hitchhiking. We'll discuss the tours and other transportation options later in this chapter. For now, we'll assume you've settled on some sort of ground transportation and that you're starting off from Eilat to see the Sinai. You'll be heading south to Sharm-el-Sheikh (redubbed **Ophira** by Israel), with a lot of veering off the course along the way.

FROM EILAT TO SHARM-EL-SHEIKH: As you begin your journey, you pass the center of Eilat, the port and the marine center, and in a short time you find yourself sandwiched squarely between rugged, bare mountains on your right and the blue-green coral sea on your left. Within about 15 minutes, you'll

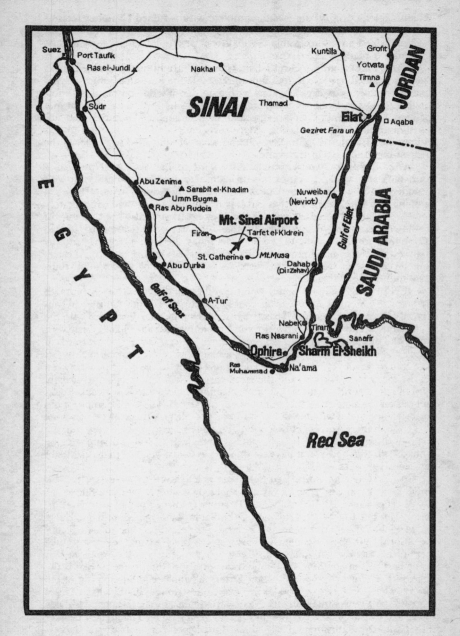

be approaching a fairy-tale island, complete with a ruined Crusader fortress which the Christians called Isle de Gris and Mamelukes dubbed el-Karrie. This is **Coral Island** and is accessible by small boat or amphibian. Try not to miss it because it really is impressive.

Three miles south of Coral Island is another traditional favorite, Israel's **Fjord,** so named because it does indeed resemble the beautiful fjords of Scandinavian countries. A deep blue bay with a border of white beach, it is almost totally enclosed by harsh, angular, high red rock formations. This is a good spot for sunning, swimming, skin-diving and such; actually, the entire Red Sea coastline of Sinai is a mecca for water-sports enthusiasts. From Eilat to Ras Muhammad (south of Ophira), you'll find what's been called (by experts) the greatest coral activity in the world.

After the Fjord, you continue southward to the oasis of **Nuweiba,** a flourishing strip of land, complete with palm trees and soft breezes, but with a modern moshav (communal farm settlement) instead of tents. There's a camping area here, where tourists can stay for minimal costs, and a moderately priced refreshment stand as well. In the oasis area you'll also see the ruins of an old fortress, built during the Ottoman Empire, where caravans stopped during their journeys along the coast. Even today, Bedouin tarry to spend the night within the crumbling walls of its enormous courtyard, and you'll easily find traces of their frequent visits here, as well as in some of the small ruins surrounding the old edifice.

If Nuweiba delights you, just wait till you reach the oasis of **Dahab,** much further south along the shore. This spot has been called Sinai's most beautiful scene by travelers who know the entire peninsula quite well. Sprinkled with the crude houses and shelters of a thriving, friendly Bedouin village, lush with palms and dunes, shell-strewn sands and warm waters, Dahab indeed revels in nature's bounty. Overnights here can be a real treat. Your guide probably will take care to direct your eyes, as the sun begins to set, to the color play between nearby mountains, the sea, and the large oasis. When we were last in Dahab, most of our group slept under the stars, cushioned by blankets or sleeping bags laid out on the sands, the surf lulling them to sleep. If you do the same, you'll perhaps understand why moon-worship was prevalent in this area in ages gone by. (Though there's no conclusive proof, certain experts go so far as to link the name of Sinai with Sin, the Mesopotamian moon god.) Sun worship was big around here too, and you'll have no doubt why when you see that desert sun and feel its powers.

By the way, the entire Red Sea coast is a Nature Reserve (see below), which means you can't haul away the shells or whatever else you find.

West of the coastline is Egyptian territory (returned to Egypt in November, 1979), but tourist sites, including the Santa Katarina Monastery, Zukei David Field School, and Bedouin Center, have remained open to Israeli tourists. Local tour operators offer various tours of the area, and it's best to take them rather than go on your own. If you arrive by car, you'll have to leave it at the border and continue via public transportation. First place to visit is the huge, impressive compound of **Santa Katarina Monastery** fanning out at the foot of what the Greek Orthodox believe to be **Mount Sinai,** where Moses received the Ten Commandments. Nearby is **Mount Horeb,** the site of **Elijah's Cave,** and a church erected in honor of his journey there. The highest peak of these fissured granite mountains is **Mount Catherine.** Yoram Tsafrir, a Hebrew University archeologist, has written that the mountains' ". . . diversity of form and color . . . height and steepness lend an impressive power to the landscape, inspiring religious feeling . . . the overwhelming might of the Sinai landscape

. . . providing . . . a tangible demonstration of the ephemeral quality and insignificance of Man against the timelessness of primordial creation."

On the subject of monasticism at Mount Sinai, Tsafrir writes that the ". . . distinctive feature of early monasticism in Sinai lies in the firm belief in the Mount of the Lord and in the mystic tendency to become one with the surrounding mountains."

We quote Tsafrir here because we can think of no better way to prepare you for the experience of being in this particular spot of the world.

The devout pilgrim Etheria visited this area around 400 A.D., and her writings tell of seeing these mounts, as well as the **Burning Bush** (more about this later). She visited the monks in the area and was shown where the **Golden Calf** stood on **Mount Aaron (Jebel Haroun); the Valley of Repose,** where the Children of Israel camped, plus **Monastery Stream (Wadi El-Deir),** where, another tradition says, the Tablets of the Law were hurled down by Moses. She described two churches, and scholars now say the one at the base of the peak was probably built by a fourth-century Syrian monk, Julianus Sabas, while the one adjacent to the Burning Bush site was probably the earliest part of Santa Katarina, even though some people insist on attributing it to Constantine's mother, Helena.

Under constant attack from Saracens (a term describing all Arab tribes of the area until the Middle Ages), the monks needed defensive fortifications, especially since their lifestyle proscribed violence. Thus Justinian, in the Byzantine era, built the walls you'll find surrounding the monastery now. At that time, it seems, the enclosure was relatively empty, including little more than the church and a hostel, which were very famous throughout the Christian world. The monastery was a caravanserai and rest stop for pilgrims, even as it is today, and one of the more important monasteries through religious history. After the Moslem conquest in the Middle Ages, a mosque was built over the ruins of the hostel, and the mosque still exists, squatting among the tightly squeezed buildings that now fill the compound's space.

Today's tourist or pilgrim will probably be most interested in two of the buildings: the one that houses the **library,** and the **Church.** In the library is a vast collection of icons, many representing the priceless few to escape eighth- and ninth-century iconoclasts; and something on the order of 3,300 manuscripts, some executed by monks through the centuries, but most brought as gifts by pilgrims since the days of the 12th century. This virtual treasure trove is regarded by scholars as the second-greatest religious library in the world, the Vatican being the first. Not for nothing have the monks of Santa Katarina ardently guarded their possessions through the centuries. Since 1967, everyone has had free access to the monastery, and scholars have been running in and out, exclaiming over what they've found. What has attracted most attention of late is something called the *Psalterium Sinaiticum,* the oldest known Slavic translation of the Book of Psalms, in Glagolitic script, dating from the 11th century and rated as exceedingly important. Tourists are not allowed to wander through the library at will, but there are many glass-enclosed icons and documents to see here.

The **Church of the Burning Bush** (sometimes called a chapel, sometimes a cathedral with nine chapels), though small, is filled to the brim with gilt and paint, carved wood and enormous brass lamps, paintings and art treasures in great abundance. Some say that the church is the oldest structure in the monastery compound; others say it dates "only" from the Middle Ages. But there is no question that its most significant treasure is a huge mosaic, executed shortly after the building was completed, and said to be one of the earliest and most beautiful in the Orient. Within recent years the mosaic had been restored and cleaned by a team of Americans.

By now some of you might be wondering who Saint Catherine was, and why there's a monastery in her name in the middle of the desert. Most stories about her agree that she was a wealthy and noble Egyptian who converted to Christianity, then went about converting others. It seems that when she chided the converted king (Maximinus) about his rather un-Christian morals, she was tortured to death, her body subsequently disappearing. Some time later, a monk in this vicinity dreamed of finding a great treasure atop the highest peak of Sinai. He promptly scaled the mountain, and there he found the remains of Catherine. On the spot he built a memorial chapel, and her bones were taken down to the monastery to be enclosed in a golden chest buried in the church. Saint Catherine became a favorite in Europe during the Middle Ages, which had much to do with the constant flow of pilgrims to this site.

Though you can't see Saint Catherine's bones, you will be able to see the bones of some 1,500 monks who've died in the monastery. These are carefully arranged by type of bone (leg bones with leg bones, skulls with skulls) in the **Skull House** in the gardens outside the enclosure. Only one skeleton is intact, and this one is now preserved inside a glass case in the middle of the rather creepy crypt. It's St. Stephen, still dressed, seated. Until very recently St. Stephen's remains sat before the door of the building, guarding the bones within from all harm. (This bone preservation may seem strange to you, but experts say it's a common desert monastic practice, reflective of the lack of burial space in the rocky terrain.)

More to see at the monastery: a raspberry plant behind the chapel which monks point out as the **Burning Bush,** itself overshadowed by a tree called **Aaron's Rod.** That tree produces whitish papery pods, roughly crescent-shaped, that the monks here consider the "almonds" that grew overnight, according to the Bible; they consider as well the tree's long branches the source of the rod that became a snake and then a rod again. You can also see three entrance gates to the monastery. According to a booklet produced by the monks, the original gate "has been closed for centuries without any reason." Another gate was opened for the visit of an archbishop about 100 years ago and subsequently closed again. The one you'll enter is quite old. There's another way of getting into the compound, but nobody uses it much any more—a basket hoisted up by muscle power.

Most of the people you'll see hereabouts are either monks or Bedouins, the latter performing the physical tasks about the monastery and its nearby gardens and plantations. These Bedouins are of the Jebaliyeh tribe, and it is thought they were originally brought here from Rumania by Justinian to guard the monastery. As time passed and various conquerors claimed the land, the tribe converted to Islam, and they are Moslems to this day. Despite their own religious beliefs, however, they are fiercely proud of having been chosen as protectors of this holy Christian site. You'll see their village of stone houses nearby.

THE RED SEA COAST: The entire Sinai Red Sea Coast has been proclaimed a Nature Reserve. You can obtain substantial information about the region from the **Nature Reserves Authority,** 16 Hanatziv St., Tel Aviv, tel. 03-30841. Do keep in mind that the corals are inviolate, that you are expected to clean up the area after camping or picnicking, that the refuse containers all along the highway are there for a reason. And while hiking is a great sport, don't do it alone, and make sure you're in camp by nightfall.

Scuba-Diving and Snorkeling

The whole region from Eilat southward is a diver's paradise. A strip of coral runs all along the coastline and the fish life is unbelievably profuse. One reason cited for the name of the Red Sea: "When a perfect calm meets the setting sun, its light reflected from the red mountains of Edom and Median in Jordan and Saudi Arabia, the deep steel-blue water turns crimson shade, making it, indeed, a red sea."

We detail the various schools and diving centers in Chapter XI; here we'll provide a few words of sage advice. Corals sting and cut. There is a spiny rock fish which is highly poisonous to the touch. If you step on a sea anemone, you'll wish you hadn't. We've heard of only two fish-bite incidents in the history of the region, but if you're spearing, keep your piscatorial catch on a free-flowing string a distance from you—blood attracts sharks and barracudas, and there are plenty of them (usually sated and docile) in the area. Nor will the water protect you from sunburn, so, as the Arabs say, "Shwaya, shwaya"—go easy.

2. Transportation and Tours

If you're flying—and the spectacular view of the desert from the air is an extraordinary sight—the name of the game is **Arkia.** Full information can be obtained from the inland carrier's office at 88 Ha'hoshmonaim St., Tel Aviv. Special taxis leave for Ben-Gurion Airport one hour and 15 minutes before check-in time, and the cost is SH3.80 ($1.10). Flight time to Sharm is about one hour, 15 minutes. Fare from Tel Aviv to Sharm is SH274.40 ($80.70), and from Tel Aviv to Eilat SH189.50 ($55.75). Arkia operates five to eight flights daily (except Saturdays) to Eilat. On Saturday there are only tour flights. During the week flights leave from 6 a.m. to 7/8:30 p.m., although there is a 9:45 p.m. flight once a week. There is one flight to Sharm-el Sheikh every day, except Saturdays. Flight time from Tel Aviv to Eilat is under one hour.

There is one scheduled bus from Eilat to Sharm, leaving the Central Bus Terminal at 2 p.m. and taking four hours. Fare is SH29.90 ($8.80), and you have to buy your ticket in advance. There are many buses daily from Tel Aviv to Eilat; the ride takes six hours and costs SH25.70 ($7.55) one way. Again, you must buy your ticket in advance.

TOURS: The pioneer of the Sinai (and Negev) desert tours is **Neot Hakikar Desert Safari Tours,** 28 King David St., tel. 02-221624, Jerusalem; in Eilat, **Kopel Tours,** at the Tourist Center, tel. 059-4105.

The company owns eleven 20-seater Reo vehicles, specially tailored and outfitted for the roughest terrain and offering maximum possible comfort to the traveler. Cars are open on the sides for direct contact with the desert trails and scenery, and guides have a wide knowledge of desert flora and fauna, geology, history, and the Bible. You'll rough it a bit on these tours—overnights are spent in sleeping bags, meals are cooked over a bonfire, there are short hikes, and mountain climbs—but you'll find that they're exciting and unforgettable.

Johnny Desert Tours, Eilat Commercial Center, tel. 059-6777, offers seven regular tours. There's a half-day tour to Ein-Netafim and the Canyon of Inscriptions for SH64.60 ($19); a six-hour tour to the Canyon of Inscriptions and the Red Canyon for SH85 ($25); a half-day tour to Coral Island in a glass-bottom boat, the fjord, and a visit with Bedouins for SH78.20 ($23); and a three-day tour to Santa Katarina Monastery and Sharm-el-Sheikh for SH374 ($110), plus SH139.40 ($41) for meals and sleeping bags. There's a 20% reduction for children under 12, and a 10% reduction for honeymooners and students on all tours except those to Mount Sinai and Santa Katarina. There are a few other tours offered; check at the office.

Egged Tours also reach out into Sinai. Their one-day coastal tour from Eilat to Sharm-el-Sheikh costs SH102 ($30). The half-day tour of Coral Island and the Fjord region runs SH51 ($15). Children up to the age of 12 and students with an ISSTA card pay 20% less on both Sinai tours. All the buses are air-conditioned.

One of the very best ways of not only seeing but getting to know Sinai is through the **Society for the Protection of Nature in Israel,** 4 Hashfela St., Tel Aviv, tel. 03-335063. Special nature-lover tours are organized, often using large, heavy-duty, refurbished trucks. Yearly membership fee is $10, and the prices that are usually quoted do not include food or sleeping equipment (which can be rented for each tour). All the guides are experts—many live in the Sinai. They will lead you through wadis and canyons, across high sandstone mountains shaped into strange erosive formations, mountains that are pink, ochre, red, white, and green, and that reach 8,500 feet into a cloudless sky. You will be taken to coral reefs endowed with some of the world's most exquisite marine life. At night you sleep under the stars. Tours range from two-and-a-half to nine days; some include full board, some you bring your own food; some are kosher, some not; some are easy, some rugged and difficult. Find one that suits your needs best.

3. Meals and Accommodations

MEALS: Sharm-el-Sheikh or Ophira (take your pick) is not yet a culinary paradise, but the mere fact that eating places exist here is a small miracle. Just to get the names straight: the airport of Sharm-el-Sheikh is called Ophir, a residential area is named Ophira, and Na'ama is a vacation area on the bay.

The new **Fisherman's Village,** just a few miles south of Neviot in the area of el-Muzzeina Bedouin, offers all the fried fish (of various kinds) you can eat, plus salad and wine or a soft drink for SH20.40 ($6). Open for lunch and dinner. You can also swim here, though there is no lifeguard is on duty.

Then there is the **Simona Milk Bar,** in the Ophira Commercial Center, tel. 057-99235, open from 9 a.m. to 1 p.m. and 4 p.m. to 1 a.m. There are colored sun umbrellas on the patio outside and a wood-finished bar on the second floor. Taped music is played. Humus and tchina in a pitta is SH2 (60¢), ice cream is SH1.50 (45¢) and up.

The **Karchon Buffet,** tel. 057-99231, also in the Commercial Center, is open from 7:30 a.m. to midnight and has a light dairy menu listing such items as cakes for SH1.50 (45¢) to SH2 (60¢), sandwiches from SH2 (60¢), milk-shakes for SH4 ($1.20), humus and salads for SH2.50 (75¢).

The last eatery in the Commercial Center is the **Tiran** and it has staggered hours—7–10 a.m., noon–3 p.m., 6–9 p.m. A good Israeli breakfast costs SH8 ($2.35); main course meat meals of chicken, liver, turkey, or hamburger with extras run SH9 ($2.65). For SH12.50 ($3.65) you can purchase a box lunch of vegetables, fruit, chicken, chips, and humus. The restaurant is large, high-ceilinged, air-conditioned, and it seats up to 100 people.

ACCOMMODATIONS: You can stay in Sinai totally free—the stars form a canopy, the sea is your antechamber, and the wind provides total air conditioning. But for those of us who prefer a bed to a sand dune, here are some alternatives:

Moving in the direction of Eilat, there's a holiday village at an oasis. **Neviot** is located at Nuweiba, and it has 85 rooms which have running water, showers and air conditioning. Single occupancy costs SH104.04 ($30.60), double occupancy SH86 ($25.30) per person, those prices including half-board. There is considerable greenery around Nuweiba. In contrast with the stark mountains behind you, there are flowers and vegetables growing everywhere. It is also the principal site of the main Sinai Bedouin tribe, the el-Muzzeina. In addition to free films, Neviot offers guests a variety of reasonably priced tours, including a seven-day diving course, diving seafaris, and more. Guests of the Neviot Village also get free use of tennis and basketball courts, free trips in a glass-bottom boat, kayaks, snorkel and wind-surfing equipment, etc. Skin-diving equipment can be rented.

Cliff Top Village Motel, P.O.B. 29, Ophira, tel. 057-99333, has 27 very clean air-conditioned rooms, all carpeted and quite attractive. It's quite new, having opened in September of 1977. Rates for a room with toilet and private shower are SH78.20 ($23) single, SH102 ($30) double; meals are about $8 each. As the owners are Americans, English is, of course, spoken. There's a rustic restaurant on the premises where meals are served, and a disco/bar nightly.

Israel's newest, most modern and beautiful hostel opened in Ophira in 1976. It's called the **Louis Price Youth Hostel,** tel. 057-99288, and it offers air-conditioned dorms and family rooms at Youth Hostel prices. Details in the next chapter.

Finally, the **Aquamarine International Diving Club Nautic Center,** Na'ama Bay, Sharm-el-Sheikh, tel. 057-99237, has a motel where full board costs SH102 ($30) per person, half-board SH74.80 ($22). During June, July, and August, students get a 25% reduction.

Chapter XI

ISRAELI ADVENTURES

1. Hitchhiking
2. Offbeat Accommodations
3. Adventure Activities
4. Remote Sights
5. Language Schools

ALL OF ISRAEL is an adventure, true. But it also offers adventurous adventures, if you know what we mean. You don't . . . well, how about jumping on a horse and hot-footing it over to a Bedouin tent for a cup of coffee? Or dunking in a mineral bath for a special underwater massage? Or joining an archeological dig? Or being adopted by a school of Red Sea fish? Or hitchhiking, or camping, or hosteling? Or taking a live-in language course so you'll be able to come up with something more original than *shalom?*

Tantalizing? Read on.

1. Hitchhiking

'Afoot and lighthearted I take to the open road,
Healthy, free, the world before me,
The long brown path before me leading wherever
I choose . . .'

When Walt Whitman wrote these lines, he might have been composing an anthem to hitching in Israel (and not to hiking from Brooklyn to Montauk Point). For in his verse lives the spirit of hitching in Israel, an adventurous, economical, and generally safe practice for the young.

Hitchhiking in Israel is called "tramping," and the method of solicitation is unique. Forget about sticking your thumb out. The procedure here consists of holding your arm out stiffly to your side with the forefinger pointed toward the ground as if notifying the driver precisely where to stop.

Unlike certain countries in Europe, vandals and highway robbers haven't yet made it unsafe for an Israeli driver to give a hitchhiker a ride. Consequently, you won't have to wait very long until someone stops, for hitching is an old and widely accepted means of transportation in Israel, where, until recent years, motorized movement was at a premium. Remember, however, that soldiers always have priority, and that you'll invariably find them, as competition, hitching along the main roads.

Be sure, by the way, to wear a hat while you're out hitching. The sun beats down awfully hard while you're waiting for a car to stop. And though it's safer in Israel than anywhere else in the world for women hitching alone, there's still the occasional molester—best to get a partner if possible.

2. Offbeat Accommodations

YOUTH HOSTELS: Age is no barrier, nor is membership, when you want to stay at one of Israel's 32 comfortable and well-scattered hostels. They offer real rock-bottom prices and friendly welcomes to all. Clean, well tended, usually modern, and with kosher kitchens, they're highly thought of in these parts, even if some of them enforce the youth hostel hours strictly: arrive by 5 p.m., lights out by 11 p.m., quiet till 6 a.m., checkout by 7–8 a.m., and offices closed between 9 a.m. and 5 p.m. Usually the maximum stay at any given hostel is three days, but this can be extended with the manager's approval.

Only hostels bearing the triangular sign are authorized by the Israel Youth Hostels Association. It is advisable to book in advance.

Having a youth hostel membership card does give you certain advantages —like better rates at the hostels, plus discounts at some restaurants, national parks, historical sites, museums, and on buses and trains. In Jerusalem the **Israel Youth Hostels Association** is located at 3 Dorot Rishonim St., P.O.B. 1075, tel. 02-225925. Tel Aviv address is 32 Bnei Dan St., P.O.B. 22078, tel. 03-455042. You're welcome to write here for detailed membership data, and for information on present offerings of the **Youth Travel Bureau.** You can also check your home town for a branch of the association, or write for data to American Youth Hostels, Inc., National Campus, Delaplane, Va. 22025.

Prices at hostels vary slightly for members and non-members. In the figures to follow, the higher price is for non-members. Overnight fees are $2.80 to $3.80; if you want a small room with up to four beds rather than the larger dorm arrangements, it's $3.40 to $4.50. In the self-service kitchens, there's a 30¢ fee to cover gas used for cooking, per person, per meal. Most hostels provide cooking utensils only; you bring along your own plates, cups, cutlery and towels. Meals go for the following rates: breakfast is about $1.30, light lunch or supper $1.60 to $1.80, lunch or supper with meat or fish $2.50 to $3. As you can see, the prices are hard to beat, as are the friendships made in these places.

Note: Not all youth hostels take foreign currency, and it's a good idea to check availability of space (especially in summer months) before arriving.

The Israel Youth Hostels Association also has 14-, 21-, and 28-day bargain-priced tours; inquire at the Jerusalem office.

Following is a rundown of the country's hostels.

In or Near Jerusalem

Louise Waterman Wise Hostel—Jerusalem, Bayit Ve'gan Quarter, 8 Pisgah Rd., tel. 02-423366, 02-420990. Adopted as a project of the Women's Division of the American Jewish Congress, it has 250 beds, hot showers, central heating, a self-service kitchen, and also provides three daily meals. There's a beautiful new wing with lecture halls, a library, and a music studio. Buses 12, 18, 20, 24, and 6/2, Mt. Herzl stop.

Ein Kerem Hostel—P.O. Box 17013, Jerusalem, tel. 02-416282; in Ein Kerem, just 15 minutes from the L.W. Wise Hostel via bus 6/2. This one has 90 beds, hot showers, heating, and provides meals if ordered in advance. Set in a flower garden in front of the woods, Ein Kerem offers superb mountain views.

Jerusalem Forest Youth Recreation Center—P.O. Box 3353, Jerusalem, tel. 02-416060, overlooks Ein Kerem, but there's limited public transportation. For groups only, it has excellent facilities which include a swimming pool, restaurants, classrooms, libraries, a 240-person-capacity building and stone bungalows with 100 double bunks in total. The hostel has hot showers, heating, and offers three meals daily.

Beit Bernstein—1 Keren Hayesod St., Jerusalem, tel. 02-228286. This one has 95 beds, heating, hot showers, and provides two meals a day. There is a supermarket across the street, and a coffee house on the premises open from 8:30 a.m. to 5:30 p.m. and 7 to 11 p.m. A library and grapevine-covered terrace are other pluses. Various entertainment is offered free most nights. Friday night dinners are conducted in a religious atmosphere, and you will not be admitted as a guest from Friday afternoon till Saturday evening or the eves of holidays. Buses 4, 7, 9, 15 and 22.

Ramot Shapiro Beit Meir—P.O. Box 7216, Jerusalem, tel. 02-913291; in the Judean Hills, 20 kms west of Jerusalem and reached via five daily buses from Shoeva junction. Offers 150 beds, including family accommodations, self-service kitchen, hot showers, heating, and three meals if ordered in advance. Hostellers must arrive before the Sabbath or Jewish holidays, and have regard for the sacredness of these days. It's used largely for groups, so phone ahead to make sure there's room.

Moreshet Yahadut Hostel (Jewish Heritage Hostel)—in the rebuilt Jewish Quarter of the Old City, P.O.B. 7880, tel. 02-288661. Accommodations for *groups only* in 70-bed dormitory facilities. Breakfast and light evening meals are served. Respect of Sabbath and Jewish holidays requested.

Kfar Etzion—tel. 02-942477; 22 kms south of Jerusalem, halfway between Bethlehem and Hebron, reached by buses from Jerusalem or Bethlehem. It has 150 beds, heating, a self-service kitchen, all meals, and hot showers, but is also for *groups only*. Unless you're already staying there, you can't get in from Friday afternoon to Saturday evening, and the same afternoon-before rule applies to Jewish holidays.

Bar Giora—tel. 02-911073; 22 kms southwest of Jerusalem, reached via buses from Jerusalem on the Ein Kerem–Bet Govrin highway. Attached to the immigrant village of Bar Giora, it has 250 beds, family accommodations, heating, hot showers, self-service kitchen, and provides all meals. Often used for school outings.

Haezrachi Hostel—Kiryat Anavim, tel. 02-539770, 12 kms west of Jerusalem. In the heart of an extensive wooded area, it's on the grounds of Kibbutz Kiryat Anavim and has family accommodations among its 80 beds, plus self-service kitchen, hot showers; serves meals if ordered in advance. It's used mainly by groups, so call first. Take the Inter-Urban bus.

Jerusalem hostels tend to be crowded all year round and overcrowded during July and August. If you arrive and find them all full, call the Israel Youth Hostels Association, tel. 02-225925; sometimes they can arrange for emergency hostels to open their doors.

In the Galilee Area

Tel Hai—Upper Galilee, 60 kms north of Tiberias, tel. 067-40043. Has 190 beds, including family accommodations; self-service kitchen, hot showers; all meals are provided. There are seven two-bedded rooms with private shower and toilet, and refrigerator; they cost SH32 ($9.40) a night for two people. The adjacent Anne Frank House serves as a cultural center for the district and guests.

Bet Benjamin—in Safed, tel. 067-31086. Has 160 beds, family rooms, hot showers, and self-service kitchen. Perched on a hill with a view of the Sea of Galilee, it is served by buses or can be reached after a 15-minute walk from the Egged Station. No meals are served, but there are restaurants nearby in town.

Nature Friends Hostel—Rosh Pinna, tel. 067-37086; 26 kms north of Tiberias and 10 kms east of Safed. Good base for trips to Galilee, the Jordan's sources, and Golan Heights. Fully equipped, it has 100 beds, family accommodations, self-service kitchen, and heating. Breakfast is obligatory, dinner served if ordered in advance.

Yoram Hostel—at Karei Deshe, Mobile Post Korazim, tel. 067-20601; 17 kms north of Tiberias, in a beautiful park right on the banks of the Sea of Galilee. Near Tabgha site, Capernaum, Korazim, and the Mt. of Beatitudes; bus stops on the Tiberias–Rosh Pinna highway. Fully equipped, including air conditioning; has 185 beds; serves all meals.

Taiber Hostel—P.O. Box 232, Tiberias, tel. 067-50050; in Poria, above the Sea of Galilee. The bus from Tiberias takes you within 1½ miles, then you walk. With 140 beds, it's fully equipped and has a splendid view of the lake and valley. Family rooms, self-service kitchen, breakfast and dinner. A recreation building was recently added. Highly recommended.

Meyouhas Hostel—in the center of town on corner of Alhadif and Yarden Sts., P.O.B. 81, Tiberias, tel. 067-21775. The hostel is located opposite the central post office, has 235 beds, mostly in family rooms of three or four beds. Some of the rooms are air-conditioned; hot showers, self-service kitchen, TV room, lecture room, music room. Films are shown occasionally, and three meals a day are provided.

Hispit Youth Hostel—near Ramat Magshimim in the Golan Heights, tel. 067-21655, is a religious settlement; you must register before the Sabbath or religious holidays. It has 18 small rooms with 100 beds, kitchen, toilets and showers for every three rooms. Meals must be ordered in advance. There's bus transportation from Tiberias and Rosh Pinna.

In and Around Haifa

Hankin Hostel—Mobile Post Gilboa, 10 kms east of Afula, tel. 065-81660, in the Jezreel Valley, bordering Maayan Harod National Park, where there's swimming. Some rooms are air-conditioned, 150 beds. It is a ten-minute walk from the bus stop.

Kiryat Tivon—17 kms east of Haifa, at 12 Alexander Zaid St., tel. 04-931482, near the bus stop; buses from Haifa (73, 74, 75). Has 100 beds, family rooms, and self-service kitchen. Breakfast and supper served if ordered in advance. This hostel is of the no-frills variety.

Yad Layad—a short distance north from the seaside town of Nahariya, tel. 04-921343. Has 254 beds, hot showers, serves three meals and has family accommodations and self-service kitchen. Good swimming nearby at Achziv National Park. Frequent bus service to Nahariya.

Carmel Hostel—Mobile Post Hof Hacarmel, tel. 04-531944, 8 kms south of Haifa (bus 45) on the Tel Aviv–Haifa highway. It is a ten-minute walk from the highway bus stop and more than a 20-minute walk from the municipal beach. Has 360 beds, family accommodations, hot showers, self-service kitchen, lunch can be ordered in advance, marvelous sea views, laundry, sports facilities. High recommendation.

Acco Youth Hostel—P.O. Box 1090, near the lighthouse in the Old City at Acre, tel. 04-911982; local bus 2 will take you there. Has 120 beds, family accommodations, hot showers, self-service kitchen, and serves all meals. Swimming at the municipal beach Hof Argaman. It is a ten-minute drive from Nahariya and half an hour from Haifa. Guests are advised not to leave the grounds after dark.

In the Tel Aviv Area

Emek Hefer Hostel—at Kfar Vitkin, tel. 053-96032, 40 kms north of Tel Aviv. The hostel is situated in a green area of lawns and trees. There are family rooms, hot showers and a self-service kitchen; during July and August (when the hostel doubles as a children's camp) meals are obtained in main dining room only. The rest of the year breakfast and supper are served if ordered in advance. There's swimming at the Beit Yannai Beach a short distance across the highway.

Tel Aviv Hostel—at 32 Bnei Dan St. (P.O.B. 22078), tel. 03-455042, opposite the municipal park on the banks of the Yarkon River. The hostel is well equipped, offers three meals a day, hot showers, some rooms with air conditioning. There is an evening of singing and dancing once or twice a week. Take bus 5 or 25.

Yad Labanim Hostel—P.O.B. 786, in Petah Tikva, tel. 03-926666, eight miles northeast of Tel Aviv; take bus 51 or 62, bus 249 from Ben-Gurion Airport, bus 75 from the bus station in Petah Tikva. Breakfast is included in your overnight fee; lunch and supper can be ordered in advance. The hostel is set in a lovely flower garden, rooms have two to eight bunks and electric heaters.

In the Negev

Beit Yatziv Hostel—P.O.B. 7, Ha'atzmauth St., Beersheba, tel. 057-77444. Located on the main road north of Beersheba, it is a short walk from the center of things. The hostel has family accommodations, a self-service kitchen, serves three meals a day, and has hot showers.

Beit Noam Hostel—P.O.B. 2, Mitzpe Ramon, tel. 057-88443. It is situated near the Ramon Canyon (Machtesh Ramon) which overlooks the ruler-straight road leading to Eilat. The hostel has 160 beds, and offers family accommodations, hot showers, three meals a day, and kitchen facilities. It is a good starting point for tours to the Nabatean city of Avdat and the Ein Avdat spring.

Beit Blau-Weiss Hostel—P.O.B. 34, Arad, tel. 057-97150. Named for a Central European Zionist youth movement, and situated in one of the youngest towns in Israel, it is an ideal starting point for desert hikes to Masada and the Dead Sea. Has 250 beds, a self-service kitchen, hot showers, family accommodations, sports facilities, swimming; serves three meals a day.

Isaac H. Taylor Hostel—Mobile Post Dead Sea, tel. 057-90649. At the foot of Masada, it is 90 kms from Beersheba via Arad, 42 kms from Arad, 90 kms from Beersheba via Sodom, and 97 kms from Jerusalem via the new road. It is air-conditioned and has hot showers. A current renovation is adding new facilities. Highly recommended.

Beit Sara Youth Hostel—Mobile Post Dead Sea, tel. 057-90871. Near Ein Gedi, Roman ruins, and an excavation of a third-century A.D. synagogue, it is 400 meters below sea level in a verdant oasis with sweet-water pools. Well kept and homey, it has air-conditioned family accommodations, serves three meals daily, offers swimming, and use of the self-service kitchen. Buses come from Beersheba via Arad and from Jerusalem.

Youth Hostel—P.O.B. 152, Eilat, tel. 059-2358. Air-conditioned, it offers two meals a day, if ordered in advance, and self-service kitchen facilities. No family accommodations. Swimming, skin-diving and boating in the Red Sea. Scheduled for total renovation by 1981.

Louis Price Youth Hostel, Ophira, tel. 057-99288, is Israel's newest, most modern and beautiful hostel. Built high above a coral reef, with a splendid view of the Sinai mountains and the bay. There are 120 beds in air-conditioned rooms; it's in walking distance of the beach, supermarket, cafes, post office. Flippers, snorkels, and masks can be rented. Rates are a bit higher at this youth hostel showplace. Members pay $4 a night, non-members $5; breakfast is $1.50, lunch $2, and meat or fish dinner $3.50. Write far in advance for reservations, especially in summer and on holidays.

CHRISTIAN HOSPICES: As we mentioned earlier, there are no better bargains than the Christian hospices which dot the country from north to center. We've listed some under their respective locations throughout the book. Additional information can be obtained from the Ministry of Tourism, Christian Information Centre, Omar Ibn El Khatab Square, Jaffa Gate, P.O.B. 14308, Jerusalem, tel. 02-287647; or by writing the hospices directly.

With the latter consideration in mind, we're now providing you with a list of hospices in the country.

Jerusalem

St. Charles Hospice, German Colony, P.O.B. 28020, tel. 02-37737.
Sisters of the Rosary, 14 Agron St., P.O.B. 54, tel. 02-228529.
Ratisbonne, 26 Shmuel Hanagid St., P.O.B. 768, tel. 02-227068; and Ratisbonne Monastery, same address, tel. 02-223847.
Dom Polski, near Damascus Gate, Old City, tel. 02-282017.
White Sisters (Franciscains de Marie), Nablus Rd., P.O.B. 19049, tel. 02-282633.
St. George Hostel, Nablus Rd. and Saladin St., P.O.B. 19018, tel. 02-283302.
Evangelical Lutheran Hostel, Old City, St. Marks St., P.O.B. 14051, tel. 02-282120.
Maison d'Abraham, Mount of Offense, P.O.B. 19680, tel. 02-284591.
St. Andrews Hospice, near the railway station, P.O.B. 14216, tel. 02-717701.
Casa Nova, P.P. Franciscains, 10 Casa Nova St., Old City, P.O.B. 1321, tel. 02-282791.
Christ Church Hospice, Jaffa Gate, P.O.B. 14037, tel. 02-282082.
Ecce Homo Convent, Via Dolorosa, P.O.B. 19056, tel. 02-282445.

Tiberias

Ospizio Monte di Beatitudine, Mt. of Beatitudes, P.O.B. 87, Doar-Na, Hevel Korazim, tel. 067-20878.
Terra Sancta, Old Town (on the shore of the Sea of Galilee), P.O.B. 179, tel. 067-20516.
Franciscan Sisters, P.O.B. 207, tel. 067-20782.
Peniel-by-Galilee, P.O.B. 192, tel. 067-20685.
Church of Scotland Centre, P.O.B. 104, tel. 067-20144.

Mount Tabor

Franciscan Convent of Transfiguration, Mt. Tabor, tel. 067-67489.

Nazareth

St. Charles Borromaeus, 316 12th St., tel. 065-54435.
St. Joseph Seminary, P.O.B. 99, tel. 065-54224.
Religieuses de Nazareth, Casa Nova, P.O.B. 274, tel. 065-54304.
Casa Nova Hospice, P.O.B. 198, tel. 065-71367.
Franciscan Sisters of Mary, P.O.B. 41, tel. 065-54071.

CAMPING SITES: Beautiful, interesting sites, and good facilities—plus low tariffs—mark Israel's well-scattered and well-tended camping sites. And at these fresh-air places you're not restricted to tents, but can choose to live in a rather romantic thatched hut or caravan, complete with electricity. Modern showers and conveniences are always nearby, and kiosks supplement or provide all your food needs. There's usually good transportation to each location.

Wherever the sites are, their prices are the same, per person or per vehicle. All camps have day and night watchman service, bonfire sites, picnic areas, garbage collection, lighted pathways, full sanitary facilities, bus connections, and a camp office.

During July, August, on weekends, and on holidays, adults with their own equipment pay SH6.50 ($2.50) a night, children up to age 13 SH3.40 ($1); a bed in a rented tent is SH8.50 ($2.50); a bungalow with two beds is SH40.80 ($12), SH54.40 ($16) with three beds, SH64.60 ($19) with four beds; a caravan with four beds is SH81.60 ($24), SH100.30 ($29.50) with six beds. You can avoid paying VAT if you pay in foreign currency. There's a minimum three-day charge on Rosh Hashanah and Shavouth. Rates at other than the above-indicated times are lower.

Some camping sites offer mobile homes—fully furnished units with a living room, two bedrooms, kitchen, bath, and toilet. These can accommodate up to six people. Bed linens are supplied, but no kitchen utensils. Rates are SH100 ($29.40) to SH120 ($35.30) per night for four people, SH15 ($4.40) a night for each additional person.

Package deals including airport transfers, auto rentals, etc., are available. Contact the **Israel Camping Union**, P.O.B. 53, Nahariya, tel. 04-923366 (or in New York, U.S. Student Travel Service, 801 Second Ave., New York, N.Y. 10017, tel. 212/223-7732) for rates, literature and further information.

As of this writing the sites include:

Tal, owned by the Upper Galilee Regional Council and the National Parks Authority, Post Kiryat Shmona, tel. 067-40400. Near Tiberias and Kibbutz Hagroshrim, it's a good spot for seeing the Galilee, Safed, Baniyas, the Jordan River, and Mt. Hermon. Open all year round (though a bit wet, cold, and dreary in winter), it accommodates cars and trailers, has tents and cabins, and a restaurant, plus cooking facilities, refrigerators, and sinks. There are hot and cold showers, telephones, gas pumps, a children's playground, and a provisions store. Campers here can swim and fish.

Lehman, owned by Moshav Lehman, Mobile Post W/Galilee, tel. 04-926206, is near Haifa and affords good touring of the Western Galilee, the Mediterranean, and Grotto Sulam Tzor. Open year round, it offers diving and fishing, a playground for children, a lounge for guests, a refrigerator for them, a provisions store and a kosher restaurant.

Achziv, owned by Sulam Tzor Regional Council, Mobile Post W/Galilee, tel. 04-921792, is in the same area as the above and is open April through October or November. One of the better-equipped sites, it has fishing, swimming, diving, a playground, and a kosher self-service restaurant. In addition to regular camping facilities, there are ten mobile homes.

Ein Gev campsite is owned by Kibbutz Ein Gev, Post Ein Gev, tel. 067-50167. Near Tiberias, Al-Hama, Sea of Galilee, Tabgha, Mt. of Beatitudes, and Capernaum, it is open all year. Ein Gev has straw bungalows, mobile homes, an area for pitching tents, and caravans—all on an excellent beach. And the nearby kibbutz has one of the area's finest restaurants.

Ha'on, owned by T.H.M. Co., Ltd., Haon, Mobile Post, Jordan Valley, tel. 067-50444, is near Ein Gev's location and is open April through October. Here there are bungalows, a restaurant, and swimming, as well as the usual facilities.

Ma'agan, owned by the kibbutz of the same name, Mobile Post Jordan Valley, tel. 067-50360, is in the same area as Ein Gev, has a restaurant, a sandy beach, and refrigerators. Open April to November. Ma'agan has mobile homes.

Ein Gedi, under the management of Production and Development, Mobile Post, Dead Sea, tel. 057-90264, is a more recently opened campsite. It's situated about 3½ miles from the famous sulphur springs in Ein Gedi. Open year round, it consists of 20 mobile homes, tent sites, and rows of four-bedded rooms with air conditioning, hot water, and kitchenettes with refrigerators. A self-service restaurant is nearby.

Harod belongs to the Gilboa Regional Council and the National Parks Authority, Post Gidona, tel. 065-81777, 81660. At Mt. Gilboa, it's within easy reach of the Jezreel Valley, Beth Shean, Nazareth, Genin, and Gan-Hashloshah. Open year round, it has a wide range of camping facilities, including a restaurant. There's swimming in a natural pool at the campsite.

Neveh-Yam is owned by Neveh-Yam Kibbutz, M.P. Hof HaCarmel, tel. 04-942236, and is near Caesarea, Athlit, Elijah's Cave, Ein Hod, Mt. Carmel, and it's right on the Mediterranean. Open all year (you can stay in winter, but there are no provisions), it offers the works and a playground.

Beth Zayit, owned by Moshav Beth Zayit, Mobile Post Harei-Yehuda, tel. 02-527929, is situated about four miles west of Jerusalem near Kibbutz Kiryat Anavim and Kibbutz Ma'ale Hahamisha. Open all year. There are bungalows for rent, a playground for children, a swimming pool, restaurant, and provisions store, plus refrigerator boxes and cooking gas containers.

Mevo Beitar Moshav, 11 miles southwest of Jerusalem, tel. 02-912474, is new (opened in 1979). There are tents, bungalows, and mobile homes, as well as a swimming pool and a place to buy groceries.

Ramat Rachel, owned by Kibbutz Ramat Rachel, P.O.B. 98, tel. 02-715712, is about 1½ miles from the center of Jerusalem. No caravans or tents here—just bungalows. There's a swimming pool, a restaurant, and a place to buy groceries.

Ashkelon is owned by Ashkelon Regional Council and the National Parks Authority, P.O.B. 5052, tel. 051-25228. Near Yad Mordechai, it's on the Mediterranean, open year round, and has all possible facilities.

Neveh-Zohar, owned by Tamar Regional Council, Post Sodom, tel. 057-90906, is right on the Dead Sea near Masada, Sodom, Ein Gedi, and the Judean Desert. It offers everything except fishing, lounge, boating, diving, or tent rental. Open the year round.

Eilat is owned by Ya'alat, Sun Bay Hotel, P.O.B. 22, Eilat, tel. 059-2362. It's within easy reach of King Solomon's Pillars, the underwater world of the Red Sea, and of course the desert. Open year round, it has a lounge but no provisions store; a sandy beach, fishing, boating and diving, but no gas, no tents to rent, and no refrigerators.

Kfar Hittim, Post Tiberias, tel. 067-92921. Two miles from Tiberias and owned by Moshav Hittim, it is an easy distance from all the sites on and near the Sea of Galilee. Open from April to October it is well equipped—close to a swimming pool, outdoor cinema, and playground.

3. Adventure Activities

HORSEBACK RIDING: There's an honest-to-goodness dude ranch, **Vered HaGalil,** in the Upper Galilee, tel. 067-37785. At the Korazim–Almago cross-road between Tiberias and Rosh Pinna, it is easily reached by car or bus. And whether you arrive in a limousine or attached to a backpack, you'll be welcomed just the same by owner Yehuda Avni, a Chicago boy who came to fight in the late 1940s, stayed on to give kibbutz life a whirl, finally dreamed up this place and settled down for good. Yehuda and his wife Yonah (fantastic cook!) run a relaxed and informal place, calm and serene. Aside from the rustic accommodations and American-style cooking, horseback riding is the big attraction here, for beginners as well as skillful riders.

Yehuda offers trail rides by the hour, day, or week, into the hills or down toward the Sea of Galilee. Up into the hills means Safed, Tel Hai, across kibbutz fields, along wadis (dried-up creek beds), over slopes strewn with black basalt rock, and through Arab villages. One of the best rides stops at an Arab village where the mukhtar (village chief) serves you lunch. Trips heading downwards stop at the Mount of the Beatitudes, Migdal, Tabgha, and Capernaum, and usually there's a break when you tie up your horse under a eucalyptus tree and go for a swim in the Sea of Galilee. Other planned tours last several days, exploring places such as Nazareth, and combining camping or hotel overnights with Arab meals and scenic extremes.

Yehuda tends to wax poetic about his rides: "When a tiny black speck in the distance becomes a Bedouin tent where you're welcome to dismount and have coffee; when a winding trail suddenly opens up into the fertile valley of Ginosar; when you're riding through the vineyards along the ridge overlooking the sky-blue Sea of Galilee and you suddenly understand why the Sermon on the Mount was given here . . . well, then you know you're visiting the Galilee as it should be visited, on horseback."

There's always something new in the offing. "We haven't ridden all the trails, yet," says Yehuda, "so we're always ready to be flexible, fill up the saddlebags with provisions, and just go out and explore new trails."

If you're a cowboy more in spirit than capability, the ring is the place for you. Here you can learn everything from holding on for dear life, to cantering prettily, to jumping like a pro. Your teacher may just be Yehuda's son Ranaan, who learned his skills in an English riding school.

The dozen or so horses here are Arabian, fine stock with temperaments suited to riders' preferences. Yehuda's prize purebred was acquired from a West Bank (formerly Jordanian) family that's bred this stock for some 500 years. The little folk have the Shetland pony all to themselves.

Horseback riding will cost you the following: SH10.20 ($3) for a half-hour, SH68 ($20) for a half-day on the trail, SH112.20 ($33) for an entire day with lunch. All rides are accompanied by guides.

In addition to the stables, Vered Hagalil has rooms for changing and showers, an outdoor grill, picnic tables, a rustic restaurant, and a bar and grill.

There are also accommodations for 28 persons in beautiful double-roomed stone cottages that look like Swiss chalets. We have been here often, and we recommend it highly. Cost per night per person varies from SH68 ($20) to SH122.40 ($36) for a couple. Up to two children can be accommodated in the cottages for an additional charge of SH34 ($10) per youngster.

The restaurant, though expensive, is certainly one of the best in Israel and, for the American palate, it's a dream. A meal consisting of real chicken-in-the-basket, lemon meringue pie, and old-fashioned Yankee coffee costs SH24 ($7.05).

Incidentally, if you want to economize on the accommodations, there are bunk-house beds to rent for SH34 ($10) an evening, breakfast included. Students can bring sleeping bags and camp free on the lawn.

When Avni first began, the whole proposition of horseback riding was in its infancy (except with the Bedouins, of course). Now there is a steady proliferation of stables—about 700 of them—mostly in kibbutzim. Other than the above, notable stables include the **Abir Riding School,** 33 Hakana'im St., Arad, tel. 057-97147; the **Green Beach Ranch,** Green Beach Holiday Village, Netanya, tel. 053-38141; and **Kfar Hanofesh Neve Ativ,** on Mt. Hermon, tel. 067-31103.

Havat Klas, 2 Hamesilah St., Herzlia, no phone, has 15 beautifully groomed horses. You can take lessons on Sunday or Thursday at 4 p.m. for SH20 ($5.90) an hour. Riding tours in the area cost the same.

For further information about horseback riding, write to the Secretary, **Israel Horse Society,** c/o Ministry of Agriculture, Galil Ma'aravi, Doar Na Ashrat, Israel.

In 1966 a bunch of amateur horse-lovers—from the moshavim and kibbutzim, from the cities, even from Bedouin encampments—got together for a fun-and-games competition called the **Sussiyada.** It's now an annual thing and most popular. Check with I.G.T.O. for where/when details, but it's usually held in Afula.

SPAS FOR FUN OR PHYSICAL FITNESS:

SPAS FOR FUN OR PHYSICAL FITNESS: Throughout history, many people have found natural mineral waters physically beneficial in several ways, depending on which minerals were present and to what degree. Fabulous resorts were created at spots where people could "take the cure" or "take the waters"—which meant drinking the stuff, immersing oneself in it, or both. Israel, as it happens, has two historically and internationally known "watering places," otherwise known as spas. As in Europe and other lands, doctors frequently send their patients for treatments in these waters. There must be something to it, or the practice wouldn't have perpetuated since pre-biblical days. Though the whole "watering" bit isn't taken too seriously in the States, it has supposedly been a boon to others medically and cosmetically. Why, even Cleopatra sent her slaves from Egypt to the Dead Sea (they walked!) to bring back jugs of the precious potent waters and muds, so she'd become healthier and even more beautiful. If you're willing to give it a go, head for **Tiberias** and the **Dead Sea.**

Ein Gedi Sulphur Springs

The kibbutz-run Ein Gedi Sulphur Springs, tel. 057-90880, on the shores of the Dead Sea, isn't as posh as the other places, but it's managed by a most likeable kibbutznik. Located in rustic cabin-like structures near Kibbutz Ein Gedi, it is easily accessible by regularly scheduled buses. On the grounds are two buildings, one with four pools for men and women and shower rooms, the other housing the snack bar and two lounge areas. (Please check food and accommodations details in Chapter IX.) There are private beaches along the Dead Sea, pools, and showers.

The waters here are known among spa aficionados for their curative powers for such afflictions as rheumatism, lumbago, back, bone, and muscle problems. Good for common scalp complaints, dandruff included. But the water is too hot and the sulphur content too high to help chronic skin diseases such as psoriasis, and if you have any heart problems, you need a medical certificate stating how long you can stay in the waters. (That's because the waters are 98°, 100°, and 102° hot, and this heat, plus the minerals, which increase the oxygen content in the blood, steps up the pulse rate.)

The heat and minerals are cleansing but tiring, so keep as still as possible, and try not to splash around. Some folks take the treatment for an hour; most stay in for 15 minutes. We found it desirable to surface and perch poolside with legs dangling twice during our watering. There is a large wall clock to remind you of the minutes (most people here have strict instructions), but in case you lose track, the staff of kibbutzniks will pull you out at the right time. Once out you can either shower right away or leave the fine film of minerals and oils clinging to you till bedtime (that's what the Israelis do; they say it's the only way to get the maximum benefit). Whether you shower or not, do your body a favor and reward it with a cool drink and a rest in the lounge area for at least 15 minutes, to slow down your pulse rate. You'll be quite relaxed afterward, ready for a sound sleep. Admission is SH6 ($1.75).

The staff here recommends that you drink 2½ gallons of water a day while in this part of Israel; they're all too familiar with heat sicknesses.

Note: These waters will make a black mess of any jewelry that's silver, copper or white gold.

Zohar Springs

Unlike the waters of Ein Gedi's spa, those at nearby Zohar Springs, tel. 057-90261, can be very helpful for skin diseases like psoriasis. These were Cleopatra's favorite waters for her beauty needs, and today the waters are said to be cleansing for skin and scalp, improving skin texture and even smoothing wrinkles. Experts came out here 16 years ago, investigated the waters, had them analyzed by Hadassah experts, and found that the waters contained the highest mineral content of any waters in the world: 300 grams per liter. "Also, in the baths here," they explain, "you take 10-14% more oxygen than in any other water in the world, and that's more purifying. Tired and nervous people come here for a week and it changes their lives. They calm down, get quieter and more settled."

People with doctors' notes can take advantage of a weight-loss program devised by the local medical team—but the current management prefers to emphasize the strictly curative powers of Zohar Springs. The young professional behind the desk said that the experts here will cater the treatment baths according to what complaints you have—spine, joint, bone, or muscle problems, etc. If you want the whole spa treatment, though, you'll have to have a medical okay. For an on-the-spot check-up, there is a resident physician. You can skip all this by bringing along a note from your own doctor certifying that your blood pressure can stand the stimulation of the waters.

This is quite a luxurious place. It is equipped with a central air-conditioning system, excellent facilities in the sulphur baths and pools, mud baths, vibration and electro-galvanized baths, underwater massages, and cosmetic treatments. Prices are SH14.90 ($4.40) for a mud bath, SH12.40 ($3.65) for an indoor sulphur bath, SH6.80 ($2) for the indoor sulphur pool; SH16.80 ($4.95) for underwater massage; SH17.20 ($5.05) for regular massage; SH7.40 ($2.20) to SH12.40 ($3.65) for vibration baths. The baths are open every day of the week from 7 a.m. to 3 p.m. At both of the above spas it's advisable to check your valuables.

Tiberias Hot Springs

On the shores of the Galilee, Tiberias Hot Springs have been the source of soothing gratification for centuries. Called "medicinal mineral springs," they are said to contain 33 grams of medicinal salt per liter of hyper-thermal water. Tiberias Hot Springs Co., Ltd. runs the show, and you can call them at 067-91967 in Tiberias.

This is by far the largest and most elegantly appointed watering spot in Israel. Aside from doctors and nurses, it employs a huge number of people just to service the crowds who frequent the complex of modern buildings, installations, and conveniences.

Among the offerings are physiotherapy, electro-hydrotherapy, underwater and regular massage, various baths, mud packs, inhalation therapy, mineral pools, and more. There are also indoor and outdoor swimming pools, a restaurant, and a cafeteria on the premises. Prices begin at SH10 ($2.95) for hot spring mineral water pools, SH7.50 ($2.20) for children ages three to ten; prices are 20% higher on Saturdays and holidays. Towels, lockers, bathing suits, and robes can be rented. Open 7 a.m. to 1 p.m. with additional hours in winter from 3 to 5 p.m.; some buildings are closed on Saturday.

SKIN DIVING: The new **Red Sea Divers Center** in Na'ama Bay, tel. 057-99295, has the most up-to-date equipment and facilities. Located on the shore of Na'ama Bay, it has all desirable equipment for rental or sale, as well as dressing rooms, showers, a bar and snack shop, lockers, and an adjacent campground. There is a 50-foot-long diving boat with deck space for 20 divers, 40 air tanks, kitchen and toilet facilities, even stereo tapes. And the center also has four-wheel drive vehicles and motorboats to transport divers to new sites. You can learn diving here, hire the equipment if you already know how (including underwater photography paraphernalia), do archeological diving, night diving, or whatever else divers do.

There's another **Red Sea Divers Center** in Eilat at the Caravan Hotel, Coral Beach, tel. 059-2776.

Also in Na'ama Bay is the **Aquamarine International Diving Club Nautic Center,** tel. 057-99237, where you can rent diving equipment. A full day diving trip with a guide, tank, air refill, weight belt, and regulator—including two dives—costs SH85 ($25) per person. The center supplies a box lunch for SH15.30 ($4.50). They also rent cameras, including movie cameras, for underwater photography.

Lucky Divers Eilat Scuba Center, in the Moriah Hotel, Eilat, tel. 059-5749, and in the Marina Hotel in Na'ama Bay, tel. 057-99365, rents all equipment for diving. For SH197.20 ($58) they offer a package that includes one night's stay at the Marina Hotel, two meals, two dives, a guide, equipment, and transportation; non-divers can take the same package with snorkeling gear for SH153 ($45). Lucky Divers also rents speed boats for fishing, diving, or water skiing.

At the **Aqua Sport International Red Sea Diving Center,** near the La-romme Hotel in Eilat, tel. 059-2788, Willie Halpert, an expert on the sea and its denizens, gives lessons in English, French, German, or Hebrew. Five- to eight-day courses at all levels are in the SH340 ($100) to SH428.40 ($126) range. They also rent equipment and offer tours and underwater safaris.

You can also rent all the requisite equipment at the **Euro-Diving Safari Club** at the Sharm Hotel in Ophira, tel. 057-99226, and the **Sea Sport Center Eilat Ltd.,** at the Fisherman's House, near the Red Rock Hotel, tel. 059-5554. The latter also rents out kayaks, yachts, and water-skiing boats, and offers underwater safaris and fishing trips.

Andromeda Yachting Centre, Old Jaffa Port, tel. 03-827572, conducts diving activities and maintains a diving school in the Old Jaffa Port. They also sell and rent skin-diving equipment in their store on 83 Salame St., corner Herzl St., Tel Aviv, under the name of **Morris Greenberg, Ltd.** They possess a special fully equipped vehicle which carries an air compressor and all necessary diving equipment for driving divers to various sites along the Red Sea coast from Eilat to Na'ama Bay.

A scuba-diving center has been established in Achziv National Park, managed by Mr. Danny Birnbaum, a professional diver and instructor in underwater archeology and a former lecturer in underwater life at Haifa University. All diving gear and equipment can be rented here. For information and rates contact: **Achziv Scuba Diving Center,** c/o Regional Council Sulam Tzor, Mobile Post, Western Galilee, tel. 04-926785.

In addition to the above there is a club in Ashkelon on 45 Hadror St.; in Haifa: the Shikmona Club, 78 Hatichon St., tel. 04-926671; in Achziv, P.O.B. 404, Nahariya, tel. 04-926671; and in the Moon Valley Hotel, Eilat, tel. 059-51111.

Serious divers should also look into package programs offered by hotels in areas where a lot of diving is done.

Finally, enthusiasts may wish to get in touch with the **Federation for Underwater Activities in Israel,** 37 Shtreeker St., Tel Aviv, tel. 03-443785.

Note: Arkia offers divers 20% off regular rates on flights to Eilat and Ophir. . . . Novices must have a chest X-ray and an examination by a medical doctor before they're allowed to dive.

CYCLING: Ever consider seeing Israel on two wheels? **The Israel Cyclists Touring Club,** P.O.B. 339, Kfar Saba, promotes guided tours between March and October. Generally, the tours are eight, nine or 14 days, and packages include bike rental, accommodations, meals, a guide, bus transportation when necessary, entrance fees to sights on the itinerary, and insurance. Contact the I.C.T.C. for further information.

Also check with the **Jerusalem Cyclists' Club,** P.O.B. 7281, Jerusalem, tel. 02-248238. They rent out bicycles for SH34 ($10) a day, and offer low-priced tours with hostel accommodations.

SKIING IN ISRAEL: The snow season in Israel usually begins in December or January and lasts until about mid-April. Skiers should check with the daily newspaper or radio weather reports before starting out. It is advisable to ski on weekdays when the slopes are less crowded.

The Mount Hermon Ski Center, about 40 miles from Tiberias, is located on the northeastern slopes of Israel's highest mountain. From the heights, you'll see all of the Golan, the Upper Galilee, the Hula Valley, Baniyas Springs, and the Crusader fortress. There's parking for 800 vehicles, and on a good, crisp Saturday, that's not enough.

Services offered include: Long-distance cable cars with 76 seats; a ski school under the supervision of experienced international instructors; equipment rental shop; shop for the purchase of ski accessories; facilities such as washrooms, first aid, information desk; baggage storing areas; and a buffet for light meals and drinks. Tel. 067-31103 for general information about the site.

Visitors to Mt. Hermon Ski Center who stay at the **Neve Ativ Holiday Village,** tel. 067-41744, receive free entrance to the ski center, free skiing lessons, and free use of all chair lifts. Accommodations are in member's homes, and all have private toilet and shower. Meals are served in the Guest House dining room, a warm, country-like place with a large fireplace and a picture window overlooking Nimrod Castle, Hula Valley, etc. A disco/bar, swimming pool, and billiard room are other facilities; horse rental is available. Rates, including breakfast, are SH58 ($17.05) Sunday to Wednesday, SH65 ($19.10) per person Thursday to Saturday. Rates with half or full board are available and mandatory in busy season.

Accommodations are available at the following nearby guest houses: **Ayelet Hashachar, Hagoshrim, Kfar Blum, Kfar Giladi,** and **Nof Ginossar.** You can also stay at hotels in Metulla, Qiryat Shmona, Safed, and Tiberias, or youth hostels in Tel Hai, Rosh Pinna, Safed, Karei Desh, Poria, and Tiberias.

HUNTING: The really serious hunters in Israel are the Arabs and Druze, the latter being particularly obsessed by the sport. There is game in the country—duck, hare, partridge, porcupines, wild boar, quail, and even a few wildcats in the Negev—and there are a couple of hunting clubs, like **The Israel Hunters Association** in Tel Aviv and the **Partridge Club** in Haifa. The season runs from September until the end of January and is sometimes extended until March; additional details are available through the I.G.T.O. You must check with the Israeli Consul and apply for your license *before* you come.

ARCHEOLOGICAL DIGS: You can volunteer to work at an archeological dig if you are 18 or older, prepared to stay for at least two weeks, and physically fit and capable of doing strenuous work in a hot climate. You will have to pay your own fare to and from Israel. Most excavations take place between June and October, but there are off-season digs. Lectures are given at some sites, and some offer academic credits for the work. If you'd like to join a dig contact Mrs. Rachel Stolar at the **University of Tel Aviv,** Department of Archeology, Gilman Bldg., Room 225, tel. 03-420417; or the Youth and Student Division of the **Ministry of Tourism,** P.O.B. 1018, Jerusalem, tel. 02-237311, ext. 377; or Mrs. Martha Rettig, Assistant to the Director, Department of Antiquities and Museums, **Ministry of Education and Culture,** P.O.B. 586, Jerusalem, tel. 02-285153. It's best to inquire as far in advance as possible.

ARCHEOLOGICAL SITES AND NATIONAL PARKS: The northernmost park is **Hurshat Tal** near Kiryat Shmona (open from April 1 to September 30). It has an artificial lake fed by the icy waters of the river Dan, and huge oak trees revered by the Moslems. There's a camping site on the grounds. . . . **The Synagogue of Bar'am** near Safed is one of the oldest (second or third century A.D.) and best preserved in the country. Much credit is due to Prof. E. L. Sukenik for his part in its restoration. A lintel of the facade is in the Louvre Museum. . . . The ancient city of **Hazor,** recorded in the Book of

Joshua, is open to the public. Large-scale excavations led by Prof. Yigael Yadin were undertaken from 1955 to 1958 and again in 1968. No less than 21 levels of settlement were uncovered. The fine Hatzor Museum is located at Kibbutz Ayelet Hashachar nearby. . . . The largest park in Israel, comprising 25,000 acres of eucalyptus, pine, and cypress trees, is on the **Carmel Mountain Range.** Entrance is free, points of interest are well marked, and there are picnic and play areas. . . . In Zichron Yaakov, just north of Caesarea, is **Ganei Ramat Hanadiv,** the burial tomb of Baron and Baroness Benjamin Edmond de Rothschild. It's set in beautiful gardens; entrance is free. . . . The park of **Achziv** is on the beach north of Nahariya. Many relics and remains of early settlements have been unearthed, and the little coastal village still clings to a medieval atmosphere. . . . A bit inland is **Yehi'am,** the ruins of a 12th-century Crusader castle. Still standing from the original structure are two lower stories of the large eastern tower. . . . Close to the Sea of Galilee are the **Ancient Synagogues of Hamath Tiberias.** Four main strata, dating from the second century B.C. to the eighth century A.D., have been uncovered. Most interesting are the three mosaic panels. . . . South in the Jordan Valley is **Belvoir,** a 12th-century Crusader castle. The Knights of Belvoir were defeated by Saladin in the crucial battle of the Horns of Hattin in 1187. . . . Farther south is the **Roman Theatre of Beth She'an.** Built to seat 5,000, it is the best preserved and most elaborate Roman structure in Israel. . . . Traveling west you'll find **Gan Hashlosha (Sachne)** at the foot of Mount Gilboa. With its natural pool and gentle waterfalls, it is very popular with Israelis for picnics and family outings. . . . The sixth-century A.D. **Beit Alpha Synagogue** in Heftziba was fully excavated by Prof. E. L. Sukenik, and virtually the entire elaborate mosaic floor is intact. **Ma'ayan Harod,** the site of Gideon's celebrated "water test" (Book of Judges, Chapter VII,) is now a beautiful park wherein a youth hostel.

Megiddo (Armageddon) lies at the head of a mountain pass at the western end of the Jezreel Valley. Commanding a key road between Egypt in the south and Syria and Mesopotamia in the north, its history goes back to 4,000 B.C. Twenty distinct historic periods have been uncovered. The ruins of ancient stables, a grain silo, and a ninth-century water system (which you can walk through, except during winter when it may be closed) are a few of the more spectacular remains. . . . **Beth She'arim** is the site of a remarkable group of catacombs cut into a limestone hill. Its vaulted chambers are ornamented with bas reliefs and frescoes. It was a favored burial place for the Jews after the fall of the Second Temple and the end of the Bar Kochba revolt. . . . **Caesarea,** on the sea about midway between Haifa and Tel Aviv, was a small Phoenician anchorage in the third-century B.C. Built by Herod in honor of the Roman Emperor, it became a great Roman city towards the end of the first century A.D. Crusaders and Byzantines came in turn, each leaving their mark. Of the Roman times, still to be seen are the remains of the bath, aqueduct, hippodrome, and theater (where the summer concerts of the Israel Festival are held). Crusader walls, tower and moat give you a good idea of what it looked like then. . . . **Samaria-Sebaste** was the home of Omri, an ancient king of Israel. Its history too is long and the ruins give evidence of its Israelite, Assyrian, Persian, Greek, Roman, and Christian inhabitants. . . . **Hisham's Palace** in Jericho dates from the Omayyad dynasty. The palace has a two-story living area surrounding a large courtyard, a bath-house with mosaics, bathing rooms, and heating installations. Two mosques and a pool with a decorated tower are within the palace grounds. Most of the excavated finds are on display at the Rockefeller Museum in Jerusalem.

Khirbet Qumran is believed to be the center of the sect (usually identified as Essenes) who wrote the Dead Sea Scrolls. The site has the remains of assembly halls, dining room, kitchen, pools, laundry, watch tower, a pottery, and stable. Of great interest are the desks and inkstands found there and believed to be those used by the scribes in the writing of the scrolls found in the nearby caves. . . . **Ein Hemed (Aqua Bella)**—named, no doubt, for the nearby springs—is the site of a 12th-century Crusader convent. Its remains are formidable and impressive. Today the area is the most attractive recreation, camping, and picnic spot in the Jerusalem region. . . . **Herodion** was one of the several wilderness fortresses built by King Herod. Some of the structures are in a good state of preservation; they show evidence of destruction in great fires and battles and bear out the descriptions of Josephus. Built in the last decade of the first century B.C., was inhabited by Christian Monks in the fifth and sixth centuries. . . . In Ashkelon you will find remnants of history from the Canaanite and Philistine civilizations on. It was one of the five major Philistine cities, mentioned in several places in the Bible; and with the ruins to see, a camping site with all facilities, swimming, and being in all a much favored park, it has something for everyone. A mile to the north of the park is a third-century A.D. frescoed tomb.

Masada would require many a good book to explain. It was the site of a magnificent palace built by Herod about 40 A.D. and the last stronghold of the Jewish rebellion after the fall of Jerusalem in 70 A.D. It should be a must for everyone. . . . **Ein Avdat** is one of nature's surprises. In the hot, sandy central Negev is the icy spring. It lies at the foot of a canyon that splits the plateau beneath the Nabatean acropolis of Avdat, which guarded the caravan route from the Red Sea to the Mediterranean. The city was founded in the third century B.C., and the handsome ruins show what a high civilization it must have been. The vast irrigation systems indicate extensive agricultural development. . . . The ruins of another Nabatean city, **Mamphis (Kurnub),** are to be found midway between Beersheba and Sodom. Excavations have unearthed several large groups of handsome buildings with halls, courts and balconies, and walls of finely dressed stone, skillfully constructed arches and well-formed columns and capitals. Mamphis dates from about the same time as Avdat. . . . **Shivta (Subeita)** is the site of yet another Nabatean city, established in the first century A.D. Much is to be seen here of the Nabateans' successors, the Byzantines, among them three churches of the fifth and sixth centuries.

A few of these sites and parks are free; where admission is charged it ranges from SH2 (60¢) to SH6 ($1.75) for an adult, SH1 (30¢) to SH2.20 (65¢) for a student or child. You can also get a SH11.90 ($3.50) ticket which admits you to any site during a 14-day period. All sites, with the exception of Masada, are open daily as follows: April to September from 8 a.m. to 5 p.m.; October to March from 8 a.m. to 4 p.m.; on Friday and holiday eves they close one or two hours earlier; all sites and parks are closed on Yom Kippur. Visiting hours for Masada are 7:30 a.m. to 3:30 p.m.

FOR NATURE-LOVERS—HIKING AND OTHER ACTIVITIES: On a
plateau above David's Spring—the oasis of Ein Gedi—there's a cluster of bright modern buildings that house the **Ami Asaf Field School.** This isn't a regular tourist stop, but you're welcome to have a look around—and by all means ask about the hiking tours. The hikes are ordinarily organized for Israeli high school students, but there are occasional hikes for others as well. You can call 057-90118 to see if there's anything planned, or simply ask when you stop by. Though arrangements usually have to be made in advance, the staff here is very accommodating to drop-ins.

There are several hikes available, and they last anywhere from one to eight hours. One hike covers the length of David's Spring and takes in the Shulamite waterfall, another goes to Mount Jesse, another to the Ein Gedi Observation Point, and there were four others on the agenda last time we stopped by. You'll learn a great deal about the desert on these walks—everything from, geology to plant and animal life, archeology, religion, and history.

But if you're not able to join one of the hikes, do take a look at the small museum on the grounds. In the school's main building, it houses a fascinating collection of stuffed birds and creatures of the desert, a model of the recently excavated Tel Goren, showing the town as it was during the Chalcolithic Period (4,000 B.C.), as well as finds and curiosities from this excavation.

Joining **The Society for the Protection of Nature in Israel,** 4 Hashfela St., Tel Aviv, tel 03-335063, is a wonderful way to discover Israel with Israelis, and we highly recommend that you do so. A yearly membership is about $10. Most of the guiding is in Hebrew, but guides and members alike often speak English and other languages. There are walking tours involving about six to 15 miles a day, and they are meant for good hikers. But there are others easy enough for children over six, as well as vehicular tours of three to eight days. You are expected to bring along your own equipment, supplies, and food, and to pay for transportation when used. Their trips and tours are far too numerous to list, but you'll be well rewarded if you do investigate the options. There are many local trips into city outskirts and the countryside.

When you become a member of the S.P.N.I. you will receive their periodical listing of outings, trips, and hikes, plus an English-language quarterly called *Land and Nature.* This journal provides fascinating information on Israel's wildlife, flora, ethnology, archeology, history, geography, etc.

Besides the one at Ein Gedi, there are a number of Field Schools in the country—in Eilat, Na'ama and around Nature Reserves. Some have guest accommodations. The Society for the Protection of Nature in Israel will provide all the information. In addition to the Tel Aviv office they have a branch in Jerusalem at 13 Heleni Hamalka St., tel. 02-222357.

The **Keren Kayemet** has opened 20 newly planted forests for picnicking—all with children's playgrounds, barbecue grills, piped drinking water, sports facilities, toilets, and parking. Many are located in areas of historical interest. For details and maps contact the Keren Kayemet office at 96 Hayarkon St., Tel Aviv, tel. 03-234367; in Jerusalem on King George and Keren Kayemet Sts., tel. 02-635261.

Nature Reserves

A Nature Reserve is an area in its natural state, where man and civilization have not penetrated. It is not a recreation park planned for visitors, and laws and rules are in effect to protect the flora and fauna. A descriptive pamphlet and information can be obtained from the **Nature Reserves Authority,** 16 Hanatziv St., Tel Aviv, tel. 03-330841. Here is a list of locations and acreage: **Nahal Hermon** (Baniyas), 210 acres; **Yahudiya Forest Reserve** (above Bit'ha, Btei'ha Valley), 19,000 acres; **Nahal Gilbon Reserve** (Wadi Jalabina, south of Ashmura), 390 acres; **Nahal I'yon Reserve** (near Metulla), 100 acres; **Hula Valley Reserve** 800 acres; **Tel Dan Reserve** (near Kibbutz Dan), 98 acres; **Pa'ar Cave Reserve** (west of Kibbutz Sasa), 3½ acres; **Mount Meiron Reserve,** about 25,000 acres; **Nahal K'ziv Reserve** (between Ma'alot-Tarshi'ha and Moshav Goren), 2,239 acres; **Nahal'Amud Reserve** (between Meiron and Safed and Kibbutz Huqoq), 1,997 acres; **Nahal Arbel Reserve** (south of Migdal), 400 acres; **Harei Gilboa Reserve,** 1,820 acres.

Mount Carmel Reserves: **Ashdot Yagur** (northeastern Carmel), **Horshat Ha'Arba'im** (near Nesher junction). Western Carmel: **Qeren** (Horn of) **Carmel** (vicinity of the Muhraqa); **Nahal Me'arot Reserve** (Haifa–Hadera Rd. opposite Kibbutz Ein Carmel), 375 acres; **Nahal Taninim Reserve** (south of Kibbutz Ma'agan Michael), 16 acres; **Tel Poleg,** "The Roman Gate" (east of Wingate Institute, Tel Aviv–Haifa Rd.), eight acres; **Nahal Poleg Reserve** (north and west of the Wingate Institute), 125 acres; **Imam 'Ali Reserve** (road to Jerusalem, east of Shaar Ha'gai), 2½ acres; **Ha'masrek,** "The Comb" (next to Moshav Beit Meir), 29 acres; **Hurvat Se'adim** (west of Moshav Aminadav and the Kennedy Memorial), 2½ acres.

Ein Gedi, 1,125 acres; **Umm-Ri'han** (west of the Arab village Ya'bad), 750 acres; **Nahal Perath-Wadi Qelt** (between Anathoth and Jericho); **Einot Tsuqim** (Ein Feshkha), **Einot Qaneh** (Ein el-Ghuweir); and **Einot Samar** (Ein Turaba; on the side of the Einot Tsuqim–Ein Gedi road), 750 acres; **Hai Bar** (wild animals) **Reserve,** in the Arava near Yotvata Kibbutz.

Eilat region: **Coral Reserve,** 29 acres; **Coral Island,** and **Fjord, Ein Netafim, Canyon of Inscriptions, Gay Shani,** and **Timna Crater.**

Soreq Cave, west of Jerusalem past the American Bicentennial Park.

Note: Sometimes an entrance fee is charged ranging from about SH2.60 (75¢) to SH5 ($1.45) for adults, SH1.20 (35¢) to SH2.60 (75¢) for children.

4. Remote Sights

Israel offers several wonderful opportunities for sightseeing off the beaten path. For example:

REMOTE GALILEE SPOTS: Ten miles from the sea, skirting the Lebanese border along the northernmost road, you'll spot a distant castle. There is then a dirt road, about two miles long, leading to the **Montfort Castle,** built by the Order of the Teutonic Knights in the 13th century. (The New York Metropolitan Museum of Art excavated the site in 1926.) The jagged castle, viewed from the thickly wooded glen as you approach, looks as medieval and incongruous as anything you could find in modern Israel. You can see the thick outer wall, the moat encircling the castle, the quarters of the knights, the cistern, chapel, and vaulted halls.

A few miles further south, and closer to the sea, stands another **Crusader Castle** built by the Teutonic Knights, this one at **Kibbutz Yechiam.** It is in better condition than the Montfort Castle, largely because it was restored in the 18th century by the local emir. Experts consider the fortress a good example of an Ottoman ruler's feudal residence. (Actually, the best-preserved Crusader fortress is **Nimrod,** near Banyas, in the Golan Heights.)

Nearby, on the next-lower road that skirts the southern flank of Mount Meiron on the way to Safed, you pass through the historic village of **Peqiin,** nestled among hills of orange earth and whitish rock. It is here that the famous Zenatis live, the family which has resided in Peqiin continuously since the destruction of Solomon's temple in 70 A.D. (They actually left twice in recent years, in 1936 and 1947, but only for a short period, due to Arab riots and ambushes.) The family has a synagogue adjoining their home, which distinguishes the members of this clan from their Arab neighbors, whom they clearly resemble.

It was also in Peqiin, in a cave just under the main road, that Rabbi Bar Yochai hid out while composing portions of the Zohar, the Cabalistic Book of Light.

Just past Peqiin, a few miles toward Safed, you'll come upon a really strange landscape, the largest plantation of olive trees in Israel. It is one of the oldest known olive orchards in the world; some claim the roots of the trees were young in the days of the Bible.

RAMLA CISTERN: The town of Ramla is just a few minutes from Ben-Gurion Airport, on the main Tel Aviv–Jerusalem road. Its bland facade hides quite a few secrets. Here, for instance, you'll find an eerie underground reservoir where you can take a gondola ride along a waterway built by the Caliph of the Thousand and One Nights, Haroun el Raschid, in the eighth century.

The entrance is in a small park off a tree-lined lane. You coast along the damp grotto channels, bumping into thick pillars that support the great vaulted ceilings. You really can't see too much else, because it's very dimly lit down here—and the resulting effect is all you'd want it to be. Open daily from 9 a.m. to 4 p.m.; entrance fee is minimal.

Just a couple of miles past Ramla, you'll pass signs for the **Valley of Ayalon,** where Joshua made the sun stand still and then defeated his hysterical enemies with the help of a hailstone barrage.

AVSHALOM NATURE RESERVE: About 12½ miles southwest of Jerusalem, you'll want to visit this reserve and see the famous caves, only recently opened to the public. It's open from 8:30 a.m. to 3:30 p.m., Friday till 12:30 p.m. Admission is SH5 ($1.45).

DAVID AND GOLIATH: An hour's drive from Jerusalem, in a southwesterly direction heading toward Beersheba, takes you to the **Valley of Elah (Emek Elah),** where David and his slingshot brought down the giant Goliath. You reach it by going out of Jerusalem on the road heading toward Herzl's tomb, continue straight on (don't go on the road to the Hadassah Hospital), and when you come to the first crossroad, follow the sign toward Bar Giora. You then wind and twist into the Judean Hills, passing scrubby hillsides and young settlements, coming finally into a more fertile region of abundant grain fields and pine woodlands. You pass a dense forest, and then the **Netif Halamed Hey Memorial,** recalling the 35 Israeli soldiers who were ambushed while going to the defense of the besieged settlers of Etzion in 1948.

In another couple of miles you'll arrive at the Valley of Elah, in the foothills of the Hebron range. An I.G.T.O. placard quotes from I Samuel 16, which tells the story of the famous slingshot battle that took place on the two hills in front of you, an area now heavily cultivated. The Philistines were encamped on the hill to the southwest, the Israelites on the hill to the northeast.

IN THE NEGEV: The Negev is part of the area in which the Children of Israel wandered for 40 years. Even a couple of hours of modern wandering can prove to you how much faith the ancients must have had to wait out the divine promises in this desolate country.

The Negev has many bizarre sights worth seeing, and there follows now a description of a few that are more or less conveniently reached yet off the tourist circuit. If you are caught by the spell of these sands, remember the invocation of Moses when he sent his two men out for reconnaissance: "And he told them to 'Go up, then, into the Negev, enter the highlands, and see what the land is like, and whether the natives are strong or weak, few or many; see whether the country is good or bad, and whether the inhabitants live in camps or in strongholds; and whether the land is rich or poor, and whether it is wooded or not. Bring back some fruit of the country.' "

If you have a car, you may want to see three unusual sites in the Negev—**Arad, Shivta,** and **Avdat.**

Southwest of Sodom, at Arad, archeologists have found an important tel (archeological hill) containing the ruins of a Canaanite town from the early Bronze Age (about 2,800 B.C.), strewn about with earthenware pots filled with grain, an indication that this region once supported agriculture. Since the soil here doesn't absorb water, scientists believe that these ancient residents conserved the rainfall by a run-off into reservoirs. Exactly how, with an eye toward future agricultural development, remains to be seen.

Also discovered here, in 1963, was an Israelite sanctuary dating from the time of Solomon. This is considered an especially important find, since, for the first time, it will now be possible to visualize the Temple of Solomon described in the Bible.

Modern Arad is covered in Chapter IX.

Twenty miles south of Beersheba the main road forks, the western route branching to the ruins of the Byzantine city of **Shivta,** where extensive landscaping and restoration have been carried out by both Israeli and American agencies. A former Nabatean city, with a clever network of water-saving dams and channels (for which the Nabatean farmers were famous), Shivta has three well-preserved churches and many streets of restored houses to remind you what life was like here 1,500 years ago.

As you pass the Sde Boker kibbutz, take a left at a fork in the main road, proceed to the Gadna camp, and take a right just after it. You will then be at **Ein Moor** and **Ein Avdat.** This is an oasis with a natural swimming pool, an area of steep red canyons. A macadam road leads in, so you don't necessarily need a jeep. But during the rainy season (November to March) you should ask first before making the trip. Heavy rains have been known to turn the region into a bleak mud bath.

On the main road from Beersheba to Eilat, just seven miles south of Kibbutz Sde Boker, you'll find the most famous Nabatean city in Israel, **Avdat,** perched on a hill above a gas station. It is here, among the tall Corinthian columns and reservoir channels, that Israeli scientists are trying to discover the ingenious methods that were employed by the Nabateans to support agricultural life in this wilderness. One Hebrew University scientist actually recreated the Nabatean system of dams, cisterns, and hillside channels, and by reviving their ancient waterworks, was successfully able to grow grain on a nearby desert site.

At Avdat, the sands drifting over the once-immense colonnades and fortress walls recall the words of Shelley's traveler who stumbled upon the plaque of Ozymandias.

> "My name is Ozymandias, king of kings:
> Look on my works, ye Mighty, and despair!"
> Nothing beside remains. Round the decay
> Of that colossal wreck, boundless and bare
> The lone and level sands stretch far away.

5. Language Schools

Should you plan an extended visit to Israel, you should know that a good many kibbutzim operate language schools called **ulpanim** which are based on the principle of working for your education, room and board. In exchange for a half-day of Hebrew language classroom instruction, you work the other half-day in a job assigned by the kibbutz—in the fields, kitchen, or wherever you are needed.

The **Jewish Agency**—here in America, abroad, and in Israel—makes the arrangements for you. Classes are mixed, and your classmates may be Argentinian, Polish, Romanian, Moroccan, Persian, and Russian.

The three big cities have ulpanim where you just pay a low fee and don't have to work for your keep. These are five-month courses, very reasonably priced. If you're interested, apply to the Jewish Agency, either in your own country, or in Israel. In America, their main office is at 515 Park Avenue, New York, N.Y. 10022.

If you prefer to make your own arrangements while in Israel, then here are a few addresses that might be worth noting: **Beit Ha'am,** Bezalel St., Jerusalem, tel. 02-224156; **Beit Meir,** 37 King George St., Tel Aviv, tel. 03-244195; **Ordenstein Center,** 20 Y.L. Peretz St., Haifa, tel. 04-662044. In addition, there are intensive language courses given at the **Jerusalem Language Center,** 6 Hazanowitz St., Jerusalem, tel. 02-234131; **Neot Rachel,** Holon, tel. 03-856366; and in Netanya at 5 Shmuel Hanatziv St.

The above ulpanim, except Beit Meir, are under the auspices of the local municipalities. The list below refers to language courses under the aegis of the Jewish Agency which are for new immigrants and temporary residents: **Ramat Yosef,** Bat Yam, tel. 03-867147; **Beit Millman,** Ramat Aviv, tel. 03-418964; **Beit Brodetzky,** Ramat Aviv, tel. 03-417461; **Kiryat Gan,** Ramat Gan, tel. 03-767447; **Lod,** 9 David Hamelekh Blvd., tel. 03-964404.

The granddaddy of the Israeli ulpanim is **Ulpan Akiva.** Privately run, and quite expensive, it accepts families and children over 12. Further information can be obtained from Ulpan Akiva, Green Beach Hotel, P.O.B. 256, Netanya, tel. 053-38344.

As far as students are concerned, the following Israeli institutions offer accredited summer courses in the Hebrew language which can earn from six to 12 credits: **Hebrew University,** Mt. Scopus, Jerusalem, tel. 02-273602; **Tel Aviv University,** Ramat Aviv, tel. 03-420111; **Bar Ilan University,** Ramat Gan, tel. 03-752103; **Haifa University,** tel. 04-254111, and **Ben-Gurion University,** Beersheba, tel. 057-71241.

And for those willing to spend at least 5½ months in a kibbutz working and studying, a huge, comprehensive list exists. The best source of reliable information is Mr. Allen Pakes of the Jewish Agency, 12 Kaplan St., Tel Aviv, tel. 03-258311.

Chapter XII

LIFE ON A KIBBUTZ

1. The Kibbutz Movement
2. Stay and Pay
3. Stay and Work

AT SOME POINT in your visit, you'll undoubtedly want to stay on an Israeli kibbutz. A kibbutz (in the plural, kibbutzim) is Israel's unique version of the collective farm, and it's been the mechanism whereby the greater part of the country's territory was first cultivated and developed. If you are simply touring Israel and want to spend a day or two in a rustic, kibbutz atmosphere, then you can take a room in one of the many modern kibbutz guest houses. If you're young, healthy, and have at least a month to spare, you can earn your keep on a kibbutz as a volunteer worker. Of, if you want to learn Hebrew, and can spend six months at the course, you can attend a kibbutz language school, going to classes for half a day and working for your board and room the other half. Anyway you choose to do it, seeing kibbutz life firsthand is a stimulating, thought-provoking experience.

The kibbutz is, of course, a major conversational topic of tourists in Israel, largely because its accomplishments, ideals, and unconventional living patterns have been spread far and wide and romanticized in fiction. A friend of ours in the Israeli foreign ministry, who often chaperones visiting guests to various kibbutzim, once remarked that few people are passive to the kibbutz idea. "They are either all for it or violently against it."

Try to keep an open mind during your visit. The kibbutz movement is a complex subject which has been dissected, analyzed, laughed at, misunderstood, and reevaluated every year for the past few decades. Though all kibbutzim are basically similar, each has individualities, and the only way you can properly understand what a particular kibbutz is all about is to live on it; even then you must have a knowledge of the underlying ideology and machinery guiding the community in order to properly understand all that you see.

If you go to a kibbutz, here's some background information to keep in mind:

1. The Kibbutz Movement

This strange new world of collective farm ownership had its origins in the beginnings of the 20th century, when pioneers from Eastern Europe envisioned the kibbutz ("group") as the instrument of colonization for the national rebirth of the Jewish homeland. Its early establishment involved a socialist-Zionist dream, as well as a reaction against the slow-footed orthodoxy of European

Jewry. The early pioneer ideologists saw the collective as a utopian vanguard of social and economic equality based on free choice and democratic principles.

Down through the years, however, the role of the kibbutz has undergone drastic and evolutionary processes. From its first role of resettling and reclaiming the land, it moved immediately into the forefront of the country's defense, and was a key factor in the protection and absorption of new immigrants. When it finally was freed from do-or-die crises, the kibbutz had an opportunity to examine itself, to look within and analyze this segment of people which had never totaled more than one-fourth of the country's Jewish population. Subtle, and not so subtle, changes began to be noticed. Ideological problems notwithstanding, the kibbutz continued to increase output, adding factories and new industries even though it already produced one-third of Israel's total agricultural products and 8% of the nation's gross national product. In all, kibbutzniks have had a profound effect on their countrymen. For example, 10% of the Knesset (Israel's parliament) is composed of kibbutzniks.

The simplest way to define kibbutz ideology is to quote the kibbutznik's motto: "To everyone according to his needs, and from everyone according to his abilities." The underlying principles of any kibbutz are social and economic equality, collective responsibility for the needs of the membership, and communal ownership of the means of production, with the corresponding elimination of private property. On an individual level, this means that each member has no need for money of his own. His work is primarily determined by the needs of the commune, and his children, in most settlements, are raised by experts.

In addition to the ideological conviction behind this pattern of life, it arose also out of the necessity of conditions in early Israel. It was obvious to the settlers of the '20s and '30s that the character of the land was such that it could be most successfully cultivated by group effort, not only because of geography, but because of the military needs of the times—self-defense of the country by citizen soldiers, farmers, and watchmen, who would surely have perished outside the strength of the group. And once within the group, it was felt, the individual would be subordinated to the greater goals of the collective. A kibbutz is work-oriented, and people are judged by their work ability. It is a society in which a person must prove himself or herself as a worker, since the society stands or falls on the success of its physical laborers. Because of the nonphysical labor background of the members, it was necessary to establish a new criterion of achievement. A tremendous emphasis—a glorification even— was placed on the idea of manual labor, and in many instances "work" itself became elevated to a mystical, holy ideal.

2. Stay and Pay

Though the kibbutz guest houses are popular with tourists nowadays, time was when they catered strictly to Israelis. The whole idea of such places was born during World War II, a time when food was scarce and the agricultural kibbutz communities had better food and fruits, and more of both, than the town workers. So it became a custom for kibbutzniks to invite town friends to visit, eat, and relax whenever they could—which wasn't often, as town businessmen and factory workers didn't even get an annual leave then. But in 1945 annual vacations were instituted, and the first actual guest house opened to give city people a week of peaceful, rural rest. The peace and quiet still appeal to kibbutz guests. Today the kibbutz guest houses enjoy high ratings among hotels, and seem to offer at least as many or more comforts for holiday guests. One thing's certain, the service is always better—maybe because the kibbutzniks who are serving aren't hired help—they're either volunteers or members who live on the kibbutz, and the visitors are like guests in their home.

Today numerous kibbutzim have built accommodations for tourists on their premises. They all have good dining rooms, and most of them have swimming pools or beaches. Spending a few days in a kibbutz is a restful affair and certainly a splendid educational experience. In addition, you don't have those diesel-chugging noises outside your window, as you often do in the city hotels. Here you are out of doors most of the time in a refreshing, relaxed setting.

As kibbutzniks are well aware of the outsider's curiosity, they frequently sponsor lectures, hold question-and-answer sessions, and take you touring on the kibbutz grounds. Feel free to ask any questions you wish.

The **Kibbutz Rest and Guest House Association**, 100 Allenby Rd., P.O.B. 1139, Tel Aviv, tel. 03-614879, publishes a small booklet listing all the guest houses, with prices, amenities, and a map. You can pick up this booklet at any I.G.T.O. or write to the association.

THE PRICES: Ayalet Hashachar and Nof Ginossar charge the most: single occupancy with breakfast is SH91.80 ($27) single, SH61.20 ($18) per person double. The others charge between SH35.70 ($10.50) and SH57.80 ($17) per person double; between SH49.30 ($14.50) and SH85 ($25) single. Rates go up during Jewish holidays by 10-20% and a 15% service charge must be added to all rates.

AN ALPHABETICAL RUNDOWN: Herewith, for quick reference, a list of all the guest houses.

Ayalet Hashachar, Upper Galilee, tel. 067-37364.
Beit Chava, Shave Zion Post, tel. 04-922391.
Beit Oren, Mt. Carmel, Post Haifa, tel. 04-222111.
Beit Yesha, Post Givat Brenner, tel. 054-50076.
Ein Gedi, Dead Sea, tel. 057-90253.
Ein Gev, on the Sea of Galilee (camping grounds), tel. 067-51167.
Gesher Haziv, Western Galilee, tel. 04-927711.
Hafetz Haim, Post Tel Aviv, tel. 055-92681.
Hagoshrim, Upper Galilee, tel. 067-40138.
Hof Dor, Post Hof Hacarmel, tel. 063-99121.
Kayit Veshayit, Sdot Yam, tel. 063-61161.
Kfar Blum Upper Galilee, tel. 067-40468.
Kfar Giladi, Upper Galilee, tel. 067-41414.
Kiryat Anavim, Judean Hills, Post Kiryat Anavim, tel. 02-539691.
Lavi, Lower Galilee, tel. 067-21477.
Ma'ale Hahamisha, Judean Hills, tel. 02-539591.
Meiron, Upper Galilee, tel. 067-39361.
Mizpe Rachel, Ramat Rachel, Jerusalem, tel. 02-715712.
Neviot, on the Red Sea, tel. 059-6192.
Neve Ilon, Judean Hills, tel. 02-522053.
Nir Etzion, Carmel Beach, tel. 04-942542.
Nof Ginossar, Lake Kinneret, tel. 067-92161.
Shefayim, Post Shefayim, tel. 03-930171.
Shoresh, Judean Hills, tel. 02-528030.

A GEOGRAPHICAL LISTING: Starting in the Upper Galilee, we'll stop at each of the guest houses and offer some comments.

Upper Galilee

Some of the country's best kibbutz guest houses are located in northern Galilee, where they make excellent jumping-off points for trips in the upper and western reaches of that lush area, as well as to the Golan Heights.

One of the handsomest (though expensive, by kibbutz standards), is **Ayelet Hashachar,** Upper Galilee, tel. 067-37364, which is a veritable paradise surrounded by beautiful gardens; every conceivable type of flower seems to be blooming on your front lawn. In addition to the gardens, the kibbutz sports a first-rate kosher restaurant, a public relations officer for sightseers, a fine swimming pool, an artists' gallery, and *duty-free* gift shops—all of them branches of reputable Israeli firms. The 124 rooms, all with private shower or bath, are air-conditioned in summer, centrally heated in winter. Sounds fancy for a kibbutz, but a kibbutz it is—one of the oldest in the country (founded in 1915 by Russian pioneers), and so proud of the kibbutz ideal that it runs regular lectures (French and English) on kibbutz life. Ayelet Hashachar is north of Safed, a 45-minute bus ride from Tiberias. The fine Hatzor Museum is here, and the kibbutz can arrange connections for tours of nearby Hatzor excavations.

In the extreme northeastern corner of the Galilee is another guest-accepting kibbutz, **Hagoshrim,** Upper Galilee, tel. 067-40138, whose grounds are interlaced with running streams that form the sources of the Jordan River. Tall eucalyptus trees offer afternoon shade while you sit and watch the swift cold water rush by at your feet. In addition, you have a swimming pool, tennis court, and nearby fishing. You're close to the Hula Nature Reserve and Mount Hermon. A special Hagoshrim feature is a modernistic concert hall and dining room, where you can enjoy the tranquility of this pastoral setting in a little patio cafe, comfortably shaded by mulberry trees and drenched with the rich sweet smell of the figs that grow nearby. All of the rooms have private toilet, bath, and shower. Food served here is kosher.

A personal favorite of ours is **Kfar Blum** guest house, Upper Galilee, tel. 067-40468, 45 minutes north of Tiberias and ten minutes southeast of Kiryat Shmona. This is a warmhearted, friendly kibbutz, settled mainly by English-speaking people (American, English), and it doesn't take much time to get on first-name terms with the staff at the guest house. The rooms are situated in two double-decker, motel-style buildings facing out on a lawn with deck chairs and backed by pine trees. The hills of Galilee ring the kibbutz and the Jordan River runs by it. This kibbutz has tennis courts and one of the finest swimming pools in the country, Olympic-sized and used by Israel's Olympic swimming team for workouts. The view of the distant hills from the pool is magnificent. You're free to wander at will through the kibbutz grounds, the orchards, and along the river (you can fish here). If you want to tour the kibbutz, someone can usually be found to guide you. The food at the guest house is kosher and excellent, and the hospitality couldn't be more cordial.

Further north, ten minutes above Kiryat Shmona and an hour's drive from Tiberias, is **Kfar Giladi** Upper Galilee, Mobile Post, tel. 067-41414. Here, too, there are comfortable accommodations, heating in winter, air conditioning in summer, tennis courts, basketball courts, a terrific library with books in many languages, a swimming pool, and lovely rustic surroundings. All the rooms have private toilet and bath or shower. Kosher food; three stars.

Near Tiberias

In the lower Galilee, close to Tiberias and the Kinneret, there are three guest houses. Directly on the Sea of Galilee is **Nof Ginossar**, Lake Kinneret, tel. 067-92161. The two-wing hotel, five minutes north of Tiberias, provides air-conditioned rooms with phone and bath or shower. Fishing and swimming are the principle pastimes for guests at Nof Ginossar. Four stars; kosher food.

And don't forget the beautiful campgrounds at **Kibbutz Ein Gev**, described in Chapter VIII.

About 15 minutes south of Tiberias is **Kibbutz Lavi**, Lower Galilee, tel. 067-21477, and it's best to telephone and confirm a room before traveling out here—not just because the guest house is popular, but because once you arrive to find all 54 rooms taken, you'll have a difficult time finding another place to stay. The rooms are scattered along flowered walkways atop a mountain that offers breathtaking views. The constant breezes here make air conditioning unnecessary, even on hot days, but most rooms are air-conditioned, nonetheless, and centrally heated for cool nights. Each has private bath or shower, a coffee-making unit, and a sofa that converts into a third bed. The kibbutz has a large and attractive swimming pool, and guests are treated to frequent films and lectures. Lavi is an Orthodox religious kibbutz, but guests are relatively free from restrictions. You may dress and do as you please—but please respect the Sabbath (don't smoke publicly, etc.). The kibbutz synagogue is situated beautifully on a carpet of greenery, and services are held there each morning and evening. The dining room is airy and neat, and anyone is welcome to stop in for refreshments or full meals. You can buy postcards, shaving cream, paperback books and such at Lavi's souvenir shop. The majority at Lavi work mainly at agricultural tasks (the topsoil had to be imported to this bare mountain). A secondary industry is the making of synagogue furniture; in fact, the kibbutz has become the main supplier of such throughout Israel. You are welcome to visit the workshops. You may also take a look at the Holstein dairy cows, or sit and watch TV in the wood-paneled guest lounge/bar. There is bus service to and from this three-star guest house.

On the Mediterranean Shore

Five kibbutzim with guest houses are located directly on the shores of the Mediterranean, spaced from just above Herzlia in the south to just above Nahariya in the north. All of these boast excellent beaches.

On the northern Mediterranean coast, 40 minutes north of Haifa and close to Lebanon, stands **Kibbutz Gesher Haziv**, Western Galilee, tel. 04-927711, founded in 1949 by a group of Americans and Israelis. You wouldn't suspect, judging from the present evidences of prosperity, that the members started out living in tents! At any rate, this kibbutz is situated on a high hill with a wonderful view of the sea below. It has a swimming pool, not to mention access to one of the best beaches in the country, at Achziv. Built in 1962, the motel cabins are modern and bright. The majority of the rooms are air-conditioned, and all are heated in winter. Gesher Haziv accepts Diners Club cards, which always strikes us as a pretty remarkable inroad on kibbutz ideology. Kosher kitchen; three stars.

One of the kibbutz members here—the principal of the high school—wrote a fine account of the Israeli collective system, called *Life in a Kibbutz*. The book is on sale in the office, and it goes a long way toward helping a sightseer understand this radically different kind of society. You'll also be interested to know that Gesher Haziv was an experimental kibbutz, since it challenged the normal kibbutz practice of having children live in separate quarters from their parents, and was one of the first to start a new trend by insisting that the children live at home.

Working south down the seaboard, we come to **Beit Chava,** Shave Zion Post, tel. 04-922391, just five minutes from Acre and 25 minutes north of Haifa. The beach is a big attraction here, as is the new swimming pool. Kosher kitchen; air conditioning; three stars.

A bit south and sharing the same stretch of golden beach is **Hof Dor,** Post Hof Hacarmel, tel. 063-99121. This kibbutz operates both a guest house and a vacation village. Rooms have showers and are directly on the beach; dancing and Israeli folk evenings are often featured. Non-kosher kitchen.

Close to the historically fascinating ruins at Caesarea, and on the beautiful Caesarea beach, is **Kayit Veshayit,** Sdot Yam, tel. 063-61161. Another vacation village, this one is within easy reach of all Caesarea's attractions: Roman ruins, beach with water sports equipment, 18-hole golf course, non-kosher kitchen. Music and drama festivals take place nearby in summer.

Shefayim, Post Shefayim, tel. 03-930171, is a beachside guest house above Herzlia, about 20 minutes north of Tel Aviv. All rooms have private showers and air conditioning at this large place, which features all sorts of sports on the beach and grounds as well as occasional entertainment. Kosher kitchen; three stars.

Inland—South of Haifa

Located on Mount Carmel, a 20-minute drive from Haifa, the **Beit Oren** guest house, Post Haifa, tel. 04-222111, has rooms with bath or shower, plus an impressive swimming pool. This is an excellent base for touring the Haifa area and the lower Galilee, and it offers a breathtaking view of the Mediterranean coast. Three stars; kitchen.

Nir Etzion, Carmel Beach, tel. 04-942542, has neither private beach nor swimming pool but does take guests on daily jaunts to nearby Tantura Beach, one of the loveliest in Israel. Situated above the artist's village of Ein Hod, it is charmingly rustic and comfortable; all rooms with shower. Kosher kitchen; three stars, synagogue on premises.

Inland—South of Tel Aviv

Two kibbutzim lie close together off the road that runs south from Rehovot. Kibbutz Givat Brenner, Post Kibbutz Givat Brenner, tel. 054-50076, operates the three-star **Beit Yesha** guest house, which offers air-conditioned rooms with central heating and private facilities. It is not kosher, and there's a swimming pool on the grounds. Good location for touring both the Tel Aviv and Jerusalem areas. Ultra-Orthodox **Hafetz Haim,** Post Tel Aviv, tel. 055-92681, is equally well situated and has its own private whirlpool and swimming pool. Each room has a bath or shower, air conditioning and central heating. This is a three-star place.

Near Jerusalem

There are three guest houses in the Judean Hills hereabouts, all within 15 to 20 minutes of Jerusalem. **Kiryat Anavim,** Judean Hills, tel. 02-539691, accommodates its guests in houses built along a hillside. Most rooms have private baths or showers, but some share facilities; all have air conditioning, heating, and phones. Activities include swimming in the private pool, occasional dances and special programs. Kosher kitchen; three stars.

At **Ma'ale Hahamisha,** Judean Hills, tel. 02-539591, all rooms have private bath or shower. The grounds here are lovely, and there's a swimming pool and entertainment for guests. Kosher kitchen; three stars.

Shoresh, Judean Hills, tel. 02-528030, makes an equally good base for seeing Jerusalem and the West Bank. All rooms with private showers; swimming pool and sports facilities; kosher kitchen; three stars.

Neve Ilan, Judean Hills, tel. 02-522053, offers fully furnished five-room cottages with all amenities. A mini-market and laundromat are on the premises. Neve Ilan is about a 15-minute drive from Jerusalem.

Finally, don't forget the aforementioned three-star **Ein Gedi,** on the Dead Sea, tel. 057-90880 (see Chapter IX); the **Neviot** (Diving Center) on the Red Sea, tel. 059-6192 (see Chapter X); and **Mizpe Rachel,** at the Ramat Rachel Kibbutz, Jerusalem, tel. 02-715712 (see Chapter III).

3. Stay and Work

If you have the time, this is the best way to experience kibbutz life—and awfully cheap as well. We know of no other country in the world where the traveler who is low on funds can arrange to work for his keep in an invigorating outdoor atmosphere, and be assured of clean quarters and good food. Many young people who come to Israel for the first time get to know the country in depth this way—working for a while at a kibbutz in the north and then heading south to work in another neck of the woods—almost without spending a dime for the entire trip. All you need is a cooperative spirit and the willingness to work hard six to eight hours a day, six days a week, wherever the kibbutz might need you—from the apple orchards, to the fish ponds, to the dish-washing sinks in the kitchen.

In exchange for that work, you're given your bed, clean sheets, normal room amenities, and three big meals a day—the fuel for your inner fires. You will also be given work clothes, some personal items, and pocket money—about SH24 ($7.05) a month. It is recommended that you bring along your own toiletries and work clothes at the start. Hospitalization insurance costs SH16 ($4.70) and is mandatory.

The kibbutzniks, incidentally, are happy to have you, especially at harvest time when they need extra hands. You'll labor beside them, dine with them, share in the kibbutz activities with them, and be invited to their rooms for tea. You may learn a little Hebrew and make some life-long friends. In all likelihood you'll meet people like yourself from all over the world. You'll gain an incomparable insight into kibbutz life this way, and you'll also perspire a lot and get a few more muscles.

There are certain requirements for working on a kibbutz. You must be between 18 and 32 and healthy (they prefer you bring along a medical certificate). You must plan a minimum stay of one or two months, as required. Although you can request to be placed on a particular kibbutz—and this request will be honored if possible—you will be placed where needed and given whatever work the kibbutz needs to get done. This means that you have to be willing to shovel manure if asked, scrub dishes, or spend your days in the fields. Remember that the kibbutz is a work-oriented society, and you are accepted in direct ratio to your willingness and ability to work. In September, October, and March through June there are places on many kibbutzim. Be sure to register far in advance if you plan to be there in July or August, when Israel's youth movements are out on the kibbutzim.

To apply for work on a kibbutz, you can't go directly to any individual kibbutz—you *must* go through the Jewish Agency or one of the federation offices, listed below. Write ahead, giving the date of your arrival, and they will make all arrangements. If you're already in Israel, try your luck at one of the four major kibbutz federations. Each is associated with a political movement—three are socialist, and one is affiliated with the religious parties. It is, however, difficult to find a place open on a religious kibbutz. Following are the Tel Aviv addresses of the various kibbutz federation offices. As we said, write in advance:

Ichud Hakvutzot Vehakibbutzim (Mapai), 53a Hayarkon St., tel. 03-51710.

Kibbutz Haartzi (Mapam), 13 Leonardo da Vinci St., tel. 03-253131.

Kibbutz Hameuchad (Achdut Haavoda), 27 Sutin Street, tel. 03-245271.

Kibbutz Hadati (religious), 7 Rehov Dubnov, tel. 03-257231.

Ichud Hakvutzot Vehakibbutzim has daily hours from 8 a.m. to noon and from 2 to 4 p.m., Friday from 8 to 11 a.m. Kibbutz Haartzi is open Sunday to Thursday from 8 a.m. to 3 p.m., sometimes open Friday till 11 a.m. Kibbutz Hameuchad has daily hours from 8 a.m. to 3 p.m. and from 8 to 10:30 a.m. on Friday. Kibbutz Hadati requests you phone for an appointment.

The **Jewish Agency** has a Volunteer Department in New York. The address is Kibbutz Aliya Desk, Jewish Agency, 575 Sixth Ave., New York, N.Y. 10011. In Tel Aviv their address is 12 Kaplan St., tel. 03-258311, extension 14, 20 or 24. The Tel Aviv office is open from 7:30 a.m. to 3 p.m., Tuesdays until 2 p.m., Fridays until noon.

You can also work in a moshav, which differs from a kibbutz in that land is owned by each individual family and worked for profit by each. Production, distribution, etc., is collectively planned. Most moshavim are agricultural, and since they are smaller than kibbutzim, and based more on family units, more contact is made between volunteers and hosts. You can easily be placed on moshavim most of the year, though it's difficult in summer. You get work clothes, a place to sleep, food, and pocket money—about SH100 ($24.40) to SH150 ($44.10) a month. If you want to work in one contact the Jewish Agency Volunteer Department in Tel Aviv or New York at the above addresses.

Chapter XIII

SHOPPING IN ISRAEL

1. Only in Israel
2. Shopping Tips

ANY HARD-CORE SHOPPER will adore plying his or her skills in the flea markets and local shops or stalls—where buying becomes a real art, involving sharp-eyed scouting and recognition of an item's value, plus a near-ceremonious bargaining rite. Many people don't know, though, that Israel is a land of modern discount and department stores, diamond and fur marts, and a souvenir wonderland of gold as well as gilt. Some disappointed travelers come home saying that goods in Israel are expensive—they're the folks who didn't know what to look for or where to go. In this chapter we'll give you a rundown of particular types of bargains and goods found only in Israel; then we'll give you a few useful shopping tips.

1. Only in Israel

Without too much looking, you'll easily find most any item you could ever imagine buying. Products from around the world abound in Israel's shops. What is of more interest to us here, and what are the real "finds," are those items which are uniquely Israeli—made in Israel by Israelis, be they kibbutzniks, individual craftsmen, large manufacturers, or Bedouins. The descriptions in this section are of goods tourists seem to fancy most, and we'll try to tell you how to recognize their quality.

HAND-STITCHERY AND WOVEN CRAFTS: Today's shopper in Israel seems to share the current international mania for anything hand-stitched or woven—and in Israel such work is about the hottest of all market items. It's produced in varying quality by Yemenite, Bedouin, Arab and Druze craftspeople. All of it tends to be expensive by Israeli standards, but much of it is quite low or reasonably priced by U.S. standards.

Most of the Yemenite work is done with fine threads, frequently metallic silver or gold, and always with great care, delicacy, and finesse in both stitches and patterns. Items produced by Bedouin, Arab and Druze are quite different from Yemenite work, but similar to each other—generally in bright colors, and sewn with thick threads that are often handmade from sheep or goat fleece. The patterns are usually bold, in keeping with the rougher textures of fabrics and yarns. Whereas Yemenite work customarily decorates fine gowns of silky fabrics, elaborate religious items and garb, beautiful linens, blouses, shirts, dresses, and children's outfits, you'll find Bedouin stitchery covering small pouch-purses that swing from the hip; cotton, heavy wool, or velvet dresses of red, black or dark hues; elaborate men's vests, jackets and shirts, and small "picture pieces" for use as rugs or hangings.

For quality, the Yemenite stitchery is outstanding, consisting usually of sturdy fabrics and colorfast threads, easily washed or cleaned and lasting for years. When you buy the work of the Bedouin, Arab, and Druze, you should be more careful. Much of the most gorgeous stuff is stitched into ancient, rotting or dirty cloth; some of the vivid, fabulous colors will run if washed or cleaned. The former have learned more about public demand, and the latter are learning fast. Much of the Yemenite work is done by standard for factories and marketing outfits; most of the Bedouin, Arab, and Druze work is individually produced according to ancient ways. However, there are shops and cooperatives now selling top-quality work of both types; if you buy at these shops you'll pay slightly more, but you will get better value.

The woven work is usually a safe and good buy, no matter where you get it. But when you buy it, the further you are from its origin, the more it'll cost. This means your best buys will be in the Druze villages near Haifa, the Beersheba Bedouin Market (every Thursday morning—the earlier the better), the Old City in Jerusalem, and in the predominantly Arab towns such as Nazareth, Bethlehem, Hebron, Acre and so forth. Where the woven work abounds, you'll also find good selections of stitchery. As for the Yemenite work, though some say there's more in Jerusalem than elsewhere, we have found it abundant everywhere, and at rather standard prices. By the way, if you look at some of the woven items with a total disregard for their actual purposes, you'll often see things you can use effectively in ways the craftsman never dreamed of. For example, some of the donkey and camel harnesses and saddles can make belts, trims, wall hangings, and so forth.

Since the whole stitchery bit has become so overwhelmingly popular, some clever folks have begun imitating it in mass-produced machine-stitched items. Today, these are much more abundant than the handwork, and much less costly. Many times these products are excellent buys, but we've been often disappointed by the poor quality of the fabrics and threads. Our advice is to be careful where you buy them. At shops like **Maskit, Batsheva, WIZO,** etc., the machine or handwork is more expensive but totally reliable. Also excellent in every respect is the **Elder Craftsman's Shop,** 14 Shivtei Israel St., in Jerusalem, tel. 02-287831. It sells handcrafted articles made by the elderly from almost every ethnic group in the country. Open daily except Friday afternoons and Saturdays from 9 a.m. to 1 p.m. and 4 to 7 p.m.

JEWELRY AND ORNATE METALWORK: It's everywhere, all kinds, from cheap to expensive, mass-produced to one-of-a-kind. But if you want the best buys in fine diamonds, gems, and jewelry of internationally recognized top quality, try the **Diamond Mart** in Haifa. Also, scout the fine jewelry stores in each key city and I.G.T.O.-recommended **Tourist Discount Center.** You can really make dazzling buys of fine jewelry in Israel.

Israel is also famous for its Yemenite jewelry—another fine and delicate art produced by these craftsmen. Usually it's characterized by fine filigree work with thin wires of metal intricately joined and meshed to create almost-solid designs. The metal is ordinarily silver, sometimes hand-dipped gold. Whether plain metal or stone-studded, the work is quite ornate and leans toward the ceremonial and quite dressy—not sporty. Probably the best-known pieces are the earrings with one or several drop levels, executed of metal or set with stones or tiny bangles. There are also large quantities of necklaces, bracelets, rings, cufflinks, and pins, as well as numerous small items for display or religious use, including birds, boxes, dishes, ritual herb and spice holders, filigree cases or covers for cigarette lighters, compacts, Torahs and Bibles, etc., etc.

Growing greatly in popularity is the Bedouin, Arab, arid Druze jewelry. Unlike the Yemenite work, these pieces are usually heavy or massive and roughly executed. Sometimes the metal is silver, but often it's tin or copper; most of the stones are roughly cut or shaped shards from desert mines, semi-precious bits highly valued here since the time of Cleopatra. This jewelry often incorporates coins—old and new, fake and real, large and small—pierced to dangle, often pounded and stone-studded, and usually very worn. These are often supplemented with roughly cut and tooled bits of metal, usually in triangles and diamond shapes. Another interesting item used in jewelry here is the clove bud; cloves frequently are strung into patterns with tiny beads and a dangling coin or two, because the women who make them find the aroma quite pleasing to themselves and their men.

Some of the items are very, very old, as is much of the Yemenite work you can buy, but there are so many good copies being turned out today, it's almost impossible to tell the ancient from the new. We thought we had it solved when we learned which types of chains and engravings were done in different times— later we learned that virtually every style is being hand-copied today. So we began looking for what would strike our fancy, rather than what was supposed to be valuable. The one thing we can pass on—for your protection—concerns some of the stones. Amber is a great favorite in such jewelry, and fake amber is common. Either of two simple tests will spot a fake immediately—the rub or the burn. Fake amber, when rubbed briskly against your clothing, will gather enough electricity to pull at paper or hair if immediately placed near either. And, since fake amber is plastic, it burns easily when touched with the lit end of a cigarette. Another, even more expensive stone, is called atik, which means old. It is usually roughly cut, then polished, and made into beads of about a quarter-inch diameter; the color is a marbled combination of red and beige-white streaks. Try the burn treatment on this too, should you have any doubts. Both stones appear in necklaces, earrings, rings, and bracelets as well as in strings, and they are occasionally set into knives, small objects, etc. They can also be bought single for your own settings.

A popular style of jewelry and small objects is the interesting Persian miniature work that's found in large quantities nowadays, especially in Jerusalem. The jewelry takes the form of bracelets, brooches, pendants, cufflinks, tie bars, rings and such, and is made of small pieces of ivory, bone, ceramic, or plastic, delicately hand-painted with figures, flora and fauna. The colors are usually bright, and the prices vary according to the finesse of the painting rather than the material employed, or even the age. Most often, the pieces are square or oblong, but sometimes they're cut as circles, ovals, triangles, hearts, or intricate designs. Aside from the jewelry, you can also buy miniature paintings. Then, too, the hand-painted Persian work is available in fine porcelain and ceramics, fashioned into thin cigarette holders, small pipes, many small boxes and jewelry items, as well as large pieces such as hanging lamps. It really is beautiful work. Other items to look for in shops that have this type of ware are small inlaid metal statues, usually of birds, made of brass, copper, or chased silver, and set with aqua and coral semi-precious stones. These small objets d'art would sell for at least double the price if bought Stateside. In Israel, you'll find them mostly in Jerusalem, and in Oriental shops and stalls throughout the country. The least expensive we saw were at the Beersheba Bedouin Market, though they certainly didn't originate there.

In either traditional or modern styles, shoppers will find a plethora of religious jewelry throughout the Holyland—in metals, woods, ivory, real and fake, elaborate and simple, expensive and very, very cheaply priced, and in designs for every religion.

Modern jewelry, made by Israeli craftspeople, is also to be found everywhere in Israel. Some of it is mass-produced and quite inexpensive; there's also an excellent selection of special designs and one-of-a-kind pieces. The modern jewelry-makers work in all sorts of media—metals, ceramics, stones, seeds, leather, you name it. And most of the modern work is clearly influenced by the more ancient jewelry of the land, which gives it a special character. You'll often see bits of ancient glass embedded in a new necklace or bracelet, age-old symbols etched into new pins or earrings, modern adaptations of ornaments thousands of years old.

OLIVEWOOD: Some of the most beautiful and unique items you can buy here are made of olivewood. Whether it's intricately carved or simply smoothed, it remains a richly veined light wood, very decorative. And it's used to make souvenirs for all budgets, from $1 to $100 or more. Some of the most popular items are the necklaces and belts fashioned largely from polished olive pits or small carved beads. Many vases, jugs, bowls and such are easily found and very well priced, and the carvings range from highly styled to primitive. Many people buy the carved figures of biblical characters or the sets of Nativity scenes, but the very best-selling item is probably the camel. Then there are rings, earrings, bookmarks, letter openers, buttons, bead curtains, desk sets, whatever. Though works of olivewood are available everywhere, the best buys are in the Arab and Christian shops in Jerusalem, Bethlehem, and Nazareth.

COPPER AND BRASS: Most of these items are difficult to transport. However if you are flying for the United States *directly* from Israel, you may be able to take a large piece with you.

Don't, incidentally, buy copper and brassware in a shop on the main streets of any of the cities, if you want to pay a realistic price. Instead, look for these pieces in the Flea Market in Jaffa, in Acre, in Jerusalem's Mea Shearim, or Nazareth. And if you find something that you *must* have (don't let the shopkeeper know this), switch immediately to an attitude of detachment; it will start the process of bargaining in your favor.

One of the ways to tell if a copper vessel is good or not is by its weight. The heavier the object, the greater amount of copper in it. If the piece is black and dirty, you can scrape it and see the copper underneath. And when you're back home, you can clean it yourself with fine sandpaper, steel wool and a great deal of patience. The large trays make beautiful cocktail tables, and can also be hung on your living room wall as an ornament.

EILAT STONES: "And King Solomon gave unto the Queen of Sheba all her desire, whatsoever she asked . . ." (I Kings, 10:13). The Old Testament doesn't say which gifts Solomon gave to his royal guest; possibly some were those green stones from his mines—pendants and brooches of turquoise green streaked with malachite and shades of blue, pink, and purple.

A beautiful aquamarine-to-dark-blue color, these stones are sold all over Israel—either as stones, or as pendants, and set in either modern or traditional settings. The best place to purchase them is of course in Eilat itself, where they are mined, and where the selection is enormous and the prices the lowest in the country. Go to the factory where the stones are cut, polished and set, and you will have a wonderful time trying to decide which one of these stones you want—since each has a slightly different design and color scheme.

POTTERY: Here again is a craft available in contemporary or ancient styles, with the contemporary work seen everywhere, varying fantastically, and priced in every range. The ancient-style work generally comes from the Arab, Bedouin, and Druze villages, and is always priced much lower there. Paints, glazes, texture, sizes, quality, and craftsmanship vary greatly, but you're certain to find something that pleases you. Probably the most outstanding work comes from Hebron, where craftspeople sell their wares in their own little shops.

Besides the Eilat stones mentioned above, a new product has appeared here—the clay from King Solomon's copper mines at Timna is made into pottery. The clay contains iron and copper, and after the pottery is fired the finished product resembles metal. When it is glazed with a transparent glazing and fired, the blue-green color of the copper appears and looks like malachite stone. A workshop where one can witness the whole production process is situated on Ha'arava Road, near the Sonol and Delek gas stations. It's called **Eilat Art Centre.**

KNITWEAR: Israel is as famous for its knitwear as for its fur products, and its knits are sold throughout the world. There are several shops and manufacturers specializing in fine knits; **Iwanir, Aled, Maskit,** and **WIZO** are among those where the quality is always superb. You'll see shirts, suits, dresses, slacks, ensembles, coats—and though these are often high-priced for Israelis, they do remain one of the foreign bargain shopper's best local buys.

LEATHER AND FURS: Israel is unbelievably furry for so hot a climate. In this land you'll find fabulous furs and leathers for prices that would seem absurd back home. For elegant, well-tailored, fine-quality, and personally fitted coats and such, you can save many dollars—even hundreds of dollars—depending on your selection. If suede is your favorite, or leather, you'll find great buys in suits, coats, jackets, slacks, bags, baubles and trinkets—from the finest quality to medium and low, with prices varying accordingly. All key cities sell these goods and they're also exported around the world. The styles are all you'd want them to be, from traditional to avant-garde. Gloves and small leather items are also good buys in Israel, and available everywhere, as are luggage pieces.

Products of sheep or goat skins are much lower in price—also in quality. Though the small skins, throw rugs, hangings, jackets, and hassocks sell very well, you'll also find slippers, hats, gloves, suitcases, boxes, bags and so forth, all in these skins that are treated according to ancient customs. We do suggest you take a good whiff of these items before buying, because sometimes they do reek, and it's almost impossible to remove or hide the odor. Also, the sheepskins are usually a bit higher, for their durability is supposed to be greater. You'll see most of these items in the Arab markets and stalls of Jerusalem's Old City, Nazareth, Acre, Bethlehem, and Hebron. Prices are best in Hebron and other West Bank areas, as most such work comes from there. The very best buys will be at various factories scattered through the West Bank areas.

GLASSWARE: Plenty of glassware in Israel, and the two most distinctive types are either contemporary or Hebron. The contemporary glassware is made in factories and by individual artists and often simulates the looks of ancient Israelite work. This stuff is beautiful indeed, but it's costly and hard to ship or take home because of breakage. We've seen excellent tiny copies of ancient vessels, handmade, that make good collection pieces, and even hold miniature flower arrangements (you can buy dried flowers to take home with you, if you're interested).

Hebron glass almost always comes from one of five factories (small shops, really) operated in Hebron by members of one family. The most popular shade is blue with a bit of green in it, but it's also made in dusty yellows and golds, greens, purples, silvers, and clear shades. Vases come in all shapes and sizes, and there are mugs, beads, ornaments for camel and donkey saddles (these make great napkin holders), and pendants about the size of a half-dollar that are quite eye-catching when strung with raw leather and hung around the neck. Impressed with many religious and simple designs, they're cheap and make interesting, appreciated gifts. Though the Hebron glass is sold throughout Israel, it's naturally much less expensive when you buy it in Hebron—and the selection's better there as well.

You'll also find many places that carry authentic ancient glass pieces, from hundreds to thousands of years old—they are of course high in price, but not as high as you'd think.

BASKETWARE: Gay baskets, trays, and pots of all shapes and sizes can be bought in the Druze villages near Haifa or in the markets of Nazareth, the West Bank, the Old City of Jerusalem, Beersheba, Acre, and many city shops as well. All of these items are light and durable, make wonderful decorative pieces for your home, and will be easy to transport. The color schemes of the heavy-woven baskets and trays are unusually animated—reds, blues, greens, oranges, purples, all mixed and expertly woven together, making them one of the best folk crafts in Israel. Some are made of rushes, some of raffia . . . some of porcupine quills!

2. Shopping Tips

DISCOUNTS: Another important tip—if you're buying certain items—is to look for shops that display a red certificate of recommendation by the Ministry of Tourism. Here, you'll get a 15% reduction on prices of particular items when you pay in foreign currency. Included in the discounted list are jewelry, clothing, giftware, rugs and footwear. And a reduction of 30% is given in some other stores selling leather goods, if these items are delivered to the airport and can be qualified as "duty-free" purchases. However, do know that all shops that give discounts usually charge a good bit more for the merchandise to begin with, and frequently you can get better buys by shopping around. In any event, we suggest you price items in more than one place before buying anything anywhere.

BARGAINING: When you shop in markets and stalls, you should understand that you're deep in Arab culture, where bargaining is an accepted way of life. You'll find a friendly haggle over price is part of the shopping ritual. And in the Old City of Jerusalem, the bargaining game becomes quite a sport, much like a poker bluff. You pretend a passing interest in an item. The shopkeeper makes you an offer. You give him a look of displeasure and note that you are interested, yes, but not at *that* price. What is your best price, you ask? He gives you a price about ten per cent lower than the first. Then you offer him 50% of the first price. Impossible, he tells you. And so is your best price, you tell him. Given five minutes of this backing and filling, you'll probably hit a price about 20-30% lower than the original price. This approach only works if the item is costly enough to start with. Only a few shopkeepers will bother with all that ritual arguing over an SH25 purchase. Should you be interested in two items at the same shop, you'll generally get a better price. It takes practice at this sort of thing. Also, don't let your heart get set on something and find yourself forced to meet a high price. You can usually find that same item elsewhere, and try the bargaining game with someone else.

And although the general rules of the game outlined above are accepted in Jerusalem's Old City market, remember there are great individual differences. Some shopkeepers just won't budge more than an agorot or two, no matter how wily you think you are. They are the merchants who feel that eventually they can get the higher prices, and they might just as well hold out for them. They have learned that the world contains an inexhaustible supply of shoppers who manage to make their way into the bazaar.

SPECIAL SHOPS: Located in all key cities are two stores that you should visit without fail. They are **Maskit** and **WIZO,** and both of them carry native crafts, everything from jewelry, pottery, fabrics, embroidery, and clothing, to glassware and religious articles. All merchandise is of the highest quality and workmanship. You will find clothing, for instance, that is not only elegant and high fashion but also anticipates future trends.

It is not only the merchandise that makes these places special. Supported by the Ministry of Labor, the Maskit shops are the outlets for the Maskit home industries program, which provides work for immigrant women. Workers are supplied with materials and trained by expert instructors. They earn money as they learn new skills. WIZO is sponsored by the Women's International Zionist Organization. Its items are handmade by the needy and profits go right back to help others.

Neither Maskit nor WIZO is what you'd call "cheap." Neither is the quality. And you would pay twice as much for the same items back home, since both organizations export to the States—to Neiman-Marcus and its ilk.

Some other shops for which "special" is an appropriate designation:

Batsheva, 38 Frishman St., Tel Aviv. Jewelry, ceramics, glassware, olivewood and rugs are the specialties here. Everything is handmade.

Hutzot Hayotzer, Arts and Crafts Lane, near Jaffa Gate in Jerusalem. This is not one shop but a complex of shops, offering a wide variety of arts and crafts. For sale are semi-precious stones in hand-crafted settings, paintings, tapestries, silver, clothing, ceramics, and more.

Jerusalem House of Quality, 12 Hebron Rd., Jerusalem. This is a center for the production, exhibition, and marketing of original works of art and handicrafts. Workshops are above the shop, with permanent exhibitions.

SHOPPING HOURS: Some stores in Israel are closed Tuesday afternoon all year round. In some places they're also closed Wednesday afternoon in July and August. Department stores are usually open 9 a.m. to 7 p.m. Sunday to Thursday, closing early Fridays. Stores in Jerusalem's Old City are open Saturdays as are stores in East Jerusalem.

Chapter XIV

A LANGUAGE GLOSSARY

1. Hebrew Terms and Expressions
2. Arabic Terms and Expressions

OUR FINAL TASK in *Israel on $20 a Day* is to provide a few guideposts to the language of the country.

The Hebrew alphabet is, of course, entirely unlike our Latin ABCs. Fortunately for us, however, Israelis use the same Arabic numerals that we use: 1, 2, 3, 4, etc.

Hebrew has a number of sounds which we don't use in English. They are difficult to communicate in writing, and until you hear them spoken correctly, you may not get the flavor of them. The first is the "ch" sound—which you'll find repeatedly in many words throughout the vocabulary. This is not the sound of "ch" in either "change" or "champagne." We don't use this sound in English, and the closest to it are the "ch" sounds in the German exclamation "ach," and in the Yiddish-Hebrew toast "le-chaim." It's a raspy, hacking sound that comes from the back of the mouth.

Another difficult sound, and also very common in Hebrew words, is the "o" sound. The best advice for practicing this sound is to say the word "oh" and halfway through saying the word suddenly cut your voice off. That's what many call a short "o." You get an approximation with the "o" sound in the word "on" and the German word "Von," although they're not exactly it either. You just have to cut the "o" short, so when you say the Hebrew word "boker," meaning "morning," you don't "bowker."

Now that you're sufficiently confused, here are some of those words:

1. Hebrew Terms and Expressions

USEFUL WORDS

hello	shaLOM	yes	ken
goodbye	shaLOM	no	lo
good night	lie-la-tov	good morning	BO-ker tov
see you later	le-HIT-rah-OTT	good evening	Erev tov
thank you	to-DAH-rah-BAH	I speak English	AH-NEE m'dah BERH angLEET
please	be-va-ka-SHA		
you are welcome	al low da-VAAR	I don't speak Hebrew	AH-NEE lo m'dah-BEHR ee-VREET
friend	cha-vare		

excuse me	slee-Cha	**yesterday**	et-MOHL
I	ah-NEE	**right (correct)**	na-CHON
you	ah-TAH	**too much**	yo-TAIR mee-DIEE
he	hoo	**patience**	SAV-la-NOOT
she	hee	**hands off**	BLEE yah-DIE-IM
we	an-NACH-noo	**what**	mah
there is	yesh	**why**	llama
there isn't	AIN	**how**	eich
little	m'AAT	**when**	mah-tiee
much	har-BEH	**movie**	cine-MA (also KOL-no-AH)
very	m'OD	**house**	bah-yit
so-so	KA-cha-Ka-cha	**white**	lahVAAHN
good	tov	**black**	sha-CHOR
hot	chAAm	**synagogue**	bait k-NESS-et
bad	rah	**school**	bait-say-FER
cold	car	**newspaper**	ee-TAHN
today	haH-yOM	**healthy**	ba-REE
tomorrow	ma-char	**sick**	cho-LEH

HOTEL TALK

hotel	meh-LON	**where is**	AY-fo
room	che-der	**money**	KES-sef
water	my-im	**bank**	bank
toilet	bait key-SAY, no-chi YOOT, she-roo-TEEM	**do you speak English?**	ah-TAH m'dah-BEHR ang-LEET?
dining room	CHE-der oh-CHEL	**key**	MAFF-tay-ACH
bill	CHESH-bon	**manager**	min-ah-HEL
Mr. (sir)	ah-don-EE	**accommodations**	ma-KOM
Mrs. (madam)	g'VER-et	**balcony**	meer-PES-eth

LOCAL TRAVELING

station	ta-cha-nah	**which bus goes to . . . ?**	EH-zeh auto-boos no-SAY-ah le . . .
railroad	rah-KEH-vet		
airport	sde t'uFAH		
bus	auto-boos	**stop here**	ah-TSOR kahn
taxi	taxi	**north**	tsa-PHON
taxi (sherut)	shay-ROOT	**south**	da-ROM
straight ahead	ya-SHAR	**east**	miz-RACH
street	re-CHOV	**west**	m'ar-AV
to the right	yeh-meanah	**near**	ka-ROV
to the left	smol-AH	**central**	MER-KA-ZITH
far	rah-CHOK	**from**	me
bus stop	ta-cha-NAHT ha-auto-boos	**to**	le
		wait	REG-gah

RESTAURANT AND FOOD

restaurant	MISS-ah-DAH	wine	YAH-yin
food	OCHEL	milk	cha-LAV
cafe	caFE	ice	ker-ACH
breakfast	ah-roo-CHAT BO-ker	tea	tay
lunch	ah-roo-CHAT TSA-ha-RYE-im	coffee	cafe
		vegetables	YEH-rah-KOHT
dinner	ah-roo CHAT Erev	salad	saLAT
waiter	mel-TSAR	fruit	pay-ROTE
menu	taf-REET	apple	ta-POO-ach
butter	chem-AH	orange	tapOOZ
cheese	g'VEE-nah	tomatoes	AG-von-ee-OAT
egg	bay-TSA	cucumber	mah-la-fe-FON
hard-boiled egg	bay-TSA ka-SHA	pepper	pil-PEL
		salt	me-LACH
soft-boiled egg	bay-TSA rah-KAH	sugar	sue-CAR
		omelet	cha-vi-TAH
scrambled eggs	bay-TSIM m-bull-BELL-et	sour	cha-MUTS
		sweet	mah-TOK
fried eggs	bay-TSEE-ah	bread	LECH-hem
soup	ma-ROCK	satisfy	saVE'a
meat	bah-SAHR	hungry	ra'EV
veal	e-gel	pleasant	nah-IM
chicken	tar-ne-GOL-et	excellent	met-soo-yAN
fish	dag	to eat	le-eh-CHOL
ice cream	glee-DAH	to drink	lish-toth

POST OFFICE

post office	dough-are	postcard	gloo-yah
letter	mich-tav	telegram	miv-rock
stamp	bool (bool-im pl.)	air mail	dough-are ah-veer
envelopes	ma-ata-FOTH		

SHOPPING AND STORES

how much is it?	KA-mah zeh oh-LEH	manicure	MAH-nee-KOOR
		appointment	p'gee-SHAH
store	cha-NOOT	doctor	row-FEH
pharmacy	bait mer-kah-CHAT	dentist	row-feh shin-eye-yim
barber, hairdresser	mahs-peh-RAH	expensive	ya-KAR
		cheap	zol
shampoo	ha-fee-FAH		

THE COUNTRYSIDE

sea	YAAM	village	K'far
sand	chol	road	der-ech
desert	mid-BAR	mountain	har
forest	yah-ARE	hill	giv-AH
farm	mesh-ekh	spring, well	ayn, ma-ay-in, ay-in
valley	EH-mek	trip	tee-YULE

DAYS AND TIME

Sunday	YOM ree-SHON	minute	da-KAH
Monday	YOM shay-NEE	hour	sha-AH
Tuesday	YOM shlee-SHEE	seven o'clock	ha-sha-AH SHAY-va
Wednesday	YOM reh-vee-EE		
Thursday	YOM cha-mee SHEE	day	yom
Friday	YOM shee-SHEE	week	sha-voo-ah
Saturday	sha-BOT (as in "hot")	month	CHO-desh
what time	MA ha-sha-AH	year	sha-NAH

NUMBERS

1	ah-CHAT	20	ess-REEM
2	SHTA-yim	21	ess-REEM v'ah-CHAT
3	sha-LOSH	30	shlo-SHEEM
4	AR-bah	50	CHA-mee-SHEEM
5	cha-MAYSH	100	MAY-ah
6	shaysh	200	mah-tah-YEEM
7	SHEV-vah	300	shlosh may-OAT
8	sh-MO-neh	500	cha-MAYSH may-OAT
9	TAY-shah	1,000	Elef
10	ESS-er	3,000	shlosh-ET elef-EEM
11	ah-CHAT ess-RAY	5,000	cha-maysh-ET elef-EEM
12	shtaym-ess-RAY		

2. Arabic Terms and Expressions

please	min fadlach	coffee	cha-hawy
how much is this?	ah-desh hadah	Jerusalem	al-kutz
thank you	shoo-khraan	hotel	'otel
goodbye	salaam aleichem, ma-ah-salameh	right	yemine
		left	she-mal
hello	a-halan, machr-haba	straight	doo-ree
do you speak English?	tech-kee Ingleesi?	pardon	sa-mech-nee
		where is?	wen?
yes	ay-wah	one	wa-had
no	la	two	tinen

three	talatay	**twenty**	eshreen
four	arbaha	**fifty**	chaamseen
five	chamseh	**one hundred**	mia
six	sitteh	**scram; beat it**	rooch min-hon
seven	sabah	**never, baloney, that'll be the**	
eight	tamanyeh	**day (literally "tomorrow's**	
nine	taisah	**apricots")**	boo-khra meesh-
ten	ahsharah		meesh

Day 1 Tel Aviv

Day 2 Nazareth, Tiberias, Sea of
      Galilee
  3 Dead Sea, Qumran, Massada, Jericho
  4 Caesarea, Haifa, Acre, Rosh
  5 Old & New Jerusalem   Hanikra
  6 Tel-Aviv, Jaffa,
      Carmel Cellars wine Tasting

  7 Leisure Day Tel-Aviv

THE FROMMER/PASMANTIER PUBLISHING CORP.
380 MADISON AVE., NEW YORK, NY 10017   Date_____

Friends, please send me (postpaid) the books checked below:

$-A-DAY GUIDES
(In-depth guides to low-cost tourist accommodations and facilities.)

☐ Europe on $15 a Day $6.95
☐ Australia on $15 & $20 a Day $4.95
☐ England and Scotland on $20 a Day $5.95
☐ Greece and Yugoslavia on $15 & $20 a Day $4.95
☐ Hawaii on $25 a Day $4.95
☐ Ireland on $15 a Day $4.95
☐ Israel on $20 a Day $4.95
☐ Mexico and Guatemala on $10 & $15 a Day $5.95
☐ New Zealand on $15 and $20 a Day $4.95
☐ New York on $20 a Day $4.95
☐ Scandinavia on $20 a Day $4.95
☐ South America on $15 a Day $4.95
☐ Spain and Morocco (plus the Canary Is.) on $10 & $15 a Day ... $4.95
☐ Turkey on $10 and $15 a Day $4.50
☐ Washington, D.C. on $25 a Day $4.95

DOLLARWISE GUIDES
(Guides to tourist accommodations and facilities from budget to deluxe, with emphasis on the medium-priced.)

☐ Egypt $4.95
☐ England & Scotland $5.95
☐ France $5.95
☐ Germany $4.95
☐ Italy $4.95
☐ Portugal (plus Madeira & the Azores) $4.95
☐ Canada $6.95
☐ Caribbean (incl. Bermuda & the Bahamas) $6.95
☐ California & Las Vegas $4.95
☐ New England $4.95
☐ Southeast & New Orleans . $4.95

THE ARTHUR FROMMER GUIDES
(Pocket-size guides to tourist accommodations and facilities in all price ranges.)

☐ Athens $2.50
☐ Boston $2.50
☐ Honolulu $2.50
☐ Ireland/Dublin/Shannon .. $2.50
☐ Las Vegas $2.50
☐ Lisbon/Madrid/Costa del Sol $2.50
☐ London $2.50
☐ Los Angeles $2.50
☐ Mexico City/Acapulco $2.50
☐ New York $2.50
☐ Paris $2.50
☐ Rome $2.50
☐ San Francisco $2.50
☐ Washington, D.C. $2.50

Special Editions

☐ The Caribbean Bargain Book $6.95
(Guide to "off-season" Caribbean—mid-April to mid-December—and the resorts that slash rates 20% to 60%; includes the Bahamas.)

☐ Where to Stay USA $4.95
(Guide to accommodations in all 50 states, from $3 to $20 per night.)

Include 60¢ for first book, 25¢ for each additional book for postage and handling.

Enclosed is my check or money order for $ _____

NAME _____

ADDRESS _____

CITY _____ STATE _____ ZIP _____